WEEKENDING
in
New England

By Betsy Wittemann and Nancy Webster

Wood Pond Press
West Hartford, Conn.

Readers should bear in mind that prices, especially in restaurants and lodgings, change seasonally and with inflation. Prices quoted in this book were correct at presstime. They are offered as a relative guide, rather than an absolute.

Rates quoted are for peak periods; weekdays and off-season dates may be lower.

The authors have personally visited the places recommended in this book. There is no charge for inclusion.

The authors invite readers' comments and suggestions.

PLEASE NOTE: The area code for telephone numbers for the publisher and all Connecticut chapters except Lower Fairfield County changed from 203 to 860, effective September 1995.

Cover design by Bob Smith the Artsmith.

Cover photo by Hanson Carroll/Vermont Hiking Holidays: Champlain Valley.

Contents

About the Authors

Betsy Wittemann is assistant lifestyle editor and travel writer for the Journal Inquirer in Manchester., Conn., and formerly was a reporter for daily newspapers in Rochester, N.Y., and Hartford, Conn. For many years she wrote a travel column called "Day Away" for the West Hartford (Conn.) News. That column was the inspiration for the book, *Daytripping & Dining in Southern New England,* written in 1978 in collaboration with co-author Nancy Webster. Besides that book and *Weekending in New England,* they have collaborated on *Waterside Escapes in the Northeast.* A native of Bridgeport, Conn., she has lived in Athens, Greece, and San Juan, Puerto Rico, where she was associate editor of a Caribbean travel magazine. Her travel articles have appeared in major newspapers in the Northeast. She and her family reside in Glastonbury, Conn.

Nancy Webster and her family are such inveterate travelers that when they moved to Connecticut, they spent their first weekend exploring New York City while others would have been unpacking. A native of Montreal, she traveled extensively in Canada and hitchhiked through Europe on $3 a day before her marriage to an American newspaper editor. In 1972, she started writing her "Roaming the Restaurants" column for the West Hartford News, which led to the other half of the *Daytripping & Dining in New England* series. She and her husband, Richard Woodworth, are co-authors of *Getaways for Gourmets in the Northeast,* two editions of *Inn Spots & Special Places,* one for New England and one for New York and the Mid-Atlantic, and *The Restaurants of New England.* She and her family live in West Hartford.

Books by Betsy Wittemann and Nancy Webster

Daytripping & Dining in Southern New England
Weekending in New England
Daytripping & Dining 2 in New England
The Best of Daytripping & Dining in Southern New England and Nearby New York
Waterside Escapes in the Northeast

To Our Readers

Americans are inveterate weekenders. Long gone are the days of summer-long sojourns at full-service resorts, for even if such a vacation were affordable, time constraints would prove prohibitive for most. The two-week or month-long vacation is becoming an infrequently indulged-in luxury, as well.

Instead, the short trip is proving to be the ideal break from our daily duties. A short or long weekend away refreshes and relaxes, returning us to the workaday world with a new outlook. It is a true stress-reducer. And, because it doesn't draw on too many "vacation days" for those of us with limited holiday time, it can be more frequently enjoyed.

New England is an ideal place for the weekender. Distances are relatively short and diversions many. Hop in your car and you can reach most weekend destinations within a few hours.

We recognized this years ago, publishing the first version of *Weekending in New England* in 1980. And what was true then is even more so now. Stung by the recent weak economy, many travelers have turned to the weekend trip as the most sensible way to take a mini-vacation.

While the original eighteen destinations chosen for the 1980 book are still viable, and included in revised forms in this edition, we have decided to add several destinations as well. New to this book are six chapters on Franconia and the Monadnock region of New Hampshire; Freeport, Maine; Middlebury and the Champlain Valley, Vt.; Bennington, Vt., and Williamstown, Mass., and Northeastern Connecticut.

What all of these weekend destinations have in common are a good selection of accommodations, dining options, and things to see and do. Some are relaxing, others invigorating. All are delightful in their own way and are favorite places of ours to spend time away from home. We hope you'll make them your favorites, too.

A word about our research methods. We do not rely on questionnaires or telephone calls to determine whether an inn, a restaurant or a tourist attraction is up to par. We visit in person, talk to the innkeepers, inspect rooms, sample foods. We try to bring you the best and latest information available so that your trip will be successful.

Now, we invite you to share in our discoveries. We wish you good travels and we welcome your comments. We're happy to have you write to us at Wood Pond Press, 365 Ridgewood Road, West Hartford, CT 06107. In the meantime, here's to great weekends!

Betsy Wittemann and Nancy Webster

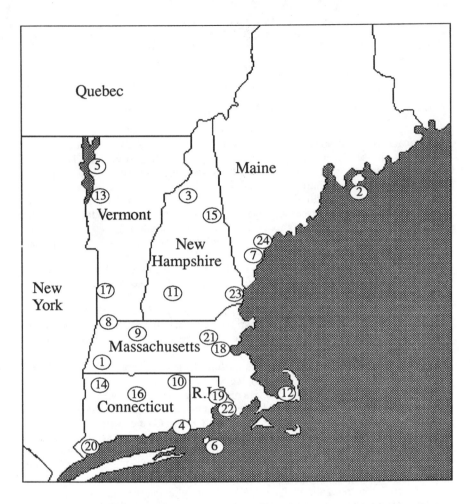

1. Southern Berkshires, MA
2. Mount Desert Island, ME
3. Franconia-Bethlehem, NH
4. Southeast Connecticut
5. Burlington-Champlain Islands, VT
6. Block Island, RI
7. Portland, ME
8. Bennington, VT - Williamstown, MA
9. Pioneer Valley, MA
10. Northeast Connecticut
11. Monadnock Region, NH
12. Cape Cod, MA
13. Middlebury-Champlain Valley, VT
14. Northwest Corner, CT
15. Mount Washington Valley, NH
16. Hartford, CT
17. Manchester and Mountains, VT
18. Boston, MA
19. Providence, RI
20. Lower Fairfield County, CT
21. Concord-Lexington, MA
22. Newport, RI
23. Portsmouth, NH
24. Freeport, ME

Music lovers relax on lawn outside Shed at Tanglewood.

A Sophisticated Summer Sojourn

The Southern Berkshires, Mass.

Ah, the Berkshires! The word conjures up thoughts of New England to anyone west of the Hudson River, of Tanglewood to the knowledgeable music lover, of quaint villages and country inns to generations of travelers, of sylvan retreats that have inspired the artists and authors who have called the Berkshires home.

And ah, the greens! When our lawn is dry and hay-colored and the summer humidity oppressive, the soft emerald lawns of the Berkshires delight the eye, with the contrast of wooded hills and dark evergreen forests refreshing, verdant and cooling at every glance.

The Berkshires mean many things to many people: at least three mountains worthy of the name, lakes and streams, fall foliage tours, culture and arts, ski areas and hiking trails, classic New England villages, historic homes, and places and names associated with the best of Americana.

For the summer visitor, the number of attractions is mind-boggling — enough to keep one busy for a week, if not longer. And yet the lesser known, unexpected discoveries in almost every nook and cranny of the mountain mosaic that is the Berkshires account for much of their unfolding appeal, even to those who know them well.

Summer simply wouldn't be summer in New England without a Sunday afternoon at Tanglewood. We have often made it a day-long outing, stopping for a morning swim in a secluded stream and then spreading our blanket on the lawn outside the music shed for a picnic (usually gazpacho, chicken salad and chardonnay) and an afternoon with the Boston Symphony, Beethoven and the New York Times.

And New England simply wouldn't be New England without a visit to picturesque Stockbridge and the countryside of the southern Berkshires. This is the inland route we take with visitors who want to see and sense the real New England in a short time.

For purposes of this guide, we've focused on the southern Berkshires and three inter-related themes: the arts, history and nature.

The arts are centered in Lenox and Stockbridge, which attracted literati of such name and number in the mid-1800s that the area became known as "America's Lake Country." Herman Melville, Nathaniel Hawthorne, Henry Adams, Edith Wharton and Henry Wadsworth Longfellow all lived here. Today, the Berkshires are unrivaled as America's summer cultural center with the foremost in music, dance and theater festivals.

Lenox remains an architectural showplace with vestiges of its days as "the inland Newport." For some of America's 400 who built palatial villas there around the turn of the century, the mountains were the summer equal of sand and surf or an autumnal transition between shore and city. "The well-regulated society person," according to an 1893 magazine quoted in an exhibition at Chesterwood, "can no more neglect a visit to Lenox during some part of the season than he can to observe Lent or to speak French at dinner."

Stockbridge is the storybook village whose scenes and residents were depicted by the late resident artist Norman Rockwell. Its New England-perfect nature is epitomized by the saga of its train depot: In 1892, townspeople were upset over the railroad's plans and commissioned architect Stanford White instead. Today, his architectural gem is the setting for a Japanese natural-foods restaurant, one of a number of such reincarnations throughout the Berkshires. Recently, the town experienced something of a battle over plans for expansion of the Norman Rockwell Museum.

Lenox and Stockbridge, with their thriving arts and hidden estates and manicured landscapes, are the Berkshires at their most sophisticated. They stand in startling contrast with the Berkshires of yesteryear, much of which still slumbers off the beaten path a few miles away.

Pages from the past are places like West Stockbridge with a vaguely Old West air, the lovely community of South Egremont, the covered bridges and tree-lined green of Sheffield, the remnants of the Shaker community still visible at Tyringham, and tiny towns like New Marlboro and Sandisfield, the forested settlement where Edmund Sears wrote the Christmas carol, "It Came Upon a Midnight Clear."

The natural beauty prompted Oliver Wendell Holmes's quote: "There's no tonic like the Housatonic," a reference to the river that snakes through the southern Berkshires. Waterfalls, ponds and hidden lakes abound. The flora of Bartholomew's Cobble, the Berkshire Botanical Garden and even the Tanglewood grounds vie with the foliage for visitors' attention.

History and nature focus in a place like Mount Washington, the old "town among the clouds," whose 60 or so permanent residents used to cast the first votes in presidential elections. Now, blueberrying is the chief occupation in the Bay State's least populated and highest town; near the top, sky-high Guilder Pond is flanked by the Berkshires' best show of flowering mountain laurel in June. Beyond the meandering roads and old buildings is the summit of Mount Everett, the state's second highest peak, with a three-state view of the Berkshires, the Catskills and the Litchfield Hills.

The views are sublime — and so are the Berkshires

Getting There

The Berkshires present unfolding panoramas on both sides of the Massachusetts Turnpike (Interstate 90), which connects with the New York Thruway at West Stockbridge and heads east to Springfield and Boston. U.S. Route 20 and State Route 9 are other east-west roads. U.S. Route 7 is the principal north-south highway; the locals call State Route 41 the "Scenic Route" and State Route 8 is both scenic and historic.

Bonanza Bus Lines and Greyhound Lines provide frequent bus service to and through the area, especially to Pittsfield, the region's major city.

Amtrak trains serve Pittsfield from Boston and the west.

Pittsfield Airport, Albany Airport and Bradley International (Springfield-Hartford) serve the area.

Seeing and Doing

The Arts

Nowhere else is so much music, arts and theatrical activity concentrated in one area every summer (in fact, Lenox was being touted in 1992 as the logical site for the National Music Foundation's proposed new national music center). People come from near and far for one or more performances; serious students and noted performers are in residence the entire season, which is roughly the last week of June to Labor Day.

Among the offerings:

Tanglewood, West Street (Route 183), Lenox, (413) 637-1940. The summer home of the Boston Symphony Orchestra and its Berkshire Music Center programs, Tanglewood is synonymous with music and the Berkshires. The 210-acre estate overlooking the shimmering waters of Stockbridge Bowl in the distance is a perfect setting for the BSO, which started presenting nine weekends of concerts each summer back in 1936. The acoustically excellent open-air shed seats 6,000 and is the place for the connoisseur who wants to see or be seen. Up to 10,000 more find spots under the sun or stars outside on the lawn, where you can't see but can hear just fine. We like to

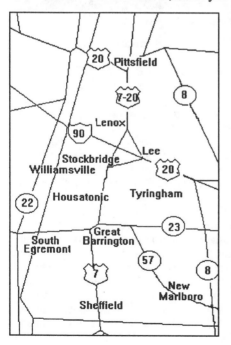

arrive when the gates open two hours prior to the performance and pick a spot under the biggest tree just outside the shed. Some of the picnics with wicker baskets, checkered tablecloths and candelabra are as elaborate as the tailgating parties at the Yale Bowl. The cafeteria also doles out food and wine amid abundant hanging fuchsias; the adjacent gift shop specializes in music, naturally. The grounds are made for strolling, and you can view the replica of Nathaniel Hawthorne's house across Hawthorne Road from the Friends of Tanglewood tent. Come early and stay late to avoid the traffic which, despite the volume, moves quite expeditiously. Special events featuring visiting performers are scheduled Thursdays in the Theatre. Concerts are held Friday at 8:30 (with 6:30 preludes, short concerts free to evening ticket-holders), Saturday at 8:30 and Sunday at 2:30. Reserved seats cost from $12.50 to $63.50; admission to the lawn is $9.50 to $10.50. The open rehears-

Daniel Chester French created Seated Lincoln in studio at Chesterwood.

($10.50) every Saturday morning at 10:30 is an excellent and intimate way for budget-watchers to get up close.

Berkshire Theatre Festival, Main Street, Stockbridge, (413) 298-5536. This summer institution has been described by the New York Times as "one of the most adventurous and exciting theaters in the country." Dedicated exclusively to the American repertoire, the festival brings top talent and four shows each summer to the 440-seat playhouse. A Children's Theater Company performs scripts written by local school children Thursday-Saturday at 11 a.m. under the tent. The Mainstage Playhouse, designed in 1886 by Stanford White as the Stockbridge casino, was the social center of the community until it became the nation's second summer theater in 1928. Mainstage performances are Monday-Friday at 8:30 and Saturday at 5 and 9; matinees Thursday at 2. Tickets, $20 to $30.

Jacob's Pillow Dance Festival, George Carter Road off Route 20, Becket, (413) 243-0745. The oldest and foremost summer dance festival in America, the "Pillow" offers everything from classic ballet to folkdancing and is known for its 300 world premieres. The rustic 100-acre wooded setting (upgraded in 1992 for the 60th anniversary season) includes several restored 18th-century barns. One is named for founder Ted Shawn, who launched the full-fledged festival in 1942 after ten experimental summers. A ten-week season is presented Tuesday-Saturday at 8 or 8:30; Saturday matinees at 2. Tickets, $24 to $28. A corollary series is presented Friday at 8, Saturday at 5 and Sunday at 7 in the Studio-Theatre; tickets, $10. **Shakespeare & Company,**

The Mount, Route 7 at Plunkett Street, Lenox, (413) 637-3353. The evening sky and the gardens of Edith Wharton's former estate above Laurel Lake yield a natural amphitheater for classical Shakespearean theater. Nineteen productions were mounted during the 1992 season in four theaters, including the newly renovated Stables Theatre and the outdoor Oxford Court Theatre, tucked in a quiet glen that was once a grass tennis court. The mainstage headliner, presented outdoors Tuesday-Sunday at 8 for six weeks, was "The Taming of the Shrew" (tickets, $15 to $22.50).

South Mountain Concerts, Route 7, one mile south of Pittsfield, (413) 442-2106. Chamber music emanates to national notice from a barn-like shed in a clearing up a dirt road off Route 7. It's been the site for 75 years of a host of chamber groups and soloists from around the world. Elizabeth Sprague Coolidge founded the chamber music festival in 1918 on the grounds of her summer home; the concert hall now is listed on the National Register of Historic Places. The straight-back pews are the only discomfort (bring a cushion to soften the seat) in an idyllic setting, where on five late-summer Saturdays and Sundays you can enjoy the balm of leading chamber music lights. Tickets, $16 to $18.

More Music: The **Aston Magna Festival,** considered the mecca of baroque, marked its twentieth season in 1992. Five concerts are given Saturdays at 6 from early July to mid-August in St. James Church, Great Barrington. The **Berkshire Opera Company** presented two operas during its eighth season at the Cranwell Opera House, Lenox. The **Berkshire Choral Festival** pairs a 200-voice chorus with the Springfield Symphony Orchestra for summer concerts Saturday at 8 in its concert shed at the Berkshire School in Sheffield. There are also weekly **Stockbridge Chamber Concerts** at Searles Castle, Great Barrington, and eight Monday evening concerts in the **Stockbridge Summer Music Series,** preceded by a buffet supper, at the DeSisto Estate, Stockbridge.

Norman Rockwell Museum at Stockbridge, Main Street, Stockbridge, (413) 298-4100. The world's largest collection of original art by America's favorite illustrator is on display in the new and expanded Norman Rockwell Museum. The museum moved in spring 1993 from the Old Corner House in town to a new $5 million building on the 40-acre Linwood estate along the Housatonic River in the Glendale section. Its nine galleries can display 150 works, about one-fourth of the musuem's collection of paintings by Rockwell, who lived his last 25 years in town and made its scenes and people his subjects. Both guided and unguided tours are scheduled. A new highlight will be the opening of the artist's studio, which was moved to the site from the center of Stockbridge and was re-created as he left it. The museum also includes changing exhibits of Stockbridge memorabilia and a gift shop that does a land-office business, including the sale of some 30,000 reproductions of Rockwell's painting of Stockbridge's Main Street at Christmas. Open May-October, daily 10 to 5; November-April, 11 to 4. Adults $8, children $2.50.

Chesterwood, Route 183, Stockbridge, (413) 298-3579. The secluded estate of sculptor Daniel Chester French, famed for the Minute Man in Concord and the Seated Lincoln in Washington, has been open to the public since his daughter donated it in 1969 to the National Trust for Historic Preservation. Visitors start at a gallery in the old cow barn, where many of French's sculptures are shown. A display of works by his daughter, Mary French Cresson, a sculptor in her own right, was on when we were there, as was a fascinating photo exhibit of the great Berkshires estates.

But it's the house and studio that are the gems of Chesterwood. The 30-room Colonial revival built in 1900 is where French spent six months a year until he died there in 1931. Gracious rooms flank the wonderfully wide, full-length hall in which a summer breeze cools the visitor. One interesting item among many is a rose from Lincoln's casket. We happened to be guided around the 22-foot-high studio a few years ago by retired school teacher May Flynn, a Stockbridge selectman and a font of knowledge. Said she: "I was eleven when he died — I'm ashamed I didn't know him — I was too busy playing baseball. But my mother did, and said he was gentle and kindly." Here you can see his plaster-cast models of the Seated Lincoln and a graceful Andromeda, which he was working on at his death. It's placed on a flatcar on a 40-foot-long railroad track and wheeled outdoors occasionally so schoolchildren can see, as French did, how a sculpture looks in natural light. The front of the studio with a corner fireplace, couch and piano is where he entertained frequent guests; in back is a piazza with wisteria vines and concord grapes framing a view of Monument Mountain. Chesterwood's gift shop is worth a visit; you also may stroll along easy trails in a hemlock forest carpeted with needles. A picnic area overlooks a large cutting garden. Open May-October, daily 10 to 5. Adults $5, children $1.

Tyringham Art Galleries, Tyringham Road, Tyringham, (413) 243-3260. It's worth a detour just to look at the outside of this fantastic place, once the studio of Sir Henry Kitson, sculptor of the Minute Man in Lexington. Called the Gingerbread House and looking as if it's straight from Hansel and Gretel, it is certainly the most unusual gallery in an area that has many. The roof, fashioned to resemble an English thatched roof, is itself a sculpture, weighing 80 tons and resting on a frame of chestnut beams. Do go inside — you'll marvel at the stained-glass windows, stone floors and some very interesting art. Out back, you can wander around a sculpture garden with surprises at every turn; sit beside an idyllic pond and admire the wildflowers and birds. Open Memorial Day to mid-October, daily 10 to 5. Adults, $1.

The History

History reveals itself everywhere in the Berkshires. Perhaps it's not so "old" nor so prominent as in the historic areas to the east, but for certain people and periods of Americana this area is supreme. Behind almost every pleasure of the moment lies an interesting tale of the past, if you pause long enough to pursue it.

The Mount, Plunkett Street, Lenox, (413) 637-1899. With four theaters, lush gardens and guided tours, the 50-acre estate built by writer Edith Wharton in 1902 offers a day's worth of activities for the visitor. The Shakespeare & Co. productions are foremost, but those with an interest in Wharton will enjoy tours of her Neo-Georgian home, which is very much a restoration in progress. Only a few rooms on the first floor are fully restored. The tour guides' information about the writer is more interesting and complete than are the rooms of her house. Her niece, landscape architect Beatrix Farrand, designed the lawns, woodlands and formal gardens. Open Memorial Day to Labor Day, Tuesday-Friday 10 to 5, weekends 9:30 to 4; through October, Friday-Sunday 10 to 5. Adults $4.50, students $3.

Colonel Ashley House, Cooper Hill Road, west of Route 7A, Ashley Falls, (413)

229-8600. The oldest house in the Berkshires (1735), this restored beauty off by itself in a meadow looks up to Mount Everett. Col. John Ashley was a judge and legislator; because of his position, our guide pointed out, the structure was somewhat elaborate for its day. In the lovely meeting room on the second floor (note the original paneling and built-in cupboard), the Sheffield Declaration of Independence was signed three years before the country's. Early furnishings and the pottery collection make this a good companion to the tour of nearby Bartholomew's Cobble (see Nature). Guided tours in summer, Wednesday-Sunday and holidays 1 to 5; weekends only, Memorial Day to Columbus Day. Adults $3, children $1.

Stockbridge's Main Street is an historic area in its own right. West of the famed Red Lion Inn, built in 1773 as a small tavern, is the **Mission House,** the town's first house and moved to the site in 1927 from Prospect Hill. Built in 1739 by the Rev. John Sergeant, the first missionary to the Stockbridge Indians, it is full of American furnishings prior to 1740. The rear of the house was Sergeant's domain, where the Indians visited. His wealthy wife Abigail entertained in front. The landscaped gardens are notable for herbs and plants of the period. Open Memorial Day to Columbus Day, Tuesday-Sunday and Monday holidays, 11 to 4. Adults $3.50, children $1.

Across the street is the **Merwin House** ("Tranquility"), built about 1825 and shown by the Society for the Preservation of New England Antiquities. Furnishings reflect the elegant life of its wealthy Victorian-era residents. Open June to Oct. 15, Tuesday, Thursday and weekends noon to 5 (adults $4, children $2). Near the end of Main Street is First Congregational Church, a striking, deep-red brick edifice built in 1824 and once the pulpit for Calvinist Jonathan Edwards. It's fronted by the stone **Children's Chimes Tower,** erected by town father David Dudley Field for his grandchildren and still rung from 5:30 to 6 every afternoon, per his directions, "from apple blossom time until frost." Just beyond are the Village Cemetery, where the epitaphs tell the story of early Stockbridge, and the Ancient Indian Burial Ground.

The Nature

The wealth of the Southern Berkshires is not all in its arts or its moneyed past. Residents and summer-home owners know it best for its beautiful and varied natural attractions, which range from wildlife preserves to mountain vistas, from waterfalls to secluded lakes. A sampling:

Bartholomew's Cobble, Rannape Road off Route 7A, Ashley Falls. A cobble is an old Yankee word for a limestone outcropping above a meadow and this National Natural Landmark nestles close by the Housatonic River. The peaceful setting of meadow and woods offers 200 acres of rock garden, where no fewer than 500 species of wildflowers, 100 species of trees, shrubs and vines, and 40 species of ferns have been catalogued. All over the cobble you can follow clearly marked trails and rest on rustic benches; although there are no tables, you can spread your picnic blanket and drink in a goodly portion of nature with your repast. The small Bailey Museum of Natural History displays local flora and fauna, plus a few Indian artifacts. Museum open April 15-Oct. 15, daily 9 to 5; grounds open year-round. Adults $2, children $1.

Berkshire Botanical Garden, Junction of Routes 102 and 183, Stockbridge, (413) 298-3926. Wonderful aromas fill the herb garden at this fifteen-acre, mostly outdoor botanical showplace with a pond, shrubs, trees, perennial borders, wildflowers, annuals, experimental plantings and more. A busy program is provided for members and children, but visitors may stroll the gardens from dawn to dusk. The solar greenhouse attracts special attention, and we loved the maple syrup house, the magnificent rose garden and the prolific vegetable garden with its own weather station. Inside are a good small library and gift shop, both with a stress on things botanical. The Herb Associates sell their wares in an outdoor shed for the benefit of the non-profit center, which stages a popular Harvest Festival the first weekend in September. Open mid-May to mid-October, daily 9:30 to 5. Adults $5, children $1, family rate $12.

Naumkeag, Prospect Hill, Stockbridge, (413) 298-3239. Many admire the interior of this 26-room, Norman-style gabled mansion built in 1885 by Stanford White for Joseph H. Choate, lawyer for the Rockefeller family and ambassador to the Court of St. James. But we like it best for the lavish hillside landscaping and gardens fashioned by Choate's daughter Mabel, who devoted her life to philanthropy, collecting art and nurturing Naumkeag. Here she produced a private world of terraces, walkways, sculpted topiary, fountains and even a Chinese pagoda. In a cool Venetian garden, water trickles from a tiny fountain; a stream cascades beside the steps in a grove of birch trees. The sculpture in the gardens befits Miss Choate's interest in the arts. Tours, Tuesday-Sunday 10 to 4:15, Memorial Day to Labor Day, weekends only to Columbus Day. Admission $6; gardens only, $4; children, $1.

Pleasant Valley Wildlife Sanctuary, West Mountain Road off Route 7, northwest of Lenox. Up a mountain road atop Lenox Mountain next to Yokun Brook is the 680-acre preserve established in 1929 by the Massachusetts Audubon Society. Seven miles of trails wind throgh 1,150 acres of uplands, fields and beaver swamps. A small trailside museum contains live exhibits. Sanctuary open Tuesday-Sunday, dawn to dusk. Adults $1.50, students 75 cents.

Mount Washington. Rising above the picturesque, historic community of South Egremont and towering above the sylvan valley floor is the town of Mount Washington, which occupies Mount Everett, the second highest mountain in Massachusetts. The town is a veritable treasure of scenery acknowledged by few other than its 60 or so year-round residents. Start your driving tour at the junction of Routes 23 and 41 next to **Smiley Pond,** a busy bird refuge and wildlife preserve. Following signs for Bash Bish Falls, you start the climb, passing an occasional house or an abandoned inn along the way. Eight miles up is **Mount Everett Reservation,** with Guilder Pond and its showy June display of mountain laurel, which blooms all over the mountain; it takes fifteen minutes to hike to the summit from the upper parking lot. Continue past the 1876

Umpachene Falls.

Town Hall and the 1874 Church of Christ down a road through a 400-foot-deep gorge like those in the Rockies to **Bash Bish Falls,** a 50-foot plunge that is the Berkshires' most dramatic. A good trail leads from a parking lot to the top of the falls. Cable fences on both sides of the crystal-clear creek keep one from seeing much of the falls, but the view through the gorge toward the Catskills is rewarding. Farther down the road, just before the New York State line, is a short road leading to the base of the falls. Several other waterfalls and mountain peaks in Massachusetts' southwesternmost town make it a haven for lovers of the wild and remote. The high-bush blueberries that make Blueberry Hill Farm the town's commercial livelihood sometimes go begging for lack of pickers.

8

New Marlborough-Monterey-Tyringham. These sparsely populated towns offer history and scenery in a choice package. Poke along back roads or follow a Circle Tour map provided by the Berkshire Visitors Bureau. We enjoyed the abandoned mills in the Mill River area and the Bucks County look of the Clayton area. Umpachene Falls, if you persevere long enough to find it, has a lovely park and a falling stream that you'll likely have to yourself. York Lake in Sandisfield State Forest offers delightful picnic groves on both sides of a small beach. The hamlets of Southfield, New Marlborough and Monterey are particularly quaint. An enchanting valley cutting between hills in Tyringham reminds some of the Austrian Tyrol. Mark Twain and Grover Cleveland summered here, and Sir Henry Kitson built his fantastic "Gingerbread House" in the valley. We like not only the Tyringham Main Road but the parallel side road along the hillside past Shaker Pond and beside some colorful old Shaker buildings, the last remnants of the once-thriving Shaker community overlooking Tyringham Cobble. These really are back roads — some of them dirt and most of them bumpy. Don't go without a detailed map.

Swimming. What's a summer day without a swim? Despite all the water, the pickings for the public seem rather slim — or is it simply that most visitors are too busy to stop for a dip? Pittsfield folks crowd the beaches of Pontoosuc Lake at Lanesboro. We prefer out-of-the-way spots like York Lake in New Marlborough, Spectacle Pond in Sandisfield, Benedict Pond in Beartown State Park near Great Barrington, Prospect Lake in North Egremont and tiny Lake Mansfield, with its interesting playground and hidden beach tucked away at the northwest edge of Great Barrington. Wahconah Falls State Park east of Dalton comes highly recommended, and the natives may guide you to their secret swimming holes.

Where to Stay

Large and small country inns, motels, B&Bs and resorts (and even the new spa, Canyon Ranch in the Berkshires) are dotted across the area. Many are booked months to a year in advance for the Tanglewood season. Some require stays of three or four nights on weekends, and some insist on prepayment of the entire bill. Rates vary widely, highest on summer and foliage weekends, often lower weekdays and much lower out of season. Because the Berkshires inns are so special, we concentrate on them here.

The Red Lion Inn, Main Street, Stockbridge 01262, (413) 298-5545. The granddaddy of them all, this big white wood structure immortalized by Norman Rockwell in his painting of Main Street is the essence of a New England inn. The site has held an inn since 1773; the present building, erected in 1897, was enlarged in the 1960s. Summer guests sit and rock on the front porch, which seems a block long, and watch the bustling activity all around. The spacious public rooms are filled with collections of antiques, and the **Pink Kitty**

gift shop in the corner has a fine selection for impulse buyers and doting grandparents. Also here is **Country Curtains,** the first in the retail chain launched by Jane Fitzpatrick, who took over the inn in the late 1960s with her state-senator husband and has restored it with taste. Rates for the 110 rooms and suites (some with color TV and 80 with private bath) vary widely, depending on the season and day of the week. The dining room is popular and pleasant, if unexciting; we prefer the adjacent **Widow Bingham Tavern** for its cozy, rustic atmosphere. Dinner entrees go from $16.50 for grilled chicken or brook trout amandine to $24.50 for prime rib. In warm weather, the vast, impatiens-bedecked patio behind the inn is fine for a drink or lunch, perhaps quiche of the day ($7.50) or creamed chicken over puff pastry ($10.50). Light food is available until midnight in the downstairs **Lion's Den** lounge. Doubles, $85 to $155, EP.

The Inn at Stockbridge, Route 7 (Box 618), Stockbridge 01262, (413) 298-3337. Staying here is like staying with friends in a country mansion. Don and Lee Weitz bought this handsome pillared house with twelve acres and converted it into a sumptuous bed-and-breakfast inn with eight guest rooms, all with private baths. The guest rooms are expensively furnished, each with its own motif; most have kingsize beds. The Weitzes offer wine and cheese in the afternoon to guests, who have the run of luxurious sitting rooms and the large outdoor pool. A full breakfast (perhaps souffles or baked french toast topped with fruit) is served in the dining room or on the back patio. Doubles, $90 to $215.

The Gables Inn, 103 Walker St., Lenox 01240, (413) 637-3416. One of the original Berkshires cottages built in 1885, this was the home of the mother-in-law of Edith Wharton, the writer who lived here while her own cottage, The Mount, was under construction. These days the Queen Anne Victorian has been grandly upgraded and expanded by Frank and Mary Newton, who offer some of Lenox's most lavish accommodations among their eighteen guest rooms and suites. Particularly stunning are the Jockey Club Suite and two new cathedral-ceilinged suites in a second-floor addition. Frank likes to show guests the eight-sided library where Edith Wharton wrote some of her short stories and the Show Business Room, full of signed photos of old stars and shelves of showbiz volumes with which to curl up on the chintz loveseat in front of the fireplace. Ever-improving, the Newtons have added a tennis court and an enclosed, solar-heated swimming pool with a jacuzzi in the back yard. Continental breakfast is served in the morning. Doubles, $80 to $145; suites, $195.

Rookwood, 19 Stockbridge Road, Box 1717, Lenox 01240, (413) 637-9750 or (800) 223-9750. This striking Victorian inn painted in shades of blues and plums, in front of which are gorgeous beds of perennials and impatiens, has nineteen rooms, all with private baths and seven with fireplaces. Owners Betsy and Tom Sherman welcome children and have cribs for babies. Bedrooms were redone in 1987, and vary from small and cozy to a two-level turret room on the third floor. Three new rooms in an addition across the back are unusually spacious. "We're still buying things at auctions," say the young and personable owners, who have an eclectic assortment of furniture from around the world. On the main floor are a Victorian parlor with a grand piano, a screened porch, wicker furniture on the veranda and a breakfast room with half a dozen tables where a full buffet breakfast (boiled eggs, cheese, fruit compote, cereal and the like) is served. Doubles, $120 to $190.

Thornewood Inn & Restaurant, 453 Stockbridge Road, Great Barrington 01230, (413) 528-3828. A pillared gray building with a curving brick walk, this fairly new inn has nine bedrooms, all with private baths, done in chintzes, mahogany antiques and plush carpeting. There are a sitting room with a big rust velvet sofa, a TV room and a swimming pool in back. The attractive dining room with bay windows onto a deck is

Suite at The Gables Inn provides elegant accommodations.

open for dinner to the public, Thursday-Sunday 5 to 9:30. Norwegian salmon, lamb chops or mixed grill might be the dinner fare. It is also the scene of a full breakfast for overnight guests — perhaps apple pancakes or sausage-egg scramble. Doubles, $95 to $155. No smoking.

Merrell Tavern Inn, Route 102, South Lee 01260, (413) 243-1794 or (800) 243-1794. One of the first properties in the Berkshires to be listed in the National Register of Historic Places, this 1800 building was saved early in the century by Mabel Choate of Naumkeag in Stockbridge, who eventually donated it to the Society for the Preservation of New England Antiquities. Upstate New Yorkers Faith and Charles Reynolds have restored it with ten guest rooms on three floors, all furnished with canopy or four-poster beds and antiques they've collected over 30 years. Guests register in the old tap room at the only surviving circular Colonial bar still intact. A grandfather's clock from 1800 graces the central hallway; the upper stairway retains its original smoke painting, an imitation of marble. Charles Reynolds delights in showing the building's prized possessions. Despite its age, however, this inn is elegant and comfortable. Common rooms have oriental rugs and guest rooms are carpeted; some have fireplaces and all have new plumbing. The old keeping room with an enormous beehive oven has been converted into a parlor. Guests are served a full breakfast and have the run of the grounds, which stretch back to the Housatonic River. Doubles, $75 to $135.

Williamsville Inn, Route 41, West Stockbridge 01266, (413) 274-6118. An elegant and quiet country inn built in 1797, this has fifteen rooms with private baths — in the inn, a remodeled barn and two cottages. Third-floor rooms have skylights, and all are named after literary notables in the Berkshires. New innkeepers Gail Ryan, her mother Kathleen and her brother Will have added a sculpture garden and a sheep's meadow on the extensive grounds, which include a clay tennis court and a swimming pool. The inn's main floor contains a handsome bar with pegged floors and a restaurant with four pretty dining rooms; one, the library, has tables on old sewing-machine bases and walls

11

of books. Dinner entrees run from $18.50 for chicken paupiette to $25.50 for rack of lamb and include popovers and salad. Atlantic salmon grilled with lime and ginger and served over a bed of sauteed arugula is a summertime favorite. A continental-plus breakfast is served in the morning in the cheery garden room with windows on three sides. Dinner nightly in summer, 6 to 9; Wednesday-Sunday rest of year. Doubles, $115 to $150; suites, $165.

Weathervane Inn, Route 23, South Egremont 01258, (413) 528-9580. This venerable inn has been much upgraded by innkeepers Anne and Vincent Murphy, she a former Long Island school teacher and he a private detective who loves to chat. The 1785 farmhouse with a Greek Revival addition has eight rooms, ranging from Colonial to contemporary, all with private baths; two more rooms are available in a coach house in back near the pool. The inn's serene, many-windowed dining room is graced by a large and striking mural of the inn and its neighbors, newly painted by a Connecticut artist. This is the setting for elegant dinners prepared by Anne, who changes her menu nightly. Entrees range from $16 to $20 for the likes of shrimp scampi, pork tenderloin dijonnaise, roast duckling with orange-raisin sauce and steak kabobs. Many are set down for posterity in Anne's new cookbook, *There's Always Another Meal at the Weathervane Inn.* Dinner by reservation, Thursday-Sunday 6:30 to 8:30 in summer, Friday and Saturday rest of year. Doubles, $170 MAP on weekends, $95 B&B.

Ivanhoe Country House, Route 41, Sheffield 01257, (413) 229-2143. Literally under the mountain on Undermountain Road is this attractive 200-year-old guest house, white with black shutters and a red door. Carole and Dick Marghery raise golden retrievers and shelter guests in nine spacious and nicely decorated, pastel-pretty rooms, all with private baths and refrigerators. One suite of two bedrooms shares the deepest bathtub imaginable — "you can really soak your cares away," says Carole. Can you believe she also delivers guests their breakfast (coffee or cocoa and muffins) via tray to their door? "I wouldn't want to drink my first cup of coffee in the morning with perfect strangers," she explains, "and I don't expect my guests to." If they want to mingle, they can use the large game room paneled in chestnut with fireplace, library, television and piano, or a pool out back. Doubles, $55 to $75; suite, $110.

Red Bird Inn, Route 57, Box 592, New Marlboro 01230, (413) 229-2433. A huge screened side porch full of lounging furniture and spectacular gardens enhance this white 1791 Colonial with gray shutters in a rural setting. Its name emanates from its status as a coach and carriage stop for the Red Bird Stage. Innkeepers Don and Joyce Coffman restored the National Register landmark inside and out for opening as a B&B. Common rooms and guest rooms are outfitted with antiques, original wide-board floors, fireplaces and panel doors. The ten-acre property includes a babbling brook and a rear cottage. A full breakfast is served. Doubles, $90 to $105.

The Old Inn on the Green, Route 57, New Marlboro 01230, (413) 229-3131. Known for inspired dining by candlelight, this 1760 stagecoach inn has been attracting well-heeled overnight guests lately. That's due mainly to the addition of luxury accommodations in a huge Normandy-style barn called Gedney Farm down the street. Beneath the barn's soaring 30-foot-high ceiling is a lineup of three rooms and eight two-level suites, their second floors fashioned from the old hayloft and reached by private staircases. Most come with fireplaced sitting rooms and double whirlpool tubs. Rooms are decorated simply but with panache in motifs from Moroccan to French provincial. Upstairs in the main inn are six rather spare bedrooms, two with private baths. A continental-plus breakfast is served in the stenciled dining rooms. The prix-fixe dinners ($45) are a Saturday tradition worth driving miles for. A short and with-it a la carte menu is offered other nights on the canopied, candlelit terrace or inside beside the

1893 Italian palazzo is home of Wheatleigh, an inn and restaurant.

hearth. Dine casually on interesting salads, pastas and entrees priced from $14 to $19.50. Dinner by reservation, Sunday-Friday 5:30 to 9 (closed Monday-Wednesday in winter); Saturday (prix-fixe only), 5:30 to 9. Doubles, $80 to $125 in inn; $150 to $225 at Gedney Farm.

The Turning Point, Route 23 at Lake Buel Road, RD2, Box 140, Great Barrington 01230, (413) 528-4777. A nice-looking old house (part wood, part brick) dating to 1800 has six guest rooms and a cottage and bills itself as "a naturally friendly inn," a reference partly to the owners' predilection for things natural. Architect Irv Yost and his wife Shirley renovated the structure, which he said was a shambles, to run a B&B. Down comforters and quilts make colorful the six guest rooms, some created out of alcoves or attic and four with private bath. An attached two-bedroom cottage comes with living room, kitchen and heated porch. The Yosts and their daughter Jamie serve a vegetarian breakfast with pancakes, pastry, herb teas and grain coffees, and treats like eggs frittata. Several common rooms include fireplaces, sofas and a piano. Irv says the inn's name originated from its location at a turning point in the road across from the Appalachian Trail and "in the lives of many people who come here." Doubles, $80 to $100; cottage, $200. No smoking.

The Black Swan, Laurel Lake, Route 20, Lee 01238, (413) 243-2700 or (800) 876-7926. You might think this is just a motel beside the lake, but with the addition of a twelve-room wing, it's considerably more. Half of the 52 rooms face the lake and have private decks. Nine of the new rooms have fireplaces and cast-marble hydrotubs, some have queen or king four-poster beds, and all are smartly decorated, most with two velvet armchairs. Some contain refrigerators, and the Lincoln Room has a log cabin quilt and a framed copy of the Gettysburg Address on the wall. In this wing is a handsome lounge/bar with an old English service bar the owners found in New Hampshire and a fireplace, as well as an exercise room and a Finnish sauna. The original motel rooms are nice, too, with cable TV, telephones and full baths. The glamorous pink dining room has large solarium windows overlooking the lake. The American menu is priced from $12.95 to $18.95 for dinner. Although there is no beach at this part of the lake, the Black Swan has a swimming pool, and pontoon and paddle boats to take out; it's obviously a favorite with families (no children in the new wing, however). Doubles, $70 to $185.

Chambery Inn, Main and Elm Streets, Box 319, Lee 01238, (413) 243-2221 or (800) 537-4321. Big bucks went into the 1990 restoration of the old St. Mary's School, which was closed and moved a block away to its final resting place. Lee businessman Joe Toole, the town moderator, and his wife Lynn, a registered nurse, created three guest rooms and six suites, notable for eight-foot-high windows and twelve-foot-high embossed ceilings. All have whirlpool baths and cable TV; suites add fireplaces, sitting areas and a desk. They contain king or two queensize beds. The school's wall-length blackboard was incorporated into the decor of one room. A continental breakfast buffet is served by staff in the morning. Doubles, $95 to $150; suites, $155 to $210.

Wheatleigh, West Hawthorne Road, Lenox 01240, (413) 637-0610. Tired of country inns? If you'd like to stay in an Italian palazzo, this may be for you and, added bonus, you can walk to Tanglewood. Built in 1893 for the Countess de Heredia, Wheatleigh is romantic, dramatic and ornate. From the moment you drive up to the imposing entrance of the honey-colored brick building framed in wrought iron, you are in a different world. All seventeen guest rooms are different. Some have terraces and fireplaces and are huge; others were former maids' quarters and suffer accordingly. Chef Peter Platt oversees the exceptional new American cuisine served in a gracious dining room and a large enclosed porch. Dinner is prix-fixe, $65 for three courses; a special tasting menu allows a sampling of more dishes for $90. The new Grill Room in the old library dining room offers an a la carte menu, priced from $9.50 for a smoked turkey sandwich to $24 for grilled sirloin with pepper nasturtium butter. For the clientele here amid surroundings that the Berkshires' most lavish resort brochure understates as of "noble proportions," price is no object. Lunch in summer, noon to 1:30; dinner nightly, 6 to 9; Grill Room, 5 to 9 or 9:30. Doubles, $165 to $425, EP.

Where to Eat

The Berkshires have their share of smart and expensive restaurants — a few, we feel, rather pretentious. As with the inns, you should reserve well ahead, especially on weekends. There also are casual and reasonable spots that are fun (and good), and more seem to spring up every year.

The Old Mill, Route 23, South Egremont, (413) 528-1421. This restored 18th-century grist mill, which opened as a restaurant in 1979, is one of our favorites anywhere. The atmosphere is a cross between a simple Colonial tavern and a European country inn — homespun and friendly, yet sophisticated — a happy combination created by owners Terry and Juliet Moore. Most entrees, which always include the freshest of fish, are in the $17 range, with prime New York strip steak the priciest item at $22. The sauteed calves liver with Irish bacon is a masterpiece. We also liked the oven-roasted poussin with garlic and the roast duck with poached pears and port sauce. If black bean soup is on the menu, try it, but save room for the mocha torte. The house salad is better than most. An addition to the smaller of two dining rooms provides large windows looking over Hubbard Brook in back. No reservations are accepted except for parties of five or more, so arrive before 7 on weekends if you don't want to wait; the creative food and relative value make the Old Mill very popular. Dinner nightly, 5:30 to 9:30 or 10:30; Sunday brunch, 11 to 3. Closed Monday or Tuesday in off-season.

Church Street Cafe, 69 Church St., Lenox, (413) 637-2745. This early (1981) "American bistro" that preceded the trend is among everybody's favorites in Lenox. Owners Linda Forman and Clayton Hambrick, once Ethel Kennedy's chef, specialize in fresh, light cafe food served inside beneath a ficus tree or outside on two decks. Dinner ($13.95 to $17.95) might bring pan-roasted salmon au poivre with basil-walnut pesto, sauteed Maine crab cakes with tomato concasse and grilled lamb loin with a shallot sauce. An appetizer of grilled fried corncake with chipotle chile sauce and an entree of grilled game hen Santa Fe marinated in tequila and cilantro show Clayton's interest in the Southwest. His chocolate mousse loaf was written up in the first issue of Chocolatier magazine, but we're partial to the chilled cranberry souffle topped with whipped cream. Our latest lunch ($6.95 to $8.50) included a super black bean tostada with three salsas and the colorful Church Street salad laden with goat cheese and chick peas. Lunch, Monday-Saturday 11 to 2; dinner nightly, 5:30 to 9; Sunday brunch in summer. Closed Monday and Tuesday in winter.

Albion Restaurant, 16 Church St., Lenox, (413) 637-0021. This was an immediate winner upon its opening in 1992 in the Village Inn's dining room. Young local chef Paul Mason changes his inventive menu frequently. Main courses on one summer menu ranged from $17.75 for walleye pike in parchment with lobster butter and cognac to $24.50 for salmis of young pigeon in the style of Rouen. Start with chilled avocado-shrimp soup with creme fraiche or a ragout of Vineyard snails and wild mushrooms with garlic and ginger. Finish with chocolate mousse-filled crepes with cointreau sabayon or a chocolate torte flavored with cassis creme anglaise for a meal to remember. The main dining room and the long side sun porch are pristine and the atmosphere elegant. The venerable inn harbors 30 rooms with private baths (doubles, $95 to $155, EP). It's known for its English tea, a variety of spreads offered Wednesday-Sunday from 2:30 to 4:30 for $5 to $9.50. Dinner, Tuesday-Sunday 5:30 to 9:30.

Cafe Lucia, 90 Church St., Lenox, (413) 637-2640. Authentic northern Italian cuisine is served with flair by Dianne and Jim Lucie in this former gallery transformed into a restaurant that shows and sells art. The pastas ($11.95 to $17.95) are great, and the chicken dishes, baked polenta with homemade sausage and the osso buco pack in devotees. Desserts are delectable: how about a cold chocolate souffle cake with almonds and amaretti or a sauteed apple, cinnamon and sour cream pie? Dinner nightly from 5; closed Sunday and Monday in winter.

Zampano's, 579 Pittsfield-Lenox Road, Lenox, (413) 448-8600. "We can cook" is the slogan for this casual new eatery. And they sure can, based on our summertime lunch on the canopied deck, totally screened off from busy Route 7. With rolls came a sweet red pepper and cheddar soup, chosen from an array that included chilled creamy passion plum, pink tomato and ginger-pear-nectarine and hot chicken vegetable with orzo, Senate bean and mushroom fennel. These were followed by a trip to the salad bar ($6.50 at lunch, $7.99 at dinner) that wins over even those who turn up their noses at salad bars — a gourmet (and all vegetarian) layout of twenty treats, from three kinds of potato salad to noodles, black beans, lentils and rice, with balsamic vinegar, extra-virgin olive oil and raspberry vinaigrette among the dressings. Everything appealed, so one of us went back to the salad bar for a dessert of fresh fruits and a whole poached pear in cinnamon sauce. We also found the grilled chicken sandwich on a sesame roll, served with a small salad, very tasty and exceptionally priced at $3.79. The same menu is available at dinner, when you also can get blackboard specials like oyster stew or prime rib with onions for $10.95 to $12.95. The desserts and wines are delectable, too. The simple decor is as appealing as the prices. Lunch daily, 11 to 5; dinner from 5.

La Bruschetta Ristorante, 1 Harris St., West Stockbridge, (413) 232-7141. The place where Truc Orient Express got its start gave way in 1992 to this wildly popular family-style Italian eatery, opened by Steven and Catherine Taub, he the former executive chef and she the pastry chef at Blantyre and Wheatleigh. The fare is robust, the cooking exciting and the prices down to earth: pastas in the $8.50 to $11.50 range (except $13.95 for a straw and hay masterpiece with shellfish and cognac), entrees from $8.95 to $16.50 for the likes of roast pork tenderloin with grilled polenta, cioppino, scallops sauteed with sundried tomatoes and grilled New York strip with gorgonzola polenta. The namesake bruschetta ($4.25) comes with chevre, grilled radicchio and basil olive oil. We know a party of four who dined very well here for $130, including two bottles of a good little $11 wine. Except for artworks on the walls, the decor in two small rooms remains the same as when it was Truc's, from whom the Taubs lease the space since the Vietnamese restaurant moved to sleeker, larger quarters next door. Dinner, Thursday-Monday 6 to 9.

Truc Orient Express, Harris Street, West Stockbridge, (413) 232-4204. This engaging restaurant was started in 1979 by Trai Thi Duong, who is from Vietnam by way of Hartford, where she used to run Truc's Restaurant. It features patio and indoor dining on two elegant floors amid oriental rugs, well-spaced tables set with white damask linens, sleek modern chairs with upholstered seats, gorgeous screens and huge black vases inlaid with mother of pearl. Haunting Vietnamese music plays in the background, and haunting aromas based on garlic waft from the kitchen. Dishes are perfectly prepared and prices are moderate (about $9 at lunch, $11.50 to $17 at dinner). Try the Vietnamese egg rolls, sweet and sour fish, singing chicken, duck with lemon grass or the house specialty, beef in four dishes (soup, appetizer, salad and fondue), $45 for two. Lunch daily, 11 to 3; dinner, 5:30 to 9 or 10. Closed Monday in winter.

John Andrew's, Route 23, South Egremont, (413) 528-3469. We don't know which is more appealing: the inspired cooking and presentation at affordable prices, or taking it all in on the expansive rear porch, artily decorated with black and white runners flowing from the roof out toward the deck. We'd dine there any time the weather cooperated, although the mod interior in black and white with splashy pink stenciling on the walls entices, too. These are perfect settings for chef-owner Dan Smith, who pairs red snapper with tomato coulis and zucchini cake, pan-roasted chicken with black bean cake and spicy tomatillo salsa, grilled pork tenderloin with pineapple mint chutney and braised red cabbage, and grilled leg of lamb with straw potato pancakes. Every accompaniment is different. We'd start with peasant bread with whole roasted garlic, sundried tomatoes and black olives and one of the great little salads, and finish with a chocolate-hazelnut torte or espresso ice cream. Pastas are $10.95 and $11.95 and entrees, $13.95 to $16.95. Dinner nightly, 5 to 10; Sunday lunch-brunch, 11:30 to 2.

Castle Street Cafe, 10 Castle St., Great Barrington, (413) 528-5244. Chef-owner Michael Ballon has attracted quite a following since returning to the Berkshires after several years at upscale restaurants in New York. The storefront space next to a movie theater is the perfect setting for his gutsy cooking, perhaps fillet of salmon with a dill pepper sauce, grilled veal chop with fresh rosemary or grilled cornish game hen marinated in lemon and garlic ($14 to $19). Try a pasta dish like fettuccine with bacon, red onion, wilted greens and garlic sauce, or an appetizer of veal and apricot pate or smoked brook trout. Save room for the world's best chocolate mousse cake (as rated by New York Newsday), frozen lemon souffle or a selection of homemade ice creams and sorbets. Dinner nightly except Tuesday, 5 to 10 or 11.

La Tomate, 293 Main St., Great Barrington, (413) 528-3003. Born in the south of France, chef Jean Claude Vierne has established a "bistro provencal" in the heart of Great Barrington. Two side-by-side dining rooms contain tables covered with white butcher paper over linens and walls of pine wainscoting beneath vivid wallpaper. The cooking is traditional French, with entrees in the $15 to $17 range except for marinated loin of lamb or lobster bouillabaisse (both $22). The locals go for the broiled chicken brushed with garlic and olive oil. Scallops and shrimp cardinal and braised striped bass also come highly recommended. For starters, how about mussels, onion tart, grilled garlic sausage or escargots? Creme caramel and chocolate mousse head the dessert list. Open Wednesday-Sunday, lunch noon to 3 (Sunday brunch to 3), dinner 5 to 10 or 11.

Embree's, Main Street, Housatonic, (413) 274-3476. The little hamlet of Housatonic, where Alice of Alice's Restaurant fame had her second restaurant, is home to this unusual spot, fashioned from an old hardware store. Hand-carved wooden trees bearing tropical fruits brighten the prevailing expanse of wood floors and tables, with the old store shelves still highlighted at either end. Out back is a marvelous garden courtyard, accented by sculptures and with high stone walls on three sides. The menu features seafood, pasta and vegetarian dishes with a Middle Eastern influence. Except for "the world's best hamburger" for $7.25, prices go from $10.75 for falafel with tahini in grilled flatbread with baba ghanoush and mint chutney to $20.25 for cajun blackened salmon or steak au poivre. We particularly like the ravioli with chevre and the African babotie. Tabbouleh, hummus with grilled flatbread and spicy vegetarian spring rolls are winning appetizers. Dinner, Wednesday-Sunday from 6.

Martin's Restaurant, 49 Railroad St., Great Barrington, (413) 528-5455. At the top of the most offbeat retail street in the Berkshires stands this storefront proclaiming "breakfast served all day." Martin Lewis, formerly a chef at the Waldorf-Astoria, packs them in with potato omelets, corned-beef hash with poached eggs and toast and a "tower of bagel," at $5.50 the priciest item and loaded with smoked salmon, cream cheese, tomato and bermuda onion. The lunch menu adds a few salads and sandwiches in the $2.50 to $5.50 range. Breakfast daily from 6 or 7; lunch, 11 to 3.

The Back Porch Restaurant, Stockbridge Road (Route 7), Great Barrington, (413) 528-8282. Ensconced in one of the red barns at Jenifer House Commons, this cheerful eatery is billed as a restaurant for the '90s. That translates to healthy international fare at reasonable prices — dinner selections ($8.95 to $12.95) including chicken fajitas, Indonesian chicken, seafood quesadilla, spanakopita, steak burrito and mixed seafood grill. Six hefty salads are offered at lunch or dinner. Desserts could be gingerbread with warm spiced peaches or chocolate mousse cake. Farm artifacts and a beamed ceiling yield a country look; a new back porch was in the works at our 1992 visit so the setting would live up to the name. Open Thursday-Monday 9 to 9 in summer; dinner served year-round.

Boiler Room Cafe, Buggy Whip Factory, Southfield, (413) 229-3105. Caterer Michele Miller, once a chef at Alice's Restaurant, runs this little cafe with a handful of tables inside and out in the rear of the Southfield Outlet and Craft Center. Her kitchen caters some of the Berkshires' best parties, but also puts out a short dinner menu — things like pan-fried duck breast in bacon with sweet and sour sauce, grilled lemon chicken with portobello mushrooms, and grilled loin lamb chop with white bean compote ($16 to $19). Basque tuna and tomato soup or chevre and shrimp tart make good starters. For dessert we'd choose Michele's superb dacquoise, although the blueberry-lemon tart and the plum crumb pie sound good, too. Soups, omelets, salads and such are featured at lunch ($6.50 to $9). Open Thursday-Saturday, lunch 11:30 to 3:30, dinner 5:30 to 10; Sunday brunch to 3.

Shopping

Obviously there are too many shops in this sophisticated, far-flung area for us to give a comprehensive guide. There are so many things to do here that we've never found much time to shop, anyway, but here are some of our favorites.

Lenox has probably the area's most exclusive shops. **Elise Farar Inc.** on Route 7 north of town stocks classic apparel and designer labels, and the small branch of **Talbots** on Walker Street has timeless but timely fashions. Nearby is **Evviva!** for contemporary designer clothing. **Mary Stuart Collections** at 81 Church St. purveys exquisite accessories for bed and bath, fine china and glass, plus gifts and children's things.

Berkshire Cottage sells solid cooking utensils and dinnerware for the country chef. For handknits, English cashmeres and imported yarns, head for **Tanglewool;** for contemporary crafts, the **Hoadley Gallery.** Handsome weavings, from pillows to coats, are displayed at **Weaver's Fancy.** The exquisite best of Britain is offered at **White Horse Hill,** 17 Housatonic St. Cross the street to **Bev's Homemade Ice Cream** for an ice cream fix. **Crosby's,** 62 Church St., is a catering service where you can pick up the makings for a super Tanglewood picnic.

In Stockbridge, don't miss the small shops in the Mews, a skip over from the Red Lion Inn. The tiny **Books & Things** has a noted collection of Norman Rockwell memorabilia with some original Saturday Evening Post covers, as well as books about local lore, cards and gifts. **Currier & I** displays colorful summer skirts among other clothing and gifts. Adorable clothes for children, including hand-smocked dresses, are to be found at **Hodge Podge,** as are frilly nightgowns for grownup ladies, sportswear and nifty gifts. We can't even begin to tell you the things in **Williams & Sons Country Store** just around the corner on Main Street. It's a true, jumbled-up country store operating since 1795 — amble in and enjoy the aromas. Nearby is the **1884 House,** an unusual Flemish-style building that once housed the town records and now stocks imports for men and women from the British Isles. We are enchanted by the **Dolphin Studio** on Main Street west of the Mission House; here are the home and studios of Primm and John ffrench, with a colorful melange of ceramic villages, batik pillows, silk-screened cards, hanging birdmobiles and fanciful necklaces. Primm will knit all kinds of sweaters to order, and John will make a small ceramic reproduction of your house for about $300.

A mile north of Great Barrington on Route 7 is the **Jenifer House Commons,** successor to the late Jenifer House and now a variety of enterprises from **Olde,** an antiques market with 60 dealers, to **DeWoolfson Down and Bed Feather Company,** claiming America's largest collection of duvet covers and imported bed linens, along with comforters, pillows and featherbeds from its own workshop. **Jillifer's Emporium** features old-fashioned gifts and goodies from books to bath salts. We admired almost everything at the stylish **Tokonoma Gallery.**

Great Barrington Pottery, actually on Route 41 in Housatonic, is worth a visit to see the Richard Bennett pottery that merges East and West, the first authentic Japanese woodburning kiln built in the United States, and a collection of beautiful silk flowers that can be custom-arranged. Tea is served daily from 1 to 4 in a ceremonial tea house amid formal Japanese gardens. Toward West Stockbridge on Route 41 is the fascinating **Undermountain Weavers** workshop and showroom. Dutch and Anne Pinkston design and make cloth on century-old looms, using fine wools from the Shetland Islands and rare Chinese cashmere. Jackets, scarves, ponchos, vests, hats and blankets are displayed.

The **Southfield Outlet and Craft Center** operates in the old Buggy Whip Factory in out-of-the-way Southfield. Started as an outlet center for the sweaters of ex-New York designer Neuma Agins, it evolved like topsy into a specialty outlet, crafts and antiques center. With occasional entertainment, pushcarts in a farmers' market, the Boiler Room Cafe and about twelve shops in the restored factory and outbuildings, it's the kind of place where you go for an hour — and end up spending the afternoon.

Antiquing is big business in the Berkshires, and all the Berkshires towns contain antiques stores. The biggest concentration is around Sheffield, where every second house seems to have an antiques sign in front of it. Many are clustered along Route 23 in South Egremont, where we were impressed by **The Splendid Peasant.**

FOR MORE INFORMATION: Berkshire Visitors Bureau, The Berkshire Common, Pittsfield 01201, (413) 443-9186 or (800) 237-5747. Individual chambers of commerce have information booths in Lenox, Stockbridge and Great Barrington.

 **Summer**

Somes Sound at sunset, as viewed from The Moorings in Manset.

The Cadillac of Islands

Mount Desert and Bar Harbor, Maine

It's August, and the city pavements and the dried-up lawns begin to seem mighty unenticing. The mind wanders to the eastern shores of Maine — memories of misty fogs and sparkling blue waters, noble rocks, thundering surf, and succulent lobsters to be eaten on a wharf.

The epitome of this vision for us is Mount Desert (pronounced "dessert") Island. Although seemingly a long way from just about anywhere, the trip is worth the effort — for a long weekend or a week (the four million who do so annually make Acadia National Park the nation's second most visited national park). Mount Desert has the most of everything we love in Maine. It is the kind of place where you can be as active or as idle as you like.

Families camp, millionaires summer in their "cottages," and trippers can find a hundred motels, inns and B&Bs. Palatial yachts and cruisers dot the inland harbor. Older folks relax on benches and watch the activity.

Bar Harbor is the largest, best-known town on Mount Desert Island and is its focal point. But it is of strollable size, with many shops and restaurants to investigate and, especially in August, it's crammed with tourists.

More rewarding for a feel of old Maine are visits to the towns of Seal Harbor, Northeast Harbor, Southwest Harbor, Manset, Bass Harbor and Somesville, one of the prettiest New England villages and the island's first settlement. With an unrivaled location at the head of Somes Sound, the Eastern Seaboard's only natural fjord, Somesville is a joy — the whites of its houses brightened by petunias, geraniums and morning glories filling flower boxes that line the street.

The draw for most island visitors is Acadia National Park, the first national park established east of the Mississippi. Situated where northern and temperate zones overlap, the park has an amazing variety of flora and fauna — including plants of the

Arctic tundra — on its 40,000 acres of unspoiled beauty. Most of the park is on Mount Desert, but part is to the northeast on Schoodic Peninsula and part offshore on Isle au Haut and other islands.

Just about everyone drives the Park Loop Road, twenty miles covering the park's major points of interest. Most visitors also consider a drive to the summit of Cadillac Mountain a must. Park rangers sometimes lead a 4 a.m. hike to the 1,530-foot-high summit, the highest point on the Atlantic coast; those hardy enough to participate can be among the first in the United States to see the rising sun.

The park offers guided walks, self-guided nature trails, carriage roads, cruises, campground talks, scenic spots, beaches and picnic areas. It's hard to find time to take advantage of everything available. And don't think that because Mount Desert is a fairly small island, it's easy to explore. Roads are convoluted, driving times between towns are longer than you would think, and there is much to see along the way.

Whether you stick to the main roads of the park and Bar Harbor, or strike off to the less crowded side of the island, climb mountains, swim in the 55-degree ocean at Sand Beach, observe beaver ponds or make your own discoveries, Mount Desert Island offers rewards to those of all ages and inclinations.

Getting There

Most people arrive by car via U.S. Route 1 through Ellsworth, the entry point for Mount Desert Island, or by ferry from Nova Scotia. The Bangor airport has commercial flights, Continental Express flies into a small airport in Trenton, just off the island, and Greyhound offers bus service from Bangor.

Incidentally, the **M.V. Bluenose,** a ferry operated by Canadian Marine Atlantic, (800) 341-7981, leaves Bar Harbor for Yarmouth, N.S., at 8 a.m. and returns at 9:30 p.m. daily

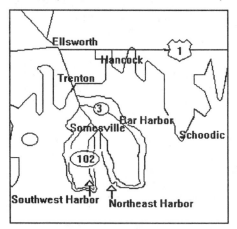

from late June to mid-September (three times a week, rest of year). The one-way trip takes six hours and saves hundreds of miles for those visiting Canada's Maritime Provinces. The ferry carries 1,100 passengers and 250 vehicles, has a duty-free shop, a bar and slot machines, and costs $75 per auto, $45 per adult and $22.50 for children, each way. We recommend taking a dramamine before this trip, for it can be quite rough; the last time we crossed, we did not envy those on the daytrip package ($59.95, including two meals) who had to face the return trip after getting seasick on the way over.

Acadia National Park

Your first stop should be the Visitor Center, three miles northwest of Bar Harbor at Hulls Cove and open daily from 8 to 6 in season (mid-June to early October; closed November-April). Atop a rather long stairway, the center has a huge picture window overlooking Frenchman Bay — a stunning view, except that on several visits we were unable to see much but fog, a frequent hazard here. Watch the fifteen-minute film

"Search for Acadia," shown on the half hour, which gives the flavor of the area.

Pick up the folder on the naturalist programs — you will discover a marvelous variety. Sea cruises, nature walks (some at dusk or at night), mountain hikes, bike trips, orienteering and astronomy watches are among the offerings. Our family chose a sunset program at the outdoor amphitheater of the Seawall Campground where the ranger, a geology professor in Kentucky, gave an informative, slide-illustrated talk on how a glacier shaped the island two million years ago. A full moon rose over the shed that housed the screen as he talked, and afterward, campers with flashlights trekked quietly through the woods back to their tents.

Admission to the Park Loop Road is by weekly pass, which costs $5 per car or $2 per person by any other kind of transportation. A $15 season pass also is available.

The Park Loop Road

Starting at the Visitor Center, this 27-mile loop can take three hours or a day, depending on the number and duration of stops, and may be entered and exited at several locations. The first two overlooks provide good views of Frenchman Bay, Bar Harbor and the area burned by a disastrous 1947 fire.

One of our favorite stops is **Sieur de Monts Spring,** named after the first French governor here and covered by a small octagonal structure. You can drink its waters from a fountain in the adjacent nature center. The **Abbe Museum,** a short stroll up a hill, tells most of what you could want to know of the area's history, especially of the Indians (adults $1.50, children 50 cents). The **Wild Gardens of Acadia** maintained by the Bar Harbor Garden Club are a special treat. All the native plants of the forests, bogs, mountains and shores are labeled and grouped in thirteen different areas, from deciduous weeds to dry heath and bog. Beautifully maintained gravel paths lead from horned bladderwort to grass pink to baked-appleberry to pickerel weed to fragrant waterlily, with benches for relaxation along the way.

The Champlain Mountain overlook offers the steep, 1.4-mile **Precipice Trail** up the side of the mountain, which the intrepid members of our family climbed, picking wild blueberries for sustenance along the way. They reported it took an hour and a half to get up, forty minutes to come down and there were two tunnels and countless firemen-type ladders to traverse, with sheer drops to contemplate. Although the trail is well marked and protected with railings, do this only if you're in good shape, don't mind precipices and have appropriate shoes. (The trail was closed throughout most of the summer of 1992 while a pair of rare peregrine falcons nested their young.)

After the climb, you may be hot enough to brave the waters below (usually 55 degrees at their warmest) at **Sand Beach,** the only saltwater beach in the park. Changing rooms are provided, the surf is fun and you'll feel exhilarated if not numb after a dip. By the way, the sand is really crushed stone and seashells, which give it a gray tint. For the non-swimmers, an easy 1.8-mile trail, **Ocean Path,** goes alongside the water here.

Youngsters love **Thunder Hole,** where the waves rush into a small cave and roar out with a sound of distant thunder if tides and surf are right. A small gift shop here has all kinds of Maine memorabilia, including calendars, cookbooks, aprons decorated with lobsters, T-shirts and pine sachets.

From **Otter Cliffs,** look out to sea from the highest headlands on the East Coast. At **Otter Point,** take your cooler and walk down through the evergreens to the rocks for a picnic enhanced by the crashing surf, hundreds of colorful lobster buoys and the occasional bold seagull looking for a handout.

Near Seal Harbor, the Park Loop Road turns inland toward the venerable Jordan Pond House, a good restaurant and an island tradition for its service of tea and popovers on the lawn. Stop and enjoy the fine view of **Jordan Pond** and the two rounded mountains known as the Bubbles (named by a summer youth for the bosom of his amour).

High at the end of Jordan Pond is a huge boulder (you can climb up to it, and rangers lead groups up) called a glacial erratic, which looks as though it will topple off at any moment. Then you pass beautiful deep-blue **Eagle Lake** and on your way up **Cadillac Mountain** you keep seeing it below, getting smaller and bluer.

Even the ashen-faced Annie in our group doesn't flinch on the road up Cadillac — it is so well designed that you hardly know you're on a mountain. The view from the top is stupendous in all directions; at dusk, watch the sunset from the Sunset parking area. At any time, take the short trail at the summit with interpretive signs and maps. There are also a gift shop and restrooms.

Other Activities

Besides the Park Loop Road tour, there are many other drives on the island. Take **Sargent Drive,** which borders the fjord-like Somes Sound, out of Northeast Harbor to Somesville for some of the best views. Across the sound is **Echo Lake,** with a fine beach and changing rooms, and water far warmer for swimming than the ocean. Head down the west side of Echo Lake for a short hike up to **Beech Cliff,** which has a great view down to the lake below (yes, you can hear your echo).

The park's **Carriage Roads** rate special mention. Fifty miles of winding gravel paths were built early in the century by philanthropist John D. Rockefeller Jr., a summer resident of Seal Harbor, who sought to preserve the horse and carriage lifestyle in the face of automobile encroachment. The remarkably designed roads, complete with seventeen stone bridges, take walkers, horseback riders and bicyclists past dazzling scenery.

Camping

The national park operates two campgrounds, **Blackwoods,** five miles south of Bar Harbor on Route 3, and **Seawall,** two miles south of Southwest Harbor on Route 102A. Both are in wooded areas near the ocean. Fees are $6 to $12 a night, and there's a fourteen-day limit. The season is generally late May through September, but Black-woods is open year-round on a limited basis. You can reserve well ahead a site at Blackwoods between mid-June and mid-September through Ticketron; Seawall is on a first-come, first-served basis. Write National Park Service, Acadia National Park, RD 1, Box 1, Bar Harbor 04609.

Privately owned campgrounds abound in the area, and we stayed at one near Ellsworth when Seawall was sold out. **Bar Harbor Campground** at Salisbury Cove is the closest to Bar Harbor. **Mount Desert Narrows Campground** is the only one on the ocean. Rates from $12 to $20 for a family of four are typical.

Old fishing boats moored off Bernard present typical scene on Mount Desert Island.

Where to Stay

It seems as if hundreds of motels and cottage colonies line Route 3 into Bar Harbor. With all the accommodations, you wouldn't think you'd need reservations — and we've always been able to find something — but in season (July to Labor Day and especially August) the good motels fill up fast with people reserving for arrival on the Bluenose Ferry from Nova Scotia in the evening or planning to board the next morning. It's wise to book for at least the first night; you can always look elsewhere the next day if you aren't satisfied.

In Bar Harbor itself are plenty of inns, motels and B&Bs, and on the other side of the island, more of the same plus a couple of grand old hotels — the kind to which rich widows used to come for the entire summer.

Motels and Cottages

Park Entrance Motel, Route 3, Bar Harbor 04609, (207) 288-9703 or (800) 288-9703. Sequestered in a quiet location across from the National Park Visitor Center, the 57 rooms here overlook manicured lawns leading down to Frenchman Bay. Each has a terrace or balcony with chairs to lounge on; some have a view of the heated swimming pool and hot tub. At the foot of the grounds are a picnic area, mooring facilities, rowboats, a small beach and so many mussels on the rocks that one of our party thought he was in seafood heaven. Doubles, $99 to $149. Open May to late October.

Bar Harbor Motel, 100 Eden St., Bar Harbor 04609, (207) 288-3453 or (800) 388-3453. Reasonably priced family units, a location near the Bluenose ferry terminal and within long-walking distance of town, and a heated pool as warm as bath water (great for tired bones and chilly days) make this a good bet. Vastly upgraded since our first stay here in budget quarters, the 70 rooms are spread out in buildings of four units each up the side of a hill; set back from the road, it's quiet until the Bluenose horn blows rather early in the morning. Tucked away in the woods at the top is the refurbished "patio section," where tall windows in our spacious room looked onto a shady common patio and the back yard was Acadia National Park. Two-bedroom family units go for $122. Complimentary coffee is served in the attractive lobby. Doubles, $88. Open mid-May to mid-October.

Hinckley's Dreamwood Motor Court, Route 3, RD 1, Box 1180, Bar Harbor 04609, (207) 288-3510. Cabins in a grove of high pines, some with screened porches and fireplaces, and a heated keyhole-shaped pool make this an appealing place. Three two-bedroom, twelve efficiency and eight motel units all have TVs and wall-to-wall carpeting. Two four-bedroom units are available for large families. Doubles, $50 to $60. Open mid-May to mid-October.

Atlantic Oakes By-the-Sea, Route 3, Bar Harbor 04609, (207) 288-5801 or (800) 336-2463. Right beside the ferry terminal on the estate that belonged to Sir Harry Oakes is this good-looking 153-unit motel, which includes 43 oceanview units in a new four-story addition. We're partial to the older, low-slung units right beside Frenchman Bay, their balconies or patios enjoying privacy as well as peace and quiet. The ten-acre complex has an indoor and a heated outdoor pool, five tennis courts, a pebbly beach and a pier where you can rent boats. Doubles, $110 to $143. Open year-round.

Holiday Inn/Bar Harbor Regency, 123 Eden St., Bar Harbor 04609, (207) 288-9723 or (800) 234-6835. What's this luxury building doing in little old Bar Harbor? Providing all the creature comforts of a resort hotel, that's what. Erected in 1986 by Ocean Properties of Florida, its four floors contain 180 rooms, all rather sophisticated for Down East Maine (there's even a glass-enclosed elevator from which to view Frenchman Bay). A 60-room Fairfield Inn by Marriott was rising in 1992 to complete the Ocean Properties project, and the owner also had taken over the motel across the street and rechristened it the Days Inn. The Regency grounds include lighted tennis courts, a jogging path, a small pool and a jacuzzi. The **Edenfield** dining room, which has windows onto the ocean, specializes in seafood, with entrees from $12.95 to $21. The new **Stewman's Lobster Pound** beside the marina features a New England clambake. Doubles, $119 to $149. Open mid-May to mid-October.

Kimball Terrace Inn, Huntington Road, Northeast Harbor 04662, (207) 276-3383. This modern, three-story motel contains 72 rooms, 50 with balconies looking across a small pool to the busy marina and harbor across the way. The rest offer what euphemistically are called "forest views." Our large room was notable for a separate vanity area and a private balcony, which helped compensate for towels that were as thin as the walls and floors between the units. Off to one side are a cocktail lounge and the **Main Sail Restaurant** serving three meals a day in three dining rooms. Doubles, $95 to $104. Open year-round.

Inns and Resorts

Bar Harbor Inn, Newport Drive, Box 7, Bar Harbor 04609, (207) 288-3351 or (800) 248-3351. Right in town and right on the water by the town pier, this seven-acre compound is a particularly attractive place in which to stay. It has 54 spacious rooms in the main inn and 64 more in a deluxe oceanfront lodge that opened in 1988 on the site of the inn's former waterside motel, part of whose modest facility was moved uphill. Wicker sedan chairs and flourishing impatiens in ceramic pots greet guests at the pillared entrance. In the elegant, semi-circular **Reading Room** restaurant, you can order dinners from $14.95 for grilled chicken or broiled haddock to $19.95 for filet mignon or rack of lamb. Lunch and drinks are served at the colorful **Gatsby's Terrace** beside

Lawn chairs at The Claremont face Somes Sound.

the pier. A lounge offers entertainment and a pool overlooks the harbor. Doubles, $95 to $215. Lodge open year-round.

Asticou Inn, Route 3, Northeast Harbor 04662, (207) 276-3344. A wonderful old resort hotel popular with those who prefer to be away from the hustle and bustle of Bar Harbor is the Asticou, which dates to 1883 but is kept thoroughly up to date and elegant. Cheerful, pleasant common rooms with oriental rugs and wingback chairs welcome guests, some of whom seem to have been coming here for extended stays for the last fifty years. They stay in the inn's 50 simple rooms or in seventeen outlying rooms in Cranberry Lodge, guest houses or the circular Topsider cottages. The setting high above the harbor is exceptional with well-tended gardens and a swimming pool. The lounge, deck and dining room offer spectacular views. Dinners for the public are $30 prix-fixe (jackets required), and the Thursday night buffet dinner with dancing afterward is an island tradition. Doubles, $195 to $228, MAP. Open April-December.

The Claremont, Clark Point Road, Box 136, Southwest Harbor 04679, (207) 244-5036. A landmark for more than a century, the Claremont is the island's oldest hotel and is on the National Register of Historic Places. The gracious dining room, in which every table has a view of Somes Sound, is highly recommended by locals. Guests can have cocktails at the boathouse, on the porch or beside the fireplace. There are 24 rooms in the yellow wooden main house, all with private baths, plus twelve housekeeping cottages (for longer stays) with fireplaces and two guest houses. Doubles, $110 to $170, MAP; cottages, $142 to $163, EP. The hotel is open from mid-June to mid-September; cottages, mid-May to mid-October.

B&Bs

The Inn at Canoe Point, Route 3, Box 216, Hulls Cove 04644, (207) 288-9511. Innkeeper Don Johnson, a Midwesterner who first opened the Lindenwood and then the Inn at Southwest, both in Southwest Harbor, reached the apex with this smart five-room B&B in an English Tudor-style house set back from the road right beside Frenchman Bay. All rooms have private baths, good views and are decorated in exquisite taste. Guests partake of a full breakfast in the waterfront Ocean Room; they also luxuriate in front of the fireplace in the living room or outside on what has to be the nicest waterside deck on the island. Doubles, $105 to $195. Open year-round.

Breakwater 1904, 45 Hancock St., Bar Harbor 04609, (207) 288-2313 or (800) 238-6309. Taped classical music plays inside this impressive 1904 English Tudor mansion, grandly reborn from dereliction in 1992 on four acres beside Frenchman Bay.

Guests enjoy two elegant parlors, a second-floor sitting room with a rooftop deck beside, six fireplaced guest rooms with private baths, a library-game room with a billiards table, and a long piazza furnished in chintz and wicker, facing the Shore Path and Bald Porcupine Island out in Frenchman Bay. Innkeepers Margot and Russell Snyder serve breakfast at a table big enough for twenty in the formal dining room. They might offer pear and raspberry cobbler with an almond crust before a main dish of eggs benedict, cranberry-walnut buttermilk pancakes, cheese and cranberry crepes or apple french toast. Afternoon tea is taken by the fireplace beneath a large portrait of owners Tom and Bonnie Sawyer of Bangor, who decorated their newest inn as a showcase for Drexel-Heritage furniture and Country Inns magazine. Doubles, $175 to $295. Open May-December.

Nannau-Seaside Bed & Breakfast, Lower Main Street, Box 710, Bar Harbor 04609, (207) 288-5575. Value-conscious travelers and families like this unassuming 1904 mansion on four wooded acres a mile south of town. Listed on the National Register, the sprawling house harbors three guest rooms with sitting areas and queensize beds, down comforters and feather pillows. Original William Morris-designed wallpapers and fabrics decorate most rooms. Guests may use two enormous parlors and a great side porch. Outside are Adirondack chairs and a croquet court, and a trail leads to a small sand beach at Compass Harbor. Owners Ron and Vikki Evers serve lavish breakfasts in the formal dining room. Doubles, $75 to $115. Open May-October.

White Columns, 57 Mount Desert St., Bar Harbor 04609, (207) 288-5398 or (800) 321-6379. Bar Harbor's "guest house row" acquired yet another in 1987 when a Christian Science church was converted into as contemporary a Victorian B&B as you could find. The ten spacious guest rooms have modern baths, queensize beds and cable TVs; three on the second floor come with private balconies. Wine and cheese are served in the fireplaced parlor, where a buffet breakfast including a huge bowl of fresh fruit compote is put out in the morning. Owner Anne Geel's former mother-in-law runs the well-established Thornhedge Inn, with 24 more rooms nearby. Doubles, $70 to $105. Open year-round.

The Moorings, Shore Road, Southwest Harbor 04679, (207) 244-5523 or 244-3210. Calling itself the "Little Norway of America," the Moorings claims perhaps the island's most dazzling location at the entrance to Somes Sound in Manset, not far from Southwest Harbor. It's a delightful small, down-home, off-the-beaten-path inn with ten rooms, all named for sailing ships built in Maine, plus three rooms in a waterside motel and six units in three white cottages and a garden apartment. Some of the upstairs inn rooms have new waterfront balconies. The fireplace glows on cool summer mornings in the inn's living room, which has a color TV and lots of books and magazines. The coffee pot is on all day in the adjacent office, where complimentary orange juice and donuts are served every morning. We called our room the Agatha Christie, as several of her paperbacks were on the bureau; a nice touch was a candle in a china holder beside the bed. Towels are large and fluffy and the beds have colorful patterned sheets. Owners Betty and Leslie King provide charcoal for the grills beside the shore, a spectacular place to cook your steak or seafood dinner, and you can rent canoes, rowboats and sailboats, and borrow clamming equipment. The beach is stony; the water cold but swimmable. We're obviously fond of the Moorings — it's most unpretentious and the prices are, too. Doubles, $55 to $75; cottages, $70 to $90. Open year-round.

The Kingsleigh Inn, 100 Main St., Southwest Harbor 04679, (207) 244-5302. A wraparound porch full of wicker and colorful pillows embellishes this B&B with glimpses of water in the distance. Inside are winning common rooms and eight guest rooms with private baths. Queensize beds, Waverly wall coverings and fabrics, and

There's nothing like eating lobster with a view such as this from Hancock Point.

country accents lend character to each room. Check the view from the telescope placed between two wicker chairs in the Turret Suite. Innkeepers Nancy and Tom Cervelli serve hearty breakfasts by candlelight in an elegant breakfast room and offer tea and lemonade in the afternoons. Doubles, $85 to $95; suite, $155. Open year-round.

Island Watch, Freeman Ridge Road, Box 1359, Southwest Harbor 04679, (207) 244-7229. Floor-to-ceiling windows and a couple of spacious decks take full advantage of the panoramic view of islands and water at this contemporary ranch house atop a high ridge east of town. Maxine Clark rents six homey guest rooms (one a single) with private baths, plus an efficiency suite in a separate building. Guests enjoy TV and stereo in the spacious living/dining room, where a full breakfast is served in the morning. Doubles, $65; efficiency, $75.

Where to Eat

Lobster Pounds

When you think of Maine, you think of lobsters, and the prices are reasonable, as low as $7.95 for a lobster supper at our last visit.

The cheapest lobsters are at the tiny shacks lining Route 3 from Ellsworth. Large signs tell what the going price is, and most have picnic tables where you can dig in. Considered the best is **Trenton Bridge Lobster Pound,** a rustic, family-owned affair with dining inside and out beside the Narrows between Frenchman and Western bays. Lobster, usually $5.50 a pound or less, is served here daily from 8 to 8, May to mid-October.

A particularly scenic setting, one where we head on the first night of most trips to Bar Harbor, is **Fisherman's Landing,** on the pier just off West Street at the foot of Main. You place your order in a shack, find a picnic table on the wharf, under a pavilion or on an upstairs deck, get a beer or a carafe of wine from the adjacent bar and wait for the most succulent lobster ever to be boiled ($6.25 a pound, last we knew). The french fries are terrific, and you can get hamburgers, lobster and crab rolls, and other items as well. It's cool and quiet beside the water, and you may get to watch the brilliantly lighted Bluenose ferry glide by about 9:15.

Things are more rustic at **Beal's Lobster Pier** beside the Coast Guard Station on Clark Point Road in Southwest Harbor. You can eat on the pier at picnic tables, and lobsters, mussels and steamers are sold inside by the pound. Lobsters are about $5.95 a pound boiled, but boiling ends between 6:30 and 7:30. At the casual **Captain's Galley** out front, they had plenty of dessert pastries but were strangely out of most flavors of ice cream the last time we were there.

Oak Point Lobster Pound, just off the island on Route 230 in Trenton, enjoys a spectacular view of Mount Desert Island across Western Bay. Some think it offers the best lobster in Maine; a shore dinner last we knew was $18.95. The stews and chowders are renowned, as are the blueberry and chocolate mousse pies. It's open nightly from 5 in summer, and has a full liquor license. Another off-island setting that is positively idyllic is the remote **Tidal Falls Lobster Pound** in nearby Hancock. Picnic tables are spaced well apart beneath the trees on lawns beside the rapids, which reverse directions with the tides. Order a la carte, everything from coleslaw to lobster ($5.75) to a Harbor Bar, and BYOB. It's open daily in season from 11 to 8.

Other Choices

Bar Harbor isn't all lobster, nor are all the restaurants in Bar Harbor.

George's, 7 Stevens Lane, Bar Harbor, (207) 288-4505. This is a bit hard to find in a Southern-style house behind the First National Bank, but it offers some of the island's more imaginative food. Local history teacher George Demas has parlayed his original Greek theme into a glamorous restaurant with an ambitious menu. Eighteen entrees from seafood strudel, scallops and cashews, shrimp with black beans and paella to honey-rum duck breast with mango, loin veal chop and George's Greek-style spaghetti are priced from $14.95 to $21.50. They come with hot crusty French bread and the best little Greek salads ever. A special shrimp with feta cheese, served with crisp snow peas, was superb. White organdy curtains flutter in the breeze in several dining rooms; Greek or classical music plays on tapes, and a pianist entertains after dinner in the lounge. A bone-dry Retsina wine goes perfectly with the food and you can finish with Greek coffee. No one at our visit could resist the fresh blueberry and peach meringue — out of this world. Dinner nightly in summer, 5:30 to midnight. Open mid-June through October.

The Porcupine Grill, 123 Cottage St., Bar Harbor, (207) 288-3884. The name comes from the nearby Porcupine Islands, and owner Terry Marinke's local antiques business provided the furnishings for this trendy new grill. Downstairs is crowded and cafe-like; the small upstairs rooms are fancier and quieter. Start with the signature caesar salad topped with garlic-fried clams ($7.95), a local goat cheese and green onion tart served warm with grapes and blueberry compote, or smoked salmon and caviar with lemon-corn madeleines and fennel cream. Among entrees ($14.50 to $17.95), we liked the sauteed shrimp and peas in a garlic cream sauce over fresh egg noodles and the grilled chicken with ginger-peach chutney. Panfried halibut kiev with cold marinated vegetables and grilled salmon with orzo on a bed of sauteed spinach are other possibilities. Finish with the sublime peach ice cream and ginger shortbread if they're on the docket. Dinner nightly from 5:30; winter, Friday-Sunday from 6.

The Fin Back, 78 West St., Bar Harbor, (207) 288-4193. Pink and white material billows beneath the peaked ceiling of this intimate little restaurant, pretty in pink and green. It's a summery setting for chef-owner Terry Preble's changing menu, which runs from $14.50 for chicken with tarragon-pecan pesto to $17.95 for lamb with curry sauce and blueberry chutney. Among the great pastas are wild mushroom ravioli, seafood pernod and lobster in coral sauce with asparagus and tangy peppercorns. Start with crabmeat quesadillas or the Finback pizzelle (two tortillas brushed with pesto, reggiano cheese and sundried tomatoes). Finish with roasted nut tart with caramel sauce, creme brulee or homemade sorbet. Dinner nightly, 5 to 11. Open late May to late October.

Carrying Place Restaurant, 130 Cottage St., Bar Harbor, (207) 288-8905. This favorite of ours moved in 1992 from a side street in Ellsworth to a grand old 1882 house in a busier location in Bar Harbor. The interesting menu survived the move, producing dishes like lobster with curried cream sauce in puff pastry ($15.95) and key lime pie. There are a variety of pastas ($9.95 to $13.95) and entrees ($11.95 to $16.95), things like grilled shrimp scampi with linguini, pork with peanut sauce, beef wellington and sweetbreads with grapes and a wine-lemon sauce. The blond tables and chairs and chef/owner Mardie Junkins's fine paintings came from Ellsworth; walls in the three dining rooms are painted a ripe pear color with a strawberry border, and the curtains are lace. Upstairs, Mardie and husband Wally Higgins were readying for opening in 1993 a small B&B consisting of three large bedrooms with decks in back, queensize Shaker beds and Shaker armoires, wicker settees and chairs in sitting areas, TVs, phones and full baths. They serve some of their brunch dishes for breakfast — perhaps crepes with raspberry sauce, homemade granola or popovers. Doubles, $95. Dinner nightly from 5 in season, fewer nights rest of year; lunch hours vary; Sunday brunch except in summer.

Maggie's Classic Scales Restaurant, 6 Summer St., Bar Harbor, (207) 288-9007. Dine on the enclosed front porch overlooking flower gardens or inside at about eight tables on "notably fresh seafood," as owner Maggie O'Connor's menu puts it. We liked the spicy cheese and chiles in phyllo topped with tomato salsa as a prelude to an excellent broiled haddock in ginger sauce and Boston blue scrod encrusted with honey-dijon mayonnaise. Good salads with interesting dressings and a $12 Australian chardonnay accompanied. Prices start at $9 and top off at $18 for lobster crepes or Maine cioppino over pasta. Dinner nightly, 5 to 10:30. Open early June-December.

Quiet Earth Restaurant, 122 Cottage St., Bar Harbor, (207) 288-3696. The old Sunflour Bakery and Tearoom gave way in 1992 to Bobbie Lynn Hutchins's new venture. A noted vegetarian chef, she hastens to explain that Quiet Earth is *not* a vegetarian restaurant, although no red meat is served and smoking is not allowed. Seafood is a specialty, as in a seafood strudel incorporating scallops, crab, fish and mushrooms in an herbed wine sauce. The cajun barbecue chicken, in a sauce with fifteen ingredients, is immensely popular among entrees priced from $10.95 to $14.95. Start with smoked bluefish pate or crab bisque, and end with the house favorite, German chocolate square with coffee ice cream. Two dining rooms have a mixed decor, from funky 50s tile on the floor in one to dark burgundy booths made by the owner's brother in the other. There's a beer and wine license, and mellow live music on Friday and Saturday nights. Dinner nightly from 6, May-October; Wednesday-Sunday, rest of year.

124 Cottage Street, 124 Cottage St., Bar Harbor, (207) 288-4383. "Downeast fare, creatively prepared" is the theme of this restaurant, one of Bar Harbor's most popular and seemingly always jammed. The crowded scene and the 50-item gourmet salad bar attract many; you'll likely wait for seats in the rear courtyard or the enclosed front porch, even on weeknights. The extensive, something-for-everyone menu ($11.95 to $18.95) specializes in seafood (including bouillabaisse and four versions of shrimp), pastas and house favorites like Bombay chicken and New York sirloin. Dinner nightly, 5 to 11.

Brick Oven Restaurant, 21 Cottage St., Bar Harbor, (207) 288-3708. Families like this atmospheric place that fancied itself as a turn-of-the-century museum until it burned down in 1986. Jovial owner Freddie Pooler rebuilt it in five months, this time inside a church he moved from East Vassalboro. Today it's outfitted with everything from gasoline pumps and a 1954 jukebox to neon signs and Lionel trains. The place is a feast for the eyes as well as the stomach. The oversize menu, priced from $9.95 to $16.95, contains eight variations of lobster and a range from deep-fried clams to steak diane. The excellent tossed salads contain everything from peas and sprouts to raisins and apples, the fresh haddock flavored with herbs was one of the better fish dishes we've had and the baked sole wrapped around crabmeat in newburg sauce proved too rich to finish. We couldn't even imagine trying any of the ice cream concoctions or a wedge of pie. Dinner nightly, 5 to 10.

Jordan Pond House, Park Loop Road, Acadia National Park, (207) 276-3316. Rebuilt in 1981 following a disastrous fire, the new restaurant is strikingly contemporary, with cathedral ceilings and huge windows. The incomparable setting remains the same, with lawns sloping down to Jordan Pond. The menu is fairly standard; lobster, seafood, chicken and steak are priced from $12.50 to $18 at night. For lunch on the porch, the seafood pasta and curried chicken salad are fine. Don't try to fill up on the popover — it's huge, but hollow! Afternoon tea with popovers on the lawn remains a tradition ($5). Lunch, 11:30 to 5; tea, 2:30 to 5:30; dinner 5:30 to 9. Open mid-June to mid-October.

The Burning Tree, Route 3, Otter Creek, (207) 288-9331. This summery place is one of our island favorites, off the beaten path between Bar Harbor and Northeast Harbor. Those in the know beat a path to the screened front porch and two interior dining rooms for what the young chef-owners call gourmet seafood with organic produce and a vegetarian sideline. Our party of four enjoyed a delicious vegetarian sushi, grilled scallops and chilled mussels with mustard sauce for starters. Then we delved into grilled monkfish with tomato coulis, a spicy cioppino, grilled trout with basil and fennel, and cajun lobster and shrimp au gratin. The vegetable accompaniments were outstanding, as were the desserts, among them fresh strawberry pie and nectarine mousse cake. The good little wine list harbored a Chilean sauvignon blanc for $11. Dinner nightly, 5 to 10. Open mid-June to mid-October.

Redfield's, Main Street, Northeast Harbor, (207) 276-5283. Just what the locals ordered was provided in 1992 by Maureen and Scott Redfield. Their new commissary and restaurant, located next to his father's Redfield Artisans showroom and beneath their Village View Inn B&B, would be quite at home in the Hamptons or on Nantucket, although the prices and lack of pretensions are refreshingly Down East. The decor is simple yet sophisticated, the tiny lamps hanging from long cords over most tables illuminating some large and summery impressionist-type paintings and making the two small adjoining rooms rather too bright. We staved off hunger with Maureen's fabulous French bread, exquisite house salads and a shared appetizer of venison carpaccio as we nursed the house La Veille Ferme wine. Lemon sorbet in a lotus dish preceded the entrees ($11.95 to $15.95). Our sliced breast of duck with fresh chutney and the marinated loin of lamb with goat cheese and black olives were superb. Chocolate-almond mint tart and strawberry sorbet were worthy endings to a memorable meal. The next day we returned for a look at the breakfast and lunch fare, perfect for mix-and-match picnics of distinction. Open daily except Monday, 8:30 a.m. to 9 or 10 p.m.

Drydock Cafe & Inn, 108 Main St., Southwest Harbor, (207) 244-3886. The Drydock has expanded and upgraded its decor and prices since we first visited. Lighter fare is served in the Captain's Lounge on one side; Mexican dishes like vegetarian quesadilla and super tostada salad are popular here. At lunch, try one of the burgers served on bulky rolls — the Maine comes with cheddar and bacon — with chips and salad. For dinner you might start with tomato-basil soup and go on to baked stuffed scallops ($14.95). More than 30 entrees, from $8.95 for spaghetti marinara to $16.95

for steak topped with artichoke hearts and bearnaise sauce, include many chicken, seafood and pasta dishes. The five lobster dishes are market-priced. There's a liquor license, and upstairs are two guest rooms and five units with kitchenettes, all with private baths and TV. Lunch, 11:30 to 3:30; dinner, 5 to 10. Shorter hours in off-season.

Seafood Ketch, On the Harbor, Bass Harbor, (207) 244-7463. The favorite of many locals on this side of the island, this is an authentic, family-style Down East shanty gone upscale and run very personably by Ed and Eileen Branch. Nothing on the mostly seafood menu is over $14.95 and everything is homemade, including the loaf of good crusty French bread that precedes dinner. We liked the baked halibut with lobster sauce and the night's special of halibut imperial over rice, accompanied by crisp vegetables and excellent garden salads. Don't miss the specialty baked lobster-seafood casserole, or Ed's secret mocha pie with toasted almonds. Dining is by candlelight at white-linened tables in the rear room beside the water, each decorated with a bottle of wine. An outdoor deck is popular unless it's buggy. Open daily from 7 a.m. to 9:30 p.m., May-November.

The Deck House Restaurant and Cabaret Theater, Ferry Road, Bass Harbor, (207) 244-5044. On a hill overlooking Bass Harbor, just past the Swans Island Ferry, this is something of a local institution, marking its eighteenth season in 1993. Dinner starts at 6:30 and at 8:15, the wait staff become players and perform barbershop, show tunes and monologs in the round. Seafood fettuccine, crabmeat au gratin, filet mignon and the like are priced in the $16.50 range. Dinner shows nightly in season.

Maine-ly Delights, Ferry Road, Bass Harbor. From a van that dispensed hot dogs and crabmeat rolls, Karen Holmes Godbout has expanded over the years to the point where she now has a roof over her head, a room with an open kitchen and an outdoor deck. This is an authentic place, where a hot dog costs only $1.25 and a lobster roll, $6.50. Karen's fryolator is famous for her original O-Boy Doughboys, and she still picks the blueberries that go into her muffins and pies. Even with a beer and wine license, she stresses, "I am quaint, not fancy, Down East all the way." Open daily, 8 a.m. to 9 p.m.

Back in Bar Harbor are several other good bets: The **Parkside** at 2 Mount Desert St. has outdoor dining under a lattice-work canopy facing the Village Green. Watch the world go by at breakfast, lunch and dinner. Dinner entrees ($10.95 to $17.95) range from Haitian crab cake and blackened catfish to bouillabaisse and tournedos au poivre.

Miguel's at 15 Rodick St. serves Mexican food at lunch and dinner at reasonable prices. Try Mayan soup, or avocado or fajita salad. Dinners range from $5.95 for a burrito to $12.95 for shrimp fajita; the menu includes the usual suspects plus surprises like Maine crab cakes with crispy blue corn coating and roasted red pepper sauce.

The **Poor Boy's Gourmet** at 1 Stanwood Place is a small house with dining inside and out along lower Main Street. The food is great and the prices right (many lobster dishes for $12.95, eight pastas for $8.95 and wines for $10.95). The house favorite is shrimp and scallop alfredo, and the apricot chicken is out of this world.

A good place for breakfast is the **Cottage Street Bakery & Deli,** 59 Cottage St., where you can feast on wild blueberry pancakes for $2.25 or any number of omelets for $3.50. The luscious baked goods include a frosting-crossed blueberry megamuffin. Sandwiches are in the $4.25 range, the baked beans are cooked in a real bean pot, and fresh breads can be dunked into cheese fondue. Wine and beer are available. Open daily 6:30 a.m. to 10 p.m.

Other Things to Do

On the Water. The possibilities are endless, ranging from a Bluenose ferry trip to Canada for a long day at the slot machines, to a sunset dinner cruise to the Cranberry

Islands. Sightseeing boat tours and deep-sea fishing expeditions leave from Bar Harbor, Northeast Harbor, Southwest Harbor and Bass Harbor; the mailboat rides out to the Cranberry Islands from Bass Harbor are cheaper. Lobster fishing and whale-watch expeditions are popular. The **Acadian Whale Watcher** on West Street, Bar Harbor, which charges adults $25 and children $15 to $18 for a cruise of about four hours, posts a sign with the previous day's count — four whales and hundreds of dolphins when we were there. Northeast Whale Watch's **Whale and Seabird Cruise** is a serious all-day affair, going 25 miles off-shore to Mount Desert Rock from Northeast Harbor for $30.

Under park auspices, naturalist sea cruises leave daily at 9:45 a.m. and 12:45 p.m. from Northeast Harbor for excursions of nearly three hours through Somes Sound and the Cranberry Isles to Little Cranberry Island with a stop at the village of Islesford (adults $8, children $6). The Sea Princess also offers a two-hour Somes Sound naturalist cruise and a three-hour sunset lobster dinner cruise. Naturalists also narrate a 4.5-hour cruise from Northeast Harbor to Baker Island, where you hike with a park ranger (adults $13, children $8), and a two-hour nature cruise from Bar Harbor through Frenchman Bay ($12.75 and $8.75).

Walk the Bar. For two hours on either side of low tide, you can walk across the water on a sand bar from Bar Harbor to Bar Island, where there are trails and shoreline to explore and the clear water is considerably warmer than at Sand Beach. Bring a bathing suit (change in the woods) and a picnic, but don't stay too long or you'll have to swim back across the current. The bar surfaces at the foot of High Street. If the tide's in, settle for a walk along the quarter-mile-long **Shore Path** from the Town Pier to Hancock Street, passing shorefront mansions from the Golden Age.

Climb to the Flowers. It's a ten-minute hike up a steep but well-maintained switchback trail to **Asticou Terrace and Thuya Gardens** off Route 3 in Northeast Harbor. The hardy are rewarded with a spectacular hilltop spread of annuals, plus hardy laurel and rhododendron that you don't expect to see so far north. Other attractions are a gazebo, a free-form freshwater pond, a shelter with pillowed seats and deck chairs in the shade — just as you'd find in the gardens of a private estate, which this once was. A plaque relates that landscape architect Joseph H. Curtis left this "for the quiet recreation of the people of this town and their summer guests." Free.

Walk amid Azaleas. A showy seasonal treat is **Asticou Azalea Gardens,** at the junction of Routes 3 and 198 in Northeast Harbor. Various species were moved from the former Rief Point gardens of Beatrix Farrand in Bar Harbor, while new varieties are added each year in this showplace funded by John D. Rockefeller. Around a free-form pond are azaleas and rhododendrons at their remarkable best in June, a Sand Garden with an arrangement of sand and stones as in Kyoto, Japanese-style evergreens and bonsai. There are gravel paths raked into lovely patterns to walk and stone benches for contemplation in this, one of the most perfect gardens we've seen. Free.

Rent a Horse, Moped, Bike or Boat. The 50 miles of old Rockefeller carriage roads in the park are perfect for horseback riding and biking. Wildwood Stables, near Jordan Pond, offers guided horseback trips and wagon rides. In Bar Harbor, mountain bikes and mopeds are available for rent at Wheels of Bar Harbor, Bar Harbor Bicycle Shop and Acadia Bike & Canoe. Canoes and kayaks are available at the last, as well as at National Park Canoe Rental at Pond's End in Somesville. You can rent sail and power boats at Harbor Boat Rentals in Bar Harbor and Manset.

Music and Theater. The **Acadia Repertory Theatre** celebrated its twentieth summer season in 1992 at the Masonic Hall, Route 102, Somesville, (244-7260). Five plays are presented in two-week cycles each Tuesday-Sunday at 8:15 and Sunday at 2; tickets are $8 to $12. Also on Monday and Thursday nights at 8, the **Bar Harbor Town Band**

Famed lighthouse hugs shore at Bass Rocks.

gives old-fashioned band concerts on the Village Green. The **Arcady Music Festival** sponsors guest artists in seven concerts Monday evenings at Mount Desert High School. For 27 seasons, the **Bar Harbor Festival** has presented a month of classical and pops concerts ranging from piano recitals and brass quintets at the Congregational Church to a tea concert at the new Breakwater 1904 B&B, a string orchestra concert at the Blackwoods campground amphitheater and a pops concert finale at Kebo Valley Golf Club. Celebrating its 30th season in 1993, the **Mount Desert Festival of Chamber Music** offers concerts on five Tuesday nights in Northeast Harbor.

Museums. Housed in a solar-heated building, the **Wendell Gilley Museum** in Southwest Harbor shows more than 200 of the late local woodcarver's birds and decoys ranging in size from a two-inch woodcock to a life-size bald eagle, daily films on natural history and special exhibitions. Admission $3. Closed Mondays.

Everything you want to know about lobsters and other sea life is available at the **Mount Desert Oceanarium,** now at three locations on the island. The original is in Southwest Harbor, where there are twenty tanks, exhibits on tides, sea water and weather and a commercial fishing room. Harbor seals, Maine lobsters and a marsh walk are featured at the new Oceanarium site along Route 3 near the entrance to the island. In the Lobster Room you can touch a lobster and talk with a lobsterman. Nearly 10,000 tiny lobsters as small as your fingernail are on display in the Oceanarium's Lobster Hatchery, beside the municipal pier in Bar Harbor. Admission at the two larger Oceanarium sites is $4.75 for adults, $3.50 for children; the Bar Harbor hatchery is $3 and $2. Each open Monday-Saturday 9 to 5.

The **Bar Harbor Whale Museum** was opened by three local businessmen in 1992 in a former restaurant facility at 52 West St. A 22-foot minke whale skeleton is on display at the entry. There are three live tank displays, lifesize models of seals and sea birds, a twenty-seat theater with a film on New England's humpback whale, and a history of whaling at tour's end. Several prints and ship's models were on loan from the Penobscot Marine Museum in Searsport to flesh out the first year's exhibits. Open daily, 9 a.m. to 10 p.m. Adults $3, under 12 free.

Shopping

Bar Harbor shops range from traditional to tacky. Many are crafts shops, which are apt to change from year to year. First on our agenda in any town is a look at the latest local guides in the bookstores; **Sherman's** at 56 Main St. (also in Northeast Harbor) has books, maps, nautical charts, records and stationery. It has competition from the new **Port in a Storm Bookstore** in Somesville, a two-story treasure converted from a general store. Two cats and a pair of binoculars occupy a reading area in back beside the water. The upstairs looks like a mezzanine gallery with works of local artists, huge windows onto Somes Sound and illuminated display shelves around an atrium.

Don't miss **Island Artisans** at 99 Main St. It's a co-op, owned by the artists who are represented in the handsome shop by their quilts, pillows and napkins done in hand-screened prints, lamps, stained and blown glass, weavings and much more. **Caleb's Sunrise** is another Main Street shop selling pottery, leather goods, wooden items, jewelry, glass and china. We coveted the handcrafts selected by a Bar Harbor potter at **A Potter's Choice**, 75 Main St. The **Acadia Shops** at 85 Main St. (and at locations in the park) feature gifts, crafts and foods of Maine. The elegant grocery store, **J.H. Butterfield Co.**, has been on Main Street forever with a fine supply of gourmet foods, chocolates, picnic items and luscious fruits, plus a good selection of wines and beers. More Main Street shops include **Cool as a Moose,** with zillions of T-shirts and bathing suits; the **Driven Woman** for clothes and cards; **Bowl and Board** for cedar planters and birdhouses, and **The Blue Heron** for darling children's clothes and gifts. **The Dancing Deer** on Mount Desert Street sells cards, Salt Marsh Pottery and all kinds of miniatures. Nearby are the **Birdsnest Gallery** and **Nestegg Handcraft Gallery.**

Northeast Harbor has one of our favorite gift shops, the fine **Kimball Shop** on Main Street, with room after room full of pretty china, furniture, Cuisinart supplies and everything else that's "in." Its **Boutique** a couple of doors down the street offers zippy summer clothing. **Beal's Classics,** an offshoot of the fine Beal's clothing and gift store in Ellsworth, stocks very nice gifts and pottery, Godiva chocolates and lots of lobstery things. **Provisions** offers good meats and produce as well as a bakery and deli. **Mrs. Pervear's Shop** is a pleasant hodgepodge of painted furniture, handknit sweaters and toys. Cute T-shirts and baby things are shown at **Main Street Mercantile,** jewelry and quilts at **Fourteen Carrots,** and all kinds of lacy and flowery things at **The Romantic Room.** George Redfield's remarkable wooden sculptures of birds are displayed at **G.E. Redfield Artisans,** while Wini Smart's evocative paintings of Maine are shown at **Smart Studio and Art Gallery.**

In Southwest Harbor, **By Way of Maine** features products made in Maine, including lobster and crab earrings and a moose hatrack. Great sweaters and skirts are for sale at **Common Threads.** The window is filled with beach toys and bathing suits at **Treasure Island,** a good store for children. **Mayan Designs** imports hand-crafted jewelry from Thailand, Greece and Mexico, among other countries. Check out the handknit sweaters at **Wicker & Wool** and the Japanese-style garden in front of the expanded **A. Jones Gallery.** Hungry or need a rest from shopping? Stop at **Mrs. McVety's Ice Cream and Sandwich Shop,** where school teacher Judy McVety in summer offers heath bar and cappuccino frozen yogurt, many flavors of ice cream and good sandwiches. Another place for a quick pick-me-up is **Giffords,** where a BLT is $2.75, and desserts include fresh bread pudding and strawberry sundaes.

FOR MORE INFORMATION: Bar Harbor Chamber of Commerce, Box 158, Bar Harbor 04609, (207) 288-5103 or (800) 288-5103. Two good information centers are on Route 3 at the entrance to the island and at the Bluenose Ferry Terminal.

Kinsman Range is on view from breakfast table outside Bungay Jar B&B.

North of the Notch

Franconia-Bethlehem, N.H.

Franconia Notch. Perhaps no name other than Mount Washington better conjures up the essence of the Granite State. Here, receding glaciers from the Ice Age cut an eight-mile-long swath between the Franconia and Kinsman mountain ranges. Their legacy of beauty and adventure has stirred visitors for two centuries.

The Flume, the Old Man of the Mountains, the Basin, Echo Lake, the Cannon Mountain aerial tramway — these are the best-known attractions of New Hampshire's best-known notch, which would be called a gap or a pass in other mountain regions. They make up Franconia Notch State Park, ranked among the nation's best parks in 1992 by Money magazine.

Many tourists give the notch short shrift, pausing only to tour the Flume and get a distant look at the Old Man's profile etched in granite. Then they turn around and head back to join the hordes at Lake Winnipesaukee or North Conway.

Too bad. For beyond the notch is a different world, one of spectacular vistas, few people and fewer signs of contemporary civilization. This is the world epitomized by the words of poet Robert Frost: "Two roads diverged in a wood, and I — I took the one less traveled by, and that has made all the difference."

Frost and other literary notables were drawn by the serenity of Franconia, so named because of its resemblance to the Franconia Alps in Germany. Grand summer hotels proliferated across the hillsides of Franconia and neighboring Sugar Hill in the 19th century. The nation's first ski school was established at Peckett's-on-Sugar Hill in 1929, and soon skiers were riding the nation's first aerial tramway lift to the top of Cannon.

Beyond Franconia and Sugar Hill lies Bethlehem, which claims to be the highest incorporated town east of the Rockies, though we know others that seem higher. Bethlehem occupies a mountain ridge 1,500 feet above sea level. Thousands of hay fever sufferers came here for its pollen-free air in the 1900s; by the turn of the century the early resort village boasted four railroad stations and 30 hotels. Today it is billed as the nation's smallest town with two PGA-rated golf courses. Its low-key lifestyle has made it a favorite summering place for Hassidic Jews from the New York metropolitan area.

Gone today are the large hotels, and the crowds and the condos stop at the south side of Franconia Notch, leaving Franconia, Sugar Hill, Bethlehem and even the "city" of Littleton for those who appreciate them as vestiges of the past.

Mountain scenery, rural and village life, peaceful inns, hiking and other outdoors activities — these are the attributes that draw folks north of the notch. So venture beyond. If you relish tranquility, you'll be glad you did.

Getting There

The area is reached by I-93, which cuts through Franconia Notch via the Franconia Notch Parkway, one of two interstate parkways in the country.

Daily bus service to Littleton and Franconia is provided by Concord Trailways from Concord, Manchester and Boston. Vermont Transit provides bus service via St. Johnsbury.

Seeing and Doing

Arguably the most celebrated mountain gap in the East, Franconia Notch contains more scenic spots than any other in New Hampshire or Vermont.

Franconia Notch State Park

These 6,440 acres, the flagship of New Hampshire's state park system, are traversed by the magnificent **Franconia Notch Parkway,** a federal parkway that opened in 1988 to link completed portions of I-93 on either side of the notch. The two-lane parkway

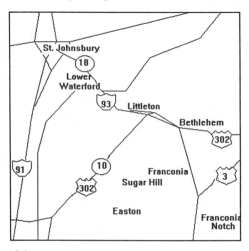

allows no stopping or left turns, and parking only in designated areas, but it gives through visitors a brief glimpse of the treasures that lie on either side. Newly posted moose crossing signs warned of 195 collisions at our visit.

Start at the **Flume Visitor Center,** a $3.2 million complex at the south entrance to the park. Here you'll see a free fifteen-minute orientation movie that gives worthwhile background on the notch, which you learn was 400 million years in the making. "Remember, when you see it today, it will never be quite the same again," the narrator intones. The visitor center contains historical displays, a cafeteria, a gift shop and, in front, a trout pond where fish leap for bread crumbs thrown by youngsters. Picnic groves are scattered around the center, as they are throughout the park. We picked some blackberries for dessert along the path from the parking lot to a picnic table not far from the car.

The Flume. When in Europe, see the cathedrals; when in Franconia, visit the Flume. A bus shuttles visitors to within 1,500 feet of a natural gorge extending nearly 800 feet along the flank of Mount Liberty. Granite walls rise 60 to 90 feet high. A boardwalk lets you look closely at the luxurious growth of flowers, mosses and ferns. A two-mile gravel nature walk displays waterfalls, glacial boulders, mountain vistas and two covered bridges. Open daily, 9 to 4:30, mid-May through late October. Adults $6, children $3; combination ticket with Cannon aerial tramway, $11 and $5.

The Basin is a granite pothole twenty feet across at the foot of a waterfall. Its sides have been smoothed by sand and small stones whirled around by the Pemigewasset River. Below the Basin is a rock formation called the Old Man's Foot.

The Old Man of the Mountains, also called The Profile and The Great Stone Face, hovers 1,200 feet above Profile Lake. Yes, they look like an old man, these five granite ledges arranged horizontally to form a human profile and keeping vigil southward through the notch. The profile measures 40 feet from chin to forehead and is 25 feet wide. Though you can make out the profile for several seconds as you drive along the parkway, it is best viewed from parking areas on either side. Of course, no one is allowed near the Old Man but for its longtime caretaker. Directly below the Old Man and nicknamed the Old Man's Washbowl is **Profile Lake,** the headwaters of the Pemigewasset River and a favorite of fly fishermen.

The **Cannon Mountain Aerial Tramway** gives 80 passengers at a time a six-minute ride 2,022 feet up Cannon, a legend among skiers. The state-of-the-art tram replaces the nation's first, a smaller model born in 1938 and retired in 1979. The tram operator points out **Artists' Bluff** and the adjacent **Indian Head** that looks like the face on an old nickel, as well as such salient sights as **Mount Lafayette,** the highest peak (5,249 feet) in the Franconia range, which is second in height only to the Presidential Range. At the 4,160-foot summit are a cafeteria of the ski lodge variety and the well-maintained Rim Trail. The quarter-mile trail leads through spruce trees and along a ledge with a sheer drop to an observation platform yielding panoramic views in all directions. New in 1992 were **summit barbecues,** served on summer Saturdays from 4:30 to 7 p.m. (adults $6, children $4). Tram runs every fifteen minutes, 9 to 4:30 daily, Memorial Day through October, til 7:30 Saturdays in summer. Adults $8, children $4.

Echo Lake, a sand and spruce-ringed beauty at the foot of Cannon Mountain, offers swimming, fishing and boating. There's a fine beach, plus grassy areas for picnicking. Canoes, kayaks, paddleboats and rowboats are rented for $6 an hour at the beach. Beach rates, $2.50; under 12 free.

Lafayette Place, just west of the parkway in the center of the park, is the camping and hiking hub of the notch. A new lodge serves as a hiking information center, offering advice and guides to miles of hiking trails. The **Lafayette Campground** provides 97 wooded tent sites.

Hiking. Park officials recommend four hikes in particular for families and novices. A 1.5-mile loop from Cannon's Peabody Base Lodge goes to **Artists Bluff,** where artists used to set their easels to paint the notch, and on to the open summit of **Bald Mountain,** a great place to watch the sunset. Another 2.5-mile round trip rises from Lafayette Place to **Lonesome Lake,** an undeveloped alpine lake some 1,000 feet above. There, a lakeside trail leads to the Appalachian Mountain Club's hut at the lake's far end and passes an active beaver lodge. The 2,557-foot summit of **Mount Pemigewasset (Indian**

Head) can be reached via a 1.4-mile trail from the Flume Visitor Center or the Indian Head Trail, which starts one mile south off Route 3. The views from the summit, both to the north and south, are awesome. The easiest and an often overlooked hike is a half-mile walk along the Basin-Cascades Trail beside Cascade Brook from the Basin to **Kinsman Falls.** The brook's basins and ledges make for a pleasant half-hour diversion.

Bicycle Path. One of the little-known treasures of the park is a paved, nine-mile bikeway running from the Flume Visitor Center north to the Skookumchuk trailhead. The bikeway is reasonably level, which makes it popular with walkers as well. A concession at the Cannon Mountain parking lot rents mountain bikes for $7 an hour, $25 a day.

Other Options

New England Ski Museum, next to the tram station at Cannon Mountain, Franconia, (603) 823-7177. Some of America's earliest skiers were introduced to the sport at nearby Peckett's-on-Sugar-Hill and at Cannon, so it is fitting that this small museum of historic ski equipment, clothing and photography occupies a lodge at Cannon's base. Founded in 1982, it marked its tenth anniversary in 1992 with "A Ski Museum Sampler," including "some of the more obscure aspects of collections not often exhibited." Obscure much of it was, but even non-skiers were impressed by the wall of old and rare skis built around the turn of the century and the antiquated ski boots that resemble the hiking boots of today. Of special interest were one of the chairs from the original single chairlift at Stowe and the old red car from the Mount Cranmore Skimobile, both of which we've ridden in our earlier skiing days. A ten-minute slide show traces the history of New England skiing. Open daily except Wednesday, noon to 5. Free.

The Frost Place, Ridge Road off Route 116, Franconia, (603) 823-5510. The rooms where Robert Frost wrote many of his best-loved poems and the sights that inspired him are on view in the farmhouse in which he lived from 1915 to 1920 and in which he summered through 1938. The house remains essentially unchanged from the 1920s. Each summer a different visiting poet occupies most of it, writing new poems as Frost did and giving poetry readings in the old timbered barn. The front room and a rear barn are open with displays of Frost memorabilia, including his handwritten "Stopping by Woods on a Snowy Evening" and a rare, large photo of Frost at age 40 working at his desk in the room. Out back, plaques along a half-mile nature trail bear Frost's poems appropriate to the site; in two cases, the poems are on the locations where he wrote them. As if the poetry and setting weren't awesome enough, the stand of woods happens to contain every variety of wildflower indigenous to Northern New England. Open July through Columbus Day, daily except Tuesday 1 to 5; Memorial Day through June, weekends 1 to 5. Adults, $3.

Sugar Hill Historical Museum, Sugar Hill, (603) 823-8142. Established by proud descendants of Sugar Hill founders, this small place displays an excellent collection in a modern, uncluttered setting. It gives a feel for the uncommon history of a unique hilltop town, named for the sugar maples that still produce sap for syrup. The life of the community is chronicled in photographs and artifacts. The Cobleigh Room recreates a stagecoach tavern kitchen from nearby Lisbon. The Carriage Barn contains a working blacksmith's shop as well as mountain wagons and horse-drawn sleighs, including one from the Butternut estate that used to belong to actress Bette Davis. Open July through mid-October, Thursday, Saturday and Sunday 1 to 4. Adults, $1.

The Rocks Estate, Glessner Road off Route 302, Bethlehem, (603) 444-6228. Boulders left by Ice Age glaciers yielded stone walls and rolling fields on this 2,000-acre

Maplewood Casino & Country Club is major presence in Bethlehem.

property west of town, donated in 1978 by the grandchildren of Chicago industrialist John Glessner, who summered here. Working woodlands, self-guided trails and a variety of entertainment and educational events can be enjoyed. This is one of more than 60 properties run by the Society for the Protection of New Hampshire Forests, which was organized to save Franconia Notch from runaway commercialism. Now a working Christmas tree, timber and maple syrup farm, it offers a one-mile woodland trail through fields and forests to an overlook onto Beaver Pond. A loop trail goes past Beaver Pond, and the return loop trail passes the Glessner children's playhouse and a bee house. Strollers and hikers give way to cross-country skiers in winter. Open daily, dawn to dusk.

Golf. Picturesque Bethlehem, astride a ridge at 1,500 feet above sea level, is the center of the area's golfing activity. The town is the smallest in New Hampshire to have two eighteen-hole courses, and the smallest in the country with two PGA-rated courses. The golf cart is the town's most popular summertime vehicle, locals say. The major presence is **Maplewood Casino & Country Club,** site of a grand hotel that burned (like most of the others around here) in 1963. The clubhouse occupies the hotel's activity building and casino, nicely restored in 1988. Basic golf-club lunches are served at the lounge, inside and out. The ball returns of what once was the bowling alley are still prominent in the long, narrow pro shop. Less of a presence than the Maplewood, but also eighteen holes, is the town-owned **Bethlehem Country Club** layout. Near the Maplewood along Route 302 is a roadside haven that locals call the **Caddy Shrine,** erected by former Maplewood caddies and dedicated "to the traveler along this way." The Chase Tennis Camp is headquartered along Main Street in the old Maplehurst Hotel.

Another summertime presence in Bethlehem are Hasidic Jews, who are much in evidence at a couple of old hotels in the center of town and in motels on the west side. Mainly from metropolitan New York and New Jersey, they come and go in large cars throughout July and August, rest on the lawns and walk along Main Street in their distinctive (and quite unsummery) attire. Otherwise Bethlehem, whose name was changed from Lloyd Hills on Christmas Day in 1779, has an interfaith Bethlehem Christian Center, a Catholic church, a Methodist church, an Episcopal chapel and a small Hebrew Congregation synagogue not used by the Hassidic visitors.

Shopping

For many, the most intriguing shopping emporium hereabouts is the **Sugar Hill Sampler,** Route 117, Sugar Hill. The large dairy barn, with nooks and crannies full of New England items for souvenir shoppers, is literally a working museum of Sugar Hill history. Owner Barbara Serafini Parker is the sixth-generation descendant of one of Sugar Hill's founders and delights in sharing her thoughts and possessions, even posting handwritten descriptions on the beams. Amid all the memorabilia is an interesting selection of quaint and unusual merchandise, from New Hampshire foods to Christmas decorations. Nearby in Sugar Hill is **Harman's Cheese and Country Store,** a tiny place selling "the world's greatest cheddar cheese" retail and through a large mail-order business. You'll also find pure maple syrup, great preserves, wildflower honey and tinned smoked salmon. In Franconia, the **Garnet Hill** catalog store displays fine bedclothes (English flannel sheets, comforters and the like), as well as pricey children's clothing, all in natural fibers, although you cannot buy anything here. The **Gale River Outlet** is an outlet for pretty cotton clothes (and stocks some of the things offered in the Garnet Hill catalog). Frogs in many guises are prominent amid the country gifts at the **Green Frog.** Friendly bears, collectibles and crafts are featured at **The Country Pineapple.** We liked the local handcrafts displayed by volunteers at **Noah's Ark,** a shop run by the Church of Christ.

Antiquing is the main shopping attraction in Bethlehem, which calls itself **Antiques Alley North.** At least six shops are scattered along Main Street. Surrounding one unnamed house in the center of town was such a mishmash of junk, both inside and out, that only the intrepid would venture in. We know a couple who did and turned up some prizes amid someone else's trash.

Littleton's Main Street has developed into an interesting shopping area, from the expanded **Village Bookstore** to the new **North Country Outfitters,** where store personnel give climbing lessons on a two-story "climbing wall" open to a rooftop skylight. **New Magoon's** is where you can find gourmet foods from Thai coconut milk to poppadums. Somewhat less esoteric fare is available at the **Garden of Eden,** which offers organic produce and ecologically correct paper goods. **Duck Soup** is a good gift and kitchen shop, purveying everything from Christmas ornaments to coffee grinders. In the same Parker's Marketplace building is **The Elephant's Trunk** for clothing. You can try on funky clothing and look at antiques at **All That Jazz.** Stop at the highly touted **Bishop's Ice Cream Shoppe,** 78 Cottage St., for homemade carrot cake ice cream (one scoop, $1.10), a banana split or a "Chill Out" T-shirt.

Where to Stay

Accommodation range from rustic cabins to luxury lodges. Most of those detailed here fall into two categories: places preferred by couples and those that cater to families.

Sophisticated Inns and B&Bs

Rabbit Hill Inn, Lower Waterford, Vt. 05848, (802) 748-5168 or (800) 762-8669. Just across the Connecticut River from Littleton, this very special inn is worth the trip

Back lawn of Adair slopes down to swimming pool with gazebo.

from Franconia or Bethlehem — indeed, from anywhere. Guest diaries in each of the nineteen rooms are long on praise: "The inn of everyone's dreams." "Your love for this inn is reflected in every detail." "An opportunity to drink in a way of life that is relaxing, enveloping and most romantic." "I feel as if I've had 24 hours of heaven." And so on. The tributes please innkeepers John and Maureen Magee, who lavish TLC on their rooms and their guests. Consider our latest stay in Victoria's Chamber, where a fire was laid (this in August), Victorian magazines filled the shelves of the nightstands beside the canopied bed, and there were a settee for lounging, a bathroom full of amenities and a wicker-filled balcony just outside. Downstairs, iced tea, lemonade and cookies were available in the parlor, and drinks were served with conviviality in the expanded Snooty Fox pub. Upon our return from dinner (see Where to Eat), a small stuffed heart had been hung on the door to use as a "do not disturb" sign and was ours to take home, the bed had been turned down, the radio was playing soft music, the lights were off and a candle was aglow, and more candles in hurricane lamps beckoned from the balcony. And the handwritten letter of welcome from Maureen, personally tailored to every guest, thanked *us* for staying with them. Breakfast the next morning was up to the rest of the experience: a buffet of juices, breads and muffins, granola and hot strawberry oatmeal in a chafing dish, followed by a choice of wonderful banana-stuffed french toast, blueberry pancakes or quiche lorraine with potatoes and mixed vegetables. Then we toddled off to see The Loft, the inn's newest room with fireplace and double jacuzzi — a companion to the Nest and the Tavern's Secret in the Magees' testaments to the ultimate in luxury. Doubles, $149 to $199, MAP; deluxe suites, $219, MAP. No smoking.

Adair, off Route 302, Box 850, Bethlehem 03574, (603) 444-2600. A hilltop mansion on a 200-acre estate was converted in 1992 into a country inn of great charm. Hardy Banfield, a former Portland (Me.) contractor, and his wife Patricia offer eight large bedrooms (all with private baths) in the house built in 1929 as a wedding gift for Dorothy Hogan Guider, who occupied it until her death in 1991. The Banfields named their rooms after nearby mountains, which is fitting considering their fabulous setting. Rooms are tastefully decorated and comfortable, particularly the Waterford in which we stayed. Public areas include a spacious living room with several sitting areas, a large sun porch beyond, a dining room big enough to hold two huge oval tables, a library on the stairway landing and a remarkable, all-stone (from walls to ceiling) basement recreation room with TV-VCR. The rear yard, landscaped by Frederick Law Olmsted, slopes down to a tennis court and a swimming pool with a gazebo. The Banfields serve an elegant breakfast, starting with fresh berries, granola and popovers and wrapping up perhaps with eggs florentine or french toast. A personal welcoming note, iced tea and cookies, Woods & Windsor toiletries, automatic closet lights and tins of Les Citrons candies are other treats. Doubles, $125 to $145; suite, $175.

The Bells, Strawberry Hill Street, Bethlehem 03574, (603) 869-2647. Bethlehem's biggest promoter is recent transplant Louise Sims, who runs this stalwart B&B with her commuting husband Bill. She and a friend researched and wrote "An Illustrated Tour of Bethlehem, Past & Present," and her drawings grace the 32-page booklet publish-ed in 1992. The much-photographed B&B is named for the eight galvanized tin bells hanging from the outside corners and **e 80 smaller carved wood bells lining the eaves of an 1892 showcase of Victorian ingenuity. A picturesque cupola tops the pagoda-style roofs. Prolific gardens, a wraparound veran-da, a small parlor, another sitting room and an enclosed porch await guests. Colorful door stops line each step of the staircase leading to the second floor and three suites  with sitting rooms, television sets and private baths. There are antiques galore and oriental rugs everywhere, as this is a showplace for the couple's assorted collections. The third-floor cupola suite, with a bathroom on the attic landing below, is clad totally in white, with windows onto the mountains on four sides. There's just enough room for a queensize bed, two armchairs and a TV. A cottage at the side includes an enclosed sitting porch. Breakfasts are bountiful, perhaps cheese souffle with scones or oatmeal pancakes with peach sauce. Doubles, $65 to $90.

Bungay Jar Bed & Breakfast, Easton Valley Road, Franconia 03580, (603) 823-7775. The mountains of the Kinsman Range loom behind this exceptional B&B, hidden on eight wooded acres and named for the legendary wind that funnels from Mount Kinsman through the Easton Valley. Innkeeper Kate Kerivan and her lawyer-husband, Lee Strimbeck, built their house from a four-level, 18th-century barn that was dis-mantled and moved to the site in 1967. The hayloft became a two-story living room holding many sitting areas, a reading corner and a fireplace. Each of three floors contains two guest rooms — the higher you go, the more remarkable the room and the more stunning the vista. The four on the top two floors have private baths, while two on the main floor share. Top of the line may be the Stargazer Suite, with a telescope aimed on the Kinsman Range. It has a kingsize bed beneath four skylights, an antique gas fireplace, a clawfoot tub under antique leaded-glass windows, a toilet behind a cloister table, and a twig loveseat and armchairs. Kate, a landscape architect, is responsible for the interesting gardens on view from the barn's various outside bal-conies. She's also quite a cook, offering breakfasts with popovers and perhaps zucchini quiche or french toast with melted ice cream. Doubles, $60 to $95. No smoking.

Sugar Hill Inn, Route 117, Franconia 03580, (603) 823-5621 or (800) 548-4748. Built as a farmhouse in 1789, this old white inn has a wonderful wraparound porch sporting colorfully padded white wicker furniture and a telescope for viewing Cannon Mountain. Innkeepers Barbara and Jim Quinn have redecorated the ten inn rooms, all with private baths and full of country charm. They also have updated the six cottage units in back, each with new baths and new front porches, stenciling, plush carpeting and television sets. Guests enjoy two living rooms in the inn and a cozy pub with a small service bar and a TV set. Dinner, which had been served only to house guests at a single seating in a country-pretty dining room, was opened to the public in 1992, $25 prix-fixe for five courses and $20 for what chef-owner Jim Quinn called "light fare." The menu allows four choices among entrees, perhaps poached salmon with dill sauce, baked stuffed shrimp, beef wellington, and chicken breast stuffed with crabmeat and topped with hollandaise. Jim's breakfasts are treats as well. We started with orange juice laced with strawberries, followed by blueberry muffins. Then came a choice of cinnamon french toast or swiss and cheddar cheese omelet, both excellent. Doubles, $135 to $150, MAP. Closed April and mid-November through Christmas. No smoking.

Lovett's Inn By Lafayette Brook, Profile Road, Franconia 03580, (603) 823-7761 or (800) 356-3802. Twenty scenic acres and Cannon Mountain are the backdrop for this venerable inn, which dates to 1794 and is listed in the National Register of Historic Places. New innkeepers Tony and Sharon Avrutine are maintaining the reputation built over 70 years by the Lovett family as they upgrade the facilities and decor. The main house holds a candlelit dining room (see Where to Eat), a lounge decked out with Civil War posters, a living room and a sunken sun porch with TV. Upstairs are nine renovated guest rooms with canopy beds and antiques. Sharon thinks the nicest is a two-room suite with kingsize bed and a sitting room. We're partial to the sixteen cottages in duplex chalets scattered beside the pool and around the lawns. Nine have fireplaces and each offers a small patio with chairs for gazing upon Cannon Mountain. All come with sitting areas and small television sets. The carriage house has a recreation room as well as six guest rooms with shared baths ($50 per person, MAP), good for budget-minded groups. A full breakfast is served in the morning. Doubles, $110 to $138, MAP. Closed April to Memorial Day and mid-October to Christmas.

The Gables of Park and Main, Park and Main Streets, Bethlehem 03574, (603) 869-3111. One of the grandest houses in town, an 1893 Victorian beauty, was converted into a five-room B&B in 1992. Barbara Ferringo, owner of Rosa Flamingo's restaurant, shares innkeeping duties here with Marcie Hornick. Beautiful woodwork graces the two sitting rooms, one with stereo and TV-VCR, and the fireplaced dining room where guests are treated to what Marcie calls "a hiker's breakfast," from fresh fruit to eggs with meat and potatoes. Guests pass a gorgeous stained-glass window on the landing on their way to four queensize rooms on the second floor (sharing one bath at our visit, but all supposed to get private baths for 1993). The third-floor suite's peaked windows show why the house is called the Gables. We like the Pool Room in the rear, with a private porch overlooking the swimming pool. Guests help themselves to port, sherry and a fruit bowl in the grand foyer. Doubles, $65; suite, $80.

The Beal House Inn, 247 West Main St., Littleton 03561, (603) 444-2661. Guests take breakfast on vintage blue willow china at a long table beside a blazing fireplace in the cheery breakfast room at this B&B reopened in 1991 by Catherine and Jean-Marie Fisher-Motheu. The fare includes a buffet of fruit, cheese, cereals and homemade baked goods, all of which are mere preliminaries to belgian waffles, made fresh daily by Jean-Marie, a native of Brussels. The local artworks and crafts here — as well as in the cozy parlor, the glassed-in front porch furnished in wicker, up the various staircases and in the guest rooms — are for sale as the innkeepers seek to support local artisans. Candies are on the pillows in the thirteen guest rooms, nine of which have private baths. Rooms vary in size and are furnished in Victorian style with antiques, charming accents and family heirlooms. They feature canopy and four-poster beds and goose down comforters. Photos of Jean-Marie's parents, who Catherine says are "old Brussels," line the stairway. Besides a cozy parlor, a second-floor game room offers television, board games (the pieces on the chess set are some of the biggest we've seen) and a collection of battery-operated toys from a generation ago. A new focal point is the carriage house, transformed in 1992 into a small restaurant serving highly acclaimed dinners to the public nightly (see Where to Eat). Doubles, $45 to $85. No smoking.

Family Resorts and Motels

Franconia Inn, Easton Road, Franconia 03580, (603) 823-5542 or (800) 473-5299. Situated amid 107 acres in the Easton valley with Cannon Mountain as a backdrop, this rambling white structure looks the way you think a country inn should look. It is the area's largest and busiest, and offers a variety of activities geared to active people. Brothers Alec and Richard Morris have upgraded the 35 rooms since acquiring the inn in 1980. Rooms vary in size and beds; some connect to become family suites, and all have private baths. Corner rooms are best in terms of size and view. The main floor has an attractive dining room where dinners are served to guests and the public (entrees, $14.95 to $21.95), a living room and oak-paneled library with fireplaces, a pool room, and a screened porch with wicker furniture overlooking a large swimming pool. Downstairs is the spacious **Rathskeller Lounge** with entertainment at night, an arcade room with pinball machines and, beyond, a hot tub in a large redwood room. Outside are four tennis courts and a glider/biplane facility. Horses offer trail rides in season; in winter, the barn turns into a cross-country ski center. Doubles, B&B, $78 to $98; suites, $113; MAP, $133 to $153; suites, $168. Closed April to Memorial Day.

The Mulburn Inn, Main Street, Bethlehem 03574, (603) 869-3389. Families are welcomed at this 1930 Tudor mansion, which once was part of the Woolworth family's summer retreat. It has been revived by two sisters, their husbands and nine children between them, who occupy the third floor and turn the rest of the very large house over to guests. The rambling second floor harbors seven guest rooms with private baths. Rooms on either end have windows on three sides and queen or king beds. The house retains its original oak staircases, stained-glass windows, rounded-corner architecture and an old elevator. The main floor contains a large, homey parlor and a gift shop for which the mother of one of the innkeepers makes many of the crafts. A huge glassed-in dining room, surrounded by porches, is big enough to feed an army. An enormous old stove at one end faces a stone fireplace at the other. In between are tables where guests are served a hearty breakfast. Outside are three acres of lawns, giving plenty of space to spread out. Doubles, $60 to $90.

Wayside Inn, Route 302 at Pierce Bridge, Box 480, Bethlehem 03574, (603) 869-3364 or (800) 448-9557. This is a homey inn of the old school, nicely located alongside the banks of the Ammonoosuc River. Sixteen rooms in the rambling main building, eight with private bath, contain period furniture and hardwood floors and trim. We're partial to the newer motel out back, its twelve units on two floors each having sliding doors onto private balconies beside the river. Decor is standard motel, although one second-floor end unit departs with a queensize bed, a sofabed and a Laura Ashley look that owner Kathe Hofmann likens to that of a city condo. The main inn also houses the **Riverview Restaurant** (see Where to Eat), a Victorian parlor, a second parlor with games and TV, plus a large lounge with TV. Outside are a swimming hole, a sandy beach, tennis court, and volleyball and basketball facilities. Doubles, $48 to $54.

Ledgeland Inn and Cottages, Route 117, RR 1, Box 94, Sugar Hill 03585, (603) 823-5341. Here's the kind of place that folks return to year after year, thanks to the extended family of Kay Whipple, proprietor for 45 years. "Everybody calls me 'Nana,'" says she. "I don't let young people call me Kay til they're 45." There are nine rooms with private baths in the main inn, originally a summer house that grew and grew. Scattered across the rolling landscape with views of Cannon Mountain are several cottages, most attached units with a maximum of four to a building. Eight are cottages for two, while five have two bedrooms each, a kitchen and a fireplace. A complimentary continental breakfast of homemade sticky buns, breads and such is offered buffet-style in the large dining room. Doubles, $62 to $100.

The Red Coach Inn, Wallace Hill Road, Box 729, Franconia 03580, (603) 823-7422 or (800) 262-2493. New in 1989 was this motor inn just above I-93, offering the most modern (and expensive) motel facilities in the area. The rooms on two floors contain kingsize or two double beds, some with poster headboards and TVs hidden in armoires. Facilities include a large indoor pool, jacuzzi and sauna. The **Coachmen Grille** serves three meals daily. Doubles, $70 to $80; suites, $100.

Hillwinds Lodge, Route 18, Franconia 03580, (603) 823-5551. This oldtimer beside the Gale River is being gradually upgraded since its takeover in 1991 by the owners of the Franconia Inn. But it still represents good value — all rooms, upgraded or not, are $39 year-round, and children stay and eat free. The 30 units are in two buildings, one with a river view and the other looking onto the pool area. Rooms are small, but each contains two double beds. Charbroiled steaks, prime rib, shish kabobs, seafood and barbequed spare ribs in the $8.95 to $12.95 range are featured in the lodge's riverside restaurant. Doubles, $39.

Eastgate Motor Inn, Cottage Street (Route 302), Littleton 03561, (603) 444-3971. Up a hill not far off I-93 is this brick motel complex that started in the 1950s and grew to 50 units. Don't be deceived by the tiny windows beside the entrances from the parking lot; the rooms we saw opened to the rear with oversize windows and sliding doors onto pretty grounds. The large and elegant white-linened dining rooms offer an extensive menu, priced from $6.95 for fish and chips to $13.95 for shrimp dijonnaise. The pool and playground as well as the on-site restaurant make this a good choice for families. Doubles, $43.70.

Where to Eat

Tim-Bir Alley, 28 Main St., Littleton, (603) 444-6142. Down a side alley is this little prize, which takes its name from owners Tim and Biruta Carr. Seven tables, plus a few stools at the counter, seat two dozen people for some of the area's most inventive fare. Glass covers the antique lace tablecloths, walls are hung with posters and macrame, and classical music plays at night. The dinner menu changes weekly. You might start with cream of mushroom-sherry soup with brie, lamb sausage with spiced pecans and sweet pepper relish or sauteed shrimp on corn pancakes with avocado-tomato salsa. Every one of the six entrees ($13.50 to $16.50) at our latest visit appealed. Who could resist a shrimp and scallop ragout with artichoke hearts on puff pastry, hoisin-soy chicken with mango chutney or tournedos on grilled eggplant with homemade barbecue sauce? Follow such assertive fare with a plum-walnut tart with whipped maple cream or chocolate-coconut bread pudding with roasted banana sauce. Dinner, Wednesday-Sunday 5:30 to 9:30; Sunday brunch, 10 to 1.

Rabbit Hill Inn, Lower Waterford, Vt., (802) 748-5168. The pad of butter that accompanies the piping hot bread here is shaped like a rabbit. It's one of the trademark details that make dining at the Rabbit Hill Inn an event. The $27 prix-fixe menu brings five courses from soup to nuts. At our latest visit, a smooth pork and venison pate and

a zesty smoked salt cod with buckwheat polenta preceded a traditional caesar salad and an unusual layered taco salad. Kiwi sorbet with champagne cleared the palate for our main courses, marinated duck breast with raspberry sauce and grilled tenderloin on an eggplant-walnut pancake, each with exotic garnishes. Blueberry cheesecake and bread pudding with raspberry sauce capped a memorable meal. A classical guitarist  played, service was polished and the ambience serene. You don't expect such style in the North Country, but that's what you get here. Dinner by reservation, nightly 6 to 9. No smoking.

Beal House Inn, 247 West Main St., Littleton, (603) 444-2661. You'd never know that new innkeeper Jean-Marie Fisher-Motheu was parking his car in what had been a carriage house only a few months before it became his "jazzy little restaurant" in 1992. The transformation is remarkable, what with rich blue and speckled beige wall coverings and a couple of ledges bearing musical instruments. Jean-Marie, former maitre-d'hotel at Boston's Locke-Ober, teamed with chef Frederick Tilton for this winner. The changing menu lists four entrees, priced from $11.95 for roasted duck with raspberry sauce to $16.95 for noisettes of lamb topped with toasted pinenuts. You might start with cold poached salmon served with homemade grapefruit mayonnaise or spinach fettuccine with a saute of shrimp. Finish with white chocolate mousse terrine, mandarin orange-kiwi crepes or maple-bourbon souffle glace. The serious wine list goes up to $200 and more. Dinner Wednesday-Sunday, 6 to 10. No smoking.

Lovett's Inn By Lafayette Brook, Profile Road, Franconia, (603) 823-7761. The traditional Lovett's offerings continue to please a coterie of regulars as well as newcomers. Before dinner, guests usually gather around the curved marble bar (obtained from a Newport mansion) in the renovated lounge for socializing. Then they adjourn to any of three beamed-ceilinged dining rooms for four-course table d'hote dinners priced at $20. A plate of pates and cocktail spreads with crackers or the chilled wild White Mountain blueberry soup make good starters. Salad and assorted relishes accompany. Entrees might be curried lamb with Lovett's grape chutney, panfried trout, blackened red snapper with creole sauce, veal marengo and shepherd's pie. Desserts are extravagant, from hot Indian pudding with ice cream to meringue glace with strawberries. We remember fondly the chocolatey Aspen crud, a fixture on the menu, from more than two decades ago. There's a choice but select wine list, and a new children's menu. Dinner nightly by reservation, 6 to 8.

Polly's Pancake Parlor, Hildex Maple Sugar Farm, Route 117, Sugar Hill, (603) 823-5575. Only in a "true" place like Sugar Hill would a pancake house be the restaurant of note. Folks pour in at all hours from all over to partake of pancakes and local color at this institution founded in 1938. Bare tables sport red mats shaped like maple leaves. Red kitchen chairs and sheet music pasted to the ceiling add color to this 1820 building, once a carriage shed. Its most appealing feature is big louvred windows with a view of Mount Lafayette and the Franconia Range. Watch the pancakes being made in the open kitchen; the batter is poured from a contraption that ensures they measure exactly three inches. Pancakes are served with maple syrup, granulated maple sugar and maple spread; an order of six costs $4.20 for plain pancakes made with white flour, buckwheat, whole wheat or cornmeal. All are available with blueberries, walnuts or coconut for $5.40. If you don't really crave pancakes in the middle of the day, try the homemade soups, quiche of the day (our ham and cheddar melted in the mouth) or a super-good BLT made with cob-smoked bacon. Eggs, muffins made with pancake batter, baked beans sweetened with syrup, salads and sandwiches are available. The homemade pies are outstanding. The coffee, made with spring water, is excellent and a glass of the spring water really hits the spot (no liquor is served). The shop on the way to the dining room sells pancake packs, maple syrup and sugar, jams and even the maple-leaf painted plates. Open daily late April to late October, Monday-Friday 7 to 3, weekends 7 to 7.

The Hilltop Inn, Main Street, Sugar Hill, (603) 823-5695. Local caterers Mike and Meri Hern serve dinner to the public as well as guests in their Victorian B&B. In season, an outdoor deck supplements the spacious dining room with its wood stove and six linened tables seating 24. Meri's limited menu usually includes a couple of starters (shrimp cocktail and cream of fiddlehead and asparagus soup) and four entrees in the $14.95 range. Pork tenderloin medallions, filet of salmon, paella and roast duck were offered at our latest visit. Desserts are to groan over, perhaps hazelnut liqueur spice cake or fresh blackberry-cinnamon crisp. Dinner by reservation, Wednesday-Saturday 6 to 8.

Lloyd Hills Country Dining, Main Street, Bethlehem, (603) 869-2141. Borrowing the original name of the town, Bill and Dianna Green have created a rustic restaurant and bar that's highly regarded locally. "We're known for our specials," says Bill, pointing to a scrapbook full of literally hundreds of variations on a theme. There are twenty kinds of eggs benedict, for instance, and a couple of pages devoted to potato skins. "We try to keep it fun," explains Bill. That they do, from breakfast through dinner. Skillet specials topped with two eggs are favored in the morning. At night, try the shrimp New Orleans, pork chops calvados, chicken chasseur, beef brochette from the printed menu, or perhaps the seafood riviera special (shrimp, scallops and crab in garlic cream sauce over linguini). Breakfast and lunch, Tuesday-Friday 11 to 2, weekends 8 to 2; dinner nightly except Monday, 5 to 9.

Riverview Restaurant, Route 302, Bethlehem, (603) 869-3364. The place to eat here is on the enclosed porch opening off the dining room onto lovely gardens beside the Ammonoosuc River. Tables covered with red and white checked cloths and oil lamps are the setting for chef-owner Victor Hofmann's American and Swiss fare. His extensive menu mixes shrimp and scallops California (with vermouth and green grapes), chicken oriental, lamb forestiere, wiener schnitzel and pork Victor, the chef's favorite, doused with wild mushrooms. Entrees start at $7.75 for chicken garnished with white asparagus tips and most are under $13. Dinner nightly except Monday, 6 to 9.

Rosa Flamingo's, Main Street, Bethlehem, (603) 869-3111. This is not the Mexican eatery that one of us expected, but rather an Italian-American restaurant in a contemporary gray wood building with dining on the main floor, a bar below and a wraparound deck. The menu is large and varied to attract families and the younger set. We can vouch for the tortellini carbonara (a house specialty) and the chicken with garlic and artichoke hearts, both $8.95 and both of which lived up to their advance billing. The rest of the menu ranges from $5.75 for manicotti to $16.95 for steak and scampi. Pizzas, nachos and sandwiches are among the possibilities. Lunch daily, 11:30 to 3; dinner, 5 to 11:30.

FOR MORE INFORMATION: Chamber of Commerce, Franconia 03580, (603) 823-5661 or (800) 237-9007.

Mystic Seaport Photo

Sailing vessels and historic structures draw visitors to Mystic Seaport.

A Whale of a Family Weekend

Southeast Connecticut: Mystic to Misquamicut

Looking for a place to keep the youngsters amused and expand your own horizons? Perhaps a place that Grandma and Grandpa or visiting Aunt Tillie from Peoria would enjoy as well?

This area is for you — the perfect summer spot for the young and young at heart, with enough diversions to keep the entire family amused all weekend or longer.

This is New England-by-the-sea. It's a place for beaching and boating, but also a place for rediscovering and reliving our early seafaring days. From the mid-1600s to the battles of the Revolution, from the whaling and shipbuilding eras to the early submarines and nuclear Tridents, this is maritime country with all its trappings.

Nowhere else in this country are so many varieties of maritime interests evident. Many are wrapped up in one appealing package at Mystic Seaport, the nation's premier maritime museum and long one of the area's leading tourist attractions. But it's not the only attraction.

To the west is Groton, "Submarine Capital of the World." The huge U.S. Naval Submarine Base keeps alive a tradition dating from before the Revolution, when the colonies launched the first naval expeditions here. Beneath old Fort Griswold, site of the bloody Revolutionary massacre where the traitor Benedict Arnold did Groton in, the Electric Boat Division of General Dynamics became famous as builder of the nation's nuclear subs.

History fairly oozes from the cracks in the bustling facade of New London, the area's largest city. The U.S. Coast Guard Academy takes full advantage of its site along the Thames River — pronounced locally "Thames," not "Tems," despite the city founders' ties with old London.

An attraction for those of a different persuasion in rural Ledyard is the Foxwoods High Stakes Bingo and Casino, opened in 1992 by the Mashantucket Pequot Indian tribe and so successful that slot machines were being added in 1993. Sometimes, fathers like to spend a few hours here, leaving the rest of their families time to explore.

East of Mystic along the shore, the pace is considerably quieter and the signs of tourism, if any, are different.

Twentieth-century life has almost passed by the coastal "borough" of Stonington, an old fishing village with Connecticut's last commercial fleet. It's still living a history that helps put Mystic Seaport into perspective.

Across the Rhode Island line, Long Island Sound opens into the Atlantic at Watch Hill, a fabled seaside society resort of the Newport-Bar Harbor ilk. Just beyond are the beaches at Misquamicut, where surf and sand are everything. This is a mecca for sun-worshipers and kids, young and old.

The whole maritime strip from New London to Weekapaug is no more than 30 miles long, but there's plenty to appeal to every taste and age.

Any child would love to board ships and submarines, ride a steamboat or a carousel, walk a boardwalk or play in the surf, explore a lighthouse museum, visit nature centers and homes dating back to the Pilgrims, see whales and seals, and even wander through a recreated 18th-century shopping village.

Most adults would, too.

See the seaport, submarines and shore. Bet you didn't know there was so much to Southern New England's maritime heritage.

Getting There

The area is easily accessible by a variety of transportation modes, more so than many New England tourist areas. Interstate 95 from New York to Boston cuts through the region a few miles inland and coastal Route 1 hugs the shore.

Train service is excellent, with frequent Amtrak runs from New York and Boston stopping at Mystic, New London and Westerly, R.I. Greyhound buses stop at all three towns as well. US Air and charter airlines serve the busy Groton-New London Airport.

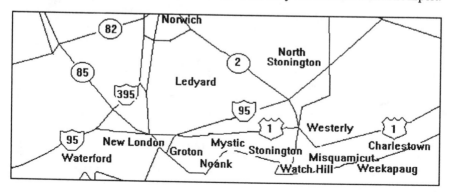

In the summer, a trolley links Mystic's tourist attractions with motels and businesses; price per boarding, adults $2 and children $1, all-day pass $6 and $2.

Seeing and Doing

The focal point for most tourists is Mystic, so that's where we'll start — with the caveat that some of the area's best features are in the twin cities of Groton-New London and in the shore towns toward the Rhode Island beaches.

Mystic

Mystic's ties with the water are epitomized by its unusual bascule bridge. Where else would busy Main Street traffic stop every hour as a 70-year-old drawbridge lifts for waiting yachts and sailboats on the Mystic River?

A diorama at the seaport shows how Mystic looked in the mid-1800s when it built more ships than any other town in America. The gleaming white homes of 18th- and 19th-century sailing captains still line the river shore across from Mystic Seaport.

Mystic Seaport, Route 27, Mystic, (203) 572-0711. Plan on at least half a day to see this seventeen-acre riverfront complex of ships and sailing memorabilia in a restored 19th-century coastal village. The old Greenman family shipyard, which launched nearly 100 vessels between 1838 and 1878, became a one-building exhibit in 1929. Now more than 40 shops, homes, work buildings and the Henry B. DuPont Preservation Shipyard give an authentic taste of the lure, the lore and the life of the sea. You can visit the old bank, chapel and newspaper office, watch shipbuilders and craftsmen at work, clamber aboard three sailing vessels and even see a planetarium show. The permanent exhibit in the Stillman Building, "New England and the Sea," is the museum's largest and most comprehensive, representing a successful effort to put the seaport's 60 other exhibits into historical context. Don't miss it or the Charles W. Morgan, the last of the nation's 19th-century wooden whalers and a National Historic Landmark. This is a low-key place where craftsmen answer questions and guides at major sites spin their tales; in between, you wander at will.

Sailors love the seaport and spend hours in each building; we know some who've gone for years and still haven't see it all. For others, all the exhibits and boats may become overwhelming after half a day, but there's plenty more: the Seamen's Inne for food and drink, the steamship Sabino for river excursions, and the vast Seaport Stores for gifts and a book shop with the best commercial collection of maritime volumes around. Open daily, 9 to 8, mid-June to September; 9 to 5, April to mid-June and September-October; 9 to 4, November to March. Adults $14, children $8.75.

Mystic Marinelife Aquarium, Coogan Boulevard off Route 27 at I-95, Mystic, (203) 536-3323. An institution with a mission (educational and scientific), this place is big on numbers — like the 600,000 visitors who make its $8-million facility the

state's single most popular tourist attraction (after the new Foxwoods Casino), or the more than 6,000 specimens in its 49 aquariums. Two sea lions greet visitors outside the gray monolith just a gull's glide from I-95. Inside, the main level contains "themed" New England, tropical and Pacific coast communities, with everything from Atlantic salmon and a rare blue lobster to sharks, a 25-pound Pacific octopus and a 175-pound jewfish. Alone worth the price of admission are the hourly demonstrations upstairs in the 1,400-seat marine theater, where Skipper, a 500-pound sea lion, joins dolphins and belukha whales in marvelously entertaining shows. On your way out, a marsh pond features a variety of waterfowl, and the indoor-outdoor Seal Island allows closeup looks at seals and sea lions in a variety of habitats. The new Penguin Pavilion is the outdoor home of adorable African black-footed penguins. Beyond is the site of the aquarium's planned $4.3 million Whale Study Center, the first in the world. The two-level gift shop is excellent. Open daily, 9 to 5:30 in summer, 9 to 4:30 rest of year. Adults $8.25, children $4.75.

Olde Mystick Village, Route 27 at I-95, Mystic. Seldom is a shopping center a tourist attraction, but this one is. Opened in 1973, it's a collection of more than 60 interesting boutiques, restaurants, services and gift shops in a well-landscaped, authentic setting — "what an old New England village should look like, and is," in the words of owner Jerry Olson. Sunday services are conducted in the Meeting House, now St. Alban's Anglican Church. Music from its carillon lends a happy air, and youngsters love to feed the ducks in a pond beside the water wheel. The old buildings and landscaped grounds are as appealing as what's inside; the kids and Dad can stroll while Mom shops. Open Monday-Saturday 10 to 6, Sunday noon to 5.

Denison Pequotsepos Nature Center, Pequotsepos Road, Mystic, (203) 536-1216. Here's a change of pace: 125 acres of wildlife sanctuary and peace with self-guiding trails, including the Four Seasons trail for the blind (with handrails, guide-ropes and taped signs in English and Braille). Near the entrance, a tree grows from a huge solid rock; red-tailed hawks and owls live in large outdoor aviaries. A sign explains one of the many stone walls winding through the sanctuary (be on the lookout in this area for the thousands of miles of stone walls made by pioneer farmers near the sea as a windbreak to prevent farmland from disappearing and to keep cattle out of the crops — the sign here explains that they also were a way to dispose of all the rocks removed from the soil). Open May-October, daily 9 to 5, Sunday noon to 5; November-April, to 4 and closed Monday. Adults $1, children 50 cents.

Denison Homestead, Pequotsepos Road, Mystic, (203) 536-9248. Just down the road is this 1717 home, authentically furnished with heirlooms from eleven generations of Denisons. The wildlife sanctuary was the bulk of a land grant given to Capt. George Denison in 1654 by the King of England; the homestead was the working farm for the family, who saved their possessions in the attic and barn. Billed as the only New England home restored in the style of five eras, it has a Colonial kitchen with fireplace, a Revolutionary era bedroom with four-poster bed, a Federal parlor, a Civil War bedroom with ornate Franklin stove and an early 1900 living room with fine Dutch china. Open mid-May to mid-October, Wednesday-Monday 1 to 4. Adults $2.50, children $1.

Boat Trips. The 1908 **S.S. Sabino,** (203) 572-0711, the last coal-fired steamboat in New England, takes 100 Seaport visitors from Mystic Seaport on half-hour summer cruises up and down the Mystic River every hour on the hour from 11 to 6 (adults $3, children $2). Even better are the 90-minute cruises at 7 out past Noank and Mason's Island toward Fishers Island; on the way you see some striking waterfront homes (adults $7.50, children $6). Best of all are the occasional evening music and Sunday dixieland jazz cruises ($11).

Longer excursions on Long Island Sound are offered by **Voyager Cruises,** (203) 536-0416, and the **Out O' Mystic Schooner Cruises,** (203) 536-4218, which include the Mystic Clipper and the Mystic Whaler, from Steamboat Wharf in Mystic.

The River Queen, 193 Thames St., Groton, (203) 445-9516, gives sightseeing and sunset cruises on the Thames River — they're especially good for seeing the submarines. Hour-long tours (adults $7.75, children $4) leave daily in the summer between 10 and 3. The River Queen II also has Dixieland jazz cruises on Saturdays at 7.

Groton-New London

Submarines and history vie for the visitor's attention in these bustling towns linked by the dual, ten-lane Gold Star suspension bridge.

Once a whaling city that rivaled New Bedford, New London barely saved itself from becoming a wasteland of urban renewal. The landmark Union Railroad Station, designed by Henry Hobson Richardson at the foot of the old State Street, was preserved as a transportation center. Out front, after some years as a pedestrian mall called Captain's Walk, the main shopping street has been reopened to traffic.

Whale Oil Row is a stretch of 1832 Greek Revival houses built by leaders in the whale oil business along Huntington Street. A couple of blocks away is Starr Street, the crowning glory of restored New London. The city and the New England Savings Bank joined to turn the ramshackle houses, most of them Greek Revival, into stunning city homes.

USS Nautilus Memorial/Submarine Force Library and Museum, at the U.S. Naval Submarine Base, Route 12, Groton, (203) 449-3174. The U.S. Naval Submarine Base, the Western Hemisphere's largest, is visible from much of New London on the east bank of the Thames in Groton. At the entrance to the tight-security installation is the Nautilus, the world's first nuclear-powered sub, which was built in Groton's Electric Boat Division shipyard. The submarine museum traces the history of underwater navigation, showing a submarine control room, working periscopes and model subs. The highlight for most is a tour of portions of the 519-foot-long Nautilus. The visitor is guided by a free audio wand that explains the torpedo and sonar rooms, the control and navigation rooms, the crew's living quarters, galley and other spaces. Open Wednesday-Monday 9 to 5, Tuesday 1 to 5, mid-April through mid-October; 9 to 4 and closed Tuesday rest of year. Closed first full week of May and first two full weeks of December. Free.

U.S. Coast Guard Academy, Mohegan Avenue (Route 32), New London. Founded in 1876, the academy trains 1,000 cadets, male and female, at its striking red brick campus on the west bank of the Thames, across the road from the gray stone buildings of Connecticut College, a private liberal-arts institution. The grounds are open from 9 to sunset; a guard at the gate issues each car a visitor's permit. A modern visitor pavilion and museum has displays and a multi-media show on cadet life; open daily 9 to 5, May-October, free. The 295-foot training barque **Eagle** may be boarded when in port on weekends from noon to 4. Military dress reviews are held in spring and fall at varying times (call 444-8270).

Ocean Beach Park, Ocean Avenue, New London. Kids especially like this city-owned property "dedicated to summer fun." It has a good sand beach, an Olympic-size saltwater pool for those who don't relish Long Island Sound with its passing tankers and subs, a triple water slide, a curving boardwalk flanked by an amusement arcade, concessions and a midway with kiddie rides and bumper cars. Ocean Beach has seen better days, but it's pleasant when not crowded; nights and weekends get hectic. Open

Cooking on the hearth at Mystic Seaport.

Memorial Day to Labor Day, daily 9 a.m. to 10 p.m. Adults $1, children 50 cents; parking, weekends and holidays $9, weekdays $7.

Fort Griswold State Park, Monument Street and Park Avenue, Groton Heights. The 135-foot-high obelisk commemorating the 1781 massacre of 67 Colonists by British troops under turncoat Benedict Arnold provides a great view of the waterfront. At its base is a free DAR museum with historic displays and downhill is the 1750 **Ebenezer Avery House,** a center-chimney Colonial with period furnishings open summer weekends from 1 to 5, free. The remains of the fort are fun to explore; kids climb the embankments and prowl through a curving tunnel and brick storeroom. Park open year-round; monument and museum, May 30 to Labor Day daily 9 to 5, weekends to Columbus Day. Free.

Hempsted Houses, 11 Hempstead St., New London, (203) 443-7949. The Joshua Hempsted House (1678), the oldest house in New London and one of the oldest in Connecticut, recreates the color and atmosphere of the Pilgrim era. The detailed diary kept by the son of the builder helped the Antiquarian & Landmarks Society of Connecticut furnish the house authentically. The colorful stained-glass casement windows, the fine pewter and the exceptional furnishings, including a primitive baby walker and folding bed, are treasures. In front, the rough stone Nathaniel Hempsted House built during the 1750s has seven rooms furnished to the period. Both are open mid-May to mid-October, daily 1 to 5. Adults $3, children $2.

Shaw Mansion, 305 Bank St., New London, (203) 443-1209. Looking quite Southern with its pillars, veranda and wrought iron, this was Connecticut's Naval Office during the Revolution — the cradle of the American Navy and headquarters for George Washington on several visits. The paneled cement fireplace walls, oil portraits and books and documents are of interest in this stone house. Visitors can see the differences a century made between the Hempsted and Shaw houses. Open Wednesday-Friday 1 to 4, Saturday 10 to 4. Adults $2, children 50 cents.

Nathan Hale Schoolhouse, Captain's Walk next to City Hall, New London. Vacation-

53

ing school children will get a kick out of this tiny, 22-by-28-foot restoration tucked between downtown buildings. Patriot Nathan Hale was schoolmaster in the two-story structure in 1775. Open weekends in summer, 2 to 4. Free.

Lyman Allyn Art Museum, 625 Williams St., New London, (203) 443-2545. A room full of Indian artifacts and a collection of dollhouse furniture and toys delight childen here. The outstanding collection of Lilliputian furniture and decorative arts is displayed in room-size cases on the lower level of this beautiful museum founded in 1932. The museum has Egyptian, Roman, Greek, Medieval and Renaissance items, and changing exhibitions are mounted in four galleries. The Primitive Gallery with native art from the South Pacific "scares the wits out of kids, but they love it!" says a staff member. The gift shop is unusual in that it sells antique silver and other collectible small antiques, not reproductions. Open daily except Monday 1 to 5, Saturday from 11, Wednesday to 9. Free, but donations accepted.

Connecticut College Arboretum, Williams Street, New London, (203) 439-2140. The magnificent mountain laurel display in June is appropriate since it's the state flower. Visitors can explore the 415-acre area via a marked trail that is about three-quarters of a mile long. The staff suggests you allow an hour or more to observe the 300 varieties of native shrubs and trees. Children enjoy the pond area and a good portion of the trail leads along its edge. This provides a cool, verdant interlude on a hot summer day. Open daily until dusk. Free.

Thames Science Center, Gallows Lane, New London, (203) 442-0391. On the grounds of the Arboretum is this small but expanding place, which offers a peaceful break for restless travelers — particularly at the giant outdoor sandbox and tire swings. Inside, youngsters spend a few happy minutes at the "Salt Water Touch Tank" where they feel sea life, fish and shells and one specimen that our young informant confirmed was a horseshoe crab. A shop sells records and many kinds of bird feeders. Open Monday-Saturday 9 to 5, Sunday 1 to 5. Adults $2, children $1.

Monte Cristo Cottage, 325 Pequot Ave., New London, (203) 443-0051. The spare cottage isn't much to write home about, but playwright Eugene O'Neill both wrote about it and called it home. This little gingerbread confection, perched at the top of a sloping lawn, is the only home he had. The living room of the cottage was the setting for both "Ah, Wilderness" and "Long Day's Journey into Night;" much of the rest of the house is empty and eerie. Nearby at 305 Great Neck Road, Waterford, is the Eugene O'Neill Theater Center, site of the National Playwrights' Conference with staged readings of new plays in the Barn Theater and an amphitheater in July. Cottage open Monday-Friday 1 to 4; closed in winter. Adults $3, children $1.

Harkness Memorial State Park, Route 213, Waterford, (203) 443-5725. The 42-room Harkness Mansion, an Italian-style villa that has been closed for renovations, and its surrounding 231 acres along Long Island Sound are a quiet refuge for beach-combers, picnickers and garden enthusiasts. The solitude is broken by evening concerts in the acclaimed **Summer Music at Harkness** series, headquartered in a white sail-like tent that's acoustically excellent. Peter Sacco, founder of the festival in 1984, conducts the Connecticut Symphony Orchestra in what has become the largest summer classical music festival in the state. Come early for a picnic supper (a catered $12 buffet is available but you must reserve) on the grounds beside the Sound. Then settle in for one of the ten Thursday or Saturday evening performances — including in 1992 a pops concert, Ray Charles, Leon Fleisher and, our happy choice, the Empire Brass. Harkness ranks right up with the Tanglewood experience and is less crowded. Lawn tickets are $12 to $17; tent tickets, $13 to $30.

Shore Towns and Beaches

Very different from the bustling cities and tourist centers are the coastal villages around Mystic and the beaches in Rhode Island.

Noank is a quaint fishing village and arts colony, so untouched by the surrounding tourism that most hardly realize its presence. We like it for Abbott's Lobster Pound and the nice public beach and picnic area nearby at Esker Point (no surf, but uncrowded and one of the pitifully few public places where you can get to the water along the Connecticut shore). To the east, Stonington is our favorite coastal village in Connecticut.

The Rhode Island shore from Watch Hill to Weekapaug harbors excellent beaches and rolling surf from the open Atlantic. It also has a variety of carnival and sedate atmospheres ranging from the ridiculous to the sublime.

Stonington. "Take a walk," advises the historical society's guide to this charming seaside community. And walking is the best way to see and savor this living anachronism jutting into the Atlantic. Connecticut's oldest borough has been cut off from the mainstream by the railroad track spanned by a viaduct. The two streets through the borough are narrow; they and their cross streets are crammed with history dating back to 1649. Around 1800, this was Connecticut's most populated town and the Wadawanuck Hotel could sleep 1,300 guests — that's long-gone and the only accommodations are at a couple of small guest houses. The last commercial fishing fleet in Connecticut is manned by the resident Portuguese community, which stages a Blessing of the Fleet festival annually in mid-July.

The Stonington Historical Society, founded in 1910 and one of the first around, has marked with signs many structures from the 18th and 19th centuries. One is the 1780 Col. Amos Palmer House at Main and Wall, where artist James McNeil Whistler once lived; it was later the home of poet Stephen Vincent Benet and since was occupied by his granddaughter. On Harmony Street is the 1786 Peleg Brown House, birthplace of Capt. Nathaniel Palmer, who at age 22 discovered Antarctica. The appeal of the old houses is enhanced by all the garden courtyards and glimpses of the harbor with its fishing trawlers. On Cannon Square are two "18-pounders" that repulsed the British in the War of 1812; beside the square, the old Ocean Bank is a replica of the Athenian Treasury at Delphi, Greece. From Stonington Point you can see across Long Island Sound to Fishers Island, N.Y., and east to Watch Hill, R.I.

Old Lighthouse Museum, 7 Water St., Stonington, (203) 535-1440. The first lighthouse in Connecticut is perched on a rise above Stonington Point, where the villagers turned back the British. Opened by the historical society in 1925, this museum is a tiny storehouse of Stonington memorabilia. Whaling and fishing gear, portraits of the town's founding fathers, a bench dating back to 1674, articles from the Orient trade and an exquisite dollhouse are included. Open May-October, Tuesday-Sunday, 11 to 4:30. Adults $2, children $1.

Watch Hill. For a staid, storied resort of the old school, things get pretty crowded on summer weekends. And costly, as you might expect from a protective place trying to retain the exclusivity it had when it was the preserve of the Carnegies, the Procters and the Harknesses. Shops still serve the carriage trade and the glossy weekly Seaside Topics is "a periodical reporting the social doings." Parking in downtown is limited and expensive on weekends. Admission to the public beach also is expensive. The beach club and yacht club are off-limits and a policeman likely will discourage out-of-town cars on a Sunday afternoon. The Flying Horse Carousel at the foot of Bay Street, a treat for kids who line up for 25-cent rides, is said to be the oldest merry-go-round in the country.

Napatree Point extends half a mile from the Watch Hill parking lot along a narrow sandy spit into Little Narragansett Bay. If you find a place to park, you can visit this privately owned conservation area, but signs warn that "Ospreys are nesting here — please aid their survival." The walk to the ruins of a Spanish-American fort at the point's far end opposite Stonington can take an hour or half a day. It's a refuge for waterfowl, tidal creatures and beachcombers — a fun adventure for the entire family.

Misquamicut. Watch Hill and Misquamicut are as different as night and day. This beachside strip is hot and honky-tonk, the state beach is crowded and the public is obviously welcome. The beaches are sandy and wide-open and the rolling surf is fairly warm — our intrepid sons when young were known to body-surf in May and September and to make sand castles in April and October. The state beach, with concession stands and locker rooms, is open daily from mid-June to early September.

Where to Stay

The area is somewhat short on classic New England country inns but it has a variety of motels — from new chains to old independents, large and small — plus B&Bs, newer inns and even a few cabins on the water. Chain motels in Mystic, a major tourist destination, charge premium prices in season: even the budget Days Inn costs $106 a night.

Hotels and Motels

The Inn at Mystic, Route 1, Mystic 06355, (203) 536-9604. Although this twelve-acre complex includes the fine Inn at Mystic in a white-pillared mansion and some deluxe inn-style rooms in its East Wing, it started as a motor inn and is, we think, by far the nicest of its kind in the area. It's the only one overlooking the water and at least looks like New England, with brown shingles and blue shutters. Atop a hill, it catches the breeze, has a tennis court, a small outdoor pool and a whirlpool, and guests can canoe out onto Pequotsepos Cove. The 67 rooms vary from good to spectacular. The newest deluxe units come with queensize canopy beds, wingback chairs, antiques, bidets, fireplaces, jacuzzis and patios or balconies with water views. Complimentary tea for guests is served daily at 4 in the adjacent Flood Tide restaurant (see Where to Eat). Definitely not for youngsters is the real Inn at Mystic, the 1904 Colonial Revival mansion with a veranda and incredible gardens atop a hill behind the motor inn. It and the nearby gatehouse have luxury accommodations in handsomely decorated rooms for $165 to $195. Motor inn, $100 to $135.

The Mystic Hilton, 20 Coogan Blvd., Mystic 06355, (203) 572-0731 or (800) 826-8699. Across from the Mystic Marinelife Aquarium, this attractive hotel is not your typical Hilton in terms of high-rise glass and steel. Its low red-brick exterior and peaked roofs emulate the look of 19th-century mills and warehouses. All is glamorous and up-to-date inside, from the grand piano and intimate sitting areas in the fireplaced lobby to the 184 guest rooms, each containing two large prints of Mystic Seaport scenes. The meandering, angled layout puts some rooms far from the elevators but contributes to peace and quiet. There are a fitness center and a small indoor-outdoor pool, as well as **The Mooring** restaurant, featuring new American cuisine at reasonable prices for lunch and dinner. Dinner entrees start at $9.95 for charbroiled pesto chicken. Treats like orange roughy over fruit chutney, cedar-roasted salmon and scallops, and grilled pork medallions with warm apple and red pepper chutney are under $15.95. We've had a couple of wonderful dinners here, but it's a grown-up treat; let the kids eat early at the McDonald's down the street. Doubles, $129 to $175.

Radisson Hotel-New London, 35 Governor Winthrop Blvd., New London 06320, (203) 443-7000. Opened in 1987, this 120-room hotel is at the edge of the city's downtown. Rooms contain kingsize or two double beds, a small sofa and-or upholstered chairs and, on the executive floor, many bath amenities, including toothbrushes. There's an attractive enclosed pool with lounge chairs, umbrellaed tables and a jacuzzi. A planter separates the two levels of **Winthrop's Grille,** in which pastas share billing with such entrees ($10.95 to $16.50) as baked cod and veal marsala. Doubles, $109 to $139.

Seaport Motor Inn, Coogan Boulevard, Mystic 06355, (203) 536-2621. Of the motels clustered around Exit 90 off I-95, this is a good bet as it's up a hill and farther from the interstate, overlooking the other motels and Olde Mystick Village. There's a large outdoor pool. The 118 rooms are pleasant and include four two-bedroom units. **Jamms Restaurant** serves lunch and dinner. Doubles, $64 to $92.

Comfort Inn, 132 Greenmanville Ave., Mystic 06355, (203) 572-8531. This brick structure with gabled windows, cupola and porte cochere is the newest of the chain motels proliferating around the main I-95 interchange. Along with the Days Inn across the street, it shares a happy distinction: a relatively secluded location back from the highway. Most of the 120 rooms are on the small side, but kingsize rooms contain loveseats. Luxury suites hold jacuzzis. An indoor fitness center and an outdoor pool are assets, as is the complimentary continental breakfast. Doubles, $84 to $96.

The Whaler's Inn, 20 East Main St., Mystic, 06355, (203) 536-1506 or (800) 243-2588. The folks from the luxury Steamboat Inn across the Mystic River have acquired this venerable inn and motel in the heart of town, which is good for walking expeditions but can get noisy. Their first order of business was to reduce the number of rooms from 45 to 41 by enlarging four in the main inn. They also modernized bathrooms and redecorated throughout. All rooms come with TVs and phones; motel units in the Noank House have showers; those in the Stonington House, bathtubs. The top of the line are in the adjacent 1865 House, where a common sitting room is available to guests in nine rooms with private baths. The ground floor of the main inn has been leased to a jewelry store, a sweets shop and Restaurant Bravo Bravo (see Where to Eat). Doubles, $74.50 to $125.

Taber Motel and Townhouse, 29 Williams Ave. (Route 1), Mystic, 06355, (203) 536-4904. Built in 1980, this pleasant motel in a residential area has rooms with kingsize or two double beds plus an 1829 guest house, where the six small rooms have private baths and air-conditioning and from the second-floor balconies you can see Long Island Sound. A family of four to six may choose the two-bedroom country guest house next door. Other rooms and configurations are available in the farmhouse. Eight townhouse suites out back offer one or two bedrooms, fireplaced living rooms, wet bars and jacuzzis. Altogether there are 28 units. Doubles, $75 to $95; townhouses, $145 to $245.

Thames Harbour Inn, 193 Thames St., Groton, 06340, (203) 445-8111. The area's only waterfront motel used to be called the Thames Botel because it allowed boats to dock overnight or longer, but new chain management has upgraded both the facilities and the name. What essentially is a two-story motel has 26 units, all but five of them efficiencies. Kids can watch the passing subs or fish from the 132-foot pier. Doubles, $68 to $96 (for two deluxe units beside the river).

The Inn at Watch Hill, Bay Street, Watch Hill, R.I. 02891, (401) 596-0665. Transformed from a rooming house with 32 rooms above stores along Watch Hill's Main Street, this row of motel-type accommodations has sixteen spacious rooms with contemporary furnishings and sliding doors opening onto small balconies above the street. The rooms are plain but pleasant, with bare wood floors, white walls, full baths and color TV. Most have a sink, refrigerator and microwave, but no dishes. Doubles, $148 to $175. Closed November-April.

Winnapaug Inn, 169 Shore Road, Westerly, R.I. 02891, (401) 348-8350 or (800) 288-9906. Erected in 1988, this three-story motor inn offers 28 rooms off central corridors and pleasant motel furnishings. Most rooms open onto balconies, the nicest on the east side facing Winnipaug Golf Course with a view of Winnapaug Pond in the distance. Rooms on the west side face a parking lot. At the rear of the property is a large swimming pool. Four more lodging units are in cottages or efficiency apartments. Doubles, $100 to $125.

Breezeway Motel, 70 Winnapaug Road, Box 1368, Misquamicut, R.I. 02891, (401) 348-8953 or (800) 462-8872. Nicely tucked back from the street in a residential section is this good-looking, two-story brick and frame motel in an L-shape around a pool. The 44 rooms contain the usual motel amenities, and a complimentary continental breakfast is served. The area is quiet, but it's a bit of a trek to the beach. Doubles, $100 to $120. Open mid-April to mid-October.

Willows Resort Motel, Route 1, Box 1260, Charleston, R.I. 02813, (401) 364-7727 or (800) 842-2181. For those who arrive by small plane, the Willows has a 1,800-foot-long grass landing strip. Its extensive grounds are at the edge of a saltwater pond for sailing, waterskiing and fishing. There are 34 units with Mediterranean decor (each has a porch and some have kingsize beds) and thirteen efficiencies, which rent by the week. The resort's restaurant features local seafood and serves breakfast and dinner. Facilities include a pool, boats, golf driving range, a tennis court, nature trails, game room and reading room. Doubles, $75.50 to $95.50. Open mid-May to mid-October.

Inns

Steamboat Inn, 73 Steamboat Wharf, Mystic 06355, (203) 536-8300. Mystic finally acquired deluxe waterfront lodging in 1990 with the opening of this small inn fashioned from a former restaurant. A local decorator outfitted the first six rooms in lavish style with mounds of pillows and designer sheets on each canopied bed, loveseats and plush armchairs in front of the fireplace, and distinctive mantels and cabinet work. All have such creature comforts as jacuzzi baths and TVs hidden in armoires or cupboards. We like best the two rooms at either end of the second floor, with big windows onto the water. New in 1992 were two deluxe ground-floor suites, both with double jacuzzis, extra sofabeds and lots of space (the front foyer in one appearing rather useless). They lack the upstairs fireplaces, however, as well as a sense of privacy because their windows are right beside the public wharf. A complimentary continental breakfast is served in an upstairs common room. Doubles, $165 to $185; suites, $250. No smoking.

Watch Hill Inn, 50 Bay St., Watch Hill, R.I. 02891, (401) 348-8912 or (800) 356-9314. A large white wooden structure with waterfront terrace and dining, the former Narragansett Inn has been remodeled under new owners. Four rooms were eliminated to provide space for private baths for all sixteen rooms on the second and third floors. Formerly advertised as rustic and quaint, they're now billed as "charming" and look more comfortable than at our previous visits. Two junior suites contain sofabeds. The

Swans entertain guests at Weekapaug Inn.

enclosed side porch serves as an office, and there are no common rooms. A packaged continental breakfast is served in the bar-lounge. There's apt to be much coming and going from the 200-seat Positano Room, a banquet facility that doubles as a dining room, and the waterfront Deck Bar & Grill. Doubles, $165; suites, $185. Closed January-March.

Shelter Harbor Inn, 10 Wagner Road (Route 1), Westerly, R.I. 02891, (401) 322-8883 or (800) 468-8883. The best choice for dining and lodging in this area is the restored 18th-century farmhouse set back from the highway (behind two paddle-tennis courts) and off by itself not far from Quonochontaug Pond. Jim and Debbye Dey have redone ten guest rooms with private baths in the main house, where they added a rooftop deck with a hot tub, from which a distant water vista must be seen to be believed. They also renovated the barn next door to include ten rooms with private baths and a spacious living room on the upper level opening onto a large deck. Their crowning achievement is the Coach House, with four deluxe guest rooms with fireplaces, upholstered armchairs, phones and small TVs. Guests crowd around the bar in the cheery sun porch after a round of croquet or a fast game of paddle tennis and, in summer, a shuttle bus takes guests to a private beach. A full breakfast is served to overnight guests in the attractive dining areas, which are open for three meals a day. Doubles, $82 to $106.

Pleasant View Inn, 65 Atlantic Ave., Misquamicut, R.I. 02891, (401) 348-8200 or (800) 782-3224. Many accommodations in honky-tonk Misquamicut are on the tacky side, but this establishment at the Watch Hill end is a cut above. A bright blue and white, three-story edifice of the Virginia Beach variety, it has 58 rooms, most with balconies facing the ocean (by far the most choice) or the pool. A lineup of lounge chairs on a grassy crest faces what, for all intents and purposes, is the inn's private beach. The fairly formal dining room overlooking the ocean serves three meals daily. Get the kids to bed early and dance in the Down-the-Hatch lounge. Doubles, $104 to $160, EP; $150 to $206, MAP. Closed late October to May.

Weekapaug Inn, Weekapaug, R.I. 02891, (401) 322-0301. The weathered brown shingles of this large inn conceal a homey and tasteful interior where guests have been

59

hosted by four generations of the Buffum family. This is an exclusive, expensive and non-commercial inn, almost like a private club and definitely not for transients. Repeat guests are drawn by the setting (it's surrounded by ocean, coves and wonderful beaches), water sports, tennis, lawn bowling, shuffleboard and good food. No liquor is served, but guests bring their own for cocktails in the Pond Room. Entertainment at night includes movies, bingo and bridge. A buffet lunch is served every day but Sunday. Lobster is often on the dinner menu, which is $25 prix-fixe for six courses to the public and jackets are required. The 65 inn rooms, all with private baths, are simple but immaculate with twin beds (some joined to form kingsize). Six are suites with sitting area and two baths. Rates are $145 to $150 per person, AP. Open mid-June to Labor Day. No credit cards.

Guest Houses and B&Bs

The Palmer Inn, 25 Church St., Noank 06340, (203) 572-9000. You can stay in the heart of the quaint seafaring hamlet of Noank in this imposing, sixteen-room mansion, built in 1907 in pillared Southern plantation style for Robert Palmer Jr. when the Palmer Shipyards were among New England's largest. Until 1984 a private home, it was restored with taste and energy by Patricia White into an appealing B&B. A mahogany staircase leads from an impressive main hall with thirteen-foot-high ceilings to six guest rooms on the second and third floors, all with private baths. A couple have balconies and views of the water and one has a fireplace. Furnished with family heirlooms and antiques, rooms also include such amenities as designer sheets, hair dryers and Crabtree & Evelyn toiletries. Guests play checkers in the library or gather for afternoon tea in the parlor; a continental-plus breakfast is served in the dining room. Doubles, $105 to $175.

Randall's Ordinary, Route 2, Box 243, North Stonington 06359, (203) 599-4540. You can harken back to the old days, enjoying hearthside dinners and historic accommodations, in this new-old inn secluded in the midst of 27 acres at the end of a dirt road. We say "new" because the inn opened in 1987 and quickly added nine rooms and suites in a renovated English barn notable for lofts, skylights, spiral staircases, modern baths, phones and TV. We say "old" because the main house dates to 1685, has three guest rooms with queensize four-poster beds and working fireplaces (although the bathrooms are so modern as to have whirlpool jets in the tubs), and is the site of Colonial hearthside meals from yesteryear. Up to 40 diners gather at 7 in the taproom for drinks and a tour of the house; they also watch cooks in Colonial costumes preparing their meals over the open hearth. The $30 prix-fixe dinner, served at old tables in two beamed dining rooms, offers a choice of up to five entrees — perhaps roast capon with wild rice, roast pork loin, hearth-grilled salmon or Nantucket scallops. They come with soup, anadama or spider corn bread, a conserve of red cabbage and apples, squash pudding, and maybe apple crisp or pumpkin cake for dessert. Open to the public, it's a memorable experience for the entire family. With similar food but less fanfare, lunch is a la carte, $4.95 to $8.50. A continental breakfast is served to overnight guests. More substantial breakfast fare is available to guests and the public. Lunch, noon to 3; dinner nightly at 7. Doubles, $85 to $140; suites to $175.

Red Brook Inn, 2800 Gold Star Highway at Welles Road, Box 237, Old Mystic 06372, (203) 572-0349. Colonial dinners (for house guests only, in November and December) also are a specialty at this elegant, expanded inn run by ex-Californian Ruth Keyes, who looked all over eastern Connecticut for a house to make into an inn. She was thrilled in 1983 to find the four-bedroom Creary Homestead, dating from about 1770, with a floor plan identical to that at the showplace 1717 Dennison Homestead

Noank and Long Island Sound are on view from widow's walk at Palmer Inn.

nearby. She was doubly thrilled three years later to find the historic 1740 Haley Tavern, which was disassembled and moved from Groton to a site behind the Creary Homestead, where it was reassembled in as fascinating an inn restoration as could be imagined. Interestingly, Nancy Creary, who was born in the homestead, married the son of Elija Haley, "so we've brought the tavern back into the same family," Ruth says. The tavern structure has seven luxurious guest rooms, all with private baths (two with whirlpool tubs) and three with working fireplaces, two common rooms full of pewter and early American glass, and a 300-year-old stagecoach room now given over to games, TV and VCR. Otherwise, Ruth is a stickler for authenticity; "people who stay here get a feel for the way life was," says she. Full breakfasts are served in the tavern's keeping room. Doubles, $95 to $159. No smoking.

The Old Mystic Inn, 58 Main St., Old Mystic 06372, (203) 572-9422. Formerly a bookstore (its sign shows a man reading a book), this red inn was built in the 1820s. New owners Mary and Peter Knight offer four rooms in the main house, plus four larger rooms with queensize canopy beds, sitting areas and air-conditioning in a newly built Victorian carriage house out back. Rooms are named for literary notables; three in the main house have working fireplaces, two in the carriage house have whirlpool tubs, and all have full private baths. The Herman Melville Room, with its rose carpeting, has twin beds and a little balcony, as well as a private entrance in back. There are a fireplaced parlor and a keeping room with television. A full country breakfast, perhaps eggs benedict or waffles, is served in a sunny breakfast room. While Mary oversees the B&B, her husband tends to the couple's newly acquired **Old Mystic Country Store** across the street. Doubles, $125.

Shore Inne, 54 East Shore Ave., Groton Long Point 06340, (203) 536-1180. This "inne on the water," facing Long Island Sound in a community of fine old summer homes, is wonderfully homey. Judith and Harold Hoyland rent seven bedrooms, three with private baths, in the summer-home style. Three across the front of the house with

61

king-twin beds look out onto Mouse Island and, beyond, Fishers Island. Guests enjoy a living room full of wicker, a dining room and a sun room with library and TV. Judith serves a continental breakfast in the mornings, urges her guests to relax on the lovely grounds, and gives beach privileges at two private beaches that are among the nicest in Connecticut. Doubles, $75 to $85.

The Queen Anne B&B, 265 Williams St., New London 06320, (203) 447-2600 or (800) 347-8818. A large, wicker-filled porch fronting onto a busy street leads into this 1880 Victorian structure that was converted into a B&B in 1987. Eight air-conditioned rooms with modern baths are nicely decorated in period style with accents of potpourri. Three come with TV sets and two with fireplaces. Two other rooms share a bath. The bridal suite has a brass canopy bed, fireplace and private balcony. Afternoon tea is served in the parlor, which is full of lace and oriental rugs. Innkeepers Julie and Ray Rutledge offer a full breakfast, perhaps apple-cinnamon waffles, ham and mushroom tarts or spinach crepes. Doubles, $78 to $155.

Where to Eat

Mystic-New London

J.P. Daniels, Route 184, Old Mystic, (203) 572-9564. A restaurant of quiet elegance in an old, high-ceilinged dairy barn, J.P. Daniels has been going strong since 1981. Tables are covered with white linens and centered with fresh flowers, and on certain evenings you may hear a harpist or a pianist in the background. Lanterns on the walls and oil lamps on the tables provide a modicum of illumination on two dining levels, as well as in the pleasant lounge area where a casual menu is offered nightly. Start with the house special, a fresh fruit daiquiri. Appetizers ($7.95 to $9.95) include grilled mussels, escargots and seafood-stuffed mushrooms. Entrees start at $13.95 for grilled lemon and herb chicken; the rest are $17.95 to $19.95. A specialty is boneless Long Island duck stuffed with seasonal fruits and finished with apricot brandy. The wine list is moderately priced and contains explanations of the offerings. Dinner nightly, 5 to 9 or 9:30; Sunday brunch, 11 to 2.

Flood Tide Restaurant, Route 1, Mystic, (203) 536-8140. This popular restaurant at the Inn at Mystic serves some of the area's best food amid fancy trappings. Past a foyer and lobby are the club-like Crystal Swan Lounge and a spacious, two-level dining room with windows onto Pequotsepos Cove. Executive chef Robert Tripp is known for a lavish Sunday brunch spread ($15.95). We were impressed with the $10.95 luncheon buffet, which ran the gamut from ceviche and lumpfish caviar through seafood crepes to kiwi tarts and bread pudding. At night, entrees are priced from $15.95 for chicken champignon or pork chops with apple-raspberry puree to $21.95 for shrimp and artichoke provencal, broiled filet mignon with mushroom cap and veal chop with lobster, morels and sundried tomatoes. Whole roast chicken, rack of baby lamb, beef wellington and chateaubriand are carved tableside for two. Grand marnier cheesecake and raspberry-kiwi parfait are among the good desserts. In season, diners on an outdoor deck enjoy a view of the water. Lunch, Monday-Saturday 11:30 to 2:30; dinner nightly, 5:30 to 9:30 or 10; Sunday brunch, 11 to 3.

Restaurant Bravo Bravo, 20 East Main St., Mystic, (203) 536-3228. This new restaurant on the main floor of the Whaler's Inn, with a sidewalk cafe spilling off to the side, captured a receptive audience upon its opening in 1991. Well-known area chefs Robert Sader and Carol Kanabis produce contemporary Italian fare. For dinner, sirloin carpaccio, chilled oysters wrapped in spinach and leeks, and interesting salads make

Stone wall surrounds 18th-century structure that houses Randall's Ordinary.

good starters in the $3.50 to $7.95 range. Creative pastas are priced from $8.95 to $14.95. The dozen entrees ($10.95 to $17.95) might include garlic shrimp sauteed with pancetta and artichokes on a bed of escarole. Dining is in a spare room at tables rather close together, or outside on a canopy-covered terrace with white molded furniture. The outdoor **Cafe Bravo** menu features brick-oven pizzas (we like the one with pesto, sundried tomatoes and goat cheese for $11.95), pastas and entrees from $8.95 to $13.95. The mainly Italian wine list is one of the area's more affordable, with all but two offerings in the teens and most under $15. Dinner, Tuesday-Sunday 5 to 9 or 10; lunch in off-season; cafe, open May-October for lunch, 11:30 to 3; dinner, 5 to 9 or 10.

    Captain Daniel Packer Inne, 32 Water St., Mystic, (203) 536-3555. This 1756 inn, once a stagecoach stop on the route from New York to Boston, was owned by the Packer-Keeler family for all its years until Rhode Islander Richard Kiley bought it in 1980 and spent three years redoing it into a handsome restaurant. The pub in the basement is especially cozy, with brick and stone walls and a huge fireplace; the two dining rooms on the main floor have working fireplaces as well and floors of wide-board pine and formal mats with pictures of sailing ships on the tables. Chowder, salads, sandwiches, pastas and entrees from $7.95 to $10.95 (for tenderloin tips or scallops Nantucket) are offered at lunch. The menu expands at night, and prices go from $12.95 for lemon peppered chicken to $18.95 for steak black jack, glazed with Jack Daniels. Both a pub menu and the dinner menu are available in the pub. Lunch daily, 11 to 4; dinner, 5 to 10, Sunday 2 to 10.

    Seamen's Inne, Route 27, Mystic, (203) 536-9649. This popular old warhorse beside Mystic Seaport has been upgraded by new owners who keep the place humming in a variety of venues. There are two main dining rooms, properly historic, and the Samuel Adams Pub. We've found the last a particularly fetching place for lunch or supper with its pressed-tin ceiling, bare wood floors and tables, and a greenhouse window filled with plants. We liked a lunch of clam chowder (thick and delicious for $3.50 a bowl), the steamed mussels in a wine garlic sauce and shrimp and oyster pasta with a spicy cajun sauce (both $7.95). The dinner menu blends Yankee with cajun and Southern; entrees are priced from $13.95 to $18.95. Yankee pot roast, red beans and rice with smoked ham hocks and cornbread, carpetbagger steak and prime rib vie with seafood specialties like shrimp creole, fillet of catfish, Maryland crab cakes, fried seafood platter and seafood pot pie. Enormous numbers of people eat inside or out, on the small front porch or in the canopy-covered riverside terrace out back. The dixieland jazz breakfast buffet ($9.95) is a festive Southern feast (from cheddar cheese grits to biscuits and honey) enjoyed by upwards of 500 patrons every Sunday. Lunch daily, 11:30 to 4; dinner, 4:30 to 9 or 10; Sunday jazz breakfast, 11 to 2.

The Fisherman, 937 Groton Long Point Road, Noank, (203) 536-1717. White tablecloth dining and views onto the waters around Esker Point are offered at this popular restaurant and lounge. The menu covers everything from fried clams to bouillabaisse, from chicken cordon bleu to veal piccata, at prices from $11.95 to $19.95. The lobster madeira over linguini is a winner. The house wines are a bargain and the others, though few, are affordably priced. Lunch, 11:30 to 3; dinner nightly, 5 to 10 or 10:30.

Kitchen Little, Route 27, Mystic, (203) 536-2122. This really is a tiny kitchen (indeed, the whole establishment is only nineteen feet square), but it serves up some of the greatest breakfasts anywhere. Chef-owner Florence Brochu's repertoire is extraordinary. Consider the three specials one time we stopped: meatloaf and cheese omelet or baked stuffed potato topped with scrambled eggs, cream cheese, scallions, sour cream and bacon (both $4.25) and a chicken-filled french toast sandwich with cranberry sauce and cheese ($3.95). The coffee flows into bright red mugs, and the people at nine tables and five stools at the counter are necessarily convivial. (A slightly larger offshoot of the same name serves breakfast and lunch plus weekend dinners at 142 Water St. in Stonington.) Breakfast in Mystic daily, 6:30 to noon, weekends to 1; lunch, Monday-Friday to 2.

Also in the Mystic area, the **Steak Loft** at Olde Mystic Village is a classic of its genre, and packed to the nines with people interested in good steak and seafood, reasonably priced, at both lunch and dinner. In Factory Square, a complex of shops in restored brick buildings, is **Margarita's,** a Mexican restaurant. On the upper level with an outdoor deck in season, it serves the usual suspects plus a strawberry margarita pie; open for dinner only. The unpretentious, noisy **Seahorse Tavern** at 65 Marsh Road, Noank, is good for local color, fresh seafood and some of the best steaks around, from $7.95 for angel-hair pasta with clam sauce to $14.95 for filet mignon; open daily, 11 to 10. **Sailor Ed's** on Old Stonington Road, Mystic, is billed as Mystic's oldest seafood restaurant (1924). It's an extravaganza of a place with touristy-nautical decor and fresh-off-the-boat seafood, most of it under $12.

O'Brien's on Bank, 52 Bank St., New London, (203) 442-3420. The Groton-New London area, seldom considered a culinary mecca, has spawned some good restaurants lately. The best is this, which made a 1992 debut in the space once occupied by the great, short-lived West Bank Bistro. A rear deck overlooks the Thames River, while the interior is sleek yet comfortable with shiny black chairs at tables topped with butcher paper over floral cloths. The short Italian menu is notable for pastas (local innkeepers rave over the angel-hair milano with sundried tomatoes and artichoke hearts), gourmet pizzas and entrees from $8.95 for sweet sausage with mashed potatoes to $13.95 for grilled ribeye steak berbere. The swordfish here is served with grilled potatoes and chile corn salsa. Desserts are few but select. Lunch and dinner daily from 11, to 9 on weekdays and 10 on weekends.

Don Juan's International Combat Style Cuisine, 405 Williams St., New London, (203) 437-3791. The name is a new one to us, but adventuresome foodies who like their ambience plainer than plain praise this newcomer where the kitchen is bigger than the dining room and the fare that emerges is distinctive. Donzell Johnson, who does most of the cooking, and Juan Madry, whose paintings adorn the rustic wood walls, feature international cooking. Portuguese-style clams with pork medallions, Jamaican jerk chicken, Mediterranean beef, Mexican seafood and cajun fillets are among the entrees (most $9.95). Can't decide? Order the combat platter ($12.95), an assortment of foods from the menu. Open daily from 11:30. BYOB. No credit cards.

Diana Restaurant, 970 Fashion Plaza, Poquonnock Road (Route 1), Groton, (203) 449-8468. Oriental rugs cover the walls and floors of this shopping-center storefront, a family operation that offers the most authentic Lebanese cooking in Connecticut. The three Saad family chefs (two of them culinary graduates of Johnson & Wales University in Providence) attract throngs from miles around for stuffed leg of lamb, beef kabob, broiled kafta, shrimp curry, half pepper and garlic chicken, and lamb and eggplant stew ($9.95 to $14.95, except $38 for a lamb feast for two). Lebanese wines are featured at this place that's true as true can be. Lunch and dinner, daily 11:30 to 9 or 9:30, Sunday 4 to 8:30.

More interesting meals are to be found at **Bayou BBQ & Grill,** 255 Broad St., New London, 443-4412, where everything is cajun or creole and decor is minimal. Dinner prices range from $8.95 for a grilled marinated vegetable platter to $11.95 for jambalaya; lunches are considerably less. In downtown New London, **Ye Olde Tavern** at 345 Bank St. is an institution operated since 1918. The kind of place where the walls are covered with pictures of local celebrities and customers, it's especially known for steaks and serves lunch and dinner. **Thames Landing Oyster House** at 2 Captains Walk is nautically decorated with nets and such; it serves a lot of seafood, including a luncheon special of lobster, clams and mussels fra diavolo. **James' Gourmet Deli** at 181 Bank St. offers good soups, sandwiches, salads and pastries among its assortment of specialty foods. Across the Thames River in Groton, and with a rear deck taking full advantage, is **Paul's Pasta Shop,** 223 Thames St., where local folks rave about the pastas, which are fresh and tantalizing, and the rest of the fare is your basic Italian; open daily 11 to 9.

Shore Towns and Beaches

Abbott's Lobster in the Rough, 117 Pearl St., Noank, (203) 536-7719. For years we've been taking visitors from all over to Abbott's, partly because of the delectable lobsters and partly because of the view of Fishers Island and Long Island Sound, with a constant parade of interesting craft in and out of Mystic Harbor. We like to sit outside at the gaily colored picnic tables placed on ground strewn with mashed-up clam shells. Kids can look at the lobster tanks or scamper around on the rocks, finding jellyfish and snails. You order at a counter and get a number — since the wait is often half an hour, we bring along drinks and appetizers to keep us going, since the portions to come are apt to be small. Lobster, last we knew, was $13.95 for a one-and-one-quarter pounder. It comes with a bag of potato chips, a small container of coleslaw, melted butter and a paper bib. Also available are steamers, clam chowder, mussels, and shrimp, lobster or crab rolls. The wholesale side sells lobsters to go, as well as cans of Abbott's own lobster or clam bisque and chowder. Open May to Labor Day, daily noon to 9; weekends only to Columbus Day.

The Harborview, Cannon Square, Stonington, (203) 535-2720. Locally considered

Tributes to the past at Cannon Square in Stonington.

the spot for a splurge, this serves classic French food from a menu that rarely changes. Dinner entrees ($12.50 to $19.95) include curried lobster, a wonderful bouillabaisse, sauteed shrimps and scallops with pea pods and ginger, and roast duckling with brandy and maple mustard sauce. We can vouch for the veal sweetbreads with crayfish tails in a basil cream sauce. The large dining room is dark-paneled with tiled fireplaces, old plates and brass sconces on the walls, and the dark blue-clothed tables bear fresh flowers. Through the small-paned windows in back, you may see sunsets over the harbor. Luncheon entrees are $7.50 to $11.50. A lavish Sunday brunch buffet with unusual hot entrees and enough food to keep you happy for a week is $14.95. The immensely popular rustic bar serves interesting tavern food all day long. Lunch, 11:30 to 3; dinner, 5 to 10; Sunday brunch, 11 to 3. Closed Tuesday in winter.

Boatyard Cafe, 194 Water St., Stonington, (203) 535-1381. Some folks so like chef-owner Deborah Jensen's scones that they are calling the borough Sconington, and her breakfasts are so popular that a section of the menu now lists "eggs all day." The tiny cafe in the Dodson Boatyard, with a great outdoor deck beside the harbor, is off to an auspicious start. Deborah, a former New York restaurateur and cooking school instructor, offers kicky "combination scrambles" like the Soho — eggs with sundried tomatoes and goat cheese — with oven fries and toast for $4.50 at breakfast, $6.95 the rest of the day. The lunch menu adds bobolis, a signature grilled chicken sandwich and some trendy salads. Fresh Stonington flounder takes top billing at dinner, prepared five ways for $10.95 to $12.95. That's the price range for the rest of the dinner options (five of them chicken), from meatloaf to spaghetti (with ham, mushrooms, roasted red peppers and sherry). Start with smoked salmon and capers ($4.95); finish with plum pie or key lime cheesecake. Everything's made here from scratch and oh-so-good. And there's no better place for eating it than on the waterside deck. Breakfast daily, 8 to 11:30; lunch, 11:30 to 2:30; dinner, Wednesday-Sunday 6 to 8:30. Closed Tuesday in off-season. BYOB.

Noah's, 113 Water St., Stonington, (203) 535-3925. This small restaurant seating 65 people in two rooms is exceptionally well-liked locally because of the refreshingly moderate prices and good, unpretentious food. Noah's opens at 7 to serve breakfast, with thick wedges of french toast made from challah bread going for $3. Chowder with half a BLT sandwich and the house pate with a bacon-gouda quiche and green salad made a fine lunch for two recently. Regional or ethnic specialties are listed nightly to supplement the dinner menu of broiled flounder, cod Portuguese, grilled breast of chicken and such, with everything except the filet mignon under $10.95. Be sure to save room for the apple brown betty, bourbon bread pudding, tangerine mousse or what a local gentleman told us was the best dessert he'd ever tasted, the fresh strawberries with Italian cream made from cream cheese, eggs and kirsch. Noah's is fully licensed and most wines are priced in the teens. Breakfast, 7 to 11; lunch, 11:15 to 2:30; dinner, 6 to 9 or 9:30. Closed Monday. No credit cards.

Skipper's Dock, 66 Water St., Stonington, (203) 535-2000. The food is reasonably priced and appealing and the location salubrious at this casual spot operated by the Harborview and located behind it on a pier over the water. On the canopy-covered deck we enjoyed a lunch of Portuguese stew and a tasty linguini with shrimp and clams (both $7.95). The bloody mary was enormous, the bread so good we asked for seconds and the main portions so ample we skipped dessert. The lunch menu is a smaller version of the dinner, when entrees are priced in the $9.95 to $16.95 range and the various catches of the day (perhaps salmon, tuna and swordfish) can be prepared five ways. Lunch daily, 11:30 to 4; dinner, 4 to 10. Closed November-March.

Shelter Harbor Inn, 10 Wagner Road (Route 1), Westerly, R.I., (401) 322-8883. Pretty as a picture are this inn's serene dining rooms dressed in white, especially the four elegant tables on the canopied outdoor deck and four more on a screened porch. The food is consistently good and equal to the setting. Dinner entrees ($12.95 to $16.95) are as diverse as seafood in puff pastry, almond-crusted salmon, finnan haddie, sauteed veal with a trio of mushrooms and grilled filet mignon with a sweet onion crust and brandied mushroom sauce. Be sure to try the Rhode Island johnny cakes with maple butter, a fixture among appetizers for $2.50. Finish with Indian pudding or sour cream apple pie. Equally interesting fare is available at lunch and Sunday brunch. Lunch, 11:30 to 3; dinner nightly, 5 to 10; Sunday brunch.

The Wilcox Tavern, Route 1, Charlestown, R.I., (401) 322-1829. Listed on the National Register of Historic Places, this weathered 1730 frame house has a large new addition and an outdoor patio; it looks bigger than its 160 seats. Dining is by candlelight on shiny black wood tables in the main house and in a more formal setting in the Sarah Jane Room addition. The extensive menu offers something for everyone, from $11.95 for Yankee pot roast to $16.95 for filet mignon. Lobster newburg, crab cakes, shrimp martinique and veal marsala are other possibilities. Desserts vary from blueberry sherbet to Vermont maple walnut sundae to cherry brandy jubilee. Dinner, Tuesday-Saturday 4:30 to 9 or 10, Sunday noon to 9.

Shopping

The **Mystic Seaport Stores,** outside the south gate so you don't have to pay admission to get to it, is a collection of marvelous shops including a book and print shop specializing in nautical books (even seafood cookbooks). It has a gallery with expensive paintings and prints, mostly of the sea, plus ship's models, a Victorian Christmas shop and much more. Lamps, furniture, scrimshaw belt buckles, a bakery — you name it, it's here.

Mystic is chock full of shops, most in the Main Street block beside the drawbridge or out at Olde Mystick Village (see above) and the new Mystic Factory Outlets, two complexes with a dozen outlets each. In the downtown, **The Bermuda Shop** and **Susan Casey Ltd.** are two nice women's clothing stores, and **William Bendett** is the place for preppy clothes. **Peppergrass & Tulip,** which makes up great gift baskets for any occasion, carries a selection of things for the boudoir, preserves, chocolates, wood carvings and such. **The Mixed Bag** offers decorative gifts and furnishings, **Whyever-not** has unique items from jewelry to fabrics, and **The Velvet Swan** is a good gift shop.

The Company of Craftsmen carries choice stock; we liked a fused-glass plate with cows marching around the rim. **McMonogram** sells personalized bags, aprons, sweaters and the like. **Good Hearted Bears** has them in all guises, even in reindeer outfits at Christmas. The best ice cream in town is made at the **Mystic Drawbridge Ice Cream Shoppe,** beside the drawbridge and also in Watch Hill.

The Emporium around the corner at 15 Water St. is a three-story Victorian landmark filled with things you don't really need but are fun to buy. A 1940s jukebox (with appropriate music) is at the entrance. The store is so jammed that many items for sale hang from the ceiling. Records, prints and unusual wrapping paper vie with such things as a T-shirt for toilet seats. We were tempted to send a relative in Florida one that said "Moon over Miami."

In Stonington at 105 Water St. is the **Hungry Palette,** where fabric silkscreened and printed by hand in "an obscure town in Rhode Island," say the owners, can be purchased by the yard or already made up into long skirts, sundresses and accessories like Bermuda bags. The colors are beautiful. Standouts among the many antiques shops are **Orkney & Yost,** which also sells oriental rugs, and **Grand & Water,** which stocks accessories and mahogany furniture as well. **Quimper Faience** at 141 Water St. has a large selection of firsts and seconds of the popular handpainted French china. The **Fun Company** is a hodgepodge of gifts, toys and collectibles, while **Anguilla Gallery** is a stunner with brass fish and flying sculptures among its handcrafts from around the world.

Watch Hill, as one would imagine, is full of expensive shops, some selling clothing and some rather intimidating. **Wm. Coppola Inc.** is of Watch Hill and Palm Beach. **John Everets** and **The Pendleton Shop** also specialize in clothing and resort wear. We quite like **R.W. Richins,** which has nice clothes and gifts, including our favorite Salt Marsh Pottery from North Dartmouth, Mass. **Finitney & Company** is a good gift and linen shop. Unique American crafts are featured at **Puffins,** and colorful handpainted dishes and furniture at **Comina.** Gifty items are available at the **Country Store of Watch Hill.** Pick up a sandwich or ice cream at the **Bay Street Deli** or the **St. Clair Annex.** For an experience of the past, stop at the **Olympia Tea Room,** where waitresses in black and white serve iced tea or lemonade along with more substantial fare.

The Fantastic Umbrella Factory on Route 1A in Charlestown has a collection of shops in 19th-century farm buildings around a maze of overgrown flower gardens. The traditional **Spice of Life Cafe & Deli** here was scaled down considerably in 1992 following a fire; chef Michael Bussey had plans to rebuild. In the large gift shop is an eccentric collection of gifts and a room full of cards, some of them rather raunchy. Children can watch the peacocks and what appear to be stray cats while parents shop.

FOR MORE INFORMATION: Southeastern Connecticut Tourism District, 27 Masonic St., New London, Conn. 06320, (203) 444-2206 or (800) 222-6783. The large Mystic and Shoreline Visitor Information Center in Olde Mystick Village, 536-1641, has materials for Mystic and environs as well as for much of Southern New England.

5 ✺ Summer

Lake Champlain looking toward Adirondack Mountains.

The Queen City and Isles

Burlington and The Champlain Islands, Vt.

"The most beautiful place in the world," William Dean Howells is said to have called it. The 19th-century novelist was referring to the lake country around Burlington, the Queen City by the lake, situated against a stunning backdrop of Adirondack Mountains across Lake Champlain.

The accolades continue for the state's largest city, which has blossomed into Vermont's downtown — "as downtown as Vermont gets," in the laconic words of Vermont Life magazine. The nation's mayors recently voted it America's most livable city. Beauty unfolds all along Lake Champlain, the 120-mile-long waterway that reaches into Quebec and, after the Great Lakes, is America's sixth largest fresh-water lake.

Just south of Burlington lies Shelburne, with its famed Shelburne Museum, Shelburne Farms and a rolling, pastoral landscape that gives new definition to suburbia, Vermont style. To the north are the Champlain Islands, a remote cluster of isles and byways lightly touched by civilization. Nowhere this side of Washington's Puget Sound are the vistas of lake and mountains quite so stunning, thanks to the Green Mountains on the east and the Adirondacks to the west.

The Champlain Islands remain in a time warp. In fact, time and transportation had pretty much passed by the entire region — old Indian country discovered by the French explorer Samuel de Champlain in 1609, eleven years before the Pilgrims landed at Plymouth Rock. The once-busy waterfront had fallen into disrepair, the Rutland Railroad was abandoned and, until the 1960s, Burlington was little more than a staid university town that happened to be Vermont's largest city. And that wasn't saying much.

The arrival of International Business Machines Corp. and General Electric Co. plus the completion of Interstate 89 changed all that. The city started renewing its lakefront, which most visitors and passers-through hadn't even realized was there, clearing rundown areas, restoring buildings and partially opening up the expanse from downtown to lake into what the mayor called "a people place." Meanwhile, a Montreal developer built Burlington Square, including a shopping mall, a 650-car parking garage, five office buildings and a hotel. Vendors and sidewalk cafes open onto the Church Street Marketplace, a downtown pedestrian mall. The result is a user-friendly downtown that works. And, after decades of neglect, the jewel of a waterfront is beginning to shine.

The area's cultural heritage has been enhanced in the summer by the outstanding Vermont Mozart Festival, the St. Michael's Summer Playhouse, outdoor Vermont Symphony pops concerts and chamber music at Shelburne Farms.

Don't think Burlington is all culture and gleam, however. Vermont author Ralph Nading Hill summed up well his native city: "Add to Burlington's natural endowments — Lake Champlain at its doorstep and the Green Mountains in its backyard — its Vermont birthright as a sensibly small but vital metropolis that has never overgrown its cultural and architectural heritage, and you have a northcountry mecca with one of New England's, and the country's, choicest futures."

Getting There

The area is reached by Interstate 89 from the southeast and north, Route 7 from the south and north, and Route 2 from the east and west.

Excellent bus service into and through the state is provided by Vermont Transit Co., headquartered at 135 Paul St., Burlington, (802) 864-6811.

Amtrak provides one train a day north and south through the Burlington area, the Montrealer between Washington, D.C., and Montreal. Burlington International Airport is served by Continental, USAir, United and smaller airlines.

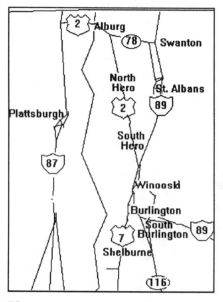

Where to Stay

The Inn at Shelburne Farms, Shelburne Farms, Shelburne 05482, (802) 985-8498 or 985-8686 (mid-October to May). The 100-room summer home of Dr. William Seward Webb and Lila Vanderbilt Webb has been refurbished into a grand inn of the old school on their 1,000-acre agricultural estate beside Lake Champlain. The rambling Queen Anne-style mansion offers 24 bedrooms and suites in interesting configurations, most with twin beds and their original furnishings from the turn of the century and fifteen with private baths. Rooms vary widely from deluxe to tiny, from corner rooms with armoires and chaise lounges and lake views to a third-floor hideaway in the front of the house (no view) where the bedroom is dwarfed in size by the bath. The main-floor public rooms are a living museum: several sitting rooms (one for afternoon tea), a library with 6,000 volumes, porches full of wicker, a game room, and a formal dining room in which breakfast and dinner are served to house guests and the public (see Where to Eat). Between meals, guests walk the grounds designed by Frederick Law Olmsted, swim at a small beach, enjoy the gardens, play croquet, shoot billiards in a game room to end all game rooms, and thoroughly savor a choice piece of property with an aura of yesteryear. Doubles, $100 to $230, EP; $192 to $322, MAP.

Radisson Hotel Burlington, 60 Battery St., Burlington 05401, (802) 658-6500. Built in the late 1970s as part of the Burlington Square retail-office complex at the edge of downtown, with a sweeping view of Lake Champlain across the road, the 256-room Radisson is for those who want all the amenities of a downtown hotel such as room service, airport limousines and a choice of eating places. The **Village Green Cafe** is for breakfast, lunch and dinner at moderate prices; **Gerard's Restaurant & Lounge** (see Where to Eat) appeals to those who want something fancier. We found the lobby austere, but the rooms are spacious and nicely decorated. The ones on the lake side and particularly those on the corners are most requested. There also are twelve suites and fourteen cabanas beside the indoor pool. The pool has a great jacuzzi on one side, a boon for aching muscles after sightseeing, and an adjacent bar and sidewalk cafe. There's also a health facility. Doubles, $95 to $135.

Sheraton-Burlington Hotel & Conference Center, 870 Williston Road, South Burlington 05403, (802) 862-6576. What started out looking like a picturesque barn on a rise near an I-89 exit is the Sheraton, which actually is built around a 150-year-old barn. It expanded like topsy in the late 1980s to the point where you need a map to find your room and to get around the campus-like complex. Enclosed pedestrian bridges and directional signs help. Some of the 309 rooms ring an interior courtyard open to the sky. Others face the indoor atrium, some of those with sliding doors onto a garden-style restaurant with an L-shaped indoor pool and fitness center beyond. Those would be fine in winter, we suppose. But, hey, this is summer in Vermont and we want a breath of fresh air; those who agree should ask for an outside room. The rooms we saw were stylish, with comfortable armchairs, and TVs tucked away in cabinets. Lunch is served in the four-story-high "summerhouse" atrium at **G's,** the aforementioned garden restaurant where diners could feel on public display. Drinks and light meals are available nearby in **Tuckaway's,** a lounge with a sun deck on the roof for swimmers who want some sun along with a splash in the indoor pool. Out front, **Baxter's** serves an appealing and varied menu for dinner (from $11.95 for chicken teriyaki to $16.75 for veal and shrimp scampi). Though rooms are attractive and comfortable, the public spaces with their garden trellises and fountains convey an artificial, Disneylandish air that some find jarring in Vermont. Doubles, $79 to $137.

Hampton Inn, 8 Mountain View Drive, Colchester 05446, (802) 655-6177. Built in 1990 at a rural location just north of the Winooski exit of I-89, this is one classy Hampton Inn. The budget chain goes upscale here with a spacious lobby, full of comfortable seating and tables with window views onto Mount Mansfield and the Worcester Range. The 188 rooms on three floors are outfitted in rich greens and burgundies; those on the third floor ensconced in dormer windows present interesting angles. Rooms facing east enjoy views of the distant mountains beyond a garden patio complete with gazebo. Even the complimentary continental breakfast here is a cut above: bagels and jars of cereals to supplement the usual. With a replica of the Colchester Reef lighthouse atop its roof, the new **Lighthouse Restaurant** displays old lake photographs and serves a steak and seafood menu from $9.95 to $14.95. Doubles, $75 to $85.

Outdoor cafes are popular along Church Street Marketplace.

Econo Lodge, 1076 Williston Road, South Burlington 05403, (802) 863-1125. In this area (Exit 14 off I-89) are many of the big chain motels, most quite near the road. But the 176-unit Econo Lodge is tucked back from the highway in a grove of trees and offers a quiet night and an attractive outdoor pool at good value. Twice in four years, the motel won the chain's national gold award as the No. 1 Econo Lodge in the nation. Next door is the **Windjammer Restaurant,** usually with a breakfast buffet and, at night, beef and seafood dishes ($8.95 to $16.95) and an extensive salad bar built into a replica of a windjammer. Families also appreciate the McDonald's across the road. Doubles, $65 to $80.

Howard Johnson Hotel, 1720 Shelburne Road, South Burlington 05403, (802) 860-6000. The newest and biggest motor inn along a strip of many is this five-story hotel, which opened in 1987 and is tiered back into the woods off Route 7. With a subsequent addition, there are now 203 rooms, all furnished in contemporary style. Billed as a hotel, it has the obligatory lobby, an indoor pool, two saunas, an exercise facility, a rooftop sun deck and a whirlpool. Next door is **What's Your Beef II,** which with its downtown original (lately renamed the Main Street Grill) calls itself Burlington's original steakhouse. Doubles, $70 to $80.

Marble Island Resort, Malletts Bay, 150 Marble Island Road, Colchester 05446, (802) 864-6800 or (800) 331-2093. This resort, down at the heels a few years ago, was transformed in 1987 into a spiffy lodging establishment and entertainment complex on an island jutting into Malletts Bay. The 34 guest rooms and mini-suites in the main building and annex, most of which have water views, are contemporary in decor and vary in size; all have private baths and TV. We're partial to the rooms in the motel annex with screened balconies backing up to the lake, but the newer mini-suites in the main building command higher prices. The sunken Hearthside dining room off the main lobby is used for dinner on weekends, but usually the action is at **Champs Fitness Center and Sports Bar** or at **Shooters Lakeside Bar & Grill.** The resort includes an eighteen-hole golf course, tennis courts, two outdoor pools, two tennis courts, three hot tubs and docking for 50 boats. Doubles, $125 to $145.

Beach and Boat Motel, 218 Lake Shore Dr., Colchester 05446, (802) 863-6577. This nine-unit motel a few miles north of Burlington is one of the few we found right on the water; it has a small pool as well as a private beach. Rooms share a common concrete balcony overlooking Malletts Bay. This is a great location, but nearby sections are somewhat honky-tonk. Doubles, $42 to $45. Open mid-April through October.

What to Do

See Downtown. Stroll along the boardwalk in the new nine-acre downtown Waterfront Park, Battery Park and through Burlington Square's lawns and shopping arcades to the Church Street Marketplace, an exceptionally nice, landscaped pedestrian mall headed by the historic brick Unitarian Church. Not for nothing is Church Street so named; close by are the spectacular Episcopal Cathedral Church of St. Paul, rebuilt after a 1971 fire and well worth a visit; the striking Catholic Cathedral of the Immaculate Conception, and the Congregational and Baptist churches with their soaring spires. A number of buildings around City Hall Park, College Street and the Battery Street waterfront are of architectural merit.

Explore the Lakefront. An 8.2-mile-long **bicycle path** stretching from Oakledge Park on the south to the Flynn Estate at the mouth of the Winooski River gets closer to the lake than any other shore route (Burlington is making good progress on opening up its waterfront to public view and access). Plans are eventually to continue the bikeway across the Winooski River through Colchester to South Hero and the Champlain Islands. Access to the path is via Oakledge and Leddy parks, North Beach, Perkins Pier and the Waterfront Park. The ribbon of tarmac winds around historic sites and breezes through verdant corridors as it offers scenic water views. It's used by walkers, joggers and roller bladers as well as cyclists.

For motorists, Pine Street south from downtown and North Avenue toward Colchester offer interesting diversions. Pine Street ends near **Red Rocks Park,** a heavily wooded picnic grove with a small beach for swimming. At the foot of Flynn Avenue, **Oakledge Park** offers picnicking, four tennis courts near the water and a rocky shoreline with good views back toward the city skyline. **Battery Park,** downtown on a crest near the lake, harbors guns that repulsed British ships in the War of 1812 and telescopes for viewing 75 peaks in the Adirondacks. Out North Avenue is the **Municipal Beach,** locally known as North Beach, with the city's best swimming, campsites, picnic tables and grills, playground and a view of the ferry (admission $1). Nearby **Leddy Park** also offers nicely wooded picnic sites near the shore. Up a winding road off Ethan Allen Parkway through **Ethan Allen Park** is a hilltop with the city's best all-around view, the Adirondacks to the west and the Green Mountains to the east. Continue out North Avenue and follow Route 127 to Colchester. Barney Point from Colchester Point Road and Marble Island Road give vistas of what the natives call "the Broad Lake," and Lakeshore Drive hugs the shore along Malletts Bay.

Take a Boat Ride. The **Spirit of Ethan Allen,** a replica of a Mississippi River paddlewheeler, leaves from Perkins Pier in downtown Burlington for 90-minute narrated cruises on Lake Champlain daily in summer at 10, noon, 2 and 4; adults $7.50, children $3.50. Be on the lookout for Champ, the legendary lake serpent; 70 passengers aboard the boat in 1984 became believers in the largest mass sighting ever. The captain's dinner cruises (adults $22.90, children $13.50) are popular with families, while the sunset and moonlight dance cruises appeal to romantics. Schedules vary, and are abbreviated after Labor Day. (The boat runs from Memorial Day to mid-October). Call (802) 862-9685 or 862-8300.

The **Burlington Ferry** leaves the King Street Dock for a scenic one-hour ride to Port Kent, N.Y., roughly every 70 minutes during the summer. Car and driver are $21 round trip, adult passengers $5.50 and children $1.50. Cheaper and more frequent ferry rides are offered from Grand Isle to Plattsburgh (crossing time twelve minutes) and from Charlotte to Essex (twenty minutes). For schedules, contact Lake Champlain Transportation Co., King Street Dock, (802) 864-9804.

Since 1988, a floating freighter known as the **Burlington Community Boathouse** has anchored the downtown waterfront. It is operated under auspices of the city recreation department as a center for water sports, renting boats and kayaks and even ice skates in the winter. There are picnic tables along the entry path, and **Whitecaps** serves basic lunches from 11:30 to 2:30. Stretching north along the lakeshore is a boardwalk promenade, where you can rest on solid wooden glider swings and look at Lake Champlain.

Robert Hull Fleming Museum, Colchester Avenue, (802) 656-0750. This expanding museum is a high point of the large and fairly nondescript University of Vermont campus. Fine, decorative and ethnographic arts are shown in several galleries in the museum, designed by McKim, Mead and White in 1931. The Egyptian mummy is usually the star of the show, as far as youngsters are concerned, At our last visit, the Frank R. Hewitt Retrospective gave a look at 75 paintings by the UVM artist after his death in 1992; a dozen bold canvases from his colorful flag series were splashed around the Marble Court. In another gallery, interesting pictures and displays depict Burlington during the Victorian era and before. The gift shop has a fine collection of cards and books. Open Tuesday-Friday 9 to 4, Saturday and Sunday 1 to 5. Free.

Ethan Allen Homestead, off Route 127 in north Burlington, (802) 865-4556. Guided tours show the restored 1787 farmhouse in which lived Ethan Allen, Vermont founder and Revolutionary War hero. Exhibits trace his life and times in the orientation center, which has a multi-media show and a gift shop. The homestead consists of the timber frame house, working gardens and several acres with hiking trails and access to the Winooski River. Open daily in summer, 10 to 5, Sunday 1 to 5; closed late October to mid-May. Adults $3.50, children $2.

Summer Entertainment. The **Vermont Mozart Festival** scheduled its 20th anniversary season in 1993 for three weeks starting in mid-July. The VMF orchestra and guest soloists give eighteen concerts at such diverse places as the Lake Champlain Ferry, the Shelburne Farms Coachyard, the Robert Frost cabin in Ripton, the Trapp Family Meadow in Stowe, local colleges and churches. Innovative programming draws thousands of concertgoers annually. The grand opening concert at the palatial lakeshore Shelburne Farms spread is a festive tradition. For schedule, contact Box 512, Burlington 05402, (802) 862-7352. Vermont's only resident stock professional theater presents performances Tuesday-Saturday at 8 throughout the summer at **St. Michael's Summer Playhouse,** St. Michael's College, in Winooski. The **Craftsbury Chamber Players** alternate concerts in the Craftsbury area with performances in Burlington at Champlain College and at the University of Vermont from mid-July to mid-August. A pre-summer highlight is the **Discover Jazz Festival** in which some 200 state and national musicians are heard in parks, restaurants, concert halls, clubs and on the streets for a week around the second week of June.

Shelburne Museum, Route 7, Shelburne, (802) 985-3344. A worthy destination in itself, this "collection of collections" depicting three centuries of Americana is truly mind-boggling. If you're a collector, you could spend day after day here. If you are a typical tourist, you may find that after six hours or so you don't want to look at another tool, quilt, painting, decoy, carriage or what have you.

Founder Electra Havemeyer Webb presided until her death in 1960 over the family collections, which are housed in 37 buildings spread over 45 acres, all beautifully landscaped with wild roses twining over rustic fences, fruit trees and flowering shrubs.

Shelburne Depot is visitor attraction at Shelburne Museum.

A free shuttle tram takes visitors from the new visitor center near the entrance to the far ends of the grounds every fifteen minutes.

The sidewheeler Ticonderoga excursion boat that cruised Lake Champlain for 47 years is what many visitors tour first; it is especially interesting to view the staterooms — some elegant and some holes in the wall — with their corner washstands; the dining room tables are set with Syracuse china. A movie that runs occasionally explains how the ship was brought overland two miles from the lake.

Among the historic structures worth visiting are a one-room schoolhouse from Vergennes, an 1871 lighthouse from the lake, a 1733 saltbox from Massachusetts, a Shaker barn filled with a fantastic collection of carriages and the last remaining two-lane covered bridge with footpath in the United States. Don't miss the Weed House, which has remarkable collections of dolls, toys, pewter and glass, and the Stencil House, with its original and very handsome stenciled walls from 1790. Our favorite is the Electra Havemeyer Webb Memorial Building, a Greek Revival mansion housing a six-room apartment taken from the Park Avenue residence of the museum founders; it is totally charming and filled with priceless paintings. The Shelburne Depot from 1890 and the private railroad car parked beside it are worth a look. The collection of wildfowl decoys here is considered the most important in the world. Altogether there are more than 80,000 pieces of Americana in this national treasure described by the New York Times as "Vermont's Smithsonian."

A cafeteria serves standard fare, and there are a couple of good museum stores.

Open daily 10 to 5, mid-May to mid-October; rest of year, guided tours by reservation daily at 1 p.m. and for families on Saturdays. Adults $14, children $6; second consecutive day free.

Shelburne Farms, 102 Harbor Road, Shelburne, (802) 985-8686. Guided tours of the 1,000-acre agricultural estate of Dr. William Seward Webb and his wife, the former Lila Vanderbilt, leave every 90 minutes from a new visitor center. Visitors board an open-air wagon to view the Farm Barn, the Dairy Barn, the Coach Barn Education Center, the beautiful gardens and the exterior of the Shelburne House, now an inn and restaurant and the delightful, Camelot-like site for concerts and special events in the summer. Shelburne Farms combines an active dairy and cheese-making operation, furniture-making, a market garden and other leased enterprises in a working farm setting flanked by lake and mountains. The cheddar cheese (we always buy a pound of the delectable extra-sharp) from a herd of cows descended from Swiss stock raised for cheese-making is sold in the fine visitor center shop, which also sells other Vermont farm products and crafts and is open daily year-round. A walking trail from the visitor center winds through woods and fields for about a mile to the top of Lone Tree Hill, which yields a superb view of Lake Champlain and the mountains. New in 1992 was a **Children's Farmyard** in the Farm Barn, where youngsters mix with the farm animals (open daily in summer, 9 to 5; adults $3.50, children $2.50). Tours daily at 9:30, 11, 12:30, 2 and 3:30, Memorial Day through mid-October. Adults $5.50, children $2.50.

Shopping

Burlington's **Church Street Marketplace,** four landscaped blocks of the main street that are closed to traffic and enlivened by sidewalk cafes, is lined with more than 100 stores and eateries as well as assorted pushcarts, from **The Cow Cart** to **Street Smart Accessories.** Off it is **Burlington Square,** an indoor shopping mall with the usual mall stores — an interesting adjunct for a lively downtown.

Church Street, which seems more thriving every time we visit, has lost two old-line stores, Abernethy's and Magrams. But trendy galleries and boutiques compensate, at least for the visitor. Here you'll find the **Peace on Earth Store** side by side with **Laura Ashley.** And **Nate's,** an old-line men's store, is next to **Kids Ink,** a children's bookstore, and across the street from **Banana Republic.** Local merchants compete head-to-head against such national retailers as **Benetton, The Lodge, Pier One Imports** and **Pompanoosuc Mills.** Among the treats for shoppers are **Chico's** for Southwest apparel, **Tempo** for home furnishings, the high-ceilinged **Chassman & Bem** bookstore with its European-style Cafe Sonata and a rack of foreign newspapers, the **Stowe Trading Post** for country apparel, **Once a Tree** for wood products and **Handblock,** purveying nifty women's wear, accessories and pottery. Other favorites are **The Penguin,** where penguin paraphernalia up front gives way to lots of clothing, gifts and accessories with a distinct adventure motif; **Frog Hollow at the Marketplace,** a branch of the Vermont State Craft Center at Frog Hollow in Middlebury; **Apple Mountain** for Vermont products, and **Nan Patrick** for classic women's apparel.

Visit **Bennington Potters North,** 127 College St., as much to see how an old brick warehouse can be restored with taste as to view the myriad items for sale: everything from aprons to egg cups to clay bird feeders to rugs and furnishings (and, of course, that good-looking pottery). **Seventh Generation** at Battery and King streets is in the vanguard of products for a healthy planet. Here you can get good ideas, from energy-efficient lighting to organic cotton clothing, and worthwhile products, from recycled materials to odor removers called "air therapy."

South of downtown is the **Cheese Outlet,** 398 Pine St., with a large selection of Vermont and imported cheeses at discount prices, wines, and luscious Vermont velvet cheesecakes. Almost across the street is the **Lake Champlain Chocolates** factory and showroom, which produces some of the best chocolates and truffles anywhere — the aroma will knock you out.

The Shelburne area has many interesting shops. The first **Talbots** store in Vermont anchors Shelburne Square, an upscale strip. The **Shelburne Country Store** has been in continuous operation since 1859, but never with more flair than lately. There are still penny candy and homemade fudge, as well as room after room full of fine crafts, toys, candles, folk art notes, lamp shades and more. Sample a taste of smoked ham and you'll probably buy some at **Harrington's,** which specializes in cob-smoked meats, pheasants, turkeys and hams, and offers "the world's best ham sandwich" for $3.75.

Factory tours are given at **The Vermont Teddy Bear Co.,** focal point of the old Jelly Mill Common, where **Chapters** teams a nature-oriented bookstore with a cafe.

More interesting shopping is found in Winooski at the **Champlain Mill,** three floors of shops and restaurants fashioned from a 1909 textile mill beside the river.

Where to Eat

In summer, Burlington appears to be one big sidewalk cafe, especially along the downtown Church Street Marketplace. And the restaurants are proliferating, with three opening within six weeks in a short block along lower Church Street at our latest visit. Outlying South Burlington and Shelburne claim good restaurants as well.

Downtown

Deja Vu Cafe & Grill, 185 Pearl St., Burlington, (802) 864-7917. Whether outside on the Spanish-style courtyard or inside on many levels or in the elegant Frank Lloyd Wright look-alike dining room, this is one beautiful restaurant (and so dimly lit that even at lunch, candles are lighted on the tables). The food is tantalizing as well. The all-day menu has lessened its traditional emphasis on crepes (now offering three in the $8.95 range) and continental cuisine in favor of more worldly fare. You might find Brazilian grilled shrimp, pasta Tuscany, Taos chicken with bean sauce, seafood Hunan, Moroccan chicken with couscous and Thai pork tenderloin as bistro plates, $8.95 to $12.95, or changing dinner specials, $14.95 to $23.95. The three-course prix-fixe dinner — including several choices of appetizer, entree and salad — is a bargain $15. We're still partial to the Breton-style crepes, one filled with smoked salmon and artichokes with jalapeno cream; another with beef tenderloin tips in a tangy demi-glace with cracked pepper and sour cream. The soupe au pistou is great, but ask for extra pistou (basil, garlic and parmesan) if you like it as much as we do. The decor is striking with all the different lamps, some wonderful glass ones fluted like lilies, and the biggest copper container we ever saw, up on a hoist and filled with plants. Even if it's not open, try to steal a look at the magnificent Wright Room, used on weekends and for private functions. Open daily, 11:30 to midnight, weekends to 1.

Gerard's Restaurant & Lounge, 60 Battery St., Burlington, (802) 864-5005. Subtitled "Windows on the Lake," the restaurant has been nicely relocated from a window-less area of the Burlington Radisson Hotel to a former disco on the hotel's lakeside second floor, where tall windows and tiered levels take full advantage. The mix of banquettes and tables is sophisticated, the service urbane, the presentation artistic and the food controversial, though generally highly regarded. The controversy stems from owner Gerard Rubaud's use of vacuum-pack gourmet food prepared at his Gerard's Haute Cuisine enterprise in nearby Fairfax. Specialties here include a creamy lobster bisque, escargots with wild mushrooms in puff pastry, poached fillet of Norwegian salmon, and roasted duck with scalloped potatoes and bordelaise sauce. Prices run from $12.90 for Thai red curry chicken or grilled turkey medallions to $19 for rack of lamb. Bouillabaisse is $26 for two. The lunch menu is similar but abbreviated in length and price, $5.90 to $8.90. Both menus are available at the new outdoor cafe, from which the Adirondacks are on bold display across the lake. A three-course sunset dinner special with beverage is $25 for two on weeknights in summer. A gourmet brunch is served for $14.95, a light brunch for $9.95. Lunch daily, 11:30 to 2; dinner, 5:30 to 9:30 or 10; Sunday brunch, 9 to 3.

Isabel's on the Waterfront, 112 Lake St., Burlington, (802) 865-2522. Growing from a catering service into a thriving lunch-brunch spot, Isabel's added dinner service three nights a week in 1992. The dinners are a great addition, inside in the high-ceilinged room backing up to a self-service counter and an open kitchen and outside on a canopied terrace not far from the lake. The short menu changes weekly. Entrees, including soup or salad, run from $11.50 for orange rosemary chicken to $13.50 for beef tournedos.

Regulars remain partial to Isabel's for lunch, when you pick your selection from the samples displayed on show plates at the counter. We enjoyed a platter of shrimp and snow peas oriental with egg fettuccine and a build-your-own salad. You might try sauteed scallops with salad, mushroom ravioli alfredo or soup and caesar salad with chicken, generally in the $5.75 to
$6.95 range. Brunch items include two kinds of vegetables benedict and "Old Mac-Donald Goes to France" ($7.95): a croissant topped with two poached eggs, sausage patties, mushrooms, brie and hollandaise. Weekday lunch and Sunday brunch, 11 to 2; dinner, Thursday-Saturday 5:30 to 9.

The Daily Planet, 15 Center St., Burlington, (802) 862-9647. Immensely popular with the university crowd, the name of this funky place reflects its global fare, which is consistent and creative. The chefs shine with things like Vietnamese shrimp patties, Thai chicken and green beans, Brazilian seafood stew, roast duck with rhubarb sauce, chicken with goat cheese, and grilled lamb loin with a salad of fennel, red onion and orange with feta flatbread, pleasantly priced in the $5 to $6 range at lunch and $9.50 to $15.50 at dinner. At lunch, try the pan bagnat, a baguette stuffed with cheese, grilled provencal vegetables and arugula. Besides an enormous bar, there are several dining rooms in which the oilcloth table coverings at noon give way to white linens at night. Lunch, Monday-Friday 11:30 to 3; dinner nightly, 5 to 10:30 or 11; Saturday and Sunday brunch, 11 to 3.

Sweet Tomatoes Trattoria, 83 Church St., Burlington, (802) 660-9533. Borrowing a page from their smash-success restaurant of the same name in Lebanon, N.H., Robert Meyers and James Reiman opened a carbon copy here in 1992. From Burlington's first wood-fired brick oven come zesty pizzas like the namesake sweet tomato pie, a combination of tomato, basil, mozzarella and olive oil ($7.75). From the rest of the open kitchen that runs along the side of the long, narrow and surprisingly large downstairs space come earthy pastas, grills and entrees at wallet-pleasing prices — $9.95 is the top price, for a mixed grill or skewers of lamb. The stark decor in white and black is offset by brick arches and stone walls — a convivial, noisy setting for what Robert calls "strictly ethnic Italian cooking, as prepared in a home kitchen." Lunch, Monday-Saturday 11:30 to 5; dinner, 5 to 10, Sunday to 9.

Coyotes Tex-Mex Cafe, 161 Church St., Burlington, (802) 865-3632. Another 1992 newcomer and a quick success is this venture fashioned from a rundown arcade. Brothers Eric and Jeff Lipkin from Kennebunkport, Me., teamed with Jim Glatz of Philadelphia to produce as authentic a Tex-Mex menu as possible (considering the far northern location) in a very authentic setting. The place is striking for its inlaid tile tables imported from Mexico, walls sponged burnt orange and shelves of pottery from the famed Goose Rocks Pottery owned by the brothers' parents. Rattlesnake beer and "ultimate" margaritas are served at a long bar converted from a bowling lane. Texas Hellfire sauce is on each table to add heat to the already hot fare; things like three-bean chipotle chili, blackened chicken fingers, a basket of corn fritters and fajitas. Main-course prices run from $4.25 for a Texas burger topped with chili to $11.95 for cowboy steak. The tortilla chips, crisp and light, come with a zesty salsa that's addictive. We also liked the black bean soup, again with its own kick, served in a heavy custom-made bowl. The Amarillo appetizer sampler (five changing choices, $5.95) was less successful, and a taco chicken salad ($4.95) proved far too much to eat. Next time we'd try the tequila chicken ($7.95), served with rice and sauteed vegetables. Lunch daily, 11:30 to 4; dinner, 11:30 to 10; late-night menu to 12:30.

The Ice House, 171 Battery St., Burlington, (802) 864-1800. Even if you don't eat here, drive by to see the charming Brueghel-like sign in front depicting ice skaters on the lake. The inside of this massive, restored stone waterfront building (it was an ice house early in the century) is charming as well, with sofas to sink into in the large upstairs lounge with its huge and rough original beams. Downstairs in the restaurant, try as an appetizer mussels pomodoro ($6.95 and enough for two). There are interesting salads, and several entrees can be ordered in small portions. Otherwise, prices range from $14.95 for grilled chicken over spinach linguini with broccoli and roasted red peppers to $20.95 for grilled rack of Vermont lamb with roasted eggplant roulade and red potato. In nice weather, dine outside on a trellised patio good for sunset-watching, with glimpses of the lake beyond the sheds of a boat yard. Lunch daily, 11:30 to 2:30; dinner, 5 to 10; Sunday brunch, 10:30 to 2:30.

Dockside Cafe, 209 Battery St., Burlington, (802) 864-5266. This casual seafood restaurant is in the Old Stone Store, built of limestone in 1825 and just as solid today with its stone walls and beamed ceiling. Its traditional fare has been updated lately. In addition to seafood chowder, fried clams and fisherman's platter, you can get smoked Vermont brook trout alfredo with sundried tomatoes and linguini or deep-fried alligator chips with cajun mango dipping sauce for starters. Black-bean stir-fry, Jamaican pork stew, grilled tournedos and lobster with brandied cream sauce, and broiled rack of lamb are among entrees priced from $9.95 to $17.95. There are glass-topped tables, a nautical bar, a slate floor and a jaunty outdoor patio with a view of the lake off Perkins Pier. Lunch daily, 11:30 to 4:30; dinner, 4:30 to 9 or 10.

Sweetwaters, Church and College Streets, Burlington, (802) 864-9800. A brick bank, built in 1926, houses one of Burlington's more popular restaurants with dining on several levels around an enormous mural in an atrium, and outside on a canopy-covered sidewalk cafe that's always crowded in summer. A cafe menu served all day offers things like potato skins, cheese nachos, chicken fingers and beer-batter shrimp ($4.95 to $6.95). Salads and Perry Farms bison burgers, from a herd raised on the Perry restaurant chain's farm in Charlotte, are featured at lunch. At night, more substantial entrees ($9.95 to $12.95) include pineapple cashew chicken, grilled duck steak and London broil. Open daily from 11:30 to 1 a.m., Sunday from 10:30 to 10.

Other downtown choices:

Sakura, 2 Church St., is authentic Japanese, from the sushi bar to the raised tatami room in which you sit on cushions and take off your shoes. More than two dozen appetizers are offered, and most offerings are numbered to help make yourself understood to the mainly Japanese staff. Prices range widely up to a combination dinner for $19.50. Lunch, Tuesday-Saturday, dinner, Tuesday-Sunday.

If you're hankering for something spicy, head for **Five Spice Cafe** at 175 Church St. The multi-Asian menu features unusual and tantalizing dishes from India, Thailand, Vietnam, Indonesia and China. Dinner entrees run from $11.95 for chicken curry to $14.50 for Thai fire shrimp. After a fiery meal, pick up a Five Spice T-shirt emblazoned with fire-breathing dragons and the saying, "Some Like It Hot." Sunday brings a dim sum brunch. Lunch and dinner daily.

Alfredo's Restaurant, 79 Mechanics Lane, expanded up front onto Church Street in 1992 with an enclosed storefront bistro and a sidewalk cafe to supplement its traditional back-alley interior and a rear trellised courtyard away from the crowds. The fare is basic Italian, $11.95 to $16.95. We'd stop late-night at one of the faux-marble tables in the sidewalk cafe and end an evening with gelato tartufo or spumoni truffle.

Desserts and pastries that turn up at the best parties in town come from **Mirabelles,** 198 Main St., a marvelous new bakery and deli created by Alison Fox and Andrew Silva and named for the golden plums grown on the Continent, where both had worked. Sandwiches are inspired, perhaps goat cheese with Mediterranean tapenade and fresh vegetables for $4.50. The ploughman's lunch ($5.95) is a sampling of cheeses, breads, fruits and a sweet. There are a handful of tables inside and out.

The breakfast special is really special at **Leunig's Old World Cafe,** a European cafe spilling onto the sidewalks at Church and College streets. It's eggs benedict and cappuccino, for a bargain $4.95. Lunch and dinner treats are equally novel, priced up to $11.95.

Sebastian's Gourmet Pizzeria & Deli, 179 Church St., was the latest place to open in 1992 in the revitalized lower Church Street area that's now chock-a-block eateries with an international flair (not counting Wendy's at the corner). Here you'll find scallops with pesto among fifteen gourmet pizzas ($8.50 to $13.50) baked in a maplewood oven. The Sunday brunch yields breakfast pizzas.

Freddy's Say Humbaby, 171 Church St., is the East's first vegetarian fast-food restaurant, according to owner Fred Solomon. Veggie burgers, veggie hot dogs, veggie sandwiches and subs, soups and chilis are available at the counter, McDonald's style. Say "humbaby" — a baseball term — and get "our version of a whopper with cheese" for $2.44, says Fred. We liked the vegetarian chili just fine, but found the miso onion soup tasted more like water and the falafel sandwich was a crumbling mix of pita and marble-hard falafel that couldn't be rescued even with a knife and fork.

The Vermont Pub & Brewery, 144 College St., combines a Victorian pub, restaurant and terrace cafe with a brewery. Up to five ales and lagers are on tap, fresh from the brewery below. Much of the menu is predictably snacky with a few dinner entrees from $8.25 for raspberry teriyaki chicken to $12.95 for black angus steak. The Sunday Welsh brunch is a surprise, authentic from oatmeal pancakes to leek omelet to baked trout with apple bacon and scones.

Ben and Jerry's (the original in the ever-expanding chain) at 169 Cherry St. serves the best ice cream cone ever. Stop in for a Heath Bar crunch, our favorite, or a white Russian or a grand marnier made with real liqueur.

On the Outskirts of Town

Cafe Shelburne, Route 7, Shelburne, (802) 985-3939. This prize of a small provincial French restaurant is better than ever following its acquisition by Patrick Grangien, a Frenchman who trained with Paul Bocuse. The copper bar, several dining areas that look as if they're straight from the European countryside and a screened and latticed rear patio all appeal. So does Patrick's updated-French menu, priced from $15 for chicken tarragon with homemade mustard-seed fettuccine to four dishes for $18.50, including shelled lobster on homemade curry fettuccine and sauteed fillet of lamb sliced over a bed of spinach and served with an herbed carrot mousse. Start with broccoli soup served with wild rice and steamed Maine shrimp or fricassee of frog's legs with shiitake mushrooms. End a memorable meal with the specialty creme brulee. Dinner, Tuesday-Sunday 5:30 to 9:30.

The Inn at Shelburne Farms, Shelburne (802) 985-8498. The lavish, landmark inn

Eating at outdoor cafes is pleasant summer pastime in downtown Burlington.

at Shelburne House harbors one of the area's more acclaimed restaurants. Dining is an event in the serene Marble Room, quite stunning with formally set tables, red fabric-covered walls and tiled floors in black and white. Chef Matt Larson, who studied at La Varenne in France, summers here and winters at Snowbird ski resort in Utah. Diners at both are the luckier for the match. His menu changes daily to feature the freshest of local ingredients. You might start with chilled avocado soup with yogurt and chives, risotto with smoked chicken, radicchio and pinenuts or marinated squid salad with ginger and scallions ($4 to $7). For a main course ($16.50 to $23.50), how about fillet of salmon with sorrel-champagne sauce or roasted rack of Vermont lamb with a grand marnier and green peppercorn sauce? Dessert could be maple creme brulee with Russian tea cakes or frozen hazelnut-chocolate terrine with raspberries. The experience is pricey, but the setting worth it for those with deep pockets. Dinner nightly, 6 to 9. Closed mid-October to mid-May.

Chaz Restaurant & Cafe, 1016 Shelburne Road, South Burlington, (802) 658-2325. Chaz Sternberg, always at the cutting edge of things culinary in the Burlington area, finally opened his own restaurant in 1992 in the front of the Best Western Redwood Inn. Here he has a main-floor cafe, lounge and espresso bar and a dramatic upstairs dining room with windows onto a lake and mountain view. His changing menu features heart-healthy cuisine (no cream, eggs or butter used in sauces). Start with his caesar salad with crispy fried oysters or a lobster and scallop sausage with tomato pasta salad. Entrees ($12.50 to $15.50) could be salmon fillet stuffed with crabmeat mousse or duck breast with a sauce of toasted fennel and peaches. Dinner begins with a complimentary baked garlic with Spanish tapenade, and a blueberry and raspberry granite prepares the palate for the main course. Finish with Chaz's specialty hot cheesecake or a chocolate torte layered with raspberries and pistachios. At our visit, a chocolate-covered strawberry garnished each large black cafe plate, overflowing with grilled swordfish, rock cornish game hen or seared sirloin steak, $7.95 to $10.95 from the cafe menu. Breakfast daily, 7:30 to 10:30, Saturday to noon, Sunday to 2; dinner nightly, 5:30 to 9:30 or 10.

Pauline's Cafe & Restaurant, 1834 Shelburne Road, South Burlington, (802) 862-1081. Pat and Robert Fuller (he was a chef at Mister Up's in Middlebury and she owned a bakery) run this fine dining spot just south of town as well as Burlington's stellar Deja Vu, which they purchased in 1987. The main floor is a cafe paneled in cherry and oak, where you can get a good meal for $5.95 to $9.50. Upstairs, all is serene and white in three small dining rooms. The printed menu changes nightly and is one of those on which everything appeals. Entrees from $13.50 to $22.95 included smoked

81

duck breast with confit leg and ginger, shrimp etouffee, venison with apples and rack of lamb with pepper relish at one visit. We fondly remember a spring dinner that began with morels and local fiddleheads in a rich madeira sauce and a sprightly dish of shrimp and scallops in ginger. Pauline's serves light and full lunches as well as bargain early dinners for $9.95, and has a pleasant little patio for warm weather. Lunch daily, 11:30 to 2; cafe menu 2 to 10; dinner, 5:30 to 10; Sunday brunch, 10:30 to 2. No smoking.

Francesca's, 2012 Shelburne Road, Shelburne, (802) 985-3373. Sophisticated northern Italian fare is the theme at this spacious establishment, expanded from the old Potting Shed restaurant and now including the Burlington area's ubiquitous outdoor dining terrace, this one hidden away from traffic in the rear and bedecked with owner Francesca Muratori's flowers. Her husband, Taste of Vermont award-winning chef Scott Vineberg, oversees the kitchen. The varied menu includes about eighteen pastas ($7.95 to $13.95) and a dozen main dishes ($10.95 to $16.95), all served with garlic bread and house salad. The fettuccine with shrimp, scallops and broccoli in a cream sauces entices, as does the charbroiled salmon with pesto-cream butter. We can vouch for a special of mussels and tuna alla panna with tomato and dill offered at one summer's lunch. Chocolate chambord torte and white chocolate cheesecake are among the luscious desserts. Lunch in summer, 11:30 to 2:30; dinner nightly, 5 to 10.

Perry's Fish House & Market, 1080 Shelburne Road, South Burlington, (802) 862-1300. The locals love this vast seafood emporium and adjacent market, as they do the local chain's Sirloin Saloons. The reasons are obvious: nautical decor (the outside, from driftwood to landscaping, looks like something you'd find in Florida; inside, maritime memorabilia hangs on walls and ceilings in four dining areas), and the "daily delivery report" on the blackboard tells species, origin and price. The large menu has all the standards, including a month-long special on lobster five ways at our visit. But the centerpiece is the nightly specials, unadulterated preparations of, say, broiled sea scallops, wood-grilled mako shark and tuna, grilled swordfish, Maryland crab cakes and king crab, $10.95 to $19.95. There's a minnow's menu for kids, who really eat this place up. Homemade key lime pie is the dessert of choice. If you're not here at dinner time, pick up a sandwich or salad or fish to go at Perry's neat new market new door. Dinner nightly, 5 to 10, weekends 4:30 to 11, Sunday 3 to 10.

The Lake Champlain Islands

Starting a dozen or so miles north of Burlington, these four pencil-shaped, interconnected islands stretch 30 miles to the Canadian border and are where you really get away from it all and revert to the long-forgotten past.

Tourist trappings have bypassed this lovely island setting (we'll never forget the Fourth of July parade in South Hero some years ago — a couple of makeshift floats and bands, plus our children's flag-waving cousins from Montreal, whose photo made the front page of the next day's Burlington Free Press; here was small-town America at its smallest).

The southern entrance to the islands via Route 2 passes the area's best lake swimming at Sand Bar State Park, where Burlington residents go to swim and picnic in a scenic grove. Beside it is the Sand Bar Wildlife Area for birdwatchers. Another recreation spot farther along is Knight Point State Park, with swimming, boating and campsites.

The Sandbar Motor Inn & Restaurant, Route 2, South Hero 05486, (802) 372-6911, is just across the Sand Bar causeway from the mainland. A simple 37-room facility with a million-dollar Hilton view, this is a motel with T.L.C. Its generally smallish rooms bear such caring touches as homemade wreaths above the beds and bouquets of

Thomas Mott Homestead, with raspberry bushes in foreground and lake in background.

fresh flowers gathered from the prolific gardens out front. There are housekeeping units as well. Sit by the fire in the locally popular restaurant (open for breakfast and dinner) and feast on mushroom caps stuffed with seafood ($3.95), followed by roast turkey ($8.95) or a steak ($11.95 to $15.25). Desserts are often made from local apples. The Sandbar has a private stony beach, rental boats and sailboards, a playground and games area on the lawn, and views of the lake and mountains from both front and back. Doubles, $45 to $52; efficiencies, $60 to $85. Open May-October.

Shore Acres Inn and Restaurant, Route 2, North Hero 05474, (802) 372-8722, is a secluded complex set well back from the highway on 50 acres of rolling grounds beside the lake. There are nineteen lakeview rooms in two motel-type wings on either side of the pleasant dining room and four new rooms in a garden house annex that operates as a B&B in the off-season. Each room has private bath, color TV, pine paneling and maple furniture. The lakeview restaurant serves breakfast, lunch and dinner daily in summer. At dinner, begin with coconut beer shrimp or grilled chicken and vegetable kabob. Entrees ($9.95 to $17.95) run from ground sirloin and grilled pork chop to an oversize New York strip steak. Doubles, $69.50 to $91.50. Open May to mid-October; B&B open all year.

The North Hero House, Route 2, North Hero 05474, (802) 372-8237, emits a homey, old-fashioned summer resort feeling. Right on Lake Champlain and good for all kinds of boating activities, it offers six simple rooms in the main inn and seventeen more in three lakeside houses with private baths; those on the lakefront come with porches. Most coveted is the Cobbler's Room, a suite with fireplaced living room, beamed ceilings and screened porch. Meals in the pleasant dining room, part of which is a fuschsia-filled greenhouse, are highly rated, although breakfast has been scaled down to continental and lunch no longer is served. The extensive dinner menu, written in English with French translations, offers everything from fettuccine alfredo to steak diane for $9.95 to $17.95. A Friday night tradition that packs in the locals is the $18.95

lobster buffet served on the pier. This is a great place to unwind, and many people book the same room for the same week every summer. Doubles, $41 to $80; suite, $95. Open mid-June to Labor Day.

The **Thomas Mott Homestead,** Blue Rock Road, Alburg 05440, (802) 796-3736 or (800) 348-0843, is one of our favorite B&Bs anywhere. Ex-California wine distributor Pat Schallert transformed an 1838 farmhouse into a homey B&B with four spacious guest rooms with private baths and a secluded lakeside location with panoramic water and mountain views that won't quit. The fireplaced living room is stocked with books and magazines, three porches invite lounging, and Pat cooks up a hearty breakfast in a spacious dining room open to the kitchen. Raspberry or blackberry pancakes, crab or shrimp omelets, and french toast spread with cream cheese and five kinds of nuts are in his extensive repertoire. Prix-fixe dinners that are quite a bargain are served by area caterers Joli Fare by prior arrangement. Other special touches that make this place a winner: a stash of Ben & Jerry's ice cream in the refrigerator, a lakeside gazebo, a patch of "stealing" raspberries and what Pat was calling (before the 1992 election) his vice presidential suite, a pen beside the barn where he raises quail. Doubles, $50 to $65.

In 1992, the islands became the summer home for the **Royal Lipizzan Stallions** of Austria, which winter in Myakka City, Fla. The fourteen purebred descendants of a line established in 1580 are known for their acrobatic leaps and other precisely executed maneuvers. From early July to Labor Day, they perform Thursday-Saturday at 6 and Sunday at 2:30 (adults $15, children $10) on a field above the lake in North Hero, where spectators occupy folding chairs beneath a striped canopy or a couple of sections of open-air bleachers. The Lipizzans are owned and directed by Col. Ottomar Herrmann, who with his father and the help of General Patton smuggled them out of Austria during World War II. The stallions can be viewed in their off-hours in their tent stable or working out on the field off Route 2, just south of North Hero.

Beside Route 2 at Grand Isle is the **Hyde Log Cabin,** considered the oldest log cabin standing in the United States and an official state historic site. Built in 1783 of hand-hewn logs, it is maintained by the Grand Isle Historical Society and displays tools, furnishings and documents Wednesday-Sunday 9:30 to 5:30 in summer, weekends only in fall; donation.

Thousands of pilgrims visit **St. Anne's Shrine** on Isle La Motte, site of Vermont's first white settlement, where the first Mass was celebrated in 1666. An open-sided chapel in a lakeside pine grove marks the spot where Samuel de Champlain landed in 1609. The shrine is primitive, in keeping with island tradition, but visitors may swim from the beach, picnic or snack in a simple cafeteria. Open free, May 15 to Oct. 15.

The **Ed Weed Fish Culture Station,** 14 Bell Hill Road, next to the ferry terminal in Grand Isle, is the newest of five fish hatcheries maintained by the state to provide fish for public waters throughout Vermont. This multi-million-dollar facility is state of the art. A visitor center includes aquaria, displays on the lake's ecology and self-guided tours. Open daily, 8 to 4.

Let's conclude with an apple a day. Why are we telling you to go to an apple stand? Well, the **Apple Farm Market** on Route 2, South Hero, isn't your everyday apple stand. You can choose from many kinds of apples, watch cider being made and get fresh apple or pumpkin pies, all kinds of Vermont cheeses, honeys, jellies and jams. A gift shop is stocked with cow and cat things, from sox to ceramics. Adjacent is a no-frills snack bar and ice cream stand, where a hot dog sells for $1 and sandwiches cost $2.45 to $2.55.

FOR MORE INFORMATION: Lake Champlain Regional Chamber of Commerce, 209 Battery St., Burlington 05402, (802) 863-3489. Lake Champlain Islands Chamber of Commerce, Box 213, North Hero 05474, (802) 372-5683.

More than 100 steps lead to ocean beach at Mohegan Bluffs on Block Island.

An Island Idyll

Block Island, R.I.

Block Island is a seascape in bright green, soft blue and touches of gray. The greens are the rolling hills; the blue, the sky and sea; the gray, the weathered houses and the old stone walls.

We first visited the island in 1970. At that time, The Block (as it's affectionately known) was barely awakening from its postwar lethargy. Big old Victorian hotels that had drawn crowds via steamer from New York City at the turn of the century were boarded-up hulks. A guest house or two — notably the 1661 Inn — were just beginning to get into the business again.

Only seven miles long by three miles wide, lying thirteen miles off the Rhode Island mainland, Block Island was more or less bypassed by those who made Martha's Vineyard and Nantucket *the* places to go. Its tiny town of Old Harbor (officially New Shoreham) didn't have much to offer: no hospital, few stores, a couple of independent groceries. The weather was occasionally so blustery that neither ferry nor airport could function. Only 500 people hung around in the winter.

Among those who spent part or all of their summers on Block Island, fierce loyalties developed. They returned year after year, and still do.

Two and three-acre zoning outside town has limited the number of houses that can be built. It's also preserved the vistas of rolling green hills with distant views of the water. The island has been likened to Ireland. It's not a bad comparison.

In 1991 The Nature Conservancy, an international organization serious about protecting biodiversity, gave Block Island its blessing. It proclaimed Block Island one of America's "Last Great Places" — and Chris Littlefield, whose family goes back to 1670 on the island, is doing his best to keep it that way. As bioreserve manager for the conservancy on the island, he works full time to acquire land and protect open space, to acquaint people with the island's history and habitats, to get them on his side: the side of the environmentally concerned.

So far, the effort is working.

Block Island is for the discriminating traveler, the kind who can be happy with a book on the beach or a bike ride to the far end of the island. He's the type who has learned to entertain himself and who doesn't expect a song and dance band to greet him wherever he goes. He might be found in cutoff jeans and a T-shirt or, at most, a pair of casual pants. He doesn't expect, nor does he want, a TV or a telephone in his room. If you're that kind of traveler, then Block Island is the place for you.

Getting There

The main port of embarkation for ferry service to Block Island is Point Judith, Galilee, R.I., from which year-round service is offered. There are eight to ten trips a day each way from mid-June to September; ferries run less often at other times. The trip takes an hour. Approximate one-way fares: adults $6.60, children $3.15, cars $20, motorcycles $12, bicycles $2. One-day round trips are available at a reduced rate. Reserve well in advance to take a car during the summer.

Daily ferries also run in summer from New London, Conn. The Anna C. takes two hours to reach the island. One-way costs: car $25, adults $14, children $9.

For information on Rhode Island ferries, contact Interstate Navigation Co., Galilee State Pier, Point Judith, R.I. 02882, (401) 783-4613. For information on the New London ferry, contact Nelseco Navigation Co., Box 482, New London, CT 06320, (203) 442-7891 or 442-9553.

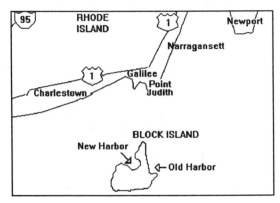

More and more people are reaching the island by air. New England Airlines offers nearly twenty flights a day from Westerly, R.I. Call (401) 596-2460 in Westerly or (401) 466-5881 on Block Island or (800) 243-2460 (outside Rhode Island). Action Airlines offers flights from Groton/New

Bicycles at the beach are characteristic of Block Island.

London and LaGuardia airports. For information call (203) 488-1646 or (800) 243-8623.

Getting Around

You don't need a car, particularly for a stay of two or three days. Getting car reservations on the ferry in midseason can be a hassle anyway. Bicycles, leisurely and quiet, are the preferred mode of travel; they can be rented for $8 to $12 a day. Walking is also recommended; if you stay in Old Harbor you can walk to just about everything, including the beach. Mopeds are noisy and often the drivers are inexperienced, making for some hairy adventures. Should you feel confident, expect to pay $40 a day for a single-passenger vehicle, $55 for a two-seater.

Where to Stay

Accommodations on Block Island are found in simple summer hotels with rocking chairs on the porches, in refurbished Victorian hostelries filled with pressed oak furniture and floral wallpapers, in small cottages and rental houses, and in increasingly sophisticated bed and breakfasts. Camping is prohibited on the island. If it's summer, it is imperative to have a reservation before you go. You may feel as if you've undergone a reverse time warp and are back at the turn of the century; in some ways you will be right. Three-night minimums are common on weekends in season.

To write for accommodations, simply address the inn as listed in care of Block Island, R.I. 02807.

The Barrington Inn, Beach and Ocean Avenues, New Harbor, (401) 466-5510. Joan and Howard Ballard are consummate and charming hosts at this six-room B&B, located high on a knoll with a view of Great Salt Pond and its inner harbors. Location is excellent: just a short walk into Old Harbor, and just down the street to a great beach. The Ballards put out fluffy striped beach towels in the parlor for guests to use. We like Room 4 with its own deck overlooking the pond. A grassy terrace with lawn furniture is good for lounging. A continental-plus breakfast is served in a large, bright room where most guests share one big table. The muffins are always freshly baked, fresh fruit is served in addition to juice, and you can scoop up the inn's own granola and yogurt. Doubles, $90 to $115.

The Atlantic Inn, Box 188, High Street, Old Harbor, (401) 466-2005. Situated on a grassy hilltop where it is sure to get the best of the island's breezes and distant views of the sea, this large Victorian hotel was renovated in 1982 and then totally redone in 1986. It is most welcoming, from the blue deck chairs and white tables scattered on the front lawn and across the large front porch to the Victorian furniture with needlepoint-look upholstery in the lobby. Check out the antique wooden phone booth with a working pay phone. The bar is one of our favorites, outfitted with bentwood bar stools, Victorian settees and sofas; it's a great place to sip sherry on a rainy evening, listening to classical music on tape. On a nice afternoon the porch is crowded for happy hour. The 21 rooms, all with private baths, feature off-white Victorian-style bedspreads with pillow shams, antique oak armoires and dressers, floral carpeting and baskets of amenities on the bureau. Resident managers keep changing, which gives us pause, but so far they seem to be doing a good job. Doubles, $110 to $160; family suite, $170. Open June-October.

Rose Farm Inn, Box E, off High Street, Old Harbor, (401) 466-2021. Robert and Judith Rose operate this comfortable B&B located off a road behind the Atlantic Inn and with the same wonderful breezes and views. Once the original farmhouse for the area, it has a marvelous stone porch that has been enclosed and turned into a multi-windowed breakfast room. All ten rooms have private tiled baths, except for two that share a bath and are popular with families. Cereal, fruit and homemade breakfast breads are the fare for continental breakfast. Guests are provided beach towels for a day at the beach; they also may use an attractive sun deck. Rooms on the east side of the inn enjoy views of the water. Double, $90 to $155. Open May-October.

1661 Inn, Guest House, and Hotel Manisses, Spring Street, Old Harbor, (401) 466-2421 or (401) 466-2063. The Abrams family of Providence took the plunge and opened the 1661 Inn, a refurbished and pleasant B&B, in 1969. Since then, they have added and upgraded, and taken over the large Victorian hotel down the street as well. Guests have a choice of accommodations, but by 1993 all were fairly elegant. The nine plush rooms in the 1661 Inn are furnished in antiques and come with private baths and refrigerators. Five have jacuzzis and eight have private sun decks. Breakfast is served daily in the oceanview dining rooms, either inside or on a covered deck. Guests at The Guest House next door and at the Manisses Hotel enjoy the same huge buffet breakfast. The Guest House offers a range of rooms; a few share baths and a wicker-filled living room, some have private baths and ocean views, and three new rooms possess loft areas and fireplaces. In the Victorian hotel, the Manisses, seventeen rooms with private baths and telephones are beautifully decorated with turn-of-the-century furniture. Some have jacuzzis. Beds are double, queen or kingsize. The large lobby with dramatic wallpaper (pink flowers on a blue background) is a great place to relax. In the evening, flaming coffees and desserts are served here. Outside are an exquisite flower garden and even a petting zoo. The main dining room downstairs is highly regarded (see Where to Eat). Doubles, $75 to $275. Some rooms are available year-round.

The Blue Dory Inn, Dodge Street, Old Harbor, (401) 466-5891. Ann and Ed Loedy run this four-building inn situated at the bend in the road where the downtown area meets the beach. Ten rooms are found in the Victorian main house with gingerbread trim; there are also The Tea Room, an efficiency with queensize bed, The Doll House and The Cottage, the last sleeping four to seven. Ann, whose background is the health care industry, is a nurturing hostess; she makes special cookies to place in a basket in the front parlor, and serves a continental breakfast in a charming room or out on the deck. Never seeming to run out of ideas, she was thinking of serving teas and spiced coffees in the afternoon to the public as well as guests. Doubles, $125 to $170.

The Surf Hotel, Dodge and Water Streets, Old Harbor, (401) 466-2241 or (401)

Atlantic Inn is typical Victorian hostelry on Block Island.

466-5990. This grand old Victorian hotel, built in 1876, is perfectly situated between the activity of Old Harbor and the glorious beach that runs for miles along the island's east coast. You can walk to everything. To some visitors the Surf is synonymous with the island itself, and the Ulric Cyr family, which has run the hotel for more than 30 years, keeps things pretty much the same from year to year. You will still find the popcorn wagon on the rocking-chair-lined front porch, where people-watchers have their fill; just about everyone on the island passes here sooner or later. The oversize chess set and a color TV in the lobby are often in use. Out back is a smaller porch for those who like to read and to contemplate the sea. All 35 rooms in the hotel share baths, but each has its own sink. The Surfside Cottage has some rooms with private baths. Views from oceanside rooms are labeled "powerful" by a friend. In 1992 the Surf stopped serving its famous full breakfasts, offering donuts and coffee to inn guests only. The Surf requires a six-night minimum stay in July and August, but seems to fill up regardless. Doubles, $70 to $120. Open end of May to early October.

The Inn at Old Harbour, Water Street, Box 994, Old Harbor, (401) 466-2212. Located not far from the ferry dock, this inn on the second and third floors above shops in Old Harbor is beautifully decorated. We love the romance of Room 1 with lilac-sprigged wallpaper, an iron Nantucket basket bed and white organdy curtains — perfect for honeymooners or second honeymooners. Many of the ten rooms yield ocean views, most rooms have private baths and all are furnished in period pieces. Continental breakfast is served in a light pine lobby, bright and sunny, which overlooks the street. You can enjoy a drink and the ocean view from the wraparound porch. Doubles, $95 to $150. Open mid-May through September.

The Harborside Inn, Water Street, Old Harbor, (401) 466-5504 or (401) 466-2693. Situated across the street from the ferry landing, the Harborside's perky red and white striped umbrellas and colorful window boxes offer a cheery welcome. Location alone makes this a good choice for those who want to be in on the action; the large, nautically accented bar is a gathering spot, and the street out front is bustling with activity. There are 42 rooms in the main inn, eight of which share baths. Rattan beds and furniture, wall-to-wall carpeting, private baths and good views of the harbor activity make several rooms in the front of the building especially appealing. The large hall baths are communal affairs with several stall showers. A full breakfast is included in the room rate in season and the dining room also serves lunch and dinner — at those umbrellaed tables in good weather. Doubles, $65 to $145.

The National Hotel, Water Street, Old Harbor, (401) 466-2901 or (800) 225-2449. This gigantic white hotel dominates the view of town as the ferry pulls into the dock.

Refurbished and restored (from several years as a decrepit, non-functioning eyesore), the hotel has been attracting crowds to its bar since its reopening in 1984. The bar is a real meeting place, in fact, and by 4 o'clock of a summer's afternoon it's sometimes all you can do to find a place to sit. If you want a quiet, off-the-beaten-track place, this probably isn't it. All 43 rooms have private baths, TVs and telephones and are appropriately decorated in the Victorian style. Suite 302 contains a Victorian day bed in one room and a double in the other. Floral blue and pink carpeting runs all through the hotel. A continental breakfast is served hotel guests in the bar. Doubles, $155 to $180; suites, $130 to $220.

Old Town Inn, Old Town Road, Box 351, Block Island, (401) 466-5958. This is the most authentic B&B on Block Island. Her British heritage gives Monica Gunter the background to provide innkeeping in the classic tradition. That means that not only are full breakfasts provided, but also tea and crumpets in the afternoon. The path to the main door of the comfortable white clapboard inn that Monica runs with her husband Ralph is lined with flowers. Eight of the twelve rooms have private baths. Rooms are simply but pleasantly furnished, mostly with pine. Breakfast is served in a pretty room off the kitchen; such goodies as blueberry muffins usually accompany a hearty main dish. Tea is served from 4 to 4:30 to inn guests. The spacious main lounge, in a newer wing, has a fireplace. There are also a deck for sunning, a badminton net, a flower garden with birdbath and a generally relaxed air. Refrigerator space — "for wine or whatever"— is offered guests and rental bikes are available. While the inn is a bit of a walk from Old Harbor or New Harbor, or even the beach, most bikers find it quite do-able. Doubles, $80 to $115. Open Memorial Day to late September.

Star Cottage, Ocean Avenue, Old Harbor, (401) 466-2842. An old-fashioned and simple B&B located at the edge of town, Star Cottage offers three guest rooms sharing one large bathroom. All are done in country style and we particularly like the room with hunter green wallpaper with pink roses. All have double beds. Guests relax on a large front porch and take continental breakfast in the parlor. Doubles, $75 to $85. Open mid-April to mid-October.

Sea Breeze Inn, Spring Street, Old Harbor, (401) 466-2275. This weathered inn is comprised of several buildings with various accommodations, from rather luxurious and pricey to more simple. Several rooms yield ocean views or glimpses. Five of the ten rooms come with private entrances and private baths. Breakfast is delivered in a basket to most rooms, although there's a common area for breakfast in one building. Doubles, $80 to $160.

Gables Inn and Gables II, Dodge Street, Old Harbor, (401) 466-2213. These adjacent guest houses with apartments, run by the Nyzio family, are across the street from the beach and not far from the shopping area. Accommodations are done simply; old-fashioned wallpaper and antique furnishings are the rule. Tea and coffee are available all day and there's a refrigerator in each building for guests' use. Barbeque grills and picnic tables in the back yard can be used for cookouts. Doubles, $73 to $100. Open May-November.

Seeing and Doing

Bicycling has long been a favorite pursuit on the island, so much so that we can't imagine the place without its bikers — some call it a Bermuda of the north. Two-wheelers and a few tandems are for rent at many spots, often at the hotel or guest house where you're staying. Mopeds also are available. Pick up a good map of the island at The Book Nook on Water Street in Old Harbor and you're in business.

Boating scene at New Harbor.

North Light at the end of Corn Neck Road (the Indians used to grow their corn there) at the northern tip of the island is a favorite destination and you can picnic once you get there. You'll also find **Settlers Rock** with the names of the sixteen hardy souls who first settled on the island.

Hardy sorts (you don't have to be *too* hardy) like to make a bicycle circuit of the island. Begin in Old Harbor and travel north along the shore to the intersection with Beach Avenue, then west past New Harbor with its marinas (you can find restrooms here), the island cemetery and onto West Side Road. From West Side Road you can take any number of dirt roads to the water; we like Cooneymus Road to reach a wild, wonderful stretch of beach, often deserted. Retrace this dirt stretch to the paved portion of Cooneymus and follow Cooneymus east to Lakeside Drive, then south to Mohegan Trail with its fabulous high views over Mohegan Bluffs (toward Montauk, Long Island) and down to **Southeast Light**, an 1874 brick lighthouse whose lantern can be seen 35 miles at sea. A small but interesting new museum at the lighthouse is operated by the Block Island Historical Society. Rooms detail the history of the island in appropriately low-key style, stressing its early families, resort status and development over the years. You can watch a couple of videos, too. Open daily in summer, 10 to 4. Admission, $3.

This end of the island has been likened to Ireland. Follow Mohegan Trail to Southeast Light Road, then to Spring Street, and back into Old Harbor.

Beaching is best along the island's east coast. There are several names for what is essentially the same strand, from Surfer's Beach to State Beach to Scotch Beach and ultimately to Mansion Beach. The whole stretch is sometimes referred to as Crescent Beach. State Beach has the gentlest section, plus a pavilion, snack bar and lifeguards; it's great for kids. You can rent umbrellas and beach chairs here. The water is crystal-clear and inclined to be brisk, especially before mid-July. Charleston Beach on the west side of the island, just southwest of the Coast Guard Station, is more rugged, less populated and better for exploring and walking than swimming. We've found good driftwood here. Reach it via dirt roads from West Side Road.

Sportfishing is big. Stripers, blues, and swordfish are caught in abundance in the waters off Block Island. Charter boats are available. You can easily find one by walking along the dock near Ballard's (see Where to Eat), not far from the ferry dock slip where several charter boats tie up. **Boating** can be approached two ways: do-it-yourself or watch others. You can rent rowboats at the **Twin Maples** on Beach Avenue, New Harbor. The marinas where you can watch graceful sailboats and huge power boats are

91

Champlin's and the Block Island Boat Basin. Payne's Dock at New Harbor is another good place for a view of the boating action.

Walking is a particular pleasure on Block Island for it's a compact place. The town of Old Harbor is fine for moseying. You can poke in the shops, watch the ferry come in, or visit the Block Island Historical Society or Island Free Library (see below). Out on the island are several good places for walking. Delightfully meandering paths cut through eleven acres of natural growth at **The Maze** in the island's northeast corner. Located atop Clay Head, it offers fantastic views out over the ocean, the surprise of hidden ponds and many birds since it's one of the Audubon Society's banding stations.

Rodman's Hollow, a wild and beautiful cleft in the rolling southwestern terrain, adjoins a 200-acre parcel of land managed by the Rhode Island Audubon Society. The **Island Cemetery** on Center Road is an interesting place for exploring, and some of the tombstones bear unusual legends.

Indoors

The **Block Island Historical Society** at Old Town Road and Ocean Avenue is open daily in summer. The **Island Free Library** on Dodge Street is surprising for its contemporary design and is a beehive of activity, especially on a rainy day. Leave a deposit and borrow a book. Flyers advertising island events are usually posted here.

You can see a movie or attend live theater on the island. The **Oceanwest Theater,** (401) 466-2971, near Champlin's Marina presents first-run movies (including matinees on rainy days) and a professional summer stock theater in July and August.

Shopping

We used to dismiss the shopping on Block Island as mundane. That has changed. Old Harbor has most of the stores and can occupy you the better part of a rainy day, if you really get into it.

Our favorite shops include **The Scarlet Begonia** on Dodge Street and **The Red Herring** upstairs above **The Shoreline,** a clothing shop, on Water Street. The former has wonderful Irish pottery, rag rugs, tablecloths and button covers. In the latter you'll find fabulous monotints by island artist Jessie Edwards, throw pillows, dried flowers, bowls and — for our patio at home — squat glass hurricane lamps in pale green.

Joan Mallick's **Block Island Blue** pottery, displayed in its own Cape Cod house on Dodge Street, is exceptionally attractive and quite affordable. Fish and cat-oriented items are to be found at **Spindrift,** a gift shop with nifty T-shirts, jewelry, sculpture and more.

The Shoreline! — with two outlets — turned up the best of all Block Island T-shirts for a college-age son. In **Eté,** which means summer in French, you can buy a T-shirt with the word for summer in just about every language, including swahili.

The women's clothing store, **Rags,** has Esprit and other good lines in casual summer wear. **Esta's** and **Star Department Store** are the venerable five and dime-style stores where you can find more T-shirts, shorts, sundresses, ceramic lobsters, kids' games and beach toys, postcards, greeting cards and wild bumper stickers.

Among the art galleries, check out **The Spring Street Gallery** (formerly The Barn), **Sea Breeze Gallery, The Ragged Sailor** and **Square One.**

Stop at **The Block Island Kite Company** on Corn Neck Road to pick out a kite for flying on the beaches. The island breezes make this a favorite pastime.

You can buy wine, beer and harder stuff at the **Red Bird Liquor Store** on Dodge

Downtown street scene in Old Harbor.

Street. We found the wine selection to be quite good. **Block Island Grocery** on Ocean Avenue has a fairly good selection of foods.

Where to Eat

Visitors to Block Island are most often looking for breakfast or dinner places. Lunch spots are plentiful, and many people simply buy a hot dog at the beach. Our listings are according to the meal.

For Breakfast

The 1661 Inn, 466-2421, serves a buffet breakfast to its own guests and those of The Manisses Hotel, and the public is welcome during the summer season. You'll feast on such specialties as corned beef hash, scrambled eggs, quiche, oven-roasted potatoes and possibly a vegetable casserole or chicken tetrazzini.

Ernie's Old Harbor Restaurant at the ferry dock, upstairs from Finn's, is popular, especially with the locals. You can order anything from pancakes to eggs, many styles, and the service is quick. Only breakfast is served here from 6:30 to noon Monday-Friday and 6:30 to 1 on weekends. Slip onto a stool at the formica counter or find a formica-topped table. Three-egg omelets are the rule and homemade muffins and coffee cake fill out a meal. "The Sunny Side" is a six-ounce steak, two eggs, homefries and an English muffin.

For Dinner

Hotel Manisses, Spring Street, Old Harbor, (401) 466-2836. The restaurant at the Manisses is well regarded. There are three locations to choose from: an inner room, with circular flowered placemats on the tables and rattan chairs; an outer room with lots of glass, and the deck, which overlooks the back yard. Fresh vegetables and herbs from the hotel garden show up in the inventive soups (often turnip or broccoli) and in many of the dishes. While prices may seem high (entrees from $14 to $22), a super-saver dinner for $13.95 (bluefish at our visit) included soup, appetizer, salad, vegetables, dessert and coffee. The menu changes nightly in summer. Appetizers ($5 to $7) might be clams casino or a black bean and feta tortilla with cilantro cream. Among entrees offered recently were flounder francaise, grilled tuna with pineapple salsa, roasted half chicken with rosemary and lemon, and veal chop with a caramelized shallot glaze. The pastry chef creates different dessert delicacies every day. Dinner nightly, 6 to 9.

Winfield's, Corn Neck Road, Old Harbor, (401) 466-5856. Next door to **McGovern's Yellow Kittens,** one of the most popular nightspots on the island, and operated by the same management, Winfield's is as romantic a dining setting as you can get here. White stucco walls, dark wood wainscoting and beams, leaded stained-glass windows and a few plants judiciously hung from the rafters make this a place for intimate dining. A small bowl of water with flowers and a candle floating in it makes an original centerpiece. Among entrees ($14 to $20) are Winfield's tortellini (chicken, shrimp and spinach tortellini in a spicy marinara sauce with a topping of saga blue cheese), fresh Block Island swordfish, veal saltimbocca and rack of lamb served with a rosemary and red currant sauce. A pasta primavera appetizer is $5.75. The dessert selection changes every day. Open nightly in season, 6 to 10; reduced schedule through New Year's Eve.

Dead Eye Dick's, Payne's Dock, New Harbor, (401) 466-2654. This low white clapboard building with window boxes is the site for some fairly good meals, especially since the arrival of new owner Jon Kodama, a well-known Connecticut shore restaurateur. We blew in one rainy, blustery Friday evening and had a great time. The place is simple and straightforward: bare wooden floors, paneled walls and each table with placemats, fresh flowers and a candle flickering. Our broiled sea scallops for $14.95 and a swordfish special for $19.95 were excellent. Appetizers are old favorites like shrimp cocktail, clams or oysters on the half shell, steamed littlenecks and — something different for the island — Maryland crab cakes with homemade salsa. Gourmet pizza is always a possibility; the ingredients change daily. Entrees include blackened swordfish with jalapeno jelly, shrimp and broccoli pasta, blackened chicken with goat cheese and red pepper jam, and scallops over linguini with a hoisin-plum-ginger sauce. Service is prompt and professional, and Dick's is popular with sailors from nearby boats anchored in the Great Salt Pond. There's a cocktail lounge, too. Lunch daily, 11 to 5; dinner, 5 to 11. Open Memorial Day to mid-September.

The Mohegan Cafe, Water Street, Old Harbor, (401) 466-5911. Located on the town's main drag, this attractive new spot with lots of nautical touches is a popular lunch stop for daytrippers. We enjoyed a salad with mandarin oranges, romaine lettuce, radicchio and toasted coconut in a light ginger soy vinaigrette at noon one day. Changing specials at dinner ($12 to $20) might be littlenecks saute, rainbow trout topped with fresh mint butter and veal napoleon. Black Forest chicken, a favorite, is sauteed with shallots, bing cherries and brandy and garnished with creme fraiche. Open daily, 11:30 to 10 or 11.

Harborside Inn, Water Street, Old Harbor, (401) 466-5504. Eat outdoors when the weather is nice or inside when it's not. Located across from the ferry dock, the Harborside is always crowded and one reason is the salad bar, which is advertised as the best on the island. Nautical touches (fish nets and such) are found above the captains' tables and chairs; red placemats and napkins add warmth. Entrees are priced from $15 to $20. Nightly specials might be grilled tuna or swordfish. Regular house specialties include scallops sauteed in a light garlic and herb butter, a grilled seafood sampler or a sirloin club steak. A good pasta menu in the $10 range is an option. Open daily for breakfast, lunch and dinner.

The Spring House, Spring Street, Old Harbor, (401) 466-5844. Getting high marks recently is the dining room at the Spring House, a venerable Block Island hotel that has been refurbished in recent years. Pink tablecloths and light wood chairs make an attractive dining environment at one end of the huge open lobby. Among entrees ($15 to $20), you might try scallops with roasted red pepper butter, broiled veal chop with a porcini mushroom sauce, rack of lamb pecan or breast of chicken pommery. The pasta selection includes calamari waterway, squid rings simmered in a fresh marinara sauce and served over black pepper fettuccine. Dinner nightly in season, 6 to 10.

Ballard's, Old Harbor, (401) 466-4231. "You haven't been to Block Island if you haven't been to Ballard's," goes the saying. Ballard's attracts boaters and daytrippers, fishermen and year-round residents and, one day when we were there, the Travelers Insurance Cos. women's club from Hartford. The place is enormous, with long tables and bentwood chairs. Flags of supposedly every nation on earth fly overhead; there are a slew of them, and we wonder how all are kept straight with the sudden changes in alliances. The famed bar is appropriately large for the cavernous dining hall. But it's not exactly atmosphere that customers here are seeking — but rather the seafood and the bustle (at night, various bands hold forth). Ballard's says its "best buy" is lobster

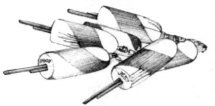

family style, where each diner gets two lobsters, a choice of potato and vegetable for $18.95. Variations are offered, including lazy lobster for $16.50 and a two-pounder for $22.95. Ballard's baby shore dinner brings a steamed lobster, a bowl of clam chowder, steamed mussels and clams, fish of the day, an ear of corn and cold watermelon for $19.75. Fried clams, fish and chips, a seafood sampler for $12.95 and a complete tuna dinner for $17 are other possibilities. You can understand why all these boaters and fishermen hang out here. Open daily in season, 11 to 10.

Finn's Seafood Restaurant, Water Street, Old Harbor, (401) 466-2473. You can't beat the freshness of the fish (from its seafood market next door) nor the prices at Finn's, especially popular with locals. The restaurant on the lower level is reached directly from the ferry dock parking lot. Upstairs is a raw bar where you can feast on clams, oysters or shrimp, sip a drink and enjoy the view of ferry comings and goings. Everything is prepared fresh and is not fancy. Lobster comes in eight sizes, all the way up to three-pounders for $34.50. Other possibilities in the $8 to $14 range: shrimp scampi, broiled swordfish and broiled yellow or bluefin tuna. Entrees can be had with coleslaw and french fries or with corn on the cob, salad and/or baked potato. Fresh baked pies and something called a chocolate suicide cake are on the dessert menu. Open daily, 11:30 to 9:30 or 10.

Sunset sipping. The best view of the sunset may be from **Trader Vic's,** at the end of the dock at Champlin's Marina. Here you sip tropical drinks and watch the sun sink into the ocean. It's a fun way to start an evening.

Finish up at **McGovern's Yellow Kittens** on Corn Neck Road, which has been attracting the beach crowd from lunchtime on for years. The current management varies the musical fare and says that even middle-aged patrons are occasionally spotted — usually for jazz. But often it's rock and usually the crowd is young. Mexican food is served on the outdoor deck at lunch. You can dance here at night and it's, well, lively.

FOR MORE INFORMATION: Block Island Chamber of Commerce, Drawer D, Block Island, R.I. 02807, (401) 466-2982.

7 ✦ Summer

Maine(ly) City

Portland, Maine

Few people think of a city as a focal point for a summer weekend, but then, few cities make the prospect attractive. One that does is Portland, which combines urban amenities with rural and coastal pursuits. The natives desert their city on weekends, naturally, to make the most of the leisure possibilities virtually in their back yards. Basing yourself in or near the city, you can do as they do and enjoy the best of both worlds — what native son Henry Wadsworth Longfellow described as "the beautiful town that is seated by the sea."

The sea is everything — or almost everything — to Portland. Although actually aside Casco Bay, the city is a peninsula ringed on all flanks by water, and the proximity of the water on every side is the first thing a visitor notices. The second may be the city's height. The downtown is on a crest that gives it something of the look of an old European town — where else in this country does one find a downtown located higher than its suburbs?

The height is fortuitous. On a clear day, the view of the shimmering waters of Casco Bay from the Eastern Promenade is breathtaking. From no other Eastern city do the blues of the water, the greens of the islands and the whites of the sailboats seem so pristine.

Other good views are the ones at sunset toward the city's skyline across the Back Cove from Baxter Boulevard, and toward New Hampshire's White Mountains from the

Western Promenade. Between the mountains and the city is the Sebago Lakes region, an inland area that vies with the sea for the attentions of Portlanders.

When they're not taking advantage of their surroundings, Portlanders are likely helping to revive — and enjoy — their revitalized city. Variously described as a big town or a little city (population, 65,000), Portland is the center of the largest urban complex in the largest state in northern New England. Its manageable size combined with a potent civic pride make it "a unique experiment in urban revival," according to one Portland newspaper writer.

Portland slumbered longer than many New England cities, so it is perhaps a surprise that it has come farther and faster than most. Ravaged by Indians and the British twice in the 1700s and destroyed by fire started by a July Fourth firecracker following the Civil War, Portland was a dying port in the 1950s. But business interests gave the city a prospering new downtown, dubbed Intown Portland, with mini-skyscrapers and plazas, landscaping and monuments, kiosks and elan. They also gave it a thriving cultural and entertainment life, including the Portland Symphony Orchestra and the expanded Museum of Art with its collection of paintings by Winslow Homer, the pride of Portland.

A lively group known as Greater Portland Landmarks Inc. is responsible for 35 years of restoration efforts that are turning Portland into what some call, on a lesser scale, "the Savannah of the North."

The crowning restoration achievement is the Old Port Exchange, a near-downtown historic district fashioned from a decaying waterfront where restaurants, boutiques and galleries flourish side by side with sailmakers and ship's chandlers.

Some of the city's best restaurants and most interesting shops are located here. The nearby waterfront is headquarters for the Casco Bay Lines, which offers a variety of cruises from morning to moonlight. They show some of the Calendar Islands (so named because they number approximately 365), four of them occupied by year-round residents.

Savor this rejuvenated city, which is compact enough to get around and see in a day (make it a Saturday, for like most cities much of Portland closes down on summer Sundays). But also get out of the city. Head north along Route 88 through suburban Falmouth Foreside and old Yarmouth. Head south through Cape Elizabeth to Two Lights, Scarborough and the coastal beaches. Head west to the Sebago Lakes region for a look at Maine's interior.

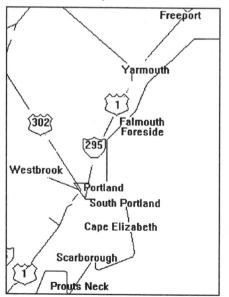

Portland, for the summer weekender, offers a little of everything.

Getting There

The Interstate 295 loop serves Portland from the Maine Turnpike (I-95) toll road, which is the fastest route into Portland. U.S. Route 1 goes through the center of the city on its way from Canada to Florida.

Greyhound and Trailways provide bus service to the city. Delta, United, Con-

97

tinental and USAir serve Portland International Jetport. Portland is also linked by ferry to Yarmouth, N.S., daily in the summer by Prince of Fundy Cruises.

Seeing and Doing

Old Port Exchange. This restored district southeast of downtown between Monument Square and the waterfront is at once the city's oldest and newest neighborhood. Settled in the 1600s, the area was ravaged by the British during the Revolution and by the Great Fire of 1866. It was rebuilt, but was going downhill until Greater Portland Landmarks started revitalizing the area in the 1960s.

An old-town restoration like those out West, Portland's is particularly successful and well done, although the accoutrements of a sophisticated city tend to overshadow what boosters describe as "a working harbor full of the sights, sounds and smells of the sea."

Exquisite architecture, landscaping, colorful signs, benches, mini-parks and a lifelike trompe l'oeil mural on a building at Middle and Exchange streets make this a fine place in which to stroll and browse as well as partake of more than 50 shops and a couple of dozen restaurants. Exchange, Fore and Middle streets are the core, but don't overlook the side streets in this approximately five-block-square area stretching between Congress and Commercial streets.

Walking Tours. Congress Street, the city's main thoroughfare from historic Stroudwater to the Eastern Promenade, is also the main shopping street and is noteworthy for its landmark buildings, from the old Romanesque public library at 619 to the French Renaissance City Hall at 389. A Greater Portland Landmarks brochure ($1) guides the way, as do others to the Old Port Exchange, Western Promenade and the State and High street area, which was added in 1971 to the National Register of Historic Places in recognition of its architectural examples. These were the grand homes of old Portland, many of them Federal and Greek Revival; they give sections of the city a red-brick look unusual for New England. On the other side of Congress Square is the often-overlooked Deering Street, an enclave of notable Victorian residences only a block removed from the city's business heart.

Cultural and Historic Sites. The **Wadsworth-Longfellow House** (1785) at 485 Congress St., where Henry Wadsworth Longfellow wrote much of his early poetry, was Portland's first brick building and is the oldest remaining residence on the Portland peninsula. A beauty it is, with original furnishings and possessions of the Wadsworth and Longfellow families. The Maine Historical Society headquarters and library are located behind the house and its lovely garden. Open June to Columbus Day, Tuesday-Saturday 10 to 4. Adults $3, children $1.

The 1860 **Victoria Mansion** at 109 Danforth St., one of the nation's most opulent Italian villas, has been described as "an encyclopedia of mid-19th-century decoration, domestic life and determined elegance." It is notable for richly carved woodwork, colorful frescoes, painted trompe l'oeil walls and ceilings, carved marble fireplaces, French porcelains and much stained and etched glass. Open Memorial Day to Labor Day, Tuesday-Saturday 10 to 4 and Sunday 1 to 5; weekends only through Columbus Day. Adults $4, children $1.50.

The **Portland Observatory,** 138 Congress St., built in 1807 as a signal tower, is maintained by Greater Portland Landmarks. Climb its 102 steps for a panoramic view of the city, Casco Bay and the White Mountains. Open Wednesday-Sunday 1 to 5 (Saturday from 10), July-August; Saturday-Sunday 1 to 5 in June, September and October. Adults $1.50, children 50 cents.

The Museum at Portland Head Light, 1000 Shore Road, Cape Elizabeth, debuted

New and old buildings co-exist in downtown Portland.

in 1992 in the East's oldest operating lighthouse. Commissioned in 1791 by George Washington, the lighthouse is said to be the Atlantic coast's most photographed. Following $600,000 worth of renovations, the Town of Cape Elizabeth opened the museum on the first floor of the lighthouse keepers' quarters. Exhibits chronicle the history of Portland Head Light and Fort Williams, a military outpost that developed for coastal defense next to the lighthouse and now is an appealing town park with trails, picnic tables and great views of the harbor. A small museum shop is housed in an adjacent garage. Open daily 10-4, June-October; weekends, November-December and April-May. Adults $2, children $1.

The historic **Lightship #112 Nantucket,** America's largest floating lighthouse, docks along the Commercial Street waterfront for guided tours between visits to other ports. Built in 1936, it is the oldest survivor of the legendary Nantucket Shoals station and screened incoming traffic to the vital Portland harbor during World War II. Today its towering light beacons and bright red hull can be seen as you board for a tour of living quarters, wardroom and galley. Open June-September, Wednesday-Saturday 10 to 4, Sunday noon to 4; weekends, rest of year. Adults $3, children $1.50.

The **Tate House** (1755) at 1270 Westbrook St. in historic Stroudwater is maintained by the National Society of Colonial Dames of America in Maine. With gambrel roof, eight fireplaces and the parlor table set for tea, it reflects an 18th-century London townhouse. Out back, a raised-bed herb garden of 18th-century plants overlooks the Stroudwater River. Open Tuesday-Saturday 10 to 4 and Sunday 1 to 4, July to Labor Day; weekends during September and October. Adults $3, children $1.

The **Portland Museum of Art,** 7 Congress Square, (207) 775-6148. This is considered northern New England's most important museum, all the more so since the opening of the $11.6-million Charles Shipman Payson Building. The local philanthropist not only sparked the museum's 1983 expansion with his gift of seventeen Winslow Homer paintings, but provided the funding for the showcase addition. The magnificent I.M. Pei-designed structure joins the original McLellan-Sweat House

(1800) and L.D.M. Sweat Memorial (1911) museum buildings and provides five times as much space. The four-story structure with its enormous elevator, a staircase that makes you feel as if you're floating upstairs and portholes through which you look outside is intriguing. So are Payson's Homer collection, the works of Wyeth and Sargent, the American Galleries, the decorative arts galleries, the Pepperrell Silver Collection and changing exhibitions. The Joan Whitney Payson Collection, a remarkable group of Impressionist and Post-Impressionist works by Picasso, Monet, Degas, Renoir, Van Gogh and others, was given to the museum in 1991. Antique cars were displayed front and center in the lobby at our latest visit, when a major exhibition called "The Elegant Auto," presenting fashion and design from the 1930s, was causing a stir in regional art circles. Open Tuesday-Saturday 10 to 5, Thursday to 9, Sunday noon to 5. Adults $3.50, children $1.

Driving Tours. Although downtown is for walking, cars are almost a necessity for the Portland visitor, and the city and surroundings are extraordinarily easy to traverse by car (with a good map). Drive out Congress Street past the landmark Portland Observatory to the Eastern Promenade, an aptly named residential street along the crest overlooking Casco Bay. It's bordered by parkland with a municipal pool, benches where you can enjoy a panoramic view and one lone picnic table where we lunched in splendor at our latest visit. Fort Allen Park boasts a cannon from the USS Maine and overlooks old Fort Gorges in the harbor. Continue your tour to Route 1 and Baxter Boulevard around the Back Cove, past more water and parks. Eventually get to the Western Promenade and its Reed Monument. From here on a clear day you see Mount Washington and tour another area of imposing, architectural-landmark residences.

Head north on Route 88 through Falmouth Foreside, home of the Portland Country Club, Portland Yacht Club and waterfront estates. Stop at **The Galley Restaurant** at 215 Foreside Road in a busy marina for lunch or Sunday brunch beside the boats and water. Beyond, Yarmouth has some of the area's earliest buildings, plus the **Cousins Island** beach, which is excellent for swimming and picnicking.

Head south on Route 77 through suburban Cape Elizabeth, with fine residential sections beside Casco Bay. A favorite stop is Fort Williams Park and the Portland Head Light and museum. Farther on are **Two Lights State Park** and the **Lobster Shack at Two Lights,** where you can feast on lobster at picnic tables with a spectacular view of he open Atlantic. Still farther are **Crescent Beach State Park, Higgins Beach** and the exclusive community of **Prouts Neck,** whose rugged cliffs inspired artist Winslow Homer and where his studio is now a private residence.

Head west for fifteen miles on Route 302 to touristy North Windham and Sebago Lake, which you seldom get to see from the main highways. **Sebago Lake State Park** is a well maintained, spectaculary situated beach and picnic grove with a setting reminiscent of the north end of Lake Tahoe. The old Songo Lock separating Sebago Lake and Brandy Pond attracts sightseers and fishermen.

Boat Tours. Nine daily sailings are offered by **Casco Bay Lines** from the ferry terminal at Commerical and Franklin streets, (207) 774-7871. Said to be America's oldest ferry service, it's the lifeline to the Calendar Islands, transporting residents, school children, mail and necessities along with visitors. The three-hour mail boat run (adults $8.75, children $4) stops twice daily at Cliff, Chebeague, Long, and Little and Great Diamond islands, giving visitors dockside views of island life. The premier cruise (adults $12.75, children $6) is a six-hour trip to Bailey Island, where you can get off for lunch or stay on board for a nature cruise. Other cruises go to Diamond Pass or involve sunset and moonlight excursions and Sunday music on the bay. Some of the islands are worthy of exploration by foot or bicycle to sample how life is lived offshore.

Portland Head Light.

The smaller **Bay View Cruises** on Fisherman's Wharf offers seal watch, island, cocktail, brunch, lobster bake and sunset cruises, daily in summer; adults $8, children $5. **Eagle Tours** at Long Wharf has good island and seal-watching cruises Monday-Thursday mornings and afternoons and Friday-Sunday afternoons (adults $7 or $8, children $4 or $5). On Friday-Sunday mornings there are cruises to Eagle Island and the site of Admiral Robert E. Peary's summer home ($15 and $9). The 24-passenger ocean racer **Palawan** gives half-day, all-day and sunset sails from Custom House Wharf through the Calendar Islands for $15 to $65 per person.

Swimming is offered at Crescent Beach State Park, where sand dunes lead to a gentle beach with locker rooms, concession stand and picnic grills (fee: $1 per person). Higgins Beach in Scarborough is fine, but parking is limited; beyond is Scarborough State Beach with good surf. Far less crowded and free, to boot, is the delightful Cousins Island Beach across the causeway from Yarmouth. There's no surf and it's a bit of a climb down (stairs provided), but the bay waters are warmer (65 degrees, compared with the ocean's 58) and the beach far less populated.

The **Scarborough Marsh Nature Center,** operated by the Maine Audubon Society on Pine Point Road in Scarborough, has a variety of naturalist-led tours of the shore and marshes as well as bird walks (most cost $3). You can rent canoes ($8 an hour) to explore the wilds of the marsh on your own. The center has rotating exhibits, aquariums and a nature store as well as 3,000 acres of salt marsh rich in plant and animal life. Open daily in summer, 9:30 to 5:30.

The Maine Audubon Society's headquarters, **Gilsland Farm,** at 118 Route 1 as you enter Falmouth from the city, has several miles of free nature trails through woods, meadows and marshes in the Presumpscot River estuary. The society's chief claim to fame here is its striking two-and-a-half-story shingled headquarters built in 1976 as the nation's first large building heated only by the sun and firewood. Designed in the old New England saltbox style, it attracts energy experts who want to see how solar heating works (a brochure illustrates a self-guided tour of the heating apparatus around the building's perimeter). The society's gift shop has all sorts of nature-related items, posters, prints, nature books and cards. Open Monday-Saturday 9 to 5, Sunday 1:30 to 4:30.

Where to Stay

Portland has its share of chain motels, large downtown motor inns, hotels and B&Bs. Two excellent inns are located on the water at the fringes of suburban Portland, but if you stay at either, you may never want to leave the inn grounds.

Portland Regency, 20 Milk St., Portland 04101, (207) 774-4200 or (800) 727-3436.

101

New in 1987, this 95-room hotel is superbly located in the heart of the Old Port Exchange, which might justify the $5 charge for valet parking. The fact that it's in the restored 1895 armory, providing some unusual architectural treatments, is a bonus. Most guest rooms go off a three-story atrium above the dining room. Rooms are plush, many with kingsize four-poster beds and minibars. Complimentary coffee and newspapers are placed at your door with your wakeup call. The health club is up-to-date, and Salutes Night Club offers nightly entertainment in a warren of downstairs rooms. The **Market Street Grill** has a with-it menu at decidedly un-hotel-like prices (belgian waffles for $2.50 and eggs benedict for $4.95 at breakfast; salads and sandwiches for $3.95 to $4.95 at lunch). Dinner entrees run from $10.95 to $14.95 for the likes of steamed lobster, grilled halibut with a lobster-basil-tomato puree and sea scallops with pernod, pinenuts and bell peppers. Doubles, $115 to $140.

Sonesta Hotel, 157 High St., Portland 04101, (207) 775-5411. Several years ago, the Sonesta chain renovated the old Eastland downtown hotel, redoing 100 large guest rooms in the old structure and adding a tower with 85 more. New owners took over in 1992 and launched more needed interior redecorating and refurbishing, the public areas looking a bit shabby at our visit. A new chef was winning accolades for the **Rib Room** restaurant, where the traditional prime rib and lobster thermidor were being upstaged by more contemporary offerings like pan-seared salmon with arugula and tomatoes, grilled pork tenderloin with leeks and capers and pepper-crusted medallions of beef with herbed cabernet sauce ($12.95 to $18.50). The prime rib with rosemary popovers and whipped horseradish cream is $16.50. The Top of the East Lounge enjoys a panoramic view of the city. Doubles, $90 to $135.

Holiday Inn By the Bay, 88 Spring St., Portland 04101, (207) 775-2311. A good location, just across the street from the Civic Center and within walking distance of the Old Port Exchange, is one reason to stay in this 240-room motor hotel that used to be called simply the Holiday Inn-Downtown. Another is the view from the higher floors. We especially enjoyed watching the Scotia Prince ferry, lit up like a Christmas tree, dock at her berth around 8 one night from our room overlooking the Fore River. If you pay a bit extra, you can get an end room with two big windows instead of one. The indoor pool room is windowless, which is fine for a rainy day, but if it's a sunny weekend you might prefer the attractive **Holiday Inn-West** out Brighton Avenue with its outdoor pool. The downtown inn's lobby and dining room are large and ornate, and a plus for a city hotel is free in-and-out covered parking. Doubles, $122 to $128.

Sheraton-Tara Hotel, 363 Maine Mall Road, South Portland 04106, (207) 775-6161. Two striking glass circular towers contain 220 guest rooms at this suburban hotel located in a busy commercial area between the Maine Mall and the Maine Turnpike. The eight-story inn hotel has a glass-domed pool area, and there's a well-equipped fitness center. The **Silver Shell** restaurant offers dinner entrees from $12 to $21. You can walk to the Maine Mall and several cinemas. Doubles, $139 to $159.

Portland Marriott Hotel, 200 Sable Oaks Drive, South Portland 04106, (207) 871-8000. Another suburban high-rise, this fancy new hostelry offers 227 guest rooms and suites with all the usual suspects. Besides a skylit indoor pool, there's a health club with sauna, whirlpool and exercise room. The eighteen-hole Sable Oaks Golf Course is adjacent. Full-service dining is available in the **Garden Court Restaurant;** snacks are served in the lounge. Doubles, $155.

Susse Chalet Hotel, 340 Park Ave., Portland 04102, (207) 871-0611. One of the budget chain, we found this 105-room, four-story motor inn off the tourist path to be quite a bargain — something like $52 for a spacious room with two double beds, comfortable chairs, good reading lights, a bathroom with separate vanity (but no

Pomegranate Inn occupies handsome 19th-century house in Portland.

amenities other than soap), and away from highway noise. There's a pint-size outdoor pool. Complimentary juice, coffee and donuts are doled out in the lobby in the morning. Another, more bare-bones Susse Chalet is at 1200 Brighton Ave. near the Maine Turnpike. Doubles, $48.70 to $52.70.

Pomegranate Inn, 49 Neal St., Portland 04102, (207) 772-1006 or (800) 356-0408. Two exotic plant sculptures (holding live plants, no less) welcome summer guests at the entrance to this exceptional in-town B&B run with T.L.C. by Connecticut transplants Isabel and Alan Smiles. The art theme continues inside the handsome 19th-century house, which Isabel's antiques collections and their contemporary artworks make a cross between a museum and a gallery. Walls in five of the guest rooms were handpainted by a local artist and are themselves works of art. The six rooms, all with modern tiled baths, come with telephone, television and a mix of antique and contemporary furnishings, not to mention prized art. A full breakfast is served at a long table at one end of the eclectic parlor. Doubles, $95 to $105. Two-night minimum on weekends.

The Inn at Parkspring, 135 Spring St., Portland 04101, (207) 774-1059. The "smallest grand hotel in Portland" is really a choice B&B in an 1835 brick townhouse. Five of the seven guest rooms have private baths. All rooms are sumptuously decorated, and fresh flowers are everywhere. A continental breakfast is available in the kitchen, and tea and cookies are served in the afternoon in the elegant parlor or outside on a small walled courtyard. Doubles, $85 to $95.

Black Point Inn, 510 Black Point Road, Prouts Neck 04074, (207) 883-4126 or (800) 258-0003. The gray shingled inn built in 1925 is not all that imposing — although very attractive and impeccably kept up — but you can tell from all the expensive cars in the parking lot that this is one elegant resort. The location not far south of the city on Prouts Neck is smashing, with Sand Dollar Beach on one side and Scarborough Beach on the other. The delightful public rooms contain overstuffed chairs, fireplaces, game tables and books to read. Breakfast and dinner are served in a pleasant pine-paneled dining room; on good days a buffet lunch is set out outside beside the large heated saltwater pool overlooking the ocean (there's also a new indoor freshwater pool). Staying in one of the 85 rooms in the inn or cottages is also one way to get to see the exclusive summer community of Prouts Neck. The famous Cliff Walk passes Winslow Homer's studio, and the pine woods between inn and ocean are a national bird sanctuary. Guests enjoy an adjacent eighteen-hole golf course and fourteen tennis courts hidden away in the woods. Doubles, $240 to $320, MAP; three-night minimum in summer. Open May to late October.

The Inn by the Sea, Route 77, Cape Elizabeth 04107, (207) 799-3134 or (800) 888-4287. If the Black Point Inn is the grand old resort, this is one for contemporary luxury. Nearly $7 million went into the place that opened in 1987 on the site of the former Crescent Beach Inn and it looks it. Handsomely designed in the Maine shingle style to blend with the oceanside setting, the angled complex has 25 one-bedroom suites in the main building and eighteen two-bedroom suites in four attached cottages. All have living rooms with reproduction Chippendale furniture, TVs hidden in armoires, kitchenettes, and balconies or patios looking onto manicured lawns and a croquet court, a pleasant pool and the ocean beyond Crescent Beach. Public rooms include a delightful rooftop library and the Audubon dining room, which serves a limited menu to house guests only. Entrees are priced from $11.95 for vegetarian pasta to $21.95 for tournedos of beef with rosemary essence or rack of lamb with shallot sauce. The breakfast prices ($6.95 for pancakes, $7.95 for an omelet) are enough to make one take cereal in the room or head off, as we did, to the local Spurwink Country Kitchen. Because all the rooms are suites, the rates seem high — except for families, of which there were few to be seen when we stayed. Doubles, $150 to $210; two-bedroom cottage suites, $270 to $330.

Where to Eat

Portland's dining scene has improved markedly in the past fifteen years. Many of the more popular restaurants, however, do not take reservations and the weekend traveler may find it annoying to have to eat at 6 p.m. or wait in a bar or outside on the street for up to an hour to get a table. On the plus side, the prices are considerably less than in Boston or New York.

Cafe Always, 47 Middle St., Portland, (207) 774-9399. This smart, new-wave-style cafe is all the rage for its walls painted with large floral designs by a local artist and its table napkins tied with black cords. And for its food, some of the best we've experienced anywhere. Boston-trained chef Cheryl Lewis changes her menu daily — it's adventuresome, the kind on which everything appeals, at least to the adventurous. Typical starters might be a scallion and cilantro quesadilla filled with three cheeses, grilled duck and wild rice nori roll with sesame tahini dipping sauce, and wild mushroom and parmesan risotto with sundried tomatoes. Then follow sensational main dishes like sweetbreads wrapped in pancetta and basted on the grill with balsamic sauce, grilled rainbow trout wrapped in grape leaves served with herb-polenta sauce and garnished with roasted peppers and fried capers, and grilled yellowfin tuna served with wasabi and pickled ginger sauce. A menu regular is steak berbere, New York sirloin coated with a toasted African spice mix. The crowning glory might be a trio of flavorful desserts: intense pineapple and plum sorbets and raspberry ice cream. Entree prices are generally $15.95 to $19.95, though there's usually a bargain like eggplant roasted with tomatoes and mushrooms, garnished with garlic aioli, for $9.95. For treats like this, we return time and again. Dinner, Tuesday-Saturday 5 to 10.

Back Bay Grill, 65 Portland St., Portland, (207) 772-8833. In its relatively short existence, this stylish establishment with two rooms and a twenty-foot-long mural of downtown Portland along one wall has become the city's most urbane restaurant — the only one we've seen lately that makes one think one should dress up for dinner on a summer's night in Portland. The menu changes nightly and the wine list every couple of weeks. To begin, you might try crab fritters with Thai vinaigrette and charred peppers or grilled duck liver brochette with white bean ragout. Move on to entrees ($16.95 to $21.95) like swordfish with tapenade croutons and sundried tomato-basil vinaigrette, grilled chicken with red onion confit and lamb loin chops with fig and raspberry compote. Pecan puff pastry napoleon with cannoli cream and toasted almond anglaise makes a fitting finale. The inspired wine list is fairly priced. Dinner, Tuesday-Saturday 5:30 to 9:30 or 10, also Sunday 5 to 9 in July and August.

Street and Co., 33 Wharf St., Portland, (207) 775-0887. Seafood, pure and simple, is the staple of this Old Port Exchange restaurant that's wildly popular with locals and visitors alike. Owner Dana Street stresses the freshest of fish on his blackboard menu. An open grill and kitchen are beside the door; beyond are 39 seats in an old basement of a room with bare pegged floors and strands of herbs and garlic hanging on brick walls. Outside are twenty more seats along Wharf Street during good weather, and the tables might turn four times on a busy night. Seafood comes grilled or broiled or served over pasta. Prices range from $10.95 for mussels marinara over linguini to $15.95. Try the scallops sauteed with mushrooms, pernod and cream; the salmon in parchment paper with aromatic vegetables and herbs, or lobster fra diavolo for two. The wine list is affordable, and there are great homemade desserts. Dinner nightly, 5:30 to 10 or 11.

Katahdin, Spring and High Streets, Portland, (207) 774-1740. There's a lot to look at in this with-it, offbeat eatery, where a creative hand is at work with the decor as well as in the kitchen. Mismatched chairs (some of them upholstered armchairs) are at tables whose tops are painted with different vegetable and fruit designs. A large 1950s mural adorns one wall; others bear quilts and changing artworks. There's a collection of mortars and pestles in one window. A variety of oldies but goodies on tape plays rather loudly. Such is the vibrant backdrop for the cooking of chef-owners Gretchen Bates and Dan Peters, who named the restaurant for Maine's highest mountain to reflect Maine home cooking and, explained the bartender, "mountains of food" and "the summit of fine dining." The ambitious menu always includes a blue plate special (lamb shanks braised with wine and rosemary the night we were there) with soup and salad for $9.95. Beef stew with salad is a bargain $7.95; nothing on the regular menu is over $12.95 (for grilled sea scallops with spicy lime and vegetable vinaigrette and grilled pork medallions wrapped in bacon and served with jalapeno butter). Meals come with buttermilk biscuits, Aunt Nina's pickles and a salad, starch and vegetable. You may not have room left for dessert, especially the chocolate mountain — a brownie shell filled with chocolate mousse fudge sauce, whipped cream and nuts. Refresh instead with mint-orange sherbet or blueberry-cinnamon frozen yogurt. A good, short wine list is priced from $11 to $21. Dinner, Monday-Saturday 5 to 10 or 11.

Alberta's, 21 Pleasant St., Portland, (207) 774-0016. Named for the mother of one of the founders, this funky cafe is short on decor and long on inspiration and value. The changing menu might feature grilled swordfish with roasted garlic and capers in a smoked tomato sauce, sauteed Atlantic salmon with chanterelles and herbed cream, and grilled butterflied lamb with rosemary and garlic ($12.95 to $16.95). Too pricey? Consider an appetizer, say sauteed chicken livers, pancetta and apples with sherry glaze ($3.95). For an extra $4, you can turn any starter into an entree that includes rice, vegetable and salad. The mix-and-match theme also works at lunch. With the owner's popular Good Egg Cafe building having burned, Alberta's was serving breakfast here. Breakfast, Monday-Friday 6 to 11:30, weekends 7 to 2; lunch, Monday-Friday 11:30 to 2:30; dinner nightly, 5 to 11.

Madd Apple Cafe, 23 Forest Ave., Portland, (207) 774-9698. Southern cooking came to Portland with the arrival of Martha and James Williamson, who took over this charming cafe beside the Portland Performing Arts Center. Jim grew up in the South, which explains all the barbecue items from secret family recipes and the fresh catfish, crayfish, boudin blanc, cornbread, bananas foster and sweet potato pie on the menu. Typical dinner entrees run from $10.95 for fettuccine pompadour through sauteed chicken livers, pork loin diablo and chicken normande to $17.95 for steak New Orleans. Carolina chopped pork barbecue ($5.95) is usually available at lunch, and barbecued Denver lamb ribs ($13.95) for dinner. Lunch, Tuesday-Friday 11:30 to 3; dinner, Tuesday-Saturday 5:30 to 9.

Hugo's Portland Bistro, 88 Middle St., Portland, (207) 774-8538. Named for the young son of the owners from Dublin, this is a pleasant room with beaucoup bric-a-brac and a short, appealing menu. Chef Caitriona Robinson says her cooking is a mix of French, Italian and American with a bit of Spanish and Moroccan, but her specialty is fresh Maine crab cakes with carrot and raisin slaw. You might start with chilled mussels on the half shell with jalapeno mayonnaise or pistachio and orange terrine before digging into fillet of sole with pesto sauce, Moroccan chicken pie in phyllo or tenderloin of pork with a garlic-maple vinaigrette over sauteed onions ($8.95 to $14.95). Dinners come with homemade Irish sodabread and salad. Creme brulee, fresh raspberry trifle, and bittersweet and white chocolate mousse are some of the good desserts, available with Irish coffee. Dinner, Tuesday-Saturday 5:15 to 10.

Pepperclub, 78 Middle St., Portland, (207) 772-0531. Among the recent entrants on Portland's Restaurant Row is this organic-vegetarian-seafood establishment, billed as a smoke-free environment and colorful as can be. It's the inspiration of artist Jaap Helper, Danish-born chef-artist who owned the late, great Vinyard restaurant nearby. He re-emerged with his paintings and a new partner, former art editor Eddie Fitzpatrick, to produce a masterpiece of culinary design. The blackboard menu lists starters like cumin corn chowder, Moroccan vegetable stew, hummus salad and smoked bluefish plate. Main dishes ($7.95 to $9.95) include Maine shrimp with pasta and pesto, Kashmiri chicken, Tunisian couscous and pinto bean burrito with salsa. Dessert could be strawberry-raspberry pie or blueberry cheesecake. Fresh flowers on the table, a crazy paint job on the walls and a bar made of old Jamaican steel drums, painted and cut in half, make for a vivid setting. Dinner nightly, 5 to 9 or 10.

DiMillo's, Long Wharf, Commercial Street, Portland, (207) 772-2216. The old DiMillo's Lobster House moved across the street onto the 206-foot-long ship Newport, converted for $2 million into one of the largest floating restaurants in the nation and probably "the busiest restaurant in Maine," according to a member of the DiMillo family. Eight hundred people can be accommodated at two outdoor cafe lounges fore and aft, in the Quarterdeck Dining Room and three private rooms, plus a very long bar, which helps those with endurance tolerate the one-hour (or more) waits on weekends. From the rare albino and orange lobsters in the tank at the reception desk to the blue and red linen, the place is incredibly nautical. The emphasis is on seafood: $11.95 for four versions of haddock to $16.95 for twin lobsters, "served to one person only," the menu advises. A shore dinner is $24.75. Open daily, 11 a.m. to midnight.

Snow Squall, 18 Ocean St., South Portland, (207) 799-2232. A cluttered view of the waterfront is offered from this California-style, fern and glass establishment overlooking the marina at MarinEast. It's named for a clipper ship built near the site during Casco

106

Weekly farmers' market draws throngs to downtown Portland.

Bay's shipbuilding era and featured in the emerging Spring Point Museum in South Portland. A large terrace with umbrellas and yellow and white furniture is as popular as the convivial bar. The dinner menu ($11.95 to $17.95) emphasizes seafood from the locally ubiquitous haddock to grilled swordfish with sundried tomato relish or sauteed scallops with a cilantro and pistachio pesto over sweet red pepper fettuccine, plus chicken, veal and three steaks. Lunch, Sunday-Friday 11:30 to 3; dinner nightly, 4:30 to 9 or 10; Sunday brunch, 11 to 2.

The Seamen's Club, 1 Exchange St., Portland, (207) 772-7311. Brick walls, arched windows, shelves of books, nice artworks and a patina of age give character to this ramble of rooms that housed small businesses and a real seamen's club in earlier times. One of the first restaurants in the Old Port Exchange restoration, it makes consistency a virtue, in the estimation of local diners-out. Dinner entrees are priced from $11.95 for chicken jardiniere to $17.95 for lobster bouillabaisse. Lobster linguini and salmon served with asparagus, a lobster claw and hollandaise are traditional favorites. The chowders are highly rated. Open daily, 11 to 11.

Christine's Dream, 41 Middle St., Portland, (207) 774-2972. Since she was 13 and a part-time dishwasher at the Madd Apple Cafe, Christine Burke's dream was to run a restaurant. Her dream came true in 1992 when, with husband Christopher (whom she met working in another Portland restaurant), she opened a breakfast and lunch spot in the stylish space vacated by Luna D'Oro. Eating here is like eating at a B&B, as one restaurateur described it. Christine is in the kitchen, her husband chats with patrons out front, and the couple live upstairs. We relished the salsa eggs scramble ($3.65), laden with cheese and flanked with homefries, and the peach pancakes ($3.55) like mother used to make. The coffee pot was bottomless. Lunchtime brings a short menu priced from $4.25 for tabouli salad with pita bread to $5.50 for rotelle with mozzarella. Other possibilities are a chicken fajita, Chinese chicken salad and a TLT double-decker with turkey. The Burkes will serve dinner of the customer's choice by reservation, for as few as two people, and we wouldn't be surprised to find them offering dinner regularly at our next visit. Open Tuesday-Friday 7 to 2:30; Saturday breakfast, 8 to 2; Sunday brunch, 9 to 2.

Other choices in this city of interesting restaurants:

Taj Mahal, 43 Middle St., imports everything from India, including T-shirts that say "India in Portland." Run by an outgoing Indian who had a Taj Mahal restaurant in West Germany, it's a good-looking place with hanging lamps, black and white posters of

India and a mobile of elephants, plus a display of the spices and breads in the middle of the room. The menu is Mughal and quite extensive, ranging from $6.50 to $13.95 for things like lamb shahi korma to vegetarian thali. Many interesting appetizers, accompaniments, vegetarian dishes and desserts like kulfi, homemade ice cream with cardamom, and mango ice cream are available. Lunch, Tuesday-Friday 11:30 to 2:30; dinner, Tuesday-Saturday 5 to 10.

Afghan Restaurant, 88 Exchange St., merits accolades for gigantic portions at teeny prices. Soups, appetizers, salads and desserts are 94 cents. Six dinner platters ($8.42 to $11.22) include soup, salad and dessert. We liked the lamb kabob but found the sampler platter, a taste of five entrees and seven side dishes, an indistinguishable mishmash that kept falling off the too-small plate. A complete dinner for four brings ten items for $42.06. Tiny white lights in the windows, little oil lamps, fresh flowers and murals make for a comfortable evening. Dinner, Tuesday-Sunday 5 to 10 or 10:30. BYOB.

Hu-Shang, 33 Exchange St., has long been touted for its Chinese fare, served up in a brick-plant-and-ceiling-fan decor. People seem to be eating here at all hours, and an outside banner at our latest visit improbably proclaimed "live Maine lobster specials: two lobsters boiled, $11, with ginger and scallion or black bean sauce, $13.95." Now that's Maine, Chinese-style. Otherwise, the prodigious Chinese menu runs twelve pages and embraces the usual dishes, most in the $6.99 to $10.50 range. Open daily, 11 to 9:30 or 10:30.

Bien Hong, 105 Exchange St., serves oriental food at a mix of copper tables and booths, plus on a spacious, shady courtyard out back. Szechuan and Vietnamese are the prevailing styles, priced from $8.95 to $11.95. At lunchtime, the oriental sandwiches ($3.50 to $4.95) served on French bread come with a cup of chicken velvet or hot and sour soup. Open daily from 11:30.

Two Thai restaurants have devoted followings. **May's Place,** 29 Wharf St. in the Old Port, serves its fare ($7.25 to $14.95) by the numbers, inside in most un-Thai-like brick recesses and outside on a sidewalk cafe. More upscale is the two-level dining room of **Thai Garden** at One City Center, a contemporary office complex, where folks marvel at the freshness and spiciness of the food ($6.95 to $14.95).

Baker's Table Grille at 434 Fore St. has slipped in locals' estimation since its glory days of a decade ago, but it's worth a stop for lunch as cooks scurry around an open kitchen and the specialty bouillabaisse ($17.95) is good as ever. During one visit, we had a memorable oriental chicken salad with snow peas, straw mushrooms and an orange and sesame seed vinaigrette dressing in the beamed Tavern beside the outdoor cafe. The weekend brunch ($3.95 to $8.95) seems to have taken the limelight lately.

Patterned after a European coffee bar, the **Portland Coffee Roasting Co.** at 111 Commercial St. draws in the locals for a coffee fix or the "eggspresso breakfast" (two scrambled eggs, bagel and small coffee, $3.25). In the afternoon and evening, tall windows reveal the passing scene as you sip cappuccino or cafe au lait in the $2.25 range. We nursed a caffe latte and caffe mocha outdoors on a ledge with a view of the waterfront and could picture ourselves back in Seattle, the latte capital of the world, where we had just been on vacation.

Chef Stuart's Foodworks, 47 India St., is a catering service par excellence. But you can stop here for four-star food out of a case, a complete box lunch ($5.40 to $7.40), healthful salads and gourmet sandwiches ($3.85 to $4.95). Peripatetic Chef Stuart Littlefield, a newcomer who has been around, was hoping to open a restaurant in town.

Della's Catessen at 9 Deering Ave. is where Della Parker, once a sous chef at Cafe Always, purveys homemade pastas, good salads, soups and desserts as well as picnic baskets to go.

For a taste of simple Down East Maine, head south a bit to Cape Elizabeth. The **Spurwink Country Kitchen** at 150 Spurwink Road, an area institution, has reopened after a brief hiatus. For breakfast, we enjoyed a fried egg with homefries and toast for $2.45 and an order of pancakes for $3.50. The pine-paneled dining room also offers a lobster roll for $6.95, and full old-fashioned dinners including soup and beverage from $5.50 to $7.95. Two lobster specials are $12.95. It's open Tuesday-Sunday from 11:30 to 8, and in summer for breakfast.

Two Lights Lobster Shack, Two Lights Road, Cape Elizabeth, is a no-frills place within the shadow of two lighthouses. Picnic tables on the bluff beside the ocean are where we like to dig into a boiled lobster dinner ($10.95) or a fisherman's platter ($11.95). There are hot dogs, hamburgers and fried chicken for the non-fish eaters. Open daily, 11 to 8, early April to mid-October.

Shopping

With the distinctive sound of seagulls all around, the shops in the Old Port Exchange draw their share of browsers and buyers. For traditionalists, the expanded Maine Mall at Turnpike Exit 7 in South Portland is anchored by Filene's and has the usual complement of stores.

In the Old Port Exchange we love to hang around **Whip and Spoon,** 161 Commercial St., a place for the serious cook. From fifteen-cent lobster picks to supplies for making beer, they've got it all. There's a section for "made in Maine" foods that are fun to buy and try. The **Paper Patch** at 17 Exchange St. carries cards for every occasion and we stock up every year. **The Ecology House** offers good tote bags, T-shirts and books about animals, and part of your purchase price goes to environmental causes. We liked the beach towel of manatees but felt that $30 was a bit much. **Covent Garden** has especially nice soaps and Caswell-Massey items, as well as MacKenzie-Childs pottery. At **Portmanteau** you can watch colorful canvas bags and other canvas goods being made. Some of the purses here are made out of woven tapestry and are really handsome. Everything at **Just ME.** is made in Maine. **Serendipity** offers lovely sweaters, mohair throws and Geiger clothes, while **Abacus** stocks unusual and very contemporary jewelry, pottery and other craft items. For years, **Amaryllis** has been the place to go for unique and trendy clothing. Windsocks shaped like lobsters, cows, parrots and carrots hang outside **Ye Old Port Kite Shoppe.** The selection of pottery at **Maxwell's Pottery Outlet** at 384 Fore St. is outstanding. For a fine selection of Maine tourmaline jewelry, visit **Cross Jewelers,** upstairs at 570 Congress St. If all this shopping (and we haven't told you the half of it) gets to be too much, stop at **Portland Wine & Cheese,** a store and deli at 188 Middle St., for a bowl of soup or a sandwich (chicken liver pate with prosciutto is $4.99, or $2.89 for a half).

Outside town, **White Pepper,** billing itself as "a summer shop by the sea," is at the end of Prouts Neck and is suavely run by summer residents Josie Scully and Patsy Timpson. Besides selling all kinds of sophisticated gifts, they continue their predecessors' tradition of selling penny candy to local youngsters.

And to the north, there awaits the huge L.L. Bean Co. and the outlet stores of Freeport.

FOR MORE INFORMATION: The Visitor Information Center of the Convention and Visitors Bureau of Greater Portland, 305 Commercial St., Portland 04101, (207) 772-4994. The Maine Tourist Bureau at the rest area on the Maine Turnpike at Kittery has information on Portland and the rest of the state.

Entrance atrium at Williams College Museum of Art.

Mountains and Museums

Bennington, Vt., and Williamstown, Mass.

Two towns on the western edge of New England — one in Massachusetts and the other in Vermont — make a charming pair for the weekender. Although situated in different states, Bennington and Williamstown are just twenty minutes apart by car. Together they offer three outstanding museums, scenic mountain vistas, good places to stay, fine dining, the presence of two well-known colleges and history galore.

It is their location amid the Green Mountains of Vermont and the Berkshire hills in Massachusetts that most influenced their development. Those mountains proved isolating, forcing the towns to develop hardy, do-it-yourself-type people. At the same time, the mountains eventually lured visitors — hikers and sightseers who were charmed by the views they offered.

All those mountain streams meant ample water power and Bennington developed as a mill town and ceramic center of note. Today, Bennington Potters still turns out attractive and sought-after table items.

Bennington is the proud site of the Battle of Bennington, an important Revolutionary

War skirmish in 1777 when the Green Mountain Boys helped to rout the British under Gen. John Burgoyne. He finally surrendered a couple of months later in Stillwater, N.Y. The event is honored by the famous Bennington Battle Monument, a granite obelisk rising 306 feet and visible for miles around; you can ascend by elevator for a 360-degree view of the area. Bennington College is located here.

Williamstown dates to 1753, when the plantation, West Hoosuck, was founded as the Massachusetts Bay Colony's front line during the French and Indian Wars. After Col. Ephraim Williams was killed in battle, his will provided for a free school in West Hoosuck — if it was named for him. Williams College opened its doors in Williamstown to fifteen students in 1793; today it has 2,000 and planned to celebrate its bicentennial in high gear.

Long known as a fine small liberal arts college, Williams was ranked tops in the country in the annual college survey in U.S. News & World Report in 1992, barely beating out archrival Amherst.

Williamstown is a true college town, the mostly red brick buildings of the college dominating the center, and the purple and gold college colors showing up everywhere. After all, the students constitute one-fourth of the town's population.

Bennington is twice as big and parts are a trifle seedy, as you might expect in an old mill town. But check out the fine old mansions in Old Bennington, the Old Burying Ground where poet Robert Frost and five Vermont governors have been laid to rest, the Bennington Museum with its stunning collection of Grandma Moses paintings, the crafts and antiques shops, and the diverse restaurants.

When it comes to art, Williamstown harbors so much, from the collections at the Williams College Museum of Art and the Sterling and Francine Clark Art Institute, that people speculate it may have the highest concentration per capita in the country.

In the fall, the hillsides flame with the colors of foliage and the roadside stands along Route 7, which connects the two towns, offer apples, maple syrup, pumpkins and cider. Cheers emanate from the football stadium at Williams on Saturday afternoons and the soccer or frisbee teams might be practicing on the fields along North Street. The aroma of wood fires from inns and restaurants fills the crisp air.

The area's eclectic mix of offerings is sure to make your weekend interesting.

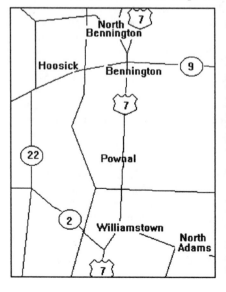

Getting There

Williamstown, in the northwest corner of Massachusetts, and Bennington, in the southwest of Vermont, lie along Route 7. The nearest major airport is in Albany, N.Y. Bonanza buses stop adjacent to the Williams campus at the Williams Inn in Williamstown. Vermont Transit serves Bennington.

Where to Stay

Bennington

South Shire Inn, 124 Elm St., Bennington 05201, (802) 447-3839. This large cream-colored Victorian house with olive trim in one of Bennington's nicer residential areas has been turned into a posh B&B. The main house was designed by architect William C. Bull, who did many stately Bennington homes. Ten-foot ceilings, a mahogany-paneled library where guests can read and relax, and fine plaster moldings are marvelous touches. All nine spacious guest rooms have private baths and seven have fireplaces. Five are in the main house and four in the Carriage House. Chippendale chairs are set at individual tables in the handsome peach dining room, where a full breakfast includes fresh fruit, muffins and a hot entree. Doubles, $95 to $150.

Molly Stark Inn, 1067 East Main St. (Route 9), Bennington 05201, (802) 442-9631. Owner and innkeeper Reed Fendler grew up in the Hartford area, graduated from the University of Connecticut and then headed north. He has turned this great old house into a welcoming B&B. Painted a deep Colonial blue with white trim, the house features a porch with wicker furniture, rockers and hanging plants. There are two front parlors for guests, one with a wood stove that Reed keeps stoked all season. Six guest rooms are furnished eclectically, the common thread being antique quilts on the beds. The top-floor room with private bath is called "really cozy" by the innkeeper, although all rooms seem warm and welcoming. Some baths are private; some shared. A full breakfast is served (apple puff pancakes were the entree at our visit). Doubles, $65 to $90.

Safford Manor, 722 Main St. (Route 9), Bennington 05201, (802) 442-5934. This big house is 218 years old and the oldest in Bennington village, according to Sandy Redding, innkeeper with her husband John. The inside is more inviting than the exterior, with lovely woodwork and three common rooms, including a game room, available to guests. Four guest rooms come in various configurations. The Rose Victorian suite contains a double and two twin beds and a private bath and rents for $68 double or $88 family. Another room has a kitchenette and its own bath; two rooms share a bath. All are clean and cheerful. A full breakfast is served in the enclosed wraparound porch, which looks onto busy Route 9. Doubles, $48 to $68.

The Four Chimneys Inn and Restaurant, 21 West Road, Old Bennington 05201, (802) 447-3500. Master chef Alex Koks is known for his food, but there are lodgings at this fine establishment as well. Seven guest rooms, rather large and elegantly furnished but not particularly cozy, are located upstairs. Another five rooms are to be added in two other buildings on the property, according to Alex. We liked Room 2 best, with a fireplace, a queen four-poster bed bearing a blue print coverlet and pink wall-to-wall carpeting. Shades of pink and cranberry dominate in the guest rooms as they do in the downstairs restaurant. All rooms come with private baths and king or queensize beds. Continental breakfast is served by tray in the bedrooms or in the restaurant. Doubles, $100 to $125.

Paradise Motor Inn, 141 West Main St., Bennington 05201, (802) 442-8351. This 76-unit motel is well-located near the center of town, on a rise behind a restaurant that it also operates. The rooms and suites offer various amenities; some have private balconies, others have patios and there are saunas, too. A heated pool and tennis courts are pluses in good weather. Rooms contain a double and a single bed, two doubles or a kingsize bed; some have just showers and some have full baths. Doubles, $56 to $91.

Best Western-New Englander, 220 Northside Drive, Route 7A, Bennington 05201, (802) 442-6311. This member of the national chain is well-situated and comfortable, although we did wish they could turn down the heat in our room. The 58 units are located on two levels of two long gray buildings with white trim. Many rooms have king or queensize beds and 35 have refrigerators. There's a small swimming pool for summer use. In the morning, pastries, donuts, juice and coffee are available in the main lobby area. Doubles, $74 to $86.

Knotty Pine Motel, 130 Northside Drive, Route 7A, Bennington 05201, (802)

Victorian mansion houses South Shire Inn in Bennington.

442-5487. Tom and Barbara Bluto have been running this small, impeccable and friendly motel for more than twenty years. The eighteen units come with either a queen or two double beds, knotty pine walls, wall-to-wall carpeting, color cable TV and in-room coffee. Doubles, $56 to $62.

Williamstown

River Bend Farm, 643 Simonds Road (Route 7 North), Williamstown 01267, (413) 458-5504 or 458-3121. Dave and Judy Loomis have opened this gorgeous Georgian Colonial farmhouse, built in 1770, to guests for more than fifteen years. The house, which is on the National Register of Historic Places, is kept as an authentic 18th-century experience (the Loomises' own more modern digs are attached at the rear). Guests sleep in five antiques-furnished bedrooms that share two baths; the bathroom on the first floor was created out of the old pantry off the keeping room and still has shelves of crockery along one wall. For breakfast, Judy serves her own granola, along with fruit, juices and homebaked breads — possibly spread with the couple's own honey — in the keeping room in front of the huge hearth. River Bend Farm offers one of the most authentic historical experiences we know of; this really *is* like going back in time. And, should you be sailors, the Loomises may share with you tales of their own transoceanic sailing experiences. Doubles, $60. Closed Thanksgiving to March.

Field Farm Guest House, 554 Sloan Road, Williamstown 01267, (413) 458-3135. This 1948 country estate was owned by an art collector, Lawrence H. Bloedel, and became available following his widow's death in 1984, when it was given to the Trustees of Reservations. The 254-acre site is stunning, with a beaver pond, views of Mount Greylock, and hiking and walking trails. And the house was perfect for conversion into a B&B, innkeepers Judy and David Loomis told the trustees when they were asked what to do with it. The Loomises, hired as management consultants, helped the organization turn it into a quite unusual B&B. Actually, there wasn't much to do, for the house was in great shape, the furnishings — right out of the 1940s and 1950s — were interesting, and all five bedrooms already had private baths. There are also second-floor balconies with ship's railings, a main-floor terrace with tables, contemporary sculpture on the grounds, and views all around from picture windows. Guests enjoy a spacious living room with tiled fireplace, furnished mostly with pieces made by Mr. Bloedel, who was a 1923 Williams graduate and onetime college librarian. The huge first-floor Gallery Room, which the owner used as a studio, contains a double bed, two twins and a separate entrance. Upstairs are four more rooms, one with tiles of butterflies around the fireplace. Continental breakfast includes fruit, granola and homemade breads. Doubles, $75.

The Orchards, 222 Adams Road, Route 2, Williamstown 01267, (413) 458-9611 or (800) 225-1517. Opened in 1985, this small hotel in the English country tradition was meant to fill a gap in terms of accommodations in Williamstown. The exterior of salmon-colored stucco is a bit confusing, but plantings are gorgeous, especially those in an interior courtyard with fountain and pool. Inside, graciousness reigns. The inn has 49 guest rooms in several different wings, all with TVs in armoires, bathroom phones and refrigerators. Pink and green predominate in the decorating scheme, both in the public rooms and the guest rooms, and some rooms have four-poster beds and working fireplaces. There's an English-style pub with fireplace and dart board and a handsome dining room with a good reputation (dinner entrees, $13.50 to $18.75), serving three meals a day. The inn's ownership by a bank following a foreclosure action made its status a bit shaky in 1992, but all seemed to be very well when we stopped by. Guests were thoroughly enjoying the afternoon tea, including several breads, tea cakes and sandwiches. Doubles, $135 to $200.

The Williams Inn, Junction of Routes 7 and 2, Williamstown 01267, (413) 458-9371. This 100-room inn is really more of a Colonial-style hotel/motel, architecturally lacking in proportion, but rather nice once you're inside. A large cocktail lounge next to a spacious dining room off the lobby attracts post-football game crowds. Guest rooms are located on three floors; all have private baths, color TVs, oversize beds and early American furnishings. There are a spacious and comfortable lobby, an indoor pool, saunas and spa. The $15.50 Sunday brunch is widely acclaimed. Doubles, $100 to $145.

Williamstown Bed and Breakfast, 30 Cold Spring Road, Williamstown 01267, (413) 458-9202. Nicely located at the crossroads of Williamstown, this big white house was turned into a comfortable and squeaky-clean B&B in 1989 by Lucinda Edmonds and Kim Rozell, who met when both were working in Boston. Kim is the cook, Lu handles the cleaning, and both are experts at what they do. There are five guest rooms and three bathrooms on the second floor, but Kim says no more than three are usually rented at one time, so guests generally have a private bath. All beds are topped with cream-colored comforters, puffy and warm. Bottled water awaits guests in each room, where braided rugs and comfortable chairs add homey touches. Kim makes the full breakfasts, which are served in a simple dining room on the main floor. "I bake bread and muffins and I always have a hot entree, sometimes cheese blintzes or blueberry pancakes," says she. Doubles, $65.

1896 Motel, Route 7, Williamstown 01267, (413) 458-825. Among a slew of motels along Routes 7 and 2, this stands out. Sue Morelle and Denise Richer joined forces seven years ago to take over the place, set back from the road and reached when you cross a tiny bridge over Hemlock Brook. Guests like to sit near the brook, which runs in front of the motel, while taking their continental breakfast in the morning. The sixteen units have knotty pine walls and wonderful old rock maple furniture with the most comfortable chairs imaginable. "Guests are always wanting to buy them," says Sue. Country-checked curtains in some rooms, Colonial prints in others, and impeccable housekeeping make this a good choice. Two airedales, Dacey May and Chelsea (mother and daughter), are also "on staff." Doubles, $68 to $75.

Keeping room at River Bend Farm conveys 18th-century heritage.

Four Acres Motel, 213 Main St., Williamstown 01267, (413) 458-8158. Another good motel, this one on the touristy outskirts east of town, has 30 large and attractive units in an L-shaped layout. It's been personally run for years by ex-Montrealers Marjorie and Keith Wallace, now enthusiastic local boosters. Combination or shower baths, air-conditioning and cable TV are among their offerings. Doubles, $54 to $70.

Seeing and Doing

A wide range of activities awaits you in this area. Of particular importance are fine museums, the out-of-doors (especially in leaf-peeping season), cultural opportunities and shopping.

Museums

The Bennington Museum, West Main Street (Route 9), Bennington, (802) 447-1571. One of the finest regional art and history museums in New England, this has the largest public collection of paintings by Grandma Moses, America's beloved folk artist. Anna Mary Robertson Moses lived just over the state line in nearby New York, but she spent three years in Bennington, making her something of a native daughter. She painted scenes that would have been familiar to townspeople and some, in fact, of Bennington. Twenty-eight of her paintings are on display here, as is the tilt-top table that she used as her easel and whose base she painted with scenes. In addition, the schoolhouse that she attended as a child was moved here from Eagle Bridge, N.Y., and contains many of her personal belongings. The military gallery in the museum features a red coat from a Redcoat along with artifacts from not only the Revolutionary War, but from every war in which Bennington men fought. An unsurpassed collection of Bennington pottery fills two galleries in the museum. Other attractions are a fine collection of American glass, a grouping of American furniture and relics of Bennington's proud past. The gift shop on the first floor is quite good. Open daily 9 to 5, March to Dec. 23; weekends and holidays only in January and February. Adults $4.50, students $3.50, family rate $10.

Williams College Museum of Art, Main Street, Williamstown, (413) 597-2429. This is one of the best college art museums in the country. It houses 11,000 works spanning the history of art, but the emphasis is on contemporary and modern art collections, American art from the late 18th century to the present and non-Western art. The neoclassical rotunda of the original structure is augmented by extensive additions designed in 1983 and 1986 by architect Charles Moore. Moore's dramatic three-story entrance atrium connects the original building with the four-story addition. The college has particularly extensive holdings of works by Maurice and Charles Prendergast. Perhaps because much of the museum is devoted to modern works, the Edwin Howland Blashfield Memorial Room, installed in 1983 and centered by an old French baptismal font from the 12th century, seems such a gem. The entire collection is staggering, though, from a 3,000-year-old Assyrian stone relief to the last self-portrait by Andy Warhol. Open Monday-Saturday 10 to 5, Sunday 1 to 5. Free.

Chapin Library, Stetson Hall, Williams College, (413) 597-2462. Nowhere else are the founding documents of the country — original printings of the Declaration of Independence, the Articles of Confederation, the Bill of Rights and drafts of the Constitution — displayed together in a simple glass case on the second floor of a college hall. This fine library contains more than 30,000 rare books, first editions and manuscripts. The lowest level of Stetson Hall contains the archives of band leader Paul Whiteman, including 3,500 original scores and a complete library of music of the 1920s. Open Monday-Friday, 9 to noon and 1 to 5. Free.

Sterling and Francine Clark Art Institute, 225 South St., Williamstown, (413) 458-9545. An heir to the Singer Sewing Machine fortune, Sterling Clark collected art avidly and, it is said, without assistance from dealers or advisers. He simply had a good eye. While living in Paris from 1911 to 1921 he laid the foundation of his own collection, buying many paintings of the old masters and the first of his favorites — Degas, Renoir, Sargent and Homer, who are well-represented here. When we visited in 1992, the exhibit "Toulouse-Lautrec at the Clark" was on view. Here were four paintings, six drawings, and 48 lithographs of works by the French artist, all owned by the Clark. But there are also extensive collections of silver, prints, drawings and sculpture. It is said the Clarks chose Williamstown because they wanted their collection safeguarded in a place where nuclear attack would be unlikely. The original building, opened in 1955, is of white marble and was designed by Daniel Perry of Long Island; it is like a little Parthenon and is quite lovely. A large red granite addition, designed by Pietro Belluschi and The Artists Collaborative, was added in 1973. The buildings are connected by a pedestrian "bridge." Open Tuesday-Sunday (and several Monday holidays including Columbus Day), 10 to 5. Free.

Park-McCullough House, corner Park and West streets, North Bennington, (802) 442-5441. For one hundred years, from the time the house was built in 1865 until Bess McCullough Johnson died, this imposing house was lived in by members of one family. One of them, John G. McCullough, was governor of Vermont and kept his office in the house, since Vermont does not have a governor's mansion. Today, the grand old place with its fourteen-foot ceilings, dark mahogany woodwork, pocket doors, parquet floors and original furnishings is a rich collection of Victoriana. In fact, it provides an unusually complete record of an important New England family. One-hour guided tours are offered. Of particular interest are the extravagant indoor plumbing, beautiful fireplace mantels and many of the clothes worn by the inhabitants. Open daily 10 to 4, early May through October, with tours on the hour from 10 to 3. Adults $4, children $2.50.

Williams College, Williamstown. Just a stroll around the campus is of interest and

White marble building of Sterling and Francine Clark Art Institute resembles little Parthenon.

the houses and buildings along Main Street (Route 2) are most beautifully sited. The old **Hopkins Observatory** is the oldest observatory in the country; on Friday nights during the school year there are programs in Milham Planetarium here.

Hancock Shaker Village, Route 20 west of Pittsfield, (413) 443-0188. Well worth a side trip is this restored Shaker village where visitors see the way the unusual Shaker religious sect lived and worked. The famous round stone barn is located here. Containing original Shaker furniture and artifacts, 21 buildings are restored and are fascinating to walk through and ponder over. Interpreters work in the kitchen making Shaker foods, in the herb garden tending Shaker herbs, in the barns caring for sheep and horses, or in the blacksmith shop forging pieces of iron. Open daily, 9:30 to 5, May-October; daily 10 to 3 in April and November. Adults $8.50, students $7.75, family rate $23.

Cultural Offerings

Williamstown and Bennington form a cultural center. In the summer, the **Williamstown Theatre Festival,** (413) 597-3399, mounts productions on the stage of the Adams Memorial Theatre at Williams College. Considered one of the best professional regional theaters in the country, it celebrates its 40th season in 1994.

In Bennington, the **Oldcastle Theatre Company,** (802) 447-0564, has just celebrated its twentieth anniversary. Performances are held from June through mid-November on the campus of Southern Vermont College.

Images Cinema, 50 Spring St., Williamstown, (413) 458-5612, is well-spoken of. This "art" cinema offers films for a few days at a time, often those that have attained a cult status but haven't been huge box-office draws. Many are foreign films. The collegians appreciate them and you may, too.

The **Williams College Department of Music** offers an ambitious schedule during the school year with appearances by the Berkshire Symphony, Williams Choral Society, Williams Jazz Ensemble, Williams Symphonic Winds, recitals with guest artists and so forth. Performances are usually given on weekends. Call Concertline at (413) 597-3146.

History

Bennington Battle Monument,, 15 Monument Circle, Old Bennington, (802) 447-0550. The tallest structure in Vermont, this 306-foot granite monument on a hill overlooking Bennington marks the site of a Continental Army storehouse that was the objective of the British Army in August 1777. That force was met and defeated by local militiamen, including the legendary Green Mountain Boys, just across the border in Wallomsac, N.Y., on Aug. 16. Many historians consider this battle the turning point in the War for Independence. Each year on the weekend closest to the date a parade is held in Bennington. The monument was dedicated in 1891 by President Benjamin Harrison on the occasion of the 100th anniversary of Vermont's becoming a state. It contains a diorama of the battle and the large army field kettle that supposedly belonged to British General John Burgoyne, surely a sweet spoil of war. You can ride the elevator to an observation area about two-thirds of the way up the monument. Glass windows allow views in all four directions and on a clear day you can see a great deal, including Mount Greylock, the highest peak in Massachusetts. A gift shop stocks made-in-Vermont items. Open daily 9 to 5, April-October. Adults $1, children 50 cents.

Bennington Battlefield, (518) 686-7109, is on Route 67 in Wallomsac, N.Y., about a mile across the Vermont-New York border. It contains markers and bronze raised maps of the Aug. 16 battle. The natural beauty and tranquility of the well-kept grounds belie the violent struggle that took place here more than 200 years ago. There are picnic benches and restrooms. Free. Closed in winter.

Old First Church, Old Bennington. The present edifice was erected in 1805 to replace the First Congregational Meeting House built in 1763-65. The existing building was designed in the Wren-influenced style by Lavius Fillmore. In the historic graveyard next to the church are buried Revolutionary War soldiers, Vermont governors and the poet Robert Frost, whose gravestone reads "I had a lover's quarrel with the world."

Two **walking tours** of Bennington are outlined in a handy printed guide and map. One takes you to **Old Bennington** and describes 27 sites, the majority of which are private residences built in the late 18th and early 19th centuries in the Federal and Colonial Revival styles. Included also are the Bennington Battle Monument and the Old First Church and Cemetery. The second, a guide to **Downtown Bennington,** covers 42 sites, some of them the big old brick mills that characterized the city. You'll also see the restored railroad station (now a restaurant) and several schools, churches and other public buildings.

Out of Doors

Getting out into the crisp fall air is a must. Many visitors like just to drive around, enjoying mountain vistas, Colonial houses and roadside stands. One trip we love is Route 43 south from Williamstown toward Hancock.

There are special places for those who like to hike or walk. **The Long Trail** is a section of the Appalachian Trail that basically runs across the ridge of the Green Mountains and the Berkshire Hills. It is accessible from a number of points off main roads, many of which provide parking areas for vehicles. There are 71 shelters along the trail, which is marked by white paint with side trails marked in blue. A detailed guide is available at local bookstores or from The Green Mountain Club, Box 889, Montpelier, VT 05602, (802) 223-3463.

Mount Greylock, at 3,491 feet, is the highest peak in Massachusetts. Much of the mountain is protected as a state reservation. Roads climb to the summit from Lanesborough, New Ashford and North Adams. The bare summit offers views in all directions and also has Bascom Lodge, built by the Civilian Conservation Corps in the 1930s and operated by the Appalachian Mountain Club. The lodge is the starting point for nature walks. Also on the summit is the 92-foot War Memorial Tower, open to the public, which affords great views. There are about 40 miles of hiking trails on Greylock.

Field Farm in South Williamstown (site of Field Farm Guest House) offers interesting walks and trails, most of them not particularly strenuous.

Hopkins Memorial Forest in the northwestern corner of Williamstown and adjacent Petersburg, N.Y., covers more than 2,200 acres. It is managed by the Williams College Center for Environmental Studies for research, education and recreation. Ten miles of trails are open to the public for hiking, snowshoeing and cross-country skiing. The Rosenberg Center is located at the eastern entrance to the forest off Northwest Hill Road. Diagonally across from the center is the Hopkins Forest Farm Museum, dedicated to the agricultural heritage of the Berkshires.

Mount Hope Park in Williamstown contains picnic sites and picturesque waterfalls.

Covered bridges. There are three in Bennington, one off Silk Street and two near Murphy Road. They're easy to find using the Chamber of Commerce map of town.

Seasonal Events. Because fall is the busiest tourist season, there are always flea markets, harvest fairs, apple festivals and the like. The Bennington Museum sponsors an annual Apple Festival at the Peter Mattison Tavern in Bennington on a Saturday in late September or early October. A big Antiques Show and Sale is staged at the Second Congregational Church in Bennington in October. Tickets are almost always available for Saturday football games at Williams College; the field is at the end of downtown at Latham and Spring streets.

Shopping

In Bennington, you will want to visit Potter's Yard at 324 County St. **Bennington Potters** is the contemporary manifestation of the historic "Bennington" pottery, which was actually made by several different firms. On-site manufacturing of the new Bennington ware, plus a retail shop, are here. There are seconds and sale items available. Also in Potter's Yard are **Cinnamons,** a kitchen store; **John McLeod,** a wood products store; **JLF Designs,** leather and nylon goods made in North Bennington, and **Terra-sua,** handcrafts from around the world. **Brasserie** is the exceptional on-site restaurant (see Where to Eat).

Hawkins House Craft Market at 262 North St. (Route 7) offers quite an array of handcrafted items. **Camelot Village** on Route 9 West is a large barn-like building with an antiques center for some 75 dealers, a dried flower shop, gift shops, a wine cellar and a restaurant.

The Apple Barn on Route 7 South, Bennington, is a good stop for cider, apples, a bake shop, cheddar cheese and maple products. Other roadside stands also are located along this stretch of highway toward Williamstown.

In Williamstown, browse along Spring Street, site of college shops like the Williams Co-op and gift and clothing stores. Don't miss **The Library,** an exceptional antiques and gift shop that takes up three storefronts and also offers lunch on weekends. On Water Street we like **Water Street Books,** a good bookstore where the college students also buy their texts; **Hey Diddle Diddle,** a fine children's store, and **The Potter's Wheel,** which backs up to the rushing Green River and artfully displays ceramics and jewelry. **The Cottage,** next to the bookstore, has funky as well as traditional clothing and gifts, too. There are antiques galore in a warehouse atmosphere at **Collectors Warehouse,** off Route 7 North.

The Store at Five Corners along Route 7 in South Williamstown, taken over in 1992 by Andy and Stuart Shatken and renovated to their specifications, is now an updated country store with gourmet items, wines, hand-scooped ice cream, a deli, baked goods, groceries and gifts.

Where to Eat

The choices for dining are quite good. In addition to solid New England fare, there is a surprising number of new, sophisticated restaurants.

Bennington

Four Chimneys Inn and Restaurant, 21 West Road, Old Bennington, (802) 447-3500. Chef-owner Alex Koks, who used to run the well-regarded Village Auberge in Dorset, Vt., took over this venerable establishment in 1987. The gorgeous old white home has three dining rooms. Those on either side of a luxurious lounge are decorated in shades of pale mauve, pink and rose with a cranberry, rose and taupe tweed carpet running through all rooms. Flickering oil lamps in hurricane chimneys and classical music in the background make this an elegant, formal setting. Dutch-born Alex concentrates on classic French fare with a touch of nouvelle. At lunch, entrees ($6 to $8) include grilled duck salad with spiced pecans, a house specialty; home-cured gravlax in a light mustard mayonnaise; sauteed shrimp with pasta in a chive and saffron sauce, and roasted quail in a port wine sauce.

Street scene in Old Bennington.

At night, the gravlax shows up as an appetizer along with a salmon and scallop terrine and what the menu refers to as "our famous mustard soup," really good and really mustardy. Entrees ($14 to $19) include a signature roast duckling served with a crisp leg and pink breast, scampi maison, double lamb chop, grilled medallion of veal and beef wellington wrapped in puff pastry and served with chestnut puree and truffle sauce. Dessert could be crepes flambes, a mocha parfait, homemade sorbets and a meringue with vanilla ice cream and chocolate sauce. Lunch, Tuesday-Saturday 11:30 to 2, July-October; dinner, Tuesday-Saturday 5 to 10, Sunday noon to 8.

Main Street Cafe, 1 Prospect St., North Bennington, (802) 442-3210. Jeffrey Bendavid and his wife Peggy oversee this intimate restaurant in a storefront location. Jeff, who hails from New Brunswick, N.J., was a musician before he turned his creativity to food and he makes beautiful music here. The sponged peach walls under a deep burgundy pressed-tin ceiling display the unusual artworks of James Kardas, a local painter, whose oversize canvases often reference patriotic subjects. Jeff was at the famous Sam's Place in Saratoga Springs before coming here in 1989. Each table sports bottles of red and white wine; you can drink whichever you'd like and pay for the amount you've imbibed. Waiters clad in tuxedoes give attentive service. Jeff and Rich Hooker work in a small kitchen open to the dining room. About half his orders are for seafood, dishes like charcoal-grilled sea scallops served on spinach linguini and topped with artichoke hearts, sundried tomatoes and basil. Also on the menu one evening were shrimp and sausage served on rigatoni, breast of chicken in marsala wine on spinach, beef and vegetable cannelloni, and pasta primavera. Entrees are priced from $14 to $18. The house caesar salad (which is made without anchovies or eggs, according to Jeff) is popular and, he says, "the semolina bread is an absolute knockout." He makes his own sausage and faithful customers sometimes buy it to take home. Desserts such as chocolate kahlua cheesecake and lemon pound cake are made by the Russian Orthodox nuns of New Skete at nearby Cambridge, N.Y. Tirami su also is sometimes offered. Dinner nightly from 6 (but Jeff says to check ahead on Sundays in football season; he's a diehard Giants fan and might be closed).

Brasserie, 324 County St. (Potter's Yard), Bennington, (802) 447-7922. David Gill has owned this wonderful little European-style cafe for 29 years since it opened, but his real genius has been in attracting fantastic chefs. Originally, it was the late, great Dionne Lucas; since the early 1970s, Sheela Harden has overseen the kitchen. "People rave about the consistency," said the manager when we stopped by. The all-day menu offers lighter lunch-type foods ($5 to $8) as well as dinner entrees ($9 to $12). One of the more famous items, one rarely seen hereabouts, is pissaladiere, a snack from Provence that amounts to a thick slice of Rock Hill bread, smothered with sweet onions cooked in olive oil almost to a jam consistency, then baked with anchovies and calamata olives on top. It is served with a tomato salad vinaigrette. The pastas are especially well-liked, and you also can get quiches, omelets, a Greek salad, a Scandinavian sampler (smoked bluefish, parslied potato salad, pickled beets and dilled cucumbers), a mozzarella loaf as luscious as the name implies, and even a chunk of chevre cheese marinated in olive oil and served with a loaf of whole wheat sunflower seed bread and tomatoes. Heartier dishes ($9 to $12) include veal and artichoke stew, chicken livers deglazed with dry sherry and steak au poivre. Creme caramel is a signature dessert. Open daily except Tuesday, 11:30 to 8; Sunday from 10:30.

Bennington Station, Depot Street, Bennington, (802) 447-1080. This converted Romanesque railroad station dates from 1897 and served trains of the Bennington & Rutland Railroad. Train aficionados love it, for it's a great renovation. Historic photos, old signs and refurbished woods and brasses make a most attractive setting. Black chairs with pink seats and matching pink napkins are at tables set with dark marble slabs over patterned cloths. We dined in what was apparently once the entryway, now glass-enclosed and off the main room. The place was packed on a Friday evening as diners selected from a large menu: everything from roast turkey and New England pot roast to seafood sampler and roast duckling with brandied peaches, most in the $13 to $17 range. We had to send a harsh glass of fume blanc back and service seemed hurried and impersonal, but clearly this is one popular restaurant. Open daily, 11:30 to 9 or 10.

Alldays & Onions, 519 Main St., Bennington, (802) 447-0043. This new restaurant, deli, specialty food shop, wine store and cafe is one of the best eating spots in town. Matthew and Maureen Forlenza serve what we'd call regional American food with lots of interesting choices. For lunch, you can build your own sandwich of traditional deli meats, cheeses, condiments and other choices, or have something like cream of golden squash soup, fettuccine with smoked chicken or tortellini with basil. Dinner menus change frequently but might include appetizers of grilled boned quail with mixed greens and peppercorn ravioli with shiitake mushrooms and bacon. Entrees in the $15 to $20 range could be roast chicken breast with lingonberries, rack of lamb with honey rosemary sauce, sauteed sweetbreads with wild mushrooms and grilled swordfish with fresh salsa. Meals come with a house salad, the restaurant's own herb bread, roasted red potatoes and garden vegetables. Fresh peach pie was one dessert choice. Open daily except Sunday 7:30 to 5; dinner, Thursday-Saturday 6 to 8.

Publyk House, Harwood Hill, Route 7A, Bennington, (802) 442-8301. This popular steak and seafood restaurant is in a remodeled barn full of dark wood, stained glass and plants. Diners arrive early for dinner and everyone seems to like the salad bar. Choice western beef is featured and prime rib is a specialty of the house. Among other entrees in the $12 to $17 range are baked scrod, grilled halibut, chicken teriyaki and sirloin steak, or you can have just soup and the salad bar for $8.95. Lunch, Monday-Friday 11:30 to 2:30; dinner nightly, 5 to 9 or 10.

Blue Benn Diner, Route 7, Bennington, (802) 442-8977. This is the place for breakfast, which is served all day. You also can get lunch and light supper. The vintage diner with blue stools and booths, blue and white ruffled curtains, and individual booth-operated jukeboxes, is a Bennington institution. We managed to snag one of the coveted booths for a Saturday breakfast, and feasted on whole wheat harvest pancakes filled with blueberries, blackberries, raspberries and strawberries ($3.50). We paid an extra 85 cents for pure Vermont maple syrup, and the meal held us until a mid-afternoon lunch. There is something of an emphasis on healthful foods and you are asked not to smoke. Breakfast and lunch daily, dinner Wednesday-Friday.

Williamstown

The Mill on the Floss, Route 7, New Ashford, (413) 458-9123. Chef Maurice Champagne, a native of Montreal, his American wife Jane and their daughter Suzanne run what most locals consider the area's best restaurant. Located just south of Williamstown, it is incongruously announced by a neon sign that also advertises the motel up on the hill in back. But inside the dark brown wood building is a cozy main dining room with white linens, rough windsor chairs and fireplace, onto which the kitchen opens with its gleaming copper pots and pans. A second wraparound garden room, looking onto the lawns out front, was undergoing redecoration for 1993. Sweetbreads au beurre noir is the most famous dish on the classic French menu. Chicken amandine, veal piccata, sliced tenderloin with garlic sauce and veal kidneys in mustard sauce are among other entrees ($16 to $25). Start with prosciutto and melon, escargots or fettuccine alfredo, among appetizers for $3 to $8. Jane's homemade desserts are impressive: chocolate truffle with raspberry sauce, deep-dish pies, creme caramel and chocolate mousse. What's really remarkable is the long tenure of most of the staff at the twenty-year-old restaurant. And the bartender makes a mean cocktail. Dinner, Tuesday-Sunday from 5.

Robin's, Latham and Spring streets, Williamstown, (413) 458-4489. Robin Mac-Donald, a young and talented chef, opened this storefront restaurant in the downtown area in 1992. The decor is simple and effective: salmon walls, white curtains draped interestingly across the front and side windows, black contemporary chairs and white tablecloths. Each table in the front room holds a small bouquet of flowers. Out back is another room for dining. There's one lone table on the tiny front porch in case you have especially fine weather. From a small but efficient kitchen, Robin turns out some extraordinary meals. For dinner we chose the grilled tuna with thyme butter and the penne pasta roasted with smoked salmon and shrimp, both scrumptious. A house salad of mixed greens with a light vinaigrette dressing was served with an edible flower on top. Starters in the $3 to $5 range included celery root remoulade, a charcuterie salad, gazpacho and a fall vegetable soup, and focaccia with brie and thyme-flavored oil. Rabbit braised with pancetta and red wine, grilled veal chop with a rosemary mustard sauce and bouillabaisse were other entrees, priced from $13 to $18 for a grilled ribeye steak with homemade ketchup and grilled onions. Changing desserts included apple-blueberry crisp, chocolate torte and white chocolate cheesecake but, alas, we had no room. Open daily, 11 to 11; Sunday, 9 to 9, when brunch also is served.

Savories, 123 Water St., Williamstown, (413) 458-2175. Here's a small restaurant with something for everyone: cozy 19th-century-style dining rooms where you can enjoy a leisurely lunch or dinner, and the new Hearth Room where you can choose from a blackboard menu at chef-owner Scott Avery's marvelous gourmet takeout store. The locals rave about the options here. We lunched in the Hearth Room on a rainy September day (we're sure a fire burns in cooler months) and enjoyed a creamy New England clam chowder flavored (a mite too strongly) with tarragon and one of the big deli sandwiches of roast beef with horseradish sauce. We've also tried a couple of standbys: the Vermonster (baked ham, Vermont cheddar and thin-sliced apple on rye) and the Smokin' Tom (sliced smoked turkey with horseradish jelly on whole wheat). The display case is filled with creative salads, and the desserts, particularly the rich, fudgy brownies, beckon. On the more formal side, you also can order hot luncheon entrees like gingered chicken with shiitake mushrooms, broiled sea scallops, salad plates or quiches, in the $6 to $9 range. At night, entrees ($13 to $19) include roast prime rib, a grilled split cornish hen, grilled Norwegian salmon topped with lime and dill butter or the pasta of the day. Lunch, Tuesday-Saturday 11 to 3; dinner, Wednesday-Sunday; Sunday brunch.

Le Country Restaurant, Route 7, Williamstown, (413) 458-4000. Academics from the nearby Williams College campus often turn up at this attractive and consistently good establishment, run for twenty years by Bev and Raymond Canales (he hails from Spain). The warm country atmosphere appeals with a beamed ceiling over the main dining room, a mix of shaded lamps and candles on the tables, and a Franklin stove to ward off the chill. Wines are especially well-priced, with nothing over $30. For lunch, you might have a salad plate, a shrimp or chicken salad sandwich, or an entree like shrimp curry, chicken fricassee on toast or chicken livers saute. At night, you could start with escargots bourguignonne, hearts of palm with prosciutto and dijon sauce, or a shrimp or clam cocktail. Coquilles St. Jacques is offered as either an appetizer or entree. Appetizers are priced from $4 to $8 and entrees, $12 to $20. Among the latter are boneless duckling with orange sauce, fettuccine tossed with cheeses and prosciutto, tournedos bordelaise, coq au vin and stuffed shrimp, a much-requested item. Lunch, Tuesday-Friday 11:30 to 1:30; dinner, Tuesday-Sunday 5 to 9.

Hobson's Choice, 159 Water St., Williamstown, (413) 458-9101. Sited in an old house, this popular eatery is furnished simply with old tools on the walls and Tiffany-style lamps. There are several blue-green booths with high backs, windsor chairs at wood-topped tables and aqua carpeting. Red, green or blue napkins add brightness. Chef-owner Dan Campbell offers blackened prime rib, many fish dishes, some Southwestern favorites like chicken Santa Fe, and a couple of vegetarian pastas. Dinner entrees are priced from about $9 to $15. At lunchtime, consider the chicken Santa Fe sandwich, fresh salmon sandwich, crab salad, seafood pasta or a cheeseburger. Mud pie and a grand fudge parfait are two signature desserts. Lunch, Tuesday-Saturday 11:30 to 2; dinner, Tuesday-Sunday 5 to 9:30.

Captain's Table, Cold Spring Road (Routes 2 and 7), Williamstown, (413) 458-2400. For twenty years, this restaurant south of town has been enticing seafood lovers. Fresh shrimp on the salad bar and a lobster pool out back are particular attractions. You'll pay $13 to $18 for such entrees as shrimp scampi, salmon, different configurations of fisherman's platters and all kinds of lobster. There are many "surf and turf" choices. You also can order filet mignon, tenderloin tips, sirloin steaks, prime rib or pasta. Baked potatoes come with the entrees, as does the salad bar. Decor is simple: captain's chairs at wood tables. Dinner, Monday-Saturday 4:30 to 9 or 9:30, Sunday 2 to 9.

The Cobble Cafe at 27 Spring St. in downtown Williamstown serves breakfast, lunch, dinner and Sunday brunch and is locally popular. For Chinese food, check out **Chopsticks** on Main Street (Route 2) heading toward North Adams. If Mexican is your thing, **Desperados** will do just fine. Located in the Colonial Shopping Center on Route 2, it has touches of Mexico on the walls, a tiled floor, and items such as fajitas, burrito platter, arroz con pollo or mariscos grande (shrimp, scallops, crab and pollock on rice).

FOR MORE INFORMATION: Bennington Area Chamber of Commerce, Route 7, Bennington, VT 05201, (802) 447-3311. The Williamstown Board of Trade, Box 357, Williamstown, MA 01267, (413) 458-9077.

123

Historic Deerfield Photo

Outstanding early structures line The Street in Deerfield.

Arts and Antiquing

The Pioneer Valley, Mass.

The Connecticut River cuts a swath through hilly west-central Massachusetts, creating rich agricultural lands that drew early settlers and turned them into well-to-do farmers. Hence the name, the Pioneer Valley.

The valley is rich not only in agriculture (Connecticut River shade-grown tobacco among other products) but in education and industry as well. In the 19th century, the bucolic setting was thought appropriate to the pursuit of higher learning. Noah Webster, the lexicographer, was one of the founders of Amherst College in 1821. In 1837, just down the road, the nation's first permanent women's college, Mount Holyoke, was founded in South Hadley.

Sophia Smith started the college that bears her name across the river in Northampton in 1875. With the huge University of Massachusetts (almost a city unto itself) and much newer, out-of-the-way Hampshire College, both in Amherst, the institutions form a five-college consortium and students benefit from their proximity.

The tourist can be a student, too, of a different sort. The valley's rich heritage is found in its examples of early architecture and antiques, and the colleges have been the center for fine art museums and cultural events. In addition, more craftspeople per capita are to be found in the Pioneer Valley than almost any other section of New England except Vermont, we're told.

There's something quite 1960s about Amherst and Northampton. It's as if they got stuck in the era of the flower children and aren't inclined to move too far, too fast. Along with young women in standard-issue jeans, you may see pigtailed lasses in batik and tie-dyed dresses and sandals, walking arm-in-arm with their long-haired escorts, eating granola and sunflower seeds. In fact, one of the great natural foods stores of all time, Bread and Circus, flourishes in the area, and Amherst harbors the area's first juice bar.

The bucolic setting is still present once you get off I-91, the major north-south highway. The rich alluvial soil that first attracted settlers now nourishes their descendants, and a patchwork of green fields stretches across the land.

A prime tourist attraction is Historic Deerfield, a walk-through museum village with an unparalleled collection of furniture, textiles and porcelain stunningly displayed in renovated houses from the 18th and 19th centuries. As much as we dislike the phrase, you really do "step back in time" when you visit the village of Deerfield, which doesn't have so much as a traffic light or a supermarket to detract from the setting. There's education here, too; tiny Deerfield is home to three private schools, including the prestigious Deerfield Academy.

Possibly the proximity of Deerfield, and perhaps the ease with which customers can get to them (via I-91 and the Massachusetts Turnpike), have encouraged antiques dealers and auctioneers to make the place their own. This is an area for serious searching as well as light-hearted browsing. Auctions, flea markets and special antiques shows are frequent.

Autumn and antiques have always had an affinity, and the valley is at its best in the golden days of Indian summer when the foliage burns brightly along the river banks and into the foothills of the Berkshires to the west, and students scuff through the leaves across tree-studded campuses. The college art museums are open, with the special enthusiasm that greets the first show of the semester.

All told, the valley has 72 towns, of which we concentrate on only a handful: Deerfield, with its history and heritage; Amherst and Northampton, with their colleges, art museums, antiques shops and galleries, and Springfield, where you find culture in a quadrangle. These towns also have good restaurants and places to stay. And if you're tired of antiquing and museum-going, remember one very special Saturday afternoon diversion — college football, played with all the intimacy that must have been there when the sport began.

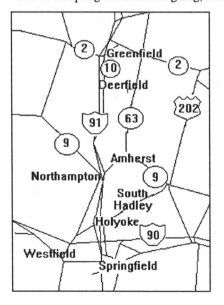

Getting There

The Pioneer Valley stretches the length of Massachusetts along the Connecticut River, from the Vermont border on the north to Connecticut on the south. Interstate 91 runs north and south through the valley and the Massachusetts Turnpike (I-90) goes east and west near Springfield.

Several bus lines serve the area, including Greyhound, Bonanza Bus Lines and Peter Pan, the largest, with offices in Springfield.

Amtrak trains serve Springfield. Major airlines fly into Bradley International Airport between Springfield and Hartford, Conn. From there, buses travel north to Springfield, Holyoke and Northampton.

Where to Stay

Accommodations in the valley range from a few old Colonial inns to modern motels and hotels with indoor pools, saunas, entertainment, the works. While you can easily find a chain hotel/motel in Springfield, we've selected places in the towns north of the city where the real ambience of the valley can be sensed.

Inns and B&Bs

Deerfield Inn, The Street, Deerfield 01342, (413) 774-5587 or (800) 926-3865. The Deerfield Inn is owned by Historic Deerfield and situated smack dab in the middle of the historic village. An obvious choice for the serious history and antiques hound, the inn has softened its somewhat formal image to take on the feeling of a comfortable country inn. Under the management of innkeepers Jane and Karl Sabo, the public rooms of the inn have been refurbished. The mahogany tables in the lovely dining room are often left bare, the better to show off their pewter service plates and white napkins. The front parlors are done in soft tones of gold and blue, and gourds and corn husks decorate the fireplace in one. There's a small tavern-type bar for a pre-dinner drink. The inn offers 23 guest rooms, several in the main building and others in the newer south wing, which has barn siding and which blends in nicely with its surroundings. All are quite spacious and have Colonial appointments. Each is named, with a card describing who the namesake is. Typical is the Samson Frary (named for Deerfield's first settler), with twin beds covered with Bates spreads and a large bathroom with complimentary toiletries. Guests may take lunch or dinner in the main dining room, or have lighter snacks in the **Stencilled Horse Coffee Shop** downstairs. Doubles, $122, B&B.

The Tea House B&B, Main Street, Deerfield 01342, (413) 772-2675. This is the only place in Old Deerfield where you can stay and live as Deerfield folks do. Natasha and Jonathan Lowe and their infant son occupy the back of their restored 1840 house and offer two spacious but spare front guest rooms that share a bath. The Cranberry Room, facing Main Street, contains a mahogany queensize bed, a fireplace beneath a vaulted ceiling and a dhurrie rug. The Jasmine Room behind it comes with queensize bed, antique pine armoire and a rocking chair. The explanations for the rooms' names are obscure; that for the B&B's name is less so. Natasha, who grew up in London, is thoroughly British; she loves tea and baking, and serves afternoon tea with shortbread, scones and homemade jams. Her breakfast includes fruit compote (perhaps blueberry-ginger), homemade granola, and maybe boursin and brie omelets, pecan waffles with fresh fruit and creme fraiche, or a rich french toast made with her chocolate-walnut butter bread. This is taken in a small dining room off a fireplaced parlor for guests' use on the main floor. Jonathan, originally from Boston and now a local real-estate entrepreneur, bought the house at age 17 when he was a student at Deerfield Academy, knowing he wanted eventually to live here. Doubles, $85 and $95.

The Autumn Inn, 259 Elm St., Northampton 01060, (413) 584-7660. This red brick inn-motel is one of our favorites. Veteran innkeeper Vince Berger refers frequently to the establishment as "the house" (which it resembles from the front), as when he points out that "the walls are insulated, so this is a quiet house to stay in." Located near the Smith College campus and set back from the main route (Route 9) leading to the quaint towns of Williamsburg, Goshen and Cummington, the Autumn Inn is one of those places to which travelers return time and again. The thirty rooms and two suites are decorated in a simple, homey style, but there are percale sheets and fluffy towels, original works of art on the walls (we liked the original framed Saturday Evening Post covers in one),

Queen Anne stick-style structure built in 1886 is now Allen House Inn in Amherst.

color TVs, some Hitchcock chairs and rockers, Stieffel lamps and the occasional poster bed. Rooms have queensize, twins or two double beds, and all have private baths. Breakfast and lunch are available in the **Harvest Room** off the lobby, a comforting space with a huge old-fashioned fireplace in which the embers glow on chilly days. The menu is comforting as well, featuring grilled cheese and other old-fashioned sandwiches for $3.15 to $4.75 and including juice or soup of the day. Downstairs is an attractive cocktail lounge. Summer guests enjoy the outdoor pool. Doubles, $82; suites, $94.

Allen House Inn, 599 Main St., Amherst 01002, (413) 253-5000. Elegant Victoriana reigns in this prized new B&B, located at the edge of Amherst in a Queen Anne stick-style house built in 1886. Alan and Ann Zieminski, he a biochemist in research at UMass and she a dental hygienist, opened it as a B&B after fifteen years in residence and promptly won the 1991 Amherst Historical Commission preservation award. Sticklers for authenticity, they offer seven guest rooms with private baths and a couple of uncommonly elaborate common rooms. The Victorian dining room, for instance, is finished in anglo-Japanese style; it harbors an ornate cherry fireplace mantel recorded in the Metropolitan Museum of Art, a stunning stained-glass window in the corner and no fewer than nine patterns of English wallpapers. The William Morris living room is papered in terra cotta, and holds a dining table in the middle for those who wish to breakfast in semi-privacy. Bedrooms feature Eastlake-style furnishings, ornate bedsteads, goose down comforters and pillows, armoires, antique AM-FM radios that work, Gilbert & Soames toiletries and more fancy wallpapers by period designers Christopher Dresser, William Morris, Walter Crane and the like. The Eastlake Room is dark and masculine, while the Peach Room is light and airy with white wicker and a queensize bed. The rear Scullery, done in authentic Laura Ashley for a seaside look, adjoins an enormous bathroom with a clawfoot tub; a puce-colored marble desk top

127

covers the scullery sink. Guests relax on wicker rockers on the small front veranda upstairs. Afternoon tea with oatmeal shortbread, cookies and cheesecake may run into the evening. For breakfast, the Zieminskis go all-out with such treats as Swedish pancakes with peach-raspberry sauce, stuffed french toast, eggs benedict and souffles. The pumpkin pancakes with maple syrup are popular in autumn. Doubles, $65 to $95.

The Brandt House, 29 Highland Ave., Greenfield 01301, (413) 774-3329. Set atop a hill on more than three acres in the high-rent district just east of downtown Greenfield, this is one magnificent, sixteen-room Colonial Revival house. Phoebe Brandt has turned it into an elegant and welcoming B&B, conveniently located just north of Deerfield. She offers eight guest rooms, six with private baths. The exceptional public areas include a fireplaced parlor, a game room with billiards and chess tables, a dining room with french doors opening onto the rear terrace, a wraparound porch and, the crowning touch, a cheery sun porch with three sofas and a TV (plus phones and fax machine) off the stairway landing. From the sun porch or terrace you can gaze across the back yard and tennis court onto woods and hills, part of vast municipal parklands containing hiking and cross-country trails and an ice-skating pond. Phoebe has furnished her attractive guest rooms with antiques, taking in the auctions every week in Deerfield. Most rooms come with king or queensize feather beds, loveseats, armoires, and good artworks and rugs. Family photos line the stairway to the third floor, where two bedrooms with twin beds share a bath and form a family suite. Energetic Phoebe used to run a B&B in Brookline before the family moved to Greenfield in 1986. At our visit, she was about to enclose part of the wraparound veranda to offer guests more common space. Breakfast — served at an expandable table for ten in the dining room, at a table for two in the bay window of the living room or outside on the terrace or veranda — is a treat. It includes fresh fruit, two homemade pastries (perhaps Danish cheese bread and streusel coffee cake) and a main course of quiche, marinated french toast or oven-baked pancakes topped with fruit. Doubles, $85 to $110. No smoking.

The Knoll Bed & Breakfast, 230 North Main St., Florence 01060, (413) 584-8164. Lee and Ed Lesko welcome overnight guests in the most imposing house in Florence, a vaguely English Tudor-style beauty on a knoll beside 150-acre Look Memorial Park just west of Northampton. The couple painted the oils that line the staircase to the second floor. Three bedrooms vacated by their grown children share two baths; two rooms contain double beds and one has twins. Decor is homey, but architectural details are fine, especially in the mahogany paneled dining room with a mahogany-beamed ceiling. The dining room is separated from a large living room by a library; the three rooms run the width of the house in the rear and look onto a back porch and seventeen acres. The Leskos serve a full breakfast of the guests' choice, including eggs, pancakes and bacon. Doubles, $45 or $50. No smoking.

Hotels and Motels

Hotel Northampton, 36 King St., Northampton 01060, (413) 584-3100. In the center of downtown, this columned, four-story brick classic has been refurbished and a new wing added to make it a more desirable place to stay. The fireplaced lobby with wing chairs and Chippendale sofa is welcoming, and all the 72 rooms have been decorated nicely, many featuring feather duvets and Laura Ashley linens and draperies. We liked one room with a kingsize canopy bed and access through french doors to a large balcony in the front of the hotel. A buffet breakfast is included in the rates. Wicker chairs add a light touch to many rooms and to the glassed-in outer lobby, which also has ice-cream-parlor tables and chairs — it's a nice spot for a drink. The **Coolidge Park Cafe** (named for Calvin, who was once mayor of Northampton) offers drinks, light fare and weekend entertainment. **Wiggins Tavern** is a quintessential Colonial dining spot pairing old favorites like yankee pot roast and Indian pudding with more contemporary fare in the $10 to $17 range. Doubles, $91 to $134.

The Lord Jeffery Inn, On the Common, Amherst 01002, (413) 253-2576 or (800) 742-0358. The "Lord Jeff" is a white brick Georgian Revival landmark in town, favored by Amherst alumni and parents of students. Owned by the college, it has been run by a succession of management groups in recent years. Of the 50 rooms, favorites are those in the Garden Wing with french doors that open onto the garden. Half the rooms have working fireplaces. Rooms are being refurbished; ask for one that has been completed. All rooms have private bathrooms, although many of them are quite small. Room 47 on the third floor is especially nice with a neat angled ceiling and a fireplace, which, unfortunately, can only be looked at. But the huge fireplace in a parlor off the lobby will probably suffice; it seems there's always a fire burning in it. Lunch and dinner are served daily in the dining room, attractive with salmon walls and napkins and a matching rosebud on each table; four lovely chandeliers light the room. Entrees are $12 to $19, and tableside preparation is featured in fettuccine alfredo, chateaubriand and bananas flambe. A light menu is available in Boltwood's Tavern. Doubles, $80 to $90; suites, $110 to $120.

Quality Hotel, 1 Atwood Drive, Northampton 01060, (413) 586-1211. Until 1992 the Northampton Hilton, this hotel under new ownership is arranged in three sections, each with its own courtyard and decor. The hacienda section has a Spanish motif; the chalet section follows a contemporary ski theme, and the Colonial village features early American decor. The real draw is the glass-domed center courtyard with an indoor pool, saunas and whirlpools. It's popular as a weekend getaway destination; we once encountered two busloads of French Canadians "sunning" around the pool on a chilly winter weekend. Besides the 123 rooms, there are eight mini-suites. The hotel's restaurant, **Morgan's,** includes a skylit loft with large sleighs and wagons on display overhead. The beef-oriented menu ($11.95 to $19) includes chateaubriand, rack of lamb, fettuccine alfredo and seafood papillotes, carved or prepared tableside. Very popular is the "Vacation under Glass" package including two nights' lodging, one dinner and two breakfasts, from $199 a couple. Doubles, $80 to $120.

Motel 6, Routes 5 and 19, South Deerfield 01373, (413) 665-7161. An unusual member of the nationwide budget chain, this was originally built as a Ramada Inn and its amenities are a notch above what you'd expect for the price. It attracts some trade from nearby Deerfield Village and guests have the use of an Olympic-size indoor pool (whose chlorinated presence permeated the entire building at our visit). There are 124 rooms, each with two double beds. Even though the office is tucked away clear around the parking lot in back, they do, as the commercial says, leave the light on for you. Motel 6 is particularly popular with families; no wonder with prices the way they are: doubles, $33.95, each additional $6, children under 17 free.

Howard Johnson Lodge, 401 Russell St. (Route 9), Hadley 01035, (413) 586-0114. This two-story, 62-room motel is standard for the chain, but is particularly well-located between Northampton and Amherst. Each room has two double beds, and comes with private terrace or balcony. There's an outdoor pool for use in summer. The restaurant next door is predictable. Doubles, $57 to $95.

University Motor Lodge, 345 North Pleasant St., Amherst 01002, (413) 256-8111. This Colonial-style, two-story motel is located about half-way between the high-rise campus of the University of Massachusetts and the center of town and you can walk to either. It's a fairly low-key place with color cable TV and in-room phones. Most of the twenty rooms are furnished with two double beds. Doubles, $52 to $87.

129

Seeing and Doing

Museums

Historic Deerfield, The Street (off Routes 5 and 10), (413) 774-5581. This village has a mile-long Main Street (called simply "The Street"), which is unique. It is lined with huge trees and outstanding examples of 18th- and 19th-century homes, thirteen of which are beautifully restored and open to the public year-round. A Connecticut couple, the Henry Flynts, whose son attended Deerfield Academy, were the benefactors. Their vision was to create a walk-through museum that would allow current generations to view and revere the architecture and furnishings of the past, while at the same time preserving that treasure. They succeeded admirably.

The houses, for the most part, are on their original sites and, as much as possible, original pieces of furniture have been obtained. The collection is priceless and contains furniture, ceramics and textiles of outstanding quality. You can't see it all in an afternoon or a day, but you can in a long weekend. If you choose carefully, you can get a taste of Deerfield in a one-day visit. Even if you don't enter any of the homes, a drive or a walk through the village is highly recommended. A first-time visitor might want to see the Wells-Thorn House, the oldest, which has been recently revamped to show seven time periods in a series of different rooms, a quite remarkable history lesson. The Jonathan Ashley House, with its matching shell-corner cupboards in the parlor, is gorgeous. The Allen House, which was the home of the Flynts from 1946 to 1974, contains their collection of needlework and period furniture, representing some of the museum's finest pieces.

Admission includes an orientation program and a walking tour of all houses. Tickets good for two consecutive days are $10 for adults, $5 for children. Single house tickets are available for $5 adults, $3 children. Don't hurry through Historic Deerfield; it deserves your attention. Open daily, 9:30 to 4:30.

Memorial Hall Museum, Memorial Street, Deerfield, (413) 774-7476. Deerfield's oldest museum occupies the original Deerfield Academy school building dating to 1798. This is the museum of the Pocumtuck Valley Memorial Association, and was one of the first museums in the country to emphasize historic preservation. The first period room in America, a kitchen, was opened here in 1880 and is still on view among the nineteen rooms open to the public on three floors. The Indian House Door, the oldest external door in America, dating from 1698, is a particularly unusual item in a most interesting museum collection. Open May-October, weekdays 10 to 4:30, weekends 12:30 to 4:30. Adults $5, children $1.

Emily Dickinson Homestead, 280 Main St., Amherst, (413) 542-8161. Arguably America's best woman poet, Emily Dickinson was born in this house in 1830 and, except for ten years when the family occupied another Amherst home, lived here until her death in 1886. The house is owned by Amherst College, which uses it as a faculty residence; open to the public are the parlor, the music room and, most important, the poet's second-floor bedroom. It was in this room that the increasingly reclusive Emily penned her poetry on scraps of paper, envelopes, whatever was handy, and stuffed them into drawers for safekeeping. In the room are a small table about the size of her writing desk (the original, alas, is at Harvard University), a Franklin stove, a family cradle and, on a mannikin, a white dress she wore during the last decade of her life (you will note her small stature). On the windowsill is a basket; a lover of children, the poet was known to lower gingerbread to her nieces and nephews and their friends when they played below. You must call ahead to reserve a tour, although we luckily were squeezed in on the day of our visit. Nearby is the West Cemetery, where Emily is buried in the family plot with her parents and her sister. Her tombstone has the simple phrase "Called Back" on it. The house is open May-October from Wednesday-Saturday for tours at 1:30, 2:15, 3 and 3:45; March, April and November, tours Wednesday and Saturday only. Admission, $3.

Jones Library, 43 Amity St., Amherst, (413) 256-4090. This small public library, arranged to resemble a luxurious private home, is notable for its fine Emily Dickinson memorabilia. The collections include some of her personal possessions, manuscripts and a model of her bedroom. Several rooms, paneled in walnut and Philippine white mahogany, are adorned with paintings and oriental rugs. Open Monday-Saturday 9 to 5:30, Tuesday and Thursday to 9:30, Sunday 1 to 5. Free.

Smith College Museum of Art, Elm Street, Northampton, (413) 584-2770. One of the most important college art collections in the country is housed in this contemporary gallery. Spanning almost all art periods and genres, the museum shows the works of world-famous painters such as Degas, Monet, Renoir, Picasso, Cezanne and Gauguin. There are also paperweights, Greek vases, pieces of Medieval and Renaissance sculpture, and a representative collection of contemporary artists. Rodin's bronze works, including "Walking Man," are also here. Just off Green Street is the prized **Lyman Plant House** and its adjoining botanical gardens containing perennials from around the world. The chrysanthemums are spectacular in the fall. Plant House is open daily 8 to 4. Art museum open Tuesday-Saturday noon to 5, Sunday 2 to 5. Hours vary in summer; closed major school vacations. Free.

Mead Art Museum, Amherst College campus, Amherst, (413) 542-2335. A smaller art gallery than Smith's, this features the works of several outstanding artists. And it has one gem: the 1611 Rotherwas Room, moved to the college from the home of an alumnus who had brought it to America from a British castle. Carved walnut paneling, an exceptionally ornate mantelpiece and fireplace, and stained-glass windows give the Jacobean banquet hall a baronial feel. Open Monday-Friday 1 to 4:30, weekends 1 to 5. Closed school vacations and August. Free.

Pratt Museum, Amherst College campus, Amherst, (413) 542-2165. This museum of natural history focuses on the geological nature of the Pioneer Valley. Home of the world's largest mastodon skeleton, the museum also exhibits meteorites, dinosaur tracks, rare minerals, crystals and fossils. Open Monday-Friday 9:30 to 3:30, Saturday 10 to 4, Sunday noon to 5; weekends only in summer. Closed school vacations. Free.

Hadley Farm Museum, Junction of Routes 9 and 47, Hadley, (413) 584-8279. Antique farm implements and tools are arranged here in a renovated 1782 barn. Exhibits include plows, hay tenders, bean shellers, spinning wheels and hand-held carpenter tools. Open May to Columbus Day, Tuesday-Saturday 10 to 4:30, Sunday 1:30 to 4:30. Donation.

Wistariahurst Museum, 238 Cabot St., Holyoke, (413) 534-2216. This huge Victorian house was the family home of the Skinners, owners of the famed Skinner Silk Mills in Holyoke. The name is for the wistaria vines that still drape the mansion. Built in the mid-1800s, the house stood originally in Skinnerville (part of nearby Williamsburg), but was brought to Holyoke in sections and rebuilt on its present site in

1874. Tiffany windows in the conservatory, an English wrought-iron balustrade on the main staircase and a checkerboard wooden parquet floor are among the architectural details. Unfortunately, none of the original furniture is in the house, although there are interesting historical exhibits. One room is filled with Shaker furniture; another has Chinese furniture. Open Tuesday-Saturday 1 to 5, Sunday 1 to 4. Donation.

Indian Motorcycle Museum, 33 Hendee St., Springfield, (413) 737-2624. Here are antiques of a different sort: early models of motorcycles made by the first American motorcycle manufacturer, Indian of Springfield. The company was started in 1901 and continued until the 1950s. The fascinating collection is displayed in an industrial building that was one of Indian's last plants. Some of the cycles are refurbished, bright and shiny and ready to ride (and the teenagers who visit wish they could)! An old gasoline pump advertises a price of 15.9 cents per gallon. The foresight of the company is apparent from its 1941 snowmobile and the motors that could be attached to bicycles, making them into a kind of moped. Open daily 10 to 5, March-November; 1 to 5, rest of year. Adults $3, children $1.

Basketball Hall of Fame, 1150 West Columbus Ave., Springfield, (413) 781-6500. Not only home to the motorcycle, Springfield was the birthplace of basketball as well. Dr. James Naismith nailed a couple of peach baskets at either end of a gymnasium so his YMCA boys would have an indoor game to play in winter. The rest, as they say, is history. This international shrine is housed in a building graced with giant murals of basketball players alongside I-91. It incorporates ingenious exhibits honoring the game's great players, teams, coaches, officials and contributors. Highlights include a cinema that places one right in the center of a rousing basketball game, the chance to shoot baskets from a moving walkway, and a locker room that displays the personal memorabilia of the game's illustrious performers. Open daily, 9 to 6 in summer, 9 to 5 rest of year. Adults $6, children $3.

Springfield Library & Museums at the Quadrangle, 220 State St., Springfield, (413) 739-3871. This downtown cultural center is marked by the statue of the Pilgrim sculpted by Augustus Saint-Gaudens. It is home to the City Library and four major museums, all open Thursday-Sunday noon to 4 (except Museum of Fine Arts, open Wednesday instead of Thursday). Free.

George Walter Vincent Smith Art Museum, (413) 733-4214, is the most exciting architecturally. Designed in the manner of a Florentine palace, it houses a rich collection of Chinese and Japanese art and sculpture — we love the cloisonne vases. Also here are 19th-century American paintings, a collection of 19th-century Ottocento Italian paintings, a hall of massive classical casts sculpted from ancient and Renaissance masterpieces, and Islamic rugs.

The Connecticut Valley Historical Museum, (413) 732-3080, is an extraneous stop if you've done Deerfield, but is quite interesting if you haven't — or if you want to see it all. Several period rooms and decorative arts collections are housed in a stone Georgian Colonial building erected in 1927. Periodically exhibits are mounted; we enjoyed a late autumn display of early Christmas ornaments.

Museum of Fine Arts, (413) 732-6092, contains works by American and European artists and manages to cover the period from 3000 B.C. to the present. You climb the broad marble staircase upstairs to twelve second-floor galleries; on the first floor are two Oriental galleries. The museum shop here is interesting.

Springfield Science Museum, (413) 733-1194, has both permanent and changing educational exhibits. Kids like the twenty-foot life-size model of Tyrannosaurus Rex and the mounted wild animal specimens, such as an African elephant and a camel. The Seymour Planetarium is the first American-built planetarium (shows, $2).

Gallery in George Walter Vincent Smith Art Museum.

The Art of Nature

Don't overlook the artistry of nature during beautiful autumn days in the valley. For the foliage freak, the place near Amherst to view the most trees from one point is **Mount Sugarloaf,** off Route 116 in nearby Sunderland. This state park has an observation tower at the summit, from which you can see the whole sweep of the river valley and the treed hillsides flanking it.

How about a hike? The **Holyoke Range State Park** off Route 116 just south of Amherst offers great hiking trails, all leading from a modern visitor center. The Mount Norwottuck Loop, four miles long, is moderately strenuous and takes two and a half hours. There are also shorter and easier trails.

If you want to get out onto the river, you can. The **Northfield Mountain Recreation and Environmental Center,** (413) 659-3714, operates special fall foliage cruises aboard the **Quinnetukut II,** a riverboat, from the Riverview Picnic Area off Route 63, Northfield. Northfield Mountain has fine hiking trails and picnic areas as well.

For a different perspective on nature, visit the historic **Montague Mill** in Montague Center, east of Deerfield across the Connecticut River. Here you can pick out a book from the Book Mill, a multi-story labyrinth of new and used books, and get a cup of coffee from World Village Coffee Merchants & Cafe, specialists in organic international coffees. Sit on one of the outdoor decks — or in a window seat inside as the sun pours in — and take in the view of the waterfall.

The Art of Football

Football in a low-key, understated way is practiced by the small but top-notch New England colleges known as the Little Ivy League, and Amherst is among them. The Lord Jeffs take to Pratt Field several Saturday afternoons in autumn; students and faithful alumni sit on low wooden bleachers, wave the purple and white, and sing the familiar college song, "Lord Jeffery Amherst." With arch-rivals Williams and Wesleyan, these teams form the Little Three and the competition is spirited. Except for Homecoming, tickets usually can be purchased the day of the game.

Across town at the larger Alumni Stadium of the University of Massachusetts on

University Drive, you can see the state universities of New England battle with the Minutemen. These games have a bit more big-league flavor.

Shopping

The area's best shopping is in Northampton, where the downtown appears thriving with serious adult shoppers (as opposed to the young people who flock to Amherst). Green Street, adjoining the Smith College campus, is home to a number of smart boutiques, art galleries and antiques shops.

In the center of Northampton, stop at **Thornes Marketplace** at 150 Main St. to see how an old department store can be recycled. The four floors here are fun to stroll through, with craft shops, art galleries, a large home furnishing and kitchen store, boutiques, a health foods store, all sorts of gift and clothing shops, and usually someone selling fresh flowers by the entryway. It has a European carnival atmosphere with awnings, bright signs and music.

Two of the better galleries along Main Street are **Pinch Pottery,** where we admired cats on bowls made by Ohio craftsmen, and the outstanding (and expensive) **Don Muller Gallery.** Colorful sweaters, sportswear and "exciting clothes" for women are stocked at a store named for its owner, **Cathy Cross.** Too exciting? Then pause next door at **Country Comfort** with great earrings, Kenya bags, warm vests and all sorts of accessories to combine for an individual look. You'll find luxurious products for body and soul at **Joia.** Mixing gifts with refreshments is **La Boutique Panthea,** a tea room with pastries, desserts and caffe latte, plus a selection of lunchtime sandwiches and platters. Satisfy your sweet tooth at **Ben & Bill's Chocolate Emporium,** two side-by-side storefronts dispensing ice cream, baked goods and truffles. If you're really hungry, stop at one of our favorite bakeries anywhere, **Konditorei Normand** at 192 Main, which has an authentic European flavor and more fancy pastries than you'll find this side of Paris. We bought freshly baked raisin bread and a delectable linzer torte. Often there's a special for on-the-street munching. Speaking of delicacies, don't miss the **Coffee Gourmet** on King Street; it has kitchenware, specialty foods and unique Christmas ornaments like the Austrian cloth Santa and angel ornaments we scooped up for $5 each.

Go under the railroad viaduct to 11 Bridge St., where you'll find **Collector Galleries,** a large and rambling collection of antiques, memorabilia, coins and just plain junk. Other antiques shops near the same corner make it worthwhile to park the car and browse.

In the **Old Deerfield Country Store** on Route 5 just south of the village, you'll find dried flowers, candy, puzzles, stoneware, hand-dipped candles, gourds, pumpkins, Indian corn and more. Speaking of candles, the **Yankee Candle Company** in Deerfield, also on Route 5, is a well-advertised stop as well. For a nice selection of history-oriented items, visit the **Museum Store** run by Historic Deerfield on The Street in Old Deerfield. You'll find many books and good little items for gifts, along with stoneware pottery and hooked wall hangings. The **Antique Center of Old Deerfield** includes fifteen shops in a barn just north of town. Quite a few antiques shops also are strung along Routes 5-10 south of Deerfield. Some of the best restaurants around are supplied by **Elm Farm Bakery,** where you can buy your own treats, in South Deerfield. **Spuds 'n' Buds** is a good produce stand and snack bar across from the Mount Sugarloaf Shoppes, which includes a small new visitor information center for the area.

The **Hadley Village Barn Country Store** and surrounding shops on Route 9 in Hadley are a destination for many.

Amherst has stores of appeal to the campus set, including an uncommon number of

134

small and specialized bookstores. **The House of Walsh** offers men's clothing and **Zanna** is a boutique for women. **Global Trader** stocks gifts and clothes from across the world. **Silverscape,** headquartered in a huge turreted yellow house, sells fine gold and silver jewelry. The **Pioneer Valley Coffee Co.** dispenses espresso, caffe latte and a special Ethiopian blend. Stop for a fruit juice cooler or a frozen yogurt at **Bananarama,** a tropical-looking place where the columns look like palm trees. There are plenty of funky boutiques in the **Amherst Carriage Shops** out North Pleasant Street. Dangles, Ecuadorian sweaters, posters, incense and wild quilt jackets are among the offerings at **The Mercantile** here (also in Northampton).

Suppose it's Indian summer and you'd rather picnic than eat indoors. Find your supplies at **Bread and Circus,** a superior health foods superstore on Route 9 between Hadley and Amherst. This is one of a pioneering Boston-area venture, newly merged with the famed Texas-based Whole Foods Market chain and about to expand at our visit. It has a great selection of teas, coffees, cereals, fresh meats, grains by the barrel, produce, even cat food. You can get salads and sandwich fixings, too.

Another food emporium that we like is the **Atkins Fruit Bowl** on Route 116 south of Amherst. Set in the middle of an orchard, this place sells exceptionally nice produce, cheeses and ready-to-go entrees, and has a bakery where you can get a cup of coffee and a treat and sit down for a while to rest your bones. You can pick out your Halloween pumpkin here, too.

The best book store of the many in the area is the **Odyssey Bookshop** in the center of South Hadley. The venerable bookstore had been forced to move because of a couple of fires, but its new home is a smashing two-story building in **The Village Commons,** a stylish complex. Among the interesting stores nearby are **Crabtree & Evelyn, Neuchatel Chocolates** and **Perfect Fit** for perfectly beautiful clothes. Serious coffee drinkers read international newspapers at tables in a flower shop called **Cafe des Fleurs.** There are tables inside and out at **Tailgate Picnic Deli-Market,** where the tailgate sampler yields three salads for $4 and all the good sandwiches (among them turkey-avocado) are $4. No wonder it was packed with folks eating early supper at our autumn visit.

Where to Eat

Northampton has long prided itself on being the dining capital of the region, but a restaurant boom was under way in Amherst, where six new restaurants opened in 1992. At our visit, the biggest was about to open as **Bertucci's Brick Oven Pizzeria,** a 245-seat facility in a former car dealership at East Pleasant and Triangle streets. At the same time, the new **Country Deli & Cafe** was packing in lunchtime crowds on three levels of a barn-like interior at Main and Pleasant Streets, Northampton.

Sienna, 28 Elm St., South Deerfield, (413) 665-0215. Transplanted New Yorker Jonathan Marohn and his wife, Kim Rosner, opened this gem of a restaurant in 1990 in a small pillared storefront that could pass for a hotel or general store on the nondescript main street of South Deerfield. They restored the high-ceilinged main floor into a subdued dining room with washed burnt sienna walls, white linens and floral tapestry banquettes they made themselves from cut-up church pews (with clay pots fastened ingeniously on the sides to use as wine buckets), and moved into residential quarters upstairs. The local produce of the Deerfield Valley was part of the attraction for this talented team, and Marohn takes full advantage. The short dinner menu ($16 to $19) might include grilled salmon with coriander, served with sauteed spinach and tomato fondue, leek and butter sauce; thyme-crusted roast halibut with arugula and cepes mushroom sauce; roast duck with pan-roasted peaches in a duck and basil sauce with a potato cake, and dry-aged New York strip steak with garlic mashed potatoes. This is serious, complicated fare, beautifully presented, and for some the side vegetable accompaniments are the stars. Others are partial to such first courses as spinach salad with baked Vermont chevre and oyster mushrooms, grilled scallops with fig vinaigrette on an endive salad, grilled medallions of eggplant topped with smoked salmon and Iowa blue cheese mousse. Stellar desserts include pistachio couscous, pumpkin crisp and a sampling of four homemade sorbets. Dinner, Wednesday-Saturday 5:30 to 9 or 10, Sunday 5 to 8.

Deerfield Inn, The Street, Deerfield, (413) 774-5587. The dining room at the Deerfield Inn is so beautiful and classically Colonial that it becomes *the* place to dine when you take a Sunday drive through Old Deerfield. Naturally, it is fine at other times, too. Dinner entrees ($16.95 to $21.50) change monthly. The November menu included fillet of salmon sauteed with sea scallops and raspberries, jumbo shrimp over linguini, roasted breast and confit of duck with spiced wild plums and cranberries, and venison medallions served over a julienne potato pancake. At lunch, you might choose quiche or ragout of the day (both $7.95), a sandwich or a main dish like ratatouille pizza or flank steak with basmati rice, $8.95 to $11.95. Indian pudding is a favorite dessert. Light lunches are served seasonally from noon to 4 in the Stencilled Horse Coffee Shop downstairs. Lunch daily, noon to 2; dinner, 6 to 9.

Spoleto, 50 Main St., Northampton, (413) 586-6313. Ask anyone in town where to eat and the first place that comes to mind is Spoleto's, an Italian high-flyer that moved to the high-visibility former location of Sze's Chinese restaurant in 1991 from smaller digs on Crafts Avenue. Spoleto Festival posters and colorful mobiles lend color to a spacious, pale yellow and green room on two levels with a tiled bar at the center and an open kitchen to the rear. Chef-owner Claudio Guerra's contemporary Italian cuisine is colorful as well. For lunch, one of us enjoyed a big bowl of tuscan fish soup ($2.50) and an appetizer of mozzarella in carozza, a high-style cheese sandwich. The other liked the penne alfredo with grilled chicken ($5.95), which came with a distinguished salad. Orange grand marnier pound cake was a decadent ending. At night, a dozen or more pastas are in the $8.95 to $14.95 range, with seafood, chicken, veal and beef dishes priced from $11.95 to $15.95. One is a great chicken rollatini with fresh spinach and fennel sausage. There's a fine, mainly Italian wine list, priced from $11 to $75. The pizza capability of the original Spoleto's is being continued by owner Guerra, operating as **Paradiso** and serving traditional wood-fired brick-oven pizzas nightly at 12 Crafts Ave. Lunch at Spoleto's daily, 11:30 to 2:30, Friday and Saturday to 3; dinner, 5 to 10 or 11, Sunday 4 to 9.

Eastside Grill, 19 Strong Ave., Northampton, (413) 586-3347. This nifty multi-level dining room offers trendy fare and a contemporary look: bare wood tables and booths, windsor chairs, white walls and skylights. The original cajun theme has been toned down to a few Louisiana overtones, as in chicken etouffee, shrimp and sausage jambalayaa, grilled catfish and crawfish in tasso cream. The surprisingly extensive menu also includes a blackened steak salad, pork tenderloin with mustard crust, shrimp and mussels with tomatoes and feta, scallops diane and barbecued salmon. Entrees are priced from $5.50 to $8.95 at lunch, $8.95 to $14.95 at dinner. Start with fried oysters, Maryland crab cakes, beer-batter shrimp or popcorn shrimp. Finish with bread pudding, mud pie or praline sundae. Lunch, Monday-Saturday 11:30 to 2:30; dinner, 5 to 10 or 11, Sunday 4 to 9.

La Cazuela, 7 Old South St., Northampton, (413) 586-0400. There is Mexican and there is La Cazuela. This is owned by a couple originally hailing from Kansas City,

Front facade of the Deerfield Inn.

Barry Steeves and Rosemary Schmidt, who say they grew up on Mexican food and like to see that it's served right. Their venture is located high off the street in what was once the old Rahar's inn and tavern — a historic plaque near the entry designates it as "long a popular gathering spot for students." Inside, everything is starkly contemporary and tables are nicely spaced. You can get enchiladas, fajitas, flautas, tacos, burritos — the full range and then some. Try the pollo en pipian — chicken in pipian sauce (pumpkin and sesame seeds, chiles, cloves, cinnamon and garlic), a bargain with rice, vegetable and salad for $10.25. Among other entrees ($6.95 to $10.50), pinon shrimp comes with green chile pesto and toasted pinenuts. An autumn favorite is chiles en nogada, two poblano chiles roasted and stuffed with a picadillo of pork, apples, raisins and spices and covered with a creamy walnut sauce. The five versions of margaritas include the La Caz super deluxe, "as good as margarita gets," says the menu. Huevos rancheros ($6.95) is a brunch fixture. Dinner nightly from 5, weekends from 3; weekend brunch, 11 to 3.

North Star, 25 West St., Northampton, (413) 586-9409. Seafood and sushi are the twin attractions at this restaurant and bar fashioned from a number of adjoining storefronts near the Smith College campus. Enter through a large bar with a prominent dance floor and nightly entertainment. Proceed to two serene, Oriental-inspired dining rooms with cane and chrome chairs and blue-clothed tables; the art on the walls is for sale. Dinner entrees run from $9.95 for grilled raspberry chicken to $17.95 for bouillabaisse. Trout grilled with sliced limes and oranges, tuna sauteed with plum tomatoes and olives and shabu-shabu are standouts on the regular menu. Specials might be catfish grilled with green chile salsa and lamb chops grilled with curried lentils and minted yogurt. Sushi is available as an appetizer or entree. Desserts follow a chocolate and lemon theme, as in rich chocolate diabolo or lemon cloud. Dinner nightly, 5 to 10; Sunday brunch, 11 to 2:30.

Green Street Cafe, 62 Green St., Northampton, (413) 586-5650. Overstuffed couches and wing chairs occupy the entry foyer, where Smith students are apt to be draped about sipping tea and coffee. Head up a few stairs to the right to an aubergine dining room with minimal decor and a counter at the back. There's more space for dining beyond, and a market was to be added in 1993. Chef John Sielski returned to his native area from running a restaurant in Brooklyn. He and a partner serve a limited but interesting menu — cafe items like chick pea crepes with provencal vegetables, sauteed shrimp and warm bean salad, Japanese chicken wings, warm chevre salad, fish en papillote, chicken with apples and hazelnuts, and beef stew with black olives. Prices are in the $4 to $6 range for appetizers and light fare, $8.95 to $13.95 for entrees. Lunch could be a pork loin and apple sandwich ($3.95) or steamed mussels with kale and pasta ($5.95). Chocolate pot de creme and creme caramel are favored desserts. Advertising a quiet, European style, the place opens at 7 a.m. with coffee and light breakfast items for students, and may end with music on the lower level at night. There's outdoor dining beside a small fountain on a brick courtyard. Breakfast, Monday-Friday 7 to 11; lunch and tea, noon to 5; dinner, Monday-Saturday 6 to 10 or 10:30. Closed Sunday. BYOB.

Paul & Elizabeth's, 150 Main St., Northampton, (413) 584-4832. Paul and Elizabeth Sustick operate this large and obviously successful natural foods restaurant in Thornes Marketplace. Regulars love the great fish chowder, hummus or cheese and sprouts sandwiches, fried tofu and omelets served with whole wheat bread and house tea. At dinner, there's a curry dip and vegetables or stuffed mushroom caps as appetizers; tabouli, spinach, watercress and hummus salads; vegetable, shrimp, scallop or scrod tempura; pastas (maybe tomato-basil pasta with cauliflower and green olives), noodles with fish tempura and specials like tofu kabobs, all in the $7.50 to $10.50 range. Open daily except Sunday, 11:30 to 9:30.

Jack August's, 5 Bridge St., Northampton, (413) 584-1197. The serious, old-fashioned fish lover need look no further. This is the original Jack August (now in its 59th year) and seafood is almost all that the August family serves — in more guises than you can imagine. The tablecloths are red and white checked, the booths are painted gray, the fish is brought in fresh daily and there's no nonsense about eating here. How about hot or cold clam juice to start, or fish chowder, clam chowder, lobster stew, clam stew, oyster stew or scallop stew? Lobster, crabmeat, tuna, shrimp and seafood are served up as salads. You can get a combination of broiled fish and shellfish on a seafood platter for $11.75, baked stuffed jumbo shrimp for $13.95 or langoustinos in drawn butter for $9.25. There are a few concessions for non-seafood eaters. Open daily except Monday, 11 to 7:30 or 8:30.

The Northampton Brewery, 11 Brewster Court, Northampton, (413) 584-9903. Ales and lagers brewed here in its microbrewery are served on an outdoor deck or inside around a semi-circular bar and on a round balcony overlooking it all. Also served is an incredibly extensive array of snack foods, sandwiches, salads, pizzas and entrees. It's enough to make one wonder, is the tail wagging the dog? Most snack foods are in the $4 to $6 range and the more serious dinner entrees like fiery chicken, grilled swordfish or filet mignon, $8.95 to $14.95. Open daily, 11:30 to 1 a.m., Sunday from 1 to 1.

La Cucina di Pinocchio, 30 Boltwood Walk, Amherst, (413) 256-4110. Mauro Aniello relocated his successful North Amherst venture of ten years into a large vacant restaurant space hidden away in the heart of Amherst in 1992. But his tradition of innovative recipes combined with the freshest ingredients continues. The front section is primarily for calzones and pizzas, priced from $3.95 to $8.25. Beyond the bar-lounge is a dimly-lit larger dining room, pretty in white and pink. Interesting nightly specials supplement an already enormous selection of pastas and entrees (nine chicken and ten veal dishes), priced from $11.50 for mussels and calamari over linguini to $16.95 for veal chop casanova. The place is big and bustling and strikes some as a bit overwhelming, but most locals love it. Lunch, Monday-Saturday 11:30 to 3; dinner to 10 or 11. No smoking.

Judie's, 51 North Pleasant St., Amherst, (413) 253-3491. Judie Teraspulsky, who was formerly at the Lord Jeff, opened her special restaurant several years ago and it remains one of the more popular in this college town. You can eat under the glass front portion and watch the passing parade of Amherst, or you can sit at one of the bare wood tables in back, above which are mounted items like colorful parrot or elephant sculptures. The all-day menu is inventive, with an emphasis on soups, munchies, burgers, sandwiches and salads (we liked the sound of the pesto popover caesar salwich, which turns out to be a caesar salad served as a sandwich ($6.99). One menu section lists a dozen sautes, among them curried shrimp and scallops over fettuccine. Dinner entrees, served with a popover and big tossed salad and priced in the $15 range, include feta shrimp, Southwestern chicken and scampi, and steak and potato. Everyone says that no matter what you order, you can't leave until you try Judie's butter-dipped popover served with apple butter ($1.99). The salad dressings and apple butter are so popular they're bottled for sale at the entry. Open daily, 11:30 to 10 or 11.

Cafe DiCarlo, 71 North Pleasant St., Amherst, (413) 253-9300. Stylish in white and black, this emerged in 1988 from one of Amherst's ubiquitous pizza parlors, owner Bonni DiCarlo anticipating the local trend to higher-style Italian cuisine (an upper-level dining room and piano bar were in the works during the local restaurant boom of 1992). Downstairs at a mix of booths and tables, regulars enjoy exotic pastas ($6.75 to $9.50) and a choice of two dozen entrees, from $12.95 for rock cornish game roasted with garlic to $17.25 for seafood ricche or veal medallions with gorgonzola. There's also a garden patio billed as the ultimate in casual Italian dining. Open daily, 11:30 to 10 or 11.

Seasons, 529 Belchertown Road (Route 9), Amherst, (413) 253-9909. A large barn formerly occupied by the Rusty Scupper is home to this local favorite, a country place with an upscale decor and comfortable seating upstairs and down. The rear windows overlooking a deck yield a great view of the hilly countryside toward the Amherst College campus. A large menu embraces the usual suspects ($11.95 to $16.95) and some not so usual. Among the latter are mixed grill, lobster and duck stir-fry, and roasted Long Island duck with black currant and pink peppercorn sauce. There's an abundant salad bar, and desserts like chocolate mousse and triple layer chocolate cake are displayed on a cart. Dinner nightly, 5 to 10; Sunday brunch, 10:30 to 3.

Amber Waves, 31 Boltwood Walk, Amherst, (413) 253-9200. An executive chef from an Asian restaurant in San Francisco teamed up with a Culinary Institute of America grad to open this bright spot in an unlikely location in 1992. We say unlikely because the kitchen is far bigger than the dining area and the prices are so low as not to be believed. If you don't snag one of the three inside tables or the picnic table out front, you're reduced to taking out. Which is what we did, bringing home green curry noodles with beef ($4.50) and pad thai with pork ($6.75), with sides of Thai-cucumber and napa cabbage salads for a late dinner in our very own private dining room. How they can survive preparing treats like happy pancakes with vegetables and pork for $2.25 is beyond us. But this is the kind of place to which we'd gravitate often, at least for takeout. Open Tuesday-Sunday, 11:30 to 10:30.

The Raw Carrot Juice Bar, 9 East Pleasant St., Amherst, (413) 549-4240. One of us chanced upon this new place in the Amherst Carriage Shops just in time for the late-afternoon juice fix she'd grown accustomed to during a just-ended vacation in

Seattle. Fruit smoothies ($1.50 to $3.50) were finding a receptive following from the college crowd, but we went all-out with a healthful wheatgrass hopper, made more palatable by pineapple and mint, for $2.75. This is where local vegetarians get vegan soups, salads and sandwiches as well as nut shakes, berry frappes and herbal teas. Chilis and a few entrees were in the works, "now that we've got an oven," said the gal on duty. Open daily, 10 to 8.

Carmelina's At the Commons, 96 Russell St., Hadley, (413) 584-8000. The food here is authentic and the ingredients the best, the owner serving "only what I was brought up on in Sicily and in Boston's North End." That means good food and lots of it, "even if we have to take you outta here in a wheelbarrel," according to the long and chatty menu. Try the crazy alfredo, "a favorite in Italian insane asylums," or the convict's pasta "served in Italian penitentiaries — no kidding," in half portions, if you hope to have room for an entree. Continue perhaps with black garlic beef, beef in a package (sirloin wrapped with prosciutto), veal orange, saltimbocca, calamari with risotto or shrimp fra diavolo. Pastas are in the $10 to $13.50 range and entrees, $10.75 to $16.50. Dessert could be chocolate chestnut cake, espresso torta or tirami su. A jazz pianist plays for the four-course Sunday brunch, which provides a good sampling of the kitchen's scope for a bargain, carry-me-outta-here $14.95. Dining is at tables with mismatched cloths amidst a jungle of philodendron plants hanging from the walls. Dinner nightly from 5; Sunday brunch, 11:30 to 2:30.

Windows on the Common, 25 College St., South Hadley, (413) 534-8222. The newish Village Commons complex across from the Mount Holyoke College campus produced this large new restaurant in 1988. Two upstairs dining rooms are the setting for a steak and seafood menu, priced from $9.95 for three chicken dishes to $16.95 for mixed seafood grill or filet mignon. All the old standbys like baked scrod, baked stuffed shrimp and prime rib are available. Downstairs are **Fedora's Tavern,** serving pub fare favored by collegians, and **Cream of the Crop,** an ice cream and espresso parlor. Lunch, 11:30 to 2; dinner, 5 to 9 or 10; Sunday brunch.

WoodBridge's, 3 Hadley St., South Hadley, (413) 536-7341. Influenced by the proximity of Mount Holyoke College (could the waitresses all be students?), this pleasant and low-key restaurant serves an all-day menu with a wide range of offerings. There are two attractive rooms with a bar in the center of the restaurant. Floors and tables are bare wood, as are the church pews used to form booths. Outdoors is a patio with white tables and chairs and bright umbrellas for dining in good weather. The menu is appropriate for the college and parent crowd with everything from sandwiches, burgers, soups and salads to hot entrees and great desserts. We ordered the seafood melt, an open-face seafood salad sandwich with mushrooms and cheddar cheese, and a delicious grilled croissant with turkey breast, Swiss cheese and Canadian bacon. For a real meal, try veal parmesan, seafood crepes, baked scallops, shrimp scampi or wiener schnitzel, all priced from $8 to $14. This was a perfect place for a victory Saturday supper following the lacrosse game one of our college kids played against Mount Holyoke. Open daily, 11 to 10 or 11.

FOR MORE INFORMATION: Greater Springfield and Pioneer Valley Convention and Visitors Bureau, 56 Dwight St., Springfield 01103, (413) 787-1548.

Stone wall fronts attractive campus of Pomfret School.

A Total Change of Pace — And Place

Northeastern Connecticut

A rolling, pastoral landscape crisscrossed by timeworn stone walls that stretch endlessly into the distance. Hill towns and mill villages brimming with history. Gracious Colonial and Victorian homes in which fascinating innkeepers lavish old-fashioned hospitality. And fall foliage creating a canopy above country lanes and wooded trails.

This is autumn in northeastern Connecticut, which lures visitors to a total change of pace — and place.

Welcome to the state's forgotten corner, or the Quiet Corner, as it was designated in a tourist bureau contest. This is Connecticut off the beaten path, a place far removed from the Hartford, Worcester and Providence metropolitan areas that threaten to encroach on its fringes like triple pincers.

The Quiet Corner wasn't always overlooked. Back in the 19th century, it was a fashionable resort area in the style of Lenox and Newport. Wealthy New Yorkers and Bostonians summered in Pomfret and Woodstock on vast country estates with dream-like names like Gwyn Careg, Courtlands and Glen Elsinore.

By the 20th century, two distinct cultures had developed. One reflected the Yankee farmers whose livelihood depended on the corn, grain and apples that grew on the gentle hillsides; the other, the mill-centered industrial workers who lived within walking distance of the river that provided the power. The more prosperous farmers and mill owners mingled with the summer elite.

Today, the mills have gone and not many farmers are left. Newcomers with means

141

and taste have followed in the footsteps of their 19th-century predecessors, imbuing the area with pockets of affluence. "The Street" in Pomfret carries much of the grace of a century ago. Substantial houses surround the picturesque commons in Brooklyn and Thompson and climb the hills of Putnam Heights. A low-key cachet is lent by Pomfret, the Rectory and Marianapolis preparatory schools and the headquarters of Crabtree & Evelyn, one of the area's largest employers.

The weekend visitor can share in the good life here. You can stay in restored inns that once were the homes of the rich and famous. You can have bed and breakfast with the aristocracy in houses filled with family treasures. Your host may be an artist, a furniture-maker, a pediatrician, an interior decorator, a puzzle-maker, a teacher or a music buff. In no other New England area have we found the innkeepers and their faciliities as a group so engaging.

Activities and sightseeing come quietly here. You will want to venture north into Massachusetts to visit Old Sturbridge Village, the region's leading tourist attraction and a restored New England village of the 1830s. But outside the museum grounds, you will be accosted by 20th-century commercialism. You'll likely be glad to return home to the Quiet Corner, if only for another day or two. Here the essence of old New England lives on, quietly.

Getting There

The Northeast Corner is bordered on the northwest by Interstate 84. Interstate 395 cuts north-south through its eastern midriff.U.S. Routes 44 and 6 serve the area on an east-west axis.

The nearest major airports are in Hartford and Providence, R.I., which are roughly equidistant, depending upon what part of the corner you're in. Amtrak trains stop at New London and Mystic to the south, as well as Willimantic and Hartford to the west.

Bonanza buses serve Danielson and Willimantic.

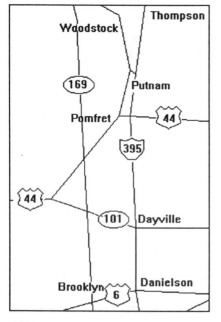

Where to Stay

The Inn at Woodstock Hill, 94 Plaine Hill Road, Box 98, South Woodstock 06267, (203) 928-0528. The heart of this full-service inn is the 1816 Christopher Wren-style home of Henry Bowen, whose shocking-pink Roseland summer cottage up the road is a landmark. Here are the main living room, a library, the morning/TV room and a small dining room, all outfitted with chintz fabrics, fine paintings, plush oriental rugs and tiled fireplaces. More Waverly floral chintzes accent the nineteen guest rooms and suites, handsome and comfortable with reproduction antiques and wicker furniture, chairs and loveseats, thick carpeting and modern baths. Television, telephones and air-conditioning come with. A wing connected to a barn leads to a cozy lounge and two elegant dining rooms (see Where to Eat). Innkeeper Sheila Becks and her

Early Woodstock home and barn house The Inn at Woodstock Hill.

partner, chef Richard Naumann, offer a continental-plus breakfast. Warm mulled cider or lemonade await arriving guests in the afternoon. Doubles, $75 to $140.

Lord Thompson Manor, Route 200, Box 428, Thompson 06277, (203) 923-3886. This luxurious inn set on 62 secluded acres has been nicely transformed from what long was a novitiate for a Roman Catholic order and, before that, the summer retreat for the Providence mercantile family of John Gladding. Built in 1917, the classic stucco English manor house offers nine guest rooms and suites, the latter with full tile baths and three with working fireplaces. Splurge, for goodness sake, on one of the suites, for the other four rooms are pint-size, retain an institutional feel amd share a single bath. For sheer elegance, book the master suite, the epitome of the masculine Schumacher and Ralph Lauren horse and hunt motif. For romance, ask for the Morgan Suite, light and feminine with apricot walls, poofy curtains, brown wicker furniture and ivy stenciling in a bathroom stocked with fine shampoos and lotions. Guests enjoy a 33-by-20-foot drawing room richly paneled in gumwood, an enormous sun porch outfitted in wicker, peach and chintz, and a downstairs billiards room with fireplace and TV. Innkeeper Jackie Sherman cooks popcorn twice a day for snacks and to offer with drinks from an honor bar in the manorial living room. She serves a full breakfast, from orange juice to fruit to Finnish or apple pancakes and waffles, on a dramatic breakfast porch with two walls of french doors to the outside. She also serves dinner by prior reservation for $20 to $25 a person. Some of the wait staff are singers and may perform a capella at breakfast or dinner. This is a manor house without pretension and with an engaging, laid-back feeling. Doubles, $75 to $85; suites, $95 to $110.

Karinn, 330 Pomfret St. (Route 169), Pomfret 06259, (203) 928-5492. Karen Schirack and Ed Wurzel put seven years of work, money and artistry into transforming a wreck of a house into a grand B&B, with common rooms as photogenic yet comfortable as any we've seen. On one side of a grand foyer is a library with modern leather recliners that invite a long read. On the other is a parlor with a 48-inch TV, more leather furniture and the biggest library of tapes and videos imaginable. Off that is a music room, where a leather sofa and leather chairs with ottomans beckon guests to listen to music afficionado Ed Wurzel's majestic stereo system. The music room opens past a sunny, plant-filled area onto a side deck overlooking restored gardens. Beyond a skylit kitchen and a chandeliered dining room is a cozy, paneled barroom that dates back to the days this was the Old Pomfret Inn. Karen, who has a master's degree in interior design, has decorated in eclectic style, mixing antiques with a touch of oriental. Upstairs are two suites. One includes a front corner room with double bed, working

143

fireplace and the oriental rugs and Thibault wallpapers characteristic of the house. Its bathroom adjoins a small room with a twin bed for another guest. Another guest room down its own hallway offers twin beds, wicker seats and a bath with clawfoot tub. Beyond it is a large sitting room with a sofabed that can be rented as a family suite. The third floor has the potential for three more rooms, but the couple seem in no hurry. They serve a full breakfast, plus afternoon tea, wine and evening cordials. Doubles, $65 to $70. No credit cards. No smoking.

Cobbscroft, 349 Pomfret St. (Route 169), Pomfret 06258, (203) 928-5560. Tom and Janet McCobb grew up in Fairfield County and lived in nineteen houses — many in New York State — while he was with Xerox, but they chose this rambling white house almost up against the road for retirement. Tom is a watercolor artist of note, and his works adorn the white walls of an airy gallery-parlor. Off the reception-library are a double and single guest room joined by a bathroom, rented as a family suite. Upstairs are three more guest rooms with baths. Janet's charming stenciling enhances a front corner room with a four-poster bed and a chaise lounge. Over the living room is the bridal suite, a wondrous affair with windows on three sides, a working fireplace, loveseat, dressing table and a bed covered in frilly white linens. Two wooden chickens and a collection of lambs are among the country touches in the dining room, where guests breakfast on eggs, quiche or strata at a long table. In the afternoon, the McCobbs serve tea with cinnamon toast or fruit bread and offer a drink. Guests help themselves to brandy in the living room after dinner. Doubles, $65; suite, $80.

Ebenezer Stoddard House, Routes 171 and Perrin Road, West Woodstock 06267, (203) 974-2552. This early 19th-century house with working fireplaces in each guest room and an upstairs ballroom-turned-bedroom caters to romance. Lynda and Don Hennigan light the fireplaces in their four guest rooms while their occupants are at dinner. Upon their return guests find a tray of candies, cookies and cordials. Each room has its own bathroom, fancy wallpaper and floral arrangements. Extra touches like a collection of evening purses, antique gloves and a christening gown abound. Guests are greeted with tea and perhaps a piece of pie, which they can enjoy on a porch or a rear patio beside a fountain. Lynda decorates two guest parlors with style and changes with the seasons — she puts up eleven Christmas trees, including one in each guest room, for Yuletide. In a breakfast room retaining its original pine floors, guests might be served a dish of fresh fruits followed by cranberry mousse and bread pudding with maple syrup tapped from a tree on the property. Doubles, $75; suite, $95; ballroom, $115.

The Felshaw Tavern, Five Mile River Road, Putnam Heights 06260, (203) 928-3467. Terry and Herb Kinsman were the pioneers in the B&B business hereabouts, opening the doors to their restored 1742 tavern in 1982. He's a Yankee, she's a Southerner and the combination is fortuitous. Herb, a woodworker of note, did most of the restoration himself. Craftsmen admire his building talents (reproduction furniture and rooms) and guests like the two uncommonly large bedrooms with working fireplaces and private baths. One with a queensize Mississippi rice-carved four-poster is full of fine French furniture. The other contains a remarkable Connecticut highboy that Herb built of cherry. Guests can watch TV in an upstairs sitting room paneled in wood. They also enjoy the keeping room/library, where the remarkable ceilings are made of stained pine, and an adjacent living room full of oriental rugs. The Kinsmans serve a full breakfast in a sunny, cathedral-ceilinged breakfast room that Herb built from scratch. They offer tea or sherry in the afternoon. Guests may lounge on the European-looking terrace or in a four-season garden with a fountain out back. Doubles, $75.

Grosvenor Place, 321 Deerfield Road (Route 97), Pomfret 06258, (203) 928-4633. Garfield and Sylvia Danenhower dispense comfort and Southern hospitality in a lovely beige house that has been in her family since it was built in 1720. They offer two large guest rooms with private baths, one adjoining a single room that makes a family suite and the other a downstairs corner room with fireplace. A focal point of the main floor is the spacious dining room filled with silver, portraits and oriental rugs. The living room contains a collection of family pictures, next to a study full of books, a piano and a jigsaw puzzle in progress. Sylvia offers her guests tea or sherry upon arrival. She and her pediatrician-husband serve a breakfast of homemade muffins and rolls, sometimes supplemented on weekends by french toast from a recipe they acquired in Malaysia. Doubles, $75.

Clark Cottage at Wintergreen, 354 Pomfret St. (Route 169), Pomfret 06258, (203) 928-5741. Four light and airy guest rooms (two with private baths and the other two adjoining as a family suite) are offered by Doris and Stan Geary in their substantial gray Victorian house, part of the old Clark estate. Most coveted is the front corner room, which has striking green painted Italian furniture, including an incredible bedstead with an oval mirror in the headboard, set off against peach walls. Plush beige carpeting enhances a rear room with a sofa, twin beds and a porch for taking in the valley view. It forms a suite with an adjoining room with a brass bed and a wood stove in the fireplace. Guests enjoy a colorful entry hall with window seats and a formal, fireplaced parlor. A full breakfast is served at a long table in the fireplaced dining room. Tea or drinks are served upon arrival, and Doris was planning to offer weekend dinner for house guests occasionally now that her professional kitchen is completed. Doubles, $65 to $75.

Samuel Watson House, 374 Thompson Road (Route 193), Thompson 06277, (203) 923-2491. Jo and Bob Godfrey raised a family in this gorgeous pre-Revolutionary home just off the large common in the center of Thompson Hill. Then they decided to put all those empty bedroooms to good use as a B&B. Four comfortable rooms, one with private bath, are on the second floor. Guests have the run of the large main floor, including a living room, a TV parlor, a back library where the shelves are full of Bob's carved birds, a formal dining room and a large and artistic country kitchen with windows onto bird feeders. Keen birdwatchers, the Godfreys invite guests to share their "sport" at breakfast, when they can look out onto a reflecting pool and all those bird feeders as they enjoy mini-muffins, popovers and omelets with bacon or ham. Check out the jigsaw puzzle in progress in the TV parlor. It's one of the remarkable handcut wooden puzzles that Bob makes out back in their fascinating studio and shop, Sea Wings. Jo helps sand the puzzles and is a sign carver in her own right. Doubles, $60 to $70.

Thurber House, 78 Liberty Hwy. (Route 21), Putnam Heights 06260, (203) 928-6776. Another local artist, in this case the late T.J. Thurber, lived in this house and the current owners, Betty and George Zimmermann, display several of his paintings on the walls. Elsie the cat parades across the wood floors and well-worn oriental rugs. All rooms have working fireplaces, and guests enjoy the keeping room and parlor as well as the view from the back porch. The Zimmermanns rent two or three rooms, one with private bath. One of Betty's breakfast specials is "fancy french toast," served in an elegant dining room. Doubles, $65 to $70.

Barrett Hill Farm, 210 Barrett Hill Road, Brooklyn 06234, (203) 779-2686. Joel Rosenberg and his wife, Beverly Burke, bought this wreck of a 1760 farmhouse and spent eighteen months renovating before opening it as a B&B in 1990. Sloping wide-board floors, exposed beams and original oak and chestnut hardwoods remain. The formal parlor is striking with a bare pine wall and blue trim that matches the wallpaper in the rest of the room. Guests also enjoy a music room and library with an upright piano, TV and wood stove, a back porch with a hot tub, and a great country kitchen and dining area with a custom-built table that looks to be twenty feet long.

Upstairs are three guest rooms, one a large, two-section room with a sleigh bed and a day bed sharing a bath with another room. The master bedroom with a TV, fireplace, dresser, two bureaus and a wooden chair has its own bath. Breakfast, served in a large dining room, includes a fruit platter, cereal, breads and perhaps an omelet or frittata. Beverly serves tea or lemonade in the afternoons. Doubles, $70 to $80.

Hickory Ridge, 1084 Quaddick Town Farm Road, Thompson 06277, (203) 928-9530. Owners Birdie and Ken Olson share with guests the spacious post and beam home they built in 1990 on three wooded acres fronting on Quaddick Lake. Guests enjoy a private entrance and two bedrooms that share a bath on the lower, walkout level right beside the lake. They also share a sitting room with a TV. A gas grill and refrigerator, fishing and canoeing are available. Birdie prepares baked goods and such entrees as quiche or baked french toast for breakfast. Quaddick State Park is nearby, and hiking is offered on seventeen private acres plus miles more of state lands. Doubles, $65.

Corttis Inn, 235 Corttis Road, North Grosvenordale 06255, (203) 935-5652. There's no other house in sight at this 1758 farmhouse, the focal point of a onetime dairy farm on 900 acres straddling two states. School teacher Herb Corttis, his wife Ginny and their toddler son moved to his family homestead to open a B&B in 1990. Theirs is obviously a lived-in house, son Justin's toy room situated between the TV room and a music room with a baby grand piano and wind-up victrola. Two bedrooms upstairs share a bath, or one room can have access to a bath downstairs. Upstairs in another section of the house is a family-suite arrangement with two more bedrooms with a bath, a formal sitting room with TV and a dining room with wood stove. The farm's 60 chickens furnish fresh eggs for the full breakfasts Ginny prepares for guests. Doubles, $65.

King's Inn, 5 Heritage Road, Putnam 06260, (203) 928-7961 or (800) 541-7304. Best of the area's motels scattered along I-395 is this recently remodeled, 41-unit establishment. The nicely landscaped grounds include a pond and a pool. **Chuck's Steak House** is adjacent. Rates include a continental breakfast, a shoeshine and a daily newspaper. Doubles, $68 to $78.

Where to Eat

The Golden Lamb Buttery, Hillandale Farm, Bush Hill Road, Brooklyn, (203) 774-4423. Possibly Connecticut's most intriguing restaurant is run with verve and personality by Jimmie and Bob Booth. Jimmie, a former Lord & Taylor buyer, is in the kitchen; Bob is the affable host on this, his family farm. He prides himself on the extensive files with photos of diners that might reappear on their table in a lucite frame. He also treats them to little touches like matchbooks with their names imprinted and tales about the 1953 Jaguar convertible, the telephone booth and a totem pole ensconced in the great barn's waiting room. Weekend dinner here is an event, booked far in advance. The evening begins with a hayride through the fields as you enjoy a pre-dinner drink and the sweet voice of folksinger Susan Lamb. Then you pass through the tiny kitchen, probably to a friendly wave from Jimmie, to get to the small and candlelit dining rooms, which — for a barn — are rather elegant in a country way. The prix-fixe meal ($60) starts with appetizers, including some knockout soups Jimmie makes with herbs from her garden. There's a choice of four entrees, always duck and often salmon, chateaubriand and lamb. These are accompanied by six to eight vegetables served family style and, for us, almost the best part of the meal. Dessert could be lemon or grand marnier mousse. Add classical music or Susan Lamb's folksongs and a bottle of wine from Bob's well-chosen wine list for a fantasy-like experience. Lunch offers a sampling of Jimmie's cooking (entrees, $9.50 to $14, like seafood crepes, salmon

Vaulted barn dining room at The Golden Lamb Buttery.

quiche or pork stew) without the evening magic. Lunch, Tuesday-Saturday noon to 2:30; dinner, Friday and Saturday, one seating from 7. Closed January-May. No credit cards.

The Harvest at Bald Hill, Route 169 and 171, South Woodstock, (203) 974-2240. A chef from the Brown University faculty club in Providence runs this highly regarded restaurant, located on the main level of a huge red barn. Peter Cooper changes the menu seasonally to reflect the restaurant's name. The screened porch is the favored place for summer dining, and is central to the **Local Bistro,** launched in 1992. Its lighter menu is served on the porch and in the bar area. For lunch, three of us enjoyed good french bread, a shared appetizer of gyoza (tasty Japanese dumplings), sauteed scrod with winter vegetables ($9.25) and two excellent — and abundant — salads, oriental seafood and tuna nicoise, $6.95 and $7.25 respectively. Dinner entrees start at $11.95 for a couple of vegetarian specialties and rise to $23.95 for mixed grill. Shrimp francaise, roast duckling with bigarade sauce and veal marsala au gratin are favorites. The new bistro menu features things like medallions of pork, seared salmon and scallops on a bed of greens, and oriental beef stir-fry for $5.95 to $9.95. Lunch, Monday-Friday 11:30 to 2; dinner, Monday-Saturday 5:30 to 9; Sunday, brunch 11 to 2, dinner 2 to 8.

The Inn at Woodstock Hill, 94 Plaine Hill Road, Woodstock, (203) 928-0528. Pink predominates in the pretty dining rooms at this inn, where German chef Richard Naumann presides over the kitchen. The restaurant, located to the side of the inn in a carriage house, contains a small dining room with banquettes draped in chintz and a long and narrow main dining room with windows onto fields and woods. Blue armchairs are at tables set with Villeroy & Boch china. Dinner entrees range from $14.50 for fillet of sole to $30 for filet mignon with green peppercorn sauce. Specials might be tuna steak with fresh basil, tarragon and dill or grilled breast of pheasant with juniper berry sauce. A few sandwiches and salads supplement a dinner-like luncheon menu, with entrees from $8.50 for stuffed chicken to $13.50 for filet mignon. Lunch, Tuesday-Saturday 11:30 to 2; dinner, Tuesday-Saturday from 5:30; Sunday brunch, 11 to 2.

Vernon Stiles Inn Restaurant, Route 193, Thompson Hill, (203) 923-9571. Chef-owner Joe Silbermann's stagecoach tavern — built in 1814 — looks exactly the way a country inn ought to: with a fire blazing in the pub, three cozy dining rooms and a great picture of the inn made with what look to be pieces of tiles. The place was named for one of its more colorful landlords, who claimed that more stage passengers dined here every day than at any other house in New England. The continental menu is well regarded locally. Appetizers include brie with apricots and almonds, crab-stuffed artichoke hearts and escargots. Among entrees ($10.95 to $17.95) are seafood strudel, lobster pie, grilled rosemary chicken, pork dijon, five versions of veal and filet mignon. The weekly Stew and Story sessions on Wednesday evenings are a winter tradition. Lunch, Wednesday-Friday 11:30 to 2; dinner nightly except Tuesday, 4:30 to 8:30 or 9; Sunday, brunch 11 to 2:30, dinner 4 to 8.

The Vanilla Bean Cafe, Junction of Routes 169, 44 and 97, Pomfret, (203) 928-1562. Eileen (Bean) Jessurun — with brothers Barry and Brian and occasionally their mom — runs this neat little cafe in a restored cream-colored 19th-century barn. You order at a counter and your choice is delivered to one of the butcher-block tables with bentwood chairs inside or, on nice days, to the patio out front, where outdoor grill items also are available. Everything — even tuna steak and lamb kabobs — is under $7 on the all-day menu, which includes chili, soups, great sandwiches and blackboard specials like gumbos, beef stew and quiches. We enjoyed the turkey sandwich which, the menu advised, is not "that awful turkey roll but the real thing, roasted here at the Bean." The desserts are decadent: rich brownies and hot fudge sundaes, perhaps, or you can order a milk shake, also listed under desserts, for $2.25. Beers and wines also are available at this fun-loving, unpretentious place, where musical entertainment starts Fridays at 8. Open Monday and Tuesday 7 to 3, Wednesday-Friday 7 to 8, weekends 8 to 8.

The Paddock, Route 101, Dayville, (203) 774-1313. Everyone locally swears by the Paddock, a nondescript place beside the railroad track in downtown Dayville. One door at the front entry leads to the bar and the other to a small dining room where captain's chairs face formica tables set with red paper mats and patio candles. Crackers and bread sticks with a zippy cheese spread come with drinks, so you probably could skip the few appetizers, which are of the chilled fruit cup ilk (the $1.50 tossed salad is big enough for two, anyway). Go for the down-home main courses like broiled scrod, ham steak with pineapple, broiled pork chops, tenderloin tips en casserole, broiled scallops and shrimp scampi. Prices range from $5.95 for fish and chips with coleslaw (Thursday and Friday only) to $15.95 for lobster casserole. Prime rib is available Saturday for $12.95. The menu and the prices seldom change here, and everybody seems to know everybody else. Lunch, Tuesday-Friday 11:30 to 2; dinner, Tuesday-Saturday 4:30 to 9.

Fox Hunt Farms Gourmet Shop, Routes 169 and 171, South Woodstock, (203) 928-0714. This specialty food shop par excellence expanded in 1992, an addition doubling its size and providing an espresso bar and tables for some of the goodies served up by partners Linda Colangelo and Laura Crosetti. Sandwiches ($4 to $4.25) include four versions of ham and cheese, roast beef with horseradish, chicken salad, smoked salmon with cream cheese and, our choice, country pate with honey mustard. We also liked a warm croissant filled with chicken and red peppers. Among vegetarian offerings is one with goat cheese and sundried tomatoes. Dessert could be raspberry rugalach or an almond truffle bar. A little deck out front with ice-cream parlor tables and chairs is used in good weather. Open daily, 10 to 5:30.

Stoggy Hollow General Store & Restaurant, Route 198, Woodstock Valley, (203) 974-3814. For a dash of local color, the aroma of coffee and a bit of history, stop at this general store where food is a big attraction. Occupying a house built in 1836, it takes its name from the pegged shoes called "stoggies" made in the valley in the mid-19th century. The aura of the old days remains here as burgers, deli sandwiches, soups, salads

Thrusting gables and vivid pink facade mark Roseland Cottage.

and more are dispensed in huge portions at prices from yesteryear — $2.95 for chicken fillet on a bun or a tuna melt on an English muffin, $1.95 for a grilled cheese sandwich. Omelets, muffins and pancakes are the fare for breakfast, when Stoggy's hearty breakfast — two eggs, pancakes, homefries, breakfast meat, a bakery basket, juice and coffee — goes for $4.95. Tea with finger sandwiches and dessert is served here by reservation Wednesdays from 2:30 to 5 for $8. Dinner specials are offered Thursday-Saturday, spring through fall. There are tables inside or on the porch. Breakfast daily, 7 to 11, Sunday to noon; lunch daily, 11:30 to 7 or 8.

Seeing and Doing

Weathered barns and old stone walls in farm fields border the roads, evidence of the agricultural character of part of the region. Once-proud mills dominating the landscape of Putnam, Danielson and Killingly testify to another aspect. The biggest annual events are the Brooklyn Fair the last weekend in August and the Woodstock Fair on Labor Day Weekend. Both are among the nation's longest-running agricultural fairs. Fast becoming another tradition is the three-day Walking Weekend staged every October.

Hill Towns and Mill Villages. A booklet of this name, prepared by the Association of Northeastern Connecticut Historical Societies, is a helpful adjunct for touring rural Woodstock, Pomfret, Brooklyn and Canterbury as well as the nearby mill towns of Thompson, Putnam, Killingly and Plainfield. We particularly enjoy "The Street" lined with academic buildings, churches and gracious homes in Pomfret, the Woodstock Hill green with a sweeping three-state view available behind Woodstock Academy, and the stunning Thompson Hill common on, yes, a hilltop. A favorite driving tour follows **Scenic Route 169,** slicing north-south through the heart of this region from the Massachusetts line to Canterbury. The buildings and land along both sides have been placed on the National Register and the 32-mile stretch is the longest officially designated scenic road in Connecticut and one of ten of the nation's most scenic as designated by Scenic America.

Heritage Corridor. The National Park Service is instrumental in an effort begun in 1988 to develop a Quinebaug-Shetucket Rivers Heritage Corridor to preserve the region's rural quality of life and protect it from encroaching development. Twenty-five area towns are cooperating to develop regional greenways and nourish historic and natural preservation. The corridor committee sponsors a **Walking Weekend** over three days each Columbus Day weekend in October. Experts guide upwards of 3,000 people on a total of about 45 walks, visiting mill towns, forests, farms, the Thompson Common, parks and more. In 1992 there were even a bird walk, a fisherman's walk, a riverside botanical walk and a dog's walk (with adults on leash).

Churches and Schools. The spireless **Old Trinity Church** in Brooklyn, the oldest Episcopal church (1771) now standing in the oldest diocese in the country, is open some summer afternoons but is used only once a year on All Saints Day. Modeled after Trinity Church in Newport and King's Chapel in Boston, it is a favorite of photographers. The gem of an interior is all bare wood, which remains unpainted. Other little treasures are the Pomfret School chapel and the Tiffany windows in Pomfret's Christ Church. Also peek into the brick one-room **Quassett School** in Woodstock. The Pomfret and Rectory private schools have pleasant campuses.

Roseland Cottage, Route 169, Woodstock, (203) 928-4074. If the Quiet Corner has an "attraction," this is it. And its thrusting gables and vivid pink facade stand in colorful contrast to the otherwise Colonial character of the attractive New England village. Woodstock native Henry C. Bowen, a New York merchant and publisher, was into roses and the Fourth of July. So he planted a formal garden with roses outside his summer house, upholstered much of its furniture in pink and named it Roseland Cottage. Such luminaries as Ulysses S. Grant, Benjamin Harrison, Rutherford B. Hayes and William McKinley came to the wild pink Gothic Revival mansion trimmed in gingerbread for his famous Independence Day celebrations. The house and its furnishings remain much as they were in the 19th century. The parterre garden, with 600 yards of dwarf boxwood edging, has survived since it was laid out in 1850. In the rear barn is the oldest extant bowling alley in a private residence; balls of varying sizes line the gutter. Victorian teas are scheduled some afternoons in summer and fall. More than 150 craftsmen and artists participate in a fall festival here the third weekend in October. Open Wednesday-Sunday noon to 5 in summer, Friday-Sunday through October. Adults $4, children $2.

Prudence Crandall Museum, Routes 14 and 169, Canterbury, (203) 546-9916. The site of New England's first black female academy has a fascinating history to reveal. Asked to educate their children, Prudence Crandall ran afoul of townspeople when she admitted a black girl in 1833. They withdrew their children, so she ran a boarding school for "young ladies and misses of color" until she was hounded out of town. Now a museum and National Register landmark, the house is interesting for its architecture and exhibits on 19th-century Canterbury, blacks and Miss Crandall. Open Wednesday-Sunday 10 to 4:30, mid-January to mid-December. Adults, $2.

Brayton Grist Mill & Marcy Blacksmith Museum, Route 44, Pomfret. At the entrance to Mashamoquet Brook State Park, this example of a one-man mill operation survives from a time when water-powered grain mills were integral to every town. The milling equipment employed until 1928 remains in its original location. The fine blacksmithing tool collection belonged to three generations of the Marcy family. Open May-September, Thursday, Saturday and Sunday 2 to 5. Free.

Mashamoquet Brook State Park, Route 44, Pomfret, (203) 928-6121. The 1,000-acre park also offers swimming, camping and an adventurous trail to the **Wolf Den,** where local Revolutionary War hero Israel Putnam killed the last she-wolf in northeastern Connecticut. Children can crawl inside and almost visualize Putnam stalking the beast in the cave. Another trail leads to a rock formation known as **Indian Chair.** Trails open free, daily to dusk. Park fee on weekends in summer.

Early blacksmith shop is home to Scranton's Shops.

Daniel Putnam Tyler Law Office, Route 169, Brooklyn, (203) 774-7728. Amid the classic churches and homesteads of the Brooklyn Green historic district stands a statue of Israel Putnam, the local Revolutionary War hero. Hidden behind is the one-room country lawyer's office where Putnam's great-grandson practiced from 1822 to 1875. It is maintained by the Brooklyn Historical Society. Open Memorial Day to Labor Day, Wednesday 1 to 5 and Saturday 10 to 2. Free.

St. Hilary's Vineyard, Webster Road (Route 12), North Grosvenordale, (203) 935-5377. Connecticut's oldest and most unusual farm winery offers free tastings in a room off the home of Mary Kerensky, wife of the late owner, and occasional tours of the vineyard he nurtured. Raspberry, blueberry and peach wines from locally grown fruit are featured. Open weekends 10 to 6, weekdays by appointment.

A Must Excursion

Old Sturbridge Village, Route 20, Sturbridge, Mass., (508) 347-3362. Just across the Massachusetts state line lies one of New England's most popular attractions, and most visitors to northeastern Connecticut take advantage. With great emphasis on authenticity, the 200-acre living-history museum re-creates a New England farming village of the 1830s. More than 40 restored buildings were moved from various sections of New England. Costumed interpreters demonstrate life as it used to be. The meeting-house dominates the common, around which are craft shops, homes and a general store. Although Old Sturbridge is special any time, we like it best in the fall, particularly around Thanksgiving time, the traditional New England holiday. The cobbler and his apprentice turn out low black boots in the shoe shop, their Shaker-style wood stove offering a pleasant blast of warmth on a chilly day. The preacher in Richardson Parsonage polishes up his Sunday sermon, while a teacher in felt top hat and black cape gives lessons at the schoolhouse. Tinsmiths are at work on small coffee pots and pepper boxes that ultimately wind up in the village's large gift shop. You can eat at Bullard Tavern, where a cafeteria dispenses chowder, chicken pot pie and sandwiches. Or snack on cider and peanut butter cookies at the Grant Store and Bake Shop. Allow at least half a day to take it all in. Open daily 9 to 5, late April to late October; Tuesday-Sunday 10 to 4 and some Monday holidays, rest of year. Adults $15, children $7.

151

Horticultural Sites

Logee's Greenhouses, 141 North St., Killingly, (203) 774-8038. Push your way through the narrow paths past a jungle of greenery on all sides. On a cold day, seeing and smelling all the orchids and begonias among 2,000 kinds of exotic indoor plants in eight greenhouses will warm your innards. Although this is a thriving commercial enterprise, it's low-key and no one may know you're there. Joy Logee Martin, owner of the 100-year-old family business, is considered one of the great horticulturalists in the country. Open daily 9 to 4. Free.

Buell's Greenhouses, 11 Weeks Road, Eastford, (203) 974-0623. Six commercial greenhouses here hold 140,000 African violets and 700 American hybrid varieties. Nearby is Buell's Orchard, where you can pick up seasonal fruits, caramel apples, homemade jams and more. Open Monday-Saturday 8 to 5. Free.

Sandra Lee's Herbs and Everlastings, 294 Hampton Road (Route 97), Pomfret, (203) 974-0525. Herbs, perennials and dried flowers are featured at this 2.5-acre herb and plant farm. There are display gardens and a retail shop. Open May-July and September-November, Tuesday-Saturday 10 to 5, Sunday noon to 5.

Caprilands Herb Farm, Silver Street, Coventry. (203) 742-7244. Worth a side trip are the 31 theme gardens, shops, herbal luncheons and lectures offered by octogenarian Adelma Grenier Simmons at this herb farm known far and wide. Most visitors book far in advance for the daily luncheons, which start about 11 o'clock with herbal tea and canapes in the greenhouse. Following a noon lecture on herbal and seasonal topics by Mrs. Simmons, visitors move to her 18th-century farmhouse for punch and lunch, where herbs flavor every dish. Dessert and more tea are served afterward in the greenhouse. Herbal luncheon programs April-Dec. 24, $18. Grounds and shops open daily 9 to 6.

Shopping

South Woodstock seems to be the focus for the kind of stores that appeal to visitors. **Scranton's Shops,** a ramble of rooms in an 1878 blacksmith shop, is full of country wares from more than 70 local artisans. The array is mind-boggling, and we defy anyone to leave without a purchase. Nearby, the new **Livery Shops** opened by Judy Cummings offer more small rooms given over to local artisans who show their wares on consignment. At our visit, the impressive, one-of-a-kind items included an amusing picnic dish set with flies and ants painted on, the striking dishes of Majilly Designs, and the watercolors of Tom McCobb.

Other shoppers like **Cornucopia Crafts** for baskets, **Brunarhans** for wood furnishings, the **Woodstock Orchards Apple Barn** and the **Christmas Barn,** all scattered about Woodstock. At the **Irish Crystal Co.** you may find exquisite Tyrone crystal of the same quality as Waterford at much lower prices. From perfume decanters to wine glasses to lamps, it all shimmers in the Woodstock showroom. A budding antiques center is emerging in downtown Putnam, where the rather elegant **Antiques Marketplace** with 200 dealers joined three smaller collectibles shops when it opened in a former department store that has been nicely restored. Opening nearby in January 1993 was the **Putnam Antiques Exchange,** a large, multi-dealer shop. **Heirloom Antiques** in Brooklyn is considered one of the area's better shops and also displays at the Livery Shops. Nearly 100 dealers show at **Pomfret Antique World.**

FOR MORE INFORMATION: Northeast Connecticut Visitors District, 62 Main St., Box 598, Putnam, CT 06260, (203) 928-1228.

Mount Monadnock is backdrop for Altar of the Nations at Cathedral of the Pines.

A Quiet Corner

The Monadnock Region, N.H.

New Hampshire's "Quiet Corner" is comprised of a group of quintessential small New England towns, most of them set out on winding back roads in the southwestern corner of the state. They're the sort of towns that come to mind when we think of picture-perfect New England, the kind often selected by landscape artists as representative.

They have the requisite white-steepled churches and town greens, the great old homes and farms with red barns, and sometimes fairly clannish townsfolk with the broad accents we associate with Yankees. Because the region is bypassed by expressways and the towns are rather sparse in population, there's an unspoiled feeling, a sense that the area has not been overrun by visitors.

Actually, the Monadnock region has been a mecca to outdoors enthusiasts, to writers and artists for more than a hundred years. Mount Monadnock, the gentle peak in its midst, is reputed to be the second most climbed mountain in the world, after Japan's Mount Fuji. A quarter of a million people hike any one of a dozen routes to its summit annually. They follow in the footsteps of Ralph Waldo Emerson, who dubbed it "The Great Inspirer," and Nathaniel Hawthorne, who described it as "a sapphire against the sky." Henry David Thoreau used to run here from Concord, Mass., for the weekend. He's known to have climbed the 3,165-foot-high mountain at least four times.

Lakes and rivers abound in the area, several of them flanked by colonies of summer homes. Dublin Lake is particularly sought after, for its shimmering waters often reflect Mount Monadnock itself.

In addition to its natural gifts, the Monadnock region has long enjoyed an active cultural life. The MacDowell Colony in Peterborough serves as a temporary refuge for writers, artists and musicians who spend quiet, creative time there. One who did was writer Willa Cather; she so loved the region that she visited several times and is buried in the beautiful old cemetery in Jaffrey.

Peterborough was the inspiration for Thornton Wilder's play, "Our Town." Today it is home to a fine professional summer theater, The Peterborough Players, as well as a new, exciting marionette theater. The Monadnock Summer Lyceum is a series of cultural events held on Sunday mornings in the summer at Peterborough's Unitarian Church; in 1992 the speakers included Mary Catherine Bateson and John Kenneth Galbraith.

Dublin is the headquarters of Yankee magazine and the *Old Farmer's Almanac* and in Sharon, the Sharon Arts Center is a top-quality home to fine artists and craftsmen and the site of classes in a variety of disciplines.

Antiques shops, gift shops and some headquarters for retail merchandising — Eastern Mountain Sports and Brookstone, among them — make the area fun for shoppers.

The real secret to the Monadnock region's richness, however, is its low-key approach. No chain motels or restaurants are located in the small towns east of Keene; the small city on the western border is a gateway to the Monadnock area, but not an integral part of it. Visitors find rooms in small bed and breakfasts and traditional, old-fashioned inns.

The Monadnock region is lovely in any season, but fall is special. The foliage is aflame, prompting Marlborough innkeeper Cal Gage to advise guests, "Turn off on any side road and it's like driving through a tunnel of color. You'll come out somewhere; you're not going to get lost."

Autumn is the time for the smell of wood smoke from inn fireplaces, for the taste of maple syrup on morning pancakes or waffles, and for the sense of well-being instilled by a walk or a hike in the crisp mountain air.

The Monadnock region is a choice for those who wish to slow down for a few days and get away from the pressures of modern life. Don't be surprised if you fall in love with the area.

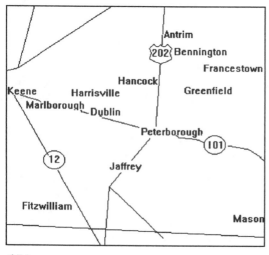

Getting There

Interstate 91 is the major north-south access from the west and south. I-93 provides access from the east, and I-89 from the north. State Route 101 is the main east-west state highway through the area.

The nearest major airports are located in Hartford, Conn., and Boston, Mass., both about two hours distant. Smaller airfields are found in Keene and Manchester, N.H. Vermont Transit buses travel from Keene to Logan Airport in Boston; there's one stop a day in Rindge.

Mount Monadnock is often reflected in placid waters of Dublin Lake beside Route 101.

Where to Stay

The Monadnock region is quite decentralized, with about fifteen small towns spread among its hills and gently winding roads. Peterborough is the largest and most important; it has the hospital, a downtown, a couple of strip shopping centers (but no malls) and a few restaurants. Surprisingly, it doesn't have an old center-of-town inn; those can be found in Fitzwilliam, Jaffrey, Hancock and Antrim. Bed and breakfasts are often the preferred accommodations; they range from small and homey to very sophisticated. Prices are lower here than in many areas.

Bed and Breakfasts

Apple Gate Bed and Breakfast, 199 Upland Farm Road (Route 123), Peterborough 03458, (603) 924-6543. Dianne and Ken Legenhausen left Long Island, where she was a music teacher and he a police officer, to open this B&B in 1990. For several years they had weekended in the area and they bring charm and enthusiasm to their venture. The 1832 white clapboard house with full-length front porch welcomes you with tiny white lights in each window year-round. Inside, Dianne has decorated with an apple theme, but she doesn't overdo it. A large poster of different kinds of apples is framed and hung on the wall; there are a wooden tic-tac-toe board with apples as playing pieces and a lamp with apples on the lampshade, for example. Two parlors, one with fireplace and the other with wood stove, piano and floor-to-ceiling books, are welcoming. Full breakfasts are served by candlelight in a large dining room where guests sit around one table and where a fire burns on chilly mornings. The four guest rooms are named for apples, naturally. Cortland, a front bedroom with queen bed and its own bathroom, is much requested. Across the way, Granny Smith is done in soft peaches and greens; its full bath is downstairs, so robes are provided. Tiny McIntosh has a three-quarter bed and a bath with footed tub; Crispin, tucked down the hall, has twin beds and also a private bath. In the fall, you can pick apples in the orchard across the way; the Legenhausens give you a bag and take the money for the farmer. For visitors staying two nights or more, a charming garage apartment is also rented out by Dianne and Ken in nearby Temple; it has a bedroom, kitchen, and living room with a sofabed so families can enjoy their own woodsy retreat. Doubles, $60 to $75.

Benjamin Prescott Inn, Route 124 East, Jaffrey 03452, (603) 532-6637. This large gold-colored clapboard house set just off the road adjoins a huge dairy farm to the rear. Innkeeper Barry Miller was in the hotel business before he and wife Jan decided in 1988 to do their own thing. All ten guest rooms in their inn have private baths. We stayed in Elder Eldad's front corner bedroom with kingsize bed, wall stenciling and private bath with stall shower. We came downstairs to Jan's exceptional breakfasts each morning: eggs benedict the first day and puffed apple pancakes with New Hampshire maple syrup the next, served at one end of a homey parlor where several small antique tables are set up. A "Gathering Room," furnished incongruously with contemporary boardroom-look conference table and upholstered chairs, was added recently for mini-conferences and business retreats and allows large groups to eat together. Doubles, $60 to $130.

Thatcher Hill Inn,, Thatcher Hill Road, Marlborough 03455, (603) 876-3361. Set way back from the road, this large white clapboard house and cupolaed 1894 barn are surrounded by open meadows, stone walls and acres of woodlands. Cal Gage, who retired from the Leo Burnett ad agency in Chicago after years as vice president of research, and his wife Marge came east in the mid-1980s and took over a place that had belonged to Cal's cousins. Thatcher Hill's seven guest rooms have private baths and come with king, queen or twin beds; one on the first floor is wheelchair-accessible. We especially liked a second-floor room with green-painted iron bed with brass finials, covered with a pink patchwork quilt, and its adjoining bathroom with a red clawfoot tub. Wide pumpkin floorboards throughout and a fireplaced public parlor add to the ambience, and Marge's home-baked breads are famed at breakfast time. There are two first-floor parlors and a second-floor sitting room. Doubles, $68 to $78.

Hannah Davis House, 186 Depot Road (Route 119), Fitzwilliam 03447, (603) 585-3344. When television's "Good Morning America" show did a segment on Fitzwilliam in 1992, the cast stayed at this beautiful 1820 Federal, and innkeeper Kaye Terpstra points out which rooms Joan Lunden and Charlie Gibson took. Kaye and husband Mike opened their inn in 1990. Now they have five rooms, all with private baths. The newest, the Loft, is a stunner created from a former carriage shed, with a private entrance from the parking area, an elevated platform reached by stairs for the queen bed and a sitting area with sleeper sofa below. The large bathroom has a footed tub, a glass-walled stall shower and brass and porcelain fixtures. Four guest rooms in the main house are compelling as well. The Canopy features a queensize pencil-post bed of cherry with antique crocheted canopy hood; Chauncey's Room has bold red floral wallpaper and a fireplace. A first-floor suite contains a fireplaced bedroom and adjoining sitting room. Breakfast is usually served in the large kitchen, which is clearly the heart of this home; in warm weather guests can take it on the rear deck overlooking colorful gardens. Stuffed french toast with ham and cheese and a dijon sauce is one of the hot entrees in Kaye's repertoire. Doubles, $55 to $80.

Amos A. Parker House, Route 119, Fitzwilliam 03447, (603) 585-6540. Just down the street from the Hannah Davis is another fabulous B&B opened by Freda B. Houpt in the mid-1980s. The owners have become good friends and they're happy to recommend one another whenever their own house is full. Freda's a dynamo who was a travel agent in Chicago before she came east to visit a son in Boston and fell in love with New England. She sold her Chicago digs and bought this big old 18th-century house. Upstairs are two front rooms with private baths and fireplaces (one has a double canopied bed and the other is twin-bedded). To the rear are two bedrooms sharing a bath, which Freda prefers to rent as a suite. On the main floor is a huge suite with private entrance containing large bedroom, sitting area with fireplace, small kitchen and bath. The dining room — with scrumptious cookies set out for expected arrivals when we stopped by — is a deep orange color; it's here that guests take a breakfast that Freda describes as "elaborate — meat and eggs and something else." Her spinach souffle with mushroom cream sauce is a favorite. Guests enjoy Freda's "great room," a special place with wood stove, barnwood walls, bookcases and dried flowers hanging from overhead beams. A porch out back looks down over her fabulous gardens; a lily pond was being added in 1992. Doubles, $65; suites, $80 to $110.

Lilac Hill Acres B&B, Ingalls Road, Jaffrey 03452, (603) 532-7278. The setting for this comfortable house, high on a hill overlooking Gilmore Pond just outside of town, is its best feature. We can imagine spending hours on the redwood loveseat that overlooks the pond, and there are great views in all directions. Ellen and Frank McNeill offer four simple bedrooms, one king-bedded room with private bath and three rooms sharing a bath. Benji, a friendly terrier, greets guests. A large porch out back is where breakfast is served in nice weather; it is also a place for guests to relax. Or they can enjoy a roaring fire in the cozy parlor. Ellen loves to cook and prides herself on serving different breakfast entrees every day; sometimes blueberry pie is on the menu. Doubles, $60 to $70.

Greenfield Inn B&B, Route 31, Greenfield 03047, (603) 547-6327. Ebullient host Vic Mangini and his wife Barbara preside over this Victorian-style B&B in tiny Greenfield. The structure is originally a farmhouse from the early 1800s, but Barbara has decked it out with teddy bears and dolls, tiny dresses hanging in the front hall, lavish curtains tied with satin ribbons and the like. Before you're barely inside you'll learn that the Manginis are friends of Bob Hope and his wife Delores, who have visited not once, but twice. The main house holds eight guest rooms, while a two-level apartment fashioned from a hayloft in the rear can handle six persons. The two front bedrooms, Delilah & Sampson and Juliet & Romeo, have private bathrooms and TV sets and are decorated with lace, fringe and floral wallpapers. Three other bedrooms come with private baths and three share. Opened in 1992 was a carriage house accommodating up to six but perfect also for honeymooners, says Vic. Two bedrooms upstairs each have a private bath; downstairs are a living room and kitchen plus a studio bedroom with bath. Doubles, $49 to $69; cottage or loft apartment, $79 to $99.

The Inn at New Ipswich, Porter Hill Road, New Ipswich 03071, (603) 878-3711. This 1790 farmhouse with attached red barn is a picture — just off the main road and surrounded by gardens with fruit trees and classic stone walls. Steve and Ginny Bankuti, who raised their family in Sudbury, Mass., opened the inn in 1988. They offer six guest rooms, five with private baths. Canopied twin beds, a working fireplace and a color scheme dominated by hunter green make the large first-floor bedroom a restful retreat. Upstairs, one room is decorated with Hungarian fabrics and artifacts in honor of Steve's heritage. Another room contains a working fireplace. A suite has a queen-bedded room plus a twin-bedded room sharing a bath. The fireplace is usually lit in the keeping room where hearty breakfasts are served; the hot dish might be an egg casserole or puff pancakes. Guests enjoy a back porch full of wicker on nice days. Doubles, $60.

Stepping Stones Bed & Breakfast, Bennington Battle Trail, Wilton Center 03086, (603) 654-9048. It's not hard to believe Ann Carlsmith is a landscape designer; her lovely gardens are the feature of this 19th-century B&B, tucked off a back road in tiny Wilton. Follow the path and find charming sitting areas amid the flora, where you'll be quite off by yourself. The interior of the large white house is light and cheery with skylights and white paint; Ann's colorful weaving loom dominates one main-floor space and guests breakfast in an airy kitchen. Three guest rooms are on the second floor, two sharing a bath and one with a queensize bed having its own. All are carpeted and nicely decorated. A reservoir across the street is a good place for walks. Our only complaint involved Stanza, a frisky young German shepherd who kept nipping at our ankles. Ann insists she's harmless. Doubles, $45 to $50.

Harrisville Squires Inn, Keene Road, Harrisville 03450, (603) 827-3925. Close to the picturesque center of the 19th-century milltown of Harrisville is this comfortable B&B. Pat and Doug McCarthy — he's a school teacher and she used to be in the hotel business — offer sumptuous breakfasts and five guest rooms. Two have private baths and three share. A peach living room with wing chairs and other comfortable furniture is a great place to relax. The dining room opens onto a pleasant grass patio; in warm weather guests sometimes eat outdoors. Pat prides herself on her five-course breakfasts that always include muffins, juice and coffee, cold and hot cereals, an entree and a hot dessert like apple crisp or peach cobbler. The inn serves as headquarters for Monadnock Bicycle Touring and Doug will plan itineraries for guests, even getting the rental bikes. Pat oversees the rustic Country Accent gift shop in the attached barn, where she sells the "official" Harrisville T-shirts (her design) as well as her own dried flowers and other tasteful gifts. Doubles, $50 to $60.

Inns

The Inn at Crotched Mountain, Mountain Road off Route 47, Francestown 03043, (603) 588-6840. This red brick inn, with white clapboard wings attached and a red and white barn, is located about 1,300 feet above sea level with a gorgeous view 40 miles across the Piscataquog Valley. The air is clear, the mood is mellow, and this is a place for getting away from it all. That is especially true since Crotched Mountain ski area, which was practically at the front door of the inn, has gone out of business. The inn keeps an erratic schedule. Basically, it's open daily from mid-June to Labor Day, and summer guests enjoy a swimming pool and clay tennis courts. It's open again for foliage season from mid-September to Halloween. Its winter season begins Christmas week, and it's open full weeks during school vacations and weekends at other times until mid-March. The inn reopens weekends from Mother's Day to mid-June. Meals in the renowned dining room (see Where to Eat) are available on Friday and Saturday nights when the inn is operating. Weekend guests are offered MAP rates; at other times the meal plan is B&B. Innkeepers Rose and John Perry offer fourteen guest rooms, five with private baths and four quite stunning with their own working fireplaces. They are decorated in comfortable Colonial style, as is the huge, attractive living room with oriental rugs. There is a game room as well. Doubles, $60 to $70, B&B; $100 to $120, MAP.

John Hancock Inn, Main Street, Hancock 03449, (603) 525-3318. Linda and Joe Johnston admit to having been miserable after departing from the New England Inn in Intervale, N.H., where they were innkeepers for eight years. They became innkeepers again in 1991, and are thrilled to be at the helm of this well-known hostelry in an especially attractive town. Their presence is being felt in the decor at the inn and in the menu in the dining room (see Where to Eat). Linda, a bundle of energy, and Joe shut the inn in November 1991 while they and a bevy of tradesmen went to work. The results are most noticeable in the pub, which now sports red and white checked Colonial swags at the windows, a mural over the fireplace by Mary Beth Sullivan showing Mount Monadnock, and cozy tavern tables, wing chairs and sofas. To the left is the more formal lobby and registration desk, and upstairs on the second and third floors are ten pleasant guest rooms. Since the the inn has catered to guests on an uninterrupted basis since 1789, Linda doesn't want to fuss with the rooms too much. The Rufus Porter room, with queensize bed and smallish private bath, contains one of the itinerant artist's famed murals. White George Washington spreads cover most beds, some of which are

John Hancock Inn has accommodated guests since 1789.

canopied. Most rooms contain a radio and simple tape player with Gershwin and other tapes. A wicker-filled lounge on the third floor is also available. Breakfast is included in the rates. Doubles, $85 to $105.

The Antrim Inn, Main Street, Antrim 03440, (603) 588-8000. The rooms at this gray mansard-roofed in-town inn are smartly decorated in a duck motif and named accordingly (Mallard, Black Scooter). All fourteen rooms are handsomely appointed and feature antique beds, sofas, wing chairs, TVs, telephones and amenities like duck-shaped soaps in the well-equipped private baths. One has a working fireplace. Innkeepers Laura and Wayne Lesperance took over in 1990; he doubles as bartender in the large first floor Tavern. Breakfast and dinner are served in a spacious, beamed dining room. Doubles, $70 to $95.

A good value — but far from up-to-date in the outfitting of their guest rooms — are **The Fitzwilliam Inn** in Fitzwilliam and **The Monadnock Inn** in Jaffrey Center. Both are better known for their food, but if you want an old-fashioned lodging experience at old-fashioned prices, consider these inns, which offer rooms with private and shared baths. Double rooms are $40 to $55 at the Fitzwilliam Inn, $55 to $65 at the Monadnock.

Motels

Jack Daniels Motor Inn, Route 202N, Peterborough 03458, (603) 924-7548. Located next to the Contoocook River, this small motel has porches and flowers and only a few units. One queen or two double beds are located in each room. Doubles, $78.

Larger chain motels are located to the west of the area in Keene.

Seeing and Doing

The Monadnock region is refreshingly uncommercial. Perhaps the most crowded it gets is on the trails leading up Mount Monadnock itself. Visitors spend much of their time out-of-doors, enjoying the mountain views, the lakes, the trails in parks and natural areas. Antiques and gift shops offer quality one-of-a-kind items, perfect for the unhurried browser but hardly alluring to the avid consumer. We've visited at the height of the tourist season and never been in a traffic jam or had trouble getting a table for dinner. The area is particularly attractive to adults. There are, frankly, not many obvious diversions to entertain children.

Outdoors

Mount Monadnock. Officially the mountain is known as Grand Monadnock to differentiate it from lesser relatives. At 3,165 feet, its summit doesn't begin to compete with the Presidential Range in the White Mountains to the northeast, but it stands well above its neighbors in the 2,000-foot-high range. The mountain boasts some 30 miles of trails and is called the second most climbed mountain in the world. Ralph Waldo Emerson climbed Monadnock in 1866 at the age of 63 with his children and their friends. Five main trails lead to the summit. That used by most visitors, the White Dot trail, leaves from the entrance to Monadnock State Park off Route 124 in Jaffrey, (603) 532-8862, where park rangers hand out maps and literature. The cost is $2.50 a head, and the average climber, we're told, takes three hours to get up and back.

Pack Monadnock Mountain in Miller State Park, off Route 101, Peterborough. We have to admit driving to the summit of Pack Monadnock and not climbing Grand Monadnock. Blame it on the heat of one particular weekend we visited or the busyness of another, but we understand it offers a great view of the giant. There are picnic tables from which to enjoy both the view and lunch.

Rhododendron State Park, off Route 119, Fitzwilliam. A pleasant foot trail of about one mile leads to views of Mount Monadnock and other peaks in the region. There's a one-mile walking path around the glen and picnic grounds in shaded pine groves. But this park is at its best when more than sixteen acres of wild rhododendrons burst into blossom annually around mid-July.

The Monadnock-Sunapee Greenway Trail is a 47-mile-long trail between Mount Monadnock and Mount Sunapee in South Central New Hampshire. The original trail dates to the 1920s when the path was laid along a series of abandoned roads. The new trail follows higher country. Many people obviously hike portions of the trail; a popular section extends 13.4 miles from Mount Monadnock State Park to Nelson Village.

The Wapack Trail. This trail leads 21 miles from Pack Monadnock Mountain to Mount Watatic in Ashburnham, Mass. It takes you through sections of Greenfield, Peterborough, Sharon, Temple and New Ipswich. For the most part, the trail follows a skyline route along the summits of the mountains.

Crotched Mountain hiking trails. Three trails lead to the summit of the 2,055-foot mountain. The Francestown Trail starts at the base area of the Crotched Mountain ski area and follows the easiest ski trail. Other trails lead from Greenfield.

Shieling Forest, Peterborough. This 45-acre area of tree-covered ridges and valleys is located off Old Street Road. Dogs are permitted and there are walking trails.

A Foliage Tour. Here's a drive suggested by the Keene Chamber of Commerce. Start in Peterborough, taking Route 101 west for five miles to Route 137. Turn south on Route 137 to Jaffrey. In Jaffrey, you might want to get out and poke around the beautiful old graveyard and restored Red Schoolhouse nearby. Head west on Route 124. This road, more than twelve miles of scenic splendor, takes you along the southern edge of Mount Monadnock to Marlborough. Turn right in Marlborough on Route 101, heading east. The road skirts Dublin Lake and bisects the town of Dublin. Turn left two miles east of Dublin on Route 137 and drive north to the picturesque town of Hancock. Continue through Hancock on 137 and turn right on Route 202 south to Peterborough.

Cathedral of the Pines, off Route 119, Rindge, (603) 899-3300. A living memorial to those who gave their lives for our country, this tranquil and inspiring spot was created by Dr. and Mrs. Douglas Sloane in memory of their son, Lt. Sanderson Sloane, who was shot down over Germany in World War II. Tall pines lead to the Altar of the Nation, behind which is a beautiful view out toward Mount Monadnock. Simple wood benches offer rest for up to 2,000 persons. Services by congregations of all faiths are held regularly during the summer months and into the fall. The Memorial Bell Tower, visible soon after you enter, is the only monument in the United States to women who died for their country. Also on the property are an attractive Mother's Chapel and a St. Francis of Assissi (sp???) Chapel, as well as a public burial area. We enjoyed peeking at a simple summer wedding one Saturday noon; the place is highly popular for such events. Open daily 9 to 5, May-October. Free.

Peterborough Walking Tour. A simple white pamphlet leads you along Grove Street in the center of town, pointing out architectural highlights and historical facts. It's an easy walk and a fun way to get to know the town.

Harrisville. Don't miss Harrisville, the only intact 19th- century textile community surviving into the 20th century with its original plan and most of its buildings. The red brick mill buildings are stunningly set around three ponds that drain into a rocky ravine, falling 100 feet in a quarter of a mile and eventually ending up in the Merrimack River. A pamphlet outlines a walking tour, and in the autumn the reflections of foliage in the water are breathtaking. Cameras are a must.

Culture

Peterborough and environs are a cultural center of note. Most famous are the **Peterborough Players,** a summer stock theatrical group. Particularly interesting is a new group, the **New England Marionettes,** which launched performances in 1992 at the Marionette Theatre on Main Street in Peterborough. Here, 32-inch puppets are manipulated masterfully to the recorded music of operas. Performances weekends, May-December.

The **MacDowell Colony** in Peterborough offers several week-long retreats to creative artists and writers for the pursuit of their art. The public can enjoy the annual day-long book sale at the colony in October.

Churches are prominent around picturesque town common in Fitzwilliam.

161

Folk music — a very ambitious schedule of it — can be heard at **The Folkway**, 85 Grove St., Peterborough, (603) 924-7484, a restaurant with a performance area where musicians of all sorts hold forth regularly. Run by a non-profit foundation, it has been called "one of the nation's most respected folk clubs" by the Boston Globe.

Points of Interest

The Barrett Mansion, Main Street, New Ipswich, (603) 878-3283. This interesting Federal mansion was built by Charles Barrett for his son, Charles Jr., and daughter-in-law, Martha Minott of Concord, Mass. Tradition holds that the bride's father said he would furnish as large and fine a house as Mr. Barrett could build. The house has twelve rooms and enjoyed one-family ownership into the early 20th century. It's now operated by the Society for the Preservation of New England Antiquities. Open Tuesday, Thursday, Saturday and Sunday, noon to 5, June to mid-October. Adults $2, children $1.

Peterborough Historical Society, 19 Grove St., Peterborough, (603) 924-3235. Guided tours take approximately one hour and include a series of galleries on three floors and visits to two restored mill houses at the rear of the property. Artifacts from the town's industries are shown in the Peterborough Room. Open Monday-Friday 1 to 4, also Saturday 1 to 4 in summer. Admission, $1.

Franklin Pierce Homestead, Hillsborough, (603) 464-4260. The boyhood home of the 14th president of the United States, a restored 1804 mansion, reflects the lifestyle of the wealthy of the early 19th century. Open Friday and Saturday 10 to 4, Sunday 1 to 4, July-Labor Day; Saturday and holidays 10 to 4 and Sunday 1 to 4, late spring and early fall. Adults, $2.50.

Jaffrey Cemetery, with the grave of novelist Willa Cather, is of interest in Jaffrey. Also found near the Cather grave in the southwest corner is the gravestone of Sarah Averill, who died at age 89 after, according to the epitaph, "She done all she could."

Friendly Farm, Route 101, Dublin, (603) 563-8444. For more than 25 years this seven-acre farm has enchanted children and their families, who get to see farm animals up close — and to pet and feed them. Baby goats, pigs, turkeys, lambs and dairy cattle are part of the menagerie. There is also a farm-oriented gift shop. Open daily 10 to 5, late April to Labor Day and weekends through mid-October. Adults $4; children $3.

Shopping

Quality crafts items and antiques shops are of particular interest in the Monadnock region.

The Sharon Arts Center on Route 123, about five miles south of Peterborough, houses an excellent gallery and a school for artists and craftspeople. Ten fine art exhibits are mounted annually, and the crafts are of the highest quality. **The Black Swan** gift shop on Route 101 in Peterborough offers dried and silk floral designs, handcrafted items and gifts. **The North Gallery at Tewksbury's** at the junction of Routes 101 and 123 in Peterborough has fine items and many pieces of art as well.

Frye's Measure Mill in Wilton has been the site of wooden-product manufacture for more than a hundred years. Today, Shaker boxes are the prize products; they are made in all different sizes and sold in the shop along with tasteful country items such as quilts, salt-glaze pottery, country folk-art pieces and Christmas ornaments. Tours of the mill, where some machinery is still water-powered, are given Saturdays at 2.

The Weaving Center at Harrisville Designs in the charming mill village of Harrisville sells outstanding weaving and knitting yarns, floor looms, beginners' looms, weaving accessories and finished woven garments. Located in one of the old brick mill buildings, the center is very attractive.

Maple sugar seems to be available at every turn. The going rate in 1992 was about  $5.50 for a pint, $9.50 to $10 for a quart. **Bacon's Sugar House** in Jaffrey Center is one place to stop. The biggest, and a destination in itself, is **Parker's Maple Barn** in Mason. It involves an early 1800s sugar house, a country store and gift shop and the Maple Barn Restaurant, which serves breakfast, lunch and dinner.

Discounts can be found in special markdown rooms at both **Brookstone** and **Eastern Mountain Sports,** whose headquarters buildings are located off Route 202 a few miles north of Peterborough. Brookstone was actually started in a garage in the town.

Smart women's fashions are sold at **The Winged Pig** on Grove Street, Peterborough. **The Toadstool Bookshop** in town is fun to browse through.

Pickity Place, Nutting Hill Road, Mason, (603) 878-1151. Located at the end of a series of horrendous dirt roads (look carefully for the small signs), this is a special spot. A 1786 house and barn are the setting for a restaurant, an herb shop, museum and garden shop. The shop smells great, with herbal teas, potpourris, pomanders, soups, dried apple wreaths and even a dill pillow. A neat catalog with unusual items is available. Pickity Place also offers herbal luncheons — five courses for $12.95. The menu is appropriate to the season; an October menu included pumpkin curry soup, broccoli strudel and Swedish apple pie. Seatings Tuesday-Saturday at 11:30, 12:45 and 2.

Where to Eat

The Monadnock region has a few fine restaurants, but tends toward simpler fare in comfortable, unpretentious surroundings. Most are quite relaxed about dress codes.

Maitre Jacq, Mountain Road, Francestown, (603) 588-6655. Robert LeJacq, born in Brittany, was working in New York City when he set out in search of a quieter life and his own place. That was seven years ago and now his restaurant is considered the best in the Monadnock region. The small clapboard house seats 55 in two charming dining rooms decorated simply with gold carpeting, blue print curtains and captain's chairs at white-clothed tables. The menu changes three times a year and stresses classic French fare. Included in the price of the entree ($17 to $23) are a choice of appetizer or soup, tossed salad, dessert and beverage, which makes the experience something of a bargain as well. Robert offers a fine selection of wines and has a large following for his special wine-tasting dinners. Dinner might start with marinated herring in sour cream, the Maitre Jacq country terrine (a veal pate with cognac and herbs), escargots bourguignonne or coquilles St. Jacques. Entrees could be shrimp scampi, saute of chicken breast with artichoke bottoms and bearnaise sauce, medallions of pork loin Normandy or roast loin of lamb with rosemary. A six-grain country bread served with all meals is so popular it is sold at the Francestown Village Store. Extravagant desserts might be chocolate mousse with curacao, frangelico cheesecake, baked alaska flambe and cherries jubilee or bananas foster for two. The restaurant also produces its own fruit sorbets. Dinner, Tuesday-Saturday 5 to 9:30; also Sunday 3 to 7:30, Easter-October.

The Boilerhouse at Noone Falls, Route 202 South, Peterborough, (603) 924-9486. This expansive second-level dining area with white-linened tables and black lacquered chairs faces huge windows overlooking the waterfall. It's part of an old mill complex that also houses a few retail shops, but the restaurant is the drawing card for many. Votive candles flicker on the tables and a romantic, relaxing atmosphere prevails. A bit higher priced than other restaurants in the area, the Boilerhouse is nonetheless praised for its food. Dinner might begin with onion soup or soup of the day, or an appetizer ($5.25 to $6.95) like sherry battered shrimp, New Orleans-style crab cakes, grilled shrimp salad or scallops sauteed with red peppers, artichokes and chives. Entrees ($12.95 to $19.95) might be rack of lamb with rosemary and shallots, grilled breast of duckling, roast pork tenderloin or New Zealand venison. New York sirloin is offered in regular and petite portions. Interesting desserts include the chef's homemade ice cream, chocolate truffle torte with raspberry cream sauce and white chocolate pate on blackberry sauce. Lunch, Tuesday-Friday 11:30 to 2; dinner, Tuesday-Saturday 5:30 to 9; Sunday, brunch noon to 2:30, dinner 5 to 8.

Latacarta, 6 School St., Peterborough, (603) 924-6878. The old Gem Theater in the center of town is the place from which the Japanese master chef Hiroshi Hayashi, who moved to Peterborough from Newbury Street in Boston, operates. He offers what he calls "Epicurean Collage" and gives seminars at his home, Sunny Forest Farm, in Peterborough. His restaurant is simple with bentwood chairs, mulberry walls, track lighting, lacy cafe curtains and a multitude of plants. The menu arrives on a huge piece of heavy paper, white for lunch, beige for dinner. The emphasis, according to Hayashi, is on "food and its preparation for a more healthful lifestyle." At lunchtime, open-face sandwiches include unusual choices. You might try Bavarian country chicken (chicken breast simmered in a sour cream-mustard sauce with wine and tarragon and served warm), Boston scrod lightly fried, hummus and cheese, or the Latacarta special (pan-grilled tofu seasoned with soy sauce, served with melted cheddar cheese on whole wheat bread), all in the $5 to $6 range. Entrees like ginger chicken and tenderloin teriyaki also are available. Specials could include shrimp salad and a pasta dish. At night, appetizers might be shrimp tempura, hummus, fresh soy beans or wild mushrooms. Entrees ($10.95 to $14.95) include the popular escallops of salmon served with snow peas, mushrooms and tomatoes in a fresh dill sauce and teppanyaki beef (tenderloin of beef, pan-grilled and served with a traditional teriyaki sauce). Other choices include pasta and shrimp, baked scrod and the Latacarta dinner, something that changes weekly but which featured spinach ravioli at our visit. Lunch, Tuesday-Friday 11 to 5, Saturday noon to 5; dinner, Tuesday-Saturday 5 to 9 or 9:30; Sunday, brunch 11 to 5, dinner 5 to 7.

Del Rossi's Trattoria, Route 137 at Route 101, Dublin, (603) 563-7195. Jaffrey natives David and Elaina Del Rossi opened this popular place in 1989 in a Colonial house out in the countryside just off Route 101. A warren of simple dining rooms is found inside, where guests choose from a multi-paged typed menu. Chef Don Gibbons's food is Italian all the way. Appetizers ($3.50 to $5.50) include shrimp scampi, calamari marinara and caponata ala Sicilian. Among salads are the vintner (walnuts, grapes and Swiss cheese) and the trattoria (fresh basil, tomato, mozzarella and scallions with olive oil and red wine vinegar). A full page of pasta selections ($6.95 to $10.50) lists linguini with olive oil and garlic, spinach fettuccine with tomato-basil sauce, linguini ala Del Rossi (artichokes, black olives, capers, prosciutto and garlic with the pasta) and several ravioli dishes. Entrees, priced from $10.95 to $14.95, include veal parmesan, pork scaloppine, chicken formaggio, haddock Italian and shrimp marinara. The desserts seem challenging: seven C's cake (chocolate-chip cream cheese topping on cocoa chocolate cake), ricotta cheesecake and Sicilian cake (pound cake layered with chocolate-flaked creamy cheese filling and frosted in chocolate), plus cannoli, Italian cookies and spumoni with claret sauce. The wine choices are quite extensive. An ambitious schedule

Large windows overlook water at The Boilerhouse at Noone Falls.

of live music is offered weekend evenings in a back room. Dinner, Tuesday-Saturday 5 to 9, Sunday 4 to 8.

The Monadnock Inn, Route 124, Jaffrey Center, (603) 532-7001. The pretty country-style dining rooms here are charmingly old-fashioned with stenciled walls, wide-plank floors, white or blue tablecloths and windsor chairs. Innkeeper Sally Roberts, a former New Jersey school teacher, has built a reputation for good food. A typical dinner menu includes the option of a caesar salad ($6) instead of the regular house salad, appetizers like skewered shrimp, baked brie or sausage and polenta for $5.75 to $6.50, and a potato-leek soup the day we were there. Entrees ($15 to $18) included chicken saute, rack of lamb, poached or grilled salmon, grilled bluefin tuna with bearnaise sauce and tortellini stuffed with mushrooms and gruyere cheese. New in 1992 was the offer of Capri goat cheese from Hubbardston, Mass., crumbled on your salad for 75 cents extra. Flans, cream puffs and Viennese chocolate cake are special desserts. We fondly recall a post-dinner hour of relaxation in the adjoining lounge while a guest played the piano one evening. The pub is particularly cozy at this inn. Lunch, Monday-Friday 11:30 to 2; dinner, Tuesday-Saturday 5:30 to 9; Sunday, brunch 10 to 1, dinner 5 to 8.

John Hancock Inn, Main Street, Hancock, (603) 525-3318. Now that Linda and Joe Johnston have taken over, the Shaker cranberry pot roast — one of the signature items at their previous inn in Intervale — is on the dinner menu. So is a roast stuffed loin of pork, and both have quickly become local favorites. Entrees ($14 to $19) also include broiled lamb rosemary, venison Hancock, raspberry duck, a pasta dish and a changing chef's choice. Appetizers might be shrimp cocktail, maple broiled scallops or smoked chicken breast. Seafood bisque is offered along with a soup of the day. The dining rooms are handsome and one has a fireplace; wood tables are set with windsor chairs in the Hancock Room. Dinner nightly, 5 to 9 or 10.

Powder Mill Pond Restaurant, Route 202, Bennington, (603) 588-2127. Two bright dining rooms and a front porch overlooking the pond for which it's named are the setting for Jerry Willis's well-liked restaurant. White tablecloths with bright red napkins, light wood chairs with bow backs, fresh flowers on the tables and spotlit art along the walls make for a most attractive setting. If the weather cooperated, however, we'd want to eat on the porch. Willis trained at the Culinary Institute of America and offers a varied menu with such simple favorites as pot roast alongside medallions of beef mignon, scampi madagascar, and chicken and Chinese vegetables, all priced from $10 to $17. Appetizers are creative: escargots casserole, Vietnamese-style shrimp and chicken satay with Java sauce, for instance, priced from $5 to $8. Willis seems to have a strong following; the place was packed early on a Saturday evening. There is a good children's menu of hamburgers, chicken fingers and "noodles and tomato sauce" ($3.50), something most kids would love. Lunch, Tuesday-Friday 11:30 to 1:30; dinner, Tuesday-Saturday 6 to 9; Sunday brunch, 11:30 to 1:30.

The Lobster Man's Family Restaurant, Route 31 and 47, Bennington, (603) 588-3000. This was a small, charming French restaurant named Petite Maison until 1990 when it closed for a few days and reopened as a basic seafood restaurant. Chef-owner Richard Ranno said the change was forced by the economy. It must have worked, because at our visit in late 1992 the place was packed at 5 one Saturday evening. There's also a take-out menu. Inside, diners still enjoy the pretty environment of the former French restaurant, a real plus and unusual for an establishment like this. The lengthy menu in the $7 to $13 range includes lots of fried seafood (clams, scallops, shrimp, haddock and sole) plus filet mignon and New York sirloin and — of course — lobsters. Hamburgers and hot dogs are offered along with clam and lobster rolls and the like. Beer and wine are available. Lunch, Tuesday-Sunday 11 to 2:30, May-October; dinner, 4 to 9 year-round.

The Inn at Crotched Mountain, Mountain Road off Route 47, Francestown, (603) 588-6840. Owner Rose Perry is in the kitchen at this handsome inn and the tantalizing smell of roasting meats greeted us as we peeked in one afternoon. The dining rooms are cheerful with white linen tablecloths, green water glasses and bouquets of flowers. The menu includes items such as roast loin of pork, liver and onions, chicken teriyaki, cheesy tofu and vegetables in phyllo and eggplant parmigiana, priced from $10.95 to $16.95. On the appetizer list were smoked mussels, shrimp cocktail and herring in wine. Dinner, Friday and Saturday 6 to 8:30 when inn is open (see Where to Stay).

The Folkway, 85 Grove St., Peterborough, (603) 924-7484. This is an interesting spread of rooms with a craft shop upstairs. The draw may be the folk music that is presented on an ambitious schedule weekend evenings, but the food is quite creative. The non-profit establishment was re-opened as such following the death of its owner in 1988 and is now run by a foundation. The cuisine includes salads and light fare as well as entrees ($9 to $15) like lemon chicken with broccoli and Thai beef with peanut sauce. Pastas ($7.50 to $9.50) might be angel hair with artichoke hearts or fettuccine with wild mushrooms. Some of the good desserts are chocolate mousse pie, chocolate peanut-butter pie and cheesecake. Lunch, Tuesday-Saturday 11:30 to 2:30; dinner, Tuesday-Saturday 5:30 to 8:30; Sunday brunch, 11:30 to 2:30; bar menu after 9.

The Fitzwilliam Inn, Fitzwilliam, (603) 585-9000. We enjoyed lunch here one late-summer Saturday — we and a lot of other diners who seemed to be out for a ride on a glorious bright day. Cold blueberry soup was being served along with shrimp cocktail (priced at 75 cents a shrimp). We liked the broccoli and mushroom quiche with salad for $5.95 and a ham, turkey and roast beef club sandwich. Two simple dining rooms are side-by-side: the rear one has baskets hanging from the ceiling and is paneled; that in front has stenciled walls. In the evening complete dinners are offered for $12.95 to $16.95 (subtract $3 if you want to order a la carte). Entrees include roast duck stuffed with apples, chicken marsala and veal oscar. But you also can get a hamburger for $4.75. Fruit cobblers and tollhouse chocolate-chip pie sound wonderful for dessert. Lunch, Monday-Saturday noon to 2; dinner, 5 or 5:30 to 8:45, Sunday noon to 8.

FOR MORE INFORMATION: Peterborough Chamber of Commerce in the Monadnock Region, Box 400, Junction of Routes 101 & 202, Peterborough, N.H. 03458, (603) 924-7234.

Hikers scale dunes at Cape Cod National Seashore.

An Off-Season Potpourri

Cape Cod, Mass.

Visitors usually feel a bit smug about being on Cape Cod after Labor Day. It's hard not to. It is a kind of "one-upmanship," we suppose, to wait until the hordes have come and gone, having jammed the sandy, surfy, sun-blessed strand for its entire length and breadth, bringing traffic to a halt and tempers to a height.

Off-season, the Cape is a different place. The clam shacks and the soft ice-cream stands are boarded up, half the motels are closed, and you can actually drive along the Mid-Cape Highway (Route 6) or beautiful Route 6A without encountering a traffic jam. The only one we confronted one October evening turned out to be a line of cars pulling into an elementary school for a Parents' Night.

The Cape settles down, off-season, to what most people find appealing in the first place: deserted beaches, slow-paced harbors, antiques shops and boutiques where the owners take the time to talk. It is an atmosphere that retirees love; the Cape rivals the South as a retirement locale for New Englanders.

The inns and restaurants that stay open are those with year-round cheer and a local following. Most have sturdy fireplaces and serve hearty meals. Not least of their attractions can be the prices. Bargain rates prevail after Columbus Day.

What do you do on the Cape in the fall? Beachwalking is a pleasure any time of year, but off-season you don't have to get up before the sun to have the place to yourself. You might climb the dunes at the National Seashore and feel as if you're the first to do it. You can sit up there, seemingly on top of the world, and watch the sun rise over the Atlantic or set over Cape Cod Bay.

Autumn on Cape Cod is, for us, the best season, mellow and moody. It is a time for moseying along the north shore route, 6A, through the Cape's oldest and prettiest towns. Here you'll see the distinctive architecture of Cape Cod cottages, weathered gray or sparkling white, hung with bittersweet in the doorways. And, because of the salubrious effect of the ocean and the bay that surround it, Cape Cod experiences autumn later than most of New England.

Others, of course, have appreciated this season on the Cape. Henry Beston, author of the classic, *The Outermost House*, came for a fortnight in September and stayed for a year. Henry David Thoreau's first walking tour was in October 1849. And the Pilgrims made landfall in Provincetown Harbor in November 1620.

Historically, the Pilgrims weren't the first to touch the Cape. Before them came Samuel de Champlain, who called it "Cap Blanc," and Capt. John Smith, who named it "Cape James" after England's ruler. Verrazzano and Henry Hudson sailed past.

And then there was Bartholomew Gosnold. He stepped ashore in 1602 and found the fishing was great. There were so many codfish, in fact, that no other name would do. He named it "Cape Cod."

Sandwich was the first town to be incorporated on the Cape, in 1637, and it is the first town of our chapter as well. If Cape Cod is like a flexed arm, the area we concentrate on stretches from the shoulder, along the biceps and forearm. Stretching along charming Route 6A after Sandwich come Barnstable, Yarmouth Port, Dennis and Brewster.

Here we find a group of bed-and-breakfast inns in historic buildings, restaurants that are rated the best on the Cape, wonderful antiques shops and other places in which to stop and to browse. There are scenic harbors, hidden beaches, fine museums. Come along with us to the best of the Cape at our favorite time of year.

Getting There

Interstate 195 and Route 6 from the west, and Interstate 495 and Route 3 from the Boston area are the major auto routes to Cape Cod.

Bonanza Bus Lines serves the Cape. Small airlines fly into Hyannis.

Bedding Down

This lovely old section of the Cape is increasingly blessed with good B&Bs. These are the accommodations of choice here for they suit the season and the surroundings. Some have fireplaced bedrooms, most have book-lined libraries or reading nooks, and all have pleasant innkeepers who serve good breakfasts before a day of exploration. For

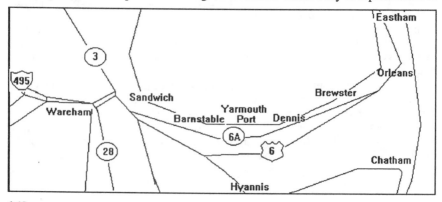

those who prefer privacy, we include a few motels and inns. Accommodations are presented in geographical order, from west to east. All are open year-round or well into the fall.

Daniel Webster Inn, 149 Main St., Sandwich 02563, (508) 888-3622. This imposing red clapboard motor inn was named after the 19th-century orator, who stayed at a previous tavern on the site when he hunted and fished in the area. While we have always found the lobby area too dark, the inn is popular for everything from a weekend getaway to Sunday dinner. No fewer than three dining rooms serve meals all day. The pub downstairs is a fun place to have Sunday brunch and maybe watch a pro football game. Colonial decor in the 47 rooms includes some canopied beds, wing chairs, ruffled curtains and the like. Twentieth-century amenities are whirlpool baths and color TVs. On one visit we remember continental breakfast delivered to the room along with the morning paper, all at the time requested. Doubles, $95 to $175, EP; $160 to $250, MAP.

The Village Inn at Sandwich, 4 Jarves St., Box 951, Sandwich 02563, (508) 833-0363 or (800) 922-9989. A grand wraparound porch is the place to relax and watch the passing action at this 1830s Federal-style home in the heart of the village. A half-dozen guest rooms feature delightfully bright decor, private baths and comforters for cozy sleeping. Innkeepers Patricia and Winfried Platz offer a hearty breakfast in the morning. The plantings on the property make it especially attractive. Doubles, $70 to $85. Closed January-March.

Spring Garden Motel, 578 Route 6A, Box 867, East Sandwich 02537, (508) 888-0710. This weathered gray motel is set back from the highway and all eleven rooms have decks to the rear overlooking a marsh. Most rooms are pine-paneled and contain two double beds; there are two efficiencies and one two-room suite. Owners Marvin and Judy Gluckman serve a homemade continental breakfast in the lobby. Out back are interesting plantings and picnic tables. Doubles, $40 to $62.

The Charles Hinckley House, Route 6A, Barnstable 02630, (508) 362-9924. Miya and Les Patrick are Pennsylvanians who have lived on the Cape for some years now. After refurbishing and running the One Centre Street Inn (see below) for a year, they found this 1809 Federal house and created a romantic B&B. All four guest bedrooms, two on the main loor and two on the second floor, come with working fireplaces. While the beds are Pennsylvania-made reproduction four-posters (three queens and a double), most of the furnishings are antique and include oriental rugs and wing chairs. Loveseats are set attractively before a fireplace in the parlor, magazines are spread on a sea chest between them, and a decanter by the window is filled with sherry. The house is named for the great-great-grandson of the last governor of Plymouth Colony, whose house it was. Miya, who also runs a catering business, makes great breakfasts — pancakes with strawberry topping the morning we stopped in. Fresh fruit, muffins, puff pastries and eggs in various styles are part of her repertoire. The Patricks love to cater to their guests on special occasions like anniversaries, and might stock the room with a bottle of champagne or deliver breakfast in bed. Doubles, $119 to $149.

Beechwood, 2839 Main St., Barnstable 02630, (508) 362-6618. An exuberant Victorian house painted in gold and green, Beechwood has six very individual guest rooms. That named Lilac is under the eaves and has a kingsize bed, full bath in lilac and pink and a separate shower room. The Rose room comes with pink walls, a canopy four-poster bed, working fireplace and oriental rug. Garret is tucked up under the eaves with a brass bed in the middle of the room and the bathroom a level below. Guests enjoy a large parlor with red velvet slipper chairs that remind us of a grandmother's house we knew. Innkeepers Anne and Bob Livermore serve a full breakfast in a charming room, where individual tables are covered with lace cloths. Bran muffins, poached pears and apple pancakes were the fare at our visit. A hammock hangs on the huge porch for your idle hours. Doubles, $100 to $135.

Liberty Hill Inn, 77 Main St., Yarmouth Port 02675, (508) 362-3976 or (800) 821-3977. Built as a private home for a shipbuilder in 1825, this Greek Revival-style house features an especially interesting elliptical staircase in the front hallway. There are five guest rooms, three on the second floor and a twin-bedded room on the first. Our room with kingsize bed on the third floor was spacious and the bathroom ample, but the steepness of the two staircases was a bit daunting. Guests have the use of a large, pleasant parlor. Breakfast is served at individual tables in the dining room. One day we had a quiche and the second day, an Irish apple pastry; both were quite tasty. Owner Beth Flanagan is a former actress who has written a book about the Cape's B&Bs and serves on the local school board. Husband Jack is a very outgoing partner who signs notes about bathroom fixtures "Jack, the plumber." Doubles, $70 to $125.

Wedgewood Inn, 83 Main St., Yarmouth Port 02675, (508) 362-5157. A romantic getaway is offered at this black-shuttered, white inn set up on a knoll overlooking the charming village. Gerrie and Milt Graham from Darien, Conn., took over in 1985 and have kept it one of the most elegant B&Bs on this side of the Cape. All six rooms have private baths and four have working fireplaces; understandably, the inn is especially popular in autumn and winter. Furnishings are somewhat formal but not stuffy. The house, built in 1812 for a maritime lawyer, has side porches for two main-floor suites, a built-in grandfather clock in the front hall, and handsome woodwork and moldings. Pencil-post beds in the rooms, floral wallpapers, wide-board floors and such touches as tea trays brought to the rooms in the afternoon contribute toward what Gerrie describes as an "elegant country" experience. Room 1 is the largest suite; in addition to its ample, fireplaced bedroom, there are a sitting room, a large bath and a porch with wicker furniture. Room 5, second-floor rear, has both a double and a single bed and a bathroom with a clawfoot tub that guests keep wanting to purchase. Gerrie serves full breakfasts in the spacious dining room, which has black windsor-style chairs and white-clothed tables. Guests help themselves to cold cereal, yogurt, muffins and pastries from a sideboard, and then are served the main dish at their tables. French toast is clearly the favorite. Doubles, $105 to $125; suites, $135 and $145.

One Centre Street Inn, One Centre Street and Old King's Highway (Route 6A), Yarmouth Port 02675, (508) 362-8910. Stefanie and Bill Wright, brave and energetic souls with four young children, provide wonderful hospitality — and great breakfasts — in what has been one of our favorite spots since 1987. The vintage Colonial main inn emits a homespun air that makes you feel welcome the minute you come through the door. Five guest rooms are in the main inn, three with private baths and two sharing a bath; two more with private baths are offered in an old ship captain's home next door. On the October night we arrived, Stefanie put out a pot of tea and cookies in the parlor, furnished with a wicker loveseat, a comfortable sofa and a full selection of magazines and newspapers. Delicious breakfasts are served at one large table and two smaller ones by the windows in a pleasant breakfast room. On our first morning we had waffles with fresh blueberry topping and whipped cream. Quiche was the main dish the next day. The inn is about a mile from a beach with a boardwalk and guests often take the trek there to build up their morning appetite. The accommodating innkeepers will do everything from making dinner reservations to toasting a prospective bridegroom with champagne the morning of his wedding (did we have fun at that breakfast)! Doubles, $65 to $100.

Weatherly House, 36 New Boston Road, Dennis 02638, (508) 385-7458. Krista and Christopher Diego used to operate the Beechcroft Inn in Brewster, a large B&B where

The Bramble Inn is known for fine dining as well as for accommodations.

the rooms were named after flowers on the Cape. Then they had two cute little boys and left the innkeeping business to raise their family. But Krista is a born innkeeper and the Diegos have turned two special rooms in their charming 1835 home into guest facilities, each with its own bath. That on the first floor has a fishnet canopy over the queen bed, and occupants enjoy the adjoining parlor. Upstairs, tucked under the eaves, is a suite with another queensize canopied bed, a small sitting room with TV and a sunny bathroom with a yellow brick wall. The hosts live in a new addition to the rear of the house, so guests have plenty of privacy. Krista serves a full breakfast and, as a native, is helpful orienting guests to activities on the Cape. Before you leave, be sure to visit the three sheep out back. Doubles, $95.

Old Sea Pines Inn, 2553 Main St., Brewster 02631, (508) 896-6114. A total of 21 rooms — fourteen in the main house and seven in the cottage out back — are offered here on the site of a former girls' finishing school. Steve and Michelle Rowan have furnished their inn like a summer house from the 1920s and 1930s with dark wicker, Mission-style oak and often bare wood floors. Some bedrooms in the main house come with tiny front sun parlors; Bickford has its own fireplace and a wicker-filled sun room as well as a high mahogany bed. The "classroom wing" contains smaller rooms sharing three full baths for a bargain $40 a night. We like the old desk with a typewriter set up in the center. Bright floral wallpaper, a fireplace and a private bath are features of one especially large room in the cottage out back. A breakfast buffet is served in a cheery front room done up in bright blue and white. Doubles, $60 to $95.

Isaiah Clark House, 1187 Old King's Highway, Brewster 02631, (508) 896-2223. Charles DiCesare, a Swiss-trained hotelier, restored this 18th-century sea captain's house and turned it into a B&B in 1986. The rambling 21-room house has five attractive guest rooms with private baths; seven more in the Rose Cottage share. Oriental-style runners in the halls and restored wide-board floors and antiques in the bedrooms all convey elegance. A welcoming parlor has a spinet piano and a comfortable sofa and chairs set around a fireplace. Another public room on the second floor features a large color TV, books and a stereo. A first-floor room, Phoebe, has a canopied queen bed and attractive adjoining bath, as well as a wildflower rug on the floor. Terrycloth robes are hung in the closets for guests to use going from rooms to private baths across the hall. A full breakfast, served in a cozy room with a fireplace or on the patio, might include pancakes or omelets. Cranberry corn muffins are one of Charles's specialties. The five-acre property includes a Norway spruce tree planted by Captain Clark, who had brought it as a seedling on his ship in the late 1700s. Doubles, $62 to $108.

The Bramble Inn, Route 6A, Brewster 02631, (508) 896-7644. Ruth and Cliff Manchester (his parents run The Old Manse Inn just down the road) struck out on their own and purchased this well-regarded establishment some years back. Ruth is the award-winning chef (see Where to Eat) and when you book a room, be sure to make a dinner reservation. Thirteen rooms with private baths are furnished with 19th-century antiques like four-poster beds. They are located on the second floor of the main house, next door in a Greek Revival known as the 1849 House and in The Pepper House, a red Colonial just down the street. A complimentary breakfast is served buffet style in the dining room of the main inn; seasonal fruit, cereal and hot dishes are offered. Doubles, $75 to $105. Open mid-April through December.

The Inn at the Egg, 1944 Old King's Highway, Brewster 02631, (508) 896-3123. Formerly the First Parish Church parsonage, the building now called by this intriguing name is run by Diane McDonald and Joan Vergnani, former school teachers. The "Egg" is actually the small, egg-shaped park across the street, which the innkeepers are interested in keeping in good shape — they produced a cookbook to benefit the park. One of the five bedrooms has a private bath and and the others share two. The Horatio Alger suite (named for the author and preacher who once lived here) has a private entrance and a porch. One of its rooms is called the Brewster Ladies Library and has a nice bookcase to prove it; the other is called the Brewster Store after the store across the street. A large upstairs room with kingsize bed has the private bath. The innkeepers also run an interior decorating business. Doubles, $63 to $105.

The Poore House, 2311 Main St., Brewster 02631, (508) 896-2094 or (800) 233-6662. Randy Guy and Paul Anderson teamed up to run this attractively decorated B&B in what really was, at one time, the town's poor house. Then known as The Alms House, it sheltered the poor until the 1930s. Five rooms on the second floor have private baths and the smallest room, with a three-quarter bed, can be had for a bargain $39 a night. The Apricot Room, with a tomato-colored floor and a peach bathroom, and the Blue Room come with fireplaces. Randy serves a full breakfast in a large sunny parlor on the main floor from 8 to noon, a luxuriously long period. The house, bright and sunny, is reminiscent of a beach house from days gone by. Doubles, $39 to $76.

The Nauset House Inn, Beach Road, Box 774, East Orleans 02643, (508) 255-2195. Route 6A ends in Orleans, but it's just a short ride farther to this very special inn. Once here, you are within walking distance of one of the Cape's great beaches, Nauset Beach. Diane and Al Johnson and their daughter and son-in-law, Cindy and John Vessella, share innkeeping duties.They offer fourteen rooms, nine in the main weathered brown inn and five in the carriage house. All are named for flowers. Rosebud comes with its own little balcony and a private bath. Three rooms in one area share a bath, including Johnny Jump-up, a cozy single that rents for $45. Iris is an especially large room with white stucco walls and a kingsize bed. Evidence of Diane's artistic creativity is everywhere; she stencils, she paints, she decorates. Breakfast is served in one of the coziest rooms imaginable with a brick floor and beamed ceiling. We also like the large fireplaced living room and the Greenhouse, where Diane puts out hors d'oeuvre at cocktail time. Curiously, breakfast is not included in the room price, costing an additional $4.50 per person. Doubles, $55 to $95.

Nauset Knoll Motor Lodge, Beach Road, Box 642, East Orleans 02643, (508) 255-2364. Fall asleep to the sound of the distant surf at this appealing little lodge, sprawled out atop a four-acre knoll above Nauset Beach. The beach is an easy stroll away, yet beachgoers and the beach parking lot in no way present an intrusion. Within

Surf is super at beaches along Cape Cod National Seashore.

the Cape Cod National Seashore, this government-owned motel is the only one in the area on the ocean. Lounge chairs are scattered across the broad lawns, from which we enjoyed a drink as we took in the ocean view. The twelve large rooms are situated four each in three separate, residential-looking buildings with cars parked out of sight in back. Each has a picture window facing the ocean, cable TV and a tiled bath with combination tub and shower. Ice and other necessities are available inside an old Cape Cod windmill, and the resident manager makes the rounds to make sure guests are happily ensconced. Doubles, $75 to $110. Open mid-April to late October.

Nickerson State Park off Route 6A, East Brewster. This is an exceptionally nice setting for campers. Tent sites are available until mid-October and facilities include drinking water, showers, flush toilets and sewer dumping. First come, first served.

Seeing, Doing and Enjoying

What is there to do on the Cape off-season? You may be surprised by the answers: beachwalking and harbor exploring, dune climbing and shell hunting, kite flying and bird watching. There are also the more traditional sports, golf and tennis, biking and fishing and — when there's snow — cross-country skiing.

Shopping is super for gifts and gadgets, books and crafts, art and antiques, especially antiques along Route 6A. There is Provincetown, a destination in itself. And there are museums and historic sites, fun to visit when the weather is foul.

First Stop: The National Seashore.

Cape Cod National Seashore, South Wellfleet, (508) 349-3785. Cape Cod's extraordinary natural resource, its ocean beaches and environs, has been preserved as a national park, for which we're grateful. The Cape Cod National Seashore, created in the early 1960s, stretches along the outer Cape from the elbow that is Chatham to the fist that is Provincetown. The wildest beaches, the highest dunes and the oldest lighthouse on the Cape are within the limits of the national seashore. It is here that you go to see the ocean, to stand at the very end of the land, as it seems, and look out to sea.

The main information center is the **Salt Pond Visitors Center** in Eastham. Open daily year-round from 9 to 4:30 and staffed by friendly, green-uniformed rangers, the center dispenses an amazing amount of information. Inside the contemporary wood building

173

you might view a color slide display of how the Cape was formed or take in an exhibit on marine life. Special events like nature walks, movies, hikes and lectures are offered daily through October. You can pick up the official map here.

A second visitor center at **Province Lands,** closer to Provincetown, is open from April through November.

Special features of the National Seashore include:

Marconi Station Area. This fascinating interpretive shelter describes the Marconi Wireless Station, the first in the United States, from which a message was successfully sent to England in 1903. There are a high ocean outlook and, in summer, a bathing beach.

Nauset Beach. This lengthy strand, reached via Beach Road in East Orleans, is a favorite place year-round. You can walk for miles and watch the open ocean.

Coast Guard Beach. The bathhouse and other manmade facilities at this favorite bathing beach were swept away during the Blizzard of 1978. For summers since, shuttle buses have been run from a new parking lot. A shower, changing facility and rest rooms have been reconstructed at the beach. A few miles north, author Henry Beston's "outermost house" was also, sad to relate, destroyed in that storm.

Pilgrim Heights. Here are the highest dunes. People like to walk up and over them to the beach. A sign cautions correctly that it's a strenuous climb. In the same area are the Pilgrim Springs, from which the Pilgrims got their first fresh water, and Corn Hill, where they found corn hidden by Indians.

Bike Trails. The national seashore has three paved trails. Nauset Trail, 1.6 miles, reached from the Salt Pond Visitors Center, is fairly easy, and so is Head of the Meadow Trail, two miles, reached from High Head Road, Truro. The Province Lands Trail, eight miles, has steep portions and sharp curves. Reach it from Herring Cove Beach parking area or Province Lands Visitors Center.

Highland Light. The oldest lighthouse on the Cape is located on the cliff above the beach and its strong beam can be seen twenty miles at sea. Henry David Thoreau said you could stand here and put all of America behind you.

Favorite Beaches, Walks, Drives

Outside the national seashore there are other great beaches and harbors, walks and drives. We like:

The John Wing Trail, Route 6A, Brewster. This mile-long trail, adjacent to the **Cape Cod Museum of Natural History,** leads through marsh and seashore vegetation to a lovely beach. The museum itself is worth a stop. A wing opened in 1987 nearly doubled the space available for exhibits, lecture rooms and the like. The whale exhibit includes the skeleton of a minke whale washed ashore at a Chatham beach in 1978. A bird room, mineral exhibit, turtle tank and weather station are other stops at this fun place, which is especially appropriate for children. There's a good gift shop. Open Monday-Saturday 9:30 to 4:30, Sunday 12:30 to 4:30. Adults $2.50, children $1.50.

Sesuit Harbor, Dennis. A small harbor with picturesque sailboats, it has a nice stone breakwater where you can sit. Reach it via Bridge Street off Route 6A.

Rock Harbor, Orleans. Follow Rock Harbor Road to a working harbor with broad clam flats. There's something we love about this place; bring a steaming cup of coffee, sit and enjoy.

Yarmouth Port Boardwalk. Follow Centre Street from Route 6A to Homer's Dock Road to Gray's Beach. A wooden pier walkway stretches to Clay's Creek, with a lookout overlooking Bass Hole. There are tidal pools, marine holes and nesting birds to be glimpsed. We recommend this spot for a picnic.

The Boardwalk in Sandwich. Sandwich also has a great boardwalk, this one rebuilt in 1991-92 after an extraordinary storm hit the western part of the Cape. Individual planks were sponsored and bear sayings like "In Memory of Granny Dowden." Wend your way north through the center of Sandwich to find the boardwalk. Take Town Neck Road off 6A to Freeman Avenue.

Brewster's Punkhorn. In 1987, the town of Brewster acquired 800 acres of an area known affectionately as the Punkhorn, one of the last great tracts of undeveloped land on the Cape. Much of it is typical Cape woodland of pitch pine and mixed oak species, but the area is ringed by a necklace of ponds, old bogs and streams. Canoeists and fishermen can have a heyday here and hikers will note that the area was once the heart of Brewster's cranberry industry. Park at the Eagle Point Conservation area off Run Hill Road. The Brewster Conservation Department offers interpretive walks in the fall.

Getting High

The Cape is essentially flat, but you can be above it all, and in the clear air of autumn your view may be exceptional.

Scargo Hill Tower, Tobey Memorial Park, Dennis. Don't be put off by the graffiti inside this stone tower; be turned on by the view across velvet-blue Cape Cod Bay, all the way to Provincetown's distinctive Pilgrim Monument. Scargo Lake, below, is a glacial gift. In the fall, there's a good view of the foliage.

The Pilgrim Monument, Town Hill, Provincetown. From the top of this 255-foot granite tower (an easy climb) you can see, on a clear day, down the Cape's forearm and across the waters of the bay toward Plymouth.

Typical Cape Cod scene at Provincetown.

The Sporting Life

Golf. The saltwater keeps the Cape warmer than most of New England, and golfers love the long season. The **Dennis Pines Golf Course** off Route 134, run by the town, is a favorite and the 18th hole is all downhill. Call (508) 385-8347 for reservations.

Fishing for flounder, striped bass, blues and giant tuna is best from late August into November. You can surfcast from beaches, jetties, bridges or boats.

Biking is popular in the National Seashore and at **Nickerson State Park** in Brewster, which has two well-developed trails. **The Rail Trail** is a seventeen-mile bike path meandering through woods, marsh and cranberry bogs from Dennis to Eastham and the Cape Cod National Seashore. It can be reached in Brewster off Underpass Road and at Nickerson State Park. Bike rentals are available at both locations. People bike all around the Cape; try to stay off Route 6A because traffic is heavy.

Tennis courts are widely available, often adjacent to schools or town facilities.

The Inside Story

Three museums in the fascinating town of Sandwich offer the opportunity for an entire museum day.

Heritage Plantation, Grove Street off Routes 6A and 130, Sandwich, (508) 888-3300. The former estate of Charles O. Dexter is famed for its rhododendrons in spring, but there's much more. Proclaiming itself "a diversified museum of Americana," Heritage Plantation displays antique automobiles in a reproduction of the Shaker round barn at Hancock, Mass.; antique firearms and military miniatures in a military museum, and a large collection of Currier and Ives lithographs. Early tools, folk art and changing exhibits add to the experience; walking the lovely grounds and picnicking are also fun. A visit takes about three hours. Open daily 10 to 5, mid-May to mid-October. Adults $7, children $3.50.

Sandwich Glass Museum.

Yesteryears Museum, Main and River Streets, Sandwich, (508) 888-1711. A retired Army colonel and his wife collected the dolls for this museum while on tours of duty in Germany, Japan and at home. There are also dolls from France, an Edison phonograph doll of 1889 and a collection of nearly 50 dollhouses at this splendid museum, housed in a former church building. A unique group of German "Nuremburg kitchens" is fascinating. American dolls are being added all the time. The shop sells antique dolls, dollhouse furniture and other appropriate items. Open Monday-Saturday 10 to 4, mid-May through October; Wednesday-Saturday rest of year; closed in January. Adults $3, children $2.

Sandwich Glass Museum, Main Street, Sandwich, (508) 888-0251. Located in the center of the town's historic district, the glass museum of the Sandwich Historical Society houses one of the most complete and comprehensive collections of glass made by the Boston and Sandwich Glass Factory between 1825 and 1888. The priceless collection contains more than 3,000 examples. Note the extensive paperweight display and the wonderful punch bowl. Open daily, 9:30 to 4:30. Closed in January. Adults $3, children 50 cents.

Other buildings of interest are the **Sturgis Library** in the center of Barnstable, which has among its collections a rare Bible brought to America in 1634 by one of Barnstable's first ministers; the **West Parish Church of Barnstable,** the oldest Congregational church building in the country, and the **Quaker Meeting House** off Spring Hill Road in East Sandwich, which has the oldest continuous Quaker meeting in the country.

Shopping

Route 6A is wonderfully scenic as it winds along the North Shore of the Cape from Sandwich to Brewster. Golden trees arch above the road; century-old houses nestle by the side, picket-fenced and proper, their doorways hung with bittersweet or vine wreaths. Antiques shops, boutiques, crafts and gift shops all hang out their shingles and as you mosey along, you'll likely find yourself stopping again and again.

Fall is the season for antiquing. **Pflock's Antique Shop** in Brewster emphasizes copper and brass. **Kingsland Manor** is one of the most elegant places we've seen and it goes on and on. How about a scale model of the Titanic, encased in glass, for a cool $10,000? There are lots more; explore and discover your own favorites.

Parnassus Book Service in Yarmouth Port is one of a kind. Old (and a few newer) books are crowded into this big gray building at the edge of Route 6A; there's an open-air book stall at which you can browse year-round. **Titcomb's Bookshop** on Route 6A in East Sandwich is another literary emporium with atmosphere galore. A wide staircase leads to the second floor where old books are shelved in wooden bookcases. On the main floor you'll find many books on the Cape (new and used), new children's books, old magazines, cards and more. The full-service **Compass Rose** bookstore in Orleans has been expanded. Adjacent is **The Haunted Bookshop,** so-called because it is "haunted by the spirits of writers past." The books, you see, are used.

Arts and crafts are in plentiful supply along Route 6A. We like the selection at **The Lemon Tree** in Brewster, with lots of pottery and other unusual gift items. Next door, the **Cook Shop** offers all sorts of things for the kitchen, many of them European imports. The **Spectrum Galleries** in Brewster represents American artists and craftsmen and the selection is fine in almost all mediums. **Don DeVita's** art gallery is located in an interesting old town hall building.

We're not as crazy about **Sydenstricker Glass** in Brewster as, it seems, almost everyone else is. Window glass is fused together with colored paints to create unusual designs for bowls, plates, vases and paperweights.

Go to the source for some great pottery. We admire the work of Steve Kemp and his attractive shop at **Kemp Pottery** in Brewster. The stoneware, porcelain and black sand porcelain (made from Nauset Beach sand) pieces are amazingly affordable, too. We especially like the lamps. In Dennis, a visit to **Scargo Pottery** is an experience. Harry Holl and his daughters — plus a couple of apprentices — hold forth in an oriental setting deep in a pine woods. Here you'll find wall art, birdbaths, whimsical teapots and cookie jars, and exceptionally ornate birdhouses that look like castles. All are displayed beneath a roof with supports but no walls so you are one with the outdoors.

Scandinavian country antiques and accessories of exquisite taste are found at **Design Works** in Yarmouth Port.

The **Brewster General Store** remains in a time warp, although it's become a bit fancier as the years go by. Stop in for coffee and your Sunday newspaper and browse among the aisles for kids' toys, kitchen knicknacks, cocktail napkins, paper goods, corkscrews, glasses or almost anything you need or might want to give as a gift.

Choose your Halloween pumpkin at the **Tobey Farm Harvest Barn** in Dennis.

Where to Eat

The Cape's restaurants offer something for everyone. You can get a clam roll, you can dine on four-star French cuisine, and there's a lot in between. Yarmouth Port has more than its share of good restaurants and two of the best restaurants on the Cape (Chillingsworth and The Bramble Inn) are in Brewster. The restaurants are presented geographically in roughly the same order as accommodations, west to east.

Barnstable Inn and Tavern Restaurant, 3180 Main St., Barnstable, (508) 362-2355. This black-shuttered, white clapboard inn is set back from the main street with a brick courtyard in front — and dining outdoors in good weather. The dining rooms, with light wood windsor chairs and mismatched tables, are cozy and welcoming. The bar is also appealing, and a good place to have dinner and watch a football game at the same time — something we did early one Saturday evening. The menu lists appetizers like mussels in puff pastry, spinach tortellini and old-fashioned fish stew ($7 to $8).

Entrees ($10 to $20) include roast rack of lamb topped with fresh pesto and herbed pistachio crumbs, chicken parmesan served over linguini, loin lamb chops with red pepper relish and roasted garlic, and loin of pork stuffed with apples, pears and almonds and glazed with a maple mustard tomato sauce. Lunch, 11:30 to 5; dinner, 5:30 to 9 or 10; Sunday brunch.

Abbicci, 43 Main St., Yarmouth Port, (508) 362-3501. A low building just off Route 6A, formerly the Cranberry Moose, provides a sophisticated setting for a great meal. Abbicci, in Italian, is "ABC." Ancient maps of Italy have been reproduced in oversize scale on the walls of one dining room by the son of owners Marietta and Bob Hickey. San Pellegrino bottled water awaits on each white-clothed table; light windsor-style chairs give a clean, uncluttered look. There is nothing spare about the food, however, and the dinner menu is quite ambitious. Appetizers ($4.50 to $10.50) include clam or mussel soup, grilled oysters with spinach, pancetta and cream, risotto fungi (with porcini and shiitake mushrooms and parmesan cheese) and fried squid on mixed greens with a garlic, lemon and parsley vinaigrette. Pastas ($11 to $19) include capellini de mare, the most expensive, with clams, mussels, lobster, squid and fish in a light and spicy tomato sauce; spaghettini basilico, with fresh basil, pinenut and garlic pesto; linguini vongole, with Wellfleet littleneck clams, and ravioli fresca, served with a fresh tomato and basil sauce. Among entrees ($15 to $24) are calves liver, sirloin florentine (marinated in lemon, oil, garlic and herbs and served with asparagus), seafood stew, lobster fra diavolo, veal saltimbocca and a sausage grill. A fine wine list with Italian and American wines includes a few less expensive selections. Lunch daily, 11:30 to 2:30; dinner, 5 to 9; Sunday brunch.

Inaho, Main Street, Yarmouth Port, (508) 362-5522. The building that housed the former La Cipollina restaurant has become the home of a Japanese restaurant that was previously in Hyannis. The night it opened in Yarmouth Port in 1992, it was mobbed by faithful fans who crossed the Cape to check out the new incarnation. Yuji Watanabe is the chef; his American wife, Alda, handles the front of the house. The Cape Cod cottage is startlingly spare and Oriental in style inside. Sushi and sashimi are featured as entrees, but you also can find chicken, salmon and beef teriyaki, several different tempuras and shabu-shabu ($36), a dinner for two cooked in a pot at the table with thinly sliced beef, vegetables and noodles, served with a dipping sauce. Appetizers ($5 to $7) include yakitori (broiled chicken on skewers), gyoza (pan-fried dumplings) and tako-su (octopus in a light vinegar dressing). Entrees from $11 to $18 include several mixed plates (sushi, tempura, teriyaki and fruit). Dinner nightly, 5 to 10.

Jack's Outback, behind 161 Main St., Yarmouth Port, (508) 362-6690. If you don't mind a little ribbing along with your spare ribs, try this establishment, located "out back" behind a large parking lot in what appears, at first glance, to be a small A-frame house. Jack Smith, a local notable, keeps up a lively repartee with the clientele as he serves home-cooked specials for breakfast, lunch and, since 1992, dinner. The locals love it and don't seem to mind writing up their own orders, pouring their own soft drinks from a soda machine and clearing their own tables. About the only thing that is done for you is the delivery of the meal, but you're encouraged to throw a tip into the huge aluminum bowl by the cash register; when you do a cow bell is rung. Food items are written on placards and posted across the front of the restaurant. The day we stopped for lunch there were three soups — "cauliflower bisk," "minnie-stroney" and "toe mater cajun," plus several pita sandwiches ($2 to $5), including roast beef, veggie and ham. An excellent cold pasta salad made of linguini, black olives, tomatoes, ham, chicken and cheese, dressed with a vinaigrette, was $3.95. Dinners include pasta dishes, scallops, scrod and prime rib for $4.95 to $9.95. Desserts look scrumptious, but beware,

Stock is on display virtually outdoors at Scargo Pottery.

Jack can give you a hard time. "What happened to the diet?" he yelled at one woman as he was about to deliver a chocolate confection. For unsuspecting visitors things can be a bit unnerving, too. One couple, obviously not regulars, left their plates on the table when they got up to leave and Jack let them know the proper procedure in no uncertain terms. But this is a fun place for those who can get into the local spirit. Breakfast daily, 6:30 to 11:30; lunch, 11:30 to 3; dinner, Tuesday-Saturday 4:30 to 8.

Marshside Restaurant, 28 Bridge St. (near the junction of Routes 6A and 134), East Dennis, (508) 385-4010. Locals like this restaurant and we do, too. Serving three meals a day seven days a week year-round, the Marshside is ready when you are. There's service at a small L-shaped counter in a rear corner as well as at calico-clothed tables. Tiny white lights on the hanging plants add to the decor in the evening; lighting overhead is from Tiffany-style lamps. Everything from a frankfurter or a teriyaki burger to chicken florentine or shrimp scampi is available. The emphasis is on fresh seafood at rational prices. We enjoyed a dinner of broiled scallops, served with boiled red potatoes and a house salad with creamy dill dressing. Entrees cost $10 to $13, which is one reason for the restaurant's popularity. Lunch is much the same as dinner with seafood platters ($10 to $12) and salads ($6 to $10); sandwiches include a chicken salad club, a veggie melt and a California croissant (with sliced turkey, homemade guacamole, swiss cheese and sprouts) in the $5 to $7 range. Wines by the glass from a variety of vineyards supplement the wine list. Desserts include apple pie, carrot cake and mud pie. From servers to guests, everyone seems very comfortable here. Breakfast daily, 7 to 11:30; lunch, 11:30 to 5; dinner, 5 to 8 or 9.

Gina's By the Sea, 154 Taunton Ave., Dennis, (508) 385-3213. Take Taunton Avenue down toward the beach and just before you reach the water you'll find Gina's. The small white clapboard restaurant with gray shutters and blue and white awnings has been on this site for more than 50 years. The original owner, Gina, has earned her heavenly reward; Larry Riley now handles the popular little spot where no reservations are taken and some people are willing to wait up to two hours for a table. The pine-paneled bar with a few booths is decorated with baseball caps left by patrons; the interior fireplaced dining room and the enclosed sun porch are pleasant places to dine. Nightly specials such as lamb chops boursin supplement the northern Italian cuisine. Eggplant parmigiana, veal scaloppine a la milanaise, fettucine alfredo and chicken dijon are among entrees ($12 to $17). You might start with mussels marinara or shrimp cocktail. Pasta dishes include baked stuffed shells, spaghetti and ravioli for $9 to $11. Finish with Mrs. Riley's chocolate rum cake or cannoli. Lunch and dinner daily in summer; dinner, Thursday-Saturday 5:30 to 9 in spring and fall.

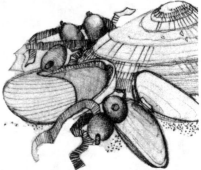

The Red Pheasant Inn, 905 Main St., Route 6A, Dennis, (508) 385-2133. People consistently praise the Red Pheasant, for the food is reliably good and the ambience great. Behind an old red Cape Cod cottage is a long addition with a new entry and two cozy dining rooms. One is a long, porch-like area with white tablecloths and hanging plants; the interior room is separated by a low partition from a waiting area with sofas and chairs placed before a fireplace. Hurricane oil lamps, wall sconces and frosted glass lights all make for subdued, intimate dining. The stuffed pheasant on the counter by the cash register is an acknowledgment, we suppose, of the restaurant's name. Chef-owner Bill Atwood Jr. features game among fall dinner entrees ($12 to $18), perhaps braised pheasant with savoy cabbage, red wine and caramelized leeks or grilled venison with chanterelles. Roast rack of lamb with a pinenut and roast garlic crust and a port and rosemary sauce is a perennial favorite. Other entrees include veal sweetbreads, tenderloin of veal wellington and grilled swordfish served with grilled polenta. For starters ($5 to $8), the signature dish is tuna pastrami, corned and smoked in-house and served with baby field greens and a green mustard-honey vinaigrette. Others include wild mushroom strudel, handcut lobster and scallop lasagna, and chilled Wellfleet oysters and littlenecks served with lime and fresh fennel. There are three seatings for the popular Thanksgiving dinner. Dinner nightly, 5 to 8:30 or 9; reduced schedule in January.

The Bramble Inn, Route 6A, Brewster, (508) 896-7644. Ruth Manchester's fame as a chef makes it imperative to have reservations at this pleasant inn, where diners are served in one of five attractive dining rooms. We especially like the small room with the single table and eight Queen Anne chairs, although Ruth says the most requested tables are on the glassed-in front porch. The entree price ($36 to $44) includes appetizer, salad and dessert. Ruth describes the food as continental and service as "fairly formal," but still likes to think of her guests as "having dinner in our home." Appetizers might be a grilled Vermont goat cheese reuben with red cabbage and maple-mustard sauce, deep-fried sage and pinenut polenta, and a country pate made with ham, pinenuts and port-macerated raisins served with cranberry-onion jam and sweet pickles. Entrees could be pan-roasted venison with a sundried cherry sauce and wild-rice pancake, seafood curry made with cod, scallops, shrimp and lobster, roast tenderloin of beef with roquefort and white wine sauce, and grilled salmon fillet served with white wine, saffron and tomato court bouillon and angel-hair pasta. Dinner nightly in summer, 6 to 9; fewer nights in spring and fall. Closed January to mid-April.

Chillingsworth, Route 6A, Brewster, (508) 896-3640. Chillingsworth is at the apex of Cape Cod restaurants. Don't be misled by the English-sounding name, though, for this is a place where French-accented cuisine reigns. The restaurant's reputation precedes its present owners, Robert "Nitzi" and Pat Rabin, who took over nearly twenty years ago after working here as apprentices. James Beard, the great gourmet, was involved in the concept, which has been refined and purified over time. In a restored 1689 house, Chillingsworth offers intimate, antiques-filled dining rooms, a greenhouse lounge and bar, a gourmet food and gift shop, and three rooms and suites for B&B guests upstairs. A harpist plays in the background as you study the menu (composed daily by Nitzi shortly before diners for the first seating arrive). He is an artist in the kitchen, serious about the quality of the food, while Pat works in the front of the house and as the pastry chef. The prix-fixe dinner ranges from $45 to $51, depending on the entree chosen. Seared salmon with sweet tomatoes, basil and orzo; tenderloin of beef with dauphinois potatoes, roasted shallots and a truffle sauce, and loin of veal with saffron risotto, garlic custard and an asparagus sauce are some of the intriguing choices. You might start with mussel bisque or chilled plum soup with port. Or how about crab cakes with cucumber julienne and lemon chive sour cream or lobster, basil and scallop mousse-filled jumbo ravioli? Chocolate nemesis with English cream has been a popular dessert for ages. Or try the plum and cinnamon tart with brandied cream or praline ice cream with chocolate sauce. A cafe menu for less formal dining in the greenhouse in the evening offers items like duck breast salad with walnut vinaigrette or grilled lamb chops with saffron risotto and beans for $11 to $19 a la carte. Cafe appetizers ($6 to $8) include grilled smoked mozzarella with prosciutto and marinated grilled shrimp with fresh fruit salsa. Lunch in summer, Wednesday-Sunday 11:30 to 2:30; dinner by reservation, Tuesday-Sunday seatings at 6 and 9; weekends only in spring and fall.

Brewster Fish House, Route 6A, Brewster, (508) 896-7867. Brothers David and Vernon Smith run this small but hugely popular spot, which they refer to as a "nonconforming restaurant." Julia Child ate here and liked it, we're told. Deep green formica-topped tables and bare wood floors are the backdrop for some inventive cuisine. Fish and nothing but fish is the order of the day, although there is the possibility of a hamburger or a chicken breast sandwich at lunchtime. "The lobster bisque is out of this world," says the hostess; fish chowder is also on the menu along with billi-bi, a mussel soup. Fried oyster and lobster salad rolls and a fish sandwich are offered. Luncheon entrees ($6 to $8) include grilled salmon with marmalade glaze, fried calamari, broiled cod with citrus butter and fish and chips. In the evening, appetizers ($3.50 to $7) could be dill and brandy-cured salmon, barbecued squid with two sauces, chilled half lobster with honey mustard and a grilled leek salad, and fried artichokes with a garlic and ginger ketchup. Entrees ($12 to $14) might be grilled sea scallops with sundried tomatoes, roast garlic and virgin olive oil, poached sole, shrimp and mussels, grilled Atlantic salmon on wilted cabbage and steamed lobster with citrus butter. Lunch daily, 11:30 to 2:30; dinner, 5 to 9. Closed Monday in the fall and open weekends only in the late fall.

Nauset Beach Club, 221 Main St., East Orleans, (508) 255-8547. Two couples, Douglas and Beth Campbell and John and Anna Salemus, have owned this restaurant since 1988. It is doing so well that in the midst of a recession they were adding a room in 1992. The addition also was to have a wood-fired oven for game and other grilled dishes. Pastas and Italian items are the rule, with entrees priced from $10 for the pizza pasta to $17 for zuppa di pesce, an assortment of shrimp, scallops and lobster in a white wine and garlic sauce with tomato provencal. Appetizers ($5 to $8) include clam cakes with sweet peppers and onions, focaccia served as a pizza rustica and a lobster tarte (chunks of lobster served atop a potato tart). Dinner nightly, 5 to 9 or 10.

FOR MORE INFORMATION: The Cape Cod Chamber of Commerce, Hyannis, (508) 362-3225, provides information but tends to boost only its members. Some towns have individual tourist organizations; write to the town of your choice.

Green Mountains and town are backdrop for Le Chateau on Middlebury College campus.

Robert Frost Country

Middlebury and the Champlain Valley, Vt.

The great poet Robert Frost spent the last 23 summers of his life in the mountains outside Middlebury. Little wonder. This gently rugged area enlivened by a college town is mountain country, Frost country, an area of rambling white houses, red barns and green fields — the essence of Vermont, if you will.

The poet who adopted New England and made it his own also adopted the Middlebury area. The small cabin where he slept is not open to the public, but there's a nearby interpretive trail where you can get a taste of his enduring poetry and the sights that inspired him. The Middlebury College library houses many of his first editions. The owner of the town's Vermont Book Shop knew the poet well and stocks many of his works. And the college's Bread Loaf mountain campus carries on his tradition with its annual summer writers' conference.

Middlebury is, for us, the epitome of the New England college town. The campus of the "college on the hill" on the west side of town is unusually picturesque, its newer gray limestone buildings complementing the older ones dating back to the college's founding in 1800. The husband of one of us first saw the campus on a snowy April day in the 1950s and decided then and there that this was to be the college for him. In summer, when the regular college is not in session, its famed Summer Language Schools turn the area into a rural United Nations as graduate students chat in almost every language except English.

The college gives the town its solid heritage and vibrant character. ("The strength of the hills is His also" are the words etched above the portals of the striking college chapel in which Robert Frost lectured to turnaway student audiences every few years.) And a returning alumnus is struck by a new dynamic — an array of restaurants and shops that is remarkable for a town its size (8,000). Except for eight annoying new traffic lights along Route 7, Middlebury somehow remains a tranquil college town.

To the east are East Middlebury and Ripton, quiet mountain hamlets, Middlebury's bucolic Bread Loaf campus and the college's impressive Snow Bowl ski area. To the west lies the Champlain Valley, a surprisingly vast and undeveloped expanse sidling up to Lake Champlain. To the north are Vergennes, which claims to be the nation's smallest city, the mountain community of Bristol and sylvan Charlotte, where mountains and lake meld in a wondrous panorama. The vistas of water and mountains are stunning, thanks to the Green Mountains on the east, the Adirondacks to the west and Lake Champlain shimmering in the middle.

This is an area of charming contrasts, one where lake and mountains, simplicity and sophistication, co-exist in peace.

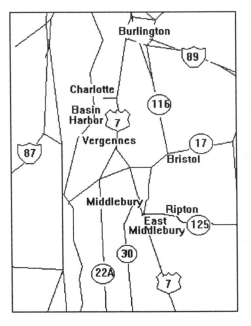

Getting There

The area is reached by U.S. Route 7 which cuts north-south through the middle, with state Routes 30 and 100 roughly paralleling to the east and west. The lake and mountains prevent direct access on an east-west axis.

Bus service is provided by Vermont Transit Co. The nearest major airport is in Burlington, 35 miles to the north.

Where to Stay

Swift House Inn, 25 Stewart Lane, Middlebury 05753, (802) 388-9925. A rambling white clapboard manse, built in 1814 and once the home of a Vermont governor, is the focal point of this exceptional, elegant inn and restaurant run by Andrea and John

Nelson. They started with nine rooms, added five more in the Gatehouse Annex and lately restored the side carriage house as the crowning touch: six deluxe rooms with fireplaces, double jacuzzis, kingsize beds, TVs and telephones. All rooms are handsomely outfitted with four-poster beds and handmade quilts, and the bathrooms are knockouts. One in the Gatehouse, done up with white wicker and purple walls, has bath pillows "so you can lie in the whirlpool tub with a good book," Andy explains. Public rooms in the inn include a wide hall used as a parlor with one of the inn's many fireplaces, a TV room and a beauty of a little cocktail lounge with five seats at the bar. Candlelight dinners are served by reservation in the inn's formal dining room (see Where to Eat). Having turned over the cooking duties to a fulltime chef, Andy has focused her attention on the lavish gardens, the fruits of which turn up in such ingenious ways as flowers in a row of baskets along the library hearth. A continental breakfast with muffins and popovers is included in the rates; more elaborate treats can be ordered from a menu. After breakfast, settle on the front porch full of wicker furniture for a look down the wide lawns toward the Adirondack mountains in the distance. Doubles, $75 to $115; carriage house, $140.

Waybury Inn, Route 125, East Middlebury 05740, (802) 388-4015 or (800) 348-1810. "The Bob Newhart Show made us famous," advertises this establishment, whose facade served as the fictional New England inn on the TV sitcom. But the inn has been attracting travelers since 1810, lately under the auspices of Middlebury restaurateurs Marty and Marcia Schuppert of Mr. Up's fame. (Marcia grew up in the inn when her parents owned it, and two of her sisters have worked here since they were youngsters. She and her husband took over the inn after it had suffered through four owners in ten years.) Away from the mainstream, the Waybury is quiet and peaceful, with a wide, shaded front porch on which to while away the hours. You can stroll up the road into the mountains or swim in a river gorge almost across the street. The fourteen guest rooms with private baths have been upgraded, some with king and queen poster beds, but are simply furnished in Vermont style. Our large room had comfy twin beds, a red velvet rocking chair, a sofa and fresh white curtains. The old-fashioned parlor harbors books, games and, the only modern touch, a small TV. Three meals a day are served in season in the dining room or rear pub (see Where to Eat). A full country breakfast is included in the rates. Doubles, $80 to $115.

Middlebury Inn, Court House Square, Box 631, Middlebury 05753, (802) 388-4961 or (800) 842-4666. This mellow red-brick inn has dominated the village square since 1827. The 45 rooms in the rambling main building have been renovated and redecorated under innkeepers Frank and Jane Emanuel, as have five in the attached Hubbard House and five more in the adjacent Porter Mansion. All have high ceilings, brass fixtures and intricate moldings as well as private baths, color TV and two telephones. The twenty rooms in a rear motel annex are large and modern, each containing a queensize sofabed for family use as well as hair dryers and coffee makers. The inn's spacious lobby, where complimentary afternoon tea is served, has nooks for reading or playing checkers. The Country Peddler gift shop offers everything from books to maple syrup. You can order cocktails and sandwiches on the screened porch in summer, or a full range of luncheon entrees in the Rose Room. The hanging ferns are strung with tiny white lights in the pillared, blue and white dining room. Dinner entrees run from $11.95 for chicken teriyaki to $17.95 for New York sirloin. Lunch, 11:30 to 2; dinner, 5:30 to 9. Doubles, $86 to $144, EP.

The Chipman Inn, Route 125, Ripton 05766, (802) 388-2390. In a real country hamlet, this expanding little inn dating from 1828 is operated by Bill Pierce and his wife, Joyce Henderson. There's lots of space to spread out — in the comfy parlor with

Exterior of Waybury Inn served as fictional inn on Bob Newhart TV show.

a big fireplace by the little bar, in a lounge full of hooked rugs, in a sitting area with magazines in the upstairs hall, and in the stenciled dining room where prix-fixe dinners are served by reservation at 7:30 for $22. The day's menu is posted with appropriate wine suggestions. The meal begins with hors d'oeuvres at 7 in the lounge; salmon mousse, marinated mushrooms and prosciutto could be the fare. Lentil or asparagus soup and salad precede the single-entree main course, perhaps loin of pork roast with rosemary and garlic or wiener schnitzel with vegetables of the day. Maple-walnut pie or chocolate pate with raspberry sauce could be the dessert. All nine guest rooms have private baths; one has a sitting room and another a skylight, and all are pleasantly furnished with antiques. Bill makes granola for the hearty breakfast, which includes a choice of egg dishes. Doubles, $93 to $108.

October Pumpkin, Route 125, Box 226, East Middlebury 05740, (802) 388-9525 or (800) 327-2007. This cheery orange and rust-colored 1850 Greek Revival house lives up to its name, but never more so than in the autumn when it's surrounded by pumpkins and cornstalks. The long rear yard backs up to an orange gazebo, near which lawn furniture is grouped around an umbrellaed table. Eileen and Charles Roeder, who used to have the Stone Mill Inn in Brandon, wanted a smaller B&B. They added pumpkin stenciling in the front hall and up the stairs leading to three guest rooms, one with private bath and two that share one with a big pink clawfoot tub. Two newer guest rooms on the first floor have sitting areas, queen beds and private baths. The house is full of character, from Eileen's quilted pieces to her husband's band boxes. Breakfast is continental, with fruit, cereals, homemade biscuits or scones and edible nasturtiums. Doubles, $50 to $75.

Brookside Meadows, Painter Road, RD 3, Box 2460, Middlebury 05753, (802) 388-6429. A gaggle of geese noisily announced our arrival at this strikingly contemporary farmhouse built in 1979 from a 19th-century design. It's nicely located in the rolling countryside three miles east of Middlebury, the Green Mountains looming in the background. Linda and Roger Cole share their family's rambling home with guests in three rooms with private baths, plus a detached two-bedroom suite. One queensize room is paneled in light barn wood; a large upstairs room with twin beds and skylights is all knotty pine. Guests enjoy a living room looking onto a brick terrace beside a small pond. A full breakfast is served at a table for six in the dining room. Doubles, $65.

Blue Spruce Motel, Route 7 South, Middlebury 05753, (802) 388-4091. A suave brochure — like that of a fancy inn — describes the best of the area's few motels, this nicely set back from the highway. Micki and Steve Paddock offer sixteen rooms in pink and blue with two double beds, a TV set on the hutch-dresser, pine furniture, two chairs and a table, shag carpeting and a vaguely Laura Ashley look. The beds bear pink sheets and two swivel reading lights are overhead. The motel contains one suite with bedroom, sitting room with a sofabed and a kitchenette renting for $85, and a couple of cabins out back, each with a double bed, for $39 a night. Doubles, $58.

Strong House Inn, 82 West Main St., Vergennes 05491, (802) 877-3337. "Park Here," says the sign directing arriving guests onto the grass in front of a thriving garden filled with corn and tomato plants. New owners have brought vitality and enthusiasm to this 1834 Federal-style house on the National Register of Historic Places, located at the west edge of town. Mary and Hugh Bargiel, transplants from Florida where both were with the Burger King headquarters, offer two suites and five rooms, all but two with private baths. Mary's handmade quilts cover the beds, which tend to king and queensize four-posters; furnishings are a mix of antiques. The Bargiels converted an attic section into a sitting room for the new second-floor Victorian suite. Samuel's Suite covers one end of the main floor and includes a fireplaced English library with TV plus a sun porch. Mary cooks dinner for house guests by reservation in the spacious dining room, where the china is color-coordinated with the teal and burgundy decor. The all-inclusive price varies from $25 to $35, depending on entree. Breakfast could be poached pears with grand marnier sauce, a four-cheese and herb quiche, croissants and sausage or bacon. Doubles, $55 to $85; suites, $95 and $120.

Basin Harbor Club, Vergennes 05491, (802) 475-2311. A friend who has traveled over much of the world says this elegant resort is the nicest, most luxurious one in which she has stayed, and generations of devoted guests over its 100 years no doubt agree. Spread out on 700 acres beside Lake Champlain with a spectacular view of the Adirondacks, the secluded resort has something for everyone. Accommodations number 40 in the two lodges and 77 in wood-paneled cottages, some with super porches overlooking the water and others with decks onto the golf course; rooms have phones but no TV. All have been redecorated over the last five years. Guests relax in brightly colored Adirondack chairs, play golf on the eighteen-hole course or tennis on five courts, swim in a large heated pool or at the waterfront, go waterskiing, and eat themselves into oblivion in the huge and fancy Lakeside dining room, or more casually at the Red Mill by the club's air strip. Dancing to a Lester Lanin quartet may top off a busy day at this many-faceted resort, where men and boys over twelve wear coats and ties in public rooms at night. There are movies, games and programs for children and teenagers; the game room has the largest dictionary we've seen. If you can't stay here, at least drop in for the lavish $16.50 luncheon buffet in the summery Ranger Room with a view of the pool. Four generations of the Beach family have run Basin Harbor since Ardelia Beach started taking in guests in her farmhouse in 1886, and they do it very well indeed. Lunch, 12:30 to 2; dinner, 7 to 9. Rates $110 to $150 per person daily by the week, AP; add ten percent for shorter stays. Open mid-June to mid-October.

Skyview Motel, Route 7, Box 1370, Ferrisburg 05456, (802) 877-3410. Set back from the highway north of Vergennes is this appealing motel of the old school. The

Basin Harbor Club lawn slopes toward Lake Champlain.

thirteen ground-level rooms offer cable TV, phones and in-room coffee. Four efficiencies are available for $8 extra. Facilities include a playground. Doubles, $46 to $54.

The Inn at Charlotte, 1188 State Park Road, Charlotte 05445, (802) 425-2934. Located just off Route 7 near the foot of Mount Philo, this started as a boutique in an old schoolhouse with the owner's living quarters behind. You'd never know it today, such is the transformation into a rambling, contemporary, chalet-style house with six guest rooms, four with private baths. Most also have private entrances via sliding doors onto a tiered rear garden around a swimming pool and tennis court. We're partial to the two rooms at the far end, one with a kingsize bed and full bath and the other with twin four-posters and a closet-size shower. Another favorite is a detached cottage with two twin beds. A thermos of Vermont spring water is in every bedroom. Besides the pool and garden area, guests enjoy a large and comfortable living room and a dining room in which owner Letty Ellinger, a caterer, serves dinner to guests by reservation (she was making delectable-smelling Chinese egg rolls at our visit). A full breakfast is served here in the morning. Doubles, $55 to $85.

Seeing and Doing

Activities range from hiking and touring the countryside to visiting museums and a state crafts center.

Hiking and Biking. The Green Mountains and the rolling Champlain Valley are a paradise for hikers and cyclists, who turn out in droves here in summer and fall. **Vermont Bicycle Touring** and **Vermont Hiking Holidays,** (802) 453-4816), busy enterprises based in Bristol, offer all kinds of bicycle and hiking tours throughout the season. You'll find countless signs identifying hiking trails, including the Long Trail, along Route 125 from Hancock through Ripton and East Middlebury. The Green Mountain National Forest maintains many of the trails. Middlebury students have their favorite waterfalls, and Bartlett Falls at Bristol was chosen by Vermont Life as the best swimming hole in Vermont.

Lakeshore Tours. For glimpses of Lake Champlain to the north and west of Middlebury, follow the rural lakeshore road, variously called Lake Road and Lake Street from Shoreham north through Bridport, Addison and Panton to Basin Harbor. You'll be surprised to discover how undeveloped such a large lake can be. About the only commercial enterprises we encountered were the Bridge Family Restaurant near Chimney Point, the Yankee Kingdom Farm Stand and Vermont's Own Products. A couple of waterfowl areas and the **D.A.R.** and **Button Bay** state parks are worthwhile stops along the way. The new **M/V Carillon,** (802) 897-5331, gives daily cruises in summer and fall on Lake Champlain from Larrabee's Point, Shoreham. **Lake Dunmore,** a small lake favored by summer cottagers and Middlebury College sailors, is another favorite destination, especially **Branbury State Park** where you can swim in Dunmore, hike to Silver Lake or the Falls of Lana, and climb Rattlesnake Point, a large rock outcrop at the southern end of Mount Moosalamoo.

Mountain Tours. A favorite mountain loop starts in East Middlebury and follows Route 116 to Bristol, a town perched on a shelf and notable for its **Lord's Prayer Rock** (the prayer is chiseled on the rock along the New Haven River just east of town). Head east on Route 17 past the entry to the Lincoln Gap (itself worth a detour) onto what's locally called the McCullogh Turnpike to the top of the **Appalachian Gap.** Continue down the east slope past **Mad River Glen** and **Sugarbush North** ski areas to Route 100 in Waitsfield. Head south through Warren to Hancock, where you turn west on Route 125 past **Texas Falls,** a beautiful little series of cascades in a chasm where Middlebury students — and their parents — cooled off in the old days before guard rails were added and swimming prohibited. At the top of the Hancock Gap is the Middlebury College Snow Bowl and, starting down the west slope, the Bread Loaf mountain campus with its old yellow wood dormitories and green Adirondack chairs scattered about the lawns. The Middlebury River alongside Route 125 below Ripton is another favorite cooling-off or picnicking spot in season. For a more spectacular option (in terms of mountain panoramas), head west through the Brandon Gap (Route 73) rather than Route 125.

Covered Bridges. Addison County possesses four of Vermont's most treasured landmarks, which are some of the best preserved in the nation. **The Pulp Mill Covered Bridge,** the oldest in the state, spans the town lines of Middlebury and Weybridge off Route 23 and the Morgan Horse Farm road. It is a two-lane bridge of three spans, one of only six remaining in the United States. Just northeast of Middlebury is the **Halpin Road Covered Bridge** above a waterfall, the highest bridge over a stream bed in Vermont. Other covered bridges are in Shoreham and Cornwall.

Robert Frost Interpretive Trail, off Route 125 between Ripton and Middlebury's Breadloaf campus. "Please take your time and leave nothing but your footprints," urges the sign at the start of this easy-to-walk, three-quarter-mile trail blazed in 1976 by the U.S. Youth Conservation Corps. Several benches are strategically placed for creative contemplation. This is a thoroughly delightful way to spend an hour or two, reading some of Frost's poems mounted on plaques en route. Meadows, woods, groves of birches and streams are traversed and identified. Frost

Robert Frost Interpretive Trail.

lived and worked within a mile of here; the fields and forests were the inspiration for his poems and mentioned in many. Nearby is the **Robert Frost Wayside Area** with picnic tables and grills in a grove of red pines that Frost pruned himself. Up a dirt road is the Homer Noble Farm, site of the cabin where Frost spent his last 23 summers. The cabin is closed to the public.

The **Vermont State Craft Center** at Frog Hollow, Mill Street just off Main Street in the center of Middlebury, (802) 388-3177. This is one of our favorite crafty places anywhere, and 150,000 visitors a year agree. With windows onto the Otter Creek falls, it's a fine showplace for sculpture and pottery. Inside the renovated mill is a 3,000-square-foot treasure trove of pottery, stained glass, pewter, quilts, pillows, wall hangings, jewelry and stuffed and wooden toys, all by Vermont artists. We managed to resist some great sculptures of dogs and bunnies ($450 to $675). We could not resist a woodcut print by artist Sabra Field, a Middlebury grad with a wonderful sense of design, and now her "Apple Tree Winter" with snowy chickadee is ensconced in our dining room. The nation's first state craft center expanded in 1991 to the Church Street Marketplace in Burlington and in 1992 to the Equinox shops in Manchester. Open free, Monday-Saturday 9:30 to 5, also Sundays 11 to 4, spring through fall.

The **Vermont Folklife Center,** 2 Court St., Middlebury, (802) 388-4964. Founded in 1984 to display the folk art and traditions of Vermont, this small but rewarding educational venture occupies the downstairs of Middlebury's historic Gamaliel Painter House. Of particular appeal to specialists, video shows and changing exhibits portray the people and places that make Vermont's folk traditions and multi-cultural heritage distinctive. The whimsical whittlings of Ed Eustace were displayed front and center at one visit and 200 years of handweaving at another. The annual Christmas "Customs of the Season" shows how various ethnic groups celebrate the holidays. Open Monday-Friday 9 to 5; also Saturday noon to 4, mid-May to mid-October.

The **Sheldon Museum,** 1 Park St., Middlebury, (802) 388-2117. Bachelor Henry Sheldon bought the brick 1829 house opposite Cannon Park and opened it as a museum in 1882, advertising it with a twenty-foot sign that read "Sheldon's Art and Archeological Museum." It was the first village museum in the country, said our guide. The place is a find, filled with all sorts of odd but interesting items like a mousetrap that kills a rodent by drowning it in a cylinder of water, a pair of shoes worn by Calvin Coolidge as a child, newspapers from the 1800s and a collection of old dentist's tools, including a primitive ether bottle. There's even a stuffed cat; it seems that Henry saved everything. Middlebury's garden clubs have created an early Victorian garden next door. The Fletcher Community History Center, a new wing connecting the museum and research center, replaced the old summer kitchen and woodshed. Open for guided tours Monday-Friday 10 to 5 and Saturday 10 to 1, June-October; Wednesday, Friday and second Sunday of each month, 1 to 4, November-May. Adults $3.50, students $3, families $7.

Middlebury College, Route 125, occupies a 1,200-acre campus on the southwest edge of Middlebury. It is notable for the consistent use of gray limestone in its buildings as well as for its summer foreign language schools. Founded in 1800, the college has evolved from the lower Old Chapel-Painter Hall row to the hillside beside Le Chateau. Now about 2,000 undergraduates are enrolled at one of the top-ranked liberal-arts colleges in the country. Hundreds of graduate students flock to the eight Summer

Adirondack Mountains and Lake Champlain are on view from picnic site atop Mount Philo.

Language Schools and the Bread Loaf School of English, where 250 writers attend the annual Bread Loaf Writers Conference, the oldest and largest in the country (Robert Frost is remembered as "the godfather of Bread Loaf"). The college library has excellent collections in its Robert Frost Room. Middlebury's $16 million **Center for the Arts** was dedicated at Homecoming '92. It's a state-of-the-art showplace for the performing arts, five galleries housing the Middlebury Museum of Art, the college's top-flight concert series and even a cafe.

Morgan Horse Farm, Weybridge Road, Weybridge (just northwest of Middlebury, past the covered bridge), (802) 388-2011. Col. Joseph Battell of Middlebury, whose name graces three college dormitories, established this farm, now managed by the University of Vermont. Most of the Morgan horses alive today can be traced to this site, where they are bred and trained. You can tour the stables on the hour, watch a slide show and observe the horses as they are trained. At the right time of day, you can even see the horses neighing and waiting for their hay, which slides down a trough into their stalls three times a day. The lush lawns include a picnic area and the 1878 barn is on the National Register of Historic Places. Open daily 9 to 4, May-October. Adults $3.50, teens $2.

Lake Champlain Maritime Museum, Basin Harbor, (802) 475-2317. This new museum is located in a complex of buildings near the Basin Harbor Club entrance. A good collection of Champlain Valley artifacts from Indian through modern times is shown in the restored 19th-century stone schoolhouse. Small boat exhibits, regional watercraft memorabilia, a working blacksmith forge and an operational boat shop are featured. Summer 1992 marked the inaugural tour of the 54-foot-long replica of the sunken gunboat Philadelphia, constructed over three years at the museum and now a traveling historical exhibit. When in port here, the 53-ton boat may be boarded for tours. Open daily 10 to 5, early May to mid-October. Adults $2, children free.

Mount Philo State Park, Mount Philo Road off Route 7, Ferrisburg, (802) 425-2390. This knob of a mountain rising from the plateau above Lake Champlain north of Vergennes offers awesome views of the lake and valley to the south. Drive up a curving road through the woods to the top, where you pay a day-use fee and park. A short walk leads to scattered picnic tables perched at mountain top's edge, great spots for a midday snack on an Indian summer day. A telescope atop a rocky outcropping brings distant panoramas up close. Sixteen tent campsites and three lean-tos are hidden away in the woods for those who wish to spend the night. Day-use fee, $1.50 each.

Vermont Wildflower Farm, Route 7, Charlotte, (802) 425-3500. Flowered pathways through six acres of field and forest at the largest wildflower seed center in the East are good for an hour's walk. Interpretive markers along the pathways explain legends and uses of the flowers. A fifteen-minute multi-media show set to music focuses on the changing seasons. The modern split-level gift shop has wildflower seeds and sachets, dried and silk flower arrangements, vases and books. Open daily 10 to 5, April-October. Adults $2, children free.

Shopping

The compact center of Middlebury is still a downtown, claiming a Ben Franklin variety store, an old-line Lazarus department store and a movie theater. The biggest store in town, appropriatelty, is the **Skihaus,** a growing enterprise that expanded into another building in 1992 at the corner of Main and Merchants Row. Two Rossignol skis are the handles on the doors to this institution run by two couples, all of whom are Middlebury graduates. Inside in a ramble of rooms on two floors you'll find summer and winter clothes, Hawaiian dresses, Austrian boiled wool jackets, cuddly Lanz nightgowns, boots for all reasons, jewelry, gifts and, of course, skiwear. They even have Lederhosen. Skihaus is the biggest single customer of **Geiger of Austria,**, whose factory is located off Route 7 on Exchange Street just north of town and where an outlet center for remainders and odd lots was about to open at our visit.

One of our favorite bookstores anywhere is the neatly jumbled **Vermont Book Store,** whose owner knew Robert Frost. It has one of the country's largest collections of Robert Frost works, including out-of-print collector's items. Also along Main Street you'll find women's sportswear at **Daffodil,** funky women's clothes at **Wild Mountain Thyme** and vintage apparel and antique jewelry at **BeJewelled.** Aromas of soaps emerge from **Teasel,** a good lingerie and bath store.

Most of the rest of the shopping action is in restored mill buildings around Frog Hollow, site of the Vermont State Craft Center. In the Star Mill, **Charlotte's Collections** carries quilts, fabrics and yarns. **Sweet Cecily** stocks great cow pottery, cow placemats and painted cabinets among its folk art and fine crafts. **Twigs** specializes in folk art antiques and found objects. **Great Falls Collection** (up a staircase beside the Otter Creek falls) has unusual jewelry, home accessories and nature and garden items. **Red Onion Clothiers** offers fashionable apparel. From here a 276-foot pedestrian bridge across Otter Creek yields a view of the falls and connects with the new **Marble Works,** a collection of specialty stores and businesses in old white marble factory buildings.

Featured are the **Vermont Only Gift Shop,** a branch of the Vermont Only Village Store in Granville, and the new showroom for **Danforth Pewterers,** where we ogled all the pewter products from thousands of buttons for $1.60 to dinner plates for $72. A dolphin on a corded necklace for $12 caught our eye. A must stop farther on in the Danforth Pewter factory complex at 52 Seymour St. is Woody Jackson's **Holy Cow,** where the artist's trademark cows are the motif on everything from golf balls to light switches, bookmarks to tablecloths. Here are many of the items available in his clever "cowtalogue" and then some.

Stop for a beer at the fledgling **Otter Creek Brewery,** 74 Exchange St., where tours are given Fridays from 4:30 to 6 and, we're told, the brews are quite good.

In Vergennes, the Kennedy Brothers Factory Store, billed as the largest gift shop in Vermont, expanded in 1987 with the opening of the **Kennedy Brothers Factory Marketplace.** Vermont products are displayed on three floors of what was once the Kennedy Brothers woodenware factory. Craftsmen offer their wares direct to the customer on the first floor, and antiques shops are scattered about other floors.

The **Dakin Farm** along Route 7 in Ferrisburg is known nationwide for fine cob-smoked ham, bacon, Vermont cheddar cheese and maple products. Maple frozen yogurt was available at our latest visit.

Where to Eat

Cafe Chatillon, Frog Hollow Mill, Middlebury, (802) 388-1040. This is the worthy successor to the late Otter Creek Cafe, which had provided one of our best dinners ever. Mary and Alec Abt, peripatetic restaurateurs who wanted a place of their own, settled on this as a culinary landmark and on Middlebury as a good community in which to raise a family. They warmed up what they considered a stark mill ambience with sand tones, white linens and accents of copper utensils in a bow window beside the outdoor deck overlooking Otter Creek. It's an engaging setting for their ever-changing fare. Dinner choices ($12 to $17) include grilled shrimp with blackberry-champagne-leek sauce, escalopes of veal with a roquefort cheese and pistachio sauce, and leg of lamb with feta cheese and roasted red pepper polenta. For starters, how about chevre

Outdoor table beside Otter Creek at Cafe Chatillon.

and nasturtium soup or tuna nicoise with green beans, new potatoes and capers? Little pots of herbs were the table centerpieces at our outdoor lunch one September day, when we sampled a delicious chevre and fresh herb soup ($1.75), country pate on French bread with onion-mustard sauce ($6.25) and grilled shrimp over black pepper pasta with tamari dressing, artistically arranged on a bed of baby lettuce leaves ($6.75). Cappuccino mousse, chocolate pot au creme and blackberry cobbler are favorite desserts. The wine list is well chosen and affordable. Lunch, Thursday-Saturday 11:30 to 3:30; dinner, Tuesday-Saturday 5:30 to 9.

Swift House Inn, 25 Stewart Lane, Middlebury, (802) 388-9925. Candlelight dinners are served by reservation in the inn's serene, gracious dining rooms. Chef Amy Parks, a Culinary Institute of America graduate, changes her menu frequently. Dinner might start with tomato and lobster bisque, smoked rainbow trout or sesame-toasted goat cheese and belgian endive salad. The ten or so entree choices ($12.50 to $18.50) could be grilled yellowfin tuna with walnut-basil pesto, grilled breast of duck on peppered tomato coulis, sauteed medallions of veal layered with brie and walnuts in a red wine sauce, or roasted rack of lamb with honey mustard. Even the lowly chicken, sauteed with eggplant, roasted peppers, onions and herbs, turns everyday dining here into a special occasion. Pastries like blueberry crumb tart and hot peach tart on a pool of caramel sauce head the dessert list, which comes with a roster of international coffees and fancy after-dinner drinks. Dinner, Thursday-Monday 5:30 to 9:30.

Woody's, 5 Bakery Lane, Middlebury, (802) 388-4182. The interior of this contemporary, multi-level restaurant with enormous windows looks like a cross between a diner and an ocean liner, its decks overlooking Otter Creek. Decor is art deco in burnt orange, black and stainless steel, the colors repeated on the covers of the various menus. Run by Woody Danforth, formerly of Mary's in nearby Bristol and the Ritz-Carlton in Boston, the place is California casual. Vegetable egg roll, caesar salad with shrimp and crabmeat, hummus salad with warm pita bread and grilled smoked chicken sandwich with french fries might be the lunchtime fare in the $2.25 to $6 range. At night, start with Woody's seafood sausage, sliced and sauteed with fresh salsa beurre blanc. Then proceed to a main course ($10.50 to $16.95) like sea scallops provencal with fettuccine, Atlantic salmon with pesto aioli, charbroiled mahi-mahi, tenderloin of beef au poivre or leg of Vermont lamb with roasted eggplant salad. Eating outside on the curved wraparound deck, right above the creek, is something like being on a cruise ship. Lunch, Monday-Saturday 11:30 to 3; dinner, 5 to 9:30; Sunday brunch, 10:30 to 3.

The Dog Team, Dog Team Road, Middlebury (three miles north off Route 7), (802) 388-7651. Generations of starving Middlebury students have been filling their little tummies here, including our aforementioned husband who used to O.D. on the sticky buns when his visiting parents treated him to a meal out. Built in the early 1930s by Sir Wilfred and Lady Grenfell, it was operated by the Grenfell Mission as an outlet for handicrafts from Labrador. Two new partners have maintained the tradition of the Joy family, longtime owners of the restaurant. It's a wonder to us how they can still serve such huge amounts of food for the price (starting at $9.75 for fried chicken with fritters and going to $15.95 for boneless sirloin — including soups, salads, buckets of relishes and vegetables served family style). The Dog Team takes no reservations, but if there's a wait, which is likely, you can enjoy the living room with its gift shop and collections of memorabilia, read a magazine on one of the stuffed sofas or wander into the large cocktail lounge where dips and chips are served with drinks. Off the bar is a pleasant, two-level deck overlooking the ubiquitous Otter Creek. You order your entree from the blackboard menu as you enter, then when you're called into the charming dining room, you eat (and eat and eat). One of us feels that far too much food is served, but the other generally is up to the challenge. Lunch, July-foliage 11:30 to 2; dinner year-round, Monday-Saturday 5 to 9, Sunday noon to 9.

Mister Up's, Bakery Lane, Middlebury, (802) 388-6724. This is a favorite with today's college students, who revel in its mix-and-match menu as well as its mix-and-match atmosphere. Try to eat here on a mild noon or evening when you can enjoy the enormous, tree-shaded deck with its ice-cream parlor chairs, right beside tumbling Otter Creek — a smashing setting. The inside is nice, too, with old brick walls and dining on several levels. The large menu embraces lots of snacky items as well as full meals, or you can just go through the salad bar (which contains sprouts, sunflower seeds and cherry tomatoes as well as about 101 other things) for $6.50, including bread. Dinner entrees run from $10.25 for basil linguini with summer vegetables and two pestos to $14.95 for Norwegian salmon. There are fajitas, a dynamite California chicken sandwich for $4.95, lobster and salmon cakes and Mediterranean grilled lamb. A Sunday buffet brunch for $8.95 is served from 11 to 2. Open daily, 11:30 to 10.

Fire & Ice, 26 Seymour St., Middlebury, (802) 388-7166. Opened by Middlebury graduates in 1974 and greatly expanded lately, Fire & Ice is a handsome establishment with all kinds of lamps and accents of copper (lanterns in copper niches on the walls and a huge copper dome in the ceiling). The rambling, candlelit dining rooms with nooks and crannies offer a mix of assertive entrees, among them spicy peanut chicken, Chinese ginger shrimp stir-fry, duckling three ways and filet mignon stuffed with oysters and smothered with melted blue cheese. Entrees run from $11.40 to $17.50. The stir-fries are famous, as is the shrimp and seafood salad bar, which includes all the shrimp you can eat. The Sunday salad bar adds crab legs. The restaurant's name comes from the title of a Robert Frost poem; the fire reflects the cooking and the ice the drink mixing that goes on here. Lunch daily except Monday, 11:30 to 4; dinner, 4 to 9:30 or 10, Sunday 11:30 to 9.

Emperor's Garden, Building 15, Marble Works, Middlebury, (802) 388-3020. Family-style Chinese cuisine in the Hunan, Szechuan and Mandarin styles is served amid a jungle of greenery in this spacious newcomer in the Marble Works complex. Plants thrive in the light from big windows and soften the sleek red and black decor. Order by the numbers; there are more than 100 choices from chop suey to shrimp with black bean sauce, from tangerine beef to Szechuan crispy pork, most priced for collegiate pocketbooks from $7.25 to $14.50 (for the sizzling seafood delight). A complete family dinner for two or more starts at $25.75. Combination meals are $6.25 at lunchtime. Lunch, Monday-Saturday 11:30 to 3; dinner, 3 to 9:30 or 10:30, Sunday 2 to 9:30.

The Vermont Country Kitchen, 3 Park St., Middlebury, (802) 388-8646. This is one of those great specialty-food and kitchen shops with a good deli and bakery that's bound to succeed in a college town. And succeeding it is, since Cathy Nief installed a few tables for eating inside or out. You can breakfast on morning glory muffins or bagels and cappuccino or caffe latte. The lunch menu adds tarragon chicken salad with sprouts, Vermont flatbread pizza and oversize sandwiches ($4.50 to $4.95), one combining Vermont apples, brie, chutney and toasted almonds. There are good soups and desserts as well. Don't miss the excellent kitchen shop adjacent. Open Monday-Friday 7:30 to 6, Saturday 9 to 6, Sunday 11 to 5.

The Otter Creek Bakery, 1 College St., Middlebury, (802) 388-3371. Ben and Sarah Wood patterned their original cafe and bakery in Frog Hollow Mill on the models they know in San Francisco. Problem was that Sarah's bakery became the tail that wagged the dog and Ben closed the cafe (the space since taken over by Cafe Chatillon) to concentrate on the growing bakery business up the street. Here the baked goods are sensational as ever, and the Woods have garnered quite a following for their mail-order cookies and dough (chunky peanut butter, maple-oatmeal-raisin and lemon-pecan among them). Now they're doing a land-office takeout business with sandwiches (we liked the Otter Creek pate and the Norwegian smoked salmon) in the $3.50 to $4.95 range. They also have a few soups, salads and pizzas to go. Open Monday-Saturday 7 to 6, Sunday 8 to noon.

Waybury Inn, Route 125, East Middlebury 05740, (802) 388-4015. Dinner and Sunday brunch are served in the pink and green dining room or on the enclosed porch of the inn pictured on the Bob Newhart Show. A pub menu is served in the Pub and Club Room out back, dark and cozy as can be. We've been going for years just for the London broil with the best mushroom sauce ever, but that specialty was missing from the menu the last time we stopped. Worthy substitutes, we understand, are poached or grilled salmon with dill hollandaise, grilled tuna with a roasted red bell pepper and garlic coulis, roasted Long Island duckling, steak au poivre, rack of lamb, lake trout stuffed with crabmeat, broiled Norwegian salmon, prime rib and steak au poivre ($12.95 to $15.95). The Waybury parfait and mousse, chocolate truffle cake and walnut torte are popular desserts. The dining room menu also includes lighter fare, and the pub menu is nicely priced from $4.50 to $6.95. Lunch seasonally; dinner nightly, 5 to 9; Sunday brunch, 11 to 2.

Mary's, 11 Main St., Bristol, (802) 453-2432. For a small and rather quirky place, Mary's has one of the more interesting menus and wine lists around and a following that drives for miles. There are different flowered cloths on every table, old kitchen chairs, six seats for lunch at a corner bar and interesting art on the walls (we liked an early painting of cows by Woody Johnson). An array of plants is overhead at the window table, where we sat for a recent lunch. The black bean soup with ham chunks and avocado cream on top was most hearty; a special of pasta with chicken, asparagus and sundried tomatoes ($8.50) delicious. A plate of chocolate-chip cookies and brownies to share was $2. Prices are reasonable for lunch or brunch and at night, when you can get light dinners for $7.50 to $9.75 and entrees from $13.50 for bluefish dijonnaise to $22 for Vermont pheasant — sliced breast and roasted leg served on a sauce of sundried cherries, chanterelles and applejack brandy. Chef Douglas Mack has a way with appetizers (country pate with mango chutney or smoked bluefish and lobster cheesecake), a renowned lamb and eggplant curry, and nightly specials for $10. Desserts like bananas foster, key lime pie, fresh raspberry and chambord mousse crepe and Vermont pecan pie are to die for. Doug and partner Linda Harmon are carrying on just fine the tradition started by Mary Bolton and Woody Danforth. At our latest visit, Doug was about to write his much-requested cookbook and lunches were to be temporarily cancelled. Lunch, 11:30 to 3; dinner, 5 to 9:30; Sunday brunch, 10:30 to 3. Closed Mondays.

Main Street Bistro, 253 Main St., Vergennes, (802) 877-3288. An ex-video store was transformed in 1992 into a nifty little bistro with red checkered cloths on the tables and plates and pictures on the walls of the two small dining rooms. Owners are Charles Kreiser, the chef who ran the esteemed Charles Restaurant for years in Saratoga Springs, and priest-turned-social-worker Tom Turley. Their handwritten menu keeps things classic, simple, honest and cheap. For appetizers, you might find chicken liver pate, cold poached bluefish and garden salad. The half-dozen entrees ($10.50 to $13.50) could be crepes, fillet of sole and New York sirloin. Among desserts are frozen mousses, creme caramel and hazelnut torte. Dinner, Monday-Saturday from 5. No smoking.

Vermont Pasta, 5 North Green St., Vergennes, (802) 877-3413. This offshoot of a popular Burlington eatery of the same name took over the space occupied on-again, off-again by Painter's Tavern in the 1793 Stevens House facing the village green. Vermont Pasta reconfigured the space into tables beside the windows and cozy booths near the bar. They added grilled pizzas, salads and sandwiches to the extensive roster of pastas "from around the planet," producing an appealing all-day menu. Pastas start at $4.95 for the Russian peasant version (simmered with vodka in a sour cream, caper and tomato sauce) and top off at $11.95 for grilled sirloin served with pasta ruffles. New Delhi chicken, Thai shrimp and San Francisco cioppino are served over pastas. Grilled tortilla omelets and huevos rancheros are on the docket at brunch. Open daily, 11:30 to 9 or 10; Sunday brunch, 11:30 to 3.

FOR MORE INFORMATION: Addison County Chamber of Commerce, 2 Court St., Middlebury 05753, (802) 388-7951.

Autumn scene in Northwest Connecticut.

A Country Sampler

Connecticut's Northwest Corner

"The Hidden Corner," New York magazine once called it, touting the virtues of the Northwest Corner as a place for city people to make their second homes.

And hidden it is, this rural panoply called the Northwest Corner by its residents and the legions of Sunday drivers who have headed here for years from across Connecticut and adjacent New York.

Less than two hours' drive northeast of New York City are the Litchfield Hills, which seem to have a corner on the state's hidden treasures. Here is an unspoiled countryside with more state parks and public lands than in any other area in Southern New England.

Much of the land not in the public domain is owned by wealthy residents and visiting New Yorkers, who have made this their weekend retreat or second home. World traveler Eugene Fodor settled outside Litchfield, the late artist-author Eric Sloane lived in Warren, playwright Arthur Miller and actor Dustin Hoffman live in Roxbury, writer Harrison Salisbury and actress Meryl Streep in Salisbury, Henry Kissinger in Kent, actress Susan St. James in Litchfield, designers Bill Blass in New Preston and Diane Von Furstenberg in New Milford, and politician James Buckley and opera singer Placido Domingo in Sharon.

The state parks and forests are relatively uncrowded and so are many of the inns, restaurants and shops that are supported by weekenders. This is a place for those who cherish nature, quiet times and a subdued sophistication — a condition somewhat removed from the neighboring Berkshires.

As in Vermont, cows outnumber people, and more deer are claimed by cars than by hunters. Litchfield County's 150,000 residents represent less than five percent of Connecticut's population but are spread across twenty percent of its land area. No town besides industrial Torrington and Winsted has more than a few thousand people.

What the truly rural Northwest Corner has most of, simply, are trees. They line the roads and hillsides and, while you'll see plenty of fall foliage up close, the longer vistas from roadsides and hilltops are infrequent and worth lingering over.

The foliage is best from Kent north and Norfolk west, according to partisans of the far Northwest Corner. The sugar and red maples and hickories present dazzling displays amid the evergreens. Bright red barns dot the landscape, and orange pumpkins grace the doorsteps of almost every Colonial home and farmhouse. Against the blues of the lakes and skies on a crisp autumn day is painted a veritable rainbow of color.

Northwest Connecticut doesn't shout its assets. You'll find few of the kinds of major attractions that beckon visitors elsewhere in New England. The area simply presents itself, quietly and quaintly, for anyone to enjoy.

The Northwest Corner is many things and many places, far too many to cover here or in one fall weekend. It's the estates of gentlemen farmers in Sharon and Norfolk, the remains of the early iron industry in Salisbury, the covered bridges and country stores along the Housatonic River, the Alpine inns around Lake Waramaug, the Indian ties of old Washington, the historic firsts of Litchfield, and the quaintness of Riverton.

It's country fairs and flea markets, the Appalachian Trail, the sports-car races at Lime Rock, whitewater canoeing and camping in state forests. It's picnicking atop Mohawk Mountain, visiting a working forest or winery, strolling through the living history of Litchfield, watching Hitchcock chairs being made. And, of course, viewing the fall foliage in all its glory.

Be advised that the Northwest Corner is rather spread out — a collection of "pockets" that extend about 25 miles from end to end. Because even the residents don't often go between them, we've dealt with each pocket individually. The whole makes up a patchwork country sampler.

Getting There

For a region so close to metropolitan areas, the Northwest Corner seems a bit inaccessible — which is fine with the natives. The only four-lane highway in the region is north-south Route 8 from Waterbury through Torrington and Winsted. Route 7 also cuts north-south; Routes 44 and 4 are main east-west roads. All are winding, two-lane highways connected by county and town roads.

Bonanza Bus Lines serves western communities on a north-south axis along Route 7. Amtrak trains serve Danbury and Hartford from New York.

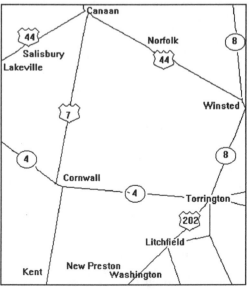

Sharon, Salisbury and the Cornwalls

The homes are larger, the shops swankier and the restaurants more expensive the farther you delve into the Northwest Corner. In this northwesternmost area, the Hotchkiss and Salisbury preparatory schools and cultural attractions have drawn residents and weekenders for the good life.

Just a few miles away is Cornwall, considered by some the most photogenic of Northwest Corner towns. Each of its sparsely populated hamlets grew separately among the hills along the Housatonic River. Skiers bound for Mohawk Mountain pass near charming Cornwall Center, unaware of its existence. The covered bridge at West Cornwall is a focus for river explorations.

Sharon epitomizes the region's quiet affluence. Historic estates line Route 41 south of town; some are the homes of the Buckley family and other "Tories" from Revolutionary days. More than 300 houses are a century or more old, giving the town a Yankee aristocratic flavor. The Clock Tower heads the long village green, where the marker says the land is "still much as it was laid out in the wilderness in 1739."

Northeast Audubon Center, Route 4, Sharon, (203) 364-0520. This is one of five national Audubon centers in the country. It's as marvelous for its abundant trees and pristine lakes as it is for wildlife (Canada geese, deer, beavers, otters and an occasional bear). A typically large old summer place houses a fine interpretive museum, a good shop and varied workshops. But "most visitors come to walk and to learn about the land and its inhabitants," reports the director. Half of the 684 acres form a natural sanctuary; the other half contain most of the eleven miles of self-guiding trails, two ponds and an herb garden. Center open daily 9 to 5, Sunday 1 to 5; trails open dawn to dusk. Adults $4, children $2.

Foliage Tours. Mount Riga is the generic name for a series of peaks stretching northwest from Salisbury to the Connecticut-Massachusetts-New York junction. Here you can hike the Appalachian Trail, swim or camp at South Pond, visit a restored stone iron furnace, climb Bald Peak or Bear Mountain, or drive (on dirt roads) across the scenic heights of Connecticut's highest area to Mount Washington in the Berkshires. The state and Mount Riga Inc., an association of 90 old-line Salisbury families who summer there, own most of the land, which you reach from Washinee Street, west of Route 44 at the Salisbury Town Hall.

Twin Lakes, just northeast of Salisbury off Route 44, is one of the most scenic places imaginable and one we've often passed without realizing it was there. Mount Riga and Canaan Mountain are backdrops for these two beautiful lakes dotted with homes and, on the east side off Twin Lakes Road, a public beach and boating area. A drive along Between-the-Lakes Road or an afternoon boat ride are good ways to enjoy the foliage.

Cathedral Pines, a centuries-old stand of gigantic pines near the foot of the Mohawk Mt. ski area, was reduced almost to rubble by a tornado. Drive along winding Essex Hill Road from the ski area access road to see the devastation, just as nature left it. You come out of the spiked forest into an open field where cows graze; just beyond is Marvelwood School and Cornwall Center. An historic marker instructs that writer Mark Van Doren "enriched many lives from his Cornwall home."

Mohawk State Forest atop 1,683-foot Mohawk Mountain is perfect for foliage viewing. Drive in from Route 4, past a couple of scenic overlooks with sweeping vistas to the west. About two and a half miles in is a wooden observation tower with 35 steep steps, which you can climb for a panoramic view in all directions.

River Expeditions. Increasingly popular pastimes on the Housatonic River are canoeing, kayaking and rafting, both whitewater and flatwater varieties. On weekends from March through October, more than 400 canoes and kayaks have been counted in

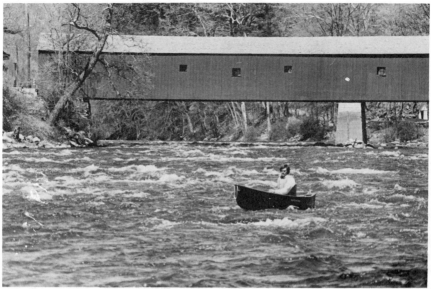

Riding the rapids near covered bridge in West Cornwall.

the 45-mile stretch from Sheffield, Mass., south to Kent — most concentrated in the twelve miles between Falls Village and Cornwall Bridge. Mark Clarke of Clarke Outdoors on Route 7 in West Cornwall, one mile south of the covered bridge, says there's no better way to view the foliage than from a canoe going down the river. Many canoeists take picnic lunches; family outings are popular, and you can get instruction, hire guides and obtain shuttle service back to your car. The standard trip takes three or four hours and canoes or kayaks can be rented by the day. Similar services are offered by Riverrunning Expeditions Ltd., Main Street, Falls Village.

Cornwall Bridge Pottery, Route 7, one-half mile south of Cornwall Bridge, (203) 672-6545. Todd Piker, the noted potter here, is helped by apprentices from everywhere. The showroom is lined with functional but beautiful and honest pottery, from tiny creamers to lamps and pots that seem too big to use for anything. Many are decorated with birds and fish. Early American, English Country and T'zu Chou are inspirations for Piker, who studied in England with the late Michael Cardew. The pottery behind his home is open daily from 9 to 5; his retail store in West Cornwall is open daily except Tuesday 10:30 to 5:30. Upstairs above the retail store is the new **Covered Bridge Gallery,** a large space leased to thirteen craftsmen in a manner similar to an antiques center. We admired the carved birds of Woodbury artist Richard Morgan, especially a tall sandhill crane and a blue heron for $55 each.

Lime Rock Park, Route 112 in Lime Rock, is billed as "the road racing center of the East," staging sports car races on summer holidays and other weekends through September. The track weaves through 350 acres around grassy knolls on a plateau beneath the hills. Actor Paul Newman has been known to race here. If that and the scenery aren't enough, there often are hot-air balloons and radio-controlled model airplanes doing their thing.

Music Mountain, off Route 7, Falls Village (Box 303, Lakeville 06039), (203) 496-2596 or 824-7126. Founded in 1930, this is the oldest continuous chamber music festival in the United States. Various string quartets from around the world present weekend concerts in the 335-seat Gordon Hall at 8 p.m. some Saturdays and 3 p.m.

Sundays from June through August. Jazz and baroque concerts are staged on other Saturdays at 8. Tickets, $15.

Room and Board

White Hart Inn, The Village Green, Box 385, Salisbury 06068, (203) 435-0030. A wide white porch full of wicker and chintz fronts the venerable White Hart Inn, several times abandoned and now handsomely restored by Terry and Juliet Moore, owners of the Old Mill restaurant in nearby South Egremont, Mass. Given their track record, we knew the food would be first-rate, but the overnight accommodations turned out first-rate as well. The Moores reduced the original 33 rooms to 26, all with private baths. Three are suites, six contain two double beds and most of the rest have queensize canopy four-poster beds. Mahogany reproduction furniture, TV sets in armoires and vivid floral wallpapers with matching comforters are the rule. The main-floor public rooms are showplaces, particularly the clubby Hunt Room with a library, bar and piano. The convivial **Tap Room,** where an excellent bistro menu is available at dinner with entrees in the $11 to $14 range, is full of dark wood. Breakfast and lunch are offered in the airy **Garden Room,** where upholstered rattan chairs flank white faux-marble tables. A friend of the Moores did the paintings of fruits and vegetables that grace the walls of **Julie's New American Sea Grille,** the serene and elegant main dining room with sponged walls of peach over green. Chef Kevin Schmitz presents changing entrees ($17 to $23) like sauteed scallops on garlic tagliatelle, grilled fillet of salmon with spaghetti cucumber, breast of duck with fresh figs and peppercorns, and grilled leg of lamb with white bean salad. Start with a tuna sashimi spring roll or beef carpaccio with arugula and parmesan, or sides of garlic potato chips or shoestring fried zucchini. Finish with a chocolate truffle macadamia torte, frozen key lime pie or a trio of homemade sorbets with chocolate-dipped cookies. The cuisine here is equal to the setting. Doubles, $110 to $160, EP; suites, $190, EP. Lunch in Garden Court, daily 11:30 to 2:30, all day on weekends; dinner in tavern, 5 to 9:30 or 10:30; Grill, dinner, Wednesday-Sunday 5:30 to 9 or 10, nightly in summer; Sunday brunch, 10 to 2.

Ragamont Inn, Route 44, Salisbury 06068, (203) 435-2372. The cooking of Swiss chef-owner Rolf Schenkel is highly rated locally. Choose one of his continental specialities from the blackboard menu, including osso buco, sauerbraten, stuffed veal breast, broiled swordfish and rack of lamb. Entrees are $13.75 to $18.50 at dinner, in the $8 to $10.50 range at lunch. Seasonal berry pies are usually on the menu, as is the chef's buttery linzer torte. One summery dining room, with green forests painted on the walls, opens onto a large covered patio; the other is a more traditional, Colonial-style room with a fireplace. Breakfast is served to overnight guests only. The inn's eight guest rooms, six with private bath, range from small singles to a suite with a fireplaced living room and have been redecorated in the last few years. The inn has a small bar on the main level, plus a living room with TV for guests. In a building out back are three modern units with kingsize beds and color TV. Doubles, $75 to $105. Lunch, Saturday and Sunday noon to 2; dinner, Wednesday-Sunday 5:30 to 9. Closed November-April. No credit cards.

Interlaken Inn, Route 112, Lakeville 06039, (203) 435-9878 or (800) 222-2909. Built in 1973, this modern resort and conference center is situated around the corner from the Hotchkiss School between Long Pond and Lake Wononskopomuc (pronounce that! — accent second syllable), which give the inn and village their names. Guests may take out a canoe or rowboat or swim in the lovely clear lake; there's also a large heated pool. The main inn is contemporary with a slate floor and leather sofas in the lobby; the 55 deluxe motel-style rooms are crisply decorated. Sunnyside, a shingled rear building which is all that is left of the original New England inn on the site, has ten rooms with brass beds and fine antiques. Contemporary buildings contain eight townhouse suites, each with fireplace, dining area, kitchen and one and a half baths. Tennis, a sauna, a game room and golf privileges at Hotchkiss's nine-hole course are available. Breakfast is served buffet-style. At dinner, continental entrees ($13.95 to $19.95) are served in the stylish **Vineyard** dining room, with its wildly colorful purple chairs, orange napkins and large ficus trees strung with tiny white lights. In season, lunch and dinner are served outside near the pool on a deck with wrought-iron furniture, globe lights and a yellow and white awning. The lounge offers dancing at night. Doubles, $105 to $160, EP; suites, $250, EP.

Hilltop Haven Bed & Breakfast, 175 Dibble Hill Road, West Cornwall 06796, (203) 672-6871. For a romantic getaway on top of the world, escape to this charmer on 64 acres almost 800 feet straight above the Housatonic River. Everett Dorn, a former Navy budget analyst whose parents built this as their summer home, offers two comfortable, paneled bedrooms with private baths. The common facilities make this exceptional: a huge, cathedral-ceilinged library with walls and floors of fieldstone and windows on three sides; a living room with grand piano, TV and another fireplace; a sun porch, and a wraparound stone veranda from which you can see New York's Catskill Mountains. Everett, who occupies a cabin on the property, puts out decanters of sherry at night and prepares a lavish breakfast of shrimp and cheese strata or grand marnier french toast. This is a much lived-in home, reflecting the furnishings and tastes of the owner's late parents. Doubles, $95.

Iron Masters Motor Inne, Route 44, Lakeville 06039, (203) 435-9844. This attractive 26-unit motel is set back from the highway over the old Davis Ore Mine. Each carpeted unit has two double beds and all rooms have been refurbished with Ethan Allen furniture, Waverly fabrics and new bathroom fixtures. The stone fireplace in the lobby dates to the 18th century and is usually ablaze for a complimentary continental-plus breakfast, which is served at tables nearby. Guests enjoy swimming in a pool in a nicely landscaped garden area. Owner Hal Meredith is well versed in the area's history and guides guests to hiking trails nearby. Doubles, $110 to $130.

Carriages, Route 44, Lakeville, (203) 435-8892. The new theme restaurant in a onetime miner's cottage at the Iron Masters Motor Inne has been called an adult McDonald's by the irreverent. Even they like the food and the prices, and have to admit there's a lot to look at. Hal Meredith offers dining in three areas: the Thirsty Garden solarium, the English Room that displays memorabilia from Britain (some of it inside the glass tables he made) and the ultimate Carriage Room, a two-story space showcasing half of a Skip Barber racing car on the ceiling, a 1957 gasoline pump, a Mercedes grill, an old cart, drive-in movie speakers and what have you. The tables here are encased in tires. Oh, yes, about the food. It's a mix of salads, sandwiches, burgers,

English Room at Carriages restaurant.

201

pastas, fajitas and about a dozen entrees, priced from $9.95 for three chicken dishes to $13.95 for New York strip steak. Open daily, 11 to 9 or 10.

The Woodland, Route 41, Lakeville, (203) 435-0578. A former coffee shop, this has been upscaled considerably and is locally favored for consistently good food. It's small and modern-looking inside, with beehive lights over the booths, interesting woven placemats and an abundance of fresh flowers. Particularly appealing is the artwork on the walls, done by the sisters of owner Carol Peters. The former outdoor terrace has been enclosed to make a small lounge. Lunch salads, sandwiches and entrees are $2.95 to $8.95 (for a shrimp platter). Entrees at night with rice and vegetable are $10.95 to $19.95, and some lunch items are available. A blackboard lists many daily specials — perhaps fried calamari, arugula salad with buffalo mozzarella, stir-fried imperial beef, cajun blackened tuna and grilled angus filet with wild mushrooms at one visit. Carol is the daughter of Anthony Peters, former owner of the Interlaken Inn, so she knows the hospitality business, and her brother Robert is the chef. Lunch, Tuesday-Saturday 11:30 to 2:30; dinner, 5:30 to 9 or 10, Sunday to 8:30. Closed Monday.

Freshfields, Route 128, West Cornwall, (203) 672-6601. This country bistro occupies the space of the former Deck Restaurant. The outdoor deck beside a waterfall, the L-shaped dining room with a view of the open kitchen, and the upstairs lounge with a huge mural of the Cornwall hills draw those who appreciate good food and drink. The menu, which used to be the area's most ingenious, was toned down in 1992 to feature "the right food at the right price." Hours were curtailed as well. Dinner entrees top off at $15.95 for the likes of grilled swordfish with cilantro-lime vinaigrette or grilled lamb with white beans and grilled vegetables. The wraparound screened deck above the roaring brook is popular for lunch or brunch. Open Tuesday-Sunday, lunch 11:30 to 2; dinner, 5:30 to 9 or 10.

The Cannery Cafe, 85 Main St., Canaan, (203) 824-7333. Canning jars are the theme at this homey little cafe. They line windows and shelves and are filled with anything from colored water to dried pastas and beans. Lemonade, iced tea and cider are served in canning jars (stronger stuff is available), and a jar of icicle pickles (cucumber, onion, and dill) is set upon your table at lunch and dinner. Chef-owner Eric Stevens, who trained in New Orleans, cooks with a Louisiana flair. His specialty, pork loin stuffed with fruit and brandy compote and served sliced with a port wine sauce ($13.25), was featured in L.L. Bean's *New New England Cookbook*. It's the lowest-priced of entrees that top off at $15.75 for grilled ribeye steak or grilled swordfish with lemon-lime butter sauce. Start with fried oysters bayou-style or fried catfish remoulade. Eric's wife, Diane, is responsible for the luscious desserts, among them grand marnier mousse and a rich, warm bread pudding with whiskey sauce. Although the cafe is homey, there's a touch of sophistication as well. You'd expect nothing less from a place that offers cajun bloody marys, cajun margaritas and good wines by the glass. Lunch, Tuesday-Thursday 11:30 to 2:30; dinner, Tuesday-Sunday 5 to 9 or 10.

Shopping

Salisbury offers a variety of shopping in a small area, which is fine for ambling around on a fall afternoon and for early Christmas shopping. **The Connecticut Yankee,** a good-looking and spacious shop, has the kind of men's and women's clothing that someone with a country home in this area would likely wear, plus a large selection of china and other gifts. Check out the ceramics, jewelry and stuffed animals at **Windemere,** an American crafts store in the Marketplace behind the bank. **Harris Foods** offers good soups and sandwiches for takeout. People used to buy the settings right off the table at Arlene Dubin's former restaurant, so she opened a shop called

Settings and sells not only table items but decorative accessories, gifts, dhurrie rugs and spectacular dried-flower arrangements of exquisite taste. Be sure to stop for tea at **Chaiwalla,** Mary O'Brien's relocated tea house in a two-story house set back from the road at 1 Main St. She offers homemade soups, tomato pie and open-face sandwiches as well as traditional tea service. Another mecca for tea connoisseurs is **Harney and Sons,** which sells exotic teas by the bag or tin. John Harney, former innkeeper at the White Hart Inn, opened a mail-order tea business in his family home across from the inn at 11 East Main St. and welcomes shoppers daily from 9 to 5.

New shops keep popping up in Lakeville, a mile away along Route 44. **Corner Clothiers** has suave apparel and **Sunflower Boutique** offers sportswear. **April 56 Extreme Cookery** carries a potpourri of gourmet foods, Junior League cookbooks and original gifts; we liked the ceramic pie plates with lids topped with berries and apples. Incredible handknit sweaters, including one bearing a flower-bedecked front porch and an American flag, are offered at **Appleyard Sweaters.**

Norfolk and Riverton

A wealthy summer colony since the completion of the Connecticut Western Railroad in 1871, the Norfolk area east of Salisbury along the Massachusetts border includes secluded estates and a lively summer music season that once gave it the title "the Lenox of Connecticut." Off the beaten track from anywhere, Riverton has become a destination in itself since West Hartford merchant John Tarrant Kenney gave up his shoe store in 1946 and restored the old Lambert Hitchcock chair factory on its original site beside the Farmington River.

Norfolk Chamber Music Festival, Ellen Battell Stoeckel Estate, Norfolk, (203) 542-5537 (or 432-1966 before June 15). The Battell family endowed Norfolk with much of its character; the Norfolk Chamber Music Festival and the Yale Summer School of Music carry on the century-old tradition with summer concerts in the redwood-lined Music Shed on the hilly grounds of the Ellen Battell Stoeckel estate west of the village green. Sixteen concerts by the Tokyo String Quartet, the New York Woodwind Quintet, the Cleveland Quartet and the Norfolk Chamber Orchestra are given on Friday and Saturday evenings from late June into August.

Great Mountain Forest, a working forest west of Norfolk atop Canaan Mountain, is a special treat for visitors. The 6,000-acre preserve is maintained with help from the Yale School of Forestry and the University of Hartford Environmental Studies Center. Enter from Wangum Mountain Road in Norfolk or, better, Canaan Mountain Road east of Falls Village. The roads through this experimental forest are lined with dozens of species — at some points, the markers come fast and furious on both sides and no matter how slowly you go, you'll miss some. Chinese imports, 90-foot hemlocks, the biggest black walnut trees you'll ever see, Douglas firs, oriental spruces and the King Boris fir are all there. Meadow sequoias are grown by the head forester from Chinese seed at the nursery.

Hitchcock Chair Co. Factory Store, Route 20, Riverton, (203) 379-4826. Hitchcock employees can be seen weaving, woodworking, rushing and stenciling behind the gift shop and furniture showroom. The authentic reproductions, sold at factory prices, start at around $50. An antique original chair with its distinctive stenciled designs of flowers and fruits with handpainted outlines of gold can sell for up to $1,000. Shop open Monday-Saturday 10 to 5, Sunday noon to 5.

John Tarrant Kenney Hitchcock Museum, Route 20, Riverton, (203) 738-4950. Antique furniture from Hitchcock and other craftsmen is shown in the Old Union Church that Lambert Hitchcock helped build in 1829. A fifteen-minute movie,

"America Be Seated," tells the early Hitchcock story. Chairs are attractively displayed; some hang in neat rows from the walls. You can view the fine stenciling and handstriping up close, and immerse yourself in other Hitchcock memorabilia. Open April-December, Wednesday-Saturday 11 to 4, Sunday noon to 4. Free.

Gilson Cafe and Cinema, 354 Main St., Winsted, (203) 379-5108 or 379-6069. Serious movie-goers flock to this cafe/theater/lounge fashioned from a 1920s movie house of grand proportions. They come from miles around to enjoy art, foreign and second-run films while munching sandwiches, salads, platters of veggies or pate and brie, chili and desserts. Tiered, side-by-side seats for two, with small tables between, face a large screen. There's a full liquor license, and no one under age 21 is admitted on weekends. With admission at $4 and food in the $4.75 range, a couple can make a night of it for twenty bucks or so. Upstairs in a new lounge, blues and jazz are performed live Thursday-Saturday nights as the flicks roll below. Movies, Tuesday-Sunday at 7, also Friday and Saturday at 9 or 9:30, doors open for dinner at 6. Lounge opens at 7, jazz at 8:30; no cover charge.

Room and Board

Manor House, Maple Avenue, Box 447, Norfolk 06058, (203) 542-5690. This grand, Tudor-style manor home on five acres has been converted into an elegant Victorian B&B by Diane and Henry Tremblay, corporate dropouts from the Hartford insurance world. All eight guest rooms have private baths, one a double jacuzzi and one with a double soaking tub. All are furnished with antique sleigh, canopy or four-poster beds covered with duvet comforters and interesting decorative touches. The Tremblays are proud to show a prized collection of old prints by a local woman, which they acquired recently at an auction. The lovely and spacious main-floor public rooms are enhanced by Tiffany windows, cherry paneling and stone fireplaces. Very comfortable are the small library, the baronial living room with a gigantic stone fireplace, a sun porch with a wood stove, and two dining rooms in which the Tremblays serve full breakfasts. The herbs come from their garden and the honey from their beehives. Doubles, $85 to $150.

Greenwoods Gate, Greenwoods Road East (Route 44), Norfolk 06058, (203) 542-5439. Guests in this small B&B in a striking white Colonial home are greeted by a gold pineapple on the door and two concrete pineapples on either side. Deanne Raymond, who used to run a sophisticated country shop in the Berkshires and now sells romantic gifts, has decorated her three suites and a single room with expensive antiques, lovely crafts and magnificent floral arrangements. Each of the lavishly furnished suites has its own entrance for privacy; check the stairs to the Trescott Suite, with antique cast-iron doorstops on each step. The three-level Levi Thompson suite with a sitting area and spa-like bath with double jacuzzi is a coveted retreat for romance. The house, including a formal living room and a family room, is "open to guests to use as though it were your own." A full breakfast is served in the pink dining room. Doubles, $150 to $195.

Mountain View Inn, Route 272, Norfolk 06058, (203) 542-5595. This big, rustic Victorian inn, built as a private home at the turn of the century, has been upgraded since

Michele Sloane took over in 1987 following a stint as a hotel manager in the Caribbean. Some of the eleven guest rooms are unusually large and most are furnished with hooked rugs, four-poster beds and old-fashioned wallpaper, but the overall effect is a bit spare. Seven have private baths. **Maxfield's** restaurant, named for artist Maxfield Parrish whose prints are on the walls, consists of a pine-paneled porch with frilly curtains and a formal inner dining room with brick fireplace and beamed ceiling. A new chef has added German specials to a continental menu priced from $13 for citron chicken on a bed of braised spinach to $21 for tournedos au poivre. Doubles, $60 to $100, including continental breakfast. Dinner, Thursday-Sunday 6 to 9; Sunday brunch, 11 to 2.

Old Riverton Inn, Route 20, Riverton 06065, (203) 379-8678. This inn opened in 1796 and was restored in 1937, but still retains a highway tavern atmosphere. Upstairs are twelve bedrooms of different sizes (some euphemistically called compact), all with private baths. The two front corner rooms are most desirable. A sitting area on the second floor contains Victorian furniture and antiques. The food served in the main dining room furnished, of course, with Hitchcock chairs, beamed low ceiling and pretty bow windows, is plain, with dinners in the $12.95 to $17.95 range. Lunch is popular with visitors to the Hitchcock factory and museum. There are also a cozy Hobby Horse bar and another dining room, the Grindstone Terrace, with a floor of Collinsville grindstones quarried in Nova Scotia, glass tables and white iron chairs. Doubles, $65 to $95. Lunch, noon to 2:30; dinner, 5 to 8:30 or 9, Sunday noon to 8. Closed Monday and Tuesday.

Catnip Mouse Tearoom, Route 20, Riverton, (203) 379-3745. Lana Wells runs this neat little luncheon spot, with dark green wallpaper on which are baskets of flowers. The handwritten menu changes bi-weekly, with soups like lobster-broccoli bisque, salads and desserts. Sandwiches in the $6.95 range might be a Peter Piper, grilled ham and chicken with homemade pepper jelly, or the Italian Delight, homemade focaccia with prosciutto, artichoke hearts and basil mayonnaise, topped with melted mozzarella and served warm. Lana makes cinnamon, baked apple and pumpkin ice creams in the fall, or you might find white chocolate pecan pie. Everything is made from scratch, even the mayonnaise seasoned with herbs from Lana's herb garden, as well as the herbal teas. Lunch, Tuesday-Saturday, 11:30 to 2.

The Hawk's Nest Pub, Route 44, Norfolk, (203) 542-5716. Crowded, casual and inexpensive — these are the attractions of this lively spot in Norfolk Center, lately taken over and being upgraded by David Davis, formerly co-owner of the famed Stonehenge restaurant and inn in Ridgefield. Sit at bare wood tables in jolly surroundings and select from a dinner menu heavy on appetizers and burgers (five versions, $4.50 to $5.95). The handful of entrees might include grilled tuna steak, grilled chicken with Thai peanut sauce and grilled New York sirloin, $10.95 to $15.95. The cobb salad ($4.75) is a standout at lunch. Lunch, Wednesday-Friday 11:30 to 3, weekend brunch to 5; dinner nightly, 5 to 9 or 10. Closed Tuesday in off-season.

Shopping

In Norfolk, stop at the **Norfolk Artisan's Guild,** where 50 local craftsmen display their wares on the main floor of the old Thurston Building. Just south on Route 272 is **Nobody Eats Parsley,** a fine shop for herbs and herb products. North of town, just across the Massachusetts line in Southfield, is **The Buggy Whip Factory,** housing antiques dealers, artisans, specialty shops and a great little cafe.

Tiny Riverton has a short street of shops, in addition to the Hitchcock Chair Factory and Store around the corner. **The Contemporary Crafts Gallery** has fine pewterware plus original works in other media; the **Seth Thomas Factory Outlet,** all kinds of clocks from America's oldest clockmaker, and the **Riverton General Store** includes a country deli. **Sarah Hubbard Putnam Antiques and Herbs** carries books, cards, new and old baskets and Carl Larsson prints. Stop at the **Village Sweet Shop** for ice cream or chocolate lace.

Lake Waramaug's Alpine Country

Nothing seems quite so European as sitting on the terrace of the Hopkins Inn for lunch or a pre-dinner cocktail and gazing down the hillside at all the boats on Lake Waramaug.

Cottage at Lake Waramaug.

Named for an Indian sachem in this old territory, the lake reminds some of those in Austria and Switzerland, and the surrounding inns capitalize on it. Off in worlds unto themselves east of the lake are quaint New Preston, a hamlet of exotic shops, and picturesque Washington Depot and Washington, the former nestled in a valley and the latter perched on a hilltop.

For foliage-viewing, the narrow road that hugs the shore as it winds around the boomerang-shaped lake is a good way to see both lake and leaves. Lovely homes and manicured lawns mark the area, and three of the four inns sit not far from water's edge. The nine-mile route is ringed by hills — when the water is calm, as it often is, the reflections of color are spectacular.

Mount Tom State Park in nearby Woodville is often overlooked. Right beside Route 202 is a 60-acre spring-fed pond for swimming; the excellent beach facilities include individual changing rooms. Picnic tables are smack dab on the shore and scattered along the hillside. A mile-long trail rises 500 feet to a tower atop Mount Tom.

The village green in the postcard-perfect community of **Washington** is as classic as any in Connecticut. Large houses and prominent churches surround it, and off to one side is the Gunnery School's interesting campus. The **Gunn Historical Museum,** housed in a 1781 wooden structure near the green, is open Thursday-Saturday from noon to 4, with a fine thimble collection, dollhouses and western Indian baskets. Routes 109 and 45 east of Washington have good panoramic views for foliage-seekers.

The Institute for American Indian Studies, Curtis Road off Route 199, Washington, (203) 868-0518. Just southwest of town is the renamed American Indian Archeological Institute, a place dedicated to Indian relics and archeological digs. Some years back it made history when a team uncovered a fluted "clovis" spear point, which they say confirms Indians at the spot 10,000 years ago. A mastodon skeleton inside the contemporary museum shows the type of animal they would have hunted; there are arrowheads, very early Indian pottery, sandstone dishes and dioramas of early Indian life. Also on the premises are an Indian longhouse, a simulated dig site and an unusual, specialized museum shop with handcrafted copies of items in the collection. A twenty-minute habitat trail takes the visitor through stages of geological and botanical development in Connecticut. Open Monday-Saturday 10 to 5, Sunday noon to 5. Adults $3, children $2.

Camping is particularly good in this area. **Lake Waramaug State Park** offers 88

Lunchers enjoy view of Lake Waramaug from terrace of Hopkins Inn.

sites in the woods and fields beside the lake, with a camp store, full facilities and a fine beach. **Housatonic Meadows State Park** in Cornwall Bridge has 104 sites in a heavily forested area beside the Housatonic River. **Macedonia Brook State Park** in Kent, known for its hiking along the Appalachian trail, offers 84 campsites. **Kent Falls State Park** south of Cornwall Bridge has twelve sites in open fields near the foot of the state's highest waterfall.

Hopkins Vineyard, Hopkins Road, New Preston, (203) 868-7954. Behind the Hopkins Inn on land the Hopkins family has farmed for more than 200 years, Bill and Judy Hopkins started planting grape vines in 1979; they now have 35 acres of French-American hybrids, from which they produce ten wines. They have converted their red dairy barn into an award-winning winery, where the visitor may taste and buy their products, including a superior seyval blanc. A winery walk extends to a new addition, allowing visitors to view the new bottling and labeling room. An art gallery with changing exhibits is upstairs, an excellent shop sells wine-related items like stemware and grapevine wreaths and baskets, and on cool days a pot of mulled wine simmers on the wood stove. You can picnic with a $10.99 bottle of chardonnay in the small picnic area with a view of the lake below. You'll probably agree with the quotation printed on the Hopkins labels: "Where the air is like wine and the wine is like nectar." Wines are $6.50 to $10.99. Open daily 10 to 5, May-December; Friday-Sunday 10 to 5, rest of year.

Room and Board

Boulders Inn, Route 45, New Preston 06777, (203) 868-0541. Innkeepers Ulla and Kees Adema of Fairfield County took over in 1988 and made an already special place even more special. "This was supposed to be our retirement," kidded Ulla, who said her husband wanted a little B&B and ended up with this grand prize. Six bedrooms and suites in the main inn and eight in contemporary, fireplaced duplex guest houses up the hill in back are most comfortably furnished. A rear carriage house adds three choice, carpeted guest rooms with plush chintz seating in front of stone fireplaces. We especially like the inn's fireplaced and paneled living room with comfy sofas and wing chairs in splashy fabrics, a library corner with stereo tapes and a big Russian samovar from which tea may be dispensed in the afternoon. It has immense picture windows overlooking the lake; next to it is a small den with a TV. The dining room with its walls of boulders and a seven-sided addition with views of Lake Waramaug has won wide acclaim. Dinner entrees in the $16 to $22.50 range might include blackened swordfish with pineapple salsa, sauteed salmon with fresh peas and cream on sorrel fettuccine, grilled veal chop with vidalia onions and port wine sauce, and grilled tournedos with shiitake mushroom compote. Start with phyllo strudels with brie and ham or grilled quail with a wild rice risotto, but save room for a dessert like mocha mousse in a chocolate cup. The outdoor patio is perfect for cocktails and dining in summer. A hike up Pinnacle Mountain behind the inn reveals abundant wildlife and birds as you work up an appetite for the excellent meals. Doubles, $225, MAP; B&B available weekdays, $175.

Hopkins Inn, Hopkins Road, New Preston 06777, (203) 868-7295. This pretty yellow inn is known more for its dining than its lodging — we often recommend it when we're asked where to take a visitor for lunch out in the country. But it does have eleven guest rooms (nine with private baths) and one apartment, unexceptional but light and airy and furnished with country antiques as befits its origin as a summer guest house in 1847. For meals, its setting atop a hill overlooking the lake, with an outdoor dining terrace shaded by a giant horse chestnut tree, is spectacular from spring through fall. One dining room has a rustic decor with barnsiding and ship's figureheads; the other is more Victorian. Chef-owner Franz Schober is Austrian and always has Austrian and Swiss dishes on the menu. Dinner entrees are $14.25 to $17.75 for classics like wiener schnitzel and sweetbreads Viennese; wife Beth Schober says the roast pheasant with red cabbage and spaetzle is especially in demand. Vegetables are always good; you may get something unusual like braised romaine lettuce. People love the strawberries romanoff and grand marnier souflee glace. The varied wine list includes half a dozen from Switzerland as well as several from Hopkins Vineyard next door. Franz designed the tile tables for the terrace and porch; he's also the inspiration for the striking copper and wrought-iron chandelier and lanterns that grace the terrace. Doubles, $52 to $60, EP. Lunch, Tuesday-Saturday noon to 2; dinner 6 to 9 or 10, Sunday 12:30 to 8:30; no lunch in April, November and December. Closed January-March.

The Inn on Lake Waramaug, North Shore Road, New Preston 06777, (203) 868-0563 or (800) 525-3466. From private home to village inn to boarding house for summer guests, this has grown since the 19th century into a destination resort with an indoor pool, whirlpool, sauna, lake beach, tennis court and 23 rooms in the main inn and guest houses, some with working fireplaces. A succession of innkeepers for the Baron Group owners keeps things busy for those who like lots of activity. The paddlewheeler Showboat takes guests on cruises around the lake. Three meals a day are served in peak season in the inn's dining rooms, on the terrace or at the boathouse beside the lake, where hamburgers are barbecued at lunchtime. Dinner entrees are priced from $16.50 for two chicken dishes to $22 for medallions of venison with peppered black plum sauce and red cabbage. Doubles, $179 to $219, MAP. Lunch in season, 11:30 to 2; dinner, 6 to 9; Sunday brunch, 11 to 2.

Birches Inn, West Shore Road, New Preston 06777, (203) 868-0229. Austrians really do love Lake Waramaug! Heinz Holl from Salzburg and his wife Christa own this inn across the lake from the Hopkins. The inn has ten rooms, two upstairs, five with private baths and a motel feeling in a guest house behind the inn and three in a waterfront

Furnishings are sumptuous in bedroom at Mayflower Inn.

cottage with its back porch right over the lake. Christa Holl is chef; her wiener schnitzel, sauerbraten and grilled salmon with dill sauce and especially her apple strudel receive high marks. Entrees in the $11.95 to $16.95 range include a Viennese platter with bratwurst, frankfurter, pork chop, carrots and potato salad. Doubles, $140 to $150, MAP. Dinner nightly except Tuesday, 5 to 9 or 10; Sunday brunch, 11:30 to 2:30.

Mayflower Inn, Route 47, Box 1288, Washington 06793, (203) 868-9466. A long driveway winds up the hill to this hidden inn on 28 wooded acres overlooking the campus of the Gunnery, the private school that used to own and operate it. New York owners Robert and Adriana Mnuchin poured big bucks into the inn's renovation and expansion in 1992, creating one of the premier English-style country hotels in America. The main inn holds fourteen guest rooms and suites of great comfort and style. Ten more are in two guest houses astride a hill beside a tiered rose garden leading up to a swimming pool. Furnishings are stately, even spectacular, mixing fine imported and domestic antiques and accesories with prized artworks and elegant touches of whimsey. The inn's main floor harbors an intimate parlor, an ever-so-British gentleman's library, an English-looking bar and three stylish dining rooms. Chef John Farnsworth, tapped as one of America's top ten chefs in 1991 by Food and Wine magazine, presents a changing menu. The night's offerings might run from $14.50 for herb-roasted chicken with cranberry ketchup and mashed potatoes to $24 for grilled veal chop with whole wheat pasta and mushroom sauce. Start with a pizza of duck confit or roasted beet salad with baby mustard greens and foie gras terrine (for a cool $10.50). Finish with double chocolate mousse cake on a pond of creme anglaise or warm raspberry tart with a scoop of raspberry ice. Work it off in the fitness club and sauna on the lower garden level. Speaking of gardens — the landscaping here is in keeping with the rest of the place, and friends who lunched on the outdoor terrace said the site was unsurpassed. Doubles, $190 to $275, EP; suites, $285 to $475, EP. Lunch daily, noon to 2:30; dinner, 6 to 9:30.

Doc's, Flirtation Avenue at Route 45, New Preston, (203) 868-9415. Everybody's favorite restaurant hereabouts is this roadside stand gone upscale. Adam Riess, a Californian just graduated from the University of Pennsylvania, opened the Italian cafe, pizzeria and bakery and named it for his grandfather, a physician who summered on Lake Waramaug for 40 years. He leased it in 1992 to his Palestinian chef, Riad Aamar, and departed for graduate school in New York. But the tradition continues: dynamite pizzas in the $7 range, super pastas from $9.75 to $13.75 and a smattering of gutsy entrees ($13.75 to $16.75), among them sauteed salmon with pesto and rack of lamb roasted with white beans, shiitake mushrooms and black olives. Most folks stick to the pizzas, pastas and salads, but you can't blame the chef for expanding his reach. The dessert chef produces a great ricotta cheesecake, torta di chocolata and tirami su. The setting is as gutsy as the food: hard green chairs at close-together tables with white butcher paper over white cloths; their only adornment is a bottle of olive oil and a big metal cheese shaker. Lunch, Friday-Sunday noon to 2:30; dinner, Wednesday-Sunday 5 to 9:30 or 10. BYOB.

Thé Cafe, Route 45, New Preston, (203) 868-1787. Another new winner is this cafe whose name plays on the French word for tea and is prounced "tay caf-fay." Folks spill out from the intimate 30-seat interior onto tables on the porch and even the asphalt. "That's the real cafe," volunteered a waiter; "the inside should be called 'the grotto.'" Anyway, classic belgian waffles, omelets and brioche french toast are featured for breakfast ($6.95). Lunch prices go from $6.95 for a burger on a focaccia bun to $9.75 for chicken pot pie; we liked the looks of the roasted eggplant, pepper and goat cheese sandwich and the penne arrabiata. At dinner ($12.95 to $17.95), cafe misto salad and smoked salmon with corn cakes and creme fraiche warm up the palate for the likes of sesame seared tuna steak with ginger creme fraiche, lamb stew in an herbed bread tureen and grilled pork loin. Tea, perhaps with one of the delectable desserts from the front display case, is served daily except Tuesday from 4 to 5. Open Wednesday-Sunday for breakfast from 9, lunch from 11:30 and dinner from 6; also Monday for breakfast and lunch. No credit cards. BYOB.

The Pantry, Titus Road, Washington Depot, (203) 868-0258. Combining many functions, the Pantry is an elegant catering service, a food and gift store for gourmets, a glorified deli and a marvelous spot for late breakfast, lunch or tea. Amidst high-tech shelving displaying everything from American Spoon preserves to red currant or green peppercorn vinegars, cooking gadgets and serious equipment, you can lunch on innovative fare. On one visit the chef was dishing up a muffaletta sandwich ($4.95), that New Orleans favorite of salami, cheese, olive oil and olives, done up inside a loaf of bread, plus salads of watercress slaw, parsnips, Italian new potatoes and gingered carrots. You might try the salad sampler for $6.95 or game pot pie ($8.50). Soups like the curried cauliflower are heavenly, and desserts are to sigh over: among them, pear-almond torte, hazelnut dream roll, linzer torte and grapefruit souffle. Open Tuesday-Saturday, 10 to 5:30.

Shopping

The hamlet of New Preston at the southeast end of Lake Waramaug is gaining small retailers of note. **Brittania Books** and **Timothy Mawson Bookseller** are two of the more distinctive. **J. Seitz & Co.** is a small paradise of eclectic clothing and furnishings with an emphasis on the Southwest. Among other choices are **Rigamarole** for decorative housewears and antiques, **The Grey Squirrel** for country furniture and folk art, **Jonathan Peters** for fine linens and lacy items, and **Black Swan Antiques.**

Washington Depot has a large and well-stocked bookstore, the **Hickory Stick Bookshop.** Authors, many of whom have homes in the area, are occasionally on hand to autograph their books. Custom handknit sweaters and imported yarns are stocked at **Nimble Fingers.** Find Canadian antiques, porcelain, painted boxes and such at the **Tulip Tree Collection,** women's sportswear at **Finula's** and gifts and jewelry at **Gracious Living.**

Litchfield

Considered Connecticut's finest example of a typical late 18th-century New England village, Litchfield is the place to which we take first-time visitors to Connecticut (we have relatives who make a beeline there almost every time they visit). You should, too, if you're anywhere in the area.

The entire center of the village settled in 1720 is a National Historic Landmark. While Williamsburg had to be restored, Litchfield simply has been maintained by its residents as a living museum. Most of the old homes and buildings are occupied. Some are opened to the public on Open House Day one Saturday in July.

The **Litchfield Historic District** is clustered around the green and along North and South streets (Route 63). The

Litchfield Congregational Church.

statuesque, gleaming white Congregational Church is said to be the most photographed in New England. Where else do a bank and a jail share a common wall as they do at North and West streets? The young attendant pointed them out proudly from the information center on the green. South Street is a broad, half-mile-long avenue where three governors, five state chief justices, six congressmen and two U.S. senators have lived. Landmarks include the birthplaces of Ethan Allen, Henry Ward Beecher and Harriet Beecher Stowe, plus Sheldons Tavern, where George Washington slept (he visited town five times). Sarah Pierce opened the first academy for the education of women in America on North Street in 1792. A good place to get your bearings is the lately renovated **Litchfield Historical Society Museum** at East and South Streets, which has four galleries of early American paintings, decorative arts, furniture and local history exhibits. Open Tuesday-Saturday 10 to 4, Sunday noon to 4, April-October; weekends only in November and December. Adults, $2.

The **Tapping Reeve House and Law School,** South Street, (203) 567-4501. America's first law school (1784) is now a museum dedicated to Judge Tapping Reeve's life and times. You can visit both the house with its handsome furnishings and the tiny school with handwritten ledgers penned by students long since gone, including Aaron Burr, John C. Calhoun and 130 members of Congress. Open mid-May to mid-October, Tuesday-Saturday 10 to 4, Sunday noon to 4. Adults, $2.

White Memorial Foundation and Conservation Center, off Route 202 west of Litchfield, (203) 567-0015. Litchfield resident Alain C. White and his sister Mary set up the foundation that established the state's largest nature center and wildlife sanctuary, and donated many other public lands in northwest Connecticut. The 4,000 acres here contain 35 miles of woodland and marsh trails — popular year-round with hikers, horseback riders and, in winter, cross-country skiers. Almost every outdoor activity is available, including birdwatching from a unique observatory in which groups can watch birds undetected, and swimming at Sandy Beach along Bantam Lake, the largest natural lake in the state. The preserve is unusual in having both managed and wild natural areas within its boundaries; on one 30-acre lot known as Catlin Woods, which has been untouched for years, a forest road winds through giant hemlocks and white pines; elsewhere, a fully operating sawmill can be observed. The preserve with eleven ponds provides environments for all manner of animals and birds. A museum in a 19th-century mansion contains collections of Indian artifacts, 3,000 species of butterflies, live and stuffed animals, geology exhibits, and an excellent nature library and gift shop. Grounds open free year-round. Museum open April-November, Tuesday-Saturday 8:30 to 4:30, Sunday 11 to 5; winter hours, 9 to 5. Adults $1, children 50 cents.

White Flower Farm, Route 63, Litchfield, (203) 567-8789. No relation to the White Memorial Foundation, this is one of the nation's more unusual nurseries. Famed almost as much for its literate catalog as for its nursery stock, it welcomes visitors to the ten acres of display gardens and a sales center from which few go home empty-handed. More than 1,000 different flowers and shrubs are offered. The gardens are especially gorgeous in late spring and summer, and the begonia display in the greenhouses is viewed from July through September. Even non-gardeners will enjoy a visit here. The catalog appears under the pen name of Amos Pettingill and readers love it. Open mid-April through October, Monday-Friday 10 to 5, weekends 9 to 5:30. Free.

Haight Vineyard and Winery, Chestnut Hill Road, Litchfield, (203) 567-4045. Housed in an English Tudor-style building, this is Connecticut's oldest farm winery, having produced its first chardonnays and rieslings in 1979 from fifteen acres of grapes planted by Sherman P. Haight Jr., master of the hounds for the Litchfield Hunt. The Haight family take pride in their Covertside white and red prize-winners as well as their chardonnay and riesling labels. There is a vineyard walk through the 25-acre property, plus a large tasting room. Open Monday-Saturday 10:30 to 5, Sunday noon to 5.

Topsmead, Buell Road, Litchfield, (203) 485-0226. Often overlooked, this 511-acre preserve on a knoll a mile east of Litchfield Center offers scenic views, picnic sites and trails for hiking and cross-country skiing. An English Tudor house that was once the summer home of the Chase brass family of Waterbury is opened for guided tours in summer. Grounds open year-round.

Room and Board

Toll Gate Hill, Route 202 (Box 39), Litchfield 06759, (203) 567-4545. This ancient-feeling inn actually is of fairly recent vintage, having opened in 1983 with six guest rooms, three dining rooms, a small tavern and a ballroom in a rural 1745 landmark home northeast of town. Four rooms and suites were added in 1986 in an adjacent "school house," and a new building with ten more rooms and suites and a lobby area was added to the rear of the property in 1990. Owner Frederick J. Zivic, who founded the late Black Dog Tavern restaurant chain in the Hartford area about 25 years ago, restored and furnished with taste the three-story house in which Capt. William Bull once took in travelers on the Hartford-Albany stage route. The bedrooms are handsomely done in custom fabrics and antiques; some have sofas, working fireplaces, goose down comforters and lighted mirrors. In the antiques-furnished dining rooms, Fritz Zivic offers a seasonal menu of regional American cuisine. The dinner menu ranges from $17 for seared pork medallions with minted barbecue sauce to $23 for shellfish

Mirrors reflect dining room at West Street Grill.

pie in puff pastry, a house favorite. We found the wine list interesting and fairly priced, the soups (like clam chowder with green chile and tomatoes) creative, and our dinner entrees of sauteed scallops in a light beer sauce and broiled salmon with a tomato-chardonnay puree and warm chive ricotta excellent. Doubles, $110 to $140; suites, $175. Lunch, noon to 3; dinner, 5:30 to 9:30 or 10:30; weekend brunch, 11:30 to 3:30.

Litchfield Inn, Route 202, Litchfield 06759, (203) 567-4503. Litchfield got a badly needed inn in 1982 when local businessman James Irwin built from scratch an authentic — if austere-looking — Colonial-style structure back from the highway about a mile west of town. Starting with twelve guest rooms and an extensive dining and bar facility, the inn expanded in 1984 with a twenty-room addition; plans for another, much larger addition have been put on hold. Nicely furnished in early American style, each room has private bath and color TV; some have wet bars. Several public rooms are studiously elegant; the long and narrow **Terrace Room** with glass roof and lots of greenery is more welcoming. Dinner is served in the large **Joseph Harris Room** with wainscoting, hand-hewn beams and wide-plank floors. Entrees run from $13.50 for chicken dijonnaise to $18.95 for tournedos of beef with roasted elephant garlic or rack of lamb coated with goat cheese. Lunches in the Terrace Room are more casual. Doubles, $95. Lunch daily, 11:30 to 2:30; dinner, 5:30 to 8:45 or 9:45.

West Street Grill, 43 West St., Litchfield, (203) 567-3885. The trendoids who pack this place at lunch and dinner seven days a week agree with the restaurant critics; the food is innovative and the sleek black and white digs quite stylish. Irish owner James O'Shea gives talented chef Matthew Fahrer a free rein. He obliges with such dinner entrees ($14.95 to $18.95) as grilled tuna japonnoise with noodle cake, wasabi and fresh pickled ginger; pan-seared cod on mashed potatoes with crispy leeks and grilled herb-crusted loin of pork with baked cannellini beans. An autumn lunch began with a rich butternut squash and pumpkin bisque and the restaurant's signature grilled peasant bread with parmesan aioli. Main dishes were a goat cheese and leek tart on flageolets with basil oil and chervil ($7.95) and a special of grilled smoked pork tenderloin with spicy Christmas limas ($8.95). Indulge in dessert, perhaps an intense key lime tart or

213

an ethereal creme brulee. The food here is as assertive and colorful as the striking mural of partying animals on a brick wall near the front. Lunch daily, 11:30 to 3, weekends to 4; dinner, 5:30 to 9 or 10.

Le Bon Coin, Route 202, Woodville, (203) 868-7763. We've always been fond of this homey and unpretentious French restaurant out in the country. William Janega, who had previously run Le Parisien in Stamford, built an addition upstairs to house his family and lives the business 24 hours a day. The two small dining rooms are most welcoming in the country French style. The front entry is decorated with wine casks, spigots and crate labels, and there are some attractive stained-glass windows. A luncheon blackboard lists such things as mousse de trois poissons, croustade de ris de veau and omelet aux champagne ($5.50 to $8.95). At night, entrees ($12.75 to $19.95) include dover sole with mushrooms and artichokes, frog's legs provencal, pepper steak and sweetbreads du jour. A plate of ice creams and sorbets, chocolate rice souffle and creme caramel are among desserts. Lunch, Thursday-Monday noon to 2; dinner, 6 to 9 or 10, Sunday 5 to 9. Closed Tuesday.

La Tienda Cafe, Sports Village, Route 202, Litchfield, (203) 567-8778. A green neon cactus beckons in the window of this two-room Mexican cafe. Colorful prints and rugs adorn the walls and cacti in small pots top the tables. A Mexican pizza ($4.95) was almost more than one could handle for lunch; an order of burritos ($4.95) also was hearty and delicious. The all-day menu has four "north of the border" dishes, but why bother when you can feast on black bean soup, Arizona-style nachos (topped with ground beef), enchiladas, tostadas and such? Dinners including Mexican rice and refried beans are $7.95 for folded tacos to $12.25 for chimichanga. Lunch, Monday-Saturday 11:30 to 2:30; dinner, 4:30 to 9 or 10, Sunday 3 to 9.

Litchfield Food Company, On the Green, Litchfield, (203) 567-3113. Lately doubled in size, this specialty foods shop, bakery and catering service has added tables for eat-in meals. Founded by transplanted New Yorkers, it was purchased in 1992 by Rick Spinell, former pastry chef at Brooklyn's River Cafe. Soups of the day could be tomato-bean-rosemary or mushroom-brie-onion. Smoked ham and turkey with cranberry-orange mayonnaise in a hard roll and the three-salad combination plate are popular for lunch. The delectable sandwiches cost about $6, and the exotic treats from the display case are priced accordingly. Open daily, 9:30 to 5:15.

Shopping

Lately, historic Litchfield has become something of a mecca for shoppers. On the green is **Workshop Inc.,** a boutique and gallery for the somewhat trendy, with Mexican and South American imports. We liked the straw hats and unusual handpainted silk earrings. Downstairs in its Gallery are many handwoven rugs and interesting pieces from Africa. **Hayseed** stocks a fine selection of cards along with sweaters, clothes and jewelry. **The Mason Gift Shop** on South Street has delightful gifts.

Cobble Court, just off the green, has several small stores including the **Litchfield Women's Exchange,** with handmade articles for infants and children, toys and linens, and homemade shortbread. **Kitchenworks** is a haven of cooking equipment and food-related gifts. The **Cobble Court Book Shop,** housed in an old blacksmith shop, recently opened the area's first espresso bar, offering treats like latte for $1.25 a cup.

West of town is Litchfield Commons, a cluster of new shops including the great **Mother Goose** toy shop, **Puddle Jumpers** for children's clothes, and **Tweeds and Tees** for colorful and classic apparel.

FOR MORE INFORMATION: Litchfield Hills Travel Council, Box 1776, Marbledale, Conn. 06777, (203) 868-2214.

Mount Washington Cog Railway is world's oldest.

A High Time

Mount Washington Valley, N.H.

If you stand in the center of North Conway's bustling Main Street and look north — admittedly a precarious venture, what with the bumper-to-bumper traffic — you can, on a clear day, see Mount Washington. The Northeast's highest mountain gives to the valley in which North Conway lies both its name and its spirit.

A rugged peak known for the perversity of its weather, Mount Washington symbolizes the challenge to hardy pioneers who forged roads through the rugged wilderness and settled towns in the valley. Not long after came sportsmen and travelers, for Mount Washington and its companion peaks in the Presidential Range are a splendid attraction.

North Conway, the largest town in their shadow, has long been a mecca for serious sportsmen and tourists who sought the mountain air, the mountain scenery and the mountain challenge. When we first visited two decades ago, we saw hardy climbers wearing hiking shoes and knapsacks on almost every corner.

The hikers and sportsmen still come, but they're more apt to be found a bit north these days — in Glen and Bartlett and Jackson, and at the Appalachian Mountain Club camp in Pinkham Notch.

North Conway has a new identity — as a serious center for discount shopping. Factory outlet stores line Route 16 south of town, bringing traffic to a crawl and often to a halt, especially on weekends in tourist season (summer, fall and winter). Canadians flock to the area to pay lower prices and lower taxes. Daytrippers from southern New Hampshire

215

and as far as Boston come in search of bargains. Fast-food stores on the strip cater to their needs.

Because Route 16 is the one main road north and south, there has been grumbling over the gridlock — even the police in town have taken to bicycles in summer to respond to calls more quickly. The age-old talk of a bypass around North Conway was heating up again in 1992. We hope it happens; we remember North Conway's earlier charm, when you could find a parking spot and shop in serious sporting goods stores, gift shops and local stores.

But there is still much to be found in the Mount Washington Valley, especially if you can avoid the commercial part of Route 16. We love the vistas of high peaks afforded by driving along Route 302 and the Kancamagus Highway (Route 112), on Route 16 north of the village, and on the 16A and 16B loop roads through Intervale and the mountain village of Jackson.

Intervale, a picturesque spot off the main road, seems to have turned every other house into an inn. A quaint red covered bridge leads to Jackson, an alpine-style mountain town, where the houses are tucked into the hillsides and you put your car into low gear to get around. It is also renowned for cross-country skiing; the Jackson Ski Touring Foundation has one of the largest trail complexes in the East.

Except for the towns, most of the area is part of the White Mountain National Forest, which protects it forever from despoilment.

Whether or not you climb them yourselves, getting up and down the mountains is one of the major diversions for visitors. The most well-known trip is that on the Mount Washington Cog Railway, but you also can go up Wildcat in a gondola or down Attitash on its Alpine Slide.

Every season in the valley has its distinct flavor. In winter, skiers flock to the downhill areas: Attitash, Wildcat, Black, Cranmore and Bretton Woods. Cross-country skiers enjoy miles upon miles of trails, especially at Jackson.

In late spring the hardiest skiers tote their gear up and then ski down the Mount Washington snowbowl known as Tuckerman Ravine, where the combination of topography and climate holds the snow latest of all. Skiing Tuckerman is, for the skier, the ultimate Northeastern challenge.

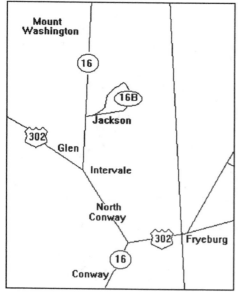

Summer visitors have long been attracted to the White Mountains to escape the heat, and for more than a hundred years they've made innkeeping a way of life in the valley. The grand old dame of summer resorts is the Mount Washington Hotel at Bretton Woods in Crawford Notch. Even if you don't stay there, you'll want to stop in and look around.

Tennis courts and golf courses are plentiful. This is the season for hikes in the woods and picnics beside mountain streams. There are swimming holes to be found as well.

Fall is short and shimmering and, for many of us, the best time of all (unfortunately, we are not alone). Our first visit to the valley was two decades ago on a late September weekend. Since

Wentworth Resort Hotel offers lodging, dining and golf.

then, whenever we think of foliage, we remember the Kancamagus Highway, a 34-mile stretch through the White Mountain National Forest from Lincoln to Conway. This is a true "high way" where the loveliness of leaf color is enhanced by the vistas over the mountains from frequent scenic lookouts.

In autumn, roadside stands are filled with cider, apples, pumpkins and New Hampshire maple syrup. Cord upon cord of wood is stacked by every house and hostelry and the smell of a wood fire greets you in the evening in virtually every inn, restaurant and lounge. The air is crisp, the sky blue, and the mountain peaks that are often obscured by clouds in other seasons are likely to be visible.

The best two weekends are the last in September and the first in October. Avoid Columbus Day weekend at all costs (no one else, it seems, does). After foliage, the valley battens down the hatches and gets ready for winter in earnest — a time for skiing and snowshoeing and stopping in cozy hostelries. Whichever season you pick, you'll love the valley.

Getting There

North Conway and the major towns of the Mount Washington Valley are located along Routes 16 and 302 in the midst of the White Mountain National Forest. Those approaching from the south can take Interstate 93 to Exit 32 and Route 112, the scenic Kancamagus Highway. Go east to Conway, then north into the valley on Routes 16 and 302.

Concord Trailways offers bus service through the valley. The nearest major airports are in Boston and Portland, Me.

Where to Stay

You'd probably be happiest staying away from the commercial strip (Route 16) in North Conway, especially if your visit is during a busy season. You can stay in Jackson, Intervale, Glen or one of the other areas to the north. These are mountain towns where you'll smell the smoke from the wood fires in the inns. For the most part we've selected personalized inns and guest houses rather than the motels that line Route 16 south of North Conway; know that these are available.

Jackson

This mountain village is traversed via a five-mile loop road, off which are located many first-class inns and resorts.

The Wentworth Resort Hotel, Route 16A, Jackson 03846, (603) 383-9700 or (800) 637-0013. Swiss-born hotelier Fritz Koeppel and his wife Diana are the new owners of this resort hotel in the center of the village. The east side of the property is bordered by the scenic Jackson Falls of the Wildcat River; to the west, the resort is framed by the eighteen-hole Wentworth golf course. Built in 1869, the large sand-colored clapboard building with striped awnings has turrets and porches and the look of a settled resident of town, which it is. Since its restoration in 1983, it has also become an elegant place to stay. The 62 rooms in the main building and six cottages spread around the property come with private baths and French provincial furnishings. Fritzie, a cockatiel, entertains guests from his perch in an ornate white birdhouse in the fireplaced lobby, where coffee is set out for guests in the morning. The Plum Room is a well-regarded dining room; dinner entrees are priced from $18 to $21. Koeppel's experience with the Ritz-Carlton and Four Seasons hotel chains is standing him in good stead in Jackson. And because his wife hails from nearby Conway, they expect to be here for the duration. Doubles, $99, EP; $145, MAP.

Christmas Farm Inn, Route 16B, Jackson 03846, (603) 383-4313 or (800) 443-5837. It's Christmas year-round at this venerable resort-inn, where Will Zeliff, son of owners Sydna and Bill Zeliff, has managed the property since his dad became a U.S. Congressman. The inn's main building, white with green shutters, was originally a farmhouse owned by the Rufus Pinkham family and built in the late 18th century. The property also includes an 18th-century red saltbox and a huge barn of about the same vintage; all now offer a variety of accommodations. When you enter the lobby and reception area of the main inn, you find a basketful of red buttons that say "We Make Memories," the inn's motto. The Christmas season is such a jolly time to be here that reservations are made a year in advance. Guests enjoy ten rooms in the main inn, all with private baths; deluxe cottage rooms, some with fireplaces, and a tiny honeymoon cottage known as The Sugar House. While all is decorated in red, green and white, it is done so subtly and tastefully that you don't feel as if you're on 42nd Street on Christmas Eve. Guests enjoy a drink in the Mistletoe Lounge — which does sport a little tinsel — before dinner (see Where to Eat). Inside the barn, they play ping-pong and enjoy other games; outdoors in good weather they enjoy a large swimming pool. Doubles, $150 to $180, MAP.

The Eagle Mountain Resort, Carter Notch Road, Jackson 03846, (603) 383-9111 or (800) 777-1700. The front porch of this imposing white clapboard hotel is longer than a football field, and a slew of dark green granny rockers is lined up along it, primed for the mountain view. Built in 1879 and totally rebuilt in 1986, the resort is busy in all four seasons, offering a nine-hole golf course, tennis courts and an outdoor heated swimming pool. There are also a health club with jacuzzi, saunas and exercise room. The old-fashioned lobby with a gorgeous patterned rug and, beyond, the Highfields dining room with its pressed oak furniture, speak of simple comforts. The 94 rooms, all with private baths, are furnished in country style. A buffet breakfast is available in Highfields; the Eagle Landing Tavern off the lobby is a pleasant spot for a drink. There's a fireplaced game room off the lobby as well. Doubles, $90 to $120, EP; suites, $120 to $155.

Front porch at The Inn at Thorn Hill has grand view of mountains.

The Inn at Thorn Hill, Thorn Hill Road, Jackson 03846, (603) 383-4242 or (800) 289-8990. New owners Ibby and Jim Cooper and their two teenagers had just arrived from Florida in 1992 at our latest visit. Jim points to his background in food and beverage with the Four Seasons, Westin and Hyatt hotels, and says he'll concentrate on the inn's dining room and kitchen to start. Wife Ibby left a teaching position to travel north. The look of the inn remains virtually the same, with the addition of a grand piano to the lobby where the manikins in Victorian dress reside. The new innkeepers very much want to keep the romantic Victorian image, says Jim. Designed by the architect Stanford White and built in 1895, the yellow inn with green trim has ten guest rooms; the Carriage House next door adds seven more, and three cottages are ideal for those who seek privacy. All accommodations have private baths. The attractive dining room with hunter green carpet and walls and oak tables and chairs is renowned for its cuisine. The front porch with its wicker furniture is much photographed and painted; while we visited, a guest was working on a pastel of the porch and its mountain view. Doubles, $130 to $200, MAP.

The Dana Place Inn, Route 16, Pinkham Notch, Jackson 03846, (603) 383-6822 or (800) 537-9276. Harris and Mary Lou Levine are innkeepers at this handsome place, the last real inn as you head north before you hit the White Mountain National Forest, Pinkham Notch and Mount Washington. The white and red clapboard buildings are perfectly picturesque. The inn is located right beside the swift-flowing Ellis River and those staying in the rustic Tree House out back can fall asleep listening to the water. More than one couple has been wed near the stream, with a view of Mount Washington towering overhead, and honeymooners are drawn to the place as well. Thirty rooms are in the rambling main inn and five in the Tree House. Above a large new dining-room addition on the main floor are seven deluxe rooms, with balconies looking toward the river. One is a corner room with two balconies. Do discuss the size, configuration and placement of your room since there's great variety. An indoor pool and a jacuzzi are popular; there are new tennis courts, too. Cross-country ski trails lead directly from the

219

property and lunch is served for skiers in winter. The four dining rooms are attractive and the food, prepared by a Hungarian chef, is well respected. Doubles, $110 to $170, MAP.

The Wildcat Inn & Tavern, Jackson 03846, (603) 383-4245. This is the most popular place to dine in Jackson and is such a convivial spot that some people like to stay upstairs on the second or third floor in one of the fourteen renovated rooms, all but two with private baths. They're not fancy and some are a bit tight, but they are clean and more than adequate with simple Colonial furnishings, pastel colors, new mattresses and thick carpeting. And you'll be oh-so-close for dinner at night. Doubles, $70 to $80; suites with sitting areas, $90.

The Village House, Route 16A, Box 359, Jackson 03846, (603) 383-6666. Two friendly dogs greet guests at this simple ten-room inn in the village of Jackson, where the central location is a draw. All but two of the New England-named rooms have private baths; two cuddly teddy bears welcome guests to Nantucket on the first floor. An ample continental breakfast with home-baked breads and muffins, yogurt and fruits gets you going in the morning. This is served at a large table in a parlor warmed by a wood stove, or you can take your food into the next door sun room, where (alas) the visuals are marred by a Pepsi machine. Facilities include a tennis court, swimming pool and a hot tub. Doubles, $60 to $80.

Crawford Notch

The Notchland Inn, Harts Location, Bartlett 03812, (603) 374-6131 or (800) 866-6131. In the nine years since John and Pat Bernardin discovered this 18th-century stone house in a state of disrepair and set about fixing it up, they have done amazing things. We found John out back constructing yet another outbuilding for the animals, and before he'd take us inside the inn, he insisted on showing the darling baby African goats and African pygmy goats in the barn. Also in residence are llamas, unusual sheep, Belgian horses that pull the wagon and sometimes a sleigh in winter, two miniature horses named Mork and Mindy, and Ruggs, an aged golden retriever. A huge pile of firewood out back is not for show; the inn's seventeen fireplaces burn about 75 cords a season. All accommodations — nine rooms in the main inn and two marvelous suites in a separate building out by the stream — have fireplaces. Laura Ashley wallpapers and fabrics, updated private baths and many decorator touches make these rooms perfect for romantic weekends. Wall-to-wall carpeting adds warmth and some rooms have wicker furniture; in others you'll find wing chairs for sitting in front of the fireplace. Several on the third floor have been expanded with large windowed dormers done so expertly you'd never know they were additions. Pat, a fine cook, serves breakfast and dinner to inn guests in a wing that John says is a part of Abel Crawford's tavern, the oldest continuously used inn building (since 1790) in the North Conway area. The fireplaced dining room with lots of windows adjoins a fireplaced sun room where guests like to lounge on chilly days. The Gustav Stickley room with lots of games and magazines is a great gathering place; the map on the floor is of the White Mountain National Forest. Bring your own wine to dinner, which is available to outsiders by reservation. It's a two-hour affair with one sitting at 7:30. Beef wellington, stuffed trout and a cajun chicken dish are among the house specialties. Doubles, $145 to $160, MAP.

Glen

The Bernerhof, Route 302, Glen 03838, (603) 383-4414 or (800) 548-8007. Long known for its dining, The Bernerhof has upgraded guest rooms on its second and third floors and some are positively elegant. Of nine guest facilities, six are "spa rooms" and two of those six are suites. These spa rooms have king or queen beds, whirlpool tubs big enough for two, and interesting appointments. We liked Room 4 with its brass kingsize bed and a separate raised area in the bathroom for the spa tub, from which a shuttered opening looks out on the bedroom. Quilts on the beds add a homey touch. On the morning of a third night's stay, you're treated to a complimentary champagne breakfast in bed. A full hot breakfast is included in the rates. Doubles, $90 to $135, B&B; $140 to $185, MAP.

The Red Apple Inn, Route 302, Glen 03838, (603) 383-9680. This really is a motel, but one that is handsomely appointed. Out back is a nice outdoor area with playscape for children, picnic tables and swimming pool. Inside is a fireplaced game room, a dining area off the lobby for a complimentary continental breakfast, and a large-screen TV for family movies. Each of the sixteen rooms contains two double beds, phone and cable TV. Doubles, $59 to $79.

Intervale

Riverside, Route 16A, Intervale 03845, (603) 356-9060. This elegant B&B is run by Anne and Geoffrey Cotter, who have been around the valley a long time. In fact, their yellow house with wraparound porch was built in 1906 as a summer "cottage" by Geoff's grandfather. It is carpeted in deep green throughout, including seven pleasant bedrooms on the second and third floors. Three have private bathrooms and four share two baths. The popular Esther room includes a brass bed, an armoire and a view of the east branch of the Saco River that flows through the property. With its wicker-furnished front porch, its side porch with bar (Auntie's Porchside Lounge) and a gracious living room with fireplace, the inn emits an elegant comfort. Anne, who ran a restaurant previously, devotes her energy to serving gourmet dinners in the pink and green dining room (an option for guests and open to the public). Breakfasts are outstanding: baked apples, eggs benedict, crepes and such. Geoff entertains guests with stories of the valley. Doubles, $55 to $95.

The 1785 Inn, North Main Street, Box 1785, North Conway 03860, (603) 356-9025 or (800) 421-1785. Becky and Charlie Mallar, who took over in 1984, have won acclaim for their dining room and we're not surprised: the aroma of roasting lamb tantalized us on a rainy afternoon visit. The seventeen guest rooms in the inn, twelve with private baths, are simple and homey. All beds have white or off-white Martha Washington-style bedspreads, lending a not-unpleasing uniformity. Some of the furniture is painted in country style. A pool out back is surrounded by a white picket fence. There are a cozy living room with fireplace and a very dark and romantic lounge for drinks before or after dinner. Rates include a full breakfast served in the wraparound dining room with views of the mountains. The old portion of the inn, built in 1785 by Elijah Dinsmore, is one of the oldest buildings in the valley. Outdoors, relax in one of the redwood chairs and contemplate an extraordinary view of Mount Washington and the Presidential Range from an area next to the famed Scenic Vista. Doubles, $99 to $129.

North Conway

Wildflowers Guest House, North Main Street (Route 16), North Conway (Box 802, Intervale 03845), (603) 356-2224. You're far enough north on the main drag to escape some of the awful traffic, but this is still North Conway — despite the P.O. address. The house, designed by Boston architect Stephen C. Earle as a summer place a century ago, remains one of our favorites. Innkeepers Eileen Davies and Dean Franke offer six guest rooms, two with private baths. In the parlor, a matching teal velvet sofa and loveseat face the wood stove and there's an oriental rug on the floor. Similarly attractive decorating is found throughout the large guest rooms on the second and third floors. Breakfast is served in a bright breakfast room wallpapered in blue with splashy white and yellow flowers. Wildflower wallpapers are used in all the guest rooms, where bouquets of fresh flowers are often displayed. A deep blue rug leads up the stairs and you'll find a nifty built-in loveseat at the landing. Eileen bakes coffee cake to go with the light continental breakfast. Three inn cats greet you from the porch, but never go inside. Doubles, $48 to $90.

The Old Red Inn & Cottages, Route 16, North Conway 03860, (603) 356-2642. Although right on the main drag in the middle of the commercial area, this is a place apart, a throwback to the old days of innkeeping with ten separate cottages and an early 19th-century inn. All are painted red with white trim and kept very nicely by owners Winnie and Don White. Winnie was previously involved in an herb business and hangs dried herb wreaths in most rooms. Of the seven rooms with private baths in the inn, we particularly like the suite with canopied queensize bed and adjacent kitchenette where you can breakfast in front of a picture window with a view of Mount Washington. It rents for $96. Four cottages have two bedrooms and two have kitchens. Winnie makes a full breakfast for everyone in the morning; it's served buffet-style in the inn parlor. Doubles, $64 to $90. Closed December-April.

Red Jacket Mountain View Motor Inn, Route 16, North Conway 03860, (603) 356-5411 or (800) 752-2538. If you want a first-rate motel, complete with a view, its own large restaurant and after-dark spot, an indoor pool and a few other things to do, this amply fills the bill. Carl Lindblade, who celebrated his twentieth year as manager in 1993, oversees the 150 rooms. They include two-bedroom townhouses with full kitchens, plus Loft Rooms that contain two additional twin beds in the loft area (and are very popular with families). The fireplaced Palmer Lounge offers evening entertainment. Champney's, the dining room, affords sweeping mountain views. A bocce court was recently added outdoors and the indoor swimming pool is quite spacious. While there are many motels in town, the Red Jacket stands (literally) above the rest. Doubles, $98 to $148; townhouses, $190.

Cranmore Mountain Lodge, Kearsarge Street, Box 1194, North Conway 03860, (603) 356-3596. This white clapboard inn with red trim is set down from one of the bypass roads in North Conway, the north-south Kearsarge Street. This allows you to stay away from midtown congestion and have a quieter time. The lodge is very close to the Mount Cranmore ski area as well. You can find traditional rooms, each with a private bath, in the main inn; modernized rooms with private bath and color cable TV in the Barn Loft, or — for economy-minded outdoor enthusiasts and groups — there are four rooms with 40 bunks that rent at bargain rates. A full country breakfast comes with the rooms. Bunks, $26; doubles, $79 to $89; two-bedroom suites, $150.

Sheraton White Mountain Inn, Route 16/302 at Settlers Green, North Conway 03860, (603) 356-9300 or (800) 648-4397. Now there's a Sheraton in North Conway, located next to one of the major discount shopping malls and surrounded by a parking lot. It offers 200 guest rooms, an indoor swimming pool, an informal restaurant and all the usual amenities. Doubles, $89 to $129.

White Trellis Motel, Route 16, North Conway 03860, (603) 356-2492. One of the best-kept motels in town is this charmer, located three-fourths of a mile north of the village center. The 22 motel rooms with knotty pine paneling are decorated in traditional Colonial style and all have cable TV. Doubles, $85 to $120.

A Special Place in Pinkham Notch

Appalachian Mountain Club, Pinkham Notch Camp, Box 298, Gorham 03581, (603) 466-2727. You don't have to be a member of the AMC to stay at this camp, which appeals to the hiker and backpacker and is often used by families. Located in the midst of the highest mountains, the camp is eleven miles north of Jackson. Trails lead from the busy base camp in all directions, including the summit of Mount Washington. Down vests, parkas and sturdy shoes are the fashion. The place really jumps in the summer and fall, so reservations are necessary. It is open 365 days a year and Christmas can be especially busy, too. Accommodations are bunk-style in spotless, rough pine-walled rooms in the Joe Dodge Lodge across from the A-frame style building containing dining room, store and meeting rooms. In the lodge are a fireplaced lounge with grand piano and Appalachian-style furniture, perfect for singalongs; downstairs is the cozy Rathskellar, also with a fireplace. Meals are served cafeteria-style in the morning and family-style at dinner in the pine-paneled dining room with soaring roof and great views from the huge  window. There's also meal service throughout the day with a chance to purchase snacks, sandwiches, trail lunches and other food supplies. Adult rates are $34 B&B, $44 MAP; children, $21 and $26.

Camping

Camping is big in the White Mountains and favored sites are those in the **White Mountain National Forest.** Most are available from mid-May to mid-October, on a first-come, first-served basis. Call (800) 283-2267 between March 1 and Sept. 30 to reserve one of the primitive sites — no hookups — offered through the forest camping system. **Crawford Notch State Park** has 30 units in its Dry River campground, twelve miles west of Bartlett on Route 302 in a wonderfully scenic area.

Private campgrounds include **Saco River Camping Area** on the Saco River in North Conway, (603) 356-3360; **Glen Ellis Campground** in Glen, (603) 383-6801, with 170 wooded and wilderness sites and a pool, not far from Story Land, and the **Crawford Notch General Store & Campground** in Hart's Location out Route 302, (603) 374-2779, advertising itself as the only private campground within the National Forest.

Seeing and Doing

Activities in the Mount Washington Valley focus on getting up and down, and hiking through, the mountains that surround it. Most people want to get to the peak of peaks — the summit of Mount Washington — the view that P.T. Barnum called "the second greatest show on earth." Mount Washington is particularly famed because of the wild weather reports issued from its observatory, which is manned year-round. The highest wind measured here set a world record, 231 miles per hour, on April 12, 1934. The lowest temperature was 47 below zero; the highest, a mere 71 above. So, if you're making the trip to the top, take suitable clothing.

Fishing, canoeing and white river rafting are other outdoor activities in the valley. A whole new clientele is drawn to the expanding array of factory outlets and discount stores in the area.

The Ups and Downs

Mount Washington Cog Railway, Route 302, Bretton Woods, (603) 846-5404 or (800) 922-8825. The most well-known and certainly the quaintest way to get to the top of Mount Washington is via the world's first cog railway, which has been operating along a 3.5-mile trestle-track since 1869. The average grade is 25 percent, although one particularly steep portion, known as Jacob's Ladder, rises at 37.4 percent. We have to admit driving to the summit via the auto road, but even if you don't actually ride the cog railway, a visit to the base station in Fabyan is a must. You can get great pictures as the feisty steam engine, billowing and snorting, disappears with its carload of passengers in a cloud of smoke. In the parking area is a display of the original railway engine, Old Peppersass. Depending on demand, up to eight trains a day can be run up the mountain. The trip takes a couple of hours, with a twenty-minute visit to the summit. The summit lodge contains a huge stone fireplace that is usually ablaze (and very welcome) as well as a neat dining area with old wood tables and windsor chairs for coffee, a sandwich or a snack. There's a souvenir shop with stuff like raccoon caps for the kids, little pine needle pillows that smell so refreshing, photographic placemats, T-shirts and a video of the cog railway for $24.95. Also on the site in a separate small building is a funky little museum with history on the cog railway and even a family of stuffed bears. Trips daily by reservation, mid-April through October. Adults $32, children $22.

Mount Washington Auto Road, Route 16, Pinkham Notch, Gorham, (603) 466-3988 or 466-2222. Opened in 1861, the eight-mile "Road to the Clouds" is used by cars and cycles. You can drive your own car (after which you can apply the bumper sticker, "This Car Climbed Mount Washington") or relax in a van driven for you. This was hardly our most frightening drive up a mountain, but it does have its dizzying moments; the average grade is twelve percent and there are frequent turnouts for taking photos or just taking in the view. The main reminder: pick a clear day or you may not see a thing. The trip takes about a half hour each way, and you should allow at least a half hour at the top. Season: mid-May to mid-October. Car and driver, $12; each passenger, $5; children, $3. Guided tour fare, adults $17, children $10.

Wildcat Gondola, Route 16, Pinkham Notch, (603) 466-3326. These enclosed two-person cars take riders on a mile-long trip to the 4,000-foot summit of Wildcat, the largest ski area in the valley. From the top you get a fantastic view of Mount Washington; there's a picnic area and some nature trails. The ride takes about 25 minutes round-trip. Open daily 9 to 4, late June to mid-October. Adults $6.50, children $4.50.

Attitash Alpine Slide, Route 302, Bartlett, (603) 374-2368. The Attitash ski area continues to expand with nearly an entire village of shops and restaurants at its base. You can take a scenic ride up the Attitash skylift, and follow it with a three-quarter-mile journey down the mountain in an Alpine Slide sled. Spectators can also ride the triple chairlift to visit the mountain's new observation tower, with its 270-degree view of the White Mountains. Open daily 10 to 5 in summer and weekends until Columbus Day. Adults $5.50, children $4.

Walking and Hiking

When you head into the mountains, know where you are going and let someone else know, too. Pick up a guide to any of the many trails in the area and study it before you take off. The AMC official guide to the White Mountains is a must for the serious hiker.

Trails lead off the road from many places in the White Mountain National Forest. Terrain varies from the mild and slightly sloping grades one finds on the ascent up North Conway's Black Cap Mountain to the wild and steep Huntington Ravine Trail, which requires lots of hand-over-hand maneuvering and is not for the faint of heart or ill-prepared.

The AMC Camp in Pinkham Notch is the center of hiking activities and offers many guided day and half-day hikes. There's good reading material and advice to be gotten here. Altogether, there are more than 1,200 miles of hiking trails in the White Mountains.

A tradition at AMC's Pinkham Notch Visitors Center is the Saturday evening lecture, a free program following the suppertime meal (adults $10, children $5). Call (603) 466-2727 for a schedule of programs.

Skiing

Downhill skiing can be pursued at four areas in the valley: Wildcat, Mount Cranmore, Attitash and Black Mountain. A bit farther west is Bretton Woods.

Wildcat is the most challenging of the areas with a vertical drop of 2,100 feet and 30 trails, nearly half of them rated for advanced skiers. The area is the farthest north, in Pinkham Notch, and from the top of the trails you get a very good look at Mount Washington. Snowmaking machines cover nearly all of its ski terrain. Five chairlifts and a gondola provide good uphill capacity. Adults, $34 Saturday and holidays, $29 Sunday, $27 midweek.

Mount Cranmore, in the center of North Conway, is the oldest ski area in these parts and one of the oldest in the country. Its famed skimobile has been retired, but its fans remain loyal to Cranmore. One of the pluses is night skiing. Another is 100 percent snowmaking. The vertical drop is 1,200 feet and there are 28 trails and five lifts. Adults, $33 weekends, $23 midweek; night skiing, Thursday-Saturday 4 to 9, $15.

Attitash is located in Bartlett and caters to families. Half of its 27 trails are rated intermediate, and the area is known for its trail grooming. Six lifts carry skiers up its 1,750-foot vertical rise. Its Children's Center advertises "some of the best kid-tested and approved programs available anywhere." Adults, $34 weekend, $27 midweek.

Black Mountain is a smaller, very comfortable downhill ski area above the mountain town of Jackson. There are 20 trails and a 1,100-foot vertical drop. The prices are lower here — a family pass allows two adults and two juniors to ski for $58 a day — and lift lines tend to be shorter. It's a great place to learn to ski. Adults, $29 weekend, $12 midweek.

Cross-country skiing is sensational in Jackson, where 64 groomed trails offer 91 miles of touring around the village and in the White Mountain National Forest. There are any number of nifty inns or restaurants to stop at for lunch. You can even take the gondola to the summit of Wildcat and tour downhill via a twelve-mile trail to Jackson, 3,200 feet below.

Driving

Our favorite road for sightseeing is the Kancamagus Highway (Route 112). Others are Bear Notch Road from the Kancamagus Highway to Bartlett, Kearsarge Road from

North Conway to Intervale and Route 16 north into Pinkham Notch. Crawford Notch Road (Route 302) is an old road passing mountain cascades and Crawford Notch State Park. Stop at the **Mount Washington Hotel** on Route 302 in Bretton Woods just to look around this beautiful old resort. Site of the Bretton Woods Monetary Conference of 1944, when representatives of 44 nations met here, the great white hotel with red roof keeps photos commemorating the event in the historic Gold Room off the huge lobby. A porch with a view of the Presidential Range stretches across the back of the hotel. You can have lunch at the hotel, but you may not be impressed with the location of the luncheon spot, Stickney's, on the lower level. More impressive are the golf course and the lobby with huge fireplaces and inviting settees.

On the Level

Echo Lake State Park, reached from West Side Road, North Conway, is picturesque. From one bank of its small lake you have a view of White Horse Ledge, sometimes with rock climbers scaling it. The large, well-kept picnic grove is good for a midday repast if the weather is not too brisk. There's swimming in summer. Parking, $2.

Conway Scenic Railway, Route 16, North Conway, (603) 356-5251. The photogenic gold and white Victorian railway station behind North Conway's green is headquarters for steam train rides south to Conway. You can ride in an enclosed coach or an open "cinder collector" car. The trip takes about an hour. Back at the station you'll find a snack bar, picnic tables and a gift shop specializing in railroad items. Trains run daily at 10,

Foliage is reflected in Echo Lake.

noon, 2 and 4, June-October; weekends in spring and late fall. Adults $7, children $4.50.

Another train ride, called **The Mountain Division,** was to be offered in 1993, if plans went as its backers hoped. This excursion would run along tracks from Bartlett to Fabyan, roughly parallel to Route 302, only a bit higher up the mountainside, and the views would be breathtaking.

Heritage New Hampshire, Route 16, Glen, (603) 383-9776. Bob Morrell, whose reputation for wholesome, well-run enterprises seems deserved, is the inspiration behind this place. A Bicentennial project, it provides a "you-are-there" approach to the state's history via dioramas, talking figures and costumed guides (some of them young adults from England whose accents are all the more authentic). Part of the fun is riding a vintage trolley from which you can trace 300 years of New Hampshire history by viewing a 120-foot-long mural, the largest outdoors in New England. Open daily 9 to 6 in summer, 9 to 5 in spring and fall; closed mid-October to Memorial Day. Adults $7.50, children $4.50.

Story Land, Route 16, Glen, (603) 383-4293. Located adjacent to Heritage New Hampshire, this is another Morrell family enterprise and is it popular! You can barely

226

find a parking space during the summer or on fall weekends. This is an amusement park-like attraction where favorite storybook characters come to life via rides, shows and exhibits. You can attend the Farm Follies Show, take a ride on Space Fantasy, or visit a South of the Border town. Open daily 9 to 6 in summer, weekends to Columbus Day. Admission, including unlimited rides and entertainment, $13; under 4, free.

Canoeing down the Saco River, golfing at the Wentworth Resort in Jackson and playing tennis at Mount Cranmore are other activities. You can rent canoes at several facilities in the valley. Among the local liveries are Canoe King of New England in North Conway, (603) 356-5280, or the Joe Jones North Shop in Intervale, which also rents rubber rafts, (603) 356-6848.

Shopping

The ever-increasing numbers of factory outlets are a great lure. Canadians who have come here in droves to take advantage of low prices, tax-free, have helped the local economy enormously.

There's no sales tax on clothing in New Hampshire. Among the names in North Conway discount stores: **Calvin Klein, Benetton, Banister Shoes, Liz Claiborne, Gorham, Polly Flinders, Eddie Bauer, Bugle Boy, J. Crew, Ralph Lauren** and **Patagonia. Anne Klein, Ellen Tracey** and **L.L. Bean** have factory outlet shops in the same small complex. We've found especially good bargains at **Banana Republic** on several occasions.

The **Jack Frost Shop** in Jackson is a preppy and expensive clothing and gift shop.

In the center of North Conway, the **Joe Jones Ski and Sport Shop** sells sporting goods for every season. **International Mountain Equipment** also draws the sportsman. **Carroll Reed** is headquartered here; check the bargains on the lower level of its Main Street store. **The Penguin** is a great gift shop with lots of ecologically-minded wares and stuffed penguins galore. **The Scottish Lion** inn runs a British/Scottish import shop. The **League of New Hampshire Craftsmen** has a large store in North Conway. **Yield House** is located here, too. And that's not the half of it.

Where to Eat

Appetites are hearty in the mountains and so is the food. Breakfast is bountiful; you'll probably like it that way, especially if you're planning a heavy day of touring, hiking, tennis, skiing or other energetic activities. Then you'll be ready for a big dinner at night.

Wildcat Inn and Tavern, Jackson, (603) 383-4245. Marty Sweeney, innkeeper with his wife Pam, oversees the kitchen at this restaurant, consistently rated tops in the area. It combines country charm and coziness with sophisticated dining at rational prices. The Wildcat's blue-gray building is located in the heart of Jackson Village. Three dining rooms offer an interesting mix of furnishings with creative placement of tables, homespun cloths and napkins, and soft candlelight in the evening. Three meals a day are served, with the emphasis at lunch on salads and sandwiches, like one with apple slices on dark bread topped with camembert cheese. A good selection of specials is available; we found the blackened red snapper with fresh fruit salsa to be excellent. The pea soup that evening was creamy and good. Entrees ($12.95 to $18.95) include Wildcat chicken (a boneless breast stuffed with capicola ham and cheese, wrapped in puff pastry and lightly topped with mustard sauce), loin of lamb with garlic rosemary sauce and pork medallions sauteed with apples and onions in applejack maple sauce. A large salad like grilled chicken salad with avocado, bacon, tomatoes, blue cheese and eggs can make a meal in the evening. Breakfast daily, 7:30 to 9:30; lunch, 11:30 to 3; dinner, 6 to 9 or 10.

The Bernerhof, Route 302, Glen, (603) 383-4414. Home of the noted A Taste of the Mountains cooking school, the Bernerhof prides itself on its excellent dining room. Actually there are three rooms plus the Zumstein Room, a dark and European-style bar named for former owners. A black bear pelt adorns one of its walls. The most requested table for dining is a deuce in front of the bay window in one room, set off by itself, private and romantic. Sometimes, we're told, a real black bear prowls around out back, looking for leftovers, and guests all run to the windows to watch. You can't fault its taste. Among favorite dinner entrees ($15 to $21.95) are the German-Swiss dishes such as wiener schnitzel, emince Zurichoise (Swiss-style julienned veal sauteed with mushrooms and onions in a white wine and cream sauce and served with rosti potatoes) and beef and cheese fondues. Also on the menu are smoked salmon pasta, Australian lamb tenderloin served with a mint and citrus vinaigrette and roast Wisconsin duckling. Lunch daily in season, noon to 3; dinner, 5:30 to 9:30.

The 1785 Inn, Route 16 at the Scenic Vista, Intervale, (603) 356-9025. The wraparound dining room at this wonderful inn yields views of the mountains all around. But you may be too absorbed in what's happening on the table in front of you to notice. Chef Peter Willis has earned an outstanding reputation for such dishes as sherried rabbit, curried chicken sauteed with shiitake mushrooms and sundried tomatoes and served over homemade pasta, and a veal rib chop with morel mushrooms and a butter sauce. Entrees are in the $18 to $23 range. For an appetizer, you might choose cinnamon spiced shrimp, blackened scallops with ginger-pineapple salsa or caesar salad for two, prepared tableside. Dinner nightly, 5 to 9 or 10.

Christmas Farm Inn, Route 16A, Jackson, (603) 383-4313. House guests already know about the food at this inn, but the dining room is open to the public as well and increasingly frequented by those who come just for a meal. A nice range of offerings includes french onion soup, "On the Lighter Side" entrees like smoked chicken and tortilla salad or grilled vegetable kabob, several seafood dishes including shrimp scampi and broiled scallops rockefeller, and meat entrees like a mixed grill of tenderloin, veal dijon and grilled pepper steak. Entrees are priced from $11 to $18. The pastry chef is known for decorated cakes and tortes. Dinner nightly, 5:30 to 9 or 9:30. No smoking.

Thompson House Eatery (T.H.E.), Route 16A at 16, Jackson, (603) 383-9341. This delightful spot is extremely popular with the locals as well as tourists. The old red farmhouse in which the restaurant is located dates from the early 1800s. There are three separate dining areas, plus an outdoor terrace in summer. Calico tablecloths in deep blue and pink are overset with burgundy placemats and topped with vases of fresh flowers. The food has a sophisticated, original bent. As you enter, check the many specials listed on a blackboard. One old reliable is T.H.E. Baked Popeye, a casserole of spinach with mushrooms and cheeses. Seafood Francesca combines fish, scallops, Maine crab and Gulf shrimp with mushrooms in a white wine sauce. We loved our dinner salads — The Currier & Ives being fresh chicken with toasted almonds and raisins and the Encumbered Crab being heavy in the Maine crabmeat department — which came with a side tray of walnuts, poppy seeds, red pepper flakes, sunflower seeds and sesame seeds for sprinkling on top. The prices are right, dinner entrees ranging from $8.50 to $15. Open daily, 11:30 to 10.

Dana Place Inn, Route 16, Pinkham Notch, Jackson, (603) 383-6822. The owners put an emphasis on the dining rooms at this inn and added a large one out back a few years ago. Pink fanned napkins atop white tablecloths are feminine and pretty, and a Hungarian chef, Bali Szabu, was getting high marks at our latest visit. Among the Dana

Place classics ($15.95 to $19.95) are brandied apple chicken, shrimp Dana (shrimp and lobster sauteed with garlic, herbs and cream and served in a puff pastry), veal oscar and roast duckling. Two items under "spa cuisine" include pasta primavera and poached sole. You might begin with lobster alfredo, baked oysters manhattan or radicchio and endive salad. Strawberry tart and bread pudding with bourbon sauce are among the good desserts. Lunch in winter, 11 to 3; dinner nightly, 6 to 9 or 10.

Red Parka Pub, Route 302, Glen, (603) 383-4344. Located near the junction of Routes 302 and 16, the Red Parka Pub has proved enormously successful over twenty years. Locals love it, skiers flock to it and travelers return time and again. A young, spirited crew staffs the place, which has a menu in the form of a newspaper. All sorts of fun drinks take over Page One, and the bar is always jammed with drinkers and popcorn eaters. Here's where you'll find appetizers like spudskins, Buffalo wings, cajun popcorn shrimp and the Pub-Pub Platter, the last a sampler of spareribs, Florida-style shrimp, jack sticks, garlic bread and Buffalo wings, enough for four people at $12.95. Among the "Top Hen Hits" are chicken dijon and the ultimate chicken sandwich (grilled boneless breast on a bulkie roll with lettuce, mayonnaise and cranberry sauce), plus chicken teriyaki. Other entrees include the royal couple (prime rib and baked stuffed shrimp), stuffed pork chops and delmonico steak. Steaks are priced from $8.95 to $14.95 but you can get a hamburger for $5.95 or the ultimate chicken sandwich for $5.50. On the children's menu, the first item is liver and broccoli for $14.95, plus an asterisk and the note "only kidding, kids!" Desserts are delectable, from mud pie to a celestial cookie (a chewy peanut butter and chocolate chip cookie lightly heated and topped with vanilla ice cream and hot fudge). Groan. Dinner nightly, 4:30 to 10.

Bellini's, Seavey Street, North Conway, (603) 356-7000. Don't be put off by the bright pink exterior. Inside you'll get the best Italian food in the area, especially veal, we're assured. The unusual decor includes a tiled floor of large black and white squares and a carousel horse mounted just inside the entrance. The menu is basically divided between pastas and veal dishes ($9 to $16). The former include ravioli bolognese and fettuccine Bellini (with imported ham and fresh tomato slices in a light cream sauce). You'll also find veal parmigiana and a special veal of the day. Dinner nightly from 5.

Horsefeathers, Main Street, North Conway, (603) 356-2687. This is a fun, young-set spot, favored by college kids and families. The lines sometimes stretch out the doors on a Thursday or a Friday night, as much because of the location in the heart of the village as for the food. But you can get pretty much anything you want, from a "bodacious burger" to lusty lasagna. Dining is on three or four different levels and we rather pity the wait staff who have to be running up and down all the time, but they're young and don't seem to mind. A dish called chicken pajamas on is boneless chicken with imported cheeses and seasoned tomato sauce; scallop pie tops scallops with mushroom and crabmeat stuffing, broiled in butter and white wine in a crock. Entrees range from $5 to $15. Open daily, 11 to 10.

The Carriage Inn Restaurant in North Conway is considered reliable for its roast beef, turkey dinners and steaks and chops. **Yesterday's** in Jackson — owned by the Christmas Farm Inn — is popular for lunch. The **Shannon Door Pub** in Jackson is highly favored by locals for its pizza and Irish entertainment.

FOR MORE INFORMATION: Mount Washington Valley Chamber of Commerce, Route 16, Box 2300-G, North Conway, N.H. 03860. For area information call (603) 356-3171. For lodging reservations call (800) 367-3364.

229

Constitution Plaza is decked out with white lights for holiday season.

A Capital Christmas

Hartford, Conn.

Any town is special at Christmastime and each has its own traditions. And, of course, it's meaningful to celebrate at home. Since Hartford is our home and a special place at Christmas, we'd like to share some of its Yuletide cheer.

For some, Hartford has a reputation as a cold, big-business type of a city with a Yankee aloofness. But along comes December and on go thousands of twinkling lights at Constitution Plaza. Up go lights in the shape of a tree and a hearty "Noel" atop the Hartford Insurance Group Tower. The top of the 38-story CityPlace is aglow with red and green wreaths, formed by more than 2,000 lights a-twinkling on each of its four sides. Voices are raised in the awe-inspiring anthems of the "Messiah" at Bushnell Memorial Hall. The Hartford Ballet's "Nutcracker" enchants children of all ages. The Mark Twain House bedecks itself with wreaths and ropes, cranberries and popcorn. Even the Travelers Insurance Companies have been known to light the windows on eight darkened floors of their Plaza Building to spell out "JOY" for passing motorists on the interstate highways.

And joyful it is, with the Civic Center coliseum offering Yuletide specials along with national entertainers and the Hartford Whalers hockey team. The area's stores have a wealth of treasures for the Christmas shopper and the restaurants offer sustenance and cheer. First Night Hartford entices folks downtown to celebrate New Year's Eve with ten hours of non-stop entertainment, a parade and fireworks. The holiday season even goes out in style, with the annual Boar's Head Festival drawing capacity throngs to Mark Twain's old church.

When the expanded Civic Center coliseum reopened following the infamous roof collapse, Hartford was thrust into the major leagues. The 16,000-seat arena is New England's largest, although the city is the smallest to have a National Hockey League franchise.

Hartford always has been big-league in finance and insurance, of course, since Jeremiah Wadsworth founded the first insurance company here in 1794. The beacon atop the 527-foot Travelers Tower has been a landmark since 1919. Aetna Life & Casualty built the world's largest Colonial edifice for its head office in 1931. Phoenix Mutual's striking green, curved-glass "hyperboloid" is the world's first two-sided building and looks like a ship.

The Yankee insurance enterprise grew out of the "Biblical Utopia" established here in 1636 by the Rev. Thomas Hooker. He and the area's other Congregationalist settlers represented the first westward migration in North America, and their homes in Wethersfield and Farmington are treasured today.

So are the literary ties of 19th-century Hartford, when Mark Twain and Harriet Beecher Stowe made Nook Farm a unique center of gracious living and lively thinking. The arts are a tradition in Hartford, led by the Wadsworth Atheneum, the nation's oldest public art museum, and including the widely acclaimed Hartford Stage Company, Hartford Ballet and Hartford Symphony Orchestra.

But while Hartford dared to turn the nation's first downtown renewal area into Constitution Plaza, built the Northeast's largest civic center, soared skyward with a new cityscape and scored with the arts, it remains Yankee at heart and capital of tradition in Connecticut, the Land of Steady Habits.

And its best tradition is Christmas. You'll want to spend Christmas Day at home, of course, but there's no better time to visit Hartford than during the holiday period from Thanksgiving to Twelfth Night.

Getting There

Hartford is in the center of Connecticut, halfway between New York and Boston. Two major interstates, Routes 91 and 84, slice through its downtown and are being widened to end infamous traffic delays.

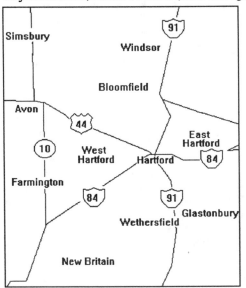

The 1914 Union Station has been revitalized into a colorful Transportation Center. Amtrak trains provide frequent passenger service to and from New York, New Haven and Springfield. Greyhound, Bonanza and Peter Pan buses offer long-distance service from the ground level, and Hartford's Connecticut Transit buses and taxis are close at hand.

Bradley International Airport, fifteen miles northwest of downtown, is served by American, Continental, Delta, Northwest, TWA, USAir and United airlines.

Although downtown is compact, Hartford and its suburbs are spread out. Some attractions in this chapter are best reached by car or bus.

Where to Stay

Although there are places to stay and things to do all across the Hartford area, this chapter focuses on the city, Old Wethersfield, West Hartford and the Farmington Valley, which are of most interest to visitors. The Hartford hotel situation was in transition as this edition went to press. The Parkview Hilton was demolished for an aborted World Trade Center. The Summit Hotel at 5 Constitution Plaza was closed and then purchased by hoteliers who planned to reopen it. A convention center and a controversial downtown casino were in the proposal stages; both included plans for major new hotels.

The Goodwin Hotel, 1 Haynes St., Hartford 06103, (203) 246-7500 or (800) 922-5006. Christened the J.P. Morgan Hotel until 1992 when it bowed to threatened litigation from the banking company of the same name, this deluxe newcomer saved face by taking the name of the historic Goodwin Building that it occupies. It retained the sumptuous J.P. Morgan Suite, a lavish, $629-a-night pad named for the Hartford-born financier who had ties with the Goodwin apartments. The only Connecticut member of the worldwide Preferred Hotels & Resorts group, this European-style urban hotel offers 113 rooms and eleven suites on six meandering floors. About half face onto the pillared atrium of the adjacent 30-story Goodwin Square office tower and seem rather cheerless for lack of daylight or access to the outside. Most rooms strike us as small, though they are nicely furnished with queensize (and a few kingsize) sleigh beds covered with down comforters, TVs on rich wood built-in shelves, corner loveseats, and marble bathrooms with pedestal sinks and hair dryers. The top-hatted doorman, the circular lobby, the marble floors, the burled wood walls and the richly paneled elevators create an elegant first impression. The sumptuous library-lounge and **Pierpont's,** the glamorous restaurant (see Festive Feasting), do not disappoint. Weekend packages start at $105. Doubles, $159 to $174; suites, $224 to $629.

Sheraton-Hartford Hotel, 315 Trumbull St. at Civic Center Plaza, Hartford 06103, (203) 728-5151. Built in 1975 with the Civic Center to which it is attached by a second-story skywalk, the Sheraton has 382 rooms, all recently renovated as part of an $8 million upgrade. Most have two double beds (some kingsize) and prints of local buildings by Hartford artist Richard Welling. There's a health club, and the large indoor pool is quite springlike with light filtering through a glass-domed roof. Three meals a day are served at **Ninety Three Church Street,** the hotel's second-floor restaurant. Singing waiters serenade guests as they sup on a broad range of American food priced from $5.95 to $19.95. Among the hotel's package plans is one called Whalers Win-Win Weekend, offering two hockey tickets, parking and overnight accommodations for two for a bargain $89. Doubles, $110 to $180.

Holiday Inn-Downtown, 50 Morgan St., Hartford 06120, (203) 549-2400. Situated — for better or worse — across I-84 from the rest of downtown, this eighteen-story hotel rose in the standings following the demise of the Parkview Hilton and Summit hotels. It has completed a $5 million renovation that added a new entrance on Morgan Street and meeting rooms. All public areas and nearly half the 343 guest rooms also were refurbished, with the rest scheduled for a facelift over the next two years. Facilities include an outdoor pool, a health club and **O'Neill's** restaurant, serving three meals daily. A weekend B&B package goes for $69 for two. Doubles, $96 to $125.

Ramada Inn-Capitol Hill, 440 Asylum St., Hartford 06103, (203) 246-6591. Except for its location fronting on Bushnell Park and the State Capitol, this is not one of the Ramada chain's more distinguished hotels. For comfort, amenities and in-and-out convenience, the Ramada Hotel just across the Connecticut River in East Hartford may be a better bet (doubles, $97 to $117). This bare-bones Ramada lacks a pool and its

Simsbury 1820 House dons its Yuletide finery.

oft-changing restaurant now is **Sharky's Restaurant and Lounge,** with a comedy club on Friday and Saturday evenings. The 96 rooms on seven floors have been redecorated. A complimentary breakfast includes danish pastries and granola bars. Doubles, $60 to $80.

Country Inns of New England, 100 Weston St., Hartford 06120, (203) 724-4667. In the shadows of downtown Hartford's office towers and not far from the jai-alai fronton is this budget establishment billed as a "country inn" on "eight acres of Connecticut landscaping." That translates to 134 motel-style units in a roundabout stucco structure with vaguely Tudor styling. The location is a commerce-park zone in Hartford's transitional North Meadows area just off I-91. Rooms are pleasantly furnished, and prices are low (doubles, $40.95 to $48.95). If you've got kids in tow, spring for a suite with an extra queensize sofa ($65).

Hartford Marriott Hotel/Farmington, 15 Farm Springs Road, Farmington 06032, (203) 678-1000. A deluxe suburban hotel just off I-84, this four-story brick structure near the end of a forested office park is one of the newest and nicest of the Marriotts. The 381 rooms, many with private patios and balconies, are spacious and individually decorated. Guests have use of indoor and outdoor pools, tennis courts, a video game room and a staffed health club. The colorful **Village Green** restaurant serves an ample luncheon buffet ($7.75) as well as a varied menu for lunch and dinner. **Nutmeg's,** a bistro-deli-tavern, serves appetizers, sandwiches and grilled fare from 11:30 to midnight. Doubles, $125 to $145; weekends, $99.

Avon Old Farms Hotel, Routes 44 and 10, Avon 06001, (203) 677-1651. A quiet suburban motel-turned-hotel, this has been renovated and expanded several times. The latest addition doubled its size to a total of 163 rooms, including a three-story atrium lobby and the new and well-regarded **Seasons** cafe-restaurant. The newer rooms are the more elegant, but all are of traditional Georgian design with poster beds, molding (and some stenciling), original watercolors by local artists of Farmington Valley scenes, and bathrooms with marble-like sinks and full-length mirrors. Besides an exercise facility and a sauna, there are a pool and a stream on the seventeen-acre property at the foot of Avon Mountain. The Brighenti family, innkeepers here, expanded their share of the suburban market in 1992, acquiring first the nearby Simsbury Inn and then the Farmington Inn. Doubles, $79 to $129.

Simsbury Inn, 397 Hopmeadow St., Box 287, Simsbury 06089, (203) 651-5700 or (800) 634-2719. New in 1988, this stylish, 100-room suburban hotel ran into financial difficulties before it was bailed out by the Brighenti family of the competing Avon Old Farms Hotel, who got it nicely back on track. Pineapples top the headboards of all the beds, which are covered with custom-designed pastel spreads that are the inn's signature. Rooms have lace curtains, antique clocks, remote-control TV, removable coat hangers and bathrooms with solid brass fixtures, mini-refrigerators, built-in hair dryers and a basket of the inn's own amenities. The indoor pool opens to the outside in summer, and adjoins an exercise room with saunas and whirlpool. The pleasant **Nutmeg Cafe** serves light fare. Twigs, a lounge with a circular bar, is notable for its bar stools carved like saddles with horse hooves for feet. From the soaring lobby, a hallway passes a wine cellar to reach **Evergreens,** the gracious main dining room with wooden pillars, brass sconces, lace draperies and a mural of 18th-century Simsbury. Dinner entrees ($17 to $26) are served at tables set with English bone china, crystal and sterling silver. Doubles, $119; suites, $175 to $350.

Simsbury 1820 House, 751 Hopmeadow St., Simsbury 06070, (203) 658-7658. A grand, wicker-filled veranda is at the entrance to this elegant inn, opened in 1986 in a restored 1820 country manor house listed on the National Register of Historic Places. The main-floor public rooms retain the remarkable wainscoting, molding and leaded-glass windows of the original; all the gilt-framed oil paintings are reproductions. In the pleasant sun room, an addition, guests may have a cocktail or play cards or other games. The 23 guest rooms on three floors in the main inn have been tastefully restored and furnished, some with kingsize four-poster beds. Many of the private baths have windows and have been tucked ingeniously into the nooks and crannies with which this fascinating house abounds. Most rooms possess comfortable sitting areas, but from them you can't watch the TVs, which are ensconced firmly in front of the beds. Garden patios adjoin a couple of suites in the Carriage House, which offers eleven more rooms and suites, all spacious and most decorated in dark and masculine tones, some with an equine theme. Some of the valley's better meals are served nightly in three serene, candlelit downstairs dining rooms, with brick archways and hunting scenes on the walls. Entrees ($15.95 to $23.95) range from Norwegian salmon en papillote to braised stuffed leg of veal. Continental breakfast is taken in the inn's sun room. Pre-Christmas shopping and Warm Up to Winter weekends are scheduled from Thanksgiving through April for $75 B&B, $135 MAP. Doubles, $90 to $130; suite $140.

The Barney House, 11 Mountain Spring Road, Farmington 06032, (203) 677-9735. If you'd like to stay in a gracious 1832 mansion, consider this. Open year-round as the Educational Conference Center of the University of Connecticut, the secluded three-story house amid formal gardens takes B&B guests by reservation. The seven spacious guest rooms, all but two with twin beds, are decorated with furnishings of the period, oriental carpets and fresh flowers, and have private baths, TVs and phones. In season, guests may tour the gardens and the Victorian greenhouse where herbs and lettuce are grown for conference dinners, swim in the pool and use the tennis court. A continental breakfast of coffee and danish is set out on the second-floor landing. Doubles, $89.

Chester Bulkley House, 184 Main St., Wethersfield 06109, (203) 563-4236. Live the way the Old Wethersfielders do in this 1830 Greek Revival home that has five bedrooms, three with private baths, in the heart of Old Wethersfield. Frank and Sophie Bottaro have furnished their home with period antiques in turn-of-the-century style. Hand-carved woodwork, wide pine floors and a Colonial brick fireplace with a beehive oven in the kitchen are original to the house. A warming fire in the parlor, fresh flowers and chocolates on the pillows at bedtime are typical of the Bottaros' caring touches. Guests take breakfast in a Victorian dining room shared by many of the owner's handmade antique dolls. The repast might include eggs, french toast or Finnish-style pancakes. Doubles, $65 to $75. No smoking.

Butternut Farm, 1654 Main St., Glastonbury 06033, (203) 633-7197. Don Reid, an enthusiastic herb grower, farmer, antiques collector and cook, opens two rooms, two suites and an apartment, all with private baths, for guests in his Colonial home. They sleep in antique beds, under antique hand-woven coverlets, surrounded by more of the same. And they breakfast on fresh eggs,

Old State House in front of bank tower.

milk and goat cheese from Don's goats and chickens. Lately, he has added a wing with a new parlor, and now has three new fireplaces, making eight in all (three in guest rooms). The cluttered keeping room of the house is quite incredible; dried herbs hang from the rafters and the lighting is as soft as if only candles were burning. You really step back two centuries in time. Doubles, $65 to $85.

Festive Feasting

The Hartford area has seen a proliferation of good new restaurants in recent years, from theme and ethnic spots to casual California-style newcomers and citadels of contemporary cuisine. There's no better time for feasting than at Christmas, when most of the restaurants are decked out for Yuletide.

Peppercorns Grill, 357 Main St., Hartford, (203) 547-1714. One of us had a birthday lunch at Peppercorns shortly after it opened and it was so good that she went back and had a birthday dinner the same day. Birthdays have come and gone, but Peppercorns remains in the vanguard of cucina fresca; our advancing age only makes us wish the place weren't so noisy. The two-section restaurant has red lacquered chairs around white formica tables, interesting art and neon squiggles on the walls, and a changing Christmas decor — individual miniature Christmas trees on each table and wrapped packages hanging from the ceiling in 1992. Our birthday lunch produced a special pizza topped with a generous portion of smoked salmon and creme fraiche, a most appetizing combination. Pastas, salads and entrees also are in the $6.95 to $8.50 range at lunch. At night, entrees are $15.50 to $19.95 (for grilled filet mignon on a bed of potato garlic sauce with roasted red and yellow pepper puree). Carpaccio and grilled portabello mushrooms with gorgonzola crostini on a bed of mesclun greens make excellent starters. Chocolate bread pudding, thick as fudge, with bourbon custard sauce is the signature dessert. The cajeta, a Southwestern flan made with goat's milk, is first-class, too. Lunch, Monday-Friday 11:30 to 2:30; dinner, Monday-Saturday 5:30 to 10 or 11:30.

Max on Main, 205 Main St., Hartford, (203) 522-2530. Calling itself a "city bistro," Max on Main is certainly that, with its rose and gray decor, dividers of glass bricks, open kitchen and young servers in pink button-down shirts and khaki pants. The floors are bare, the white cloths are covered with white paper and the chairs are lacquered. Unfortunately, it is so noisy that if you are at a table for more than two, you almost have to shout to make yourself heard. That's the price of popularity, we guess, and this is so popular that Rosenthal has opened a new Max-A-Mia in suburban Avon. The downtown Max is trendy enough to have an oyster bar, a long list of wines by the taste or glass and pizzas that have been renamed "stone pies." They bear toppings like eggplant caponata with spinach and ricotta or grilled chicken with asparagus and goat cheese and cost $8.95 or $9.25. We had another birthday lunch here, and very much enjoyed the mussels steamed with cilantro, cumin and tomato, and a salad of radicchio, watercress, arugula and belgian endive with black pepper goat cheese. The panfried catfish special with celeriac slaw, hush puppies and lime-butter sauce that one of our tablemates ordered was delicious, as was the dish of grilled homemade garlic sausages with fried new potatoes and cucumber salad. Owner Richard Rosenthal changes the menu daily. At night, pastas are $11.95 to $15.95 (for capellini with sea scallops, tomato, cilantro, chiles and lime). Entrees run from $13.95 for grilled pork loin with wild mushroom bread pudding and granny smith applesauce to $18.95 for porterhouse steak with straw potatoes and salsa fresca. Tirami su is the favorite dessert, but we prefer the white satin torte on a bed of fresh strawberry sauce. Lunch, Monday-Friday 11:30 to 2:30; dinner, Monday-Saturday 5 to 10 or 11.

Pierponts, 1 Haynes St., Hartford, (203) 522-4935. Hartford has no more glamorous dining room than this, a beauty in burled wood paneling, beige banquettes, mirrored walls, starched white linens and the most beautiful, custom-designed jaguar and parrot service plates imaginable. The restaurant at the Goodwin (nee J.P. Morgan) Hotel aims for the stars and does nicely, though its reach too often exceeds its grasp and service, while professional, can be downright slow. Since its heady opening days, it has downscaled and downpriced the menu, adding Southwestern dishes. Dinner entrees are priced from $16.75 for grilled free-range chicken with garlic mashed potatoes to $21 for grilled ribeye steak with roasted winter vegetables and barolo butter. We've liked such dishes here as pan-seared duckling with lingonberries, Maine crab cakes with jalapeno butter and pork chops with sundried cranberries and lacy sweet potatoes. The vegetables here are teamed individually with each entree and attractively presented. You might start with spicy lamb sausage with polenta, baked oysters with cornbread or lobster with basil pasta, Thai curry and lemon grass ($6.75 to $9). Or how about a "frizzy" salad with duck and crimson pears? Finish with apple pandowdy with calvados chantilly, pumpkin creme brulee or cappuccino mousse. The lunch menu here is equally wide-ranging, but not for the faint of wallet or those short of time. Lunch, Monday-Friday 11:30 to 2; dinner nightly, 5:30 to 10 or 11; Sunday brunch, 11:30 to 3.

Capitol Fish House Restaurant, 391 Main St., Hartford, (203) 724-3370. The best seafood in the city is served at this engaging, dimly lit establishment done up in brick and green. The printed menu of "faithful dinner specialties" would suffice in most places, things like baked scrod, pasta with white clam sauce, baked stuffed shrimp, coquilles St. Jacques and San Francisco cioppino ($11.25 to $24.75). But the daily specials are where it's at. At our visit, tuna was offered grilled with orange-tomato sauce,

236

broiled or blackened with herb butter or seared with capers, olive oil, lemon and ripe olives. Bluefish came grilled with curry lime vinaigrette, broiled with ginger butter or baked with bread crumbs. Grouper, redfish, rainbow trout, mahi-mahi, lobster and more were on the docket for $16.95 to $23. The only non-seafood items were grilled chicken and sirloin steak. Dessert standbys like cheesecake and carrot cake also are supplemented by nightly specials. Lunch, Monday-Friday 11:30 to 2:30; dinner, Monday-Saturday 5 to 10:30 or 11.

Hot Tomato's, 1 Union Place, Hartford, (203) 249-5100. Started in a downtown storefront, John Guerriero's Italian baby moved to larger quarters at one end of Union Station and spawned an offshoot, Hot Tamales, at the station's other end. This is one noisy and colorful cavern of a place, with floor-to-ceiling windows, neon lights, black faux marble tables, fuschia-colored booths and burgundy chairs. The staff is all in black from head to toe, except for two waiters in shorts, looking ludicrous the snowy pre-Christmas day we lunched here. Pastas are the rule; in fact, there are few other choices, beyond appetizers, grilled chicken salad, chicken and sausage stew, chicken parmesan and eggplant mascarpone at lunch. So go with the flow, as in a zesty spaghetti vongole ($8.95) with tiny manila clams in a garlicky butter sauce and cannelloni genovese ($7.95), three crepes stuffed with grilled chicken, cheese, sundried tomatoes and pinenuts, which would have been far better if they hadn't been served lukewarm. Good peasant bread with, egad, foil-wrapped butter and house salads came with. The roar of passing trains overhead occasionally drowned out the decidedly un-Christmasy music attuned to young ears. At night, pasta prices rise to the $9.95 to $19.95 range; three veal and three chicken dishes also are available for $13.95 to $19.95. Desserts run to white chocolate mousse, tirami su, carrot cake and espresso creme caramel. Lunch, Tuesday-Friday 11:30 to 2:30; dinner, Tuesday-Saturday 5:30 to 10 or 11.

Hot Tamales, 1 Union Station, Hartford, (203) 247-5544. The Southwest is enshrined in food and decor at this new, lower-key place opened by the Hot Tomato's folks at the north end of Union Station. Pastel murals of mountains and cactus bathed in violet light, tables inset with tiles, a quarry tile floor, live cactus plants and a lineup of masks above a very purplish bar provide an interesting backdrop. The chef fires things up, starting with homemade three-color tortilla chips and salsa. Try the scorpion bites (jalapeno peppers stuffed with jack cheese and shrimp, rolled in yellow cornmeal and deep-fried) or the shrimp tamale wrapped and steamed in a fresh corn husk for appetizers ($3.95 to $5.95). Red pork or green chile enchiladas, chimichangas, chicken mole, anaheim chile rellenos, aztec shrimp and a spicy swordfish ("not for wimps") are $6.25 to $8.25 at lunch, $8.95 to $16.95 at dinner. We like the sound of the hot pepper pasta — lobster, shrimp and scallops in a chipotle pepper cream sauce over jalapeno pepper fettuccine — a dinner specialty. Dessert could be raspberry-chocolate torte or kiwi sorbet in strawberry sauce. Lunch, Tuesday-Friday 11:30 to 2:30; dinner, Tuesday-Saturday 5:30 to 10 or 11.

Museum Cafe, Wadsworth Atheneum, 600 Main St., Hartford, (203) 728-5989. Poinsettias and artworks provide a modicum of color at Christmas for this serene cafe, sleek in black and gray. Large windows afford a view of the outdoor sculpture courtyard that's a lively setting for al fresco lunches in summer. Mellow, jazzy Christmas music played for a brunch made festive by three Christmasy breads in a basket and desserts like cranberry tart, dried fruit pudding with figs and a Yule log with chestnut mousse. From the short menu ($6.95 to $8.50) we tried tasty panfried crab cakes served with homefries that were barely cooked, let alone fried, and the cafe pasta, excellent pieces of chicken tossed with orecchiette pasta, plum tomatoes, calamata olives and spinach. Glasses of Hogue chardonnay and Firestone gewurztraminer accompanied. The expanded lunch menu ($4.95 to $8.50) offered by chef Paul Rossman, a painter with an artistic appreciation for food as well, is one of Hartford's more appealing. Besides the cafe pasta, you might find grilled spicy shrimp and scallops with red bean pesto and fried corn tortillas or grilled venison with chipotle sauce. Also available are a fruit and cheese board, grilled tuna sandwich with tomatoes, tapenade, roasted peppers and grilled onions on tuscan bread, and soup and salad or half a sandwich. Tea, scones and tea sandwiches are served for $5 on Sundays from noon to 4. The only downside here is that a sign at the museum entrance says cafe-goers must pay the $3 museum admission, although we managed to talk our way in. Lunch, Tuesday-Friday 11:30 to 2:30, Saturday noon to 3; Sunday brunch, noon to 3.

Congress Rotisserie, 7 Maple Ave., Hartford. (203) 560-1965. One of Hartford's "now" restaurants, this opened in 1986 and proved so popular that its takeout service has been expanded across the city and was being franchised as this edition went to press. The bar is crowded at happy hour, when the addictive homemade all-natural potato chips are gratis, and all we can say is we're thankful the music gets turned down after HH is over. Wonderful aromas come from the ever-turning rotisserie, where the cooks wear black berets. The hip crowd dines on two levels amid a stark black-and-white decor. The all-day menu ranges widely, from omelets, appetizers made for grazing, sandwiches and salads to pastas and entrees. The grilled shrimp marinated in ginger plum sauce and served over sesame noodles is the best-seller and priciest pasta dish at $10.95. Nothing else is in double digits except chicken and dumplings ($11.95) and grilled sirloin steak with onion strings and mashed potatoes ($17.95). Meat loaf and shepherd's pie are two wintertime back-to-basics for under $10. The rotisserie chicken (a half bird with choice of two side dishes) is $7.95 here, $4.95 at the takeout. Fresh yogurt of the day with fruit topping, rich pecan pie and mile-high apple pie are among desserts. The adjacent carry-out sells interesting sandwiches, many of the dishes offered in the rotisserie, and those delicious potato chips at $1.60 for a large portion. Lunch, Monday-Saturday 11 to 5; dinner nightly, 5 to midnight or 1.

Brown, Thomson & Company, 942 Main St., Hartford, (203) 525-1600. Billing itself as a food and drink emporium, this is more a place for fun than serious dining — that is, if you can even get past the mob scene at the large bar. In the old Brown, Thomson department store and built around an atrium on several levels filled with antiques and memorabilia, BT is worth a visit just to look. The menu is huge, from house drinks using ice cream like oreo cookie and peanut butter cup to desserts like mud pie and deep-fried ice cream. In between are salads ($5.95 to $8.95, including spinach, cobb, taco and blackened chicken), many sandwiches, burgers, appetizers like Buffalo wings and popcorn shrimp, and dinner entrees from $9.95 for barbecued chicken to $15.95 for filet mignon. Cajun entrees are served with herbed rice; some of the dishes are Mexican, and you can get a Philly cheese steak sandwich or a vegetable stir-fry — this place has something for everyone. Open from 11:30 to 11 or midnight; Sunday brunch, 11:30 to 3, dinner to 10.

Costa del Sol, 901 Wethersfield Ave., Hartford, (203) 560-1714. This endearing Spanish restaurant, located in Hartford's Italian South End, is consistently excellent. Its two small rooms have white-clothed tables with a red and a white carnation on each, a red carpet underfoot, and rough white plaster walls for a Mediterranean feeling. We crave the paella Valenciana for two ($10.95 each) and usually talk a dinnermate into joining us; it's an ample portion served in the traditional two-handled metal pan. At one visit a friend chose baby coho salmon served with a dill sauce; another had the red snapper, moist and succulent, which came in a dish with mussels and Spanish vegetables. The onion soup is particularly good; a creamy shellfish soup is also on the menu. While the house salad with its dijon vinaigrette dressing is excellent, the ensalada catalano includes prosciutto, asparagus, tomatoes and artichoke hearts in the house dressing. About 30 hot and cold tapas are offered for $2.95 to $4.95 nightly except on weekends. Other entrees ($11.95 to $21.95) include veal chops or beef in a Spanish sauce, but seafood is king here. Portions are ample, but save room for the delectable flan. Lunch, Tuesday-Friday 11:30 to 2:30; dinner, Tuesday-Saturday 5 to 10, Sunday 4 to 9. Beer and wine only.

Standish House, 222 Main St., Wethersfield, (203) 721-1113. One of the grandest homes in Old Wethersfield when it was built in 1790, this began a new life as a restaurant in 1984 under the aegis of the Wethersfield Historical Society, which owns the building. It has been carefully restored with soft Williamsburg colors and Axminster woven carpets. Two small dining rooms downstairs (one with Queen Anne chairs) and three larger ones upstairs seat 100 people for lunch and dinner. One of our corporate boards finds it a perfect setting for its annual Christmas dinner. Our latest outing there yielded memorable appetizers of chilled oversize mussels with apple horseradish mayonnaise ($4.75) and salmon sausage with rouille lemon sauce ($6.25). Among entrees ($13.95 to $21.95), the breast of duck with fresh pears, the sherried veal medallions with a sweetbread and mushroom ragout and the tournedos of beef with shiitake mushrooms and sundried tomatoes were winners. And the marble cheesecake, chocolate-raspberry mousse cake and chocolate silk walnut torte with creme anglaise were too much to finish. Dinner, Tuesday-Saturday 5 to 9.

Assagio, 904 Farmington Ave., West Hartford, (203) 233-4520. The owners of this enduring Italian eatery in a building that has harbored a succession of failures embody the Christmas spirit, offering special dinners to the needy and giving away holiday meals to the homeless. Their spacious dining room is a pretty space, all curves and angles and niches, set off by lattice work and opaque glass-brick partitions with endless circles of white neon overhead. Pizzas ($7 to $9), baked in a wood-burning oven, come with a crackling crust and exotic ingredients. Among other starters we like the delicate black bean and red pepper soup and the spiedini romano, a skewer of shrimp and pancetta-wrapped oysters, served with grilled garlic bread. The pastas and risottos ($9 to $14.50) are delectable, especially the angel hair tossed with shrimp, sundried tomatoes, pinenuts and salty calamata olives. The chef also shines on such entrees ($14 to $23.50) as grilled catfish with tomato-pesto aioli, grilled salmon with lemon-pinenut sauce and sauteed escarole, and grilled veal chop with wild mushroom and fresh chive cream sauce. Ricotta cheesecake with strawberries and homemade pistachio gelato topped by chocolate-coconut sauce are stellar desserts. Lunch, Monday-Friday 11:45 to 2:30; dinner, Monday-Saturday 5:30 to 10 or 10:30.

Butterfield's, 971 Farmington Ave., West Hartford, (203) 231-1922. Tucked behind the Toy Chest in the municipal parking lot is this whimsical new place with a wall of windows, a jungle of plants and a papier-mache serpent coiled in a grapevine arbor over the bar, with bunches of decorative grapes spilling from all sides. Steve Kantrowitz, former executive chef at Hartford's Max on Main, has upgraded the fare, emphasizing rustic dishes priced affordably. The small and imaginative menu produces such treats ($8.95 to $13.95) as grilled yellowfin tuna on focaccia topped with roasted peppers and arugula, and sesame roast leg of lamb with toasted pecans, Chinese cabbage, snow peas and scallions. We liked the penne with grilled chicken and sundried tomatoes. Owner Palmer Butterfield, the pastry chef, prepares the fine, ever-changing desserts. The beer and wine lists are interesting as well. Open Tuesday-Saturday, 11:30 to 10 or midnight.

Apricots, 1593 Farmington Ave. (Route 4), Farmington, (203) 673-5405. Ann Howard was known first for her cooking lessons in her home and then for her Ann

Howard Cookery in Farmington, from which are catered some of the best parties in town. So there was general rejoicing when at Christmas 1982 she opened Apricots, "a juicy pub," in an old trolley barn beside the Farmington River. Downstairs is a cozy pub with exposed pipes painted with apricots and leaves by Farmington artist Tom Rose; more apricots are painted on walls and posts in the sunny and simple outer dining room upstairs, with views of the river through old-fashioned, porch-like windows. In summer, a shortened menu is available on a terrace right beside the river. A casual menu is served in the pub, and upstairs at night entrees are $14.95 to $28.50 for dishes like lobster and sea scallops fra diavalo, roast quail stuffed with veal and wild mushrooms, roast leg of venison with pear and port wine sauce, and sauteed veal tenderloin served with prosciutto and mushrooms. For lunch over the years, we've enjoyed warm poached salmon salad served over greens, vegetarian focac-

Dining alcove at Apricots.

cia pie with salad, pizza a la mexicaine, the famous chicken pot pie, a creamy fettuccine with crab and mushrooms, and wonderful mussels ($6.50 to $12.95). The menu changes seasonally and Ann Howard keeps up on all the latest trends. The intense and lovely apricot mousse is offered only occasionally these days, but there's apricot gelato ($4.50). Lunch, Monday-Saturday 11:30 to 2:30; dinner, 6 to 10, pub from 2:30; Sunday brunch, 11:30 to 2:30.

Max-A-Mia, 70 East Main St., Avon, (203) 677-6299. This wildly popular offshoot of Hartford's Max on Main is hot. Hot as in trendy, hot in value and hot in popularity. Folks line up day and night to dine happily on crostini sandwiches, a variety of thin-crusted pizzas called stone pies, powerful pastas and a few grills, priced from $4.95 to $8.95 at lunch, $6.95 to $13.95 at dinner. A birthday lunch here became quite festive when four of us sampled the sauteed chicken livers (elaborately served with white beans, roasted shallots, arugula, plum tomatoes, porcini mushrooms and fresh herbs), the sauteed catfish topped with a cucumber salad and served over a roasted plum tomato and lavender coulis, the PLT (prosciutto, arugula, roma tomatoes and fresh mozzarella served on focaccia), and a stone pie with white clams, sweet roasted peppers, pancetta and parmigiana. An order of bruschetta and a $14 bottle of pinot grigio from the all-Italian wine list accompanied. Ricotta cheesecake with amarone cherries, chocolate polenta cake with cappuccino sauce, tirami su and chocolate-hazelnut gelato were better than any birthday cake. At night, try one of the baked pastas al forno, changing risottos, tantalizing pastas or the grilled skirt steak with watercress and tuscan peppers, served with fried leeks and matchstick potatoes. Open daily, 11:30 to 10 or 11; Sunday, brunch 11 to 2:30, dinner 4 to 9.

A few other restaurants we recommend:

Amarillo Grill, 309 Asylum St., looks like a Texas ranchhouse and conveys food to match. Borrowing a page from oyster bars, there's a buck-a-bone rib bar in the lounge.

Lone Star beer is on draught and a rustic dining room purveys platters of prize-winning Texas-style barbecue ribs for $10.95. The casual menu is true to the name, from skillet potatoes topped with cheese served right in the pan to peach cobbler Alamo.

The young professional crowd is partial to **Spencer's,** ensconced in the landmark, turn-of-the-century Linden Building at 10 Capitol Ave. The formal downstairs restaurant has been turned into a pub and billiards parlor; the action now is upstairs in the new dining room, where complete dinners are priced from $16 to $22, and the adjacent nightclub, where raucous music and dancing continue into the wee hours. Regulars make a meal out of the buffet platters set out during happy hour.

Beer is the raison d'etre at the **Hartford Brewery Ltd.,** 35 Pearl St., a new brew pub gone upscale in an open setting with big windows onto the street. The brews ($3 a pint) are first-rate. To go with are bratwursts, sandwiches (the house reuben is a favorite), a three-alarm chili, soups and salads, most priced from $4.25 to $6.25.

The old mahogany-trimmed diner incorporated into the late, lamented Shenanigans now purveys sushi. **Ichiban** at One Gold St. in the Bushnell Plaza has taken over the onetime citadel of Hartford yuppiedom. The Japanese menu is highly regarded, priced from $6.50 to $18.50.

Franklin Avenue is Hartford's "Little Italy" and restaurant row. **Carbone's** at 588 is the most formal, a gathering spot for state politicians, It has excellent veal, a famous spinach salad and great unlisted specials. An offspring, **Gaetano's,** run by the Carbone family, took the space a few years ago of the former Signature in the Hartford Civic Center. **Capriccio** at 626 is all clutter and charm with hanging bottles and grapes; the cioppino is good. **DiFiore's Restaurant** at 395 Franklin is a handsome place run by a family whose adjacent pasta shop is highly rated. **Corvo** at 494 Franklin Ave. and **Bellini** at 438 have luxurious atmospheres and food to match. **Sorrento** at 371 Franklin adds a Mediterranean cafe ambience.

Casa Portuguesa at 1999 Park St. is where we go for a dish of pork and clams, garlic soup and heavenly rolls, washed down with vinho verde. Prices are reasonable and lots of Portuguese people eat here.

We love Vietnamese food, and the stylish **Truc Orient Express,** 735 Wethersfield Ave., fills the bill. With a pretty greenhouse out front, it offers things like Vietnamese egg rolls ($4.25) and singing chicken, shaking beef, grilled quail, coral lobster and grilled duck with spiced eggplant ($11 to $16.50). But our favorite dish is happy pancakes, with many vegetables and shrimp, pork or chicken inside a rice batter crepe ($11.95). Owner Binh Duong is proud of his recently published cookbook. Two other Vietnamese restaurants we like (and with many of the same dishes) are **Que-Huong** at 355 New Park Ave. and **Pacific Restaurant** at 206 Park Road, both in West Hartford. **Isan Classic Lao-Thai Restaurant** at 278 Park Road, West Hartford, is the first eatery in Connecticut that serves Laotian food and also offers some of the best tastes of Thai around. Another Thai favorite at 2477 Albany Ave. in West Hartford is **Bangkok Cuisine,** where folks go wild over the crispy Siam duck with ginger-plum sauce.

West Hartford, which for years was a virtual dining wasteland, has come of culinary age with thirteen restaurants opening in one six-month period alone, many of them in West Hartford Center. **Panda Inn,** part of the highly rated Panda chain based in western Massachusetts, was among the first. **Osaka,** a good Japanese restaurant, opened next door, **Chengdu** added Chinese fare down the street and, around the corner, **Lemon Grass** became one of the more upscale Thai eateries anywhere. We never thought we'd be writing about a pizza parlor in West Hartford, but **Harry's** in the Center is a role model for atmosphere (sleek mod decor and a good little wine list) and his create-your-own pizzas are thin-crusted and tasty. The Mongolian barbecue restaurant, **Magic Wok,** draws crowds to 1245 New Britain Ave. Down New Britain at 1144 is **Fuji,** another Japanese restaurant with authentic, daring food. Up the street at 1509 New Britain at Corbins Corner is **Papa-Razzi,** a sophisticated branch of the Boston Italian chain, dispensing pastas, pizzas and grill items on the second floor above **Joe's American Bar & Grill.**

Christmas Shopping

Downtown Hartford has been in a state of flux since the closing of the old Sage-Allen & Co. and the landmark G.Fox & Co. department store, New England's oldest and, at one time, its largest. Following the latter's demise in January 1993, there was talk of filling the void with an emphasis on factory outlet and discount stores. The Main Street Market provides a lively farmer's and crafts market in the prime space left vacant by buildings razed for one of three planned skyscrapers up to 62 stories high — all put on hold during the recession of the early 1990s. The peripatetic Hartford Guides, uniformed in red and gray, help direct visitors and make downtown more user-friendly. A Holly Trolley shuttles shoppers on weekends in December, and a permanent downtown shuttle system was in the talking stage. An ambitious Riverfront Recapture project to connect downtown with the Connecticut River was ahead of schedule. It includes the lowering of I-91, new waterfront access by walkways from Constitution Plaza, riverside trails, parklands, water taxis, the Lady Fenwick boat cruises and a 5,000-seat amphitheater.

With the department stores gone, downtown's focus is the Civic Center Mall with 40 stores and an unhurried atmosphere. For the holidays, the vast Center Court is filled with a 32-foot-high tree bedecked with lights and a whirling wreath festooned with ribbons, topiary and carousel horses. **Luettgens Limited,** its anchor store, was the nation's first new downtown department store venture in years; it has handsome clothes and gifts in a modern setting and gorgeous holiday decor. Downsized lately, its second floor has been taken over by **T.J. Maxx,** whose success fueled speculation that discounting might be downtown's future. Other holiday favorites are **Eastern Mountain Sports, New England Craftsmen,** the **Whalers Pro Image** gift shop, and clothing stores like **Henry Miller, Casual Corner, The Weathervane** and **Ann Taylor.** The mall also contains Gaetano's, Chuck's Steak House and Margarita's restaurants, as well as a patio food court.

The most spectacular Christmas display lately has been in the soaring atrium of CityPlace (reached by skywalk from the Civic Center). "The Spirit of Christmas," eight-foot sculptures representing Santa figures from around the world, stand amid Christmas trees lit with tiny white lights.

Another skywalk from the Civic Center crosses Trumbull Street; the casual Skywalk Restaurant perched above the street yields views of downtown goings-on. **Pratt Street,** connecting the Civic Center with Main Street, has been rejuvenated with sidewalks paved with individually monogrammed bricks, gas-type lamps, benches, planters and tasteful Yuletide decorations like the costumed Dickens figures on a balcony beside the restaurant No Fish Today. Stores here include the venerable, high-fashion **Stackpole, Moore, Tryon** in stylish new digs, **Lux, Bond & Green** and **Becker's** jewelers, **Cook's Bazaar** for kitchenware, **Overland** and **The Gap.**

On Main Street, **The Richardson Mall,** the 1875 Henry Hobson Richardson-designed former Brown Thomson store between the former G.Fox and Sage-Allen, has been converted into two floors of stores and a basement food court. Nearby is the **Pavilion at State House Square** with twenty more food and fashion shops in a dazzling art-deco setting. Among the eateries are **Boonoonoonoos** for Jamaican food (how about curried goat or sweet potato pie?), **India Garden, China Express, Ben & Jerry's** ice

Flying carousel soars above holiday shoppers at Civic Center Mall.

cream, and **T.J. Cinnamons,** where the cinnamon or pecan rolls are as sticky as can be.

Old Hartford tends to shop in **West Hartford Center,** a low-key, tree-lined area with brick sidewalks, new courtyards and alleys, and outdoor dining in season. There are many longtime shopkeepers among the trendy newcomers and, still, blessedly few chains. Merchants dispense Christmas cheer and refreshments during the annual Christmas Stroll the first Sunday afternoon in December. The striking **Oneta Gallery, Comina, Finitney & Co., Papier Ink, Reigning Cats and Dogs, Nanny's** and **Scandia Down Shop** are among the specialty stores. For home accessories, consider the **Red Geranium, New Frontier/American Living, Nature's, Pompanoosuc Mills** and **The Workbench.** The expanded **Lucy Baltzell** women's shop looks straight out of Beverly Hills, and other nice apparel shops are **Appleseed's, Artichoke, Florence Travis** and **Cuzzi's.** The men at almost every Christmas party in town wear holiday attire from **Allen Collins,** with whale ties, pants with holly or patchwork — the real Hartford executive-at-leisure look.

In **Old Wethersfield,** the **Red Barn Christmas Shop** at 133 Main St. is open from August to New Year's Eve. Next door is the **Enchanted Heart,** open all year. Both are owned by Betty Veilleux, who handpaints little sleds with local scenes, which people collect for tree ornaments. She sells collectible Santas, David Winter cottages, Tom Clark's gnomes and a huge selection of nutcrackers. In the barn are many trees with exquisite ornaments, a wall of Advent calendars, lighted porcelain villages, Byers carolers, and nativities from across the world. **Comstock, Ferre & Co.** at 263 Main St., the nation's oldest seed company, has an array of gifts and materials for Christmas decorations in its rambling building filled with seeds and garden supplies. Dollhouses and quality miniatures are the forte of **Treasures in the Attic,** while dolls and bears threaten to take over the **Olde Towne Doll Shoppe.**

In Avon, **Riverdale Farms** on Route 10 is a growing complex of specialty shops in a contemporary dairy-farm setting, from the **Yellow Daffodil,** a glorious ramble of rooms full of gifts for all occasions as well as a Christmas shop, to **The Nutcracker** (toys for learning and fun), the **Spirited Hand** for handcrafts, **Neuchatel Chocolates, Oxford Baggs Outfitters** and **Jillian Thomas** for party clothes. At the new **Shops at River Park** along Route 44, you'll find party hams at **Harrington's,** gifts and toiletries at **The Secret Garden of Martha's Vineyard,** every pattern you could imagine at **The China Shop** and every earring you could possibly want at **L'Eleganza.** A more historic atmosphere pervades the shops at **Old Avon Village** next door. Situated along Route 44 just past Avon Center are **Talbots, Country Curtains** and the **Hitchcock Chair Co.**

Shopping is art at **The Farmington Valley Arts Center** off Route 44 in Avon Park North, an interesting complex where twenty working craftsmen have their studios. The annual Christmas show and sale, "The Art of Giving — The Giving of Art," features works of more than 100 craftsmen, daily 10 to 4, Sunday noon to 5, from early November to Christmas Eve. Hartford's **Old State House** devotes its main-floor galleries to an excellent Christmas craft exhibition and sale, displaying thousands of handcrafted decorations and gifts, daily from Thanksgiving to Christmas. A fascinating selection of gifts appropriate to their institutions are found in the museum shops of the **Wadsworth Atheneum, Science Museum of Connecticut, Mark Twain Memorial** and **Noah Webster House.** More commercial are the Christmas Crafts Expos, Connecticut's largest indoor crafts shows, staged annually the first two weekends in December at the Hartford Civic Center. A bit farther afield is the annual Christmas show and sale of the **Wesleyan Potters,** a post-Thanksgiving tradition at 350 South Main St., Middletown.

Holiday Treats

The theme in Hartford since 1991 has been **A Dickens of a Downtown Holiday.** Nearly 200 costumed entertainers and musicians from the pages of Dickens fill Pratt Street, the Main Street Market and the Civic Center Mall for the Dickens Stroll the Friday after Thanksgiving from noon to 5. Clad in red ceremonial garments, the Governor's Foot Guard leads the procession to Constitution Plaza. Thousands watch and sing carols as Santa arrives at 5 for the opening of the **Festival of Light.** Constitution Plaza, dull and dark most of the year, becomes a wonderland with 200,000 tiny white lights twinkling in the shapes of angels, fountains, animals and trees.

The downtown activities continue through New Year's Eve, when more thousands turn out for **First Night Hartford,** ten hours of non-stop entertainment by more than 250 artists at 25 indoor and outdoor locations from Union Station to Christ Church Cathedral. The event starts at 2 p.m. and ends with a procession through the streets of downtown to a fireworks display at midnight in Bushnell Park. Buttons admitting the wearer to all activities are sold for $7 adults ($5 if purchased ahead), $1 children.

Weekends during the holiday season are alive with special activities. London-style street vendors dressed as Victorian urchins purvey roasted chestnuts, hot cider and cherry tarts along Pratt Street. Costumed carolers from Hartt School of Music stroll the streets. The Holly Trolley may be boarded for 50 cents. Horse-drawn carriage tours ($5) offer 30-minute rides around downtown into the evening, Thursday-Sunday. The Bushnell Park Carousel gives rides, and the pond is open for ice skating daily the week between Christmas and New Year's.

Historic Holidays

Old State House, 800 Main St., Hartford, (203) 522-6766. The large blue spruce in front of the nation's oldest legislative building (1796) sports colored lights along a square linking Constitution Plaza with the downtown retail district. The Bulfinch-designed Federal structure was closed until 1994 for $10 million worth of renovations to include a large underground museum to be run by the Connecticut Historical Society, a small Faneuil Hall-style outdoor marketplace and a restored east lawn for outdoor entertainment. The Senate Chamber was being restored to its original look in 1818 and the House Chamber to the turn-of-the-century period when it was used by City Hall. The expanded museum shop specializes in Connecticut heritage — crafted items, pottery, quilts, jewelry, toys, books and stocking stuffers. Guards in Continental Army uniforms present Yankee Doodle cannon salutes Monday-Saturday at 10, noon and 5, Sunday at noon and 4. Open Monday-Saturday 10 to 5, Sunday noon to 5. Free.

Mark Twain House, Nook Farm Visitor Center, 77 Forest St., Hartford, (203) 525-9317. The best time to visit this elaborate Victorian Gothic mansion, lived in and loved by the Samuel Clemens family from 1874 to 1891, is at Christmas. Live poinsettias glow in the conservataory, which abounds with Japanese lanterns. Cranber-

ries and popcorn are strung on the Victorian Christmas tree in the library. There are wreaths on windows and doors, garlands up the massive central staircase, stockings hung in the nursery schoolroom, and partly-wrapped packages scatttered over the mahogany guest room. Next door, the Harriet Beecher Stowe House, the white brick cottage in which the author lived from 1873 to 1896, also is decorated in late 19th-century style for the holidays. The Mark Twain Memorial Women's Committee sponsors an annual **Christmas Walk** through these two houses plus five gracious area homes decorated for the season the first Sunday in December. The gift shop at Nook Farm is filled with books, Victorian toys, frog-related items in honor of the "Jumping Frog" and, in December, small loaves of sweet mincecake made from Mark Twain's recipe. Open June-Columbus Day and December, Monday-Saturday 9:30 to 4, Sunday noon to 4; closed Monday rest of year. Adults $6.50, children $2.75; combination Twain and Stowe houses, $10 and $4.50.

Butler-McCook Homestead, 396 Main St., Hartford, (203) 522-1806. Except for a temporary hiatus in 1992, the Christmas celebrated a century ago by the McCook family, headed by "Poppa," who was pastor of an Episcopal church in East Hartford, is recreated in this 1782 landmark with fine period furnishings. Spicy aromas waft from the original kitchen at the rear of the house; the rest of the house has been Victorianized. The lavish Christmas decorations are what the McCooks would have had, from the elaborate fruit centerpiece on the dining room table to the huge wreaths suspended from red velvet ribbons inside the main-floor windows. Antique toys are displayed under the Christmas tree decorated with tiny candies, dates and cookies. Open in December, Tuesday, Thursday and weekends noon to 4 through Christmas; May 15 to Oct. 15, Tuesday, Thursday and Sunday noon to 4. Adults $2, children 50 cents.

Old Wethersfield. The streets of the first historic district in Connecticut are lined with 150 houses dating before 1850. The **Webb-Deane-Stevens Museum,** three adjacent houses at 203-215 Main St., provide a good look at a late 18th-century New England town. At the Stevens House, antique toys under a Christmas tree include dolls and wind-up miniatures of venerable age. Costumed interpreters show holiday festivities from the past two centuries during **Merry Museums,** an annual holiday tour by reservation the first two weekends in December from 4 to 8 p.m.; adults $7.50, children $4. Open Tuesday-Saturday 10 to 4, Sunday 1 to 4, May-October; Friday-Sunday 10 to 4, rest of year. Adults $5, students $2.50. The Wethersfield Historical Society celebrates **Christmas in Old Wethersfield** the first Saturday in December with music, a doll exhibit and horse-drawn carriage rides at the Keeney Memorial, a museum and cultural center at 200 Main St. A Victorian Christmas is celebrated at the **Capt. James Francis House,** 120 Hartford Ave. Open-hearth cooking is demonstrated at an open house the first Saturday in December; tours of the decorated house are offered by appointment Dec. 7-19 for $2.

Noah Webster House, 227 South Main St., West Hartford, (203) 521-5362. This excellent example of an 18th-century farmhouse, birthplace of Noah Webster of dictionary fame, is furnished as it would have been in pre-Revolutionary times. Costumed docents give informative tours, and changing exhibitions are presented in the museum wing. In December, there's a Holiday Hearth open house with crafts demonstrations, but the house is not decorated for the holidays because it remains true to the Colonial period. The year's highlight is the Noah Webster Birthday Party, an annual festival the last Saturday of September. Open mid-June through September, daily except Wednesday 10 to 4 and weekends 1 to 4; October to mid-June, daily except Wednesday 1 to 4. Adults $3, children $1.

Stanley-Whitman House, 37 High St., Farmington, (203) 677-9222. Built in 1660 and now the Farmington Museum, this is one of the best examples of a 17th-century frame overhang house in New England. It has rare diamond-paned windows and is furnished with Colonial pieces, many the gifts of local residents. Open Wednesday-Sunday noon to 4, May-October; Sunday, noon to 4 in November-December. Adults $3, students $2, under 12 free.

While in Farmington, drive along Main Street to see houses dating from the 17th century. Many belong to Miss Porter's School, which has kept the exteriors unchanged.

Massacoh Plantation, 800 Hopmeadow St., Simsbury, (203) 658-2500. History comes alive during the **Three Centuries by Candlelight** programs for five nights during the first week of December at this historic complex of buildings and exhibits. Re-enactments of a town meeting and life in the 1771 Phelps House tavern and canal hotel, the Hendricks Cottage, the fuse manufactory and the school house draw capacity audiences by reservation for tours every half hour starting at 5:30 or 6:30. The Simsbury Historical Society's plantation village is open daily May-October with guided tours from 1 to 3; Phelps House, Monday-Friday 1 to 4, year-round. Adults $5, children $2.50.

Heritage Trails, Box 138, Farmington 06034, (203) 677-8867. Farmington native Ernest Shaw offers two-hour tours of sites in Hartford, leaving Hartford hotels five times daily by reservation for $12. Passengers travel in a ten-seat minibus, accompanied by taped sound effects and erudite commentary. Candlelight dinner tours daily at 5:30 include a tour of Farmington and dining in a private 1789 inn for $29.95. Shaw's 90-minute audio driving-tour cassettes are available from the Old State House.

Art-full Holidays

Wadsworth Atheneum, 600 Main St., Hartford, (203) 278-2670. This venerable art museum, the nation's oldest (150 years in 1992) and considered one of its finest, is a special place at Christmas. Launching the holiday social season is a gala preview party opening the annual **Festival of Trees;** for nine days in early December about 200 artistically and inventively decorated trees and wreaths created by area organizations and individuals are on display and for sale (the best are snapped up at the preview party). Various groups play or sing Christmas music daily. The Atheneum's 45,000-plus works are of such importance that twice recently some have been loaned for tours to Paris and Japan. The emphasis from the beginning was on American art, lately supplemented by a gallery devoted to African-American art. J. Pierpont Morgan's

Legislative chamber at Old State House.

gift of 1,325 works in 1917 added priceless European paintings and decorative arts. There also are distinguished collections of contemporary and 19th-century art, early American landscape paintings, English and American silver, period costumes and Colt firearms. The Wallace Nutting collection of Pilgrim furniture and artifacts is outstanding. The Lions Gallery of the Senses presents tactile art for the vision-impaired and the Matrix Gallery is rather avant-garde. Open Tuesday-Sunday 11 to 5. Adults $3, students $1.50. Free admission all day Thursday and Saturday 11 to 1.

New Britain Museum of American Art, 56 Lexington St., New Britain, (203) 229-0257. Visiting this 1907 mansion is like going into a private home (which it was), furnished with colorful oriental rugs and ornate Victorian furniture. The informality combined with choice art make it one of our favorite museums anywhere. It is elaborately decorated in a different theme each year — once a Wiliamsburg Christmas and, in 1992, a "Letter to Santa." One of the richest collections of American art in the country is here. An entire room is filled with Thomas Hart Benton murals. Newer wings house changing exhibitions; upstairs in intimate galleries are paintings by N.C. and Andrew Wyeth, Georgia O'Keeffe and Eric Sloane. Also of special interest are the Western bronzes by Solon Borglum and the Sanford Low Memorial Collection of American Illustration, comprised of more than 1,000 works. Open Tuesday-Sunday 1 to 5, Wednesday to 7. Free.

Hill-Stead Museum, Farmington Avenue, Farmington, (203) 677-9064. A locally beloved treasure trove reflecting the life of America's turn-of-the-century beau monde, this 29-room white clapboard home with rambling wings and a Mount Vernon facade atop a hill is a pleasantly personal masterpiece of a place anytime, but is specially decorated at Christmas. Built in 1901 from designs of Stanford White as the retirement home for the Alfred Atmore Popes of Cleveland and a showplace for their art collections, it was also the home of their daughter, Theodate, an architect who helped design it. As stated in her will, the house and its contents are maintained as she left them in 1946. In the drawing room are two of Monet's "haystack" paintings and works by Manet, Degas and Antoine-Louis Barye. The guided tour takes an hour: Hepplewhite and Chippendale furniture, Whistler paintings, rare Chinese porcelains, a Queen Anne dresser and more are seen in the homelike setting. The property's elaborate sunken gardens, designed by landscape architect Beatrix Farrand, have been reconstructed to their pre-1925 state. Open for guided tours Wednesday-Sunday noon to 5, November-April to 4. Closed mid-January to mid-February. Adults $5, children $2.

Family Holidays

"The Nutcracker." The Hartford Ballet Company has presented the classic for many years in December at Bushnell Memorial Hall. With accompaniment by the Hartford Chamber Orchestra, 30 dancers, fourteen children, 130 costumes and "lights enough to light up a country," the performance is a delight for the entire family. A Christmas tree made of ostrich feathers, 60 feet tall, grows out of Clara's house, and snowflakes fall in the "Waltz of the Snowflakes." Six evening and four matinee performances are scheduled from about Dec. 11 to 20. Tickets, $10.50 to $40.50, are available at the Bushnell Box Office, 246-6807.

Symphony on Ice. The U.S. Coast Guard Band, the Skating Club of Hartford and guest celebrities participate in the annual skating and musical performance the first Saturday of December at the Hartford Civic Center. Reserved seats are free, but require a gift for the area's **Toys for Tots** campaign. Tickets through the Civic Center Box Office.

Science Museum of Connecticut, 950 Trout Brook Drive, West Hartford, (203) 236-2961. Santa arrives by dog sled at the annual Christmas celebration in December. "Nutcracker Fantasy," a choreographed laser light show of Tchaikovsky's holiday classic, is presented twice a day during December at the Gengras Planetarium. The expanding facility, which plans eventually to move to a riverfront site in East Hartford, also has a marine-life touch tank, a hands-on discovery room, a computer laboratory and a live animal center, with an increasing emphasis on technology, from robots to micro chips and a computerized heart exhibit. Science-related items are found in the museum shop. Open Tuesday-Saturday 10 to 5, Sunday noon to 5. Adults $5, children $4.

Musical Traditions. Handel's "Messiah" is presented early in December at the Bushnell Memorial by the Hartford Chorale and the Hartford Symphony. Area choral groups present outdoor performances in the **Concert of Lights series** on weekend evenings at the Clock Tower on Constitution Plaza. Name entertainers usually perform in a Christmas show at the Hartford Civic Center; Perry Como crooned the old tunes in 1992. A **Festival of Lessons and Carols,** a candlelight service modeled after the one at Cambridge University, takes place the first or second Sunday in December (services in late afternoon and evening) in the beautiful Gothic chapel at Trinity College.

Boar's Head and Yule Log Festival. A stirring end to the holiday season is this musical pageant in the poinsettia- and banner-filled Asylum Hill Congregational Church (where Mark Twain attended services when his friend Joseph Twichell was pastor) at 814 Asylum Ave. Five performances are scheduled on Friday, Saturday and Sunday of Epiphany weekend in early January. Participants include geese, sheep, goats, donkeys and a large and recalcitrant camel; church members dress as beefeaters, woodsmen and peasant women, and little girls in jester costumes balance along the pews and do handstands up the aisles. It's an incredibly colorful experience, one that was filmed for showing nationally on public television. The music of the Brass Ring, roving musicians and the Asylum Hill Oratorio Choir is a splendid backdrop. Tickets ($12) are usually sold out well in advance — call 525-5696 for information or get a Hartford friend to order them for you in November.

We wish you a Merry Christmas and a Happy New Year!

FOR MORE INFORMATION: Greater Hartford Convention & Visitors Bureau, 1 Civic Center Plaza, Hartford 06103, (203) 728-6789 or (800) 446-7811.

Cross-country skiers are active at base of Stratton Mountain.

Hubert Schriebl Photo

Skiing in Southern Vermont

Manchester and the Mountains

Winter in Vermont. Think about it: snow that softens the edges of everything and stays white until it melts, the frosty air that turns your breath to steam, and the green-shuttered, white clapboard houses and hostelries, smoke curling from their chimneys, fires crackling in their hearths. Think about the fine country inns and restaurants where meals are hot and hearty, fortifying you for another day in the woods or on the slopes.

Protected from the warming influence of the coast by New Hampshire to the east, Vermont catches the cold and keeps it. The snow usually arrives earlier, stays later and lies deeper than it does in the rest of New England. Because so much of the winter is spent under a blanket of white, Vermonters not only put up with it, they play in it, developing Olympic-class skiers from toddlers who start in their back yards.

Eventually, of course, the word has gotten out that the state, which is cool and comfortable in summer and red and rustic in fall, is most welcoming in winter.

It happened in earnest more than half a century ago when skiers like Fred Pabst (of the brewing family) looked at Bromley Mountain and decided it would make good

249

skiing. In 1937 he founded one of the country's first ski areas in the tiny community of Peru; since then Vermont has meant skiing in the East as surely as Colorado has meant it in the West.

In Vermont, it's different. Sitting in a chairlift, being hauled up a ski slope, you're aware of snow-frosted evergreens everywhere (they are, after all, what help make the Green Mountains green). And when you reach the top and prepare for that first run, you can look across the valleys to other ski areas in the distance and the mountain villages tucked between.

Bromley was the first of the mountains in southern Vermont to become a ski destination. The development of Stratton twenty or so years later ensured that this section of the state would become a four-season recreation area.

Guest houses and inns that used to open in May and close in October are in business again by Christmas, staying open as late in the spring as the skiers come. But you don't have to be a downhill skier to appreciate southern Vermont in winter.

In 1970, the Viking Ski Touring Center opened in Londonderry and quickly became one of the largest and best in the country. As cross-country skiing caught on, more and more trails were opened, some of them through the virgin wilderness of the Green Mountain National Forest.

Winter hikers and snowshoers come to use the Long Trail, completed in 1931 by the Green Mountain Club and extending an impressive 263 miles from Massachusetts to the Canadian border; it can be entered from Route 11 east of Manchester.

There are indoor sports, too. They are for people who'd rather look at the snow than trudge through it, who prefer to poke through shops than schuss the slopes and who delight in curling up in front of the fire with a good book.

Almost every village in southern Vermont makes stopping a pleasure. There's Dorset, where nearly all the big old houses are painted white with black shutters and where the sidewalks are made of marble because that's where the state's first marble quarry was opened in 1786. The sidewalks are also marble in historic Manchester Village, where stately white homes are set well back from the street and where the restored Equinox hotel presides in columned grandeur. And there's Weston, a storybook village that's Vermont as it's pictured to be.

Shoppers can hunt for bargains at Manchester's ever-expanding numbers of designer outlet stores — a great boon for spouses while skiers are on the slopes, and for skiers when the snow conditions are less than optimum. They can buy rare books from the vault of a bank-turned-bookstore in Manchester Village and watch wooden bowls being

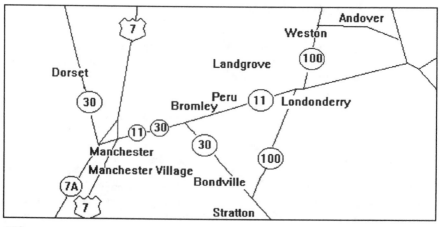

made in an old mill in Weston. Because cold weather stirs an appetite, everyone appreciates the fine restaurants in the area with their memorable meals served beside a blazing fire in the hearth.

Winter in Vermont is everything you ever remember about making the first run in untracked snow or viewing a mountain village frosted in white. It's so good that we have to spend at least one weekend of every winter here.

Getting There

Manchester is the main town in the area and there are two of them: Manchester Village and Manchester Center. The village, along Route 7, is elegant, especially with the restoration of the Equinox resort. The center is more commercial, with lots of upscale factory outlets, the original Orvis store, good restaurants and coffee shops, and a traffic problem that has led to calling the major intersection "Malfunction Junction."

Interstate 87 in New York and Interstate 91 in Vermont provide access to the area, as do U.S. Route 7 and other state highways. Vermont Transit buses serve Manchester Center. There are small airports at Bennington and Rutland. From greater distances, visitors fly into Albany, N.Y., or Hartford, Conn., and drive to Vermont.

Where to Ski

The question is: downhill or cross-country? The major downhill areas are Bromley and Stratton. Bromley, the oldest ski area in New England, still attracts families, although it has challenging runs for better skiers. Stratton is lots of glitz and glitter and New York hot shots, but you can still have a great day of skiing on the highest peak in southern Vermont. Within easy driving distance of the area are three of Vermont's largest ski areas, Mount Snow, Okemo and Killington.

Cross-country skiers have several areas to choose from. Here's the scoop:

Downhill

Bromley, Route 11, Peru, (802) 824-5522. Bromley was first and has achieved a reputation for being one of the best family-oriented ski areas in the East. With a 1,334-foot vertical drop, it is known for wide, easy skiing on manicured slopes; not for nothing is one of our favorite runs called Boulevard. The newer East Face offers some challenging runs, for example Havoc, which our kids like for its moguls, and Pabst Panic, for its steep cruising. The mountain is unusual for its southern exposure, which makes it particularly appealing on sunny, cold days. Bromley also remains low-key and personal in an era of impersonal corporate mega resorts. The traditional base lodge looks as it did two decades ago; the goal here is to be comfortable, rather than showy. Nonetheless, the area is proud of its many firsts: first slopeside nursery, first major snowmaking installation, and the first "on-the-slope testing center," which was an arrangement with a ski manufacturer. Seven major lifts take skiers up the slopes. Children 6 and under ski free always; juniors 14 and under ski free on non-holiday weekdays when accompanied by an adult. Lift tickets for adults are $36 on weekends, $25 midweek; juniors, $23 and $13.

Stratton, off Routes 11 and 30, Stratton Mountain, (802) 297-2200. Opened as a ski resort more than 30 years ago, Stratton has experienced extraordinary growth and the scene leaves some with mixed feelings. The new Stratton Village Square, a shopping complex complete with clock tower, gives Stratton the look of a European ski village. A multi-level parking garage, a multitude of condo/villas at the base, a sports center, inns and restaurants, golf courses, an orthopedic-medical clinic, and tiers of side roads hiding substantial private homes make for one beautiful, self-contained resort capable of supporting the slick quarterly magazine called Stratton. Southern Vermont's highest mountain offers something for everyone: high, steep trails for advanced skiers, and easy slopes for beginners. The Sun Bowl is a pleasant, sunny area with mostly intermediate trails. Altogether, Stratton offers a 2,000-foot vertical drop, eleven chairlifts, a unique twelve-passenger summit gondola and 92 trails — the most of any Eastern ski area on a single mountain and two-thirds of them covered by snowmaking. Stratton has tried to shake its early image as Mascara Mountain East and aims now to be a friendly, skier's mountain. It pioneers with such ploys as bargain skiing early and late in the season and frequent-skier pricing. Somewhat incongruously, Stratton also was the

Chairlift takes skiers to summit of Stratton.

first ski area to turn over its trails to snowboarders (the Burton snowboard company got its start nearby), and now claims to be the snowboarding capital of the East. Adult lift tickets are $39 on weekends, $34 weekdays; juniors, $24.

Cross-Country

Viking Ski Touring Center, Little Pond Road, Londonderry, (802) 824-3933. Established in 1970 by the Allaben brothers, Viking was one of the first touring areas in the East and has grown into one of the most extensive and best-run. It has more than 40 kilometers of groomed trails, many of them through gorgeous pine woods. The Cobble Hill trail is a thirteen-kilometer loop that meanders through woodlands and open fields past beaver ponds and brooks. The eight-kilometer Weston Village Trail connects Viking and the pretty village of Weston, where lunch or shopping can be enjoyed at the halfway point. Beginners can find easy trails and can warm up in an open field. There's also night skiing on Saturdays on three kilometers of trails. Facilities include a complete rental shop (adult rentals are $12 a day, $8 a half day), a cross-country ski shop, and a gallery cafe for breakfast and lunch (good sandwiches, soups and chili). Trail fees: adults $11, half day (after 1) $8; children, $6 and $5.

Wild Wings Ski Touring Center, Peru, (802) 824-6793. A converted horse barn with a rental shop and warming room centers this low-key, family-oriented ski touring setup within the boundaries of the Green Mountain National Forest. Tracy and Chuck Black run the center, which has twenty kilometers of groomed trails. Adults, $9.

Hildene Ski Touring Center, Route 7A South, Manchester Village, (802) 362-1788. The estate of Robert Todd Lincoln, son of Abe, has 22 groomed trails winding through fifteen kilometers of woods and meadows. The carriage barn serves hot drinks and light refreshments. Adults $8, juniors $5.

Nordic Inn Ski Touring Center, Route 11, Landgrove, (802) 824-6454. About fifteen miles of groomed trails are offered behind the Nordic Inn, which is a good place for lunch before or after skiing. These are primarily wooded trails, with most of the terrain suitable for intermediates, although there are some trails for beginners and experts. Adults, $7.

Stratton Ski Touring Center, Stratton Mountain Road, Stratton Mountain, (802) 297-1880. Twenty kilometers of groomed trails and 50 kilometers of back-country skiing are offered at the Sun Bowl touring center. Moonlight tours, lessons and rentals are available. Adults, $10.

Other Outdoor Sports

Hiking and snowshoeing are popular in the Green Mountain National Forest, but those who do it are advised to prepare carefully and tell someone of their itinerary. The source for guidebook and maps of the Long Trail is the Green Mountain Club, Box 889, Montpelier 05602. A sign on Routes 11 and 30 just north of where they converge east of Manchester Center indicates access to the Long Trail.

Sleigh rides are offered, weather permitting, through a variety of sources. They usually can be arranged by local inns and hotels. A local horsewoman teams with Taylor Farm, Route 11, Londonderry, (802) 824-3750, to offer sleigh rides day or night by appointment.

Guided **snowmobile tours** through the Green Mountain National Forest are available through Factory Point Rent All Inc., Routes 11 and 30, Manchester Center, (802) 362-2124. Experienced guides offer instruction, lead tours and provide commentary on the wilderness. Two-hour tours, including snowmobiles and equipment, cost $70 per person. Longer tours and overnight camping can be arranged.

Weather permitting, ice skating is available at the Stratton Mountain Sports Center. For information, call 297-2200.

The Great Indoors

If you want to get some exercise but want to stay warm doing so, visit the Equinox Fitness Spa in Manchester Village. You can work out on the Nautilus equipment, take an aerobics class or swim in the pool. Day use of the facilities is priced at $20.

Indoor tennis courts are available at West River Tennis on Route 100, South Londonderry, 824-5411. The Derry Twin Cinemas are located at the Mountain Marketplace shopping center at the intersection of Routes 100 and 11 in Londonderry. More movies are shown at the Manchester Twin Cinemas in Manchester Shopping Center, Manchester Center.

The American Museum of Flyfishing, Seminary Avenue, Manchester Village, displays treasures of American angling, among them the masterworks of America's best fly-tiers and the craftsmanship of fine fishing rods. Highlights include the fishing tackle of fishermen from Daniel Webster to Ernest Hemingway, Andrew Carnegie to Dwight Eisenhower. Open daily 10 to 4, May-October; weekdays rest of year. Adults, $2.

At the **Weston Priory,** Route 155 north of Weston Center, the Benedictine monks conduct an 11:30 a.m. Sunday service that packs the small and tasteful chapel with people from all denominations. You must get there at least a half hour early to claim one of the red upholstered chairs; recorded guitar music sets the mood until the monks enter, group themselves about the altar and start to sing. The Catholic Mass with emphasis on singing and reflection is stirring. Phone (802) 824-5409 to verify times.

Artists and craftspeople have long found Vermont inspiring. Most famous of the art centers here is the **Southern Vermont Art Center,** housed in a beautiful white mansion on a hill above Manchester Village and now open year-round. Perhaps the best collection of native American art in New England is shown at **Long Ago & Far Away** in the Green Mountain Shops on Main Street in Manchester Center. Billed as Vermont's largest gallery, **Tilting at Windmills Gallery** creates interesting lighting effects with oddly shaped windows and shows works of many artists. **Todd Gallery,** ensconced in an 1840 barn and carriage house in Weston, displays art by prominent Vermont artists in all media, especially pottery. **Gallery North Star** shows works of leading Vermont artists in two settings, in Village Square at Stratton Mountain and on Townshend Road in Grafton.

Shopping

Between the tows and the toddies, many skiers like to shop and Manchester offers a lot.

Children of all ages enjoy wandering through the **Enchanted Doll House** on Route 7 north of Manchester Center. We first fell in love with this place from its catalog, and mail order is still big business. But to be here and to see the twelve rooms full of all the dolls and the dollhouses and the miniatures and the trains and the books and the teddy bears is like making every day Christmas.

Youngsters also like the **Jelly Mill,** Route 7, south of the intersection with Route 30; where else can you find jelly beans in peanut butter, watermelon or cream soda flavors? This three-story emporium attracts browsers and buyers by the droves. The entire second floor and part of the third is devoted to the House Works, with all kinds of bakeware, kitchen gadgets, placemats, pillows, baskets and much more. Also on the second floor is the **Buttery,** a restaurant serving soups, salads, crepes and quiches for lunch. The first floor is a potpourri of decorative accessories, jewelry, furniture, handcrafts, candles, cards, and Vermont foods.

The most unusual book store around might be **Johnny Appleseed's** in the old Battenkill Bank building on Route 7 in Manchester Village, next door to the Equinox. The bank vault is used for storing old and rare books and the selection here is wonderful. The **Northshire Bookstore** has moved to the prime corner of Routes 7 and 30 in Manchester Center, site of the old Colburn House hotel. Now bigger than ever, it has an especially good selection of children's books.

Designer outlet stores are a big attraction in Manchester; they include **Samuel Robert, Joan & David, Hickey-Freeman, Jones New York, Ralph Lauren, Benetton, Hathaway** and **Anne Klein.** You'll note that most stores are upscale and the story is told of one factory outlet, which carried a cheaper line, that did not make it.

Landau's Icelandic Woolens offers a huge collection of Icelandic woolens and handknit woolen sweaters, plus Austrian boiled wool jackets and Scottish kilts.

The Equinox Shops, across the street from the hotel, include the **Clift Collection,** where we fell in love with the brightly quilted jackets from California and colorful sweaters from Uruguay on the first floor; the second floor is filled with fancy duds for fancy evenings. A branch of the **Vermont State Craft Center** at Frog Hollow is here, as is **Gallery on the Green** with traditional art and **The American Collector** with folk art. **Christine's** is a boutique with especially trendy and expensive women's clothes on Union Street in Manchester Village.

Orvis, Route 7, Manchester Center, with its smashing catalog, is the L.L. Bean of Southern Vermont and more. Outdoors-oriented merchandise includes fishing gear, country and hunting clothes, lamps with duck decoy bases, tie tacks in wild animal shapes, even a revolving duck-plucker. A new Orvis outlet store is located on Union Street in Manchester Village.

Mother Myrick's Confectionary is one of our favorite stops in Vermont. The best

Stratton Village offers shops and restaurants at foot of ski area.

hot fudge sauce in the world, mouth-watering candy (the buttercrunch is to die for), desserts like lemon lulu cake, ice cream and fine coffees — this is where you can indulge your sweet tooth to heart's content.

Valerie's Country Collection on Route 7 north of Manchester offers custom and ready-made quilts at prices better than any we've seen. You can also buy calico fabrics for making your own. Ski shops are everywhere; so are antiques shops.

Wood products are prominent in Vermont. The **Weston Bowl Mill,** Route 100, Weston, turns out bowls, trays, plates and spoons in a mill that looks just as it did when it opened nearly a century ago. The gift shop is open seven days a week. The **J.K. Adams Co.** on Route 30 in Dorset sells fine cutting boards, ice buckets, cheese boards and other wood accessories — we like the revolving spice racks — of the Hammacher Schlemmer class at substantial discounts. One of the niftiest items here is a true gardener's wheelbarrow, a copy of the old Buch wheelbarrow made until shortly after World War II in Elizabethtown, Pa. Hardwood and steel are the ingredients and the lines are perfect.

The **Vermont Country Store** in Weston has a large inventory of staples like long underwear and flannel nightgowns and a catalog that it sends all over the world. Ever-expanding, it opened the **Bandstand** for unusual books and art and the **West River Jewelry Company** for fine handcrafts in adjacent buildings in 1992. Across the street is the **Weston Village Store** with an attractive jumble of items. Beside it is **Mountain Stitchery,** stocking needlework and yarns. Nearby are the **Weston Toy Works** and the **Weston House Quilt Collection.**

Stratton Village offers an exceptional line of shops for a ski area. Here you'll find **Alpine Espresso,** a European coffeehouse, interspersed with **Bogner,** the posh ski outfitters, and **Von Bargen's Jewelers.** Other choice stops are the new **Stratton Arts Festival Vermont Craft Shop, Anton of Vermont Quilts, Resort Works, Country Casuals North, Stratton Mountain Sports** and **Equipe Sport.** There's even a snowboard shop here. Check out the fine selection of specialty foods, wines and deli sandwiches at **Partridge in a Pantry.** Down near the entrance to Stratton along Route 30 is another **Equipe Sport, Detail Sports** and **The Startingate** ski shop.

Where to Stay

Your choice of accommodations will depend on where you want to be located as well as the type of situation you prefer. During winter, many Vermont ski lodges and inns offer only Modified American Plan rates with breakfast and dinner included. You can find European Plan at motels and some hotels (there seems to be a trend in this direction), which allows you to try different restaurants. If you want to do your own cooking, you can rent a condominium, often the choice of families. Rates rise sharply depending on weekday, weekend or holiday period. Those quoted here, as elsewhere in the book, are for peak periods.

Bromley

Johnny Seesaw's, Route 11, Peru 05152, (802) 824-5533. This weathered clapboard building with red trim seems to sink into the hillside, as well it might, after the many years and hard use it's had. Dating from 1926, it was originally a dance hall, but soon became an institution as a ski lodge because of its proximity to Bromley. Accommodations include cottages with fireplaces (good for families or two couples), inn rooms with private and shared baths, and "The Zoo," a large room with a double bed and two twins adjoining another room with two twin beds. Innkeepers Nancy and Gary Okun have been upgrading and renovating slowly since taking over in 1980. But they retain the special feeling that makes this live up to its billing as a legendary twenties roadhouse, "everything you've dreamed a lodge should be." The main floor holds a pleasant bar, an unusual circular fireplace surrounded by the kind of sofas you'll sink into and remain in for hours, and an alcove with cushioned mats for resting, talking or snoozing. Old guest registers and bound volumes of Ski magazine are fun to pore through; the nicks in the woodwork come from years of ski boot contact. The 22 rooms retain lots of wood and interesting angles, and are simply furnished. Val and John Tsirikos, who've been cooks at Johnny Seesaw's since 1978, offer hot and hearty breakfasts and dinners; entree prices for the latter, open to the public, run from $11.95 to $17.95. Doubles, $100 to $150, MAP.

The Wiley Inn, Route 11, Box 37, Peru 05152, (802) 824-6600. Just one mile down the road from the lifts at Bromley, this low-slung inn on a hillside was rescued by from a period of neglect and disrepair in 1983 and turned into a handsome and comfortable place to stay. Owners Fred and Helga Sobek turned it over in 1992 to their son and daughter-in-law, M.A. and Manfred Sobek, he formerly a chef at restaurants in Connecticut's Fairfield County. Manfred is the cook, whipping up full country breakfasts — farmer's omelet, cinnamon-raisin french toast and apple pancakes were the choices at our visit. Dinner is served by candlelight and open to the public ($20, prix-fixe for three courses). The meal might start with roasted garlic and leek chowder or duck liver mousse with cumberland sauce, followed by scallops provencal or roast venison with juniper glaze as entrees. About 40 guests can be seated in the pleasant, fireplaced dining area, with an old enameled stove at its center, and in a smaller room. A cozy lounge with fireplace and wing chairs is an invitation to read or chat. A game room with a jukebox that plays "oldies" is another spot for relaxing, and light classical music is sometimes heard in the background while dining. There are eight rooms and four two-bedroom suites, all with private baths. Rooms in the main house built in 1835 and

256

Bromley slopes are backdrop for Johnny Seesaw's lodge and restaurant.

the fireplaced suite are the most expensive. Serving variously as a stagecoach stop and a tea room, the building is a fine example of what is called Vermont continuous architecture, with at least ten additions to date. When you approach the Wiley in the evening in winter, the candles glowing in every window are quite a sight. Doubles, $100 to $135, MAP. Closed two weeks in November and April.

Bromley Sun Lodge, Route 11, Peru 05152, (802) 824-6941. You can ski out the door and right onto the slopes at this four-story, chalet-style lodge that backs up to Bromley, almost next to the base lodge. The 51 spacious rooms have two double beds, except for four with king beds. A large photo of tropical ocean and palm trees incongruously adorns one wall of the room holding the indoor pool. Other facilities include a sauna, game room, paneled bar and lounge, and a large family-style dining room serving American and European cuisine. Doubles, $85 to $120, EP; add $25 per person MAP; three-night minimum during holiday periods.

Swiss Inn, Route 11, RFD 1, Box 140, Londonderry 05148, (802) 824-3442 or (800) 847-9477. When the longtime Swiss owners of this alpine-style motel and restaurant retired, buyers Pat and Joe Donahue didn't miss a beat. Pat retained the Swiss menu in the dining room, cooking in the style of her predecessor, Lisa Gegenschatz. The somewhat plain exterior has been given a new columned front and the interior has been redecorated. There's a fireplaced lounge with a small game room as you enter; another lounge with a couple of tables and a bar is located outside the pink and blue dining room. Pat's dinners (entree prices, $13.50 to $17.50) attract the public, although they're optional for guests since the inn has switched from MAP to B&B. The nineteen rooms with private baths and TVs are fairly contemporary and impeccably clean. In season, guests enjoy a swimming pool, a pond, a tennis court and gardens. Doubles, $59 to $88; two connecting rooms, ideal for a family of four, are $129.

Condominium rentals. Bromley Village has 300 condominium units of one to four bedrooms, some of them slopeside, others within easy reach of the mountain. Bromley Lodging Service, (802) 824-5458, handles rentals. There's a two-night minimum. Weekends, a two-bedroom condo sleeping four to six is $644; a three-bedroom, sleeping six to eight, $764. All have fireplaces and complete kitchens.

Stratton

Birkenhaus, Stratton Mountain 05155, (802) 297-2000. In the busy Stratton base area, this eighteen-room inn is a quiet oasis and remains our favorite of the inns within walking distance of the base lodge. Taken over in 1986 by a Czechoslovakian couple who had been living in New Jersey, Ina and Jan Dlouhy, it retains the Austrian "gemutlichkeit" fostered by Anne and Emo Henrich, who made it so special. Most rooms are not particularly large, but are cozily appointed; all have private bath, telephone and television. A couple of rooms contain sets of bunks for children ($32 per person). Afternoon tea and cake are served beside the fire in the upstairs lounge with its view of Stratton. The adjoining library contains a TV and VCR with a good video selection for children. In the engaging dining room, waitresses in dirndls serve highly acclaimed dinners to guests and the public (see Where to Eat). There's also a cheery lounge where tired skiers like to lift a stein and share the day's tales. Doubles, $95 to $160, EP; $164 to $232, MAP.

Stratton Mountain Inn, Middle Ridge Road, Stratton 05155, (802) 297-2500. This 125-room full-service hotel is one of two Stratton lodging establishments operated by Colony Hotels & Resorts. Rooms are modern and amenities include a sauna, whirlpool and exercise area. Guests have access to all Stratton facilities, including the sports center. Meals are available in a cafeteria and in the **Sage Hill Restaurant.** Even closer to the ski area — in fact, part of the Stratton Village complex — is the Colony-run **Stratton Village Lodge,** (802) 297-2260. This is a contemporary lodge with 91 rooms, each with small refrigerator and microwave. We found one of the two-bedroom units a good bet for a family ski outing a few years back. Doubles, $114 to $134 at inn, $134 to $144 at lodge.

Alpenrose Inn, Winhall Hollow Road, Bondville 05340, (802) 297-2750. The Alpenrose has come a long way since the old barn was converted into a bunkhouse the year Stratton opened. "It was called 'Bud's Bunks,'" relates owner Rosemarie Strine; "I've still got the sign." Under the tutelage of Rosemarie and her late husband Bob, the inn has shed all vestiges of its bunkhouse status. Off by itself in the rural countryside, it offers seven cozy guest rooms, each with private bath and furnished with period pieces, handmade quilts ("by me," advises Rosemarie) and goose down comforters. A Chippendale highboy graces the Yodeler (all rooms are named after Stratton trails), which has one of the inn's two queensize canopy beds; the Tamarack contains double and single poster beds. The common rooms are unusually alluring here: a large barnwood lounge with a wood stove in the fireplace, a snug Victorian parlor with TV, and a large dining room with hand-hewn beams, the original barn floors and a charming country look. Rosemarie advises guests to sit against the light green kachelofen to warm their bodies after skiing. The alpine-style contraption of handmade tiles covers the old fireplace and provides energy-efficient heat; who's to question Rosemarie's guess that it's the only kachelofen in Vermont? Here she provides a full breakfast of the guest's choice. In summer, a pond out back is good for swimming and bass fishing. Doubles, $95 to $115.

The Inn at Bear Creek, Route 30, Rawsonville 05155, (802) 297-1700. Calling itself a "sport hotel and condominium complex," this establishment, about ten minutes from Stratton, is nicely decorated in a contemporary style with lots of light wood. A little red bus transports skiers from the inn to the mountain. Rooms are modern and motel-like, and all have color TVs and phones. Bunk rooms are available ($30 per person), as are condominiums on the adjoining site. Meals may be taken in **The Restaurant at Bear Creek,** a paneled inner room and a windowed outer room, where entrees are priced from $8.95 for fettuccine marinara to $16.95 for veal sauteed with bacon, sundried tomatoes and brandy. Doubles, $99.

Condominiums at Stratton can be rented through the Stratton Mountain Lodging Service, (800) 843-6867. About 150 fully furnished Stratton Mountain Villas of one to four bedrooms are located as close to the mountain as you can get, with a sports center and a couple of restaurants nearby. Villas, $240 to $480, double occupancy; extra persons, $20.

Ski-Touring Inns

The Village Inn, RFD Box 215, Landgrove 05148, (802) 824-6673 or (800) 669-8466. A true country inn of "Vermont continuous architecture," this is out in the back of beyond and reached by gravel roads, not all of them marked. It's carefully run by the Snyder family, Jay and Kathy and their children, plus Jay's parents, Don and Else, who started the whole thing 30 years ago when they left New Jersey. Jay is the innkeeper, Don is the breakfast cook and Else can be found most often at the front desk. The classic red inn with white trim dates from the 1820s; add-ons include a few modern rooms and a game room with a whirlpool tub. Sixteen rooms have private baths; four more use two hall bathrooms. We like the angled ceilings and creatively arranged rooms in the older part of this complex, and we love the Rafter Room with dart board, bar, bumper pool and wood stove. You can stretch out on a lounging sofa and really relax. Dinner is "chef's choice," but special diets will be accommodated. Usually Saturday night finds some form of roast beef on the menu. A new paddle tennis court is used in winter by the hardy; there's also a pond for ice-skating. Cross-country trails enter Green Mountain National Forest from the inn property, and three touring centers are located within five miles. A few cross-country ski outfits are for rent, but you have to be early to get the right size. Doubles, $110 to $155, MAP; summer, $55 to $85, B&B.

The Nordic Inn, Route 11, Landgrove 05148, (802) 824-6444. If your party has alpine and nordic skiers, we can't think of a better compromise for both than this appealing spot not far from Bromley and with its own lovely cross-country trails. Judy and Tom Acton took over the Nordic Inn in 1983 and, despite their Irish backgrounds, have kept its Scandinavian flavor. Judy cooks the meals (see Where to Eat), which are served in most attractive dining rooms. For lunch, we like the solarium area overlooking the winter woods. The intimate, lower-level pub dispenses Swedish glogg for $3.50, which is just right for fireside sipping. The inn has five guest rooms, named for the four Scandinavian countries plus Vermont. Three have private baths and each is simply but colorfully decorated. Sweden is extra-large and has a wood stove and private bath. Judy prepares a full breakfast for guests in winter. A cross-country ski shop on the premises rents equipment and instruction is offered. Doubles, $120 to $150 MAP.

The Barrows House, Route 30, Dorset 05251, (802) 867-4455. Cross-country trails lead from the front door of this historic inn of eight buildings on twelve park-like acres. Owners Sally and Tim Brown have a cross-country rental shop and direct skiers to trails at Merck Forest & Farmland Center or the Dorset Country Club; they will pack a Brown's Bag Lunch for guests. The inn and cottage complex offers 28 comfortable rooms with private baths. The main inn has eight rooms off a long narrow hallway, simply furnished in a country inn manner. Family reunions occasionally take place in the cottages, one of which contains eight rooms. The cozy tavern, with its trompe l'oeil walls of books, is a good place for end-of-the-day toddies. Chef Tim Blackwell offers acclaimed regional cuisine for dinner in the dining room, where we love to sit in the greenhouse addition and look out at the falling snow. Entrees ($14.95 to $22) include baked Norwegian salmon and mushroom duxelle, sliced pork tenderloin with sweet and sour apples, and rack of lamb with pear-rum raisin chutney. An interesting tavern menu, available every night but Saturday, is priced from $8.50 to $11.50. Dinner nightly, 6 to 9. Doubles, $160 to $215, MAP.

The Inn at Weston, Route 100, Weston 05161, (802) 824-5804. Cross-country skiers can set out from the doorstep of this inn to avail themselves of a network of trails encircling the picturebook village of Weston or the layouts at nearby touring centers. They also can be assured of being well-fed in the inn's restaurant, where chef Jay McCoy varies the dinner fare ($14.95 to $22.50), from a basic breast of chicken with morel sauce to a complex confit of duck leg and pan-roasted duck breast with blueberry sauce. Venison medallions with a wild mushroom and black currant sauce is a winter favorite. The establishment bears antiques and elegant touches reminiscent of the English country inns that owners Jeanne and Bob Wilder enjoyed while living and traveling in England. Arriving in Weston in 1986, they set about upgrading the original 1848 farmhouse, which had been a guesthouse since 1951, and acquired the 1830 Coleman House across the street. The traffic patterns were shifted so that house guests no longer have to go through the busy kitchen to get to the dining room and now enjoy a new parlor with cozy chairs and a wood stove. Upstairs in the main inn are thirteen redecorated guest rooms, seven with private baths and the rest with lavatory facilities in the room. The Coleman House offers a living room and six more guest rooms, all with private baths. Breakfast is for hearty appetites, including a choice of different kinds of pancakes and eggs any style. Doubles, $118 to $163, MAP.

Viking Guest House, The Viking Center, Little Pond Road, Londonderry 05148, (802) 824-3933. Four bedrooms and a comfortable living room are offered in an 1860 farmhouse on the Viking Center property. Just outside are more than 25 miles of cross-country trails. Center personnel suggest putting together your own group of four couples to have the kitchen and dining room to yourselves. Rates include breakfast, trail pass and complimentary refreshments. Doubles, $110.

The Inn at High View, East Hill Road, RR 1, Box 201A, Andover 05143, (802) 875-2724 or (800) 852-4667. The old Swedish Ski Club has been turned into a relatively fancy B&B, way out in the boondocks off the Andover-Weston Road east of Weston. The club's bunk rooms gave way to a pair of two-room family suites in the front of the house. Elsewhere are six more guest rooms, all with private baths, down comforters, quilts, thick carpeting and decanters of port. Most are named after the cats in *Old Possum's Book of Practical Cats* by T.S. Eliot, whose book is on the nightstand in nearly every room. Owner Greg Bohan, whose background is hotel market research, does all the work with his chef-partner, Sal Massaro, who dabbles in landscaping and floral design. Sal concocted the stunning Christmas decorations that graced the large living room and two dining rooms at our visit. Downstairs is a bright and colorful TV/recreation room that doubles as a conference center. Skiers enjoy the sauna and three cross-country loops of five, ten and fifteen kilometers each out back. Summer guests use the swimming pool bordered by stones and a front porch affording one of the more remarkable mountain prospects we've seen. Sal cooks hearty breakfasts to order. He and Greg offer five-course sitdown dinners on weekends for $25 each. The fare could be asparagus wrapped in smoked salmon, chicory and tomato salad, fettuccine with pesto and sundried tomatoes, chicken saltimbocca and tirami su. Doubles, $90 to $105; suites, $125.

Other Choices

The Equinox, Manchester Village 05254, (802) 362-4700 or (800) 362-4747. Everyone is delighted to see the resurrection — not once but twice — of the old Equinox

Restored Equinox hotel stands proudly in Manchester Village.

House, one of the grand dames of summer resorts, now open all year for elegant lodging and dining. The hotel, dating to 1769 when it started as Marsh Tavern, was renovated to the tune of $20 million in 1985 and reopened as a year-round resort. It was acquired in 1991 by a partnership whose majority owner is Guinness, the beer company that owns the noted Gleneagles Hotel in Scotland. The hotel was closed for three months in 1992 for another $10 million makeover, this one really making a difference. It involved all 141 guest rooms and eleven suites, a new lobby, a vastly expanded Marsh Tavern and the formal Colonnade dining room. The classic and columned white hotel now opens into a world of lush comfort, starting with a dramatic, two-story lobby with a view of Mount Equinox, converted from what had been nine guest rooms. Overnighters notice the vast improvement in guest rooms, all now fully winterized and dressed in light pine furniture, new carpeting and coordinated bedspreads and draperies, and equipped with modern baths, TVs and telephones. Rooms come in four sizes (standard, superior, deluxe and premium), although anything less than deluxe may be a letdown. The former lobby gave way in 1992 to Marsh Tavern, now four times as big with a bar and well-spaced tables flanked by windsor and wing chairs and loveseats; it's all quite handsome in dark green, red and black. The grand Colonnade dining room with a barrel-vaulted ceiling, stenciled by hand by a latter-day Michelangelo who lay on his back on scaffolding for days on end, is suitably formal for those who like to dress for dinner, as is required here. A spa in an adjacent building has a pool, steam rooms, an exercise room with Nautilus equipment, massage therapy, aerobics programs, the works — and spa packages to match. The whole place is stately, pricey and refined, although the staff is friendly and accommodating. Doubles, $129 to $219, EP; suites, $250 to $325.

The Reluctant Panther Inn, Manchester Village 05254, (802) 362-2568 or (800) 822-2331. The purple house with yellow shutters continues to be one of the best located and most delightful inns in the area. Robert and Maye Bachofen, he a Swiss hotelier and she a personable Peruvian, offer first-class dining as well as some of the most sumptuous and comfortable accommodations in town. Added recently were four luxurious suites in the Mary Porter House next door; they come with kingsize poster beds, fireplaces and jacuzzis. One claims a double jacuzzi in the center of the largest bathroom you ever saw, with a fireplace opposite, two pedestal sinks and a separate shower. "If you ever find another room like this, you tell me," says Maye proudly. She

261

has redecorated the twelve rooms in the main house in a mix of styles, each with splashy wallpapers, fabrics and window treatments, goose down comforters on the beds, Gilbert & Soames toiletries and sitting areas with wing chairs. All rooms have private baths, telephones and cable television, and eight have working fireplaces. Guests find a half-bottle of Robert Mondavi red wine in their room upon arrival. A full breakfast is served at six marble tables in a fireplaced breakfast room. The inviting dining room with a greenhouse at one end, open to the public by reservation, offers a short menu that changes daily. At our visit, the seven entrees ranged from $14.95 for pumpkin-filled sage ravioli with smoked chicken and roasted garlic cream to $23 for pan-roasted veal chop on wild mushroom risotto. The Bachofens offer "country hospitality for the sophisticated traveler;" theirs is truly a place for a romantic getaway. Doubles, $175 to $195, MAP; suites, $210 to $250, MAP. No smoking.

1811 House, Manchester Village 05254, (802) 362-1811 or (800) 432-1811. There are bowls of popcorn and no fewer than 26 single-malt scotches available in the intimate pub of this B&B full of antiques, oriental rugs and charm. The soft cocoa-colored house has history, too. Mary Lincoln Isham, granddaughter of Abraham Lincoln, once lived here, and the house had welcomed guests since 1935. But its complete renovation in 1983 made it something special. There are rooms with fireplaces, some with canopied beds, and all with carefully chosen reproduction wallpapers and decor. A recently redone cottage adds three rooms to the eleven in the main inn, all but two with private baths. The new rooms have kingsize beds and fireplaces. Extensive gardens overlook a pond out back. The inn's coziest of British pubs (open nightly from 5:30 to 8) is where owners Marnie and Bruce Duff offer McEwan's ale on draught or one of their rare single-malt scotches, $4 to $7 a shot or three for $10 for a wee dram of each, if you're really into testing. Marnie serves an ample English breakfast, from fried tomatoes to fresh scones, in the elegant dining room with a mahogany table and chairs. We love the gray and white cat stretched out on the oriental rug in the front parlor and the bowl of mixed nuts ready for cracking. Doubles, $110 to $180.

The Inn at Ormsby Hill, Route 7A, RR 2, Box 3264, Manchester Center 05255, (802) 362-1163. "We don't have to sell this house — it sells itself," says Nancy Burd, owner of this engaging new B&B with her husband Don. And so it does. The sprawling manor house was long owned by Edward Isham, an Illinois state legislator and senior partner in a Chicago law firm with Robert Todd Lincoln (Abraham's son), whom he entertained here. Later, the Isham Foundation used it to house underprivileged boys. Recently restored, the house is a beauty — one that Orvis chose as the backdrop for its fall catalog in 1992. You enter from a foyer into a parlor furnished with rare antiques from both sides of the Burd family and look to the rear through a spacious fireplaced library into a sunny dining room extending 40 feet back. The total depth — in what already appears as a strikingly wide house — takes the breath away. So does the view across terrace, back yard and Hildene to mountains from the many-paned boat windows in this dining room that was constructed to resemble a ship. Look at the ornate carved fireplace mantel — which, Don says, reflects the global tastes of Edward Isham — from a snug sitting area at the far end. The Burds offer five comfortable guest rooms, four with whirlpool baths and separate showers, and all with oversize four-poster or canopy beds, plush armchairs, antique chests, fine artworks and oriental rugs. Talented Nancy's paintings, quilts and hooked rugs are on display throughout. The Burds also use their college son's room for overflow, and were thinking of adding three more guest rooms in the north wing of the house. Don cooks the breakfast entrees and Nancy does the baking and serves: juice and an exotic fresh fruit course, homemade muffins and breads, and perhaps oven pancakes with apples and sausage. For the summer of 1993, the Burds

First snow of season blankets picturesque town of Dorset.

planned to restore some of the perennial gardens and resurface the tennis court. Their 2 1/2-acre property adjoins Hildene, built by Lincoln on 412 acres behind Isham's Ormsby Hill. Doubles, $90 to $160.

Cornucopia of Dorset, Route 30, Box 307, Dorset 05251, (802) 867-5751. Innkeepers Bill and Linda Ley have turned this lovely 19th-century Colonial home into a B&B of distinction. Deceptively small on the outside, Cornucopia opens into an expansive first floor with a fireplaced library, an inviting living room with overstuffed sofas and a large central dining room opening into an airy sun room, warm and bright with plants in winter. Four sumptuous bedrooms with king or queen beds in the main house plus a cottage — perfect for honeymooners or second honeymooners — out back comprise the accommodations, all with private baths. We especially like Scallop, the front room with canopied queensize bed, corner fireplace, large bright windows and oversize bathroom. But the cottage is no slouch: a sofabed faces the fireplace in the cathedral-ceilinged living room, there's a full kitchen, and upstairs is a skylit loft with queensize bed and even a spinning wheel and cradle. The personable Leys are known for their attention to detail, from champagne served at check-in to the slice of Mother Myrick's buttercrunch on the pillow of a bed turned down ever so artistically upon your return from dinner. Their breakfast is special, perhaps fresh orange juice, hot spiced fruit compote and baked cinnamon apple pancakes. Doubles, $100 to $130; cottage, $175. No smoking.

Manchester View Motel, Route 7, Box 1268, Manchester Center 05255, (802) 362-2739. The word "motel" can be a turnoff, but this is several notches above the norm. Crowning a hill off Route 7 north of town with views in all directions, the complex scatters five deep brown buildings with white trim, each of which contains some unusual — and very individualistic — accommodations. The enormous Calvin Coolidge Room yields a fantastic view of the mountains; it has a kingsize bed plus double sofabed and large private bath, and photos of one of Vermont's favorite sons. The Norman Rockwell suite contains a traditionally furnished sitting room, a bedroom with king bed and a jacuzzi bath. Five new grand suites come with living room, fireplace, powder room, bedroom with kingsize bed, and bathroom with two-person jacuzzi and large walk-in European shower. All suites have two TVs and a VCR. Among the 29 rooms are some deluxe, charmingly decorated rooms with fireplaces and two queensize or one kingsize bed. The standard rooms, many with decks or balconies and views of the mountains that surround this site, are nice, too. Visit the simply furnished breakfast room in the early morning and for $2.50 you'll get English muffins, waffles with maple syrup, juice and a hot beverage. Owners Pat and Tom Barnett have been making improvements here for sixteen years. Doubles, $65 to $135; suites for four with two bedrooms and fireplaced living room, $165 to $175; grand suites, $175.

Barnstead Innstead, Route 30, Box 988, Manchester Center 05255, (802) 362-1619. A New England hay barn, built in the 1830s, has been converted into one of the coziest little places to stay around; a dozen rooms have wall-to-wall carpeting, cable TV, courtesy coffee and private baths. We liked our two-room suite, carpeted in a braided rug look and with nice touches like a pierced tin lamp in the hall. Another time we stayed in Room 1, paneled in barnwood, with a kingsize bed, tiled bath, a comfy chair and two old school desks that doubled as chairs and nightstands. The lamps are in brown crocks, calico wall hangings adorn the walls and rough pine furniture adds a rustic feeling. The location is good, just a quarter-mile from town and set back from the road, and the price is right ($50 at midweek in winter). Owners Peter and Cindy Conrad offer a swimming pool in summer. Doubles, $50 to $85.

The Three Clock Inn, Middletown Road, South Londonderry 05155, (802) 824-6327. Long known for fine dining under the aegis of master chef Heinrich Tschernitz (see Where to Eat), this was looking up in terms of accommodations with its purchase in 1992 by Lisa and Patrick Brown of Memphis, Tenn. Patrick was overseeing the dining operation, with assistance from Hank Tschernitz, who is retiring but only moved down the street. Energetic Lisa was redecorating the guest rooms in bright colors with chintz fabrics, tailored bedspreads and down comforters. The room configuration varies widely, from a large fireplaced room with beamed ceiling, canopy bed and a day bed to a long narrow porch of a room with twin beds placed end to end. Both of these have private baths, while two front bedrooms share a bath. Two suites, one off the main-floor parlor and another upstairs, offer accommodations for four. Guests share the main-floor living room with restaurant patrons, and have another sitting room with fireplace and TV upstairs. A full breakfast is cooked to order by chef Patrick. Doubles, $150, MAP.

The Londonderry Inn, Route 100, South Londonderry 05155, (802) 824-5226. An old dairy farm dating to the 1826 just grew and grew in the fashion of Vermont continuous architecture. The result, after 50 years of innkeeping, is a comfortable, laid-back place of uncommon value. The woodshed became a dining room, and guest rooms sprouted off narrow, twisting corridors up steep stairs on the second and third floors. Nooks and crannies turn up a tavern, a game room and a billiards room with two tables at the ready. Eighteen of the 23 bedrooms come with private baths. They are outfitted with a mix of pine and antique furniture; carpeting covers the wide-board floors in some. Eight rooms in a newer wing appear more spacious because they are square and lack the angles of the older section. Two large family rooms on the third floor contain a double bed each, plus four twin beds in one and three twins in the other; these are good values at $15 to $20 a person, including breakfast. A stone fireplace warms one end of the large living room. Innkeepers Jim and Jean Cavanagh welcome guests and the public in the paneled dining room, country-homey in blue and white with windows on three sides. The dinner menu changes daily and gets quite creative, as in curried lamb with apricots and puerco adobo (pork medallions in a chipotle pepper, tomato and orange sauce). Veal parmesan, Vermont brook trout meuniere and duckling bigarade are other choices ($10.50 to $14.95). A buffet breakfast is served in the morning. Dinner nightly, 5:30 to 9:30. Doubles, $60 to $75. No credit cards.

The Wilder Homestead Inn, RR 1, Box 106-D, Weston 05161, (802) 824-8172. One of two brick homesteads ever built in Weston, this masterpiece erected in 1827 for Judge Wilder is now an inviting B&B. Roy and Peggy Varner offer five large rooms with private baths and queensize canopy beds and two third-floor rooms with double beds and shared bath. Eight Count Rumford fireplaces and Moses Eaton stenciling on the walls lend an air of historic elegance to guest rooms and the three common sitting rooms. The Varners put decanters of cream sherry in the rooms and serve breakfast in a large paneled and stenciled dining room at a table big enough to seat ten. Roy makes the jams for the baking-powder biscuits, along with a choice of pancakes, french toast, eggs any style or a cheese omelet with Vermont cheddar. Incredibly, he also makes all the hand-dipped candles, furniture and wood crafts the couple sell in **The 1827 Shoppe** at the side of the house. At our visit, he was fashioning jet-black "Vermont flamingos," a.k.a. crows — "Florida has the flamingo, and Vermont has the crow," said he. They come in all sizes to grace mailboxes, shelves, pots and such, $14 each. Doubles, $60 to $90. No smoking.

1830 Inn on the Green, Route 100, Box 104, Weston 05161, (802) 824-6789. With a pillared, two-story veranda facing the green, this B&B resembles a small Southern plantation house. Inside, all is elegant and up-to-date. Sandy and Dave Granger share their plushly carpeted formal parlor with overnight guests. At the top of a wide, curving staircase is quite a collection of stuffed animals peeking out from an old trunk. The staircase, we're told, came from the mansion of Hetty Green, the famed "Witch of Wall Street," who summered in nearby Bellows Falls. The Grangers offer four bedrooms, two with private baths. We like the Polly Farrar room with kingsize brass bed, thick blue carpeting and sophisticated country accessories all around. A full breakfast involves a choice of eggs, pancakes, french toast or waffles. Doubles, $60 to $80.

Where to Eat

Skiers work up hearty appetites. After a long day on the slopes or trails, they often will drive some distance to a good restaurant. Families look for simpler fare.

Fine Dining

Chantecleer, Route 7A, East Dorset, (802) 362-1616. Swiss-born Michel Baumann has turned this converted dairy barn (look for the silo outside) into a renowned restaurant that's perfect for ski country. A serious chef-owner who insists on doing it his way, Baumann serves no more than 50 diners in a two-section dining room (the three tables near the old stone fireplace are the ones reserved first). The rustic interior, with beamed ceiling and lots of wood, has elegant table appointments, and crystal and silverplate gleam in the soft lighting. Swiss yodeling music may be played on tape as diners feast on the Swiss and French provincial cuisine. Among starters ($4.95 to $7.50) are a classic French onion soup baked with gruyere and emmental cheeses, a Swiss sausage plate served with horseradish-mustard sauce and sauerkraut, fresh oyster salad on a bed of greens and, our favorite, the bundnerfleisch, Swiss air-dried beef fanned out in little coronets with pearl onions, cornichons and melba rounds. Signature entrees ($16.95 to $25) include rack of lamb and frogs' legs with a garlic butter sauce. We can vouch for the veal sweetbreads morel, sauteed quail stuffed with mushroom duxelle and one night's special, boneless pheasant with smoked bacon and grapes. Bananas foster, trifle and creme brulee make worthy endings. Dinner by reservation, Wednesday-Sunday 6 to 9:30.

The Equinox, Route 7, Manchester Village, (802) 362-4700. Dinner in the main **Colonnade** dining room is fancier both in atmosphere and price than most skiers appreciate, but it's revered by the old-guard clientele who pack this place on weekends, holidays and most of the summer and fall. They don the obligatory jackets and ties to feast on such entrees ($18 to $24) as wellington of salmon, veal ribeye steak, and roasted lamb chops with whole grain mustard and walnut pesto and garlic polenta. Skiers (and other more casual mortals) prefer the clubby and masculine **Marsh Tavern,** recently quadrupled in size and seating 86 people at well-spaced tables. We found the place too bright with lights right over our heads, although the hostess said that was a new one on her — most folks thought it was too dark. We also found the dinner menu rather pricey and lacking in depth, given that it was the only restaurant open in the hotel that evening. Witness a caesar salad with a few baby shrimp for $7, a simple tossed salad for $5, a good lamb stew with potato gratin for $10 (it was called shepherd's pie but wasn't) and a small roasted cornish game hen for $13.50. With a shared cranberry-walnut torte and a bottle of Hawk's Crest cabernet for $21, a simple dinner for two turned into something of an extravagance for $70. Mind you, our reaction does not seem to be shared by the loyal clientele who love the tavern. The fare runs from $8 for a burger to $16 for baked swordfish. Colonnade, dinner, weekends only in winter, 6 to 9:30, nightly at peak periods; Sunday brunch, 11 to 2:30. Marsh Tavern, lunch, Monday-Saturday noon to 2; dinner nightly, 6 to 9:30.

The Black Swan, Route 7, Manchester Center, (802) 362-3807. This 1830 brick house set on a knoll along Route 7 is the setting for a special dining experience in the hands of chef-owner Richard Whisenhunt, whose wife Kathy takes care of the front of the house. Before opening his own place in 1985, he was at Le Cirque in New York City and the Homestead Inn in Greenwich, Conn. Here his forte is continental cuisine with a California influence. You can sample casual fare in the **Mucky Duck** bistro and lounge in the front of the house or dine more elegantly in the formal, fireplaced rear dining room where the chef is in his element. Entrees run from $15.50 for chicken and sausage bouillabaisse, a variation on the classic in a saffron-garlic chicken broth, to $19.50 for fettuccine with smoked pheasant and shittake mushrooms or scaloppine of venison with cranberry-orange sauce. Wild mushroom tart, fresh Maine crab cake and seared filet of beef are winning starters. Sweet endings might include walnut torte and white chocolate mousse with raspberry melba sauce. Dinner, Thursday-Monday from 5:30.

Ye Olde Tavern, Main Street, Manchester Center, (802) 362-3770. Just the ticket for skiers — and anyone else who likes good food in an historic setting — is this mustard-yellow building with white pillars and trim, dating to 1790. It shows its age nicely in three main-floor dining rooms with stenciled walls, bare wood floors and Williamsburg colors. But the food is up to date for candlelit, blue-tablecloth dinners. You can get any of a dozen entrees from $14.95 to $18.50 for the likes of salmon fillet with red pepper cream sauce, pork medallions with raisins and leeks, and tournedos with green peppercorn and red wine sauce. Entrees come with soup or salad, so you can probably skip an appetizer. Or you can order interesting light entrees from $8.95 to $11.95, quite adequate meals with rice or potatoes and vegetables — dishes like lime-marinated chicken, broiled rainbow trout, cajun veal stew or, amazingly, petite steak and lobster tail. Lunch daily from 11:30; dinner nightly from 5; Sunday brunch, 10 to 3.

Dorset Inn, On the Green, Dorset, (802) 867-5500. Co-owner Sissy Hicks is the chef and partner Gretchen Schmidt does the desserts for the culinary side of this venerable institution, the oldest continuously operated country inn in Vermont. They offer 34 pleasant guest rooms on the second and third floors, but are best known for their dining. You can have lunch in the cheerful sun porch or supper before the fireplace in the tavern, or you might opt for dinner in the main dining room with its flowered wallpaper and blue-clothed tables. Dinner entrees here range from $10.50 for a six-ounce apple-smoked ribeye steak with apple-sage butter to $22.50 for roast rack of lamb with minty brown sauce. We're partial to the calves liver and the fresh trout laden with sauteed leeks and mushrooms. Skiers really go for the inn's convivial tavern, where most dishes on the versatile menu are $6.50 to $8.50. Among the choices are sauteed chicken livers with madeira tomato sauce, salmon cakes with spinach-dill hollandaise, barbecued pork sandwich with coleslaw, spicy beef or turkey chili, steamed mussels and grilled basil-garlic chicken with orzo provencal. Many of the tavern dishes are available at lunch. This is Vermont country dining at its best. Lunch daily, 11:30 to 2; dinner nightly 6 to 9; tavern, 5:30 to 9.

The Three Clock Inn, Middletown Road, South Londonderry, (802) 824-6327. Up the hill past the hardware store you'll find the unimposing white house that served as a base for master chef Heinrich Tschernitz and his wife Frances for some 25 years. Very little changed in that time and, with their retirement in 1992, new owners Patrick and Lisa Brown promised few changes in the future. Even in retirement, Hank Tschernitz was staying on as chef for a year to train Patrick — no slouch himself in the kitchen, given a varied restaurant background in St. Louis and North Carolina. Dinners are served by candlelight in three simple, cozy dining rooms and, in summer, on a screened porch. There are more than three clocks that give the inn its name, plus lots of hippopotomi that the Tschernitzes collected in all kinds of guises. Our favorite piece on a cluttered fireplace mantel in the main dining room is a statue of the Austrian patron saint of wine, clutching bunches of purple grapes. Patrick retained his predecessor's printed menu, declining to tamper with a proven format. Ten entrees, priced from $14.75 to $21.50, include soup or most appetizers and dessert — an astonishing value. You might start with herring in sour cream, the house pate or soup of the day (perhaps black bean on a wintry evening). Then go on to frogs' legs provencal, scampi maison, veal marsala, duckling a l'orange, lamb chops or filet mignon au poivre. Salad follows the main course. Finish with strawberries romanoff, pear helene or a fruit turnover. The food is every bit as engaging as the ambience. Dinner, Tuesday-Sunday 6 to 9:30. No credit cards.

The Nordic Inn, Route 11, Landgrove, (802) 824-6444. Dining is on two levels in the striking solarium with brick floor, soaring cathedral ceiling and skylights, plus huge windows looking onto the lawns and birch-filled forest. Appointments have that clean Scandinavian look. Recorded classical music played during Sunday brunch as we enjoyed hot French bread, an olive, tomato and celery soup, a special shrimp and crab souffle, and Swedish hash with a fried egg, pickled beets and a distinct bite. Innkeeper Judy Acton is the chef, offering a variety of blackboard specials from $4.95 to $7.95 for lunch during cross-country season. The menu is continental at night, when entrees run from $13.95 for chicken forestiere to $21 for steak au poivre. Grilled Norwegian salmon, pork normandy and veal with two mustards are other favorites. You might start with herring Nordic, garnished with sour cream, onions and pickled beets, or fresh salmon cakes served with tartar and caper sauce. A frozen hazelnut souffle with raspberry coulis was a memorable dessert. Dinner nightly, 6 to 10; lunch in winter, noon to 2; Sunday brunch, 11 to 3. Closed Tuesday.

Red Fox Inn, Winhall Hollow Road, Bondville, (802) 297-2488. A soaring red ex-livestock barn houses a lively main-floor tavern that's popular with the apres-ski crowd and a lofty upstairs dining room dressed with white-linened tables and holding a blazing hearth at the far end. The food is highly rated, if considered locally a bit pricey. Dinner entrees run from $16.95 for chicken boursin or roast duckling with orange-grand marnier sauce to $21.95 for prime rib or rack of lamb. Salmon en papillote, swordfish with mustard beurre blanc and veal chop with herb butter might be nightly specials. For an unusual start, try the Vermont pasties — puff pastry stuffed with veal, pork, turnips, potatoes and carrots on a bed of cheese mornay sauce. Downstairs, a tavern menu offers all kinds of snacky appetizers, pizzas and pedestrian dinners ($4.95 to $6.95). The inn has ten snug guest rooms with private baths in the adjacent 18th-century farmhouse dubbed "The White House" (doubles, $60 to $75). Dinner nightly, 6 to 10. No credit cards.

Birkenhaus, Stratton Mountain, (802) 297-2000. Across the access road from the new Stratton Village and the ski slopes is this bastion of fine cuisine in an attractive alpine-style inn. Waitresses in dirndls serve patrons at paneled banquettes and sturdy chairs facing heavily napped tables in the elegant but comfortable dining room. Owners Jan and Ina Dlouhy are known for their French, Austrian and Czechoslovakian specialties, but the menu we saw (they change daily) was as contemporary American as any around. The predictable wiener schnitzel and sauerbraten were listed with such entrees ($17.50 to $19) as fresh scrod with black beans, fillet of tuna with red onions and peas, medallions of pork with braised red cabbage and beef tournedos with artichoke hearts. Hardly your classic alpine appetizers are treats like fettuccine with mussels and shrimp, grilled andouille and white beans, and braised pheasant with raisins and pecans. For dessert, there's apple strudel, of course. But you also might find macadamia nut tart, maple creme caramel and homemade banana-raspberry sorbet. The kitchen under chef Douglas Rountree knows what it's doing. Dinner nightly, 6 to 9.

Hot and Hearty

The Sirloin Saloon, Routes 11 and 30, Manchester Center, (802) 362-2600. If anything, the Sirloin Saloon only gets bigger, better and more popular. Richly colored Tiffany lamps light the old grist mill, where dining areas feature a fine collection of American Indian art and artifacts. The ornate bar, a conversation piece, was taken from a former speakeasy in Granville, N.Y. The menu suits hearty winter appetites, starring choice Western grain-fed beef; with it come rice or potato and homebaked home-grain bread. Prime rib, New York or teriyaki sirloin, wood-grilled swordfish, shrimp scampi and various combinations are priced from $8.95 to $18.95. Light entrees ($7.95 to $10.95) include a petite top sirloin and a petite chicken. Or you can just have the salad bar for $7.95. Mud pie, New York cheesecake and a variety of ice creams are the dessert choices. Dinner nightly, 5 to 10 or 11.

Garlic John's, Routes 11 and 30, Manchester, (802) 362-9843. Here's another restaurant that has found a warm welcome in Manchester. Enlarged and made more imposing by the addition of huge columns, Garlic John's maintains its reputation for pasta. From the ceiling hang hundreds of chianti bottles. Varnished wood tables are set with red placemats and surrounded with captain's chairs. Into this simple atmosphere is brought some good food. Among appetizers ($3 to $6.95) are mussels marinara, shrimp cocktail, antipasto, stuffed mushrooms Amerigo, and marinated artichokes and mushrooms. Pasta is either spaghetti or linguini and the prices are fair: from $7.95 for pasta with marinara or bolognese sauce to $14.95 for pasta with seafood. The baked ziti Amadeo has three kinds of cheeses and a marinara sauce. Garlic John's menu has expanded to include more chicken, veal, beef and seafood entrees ($10.95 to $14.95). Homemade tortoni is the dessert of choice. Next door is **GJ's Double Hex,** featuring inexpensive family meals and notable charcoal-broiled burgers for lunch and dinner. Dinner nightly, 4 to 9 or 10.

Mulligans, Stratton Village, Stratton Mountain, (802) 297-9293. This is a classic skier's establishment, with a main-floor bar and dining on various levels around a soaring atrium. Sleds, musical instruments and other paraphernalia hang from the walls and the three-story-high ceiling. There's a lot to look at, not even considering the boisterous crowd below. Actually, the different levels

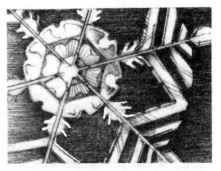

and various nooks make for surprisingly private dining, at round wood tables with fancy, ultra-high-back chairs. The extensive menu offers something for everyone, from beefalo burgers (the meat raised at Vermont's only beefalo ranch in Manchester) to salads to Mexican burritos to jalapeno poppers (jalapeno peppers stuffed with cheddar cheese, deep-fried and served with salsa) to baby back pork ribs, the house specialty. Dinner entrees are priced from $11.95 to $16.95. Much the same fare is offered at lunch, when the blue-plate corner touts baked meatloaf, beef stew and roast turkey dinner for $8.50 each. The formula obviously works, for Mulligans has opened a second restaurant in a house along Route 7A near the historic heart of Manchester Village. Lunch daily, 11:30 to 5; dinner, 5 to 10 or 10:30; breakfast on winter weekends and holidays, 7:30 to 10:30.

Haig's, Route 30, Bondville, (802) 297-1300. Billed as a mountain tradition since 1973, this cafe, restaurant, lounge, lodge and disco keeps growing like topsy. Haig and Paul Bogossian run quite the lively complex, ranging from a large sports bar with four TVs (including a fifteen-foot screen) to a club whose dance floor holds 450 people. Meals are served in the Bridge Cafe and an airy, windowed dining room with a salad bar at the entrance and an abundance of hanging plants. We once had dinner here with our teenagers and found it adequate, though no one remembered what they ate. Recently, the wide-ranging menu offered dinner entrees like lasagna, chicken teriyaki, veal parmigiana, blackened swordfish, barbecued ribs, T-bone steak, Alaskan king crab and various combinations thereof, widely priced from $8.95 to $24.95. Oh, yes, Haig's also has eighteen new guest rooms and suites with private baths, some with fireplaces and TVs, and vaguely early American decor, renting for $80 to $114 a night. Lunch daily, 11:30 to 9:30 (to 11 on weekends; dinner, 5 to 9:30 or 10; Sunday brunch, 10:30 to 2:30.

On the Lighter Side

Park Bench Cafe, Route 7A, Manchester Center, (802) 362-2557. You can hardly get into this little restaurant, located in a small gray Cape Cod-style house on the main drag between Manchester Center and Village. In fact, try as we might, we couldn't wait another half hour for lunch on the Saturday we stopped; it was already 2:30 and we were famished. Locals swear by the Mexican specialties; there are also cajun and grill items. Baked onion soup is always on the menu and so is a Bowl of Red (chili) for $4.75. You can start with a plate of crisp veggies with a creamy dressing for dipping. Better than any they've tasted, say the locals, are the super nachos ($4.95). For dinner ($9.95 to $14.95), try shrimp creole, chicken teriyaki, grilled swordfish or New York sirloin. The menu here is large and varied enough to suit all tastes, from international omelets and huevos bencheros to tortellini alfredo with shrimp. Breakfast, Friday-Monday 8 to 11; lunch daily, 11:30 to 4:30; dinner, 4:30 to 10 or 11.

The Gourmet Deli-Cafe, Factory Point Square, Route 7, Manchester Center, (802) 362-1254. Lunch only is served at this terrific spot in a small, country-style shopping center back from the street, and it's a tasty lunch indeed. You order from a blackboard menu, select a booth or table and wait for your meal to be delivered by one of the busy women who make this place hum. New England clam chowder is a staple; the split pea soup was also very good the day we were there. Deli sandwiches are available, but other stuff is too good to be missed, things like chicken and broccoli salad, Mexican meat pie, a ham and swiss quiche, hot crabmeat croissant or a hot or cold meat loaf sandwich, nicely priced from $3.95 to $5.95. Black walnut meringue pie is the dessert specialty. There are numerous beers and wines as well as soft drinks and juices. In the summer you can eat outdoors. Open daily, 11 to 4.

J.M. Noonie's Deli & Grill, Routes 11 and 30, Manchester Center, (802) 362-0005. The breads baked here are sensational; thick slices in a half a sandwich and a bowl of soup go a long way for lunch for $3.50. We were impressed with the takeout shelf of honey-oat loaves ($2.75) and the French bread ($1 regular, 75 cents for a demi-loaf). We also liked the mod seating on several levels upstairs and down in the high-ceilinged restaurant, all overlooking an open kitchen. There are dynamite french toast and omelets for breakfast, sandwiches and salad plates for lunch, and stuffed baked potatoes for any time. Owner Guy Thomas is onto a good thing, and was seeking to expand to other locations. Open daily, 7 to 4, weekends to 6.

The Village Store, Union Street, Manchester Village, (802) 362-2599. Cross-country skiers from Hildene join everyday locals for lunch at this specialty food store and deli. The short blackboard menu might list soups ($1.95) like mushroom-barley or black bean and chicken; seafood stew for $6.95, or delectable sandwiches ($3.95), perhaps chicken tarragon salad on a croissant, roast beef with garlic cheese on sourdough rye, or smoked salmon and cream cheese on a bagel. There are four tables to eat on, but most folks seem to take out. Open Monday-Saturday 9 to 5:30, Sunday 9 to 3.

Up for Breakfast, Main Street, Manchester Center. Get here early or you're apt to be lined up on the sidewalk with everyone else, awaiting seats upstairs in this L-shaped, breakfast-only spot. It's worth the wait for treats ($4.75 to $7) like belgian waffles, wild turkey hash, huevos rancheros and, our choice, "one of each" — one eggs benedict and one eggs argyle (with smoked salmon) for $6.50. These proved hearty dishes for Vermont appetites, as did the heavy Irish scone ($1.50), both garnished with chunks of pineapple and watermelon. Be sure to check out the blackboard hidden around the corner from our window table. We found out too late that we could have ordered mango-cranberry-nutmeg pancakes, rainbow trout with two eggs or scone french toast. Open weekdays except Tuesday 6 to noon, weekends 7 to 1.

Apres-Ski

Andy Avery, a folksinger whom folks rave about, appears in the tavern at The Equinox on weekend evenings, and a guitarist plays other nights in the lounge. The Stratton Mountain Boys conduct Tyrolean evenings a couple of nights a week at Stratton's Base Lodge. The Club at Haig's in Bondville is a disco with contemporary music, videos and a light show.

But if you're the way we are, after a day of skiing you're not up to a night of spreeing.

FOR MORE INFORMATION: Chamber of Commerce for Manchester and the Mountains, Manchester Center, Vt. 05254, (802) 362-2100.

New Boston Harbor Hotel at Rowes Wharf is part of changing downtown skyline.

Big-City Splurge

Boston, Mass.

New England's hub is a weekend destination to satisfy many desires. You want sports? There are the Celtics, the Bruins and the Red Sox. Interested in history? Visit the Freedom Trail, Old Ironsides, Bunker Hill. Culture? Think about the symphony, the art museums and the libraries.

Those of us who live elsewhere in New England are attracted to all of these options in Boston. But there are other lures: an elegance, an assuredness, a sense of place. Perhaps it's the age of the city that does it, the constant reminders of heritage in a metropolis that came into the late 20th century at full throttle.

We all come to Boston, even those who are visiting for the first time, as if we're already old friends. In a way we are. After all, so much of Boston's history lives in our national heritage; so many of her moments are fixed in our memories. There is Revolutionary Boston (Paul Revere, Sam Adams and the Boston Tea Party) and there is Bulfinch's Boston (the glorious gold-capped State House and so much of Beacon Hill's architecture). There is a taste of Boston (baked beans and brown bread and Boston

271

cream pie) and a sound of Boston (the Symphony, the Pops and the 1812 Overture on the banks of the Charles River on the Fourth of July).

Boston is a city of the learned and the literate. The nation's first public school, the famed Boston Latin School, was founded here in 1635; a year later Harvard opened its doors as the first institution of higher learning. And Boston is home to the oldest public library supported by taxation in the country; a grand place it is, too.

And now, for all of us who want to spend time in Boston, there are fine hotels to accommodate us. Luxury hotels have risen on the city's waterfront and overlooking her public garden; great chefs vie for star ratings in the hotel dining rooms and in independent restaurants.

And the shopping is sensational. Prompted by the great success of the Faneuil Hall Marketplace in the 1970s, the city has seen the building of the tony Copley Place, where you can shop at Neiman-Marcus and other noted emporia. Newbury Street remains the place for objets d'art, antiques and designer fashions. On Charles Street you'll find great antiques shops, greengrocers and even cowboy boots.

Boston is not an inexpensive place to visit — if you want to do it right. So grab your wallet and your walking shoes and prepare for a splurge. Boston is *the* city in New England for the traveler.

Getting There

When George Washington visited Boston he had to take the old King's Highway, Route 1. Today's traveler has an easier time of it. The Massachusetts Turnpike (I-90) leads directly into downtown from the west. Route 3 is a fast route north from Cape Cod. Interstate 93 brings visitors south from New Hampshire, and Interstate 95 comes in from Maine and Rhode Island.

Amtrak trains reach Boston from New York and commuter trains take suburbanites into the city from the west. Interstate buses serve the city with midtown terminals.

Most major airlines fly to Logan International Airport. A water shuttle takes airline passengers to Rowes Wharf (next to the Boston Harbor Hotel) on the downtown waterfront. It departs Logan frequently and runs year-round.

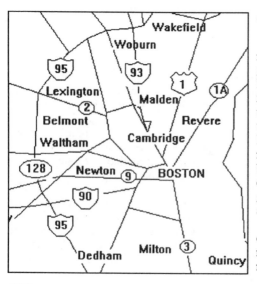

Getting Around

Boston is an impossible city to navigate by car without fortitude, good humor and just plain luck. Even Bostonians seem puzzled by the traffic. Park your car at your hotel, underneath the Boston Common or at the Prudential Center and walk. Boston's subway (the "T") is the nation's oldest but far from its grubbiest and is a bargain. Four color-coded lines (blue, orange, green and red) take you almost anyplace you want to go.

Taxis are expensive and not always easy to find. But they are sometimes necessary, especially when going to a restaurant in the evening.

272

Breakfast in the room at Ritz-Carlton Hotel.

Where to Stay

For a big-city weekend we'd choose a hotel with class and taste. The classiest in Boston, for our money, are these:

The Ritz-Carlton, 15 Arlington St., Boston 02117, (617) 536-5700. The grand dame of Boston's hotels, the Ritz-Carlton remains the ritziest. Understated elegance and an emphasis on personal service, with uniformed elevator operators who take the time to chat and afternoon tea that really is tea, are reminders of an era of gentility. Our room with kingsize bed, white French Provincial furniture, salmon and green floral draperies, bedspread and matching upholstered chairs and a view of the Public Garden (with ice skaters) was worth every penny. Breakfast in the room, wheeled in by an elderly and experienced waiter, was a memorable indulgence. It arrived on a white-clothed table with a single rose in a bud vase and coffee steaming from a silver pot. The 285-unit hotel (237 rooms and 48 suites) was taken over in 1983 by the Ritz-Carlton Hotel Company, with hotels also in Georgia, Florida and California. But this is the group's flagship, with its views of the Public Garden, of Beacon Hill and Back Bay, of Newbury Street and Commonwealth Avenue. The location is superb. The Ritz-Carlton Club, a concierge section on the three uppermost floors, offers special amenities such as telephones in bathrooms, hair dryers, room refrigerators and weekday morning limousine service to select areas. The second-floor **Dining Room** overlooking the Garden and the first-floor **Cafe** and intimate bar are favorite gathering places for Bostonians, proper and otherwise. And now there's dancing nightly in the **Lounge.** Doubles, $260 to $380; suites, $495 to $1,900.

Four Seasons Hotel, 200 Boylston St., Boston 02116, (617) 338-4400. This relative newcomer to the Boston hotel scene is nicely situated, opposite the Public Garden with a view of the gold-domed State House across the way. The brick facade is not particularly extraordinary, but inside the feeling is sophisticated indeed. The open, spacious lobby leads to a main staircase and wonderful restaurants: **Aujourd'hui,** the main dining room (see Where to Eat), and the **Bristol Lounge,** where you can enjoy afternoon tea looking out over the Public Garden or choose from an all-day menu of lighter fare including brick-oven pizzas. The 288 rooms come in several categories, but all that we saw were spacious, traditionally furnished and enhanced by such amenities as hair dryers, plush robes, minibars, telephones in the bathrooms and — if you dare — scales. For a splurge, try the Presidential Suite, overlooking the Public Garden, with a balcony from which you might wave to your adoring throngs. The bathroom is marble, a grand piano graces its parlor, and Chippendale chairs are at a mahogany table in the dining room. It's yours for $1,800 a night. Guests also may enjoy a spa with pool, fitness center, masseuse, the works. No wonder that the American Automobile Assciation awarded both the hotel and its restaurant its coveted Five Diamond Award in 1992. Doubles, $280 to $400.

Boston Harbor Hotel, 70 Rowes Wharf, Boston 02110, (617) 439-7000 or (800) 752-7077. This new hotel on the waterfront is exciting — not only for the views of the harbor from nearly everywhere, but also for its elegant appointments and its location near Faneuil Hall, the Aquarium and other fun destinations. The floors are marble and the elevator walls are upholstered in brocade. Fascinating nautical prints and fine art are hung in the public rooms. Because the airport water shuttle docks here, there's always activity at the waterfront, and you can walk outside in a lovely promenade area. The 230 rooms and suites are located on floors 8 through 16. Our oversize room had reproduction antique furniture, a sofa and an upholstered chair with good reading lamps in a sitting area, a kingsize bed and an enormous bathroom full of amenities from fine soaps to terry robes to a hair dryer. Breakfronts conceal the TV and a minibar. Soundproof windows that open and enormous towels are also pluses. A handsome, dark wood bar on the main floor and a lounge with piano overlooking the water are pleasant spots for a break from shopping or touring. The dining room on the second floor, **Rowes Wharf,** has dark wood walls, recessed lighting and a deep blue decor; its Sunday brunch buffet is particularly popular. Lunch and dinner, also highly rated, feature seafood. The Rowes Wharf Health Club and Spa has a 60-foot-long lap pool, steam rooms and saunas, hydrotherapy tub and an exercise room with state-of-the-art equipment. Doubles, $220 to $375; suites, $390 to $1,300.

The Bostonian Hotel, Faneuil Hall Marketplace, Boston 02109, (617) 523-3600 or (800) 343-0922. Located across from the Faneuil Hall Marketplace, this smallish, deluxe hotel is very special. Most of the 153 rooms on three floors are small but beautifully decorated and equipped, all with bathrooms with deep tiled tubs, French soaps and thirsty towels. French doors open from many rooms onto tiny decorative balconies with wrought-iron rails and plants. Some rooms have fireplaces. The scene for all this elegance is set when you arrive via a dramatic circular driveway with marquee lighting overhead and enter the small lobby where you check in at a free-standing period desk. An intimate cafe and cocktail lounge with piano is at one end. The gracious restaurant, **Seasons,** has served as a training ground for some of the city's best chefs. Downtown wheeler-dealers come here for power lunches. Doubles, $215 to $300.

Le Meridien, 250 Franklin St., Boston 02110, (617) 451-1900. The former Federal Reserve Bank in the heart of the Financial District can be hard to find, but it's worth the search. Run in a European manner by the Meridien group, the hotel has 326 guest rooms on nine floors, ranging from two-story loft rooms to several with mansard-roof and sloping windows on the top floors. Contemporary sofas and artworks plus live plants are found in each room. Beds are made up in the French style with an extra sheet over the blanket, and turn-down service at night comes with mints. The large bathrooms contain scales, assorted amenities and telephones. **Cafe Fleuri,** the interior courtyard-atrium restaurant, serves three meals daily. **Julien** is a fine French restaurant, and the cocktail lounge with its richly decorated ceiling and murals by N.C. Wyeth is a place to listen to soft piano music, munch on salted almonds and sip something like a brandy

Copley Plaza Hotel faces Copley Square, with Copley Place complex behind at right.

alexander. There's a full-scale health club. Weekend package plans ($125 to $169 a night) include "Boston for the Fun of It," with discounts to museums and restaurants and on Cafe Fleuri's fabled Sunday brunch. Another draw is "The Ultimate Chocolate Bar," an all-you-can-eat buffet of light and dark chocolate desserts Saturdays from 2 to 5 in Cafe Fleuri. Doubles, $220 to $250.

Copley Plaza Hotel, Copley Square, Boston 02116, (617) 267-5300 or (800) 225-7654. A refurbished elegance is apparent at the Copley Plaza, one of the city's classics, and the location is fortuitous, on Copley Square just across from the deluxe shops of Copley Place. Opened in 1912, the Copley Plaza has hosted its share of prestigious Boston events, and President John F. Kennedy stayed here on his last trip to Boston in 1963. The hotel was designed by architect Henry Janeway Hardenbergh, who also designed New York's Plaza Hotel and the Willard in Washington, D.C. The **Tea Court** bedecked in palms and greenery off the main lobby is popular for light refreshments. We love the **Plaza Bar** with its dark wood walls and subdued lighting, entered after walking through a vaulted passageway with a mosaic floor. The hotel's 365 rooms have been renovated by new owner James Daley, a native Bostonian whose lifelong dream was to own it. Suites have kingsize beds, mahogany furniture, marble bathrooms with bidets, and color-coordinated draperies and bedspreads. Doubles, $210 to $280; suites, $375 to $1,200.

The Eliot Hotel, 370 Commonwealth Ave., Boston 02215, (617) 267-1607. Located next door to the Harvard Club in Back Bay, this small hotel has been recently refurbished and made into an all-suites hotel. The Eliot Lounge is well known to marathoners around the world for it is *the* in place during the Boston Marathon. The 92 nicely furnished suites come with microwave, coffee maker, refrigerator, a stocked minibar and two televisions. Bathrooms are Italian marble. French doors divide the bedrooms from the bathrooms. A warm and inviting family-owned hotel, the Eliot seems a quiet oasis from the moment you walk into its small but tasteful two-level lobby. A continental breakfast is served each morning in the hotel's private dining room. Doubles, $175.

The Lenox Hotel, 710 Boylston St., Boston 02116, (617) 536-5300 or (800) 225-7676. This is another smallish, family-owned hotel that has been updated recently. The 222 guest rooms include several corner rooms with working fireplaces. Corridors are wide and our room was a decent size, but we did find its faux-oriental furniture a bit tacky. We like the location at Copley Square: the Boston Public Library is across the street and the Newbury Street shopping district a block away. Room rates are quite good, especially in winter, when you may get a double for around $100. Corner rooms with working fireplace cost $235. Doubles, $155 to $235; suites, $350.

Boston Marriott Hotel/Copley Place, 110 Huntington Ave., Boston 02116, (617) 236-5800. If you'd like to be right in the heart of the upscale Copley Plaza shopping area, choose this. Just walk out of the lobby and into the shopping arcade. The lobby is large and luxurious with muted colors and lots of seating. Facilities include restaurants, a health club and a glass-enclosed whirlpool and swimming pool. The hotel is big — 1,147 rooms — and many conventioneers stay here because it is close to the Hynes Convention Center. A special Two for Breakfast weekend package appeals for $129. Doubles, $169 to $230.

Copley Square Hotel, 47 Huntington Ave., Boston 02116, (617) 536-9000 or (800) 225-7062. We were delighted to stay in a large bay-windowed front room at the Copley Square, another refurbished hotel that is named for its magnificent location. It also houses the Cafe Budapest (see Dining), a Hungarian restaurant of romantic elegance. The hotel has 153 rooms and suites, a comfortable lounge for a pre- or post-dinner drink and a bright restaurant, **Pops Place,** for a quick breakfast, lunch or dinner. The best part is probably the winter rate; from mid-November through March, you can book a double room for $68. Doubles, $120 to $145; two-bedroom family suites, $188.

Several **bed-and-breakfast** reservation services operate in Boston. They direct you to rooms in private homes or townhouses, costing in the range of $60 to $100 for double occupancy. **Bed & Breakfast Cambridge & Greater Boston,** Box 665, Cambridge 02140, (617) 576-1492, advertises B&Bs in Boston, Cambridge and Lexington.

Seeing and Doing

If a Bostonian were asked what a winter weekender should do in his city, he'd probably recommend attending a concert by the Boston Symphony Orchestra. He'd be sure to suggest a stop at the Museum of Fine Arts and another at the Gardner Museum with its flower-banked inner courtyard and chamber music concerts. He'd tell you to walk around Beacon Hill and to shop at Copley Place, Quincy Market and along Newbury and Charles streets. He'd probably urge a visit to the John F. Kennedy Library and perhaps the Boston Public Library.

He might not know you can visit a lavish Victorian townhouse in Back Bay, a Bulfinch residence in the West End or a wonderful house museum right on Beacon Hill.

A first stop for the culturally minded visitor is the Bostix Ticket Booth at Faneuil Hall Marketplace, (617) 423-4454. Stop in and see the recently refurbished and reopened Faneuil Hall itself while there. Tickets are available here for cultural events, including same-day, half-price tickets to commercial theaters. You also can pick up information about museums and occasionally discounted tickets to museum services.

Music

Boston Symphony Orchestra, Symphony Hall, Huntington and Massachusetts Avenues, (617) 266-1492. The 1900 McKim, Mead and White building called Symphony Hall, with its columned facade and gilded interior, holds a warm and prideful

Seiji Ozawa conducts Boston Symphony Orchestra in Symphony Hall.

spot in the heart of Bostonians. The renowned Boston Symphony Orchestra, under the baton of Seiji Ozawa, and the Boston Pops are at home here. The BSO is on in the winter and single tickets are devilishly difficult to come by. The Friday matinee is famous. Beacon Hill dowagers, retired gentlemen and suburban matrons hold most subscriptions and in the ladies room it sounds like old home week. We remember one concert when the older woman next to us began to cough. We slipped her a cough drop and at intermission she confided, "I've been coming to Symphony for 50 years and I've lived in dread that something like that would happen. You saved my life!" The acoustics are marvelous and the audience exceptionally well-mannered. A few special "rush seats" are available for Friday matinees and Tuesday and Thursday evenings, going on sale at 9 a.m. Friday and 5 p.m. the other days. It's one ticket to a customer and you'll have to vie with Boston's music and university students to get the $6.50 tickets.

Emmanuel Church, 15 Newbury St., (617) 536-3355. It takes about seven years to complete the entire cycle of Bach cantatas but they did it at the Emmanuel Church, a city church that expresses much of its ministry through the arts, music in particular. This ecumenical church with an Episcopal base is famed for its Mozart Birthday Party concert every Jan. 27 and its Bach Birthday concert on March 21. There are also Sunday afternoon concerts in the winter and the 10 a.m. service on Sunday is filled with the sounds of music.

The New England Conservatory of Music, 290 Huntington Ave., (617) 262-1120. The conservatory has been in existence for more than 100 years and many musicians performing in the Boston area were trained here. The emphasis is classical, but other forms of music also are taught. More than 300 concerts a year are presented and it's likely you'll be able to find one when you're in town, especially on a Saturday night.

The Wang Center for the Performing Arts, 270 Tremont St., (617) 482-9393. Renovated in 1980, Boston's old Music Hall serves as home to The Met in Boston, the Boston Ballet and several theater groups. Programs are scheduled every weekend.

Tea and music. Visitors to the Museum of Fine Arts on Tuesday through Friday afternoons may want to head for the Evans wing for this Boston tradition. New England musicians play while you sip tea in the Ladies Committee Gallery. The cost is $2.

Art

Museum of Fine Arts, 465 Huntington Ave., (617) 267-9300. With its important collections, Boston's Museum of Fine Arts is a treasure. The addition in 1981 of the new West Wing by I.M. Pei with its skylighted gallery and additional amenities like a fine auditorium, restaurant and exceptional museum shop was a wise move. In 1983 the entire Asiatic Wing was renovated. We have always liked the Egyptian art, and who doesn't love the many French Impressionist paintings? The museum should be allotted plenty of time for browsing (you can pause for a snack or a meal at the restaurant). It also presents an extensive series of concerts, films and lectures. Open Tuesday-Sunday 10 to 4:45, Wednesday to 9:45; also Thursday and Friday 5 to 9:45, West Wing only. Adults $6, children $3.

Isabella Stewart Gardner Museum, 280 The Fenway, (617) 566-1401. Within walking distance of the Museum of Fine Arts, the Gardner is unique, and we use the word advisedly. Flowers, art and music were the passions of Mrs. Gardner, a New Yorker who was never fully accepted by the Boston society into which she married. She left her memorial in this replica of a Venetian palazzo, crammed with fine art objects and fascinating architectural and sculptural elements, most of them from the Medieval and Renaissance periods. Flowers, grown in greenhouses on the property, bank the exquisite interior courtyard. Musical concerts are held Saturday and Sunday afternoons at 1:30 in the handsome, tiled Tapestry Hall, a special atmosphere (adults $4, students $2). Check the concert calendar at the museum desk or call (617) 734-1359. Open Tuesday-Sunday 11 to 5. Adults $6, students $3.

Institute of Contemporary Art, 955 Boylston St., (617) 266-5152. Housed quite creatively in a renovated police station in the Back Bay area, this museum mounts changing exhibitions by contemporary artists. Open Wednesday 5 to 9, Thursday noon to 9, Friday-Sunday noon to 5. Adults $4, students $3.

Libraries

Boston Public Library, Copley Square, (617) 536-5400. The beautiful Italian Renaissance building designed by McKim, Mead and White in the 1890s has much to recommend it to the visitor. The central staircase is decorated with murals by the French artist Puvis de Chavannes (his only ones outside France) to represent the areas of poetry, philosophy, history and science. John Singer Sargent decorated the third-floor walls with murals dealing with Judaism and Christianity. In the second-floor Book Delivery Room are the Edwin Austin Abbey wall paintings depicting "The Quest and Achievement of the Holy Grail." From this room look down upon a sanctuary below — the cloistered courtyard with gardens and mosaic tiles. Open Monday-Thursday 9 to 9, Friday and Saturday 9 to 5.

Boston Athenaeum, 10 1/2 Beacon St., Boston, (617) 227-0270. Here on Beacon Street, not far from the State Capitol and behind a sooty and settled facade, are five floors of great books. Among the collections is the library of George Washington, for example. While the Athenaeum is a private shareholders' library, with shares traceable through Boston's patrician past, visitors are welcome to browse on the first two floors. It is an invitation to be accepted. At the desk where you check your parcels and coats, you're handed a large visitor's pass, which you must keep with you as you walk around. There is an impressive amount of artwork on the second floor; in fact, it was the Athenaeum's collecting of art that eventually paved the way for the Museum of Fine Arts. On the main floor, with high windows looking out on the old Granary Burying Ground, are two grand reading rooms. We leafed through some great periodicals, noted alumni magazines from most Massachusetts colleges and universities, and felt privileged indeed. Open Monday-Friday 9 to 5, Saturday 9 to 4.

John F. Kennedy Library and Museum, Morrissey Boulevard, (617) 929-4523. Dedicated to the memory of America's 35th president, the library and museum was designed by I.M. Pei and opened in 1979. Within three months more than 170,000 people had streamed through the exhibition area, and the crowds have never ceased. Visitors watch a half-hour biographical film produced exclusively for the library, and can view excerpts from President Kennedy's televised press conferences, listen to his mother's recorded recollections of his early life, and watch a short film on the life of Robert F. Kennedy. A central exhibit, showing President Kennedy's desk and rocking chair, portrays the different roles played by the chief executive. Exhibits on his personal and family interests recapture the style and atmosphere of his presidency. The introductory film is particularly stirring; you will be moved by JFK's intelligence, vibrancy, sense of humor and the tragedy of his early death. Upstairs are manuscripts and letters of the writer Ernest Hemingway, donated by his widow. A certain stark grandeur is provided the building by its waterfront setting on the Boston campus of the University of Massachusetts. A small restaurant was in the works in 1992. Open daily, 9 to 5. Adults $5, children $1.

The Way They Lived

Nichols House Museum, 55 Mount Vernon St., (617) 227-6993. Henry James is reported to have said Mount Vernon was the most proper of Beacon Hill's streets. Few tourists seem to find their way to this house, attributed to Charles Bulfinch, located at the crest of the hill with a splendid view down the street. It's been a museum for some 30 years, willed as such by the unmarried Rose Standish Nichols, a gracious hostess and a landscape architect in her own right. You'll see Flemish tapestry from 1525, the parlor where Miss Nichols hosted afternoon teas and imitation embossed-leather wallpaper in the dining room. But the bookcase-flanked window seat on the third floor, with a glimpse of other brick facades on the street, is our favorite feature. The house is still in use as a neighborhood center and as

Nichols House Museum on Beacon Hill.

headquarters for the Boston Council for International Visitors. Open Tuesday-Saturday, 1 to 5. Adults, $3.

Louisburg Square, considered the gemstone of Beacon Hill, is reached from Mount Vernon Street, the equivalent of a block or two below the Nichols House. If the hill is icy, you'll appreciate the iron handrails to help you down. The gaslights lend atmosphere, as do the statues of Aristides and Columbus in the center. Caroling and a handbell concert make the square ring on Christmas Eve.

Harrison Gray Otis House, 141 Cambridge St., (617) 227-3956. An appropriately grand location for the headquarters of the Society of the Preservation of New England Antiquities, this brick Federal mansion is typical of the kind built after the Revolutionary War for well-to-do Bostonians. Charles Bulfinch designed it in 1796 for the Otises, a social couple who kept moving up; after this house they moved to two more Bulfinch-designed houses on Beacon Hill. This is Boston's once fashionable West End, now full of motels, parking lots and stores. But the house is magnificent and its position, jammed among less inspiring neighbors, sets it off to advantage. It has been carefully restored to the period. We love the red, yellow and green patterned carpet in the front parlor, the classic revival look to the dining room and the "withdrawing room" upstairs with its flowery, feminine touches. The Otises were great partygivers and their famous punchbowl is also on display. It was a family tradition to invite friends at 4 p.m. for a drink, possibly a precurser to today's cocktail hour. Otis was a Congressman, mayor of Boston, a land developer and the father of eleven children. Open Tuesday-Friday noon 2 to 5, Saturday 10 to 5; tours on the hour through 4. Adults $4, children $2.

Gibson House, 137 Beacon St., (617) 267-6338. Now for the Victorian period. This house in Back Bay was built in 1860 for a family whose bachelor son willed it in 1954 to the private Gibson Society. He was Charles Hammond Gibson Jr., who kept the place just as it looked in its heyday. Our enthusiastic guide, a graduate student in local history at Northeastern University, said the gilt-embossed linen wallpaper in the foyer is original, and what a start! Check out the Bavarian carved wooden umbrella stand; you've never seen anything like it. The dining room, its table set with family china, is located to the rear of the house and looks out on the narrow lot. The four floors above are chock-full of original, incredible pieces, among them a velvet pet pagoda, a genuine hand-crank victrola, a stereopticon viewer and a magic-lantern slide projector. Even though the house has been open to the public for more than 35 years, it's a find. Tours, Wednesday-Sunday at 1, 2 and 3, May-October; Saturday and Sunday at 1, 2 and 3, rest of year. Adults $3.

In case you wonder how high the society was in the neighborhood, the plaque across the street cites 152 Beacon St. as the residence of Isabella Stewart Gardner before she moved to her museum on the Fenway. Once she left, the number was retired at her request.

A Boston Miscellany

The following are some traditionally favorite stops.

John Hancock Observatory, 60th Floor, John Hancock Tower, 200 Clarendon St., (617) 247-1976. New England's highest manmade vantage point affords views of Boston and surroundings. There's also a presentation detailing the history of the Revolutionary War in Boston and changes that have occurred in the city's topography in the past two centuries. Open Monday-Saturday 9 a.m. to 11 p.m., Sunday noon to 11. Adults $2.75, children $2.

Skywalk, Prudential Tower, 800 Boylston St., (617) 236-3318. Take the elevator for a 360-degree view of Boston and the surrounding area; on a clear day you can see the White Mountains of New Hampshire. Open Monday-Saturday 10 to 10, Sunday noon to 10. Adults $2.75, children $1.75.

Boston Tea Party Ship & Museum, Congress Street Bridge, (617) 338-1773. Here you combine a history lesson and a good time aboard a full-scale working replica of the Tea Party Ship. Audio-visual presentations in the adjacent museum are helpful and costumed guides are knowledgeable. Open daily, 9 to 5. Adults $6, children $3.

The **Freedom Trail** begins at the Boston Common Information Center on Tremont Street, where you may obtain a brochure to guide you. The trail is about one and a half miles long and includes sixteen historical sites, all clearly marked.

First Night is Boston's creative approach to New Year's Eve. The entire downtown area, the Prudential Center and the Common feature events like puppet shows, jazz concerts, ballet and fireworks. The Boston Pops holds forth at Symphony Hall.

Shopping

Boston is a fabulous city for shopping, from bargains to books to boutiques. Note that Massachusetts has no sales tax on clothing (up to $150 per item) and food.

The downtown department store area along Washington and Tremont streets is not the most elegant in the city, but a pedestrian mall called Downtown Crossing is flanked by a renovated **Jordan Marsh** department store and by **Filene's. Filene's Basement** is an institution; you may find $500 dresses from Neiman-Marcus going for a fraction of the original price; Brooks Brothers suits, men's quality shoes, children's items and more are discounted, depending on what the latest shipment is and how long the merchandise has been there. One of our favorite people bought her wedding gown here; we still smile to think of her struggling to try it on in the aisles (there are no dressing rooms). Incredibly, merchandise is returnable.

Faneuil Hall Marketplace, a comfortable walk from Filene's, has maintained its popularity as one of America's favored downtown renovations. Opened in stages between 1976 and 1978, it has attracted some 150 retail merchants, restaurants and even a branch of the Museum of Fine Arts. Now the most popular of Boston's visitor attractions, the marketplace has an information center where you can pick up a listing of the shops and stores and make your way among the three buildings: North Market, South Market and Quincy Market. There are a fantastic kite shop, a coffee shop, boutiques for both men and women, pushcarts with earrings, toys and jewelry, and all sorts of food shops for picking up chocolate-chip cookies, sandwiches, soups and such. Adjacent to the marketplace toward the waterfront is the new **Marketplace Center,** with still more upscale shops. You can easily spend a day around here — and a bundle.

Faneuil Hall Marketplace from shop window.

Copley Place is the trendy shopping mall anchored by **Neiman-Marcus** in the Copley Square area. **Tiffany, Ralph Lauren, Gucci** and **Brookstone** are among the tenants; you will have a wonderful time shopping here, even if it's just the window variety. There's a lovely Dimitri Hadzi contemporary sculpture and waterfall near the center of the mall.

Newbury Street has always been the place for art, antiques, furs, jewelry and fine clothing boutiques. Check out **Waterstone's Booksellers** at Newbury and Exeter streets, a three-story British-owned emporium with frequent readings and book signings. At 175 Newbury, the **Society of Arts and Crafts** carries lots of unusual handmade pieces; we also like **Sweet Peas,** a whimsical crafts shop run by Nantucket restaurateur

Liz McCutcheon. **Vose Galleries**, a family-owned art gallery for years and years, is pleasant to visit and you don't feel as if you must buy something.

Charles Street is also a fun shopping street. **Helen's Leather Shop** is known for its quality handbags and one of the best selections of Western boots in New England. Not far from Charles, on Beacon, you may want to stop in the **Bull & Finch Pub,** inspiration for the TV show, "Cheers," and a purveyor of T-shirts and other memorabilia with the Cheers logo.

Where to Eat

The home of the bean and the cod offers cuisine for more sophisticated palates, too. Hotel dining rooms are currently among the most fashionable places to dine in Boston. Here is a sampling of elegant places to eat.

Beacon Hill streetscape.

Jasper's, 240 Commercial St., (617) 523-1126. Jasper White opened his own restaurant to four-star reviews in both Boston newspapers in 1983 after training at the Culinary Institute and on the West Coast, working at the Copley Plaza and helping open Seasons at the Bostonian Hotel. Striking art is on the pastel brick walls of three small dining rooms, and there are organdy curtains, floral china and exquisite floral arrangements. Dining is calm and relaxed. Fresh bread sticks (the flavor changes nightly) begin this culinary adventure. A choice of perhaps ten appetizers (priced from $9 to $32 for ossetra caviar with johnnycakes) might include rock crab and flounder rolls or sauteed moutard foie gras with brandied peaches. Entrees ($18 to $36) might be grilled sea scallops with roasted chile sauce, corn relish and hot crabmeat tamale, mixed grill of quail and spicy duck sausage with eggplant and risotto cakes, and double thick pork rib chop with sage and apples and roasted sweet potatoes. The most expensive item is often lobster, pan-roasted with chervil and chives at our visit. Desserts include a pear upside-down cake, vanilla bean ice cream with warm dried fruit compote and maple Indian pudding custard. As you leave, you might be tempted to buy a copy of *Jasper White's Cooking from New England,* an enticing cookbook. Dinner, Tuesday-Saturday 5:45 to 9:30.

Biba, 272 Boylston St., (617) 426-7878. Lydia Shire, who once worked with Jasper White at Seasons in the Bostonian Hotel, spent some time on the West Coast before returning to Boston in 1989 to open a restaurant of her own. The two-story establishment in the Heritage on the Garden shopping and residential complex is across from the Public Garden. A bar seating 50 serves tapas and such on the main floor. Upstairs is the Biba Food Hall, with windows onto the Garden. Soft gold-yellow walls contrast with ceiling murals painted in bright patterns taken from Albanian carpets. Warm woods, white-clothed tables, chairs covered in deep green and huge bouquets of fresh flowers make for an interesting environment. Cream of onion and green garlic soup in a roasted onion skin was offered the crisp winter day we had lunch here, along with such appetizers ($8 to $12) as a sandwich of duck confit in aromatic spice on toasted fig bread and white clam pizza with charred Italian greens. Entrees ($12 to $17) were equally inventive. Choices included wood-roasted cod with greens and salt cod hash, chicken with prosciutto, spit-roasted at your table and served with pumpkin risotto, and scallop raviolis with quince and grilled chanterelles. The husband of one of us had a lamb shank flamed over fennel branches with baked lemony orzo, since pronounced the best lamb shank he's ever had; our flaky tomato, potato and olive pissaladiere was a room-temperature slab of French bread with the zesty topping, served with a great plateful of caesar salad. We made quick work of our basket of breads (the spectacular naan bread baked in the tandoori oven is both chewy and flaky), but had to forego dessert, among such possibilities as pear and persimmon swirl sorbet with hot quince turnovers, crisp blackened apple butter tart with molasses ice cream, and warm sugar-crisped spice cake with English Devonshire cream. Three career women at the next table were groaning in delight from the richness of their hot chocolate cheesecake. In the evening, entrees ($18 to $25) might include "dark roasted rack and loin of lamb with delicate cream of endive, lemon and parsley" or duck steak grilled over branches of exotic wood with "very special frittes" or braised oxtails with hot horseradish. Everything is novel and delicious, and about the only complaint relates to the high noise level. Lunch, Monday-Friday 11:30 to 3; dinner nightly, 5 to 10; Sunday brunch, 11:30 to 3.

Hamersley's Bistro, 578 Tremont St., (617) 267-6068. Along with Jasper's and Biba, this restaurant completes the triumvirate of the three top restaurants in Boston, as noted in 1992 by Boston magazine. Hamersley's is a smallish, 50-seat storefront in a South End area gradually becoming gentrified. The decor is typical bistro: white-clothed tables topped with butcher paper and rather too close together, black chairs and yellow walls. Chef Gordon Hamersley produces incredible dishes from his open kitchen. Three items have become standards and draw people again and again: the mushroom and garlic sandwich on country bread as an appetizer; the roast chicken with garlic, lemon and parsley, an entree; and the soufleed lemon custard, a dessert. Wife Fiona presides over a quite sophisticated wine list. Other appetizers ($7.50 to $11) include chicken liver pate with sweet and sour onions, spicy squid and grilled cabbage salad, and potato and onion tart with a watercress and endive salad. Pastas and main-course salads ($17 to $19) might include spiced scallop salad with couscous or pan-cooked penne and autumn vegetables with mushroom essence. Among main courses ($17 to $25) might be beef short ribs braised in burgundy with lyonnaise potatoes, gratin of mussels, country ham and potatoes, swordfish with vermouth butter, orange and fennel, and lamb chops with cider, ginger and fennel. Finish with a warm pear and ginger tart, a "big warm chocolate cookie with vanilla ice cream" or a chocolate terrine with cointreau cream and candied orange, all $6. Dinner nightly, 5 to 10.

Another Season, 97 Mount Vernon St., Boston. (617) 367-0880. This charming spot in a Beacon Hill townhouse is Odette Bery's third restaurant in the area. Opened in the late 1970s, the restaurant gives one the feeling of dining in a small art gallery, for the three small rooms have French murals on the walls and neutral, contemporary touches elsewhere. Spanking white tablecloths, fresh flowers, gray carpeting and cane chairs spell city sophistication, although at times you may find yourself sitting too close to your neighbors. The changing menu is eclectic and, given the prices of Boston food emporia, reasonable. Appetizers are priced from $5 to $8 and entrees, $14 to $20 (a special, seasonal prix-fixe menu for $22 is offered Monday-Thursday evenings). You might start with carpaccio of beef served with fresh fennel salad or roasted red pepper soup garnished with chevre. A seasonal salad ($5) might be composed of mixed greens with pears and toasted pecans, served with a roquefort or balsamic dressing. Entrees could be medallions of beef with a sauce of portabello mushrooms and thyme, salmon crusted with lemon angel-hair pasta and finished with a lemon, white wine and dill sauce, or cannelloni stuffed with butternut squash and ricotta. At lunch ($7 to $9), you might try an open-face grilled shrimp sandwich or New Brunswick stew. Lunch, Tuesday-Friday noon to 2; dinner, Monday-Saturday 5:45 to 10.

Aujourd'hui, Four Seasons Hotel, 200 Boylston St., (617) 338-4400. The location of this restaurant, on the hotel's second floor, where a window table gives you a view of the Public Garden, is one of its assets. Another is executive chef Michael Kornick, who has been turning out superb food since he arrived in 1991. An import from Chicago, where he perfected his skills at the Pump Room of the Ambassador East Hotel, Kornick is a graduate of the Culinary Institute of America. This is definitely a spot for a splurge: appetizers cost $7 to $16, entrees $26 to $36 and desserts $6.50 to $8. At lunchtime, you can dine for $12.50 to $24. Especially good choices are the corn chowder or the asparagus and crayfish bisque, breast of squab with hazelnut-crust foie gras, baby roasted chicken, sauteed soft-shell crabs and medallions of veal with calamata olive polenta. For dessert, consider vermouth and white chocolate sorbet, carrot cake or cinnamon-scented apple tart with vanilla ice cream. The dining setting is gracious: floral covered banquettes, rich oak paneling, white damask tablecloths, nicely spaced tables and a solicitous staff. Lunch, Monday-Friday 11:30 to 2:30; dinner nightly, 6 to 10:30 or 11; Sunday brunch, 11:30 to 2:30.

Cafe Budapest, 90 Exeter St., (617) 734-3388. We applaud this Hungarian restaurant in the basement of the Copley Square Hotel, which has proved its staying power in Boston's volatile dining scene. The late Edith Ban created the romantic European spot; it is now run by her sister, Livia Rev-Kurey. Our favorite dining room is paneled in oak, with red and white touches and Hungarian flasks, walking sticks, wine jugs and decorative plates on the walls. More feminine and elegant is the green and pink room off the lounge. Either way, the food is memorable. Meals are fit for royalty and the setting is so Old World romantic that you wouldn't be surprised to see Zsa Zsa Gabor (and she has been here, we're told). Most of the 25 dinner entrees ($18 to $29) are middle European — items like sauerbraten, wiener schnitzel and sweetbreads Hungarian style. One night we enjoyed a spectacular veal dish served with rice, string beans and carrots, along with a special salad of grapes and endive arranged like a star. End the evening, if you are in a romantic mood, with dessert crepes flambeed tableside while a pianist and violinist play nearby. Lunch, Monday-Saturday noon to 3; dinner, 5:30 to 10:30 or midnight, Sunday 1 to 10:30.

Rocco's, 5 Charles St. South, (617) 723-6800. Patrick Bowe, former manager of Harvest in Cambridge, opened his own restaurant in this colorful space in 1988. The high ceilings bear fanciful murals of nymphs and satyrs, huge windows are framed with sweeping draperies and gigantic bronze chandeliers hang from the ceiling. We had a fun dinner here one evening before meeting a son at Logan airport; the pre-theater crowd also finds it convenient. At lunchtime, the inventive menu includes crispy thin-crust pizzas topped with things like ham, hot peppers and grilled onions; a crab cake sandwich with grilled chicory and sundried tomato dressing on a sesame roll, pastas such as fettuccine bolognese or spaghetti with garlic and oil ($7 to 11), and entrees like steamed trout with roasted root vegetables or sauteed pork chops with artichokes, prosciutto and lemon ($7 to $12). Brunch dishes, including Italian french toast (talk about cross-cultural!) — a walnut, date and raisin sweet focaccia — are available every day at lunch. For dinner, try appetizers ($5 to $8) like grilled quail with truffles, sausage crostini or warm antipasto and entrees ($13 to $19) such as grilled leg of lamb with pepper-garlic jus or broiled sea scallops with a spinach-onion tart. Lunch, Monday-Friday 11:30 to 2:30, weekends noon to 3; dinner nightly, 5 to 10 or 11:30.

Newbury Street brownstones house restaurants and boutiques.

St. Botolph Restaurant, 99 St. Botolph St., (617) 266-3030. This turreted brick townhouse tucked into the Back Bay area looks like such a romantic spot to dine. Inside, the feeling is much more contemporary than one might expect, with bare brick walls, dark carpeting, white-clothed tables and rush-seated chairs — it's almost spartan, in fact. The main-floor cafe serves a lighter menu from noon to midnight — all of the appetizer choices from the regular dinner menu plus such main dishes ($7 to $11) as vegetable lasagna, chicken and gorgonzola pizza and a St. Botolph burger with bacon, mushrooms and cheese. You're trooped up a center staircase to the second floor for a more formal dinner at night. For starters ($6 to $9), you might try chicken livers on a stick with a pancetta and shallot demiglaze, fried calamari, smoked Norwegian salmon on rye toast with horseradish or caesar salad. Salad does not come with the entree, and rolls were delivered only grudgingly. Entrees ($15 to $23) the night we dined included swordfish in a cilantro marinade with steamed potatoes and vegetables, a pretty plateful but not an overly large portion; grilled veal steak in a chianti and onion sauce with mashed potatoes, broccoli and red beets, and Atlantic salmon in lemon garlic and olive oil with grilled asparagus, roasted red peppers and mushrooms. Sit close to one of the large windows, or — better yet — in one of the turrets for a view of the street scene below. Lunch, Monday-Friday noon to 2:30; dinner nightly, 6 to 10; Sunday brunch.

The Capital Grille, 359 Newbury St., (617) 262-8900. The reemergence of the grill restaurant typical of the 1920s and 1930s is seen in this clubby spot, sister to a restaurant by the same name in Providence, R.I. The marble floor, burgundy leather booths and dark mahogany woodwork lend a masculine, deal-making atmosphere; small brass lamps with black shades perched between the booths add soft lighting. Hunks of aging beef are displayed in a case out front. Dry-aged sirloin and porterhouse steaks lead off the dinner menu, priced at $23.95 and $24.95 respectively for a chloresterol-loading twenty- to 24-ounce portion. Filet mignon, sliced steak, steak au poivre, delmonico steak and prime rib also are available, along with a few seafood items. Potatoes and pasta are extra; a one-pound baked potato costs $2.75 and mashed potatoes, a stunning $3.75. Appetizers ($8 to $35, for beluga caviar) include panfried calamari with hot cherry peppers, oysters and clams on the half shell, smoked trout and shrimp cocktail. If you have room for dessert after all this, try the white chocolate mousse, cheesecake with strawberries, tirami su or apple Bavarian torte. Dinner nightly, 5 to 11.

Other recommended hotel dining rooms include **Seasons** at the Bostonian Hotel, **Julien** at Le Meridien and the **Dining Room** at the Ritz-Carlton. Other recommended restaurants include **Maison Robert** and **Locke-Ober.**

At the Museums

Having lunch or dinner as part of your art museum experience is a fun diversion in Boston.

The tiny **Cafe at the Gardner Museum** attempts to look larger with two mirrored walls, but it still seems rather crowded and seats only 32. You're advised to arrive early, eat first and then enjoy the remarkable museum. The food is good, if our lunch was an indication. Start with lobster bisque or soup of the day. Sandwiches ($7 to $8) might be shrimp salad, smoked salmon, turkey or English cucumber. A boursin omelet and a hearts of palm salad with tomato and feta were on the menu at our visit, as were such entrees (around $10) as Spanish paella and roast quail with polenta and wild mushrooms. The dessert selection is inviting: orange and chocolate bit cake, caramel apple pie, lemon tea cake, raspberry-almond tart and tirami su. Beers and wines are available; you can also get fresh ginger tea with lemon and honey or Italian bitters. An outdoor terrace is open in warm weather. Lunch, Tuesday-Friday 11:30 to 3, Saturday and Sunday to 4.

The spacious second-floor restaurant at the **Museum of Fine Arts** is very popular, especially for lunch on weekends (hint: reservations are taken for the 11:30 luncheon seating and for dinner). The view is outdoors to the courtyard and there's an open, airy feeling. Specials are named for paintings or pieces in current exhibitions. Recent lunch offerings included roast beef, turkey and tuna sandwiches ($6 to $7); salads were veal with tuna sauce or fresh fruit and berries served with a champagne sorbet ($6 to $11), or you could create your own from the salad bar for $5.25. Lunch entrees ($7 to $12) include pork loin roasted with caraway and lemon and herb ravioli. In the evening, entrees cost $12 to $18 for such things as rack of Virginia lamb, seafood provencal and black angus beef tenderloin served on an Indian grain pilaf. Lunch, Tuesday-Sunday 11:30 to 2:30; dinner, Wednesay-Friday 5:30 to 8:30.

The **Galleria Cafe** on the main floorof the Museum of Fine Arts is also good for something light. The fare might include sandwiches ($6 to $7) such as the Bostonian (smoked turkey with swiss cheese on a hearty grain bread with mustard). Among salads ($5 to $7) is curried chicken salad; European pastries are displayed on a cart. Wine and beer are available.

Sunday Brunch

Sunday brunch is an institution in Boston, and most hotel dining rooms and many restaurants offer it.

Cafe Fleuri in the Meridien Hotel presents a brunch that often has been voted the best in Boston by readers of Boston magazine. We found this skylit room with dark rattan chairs, deep rust banquettes, a soft rose and green patterned carpet and pink-clothed tables to be a luscious spot to devour the Sunday Boston Globe and the food. For the fixed price of $26 each, you can sample appetizers, hot foods, crepes and desserts from nine different stations. Waiters bring beverages and are good about refilling coffee cups. Soft jazz plays in the background, and there's a sophisticated, big-city feel to the experience. The hors d'oeuvre table offered pates, mixed fresh fruits, chicken liver mousse, whipped cream cheese, rolls, bagels, herring in sour cream, cheeses and a nice selection of salads. Main dishes included leg of lamb with rosemary, beef in brioche and a port wine sauce, eggs benedict, veal medallions in pommery mustard sauce, scrambled eggs, chicken with tomatoes and basil, rice pilaf, scalloped potatoes and mixed vegetables. Crepes of all sorts — served with ice cream or whipped cream and several intriguing sauces — were made to order. Among desserts were creme caramel, pecan pie, cheese cake, banana cake, chocolate layer cake and apple torte. Seatings are between 11 and 2, and reservations are advised.

Other favored brunch spots include the Four Seasons Hotel, the Boston Harbor Hotel, The Bostonian Hotel, and the Ritz-Carlton on both Saturday and Sunday.

Sunday brunch at Cafe Fleuri.

For Tea

Tea in the second floor parlor-lounge at **The Ritz-Carlton** is legendary. The room with its wing chairs, pie-crust mahogany tables, faded colors, floor lamps and wall sconces is perfect. A harpist adds just the right touch. A single red rose is on each table, and the waiters and waitresses all wear black jackets and ties. You can order full tea ($16.50), light tea ($12.50) or a la carte. On a chilly late Saturday afternoon in January we enjoyed the leisurely pace, the warming tea and the passing parade; this is a place to see mothers with their young daughters in smocked dresses and patent leather shoes or couples having tete-a-tetes. For full tea you receive two tea sandwiches, a scone, tea bread and a fruit tart; light tea omits the sandwiches. The teas include Keemum, Lapsang Souchang, Harney's low caffeine tea, Darjeeling, Ceylon and India and Earl Grey's. You also can have sherry or coffee. Tiny fruit tarts and chocolate-covered strawberries are the finishing touches to this memorable experience. Tea daily, 3 to 5:30.

Tea is also served in the **Bristol Court** at the Four Seasons Hotel.

On the Lighter Side

Rebecca's, 21 Charles St., (617) 742-9747. Rebecca Caras's restaurant at the foot of Beacon Hill continues to be a favorite of locals and visitors alike. People gladly wait in line to be seated at one of the small square tables. There's a bakery counter where you can pick up goodies to go. The creative cuisine offers such lunch items as warm duck salad with spicy walnuts served with a raspberry vinaigrette, spicy Maine crab cakes with a lemon chervil sauce or osso buco ($6 to $10). Soups are always good, as are appetizers like steamed mussels in white wine, garlic and herbs or baked polenta with wild mushrooms and fontina cheese in an herb tomato sauce. For dinner, entrees ($13 to $18) might be roasted chicken with a sauce of caramelized onions, plum tomatoes and chardonnay wine or veal scaloppini with artichoke hearts and lemon

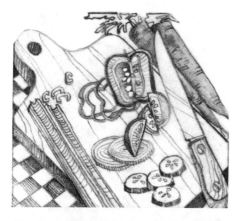

fettuccine. On the brunch menu ($10 to $15) you may find french toast with a compote of blackberries, raspberries and strawberries, an omelet with asparagus and boursin cheese, and chicken livers with roasted shallots and mushrooms in a mustard demi-glace. Desserts are well-loved as are the muffins, scones and other bakery items. Lunch, Monday-Saturday 11:30 to 4; dinner nightly, 5:30 to 11; Sunday brunch, 11 to 4.

Harvard Book Store Cafe, 190 Newbury St., (617) 536-0095. Continental breakfast, lunch and dinner are served amid the books at this fun place in the Newbury Street shopping district. Patrons eat and read or eat and chat in three small dining areas. If you're alone, this is a comfortable place to dine. For breakfast, pick up a tray and ask for a bagel or muffin or croissant, some juice and coffee; refills are free. Classical music plays in the background and you can buy your Globe or New York Times at the front of the store. Chef Moncef Meddeb once owned L'Espalier, a highly touted restaurant nearby; his partner here is Pierre Jospe. The all-day menu includes such sandwiches as smoked salmon club and lots of salads, among them nicoise, caesar, a hummus plate with pita points and a Middle Eastern antipasto. Hot entrees ($6 to $8) might be grilled capon breast or green falafel in rolled pita. Desserts include pecan or apple pie; a homemade chocolate-chip cookie goes for $1.65. Continental breakfast, daily 8 to 11; lunch, 11:30 to 5; dinner, 5 to 10; Sunday brunch, 11 to 3.

Hard Rock Cafe, 131 Clarendon St., (617) 424-7625. Probably no restaurant you choose would please young and young-at-heart fans more and we saw "kids" from seven to nearly 70 here one Sunday evening. "Love all; serve all; all is one" is the menu motto and "Massachusetts Institute of Rock" is emblazoned on a wall. Those celebrating birthdays get their names announced by intercom above the rock music. Barbecue and southwestern favorites are emphasized, but you can get all sorts of burgers and sandwiches (most items in the $6 to $8 range). The Pig Sandwich, smoked pulled pork with barbecue sauce, is a house specialty at $7.95. Root beer floats and banana splits are among the desserts. There's also a full bar. Open daily, 11 a.m. to 2 a.m.

Geoffrey's, 651 Boylston St., (617) 437-6400. This cute little bistro in the shopping district has a glassed-in area overlooking the sidewalk (for smokers, alas) and a pleasant rear dining room with red painted brick walls, square and round wood and faux marble tables, black leather-like banquettes and black chairs with deep green seats. It all works together somehow. We breakfasted here on good scones, fried eggs, hash browns and excellent coffee. Breakfast is served until mid-afternoon. Among sandwiches in the $6 to $7 range are California grill and vegetarian pita. For dinner, you might go for the pastas and bistro fare ($10 to $12), perhaps penne with lemon, spinach, parmesan cheese and cream or shrimp risotto with crisp ginger. Sides include roasted garlic mashed potatoes and sweet potato puree. Breakfast, Monday-Friday 7:30 to 3, Saturday to 4; lunch and dinner, 11 to 11.

The best burger late at night is said to be found at the **St. Cloud** restaurant on Tremont Street. It is served with aged cheddar and triple-smoked bacon and costs $8.

FOR MORE INFORMATION: Greater Boston Convention and Visitors Center, Prudential Plaza, Box 490, Boston, MA 02199. (617) 536-4100. A good book for background is *About Boston* by David McCord.

Early homes have been restored along Benefit Street's "Mile of History."

A Haven of History

Providence, R.I.

"For freedom of conscience the town was first planted,
Persuasion, not force, was used by the people.
This church is the oldest, and has not recanted,
Enjoying and granting bell, temple and steeple."

The inscription is on the bell atop the first Baptist church in America. It tells something about this city and this church founded in 1636 by Roger Williams, who started here more than 350 years ago the thrust for "soul liberty" and individual freedom that now prevails across the land.

The words cannot fully convey the legacy of Roger Williams, who fled the tyranny of Massachusetts Puritanism and named his settlement at the head of Narragansett Bay "in commemoration of God's providence." Nor can prose adequately describe the charms today for the visitor to this rags-to-riches city that calls itself — with a curious mixture of hometown pride and inferiority — "New England's Best Kept Secret."

Although seldom recognized beyond its borders, its treasures of history, architecture, arts and letters are appropriate for an over 350-year-old university town. And though not so publicized as Savannah or Charleston, in terms of historic preservation Providence takes a back seat to no city in the North.

Lately, this long-sleepy town that has had a reputation for flamboyance and tackiness is beginning to act like the second largest New England city that it is.

The views of the skyscrapers through the ivied gates of Brown University give it something of the look of Boston. The spotlighted State Capitol dome could be Washington's. The restored townhouses, close-in mansions, gaslight-type lanterns and statued squares lend the air of Philadelphia. And the East Side's near perpendicular hills could be San Francisco's.

All this is on a compact, human scale. Providence is unusual in that most of its historic, cultural and sightseeing attractions are within walking distance of downtown.

In the vanguard of the restoration movement, the city was among the first in the nation to attempt to save an entire neighborhood. The preservation of College Hill on the East Side is an achievement that began more than three decades ago and is still unfolding on its steep, tree-lined Colonial streets with providential names like Benefit, Hope, Benevolent and Power.

Today, College Hill is a lively mix of historic residences and institutions, including top-ranked Brown University with its world-class libraries and the Rhode Island School of Design with its outstanding art museum. Benefit Street's "Mile of History" has more than 200 notable homes dating back to early Providence, when this was *the* street (it still is). At the foot of College Hill are the restored South Main and North Main street areas, where the city was born along the riverfront. Boutiques and restaurants have sprung up amid old buildings. And everywhere there are churches, whose spires give this part of the city a classic New England look, as befits its religious heritage.

The downtown area is regaining some of its lost vibrancy with the pending opening of a convention center and the ongoing development of a massive retail, office, residential and hotel complex known as Capital Center on 60 acres between Union Station and the Statehouse. New buildings are rising, and interstate highway interchanges and even rivers are being moved as Providence heads into the mid-1990s.

This is a city of rarities, firsts and superlatives: America's first enclosed shopping mall (1828). A national park. The world's second largest unsupported dome. A bus tunnel under College Hill. New England's largest city park and zoo. The country's first

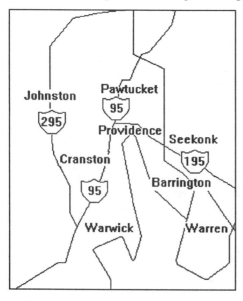

department and dry goods stores. Two of its oldest banks.

Not only is Providence a city of firsts. It's a city of today, especially in its restorations and restaurants, both of which are receiving national recognition. The mix is intriguing for a weekend visitor, especially in winter when the colleges are in session and the city seems particularly vibrant.

Getting There

Interstate highways ring Providence and cut around the downtown area from all directions. But this is not an easy city in which to drive unless you know exactly where you're going (we've managed to get lost every time we've driven in Providence). Streets are poorly signed and routes are roundabout. One-way streets, dead-ends and unmarked expressway entrances are a visiting motorist's nightmare, and the ongoing highway, downtown and river reconstruction projects were making it temporarily worse. If you stay downtown, park your car and walk.

Amtrak trains from New York and Boston stop at a new railroad station at the edge of downtown. The old Union Station facing Kennedy Square has been converted to new uses. Local buses converge on Kennedy Square, which is now a busy transit center. The bus station for Greyhound and Bonanza lines is nearby.

T.F. Green State Airport south of the city in Warwick is served by American, Continental, Delta, Northwest, United and USAir. More frequent flights serve Boston's Logan International Airport, an hour's drive north of Providence.

Where to Stay

Chain motels are concentrated south of Providence in the Warwick area and east of the city (a shorter drive) in Seekonk, Mass. For a city weekend, however, you probably will want accommodations in or near downtown.

Omni Biltmore Hotel, Kennedy Plaza, Providence 02903, (401) 421-0700. A feather in Providence's cap, this downtown hotel was restored in the grand tradition. The imposing brick dowager opened in 1922 to a special trainload from New York, a 50-piece band and a sea of roses, but fell on hard times and closed in 1973. It reopened in 1979 after local business interests renovated it for $15 million. It later was taken over by the Omni chain and another major renovation of rooms has been completed. At the top of the three-story lobby you can see the wonderfully ornate, original gilt ceiling, and the crystal chandelier and palm trees remind one of the Plaza in New York. The original 500 bedrooms have been converted into 289 comfortable, unusually large and deluxe rooms, done in soft and soothing colors. Most have kingsize or two double beds, plus armchairs and sofas in elegant sitting areas, with TVs hidden in armoires and swiveling on swing-out racks. The closets are huge, and bathrooms have separate dressing areas with vanities. Rooms on the Club Floor come with more amenities, like small refrigerators and tiny TVs in the bathrooms. The Presidential and Vice Regal suites are about the largest we've seen — each impeccably outfitted with antiques, two bathrooms, dining room, living room and kitchenette. (The price? If you have to ask, you won't be staying). Although the sumptuous L'Apogee restaurant on the 18th floor has closed except for special events like a Mothers' Day brunch, the smaller **Stanford's American Bar & Grill** serves three meals a day in a pleasant setting on the main floor. Pastas, rotisserie-grilled beef and chicken, and seafood specialties are offered in the $13 to $19 range at dinner. Choose a sandwich or salad from the deli express at lunch, and you can eat in half an hour. Doubles, $139 to $179; weekend packages, $79 up.

Days Hotel On the Harbor, India Street, Providence 02906, (401) 272-5577. Opened in 1989, this 136-room cross between a Days Inn and something more grandiose is a welcome addition to Providence accommodations. The six-story hotel faces the spruced-up waterfront park, from which the new East Bay bicycle path originates on its fourteen-mile trek along the shore to Bristol. A cocktail terrace takes advantage of the view. Rooms come in four configurations — two doubles, queensize, kingsize and king deluxe with jacuzzi. The decor is pleasant in green and beige, with light pine furniture. We regretted that our room with two double beds had only one easy chair, and that was clear across the room from the TV set. The only drinking glasses were white plastic Days Inn cups. But the room on the harbor side was quiet (not so those on the other side right next to I-95) and the price was right. A small health center includes a jacuzzi. Three meals a day are served in the well-regarded **India Point Cafe.** Doubles, $65 to $115.

Providence Marriott, Charles and Orms Streets (Exit 23, I-95), Providence 02904, (401) 272-2400. This eighteen-year-old motor inn is good for families, with its large indoor-outdoor pool, game room, sauna, whirlpool and exercise equipment. The 345 rooms on six floors are ordinary size, nicely decorated and have queen or kingsize beds; some have a view of the nearby State Capitol or face onto the landscaped pool area. The lobby is especially welcoming. **Stacy's Sea Grille Restaurant** offers three meals a day. The large **Cahoots Lounge** bustles at night. It's a long walk to downtown, but buses pass every fifteen minutes. Doubles, $125 to $163; weekends from $89.

The Old Court, 144 Benefit St., Providence 02903, (401) 751-2002 or 351-0747. You can stay on historic Benefit Street and relive today the Providence of yesteryear, thanks to the conversion of an 1863 Episcopal church rectory into an elegant B&B. Owners Jon and Carol Rosenblatt, who also have a series of small East Side restaurants, spared no expense in the restoration. Italianate in design, the Old Court has ornate mantelpieces, plaster moldings and twelve-foot-high ceilings. Each of the ten guest rooms with private tiled baths is decorated differently. Some have brass beds, some four-poster, and most have exotic wallpapers. The Eastlake Room is done with Eastlake furniture. Lace curtains and old clocks convey a feeling of the past; air-conditioning and television are concessions to the present. Because there is no common room, the Old Court seems like a small hotel. Croissants and muffins are served in a pink breakfast room, graced with an oriental rug and fresh flowers. A new two-bedroom suite in a house across the street is available for long-term guests at $160 a night. Doubles, $110.

State House Inn, 43 Jewett St., Providence 02908, (401) 785-1235. Creature comforts are well provided in this rooming-house-turned-B&B in a residential area just across I-95 from the State Capitol. Frank and Monica Hopton have furnished their ten guest rooms in a vaguely Colonial style typical of her (Parker) family's three B&Bs on Nantucket. Two rooms have canopy beds and two have fireplaces; all contain TVs, telephones, king or queensize beds topped with quilts or comforters and an overstuffed, comfy chair. Hooked rugs or carpets cover the maple floors original to the house. Stenciling and wreaths are scattered here and there. The main floor harbors a small guest parlor and a bigger, fireplaced dining room where the full breakfast might include quiche, french toast or blueberry pancakes. Doubles, $79 to $89. No smoking.

C.C. Ledbetter Bed & Breakfast, 326 Benefit St., Providence 02903, (401) 351-4699. There is artistry in Clare "C.C." Ledbetter's B&B, which occupies an historic house with a big side yard and garden in the heart of the East Side historic district. The artistry is reflected in C.C.'s amazing collection of paintings and photographs, her choice of colors (vivid green and apricot for the guest living room), and in the dhurrie rugs, Delft tiles and handmade quilts gracing four guest rooms that share two baths. The spacious third-floor front room running the width of the house contains a canopy four-poster bed and an exercise machine. Each room is decorated in eclectic style and has a small TV. C.C., who raised three children in Montana before moving back East in 1988 and deciding to settle in Providence sight unseen, serves a continental-plus breakfast of fruit, choice of juices, cheese, bagels, homemade breads or English muffins. Doubles, $67.

Holiday Inn-Providence, 21 Atwells Ave. at I-95, Providence 02903, (401) 831-3900. This 274-room, thirteen-story highrise has been refurbished, has an indoor pool and a good location next to the Civic Center, just across I-95 from the ethnic Federal Hill section. Rooms are a cut above the average Holiday Inn style, and parking is free. The restaurant serves three meals a day. Doubles, $85 to $115.

Roger Williams Memorial statue overlooks downtown Providence.

Seeing and Doing

To know Providence one must understand its evolution. Consider its neighborhoods and epochs, and pause to admire its architectural landmarks and the periods they represent.

Preservation and Architecture

The 17th-century colonists who joined Roger Williams's experiment in democracy set up shop along the Main Street riverfront. They built their homes and churches on the hill rising sharply up the east bank, an area known variously as College Hill and the East Side.

In the 18th century, the town's leading citizens were the four Brown brothers (John, Joseph, Nicholas and Moses), merchants and entrepreneurs whose funds helped build Brown University and one of the nation's most powerful business dynasties. The Brown family name and the course of Providence are interwoven to this day.

During the 19th century, the business center moved across the river to Weybosset Point and immigrants settled to the west in Victorian homes in Elmwood and Federal Hill. By 1900, Providence was one-third foreign born, and another third were children of immigrants. The ethnic ties of these groups remained stronger here than elsewhere and a few resisted assimilation; some neighborhoods still possess a foreign air.

With the flight to the suburbs in the 20th century, only College Hill retained its historic aura as a Yankee enclave, proud and aloof. Even that was endangered by university expansion in the mid-1950s, at which time John Nicholas Brown founded the **Providence Preservation Society** to preserve the past as "an asset for the future."

The **Benefit Street "Mile of History"** is the showcase of the Preservation Society's efforts. It is an extraordinary mix of 18th- and 19th-century residential and institutional treasures — more than 200 on stunning, tree-lined Benefit Street with its imitation gaslights and brick sidewalks, and more on cross streets. Benefit Street, surely one of America's most distinctive thoroughfares, is eminently walkable — and that's the best way to see and savor it. The society guides group tours by reservation, (401) 831-7440, has brochures for self-guided walks (80 cents) and offers "Stroll Through Providence" audio-cassette tours of College Hill and the downtown area in conjunction with the Greater Providence Convention & Visitors Bureau. Each walking tour takes about 90 minutes and the tapes cost $5 each, $7.50 for both. The College Hill tour starts at the

Preservation Society office, 21 Meeting St.; the downtown tour at the Visitors Bureau, 30 Exchange Ter.

Besides Benefit Street, the College Hill tour takes in **South Main Street** at the foot of College Hill, which was restored for business and residential purposes in the early 1970s. Brick warehouses along the riverfront are still being converted into restaurants and shops. Across the street are newish townhouses. At the north end of the restoration area is **Market Square,** the historic heart of the city where the Pequot and Wampanoag Indian trails met. The Woonasquatucket and Moshassuck rivers had been paved over in the 19th century by the 1,145-foot-wide Crawford Street Bridge, once the world's widest. Now the rivers have been relocated and flow freely under picturesque new bridges beside walkways and gardens, connecting eventually with the harbor near India Point Park.

Architect Joseph Brown designed the 1773 **Market House** at the end of Market Square and his own **Joseph Brown House** (1774) along one side at 50 South Main. The house was occupied in the 19th century by the Providence Bank which he founded, the oldest in New England. Next door is the gold-domed **Old Stone Bank** building, once the Providence Institute for Savings, one of the nation's first. The huge red brick **County Court House** (1933) is considered the largest Republican structure of its style in the world. It's on a hill that rises so steeply that its fifth floor opens onto Benefit Street. Buses go through the East Side Bus Tunnel to Thayer Street.

The **Roger Williams National Memorial,** 282 North Main St., is a four-and-a-half-acre plot being developed gradually for passive recreation around the site of the original 1636 settlement. National Park Service rangers preside over a small visitor center (open daily 9 to 5, May-October, and Monday-Friday 8 to 4:30 rest of year) with exhibits and a three-minute slide show, a park with gardens, and a shrine around the site of the spring that supplied Williams's water and was the true beginning of the colony. Several blocks east and almost straight up on Congdon Street is **Prospect Terrace,** site of the Roger Williams memorial statue. It yields a panoramic view of downtown Providence.

Old State House Area. An open "parade" leads from North Main Street up the hill to the **Old State House,** 150 Benefit St., and is surrounded by structures that rank among the city's oldest (the **Cushing houses,** 1737 and 1772). The state house is where Rhode Island became the first colony to declare its independence from England on May 4, 1776. Now housing state preservation offices, it was the seat of government and social life until the new Capitol opened in 1900. A block south is the **Brick School House,** built in 1769 and the city's first free school; now it is the home of the Providence Preservation Society's Revolving Fund. Across the street is **Shakespeare's Head** (1771), a restored garden and a house where Benjamin Franklin's apprentice, John Carter, published the Providence Gazette; the Preservation Society's main office is here. On Benefit Street to the north are the 1810 **Sullivan Dorr Mansion,** an outstanding example of Federal architecture designed by John Holden Greene and once home of the leader of the Dorr Rebellion for universal voting rights; the **Sarah Helen Whitman House** (1783-92), home of the poet courted by Edgar Allan Poe, and several houses built by the founder of Providence's Gorham Silver Company.

Governor Stephen Hopkins House, 15 Hopkins St. at Benefit Street, (401) 884-8337. Owned by the state and administered by the National Society of Colonial Dames, this is the dark red clapboard home of the ten-times governor of Rhode Island, first chancellor of Brown University and a signer of the Declaration of Independence. Governor Hopkins added the main part of the house in 1743 to the original two 1707 rooms. He became a Quaker after he married his second wife and the home reveals his simplicity of heart. Here is the four-poster in which George Washington slept, the wig

Rhode Island State Capitol, as seen from rear of house on Benefit Street.

stand on which he rested his wig and a decanter set he presented to his host. On display are the owner's spectacles, his baby cap, shoe buckles and a knife. Guides point out the children's room with a trundle bed, an old cradle with a cloth doll, a tiny chair used by tots to learn to walk as they held onto the back, and the weasel (a wool winder that popped every 40th revolution — hence "Pop Goes the Weasel"). Beside the house is a typical 18th-century parterre garden designed by a Hopkins descendant and centered by a sundial with a Hopkins quote: "A garden that might comfort yield." Open April-December, Wednesday and Saturday 1 to 4 and by appointment. Free.

John Brown House, 52 Power St., (401) 331-8575. The first great mansion in Providence was built in 1786 for John Brown, China trade merchant, slave trader, privateer and patriot. George Washington was entertained here, and John Quincy Adams called it "the most magnificent and elegant private mansion that I have ever seen on this continent." An outstanding example of late Georgian architecture, it is now a house museum with nine rooms and a priceless collection of Rhode Island cabinetmakers' furniture. The most prized Goddard piece is Joseph Brown's block and shell desk and bookcase. Visitors see a video show giving a good background of early life in Providence before they are guided on hour-long tours through the three-story museum, now owned by the Rhode Island Historical Society. You can tell that John Brown really weighed 300 pounds in his later years by his capacious waistcoat spread on one of the beds. The third floor displays collections of early dolls, silver and pewter (most of it the family's), plus goods brought back from the Orient by neighbor Edward Carrington. The carriage house garage has John Brown's robin's-egg-blue chariot, the earliest coach made in America (1782). Open Tuesday-Saturday 11 to 4, Sunday 1 to 4 (weekends only in January and February). Adults $5, children $2, families $12.

Museum of Rhode Island History at Aldrich House, 110 Benevolent St., (401) 331-8575. The 1822 Federal-style mansion, home of the Nelson Aldrich family, was donated by heirs of Winthrop Aldrich, ambassador to Great Britain, and is now the Museum of Rhode Island History. Exhibitions change about twice yearly and are generally excellent (one called "Harboring History: The Providence Waterfront" included a lecture series and boat tours). We like the wrought-iron benches under the huge copper beech tree at the other side of the house, where groups may picnic by appointment. Open Tuesday-Saturday 11 to 4, Sunday 1 to 4. Adults $2, children $1.

Downtown Providence, focus of an audio-cassette walking tour, is full of what a tour organizer calls "Victorian eccentricities." **The Arcade,** built in 1829 between Weybosset and Westminster streets, was cited by the Metropolitan Museum as one of the 19th century's best specimens of commercial architecture. The nation's first indoor shopping mall, it reopened in 1980 with three floors of specialty shops and fast-food eateries connected by balconies with cast-iron railings and topped by a block-long skylight. The landmark ziggurat (stepped-back) **Fleet National Bank** building is the one that, legend has it, Superman "leapt over with a single bound" before each TV broadcast. The Lederer Theater, one of several art deco theaters and movie palaces, is now the home of the well-known **Trinity Repertory Company,** one of the country's leading regional theaters. Nearby, an old Loew's showplace is now the **Providence Performing Arts Center,** site for traveling Broadway shows and big-band concerts. The former **Westminster Street Pedestrian Mall,** first in a large New England city, was too late to save two local institutions — the Shepard Co., the nation's first department store, and Gladding's, the first dry goods store. It couldn't even save the city's last remaining department store, the Outlet Co., which closed in 1982. Indeed, the pedestrian mall could not save itself and has been reopened to vehicular traffic.

Antiques shops, galleries and funky restaurants have congregated lately along **Wickenden Street** in the heart of the historic Fox Point section bordering the Providence and Seekonk rivers southeast of downtown. **North Main Street** is the scene of more business-residential restorations, which are enhanced by their proximity to the stunning **State Capitol** with its broad lawns. Built in 1900 of white Georgia marble, it claims the largest self-supported dome in the world after St. Peter's Basilica in Rome. Brilliantly illuminated at night, it is a worthy rival to the U.S. Capitol.

A massive arched gateway topped with a pineapple, symbol of hospitality, welcomes visitors to **Federal Hill,** Providence's Little Italy section along Atwells Avenue just west of downtown. Ethnic eateries, markets and shops convey a sense of the old world, particularly around the fountain and courtyard at DePasquale Square.

Elmwood, a transitional 19th-century neighborhoood southwest of downtown, is one of the latest targets for the preservationists. Here, colorful Victorian landmarks (outlined in a preservation society guide) stand amid abandoned structures that look as if they've been bombed. The fearless will find the side streets interesting on their way to or from the city's huge Roger Williams Park.

Roger Williams Park, 950 Elmwood Ave., Exit 17 off I-95 south, (401) 785-9450. One of the pleasant surprises of Providence is this 450-acre haven of greenery — the largest city park with the largest and best zoo in New England. This is a real urban park, well-maintained and a place on the way up. We know East Siders who like to rent paddleboats on Sunday afternoons and lose themselves along the meandering lagoons — "you go with the hordes and end up thinking you're out in the country," they say. Rent the boats from the restored Victorian Dalrymple Boathouse. The casino also has been restored and the excellent, 400-animal zoo contains penguins, polar bears, sea lions, pink flamingos, bison, elephants and two rare Masai giraffes. The **Museum of Natural History and Planetarium** and the Rose, Japanese and Hartman outdoor gardens are considered fine. Near the park entrance (follow the signs and the statues) is the restored 1773 **Betsy Williams Cottage,** last occupied by a descendant who deeded part of the land in honor of the city's founder. Besides miles of walks, waterways and driveways, the park has a Carousel Village with a new replica of a Victorian carousel, a train ride, and a small amusement area with an indoor pony ring. Park open daily, 7 a.m. to 9 p.m., free; zoo (adults $3, children $2), greenhouses and Carousel Village, daily 10 to 4.

Arts and Letters

The educational heritage of Brown University and the creative influence of Rhode Island School of Design (RISD, locally called Riz-D) have left their marks on Providence, particularly on College Hill.

John Carter Brown Library.

Brown University, the nation's seventh oldest, is the dominant influence. Brown was the Baptist answer to Congregationalist Yale and Harvard, Presbyterian Princeton and Episcopalian Penn and Columbia; graduates still process down the hill to the First Baptist Meeting House for commencement exercises, although the university shed its Baptist ties in 1938 and then entered a period of rapid expansion.

The original **University Hall,** patterned by Joseph Brown after Princeton's Nassau Hall, houses the administration at the head of College Street today. The admissions office is located in the 19th-century Italian villa-style **Corliss-Brackett House** (ask to see the Victorian bathroom) at Prospect and Angell streets, where students start guided campus tours on weekdays and Saturday mornings from September to December.

Brown Libraries. The huge **John D. Rockefeller Jr. Library** at 10 Prospect St. houses the university's general collections. Next door is the old **John Hay Library,** now home of the university archives and special collections. Foremost here is the McLellan Collection of Abraham Lincoln memorabilia — two small upstairs rooms with 700 Lincoln manuscripts, busts, portraits and even a lock of his hair. The curator considers it one of the finest in the country. The Lownes History of Science Collection is said to be the largest botanical collection anywhere. Open Monday-Friday 9 to 5. The beaux arts **John Carter Brown Library** across the quadrangle is a world-renowned repository of early Americana, furnished like a "gentleman's library" with huge hanging tapestries at either end. Manuscripts starting from the 15th century were shown in glass cases when we were there. The casual visitor may be disappointed, but the scholar will find such national treasures as Thomas Paine's original manuscripts for *Common Sense* and eight editions of Christopher Columbus's 1493 letters. Open Monday-Friday 8:30 to 5, Saturday 9 to noon.

Museum of Art, Rhode Island School of Design, 224 Benefit St., (401) 454-6500. One of the nation's outstanding small art museums is operated by one of its leading art and design schools. From mosaics and other treasures of ancient Greece and Rome to a fine collection of oriental art (don't miss the exquisite robes given to the museum by Lucy Truman Aldrich) to an outstanding selection of French artists (Monet, Degas, Manet, Cezanne and Matisse, among many) to changing exhibits, there is a bit of everything among the more than 70,000 works here. The famous bronze of Balzac by Rodin is one of the museum's prized possessions. The adjoining Pendleton House, housing American furniture and decorative arts, is the earliest example of an American wing in an American museum. Here is the Lucy Truman Aldrich collection of 18th-century porcelain figures, wonderfully displayed in cabinets lighted from inside. Under construction for opening in the fall of 1993 was the Daphne Farago Wing, producing

297

two large contemporary galleries and freeing up space elsewhere for a permanent gallery for the museum's Gorham silver collection, a recent gift of the Providence-based Textron Inc. A nifty little museum shop has jewelry, posters, dolls, postcards, stained-glass medallions and notes and cards. Open Tuesday-Saturday 10:30 to 5, Thursday noon to 8, Sunday 2 to 5; mid-June through August, Wednesday-Saturday noon to 5. Adults $2, students 50 cents; admission by donation Saturday.

The Providence Art Club, 11 Thomas St., (401) 331-1114. This 1790 brick-veneered house within easy walking distance of the RISD Museum has harbored the nation's second oldest art club (1880) with its parlors and private dining rooms for more than 100 years. A spacious upstairs gallery holds changing exhibits by a membership that does everything from oils to photography. Open Monday-Friday 10 to 4, Saturday noon to 3, Sunday 3 to 5; free. Two buildings down the street is the unusual 1866 Norman-Breton **Fleur de Lys Building,** former studio of Sidney R. Burleigh, dean of Rhode Island artists in the early 1900s. The Greek Revival building at 5 Thomas St. was long the headquarters of the Providence Water Color Club. Off "Artist's Row" but within walking distance is the **Bell Gallery** in Brown University's contemporary List Art Center, 64 College St., with changing exhibits throughout the school year.

Woods-Gerry Gallery, 62 Prospect St., (401) 454-6100. An Italian Renaissance-style mansion designed by Richard Upjohn houses RISD student galleries. Three sculptures, a towering copper beech tree and thick plantings of rhododendrons grace the lawns and terrace overlooking Providence. Maintained as an important example of the city's 19th-century architecture, the three-story mansion devotes its stripped-down main floor to changing exhibitions. The student works are worth viewing. Open Monday-Saturday 11 to 4, Tuesday to 7, Sunday 2 to 5. Free.

Providence Athenaeum, 251 Benefit St., (401) 421-6970. One of America's oldest subscription libraries is housed in this 1838 Greek-Doric temple-style building, which was the center of Providence's early intellectual and literary life. Many valuable books are shelved in its alcoves, within which Edgar Allan Poe wooed local poet Sarah Helen Whitman. The rare book wing has original Audubon elephant folios and changing art exhibits. Books are for members only, but the rare book displays and art exhibits are open to visitors. Open Monday-Friday 8:30 to 5:30, Wednesday to 8:30, Saturday 9:30 to 5:30 except in summer.

The Churches

Like the cathedrals of Europe and the missions in California, Providence's churches can be a destination in themselves. What better way to spend a Sunday morning in this city of churches?

First Baptist Meeting House, 75 North Main St. Members from as far away as Newport belong to the oldest Baptist congregation in America, established in 1638 by Roger Williams. Designed by architect Joseph Brown, it opened in 1775 "for the publick worship of Almighty God; and also for holding Commencement in." Its 1,300 seats represented one-fourth the population of Providence at the time; it's still filled to the rafters for Brown University's commencement. John D. Rockefeller Jr., who taught Sunday school here as a Brown undergraduate, provided funds in 1957 to renovate and strengthen the building. The woodwork was restored to the original Meeting House color — a restful sage. Note the Waterford crystal chandelier, given by Hope Brown upon her marriage in 1792 in memory of her father; it has gone from candles to gas to electrified miniature lights. The striking 185-foot spire was based on designs for the steeple of St. Martins-in-the-Fields, London. Free guided or self-guided tours are available Monday-Friday 10 to 3. Tours are given by members after Sunday services,

Waterford crystal chandelier hangs in First Baptist Meeting House.

at 9:30 in July and August, at 11 rest of year; our guide was an erudite drama professor from Brown.

Beneficent Congregational Church, 300 Weybosset St. Also called Round Top Church for its landmark copper dome, this is the city's oldest church (1809) west of the Providence River. It resembles the Custom House Building in Dublin and is one of America's earliest Greek Revival buildings. The church has had only ten ministers since its founding in 1743 and is known as the "house of ecumenicity." The first sermon by a Universalist was preached here in 1773, the first by a Methodist in 1791 and the first by a Roman Catholic bishop in 1962. The crystal chandelier — a feature of many Providence churches — came from Austria, and the splendid organ was given by Mr. and Mrs. John D. Rockefeller Jr. in memory of her mother, Abby Pierce Aldrich. Open Monday-Friday 9 to 4, Saturday 9 to noon and Sunday 9 to 1:30.

First Unitarian Church, Benefit and Benevolent Streets. Local architect John Holden Greene built this stone church, third on the site, in 1816 and considered it his best work. The always-liberal congregation was officially Congregational but affiliated with the Unitarian movement and changed the name to reflect its leanings in 1953. You can climb your winding way up the steeple (by appointment with the sexton) for a good view of the city and of the largest bell ever cast by Paul Revere and Son. Interior features are a three-tiered chandelier and the shallow oval dome, decorated with graduated panels, of Bulfinch inspiration.

The Cathedral of St. John, 271 North Main St. This Georgian building with Gothic trim, detail and tower was built by John Holden Greene in 1810 after the 1722 King's Church structure was demolished. Under the 18th-century altar is a replica of an ancient Saxon cross set in a stone from Canterbury Cathedral; the 1816 Waterford chandelier is striking. The Episcopal congregation now is racially mixed. The adjacent burial ground contains graves of famous Rhode Islanders. Open Monday-Friday 9 to 4, Sunday 8:30 to 11:30 (tours following services).

Other churches of note: **Grace Church** (Episcopal), serene amidst the hubbub of Westminster Street, was designed in 1846 by Richard Upjohn. The earliest Gothic

299

Revival church in the country, it has buttressed walls, a towering spire and a dark interior lighted by fourteen unique memorial windows. Another Upjohn church, **St. Stephen's** at 114 George St., is described as "Smoky St. Steve's" by the irreverent because it's so high Episcopal. Outstanding stained glass and a large chapel with windows onto the huge carved-wood sanctuary mark this Georgian edifice surrounded by Brown University. The green dome of **First Church of Christ, Scientist,** at Prospect and Meeting streets is a landmark visible across the city (and the Unitarian church sexton says it has a better view than his).

First Unitarian Church.

Where to Eat

It was little more than a decade ago that the Mobil Guide did not list a single restaurant for Rhode Island's capital city and on one dining foray we nearly were reduced to writing about the downtown McDonald's. That situation has happily changed, and Providence now claims some of the best and most interesting restaurants in New England. Lamentably, many of the most popular do not take reservations — we know folks who have driven from Boston and faced a two-hour wait for dinner.

Al Forno, 577 South Main St., (401) 273-9760. Moving from tiny quarters on Steeple Street to two floors of a renovated 19th-century stable near the waterfront, owners Johanne Killeen and George Germon have generated national publicity and turnaway crowds for their innovative northern Italian cuisine. Their followers love the pizzas done over the open fire with ever-changing toppings, they love the salads dressed with extra-virgin olive oil and balsamic vinegar, they love the pastas bearing such goodies as grilled squid and spicy peppers, and they love the grilled items done on the wood grill using fruitwoods and even grapevines from Sakonnet Vineyards. They also don't mind spending quite a bit of cash; pizzas (perhaps with sausage, tomato, garlic, jalapenos and two cheeses) are in the $10.95 range; pastas (how about one with ground sausage, walnuts, currants and grilled shiitakes?) $15.95, and grills and roasts from $12.95 for peppered grilled chicken paillard with mesclun, shaved parmigiano, caramelized onions and spiced olives to $24.95 for pot-roasted beef filet with onion sauce and fall mashed potatoes. Pizza done over the grill in the main-floor kitchen open to the bar is the signature dish. With a crackly thin crust and different toppings every day (ours had tomato, onion, gorgonzola, chicken, tarragon and tomato coulis), it is sensational. The choucroute garni includes three of the fattest sausages you ever saw topping mild and not-salty sauerkraut, accompanied by wide noodles sparked with fresh coriander; the skirt steak is seared right on the coals and served with wilted watercress and a green chile sauce. The exceptional desserts include tirami su and mascarpone-cream-filled chestnut crepes with persimmon and caramelized pear; the special tarts for two are $12.95 — on the menu that changes daily you might find one of cranberry-pecan or fresh quince. We tried the lemon souffle version, which was ethereal. Portions are huge and we saw many others leave, as we did, with doggy bags. This is food at its gutsiest. Tables are covered with sheets of paper, the wine is poured into stemless glasses like those used for vin ordinaire in the south of France, and the atmosphere is jolly and just right. The owners, both RISD graduates, are artists and restaurant designers as well as highly inventive cooks; their cookbook, *Cucina Simpatica,* is available for $25. Dinner, Tuesday-Saturday 5:30 to 10. No reservations; No smoking.

Pot au Feu, 44 Custom House St., (401) 273-9853. No less an authority than Julia Child is partial to Bob and Ann Burke's long-running success — twenty years in 1992, a milestone marked by the first five-star rating granted by Rhode Island Monthly magazine reviewers. A country French bistro in the basement contains old dark beams, brick and fieldstone walls, steel tables and a zinc bar. Here you can snack on pate, soups, snails, omelets, salads and crepes or feast on entrees like seafood baked in homemade French bread or Pot au Feu stew of beef and chicken (dinner entrees, $14.95 to $19.95). Upstairs, a pleasing L-shaped room houses an excellent classical French restaurant called the Salon. Panels of huge peach and white flowers on a sea green background ring two of the pale peach walls, and jet black plates contrast vividly with white tablecloths. Tables are centered with vases of carnations and baby's breath. Here you can have a five-course meal for $25.50 to $35, a good value, or order a la carte (entrees $16.75 to $26). Up to twenty nightly specials supplement chef John Richardson's regular menu. On the night we dined we were celebrating a double birthday and each ate enough for two. Fond memories of escargots bourguignonne and clams epinard dance in our heads, as do thoughts of the mushroom soup, the salad with fresh mushrooms and cherry tomatoes, the French bread served from a huge basket with sweet butter, the pink roast lamb, the tournedos bearnaise, the crisp vegetables, the hazelnut tart, the espresso. Memories are a bit blurred by a couple of the best martinis we've had and a bottle of La Cour Pavillon Medoc — well, it was a birthday! We can't wait to go back before too many more roll around. Lunch, Tuesday-Friday 11:30 to 2:30; dinner, Tuesday-Saturday 6 to 9 or 10; bistro open for lunch and dinner daily. No smoking.

Adesso, 161 Cushing St., (401) 521-0770. An old garage just off Thayer Street has been converted into a swinging, sophisticated California cafe and pizzeria by Anthony Michilitti, owner of the former Anthony's restaurant downtown, and David Drake. It's noisy and fun, with its gray oilcloth tablecloths, heavy European cutlery rolled up inside white linen napkins, and neon signs on the walls. The back room is like a greenhouse, with skylights and huge windows. From the open mesquite grill and wood oven come interesting pizzas — $7.75 to $10.50 at lunch, $9.95 to $12.75 at dinner. Asparagus with pancetta, smoked salmon with shrimp and saffron lobster sauce, barbecued chicken with cilantro and duck sausage with sundried tomatoes are some. For lunch, we tried a marvelous pizza with lamb sausage, roasted red and yellow peppers, mozzarella, wild mushrooms and a madeira sauce. We also sampled delicious grilled squid with a salsa of red peppers, onions and black olives, served with grilled zucchini, potatoes and snap peas, followed by a pear bread pudding with bourbon sauce. At dinner start with grilled shrimp with a melon, red pepper and fresh mint concasse, order something from the mesquite grill like grilled warm duck salad with radicchio, mushrooms, grapefruit, orange and grand marnier or grilled pork chops with a cranberry and walnut glaze ($13.95 to $19.95), and end with a refreshing trifle with plump blackberries and strawberries or imported white peaches with champagne sabayon, orange sherbet, raspberry sauce and crushed amaretti. Whew! Strong coffee is served in stainless steel cups, and the sleek chrome and glass salt and pepper grinders are so handsome that we bought a pair for $25. A pizza chef from Spago in Los Angeles helped open this place in 1987; Adesso means "now" in Italian and it is up-to-date indeed. Open daily from noon to 10:30 or midnight. No reservations.

Angels, 125 North Main St., (401) 273-0310. Opened by a former chef from Al Forno, this haute European bistro was taken over in 1992 by John Elkay and Guy Abelson, caterers of note who put the late Cafe in the Barn in Seekonk on the culinary map before turning their attention to In-Prov (see below). Now they have another upscale venue, intimate and handsome in black and white, in which to serve Mediterranean-influenced fare in tandem with a chef from Biba in Boston. The short, handwritten menu might offer such entrees ($17.50 to $23.95) as lobster ravioli with leeks, oyster mushrooms and three-cheese sauce; salmon roasted in potato crust with baby greens and sundried tomato vinaigrette, and grilled veal tenderloin with barolo wine sauce, mashed potatoes and grilled asparagus. Among exotic (and pricey — $6.50 to $9.95) starters are roasted clams with grilled fennel and garlic, grilled veal sweetbreads with fall vegetable confetti and balsamic maple sauce, and crostini with frisee, roasted peppers and warm goat cheese. If you have room left, try the grilled banana split; if not, at least sample the homemade ice creams and sorbets. Dinner nightly, 5:30 to 10 or 10:30.

New Rivers, 7 Steeple St., (401) 751-0350. The intimate space where Al Forno got its start is now the setting for ex-Bostonians Bruce and Patricia Tillinghast, he in the kitchen and she out front. A striking picture of red pears glistening against a dark green wall sets the theme for contemporary international fare. Fresh Nime Chow spring rolls are perennial starters, but we'd opt for one of the New Rivers sampler plates — perhaps the Portuguese, Vietnamese or Indian, $9.95 to $11.95 and planned for sharing. Then we'd move on to one of the pastas (say porcini cappelletti with grilled chicken, hot sausage and arugula, $14.95) or an entree from the grill or oven, perhaps Moroccan chicken legs, Jamaican jerk beef with oven-fried sweet potatoes or grilled pork chop with cranberry-port chutney, $10.95 to $19.95. Walnut torte with a spice-poached pear and maple cream, a fruit tartlet in a delicate pastry shell or praline ice cream might top off your meal. Dinner, Tuesday-Saturday 5:30 to 10.

Pizzico, 762 Hope St., (401) 421-4114. The owners of Il Piccolo in suburban Johnston opened an offshoot in Providence in 1991 to immediate and equal acclaim. Here is one of the more engaging regional Italian trattorias we've seen: two side-by-side dining rooms with pink painted and white brick walls. Generally well-spaced tables sport white butcher paper over white cloths and a bottle of the featured wine. Folks rave about the food. The lengthy menu starts with "center of the table" plates to be shared ($6.25 to $15.50), among them bruschetta, focaccia and a piatto rustico yielding prosciutto, sausage, venison pate, chunks of parmigiano reggiano and fresh fennel. Main courses run from $12 for penne in a vodka pink sauce to $21.50 for grilled veal T-bone with shiitake mushrooms, pinenuts and a two-mustard sauce. The extensive wine list might be supplemented by a blackboard listing "special chiantis and super Tuscans." Lunch, Monday-Friday 11:30 to 2:30; dinner nightly from 5.

Bluepoint, 99 North Main St., (401) 272-6145. Next to a railroad viaduct, this oyster bar and restaurant looks like a dive from the outside and is pretty funky on the inside, too. But we are assured that you can find the best seafood in Providence here. Swinging doors, a neon clock, a few fish on the walls, lights that look like shells beside the blue booths, orange chairs and a standup bar comprise the decor. The innovative menu changes daily. Start perhaps with oysters from the raw bar, steamed Thai spiced clams with mango and fresh cilantro, conch salad, oyster stew or the house quahog stuffies ($4.50 to $9.75). For main courses ($13.75 to $18.75), how about grilled Szechuan glazed Atlantic salmon with cool cucumber salad, seared sea scallops with shallots and pinenuts over linguini and watercress, a hearty Portuguese seafood platter with chorizo or spicy barbecued shrimp in the rough? Broiled chicken was the only non-seafood item at our visit. Creme brulee, a warm apple and cranberry tart and a chocolate, currant and pecan torte with southern comfort cream are among the good desserts. The wine list is more aptly called the wine book, accorded the Wine Spectator grand award of excellence. Its 750 entries are alphabetized, and last we knew listed no fewer than 101 chardonnays from $14 to $68. The 20,000-bottle wine cellar stretches under the adjacent building as well. Dinner nightly, 5 to 10 or 11.

Rue de L'Espoir, 99 Hope St., (401) 751-8890. Originally a Left Bank-type bistro in the university area, this neighborhood place has changed to an international menu, and now is French in name only. But longtime owner Deb Norman retains her following with an inexpensive, with-it dinner menu featuring entrees ($11.95 to $16.95) like grilled finfish with fennel and tomato relish, lime-broiled salmon with black beans, roasted pork tenderloin with capanota and grilled chicken over three-cheese ravioli. The popular Rue Rue platter ($17.50), a sampler of five appetizers, is a meal in itself. So are some of the specialty salads, among them nicoise and caesar with grilled chicken or shrimp. A large selection of beers is available, as are interesting and reasonable wines. For lunch, the grilled scallops and tomatoes on a bed of greens has a nippy citrus-thyme vinaigrette, pan-sauteed mussels are served with a champagne sauce on a bed of wilted greens, and from the dessert tray we still recall a memorable charlotte malakoff (lady fingers, whipped cream, nuts, kirsch and strawberry preserves). The unusual tables are made of quarry tiles, copper pans and plants hang from the pressed-tin ceiling, and decorative panels and woodwork are sponged in navy and cranberry colors. Breakfast, Tuesday-Friday 7:30 to 11, weekends 8:30 to 2:30; lunch, Tuesday-Sunday 11:30 to 2:30; dinner nightly, 5 to 9 or 10:30. No smoking.

Hemenway's, 1 Old Stone Square, (401) 351-8570. With a view of the river from its sleek glass quarters on the main floor of a new downtown bank building, Hemenway's appeals to those who like their seafood in stylish surroundings. There's a pricey retail market with a live lobster tank made of marble at the entrance. The tables bear huge bottles of tabasco sauce and neon fish hang from the ceiling amid the clubby decor of dark greens, etched glass, brass lamps, bare tables, leather banquettes and dark wood booths. An extensive, eight-page menu with colorful fish swimming all over it, printed every three days, starts with eighteen entries from Hemenway's oyster bar. Crab and shrimp potato skins, and oysters Hemenway (grilled with herb butter, lime juice and Absolut vodka) are favorite appetizers. Every kind of fish you've heard of — and probably some you haven't, including four "fresh from Hawaii" — are listed for main courses, from $13.95 for blackened scrod or catfish to $19.95 for baked Florida red snapper. Grilled Norwegian salmon topped with artichoke hearts and Florida swordfish topped with sauteed spinach and tomatoes were among specials when we were there. There are a few steak and chicken items for landlubbers, and fresh fruit salad and grilled chicken sandwich join the seafood parade at lunch. The house salad that comes with every entree is topped with baby shrimp, there's apple crumb pie a la mode for dessert and children have a choice of four inexpensive meals. Lunch, Monday-Saturday 11:30 to 3; dinner, Monday-Saturday 5 to 10 or 11, Sunday noon to 9.

The Capital Grille, 1 Cookson Place, (401) 521-5600. If Hemenway's is owner Ned Grace's shrine for seafood, this is his sanctuary for steaks. All is dark and elegant in the style of a British men's club, with little hint that this was once the boiler room of the old Union Station. Only the beams and ceiling are original; the rest shows what deep pockets can buy. Hobnob with the pols as you feast on the finest steaks (aged on premises), chops and roasts, priced from $18.95 to $23.95, except chicken for $13.95. This is dining of the grand old school: cold shellfish platter and beluga caviar among appetizers, French onion soup and caesar salad, and sides of potato (baked, $2.75) and vegetables (asparagus with hollandaise, $4.50). Fresh strawberries with grand marnier is the dessert of choice. Lunch, Monday-Friday 11:30 to 3; dinner nightly, 5 to 10 or 11, Sunday noon to 9.

In-Prov, 50 Kennedy Plaza, (401) 351-8770. This American bistro opening into the atrium of the Fleet Center is just the ticket for those into tapas and rotisserie foods. Frozen flavored vodka is one of the bar specialties, and up to 30 wines are available by the glass. Faux marble walls and marble floors are the backdrop for tables with rattan chairs in the lounge, the small dining room and out in the atrium. The menu lists a variety of tapas (available after 4 p.m.), from fried squid rings with chipotle mayonnaise and shrimp rolls with Thai dipping sauce to crayfish and corn fritters and juniper-smoked Norwegian salmon and grilled bagel chips ($4.50 to $8.50). Entrees of spit-roasted chicken with mashed potatoes and Jack Daniels gravy, pork tenderloin with pumpkin polenta cakes and oven-roasted salmon on a bed of creamed spinach, pancetta and onions go for $12.50 to $18.95. At lunch, chef John Elkhay's black bean soup gave new meaning to the word "hearty;" that and the barbecued duck spring rolls ($4.95) proved too much to eat, as did Le Sandwich ($6.50) of mozzarella, artichokes, sundried tomatoes and more on focaccia. Peanut-butter chocolate-chip cheesecake and chocolate-pistachio cake with fruit sauces are among desserts. There's a takeout counter where we once picked up apricot-glazed chicken and delicious salads for a late dinner at home. Lunch, Monday-Friday 11:30 to 3; dinner, Monday-Saturday 5:30 to midnight.

Leon's on the West Side, 166 Broadway, (401) 273-1055. From a funky catering shop that started serving breakfast and lunch, Leon's has upscaled and moved to a prime location just across I-95 from the civic and convention centers and theaters. Bill Andrews oversees his stylish new digs, named for his wife's late brother who was a waiter at their former Catering on Broadway. Here, striking artworks and a convivial crowd brighten what could be an austere setting of exposed beams, whirring black ceiling fans and bare dark wood floors. The breakfasts here are legendary, from scones to florentine omelets and smoked salmon benedicts; heavy eaters go for the Texas trucker (ham steak, three eggs and two pancakes, $7.25). A staggering 400 people showed up for brunch on the Sunday preceding our visit. Build-your-own burgers and create-your-own pastas are featured on the all-day menu, which ranges from a chicken souvlaki sandwich ($6.95) to grilled fish, steak or veal of the day (market price). Breakfast, Tuesday-Friday 8 to 11:30; lunch, Tuesday-Saturday 11:30 to 3; dinner, 5 to 10 or 11; weekend brunch, 8 to 3.

Raphael's Bar-risto, 345 South Main St., (401) 421-4646. In 1985, then 27-year-old Raphael Conte opened a smart Italian restaurant in the boiler room of one of Providence's many old jewelry factories along Pine Street. In 1992, the space was usurped by Johnson & Wales University, so Raphael — a bit older and wiser — moved to a more central location with a more casual ambience. A long bar, big windows onto South Water Street, sponged yellow walls and a black ceiling were being readied for opening at our visit. From an open kitchen, Raphael planned to do a lot of wood grilling, pastas and salads, with some 40 items changing weekly and priced about $3.95 for appetizers and salads, $10.95 to $12.95 for entrees. Dinner, Tuesday-Saturday from 5.

Ichidai, 303 South Main St., (401) 453-3660. This "Japanese Modern" restaurant must be seen to be believed. A curving, concrete foyer leads into an amazing space, all high-tech in black and gray. Sushi is served at an L-shaped counter, $9.95 for eight pieces at lunch, $16.95 for a combination plate at dinner. The menu is modern as well, from salmon sauteed in mirin wine sauce to Hachidai steak rolled up in red lettuce to beef and tofu stir-fried in a tobanja sauce over rice. Entrees are priced from $13.95 for five chicken dishes to $23.95 for filet mignon and lobster tail. Lunch, Monday-Friday 11:30 to 2; dinner nightly, 5 to 10 or 11.

L'Elizabeth, 285 South Main St., is the most romantic spot imaginable for a tete-a-tete drink. It has a true European feeling, with the look of a salon where there are different groupings of sofas and chairs, and is very dimly lit at night. No meals are served, but tea and pastries in the afternoon (always L'Elizabeth's torte cake with raspberry, apricot and chocolate or maybe chocolate mousse pie) are about $6. Espresso, cappuccino, international coffees, hot toddies and a large selection of liquor and liqueurs are available. Open daily from noon to 1 a.m., Sunday from 3.

Federal Hill. An entire book could be written on Federal Hill, a tight little enclave of ethnic eateries. Lately, the stress on heavy Neapolitan cuisine has been broadened with the likes of **Ristorante Toscano,** a reborn Federal Hill branch of Boston's class Florentine act; the new **Thailand Restaurant** and the Japanese outpost, **Fuji.** Traditionalists still dote on the **Blue Grotto, Camille's Roman Garden** and **Cassarino's.** Visitors mix with regulars at old kitchen tables in **Angelo's Civita Farnese,** an unlikely-looking spot where you roll up your sleeves for family-style food like Mama really did make. We like best the new action around DePasquale Square, where you can lunch on an Italian tuna sandwich ($4.50) or one of prosciutto, fresh mozzarella and tomatoes, and fine imported desserts at **Caffe Dolce Vita,** or head for an exotic homemade dessert (perhaps toffee-walnut torte or pumpkin cheesecake, $2.75 a slice) with cappuccino or caffe latte at **Pastiche,** a bakery and gourmet dessertery par excellence around the corner at 92 Spruce St. Pick out a salad or grilled pizza ($7.25 to $10.25) at **Bob & Timmy's Legendary Grilled Pizza** on the square or a salad or pasta to go from the remarkable **Tony's Colonial Food** store at 311 Atwells Ave. The natives are right when they think they have a touch of Europe here.

Shopping

In recent years, the shopping scene in Providence has shifted away from downtown, which still was hanging on until the last few years, to the malls of suburban Warwick and, lately, the upscale stores at The Village at Garden City Center in Cranston.

Most of the shops and restaurants at the restored Davol Square have given way to a jewelry center for wholesalers, and some of our traditional favorites have vanished from the restored 19th-century **Arcade** at 65 Weybosset St. Its main floor is now mostly fast-food eateries, where all of Providence seems to line up for a quick weekday lunch. About the only interesting stores left are a couple of posh apparel shops, **Crabtree & Evelyn** and **Spectrum** for crafts.

Thayer Street has college-type shops and two good book stores beside each other — the **College Hill Book Store** and the **Brown University Book Store.** Wayland Square on the East Side is the center of old-line shops for clothing, gifts and such, among them **M's** for upscale gifts, **Peter Blieden** for lovely apparel, the **Cheese Shop** and **Books on the Square.**

You'll also find several contemporary stores along South Main Street, including the **Opulent Owl,** one of our favorite gift shops anywhere; **Briggs** for men, **Nature's Comfort** for shoes and boots, and **Comina,** for international gifts and crafts. Galleries and antiques shops are proliferating along four blocks of nearby **Wickenden Street.**

FOR MORE INFORMATION: Greater Providence Convention & Visitors Bureau, 30 Exhange Ter., Providence, R.I. 02903, (401) 274-1636 or (800) 233-1636.

Dogwoods bloom in front of Greenfield Hill Congregational Church.

Spring Along the Shore

Lower Fairfield County, Conn.

It's called "The Gold Coast" and the per-capita income is among the highest in the country here in the southwestern corner of Connecticut. In many respects an elongated bedroom community for commuters to New York City, lower Fairfield County is filled with tony towns and shopping areas, fine restaurants and fancy cars, busy marinas and posh estates beside Long Island Sound. Tourism is not the chief source of income; in fact, tourists are, to some extent, ignored. That is not to say they are unwelcome. It's just that there is so much else going on here that tourism is not given much attention.

Nonetheless, lower Fairfield County is increasingly becoming an interesting place for weekenders. Here are two cities, several smart suburban towns and patches of unspoiled country. Because of its Yankee heritage, the area has many historic houses and museums. And visitors increasingly find appealing places in which to stay.

Early in our nation's history, the irregular coastline and fine harbors on Long Island Sound made settlement attractive. Good harbors meant good shipping and hence trading; Roger Ludlow arrived in what is now the town of Fairfield in 1637 and quickly realized he'd be smart to stay. Up in Hartford, where the colony's General Court met, Ludlow was granted not just Fairfield, but the area extending down the line as well, including Norwalk and Westport.

Shipping made the communities rich. Southport shared distinction with New Haven as the major harbor in Connecticut in the late 17th and early 18th centuries. By 1774 Norwalk and Fairfield were ranked among Connecticut's dozen largest communities. All the coastal towns were linked early by the venerable Boston Post Road (Route 1), the first Colonial highway and now a busy commercial strip.

It was the train that most dramatically influenced the development of lower Fairfield County as we know it today. Since the establishment of the New Haven line in the mid-19th century, joining the towns with nearby New York City, residents have looked west to Manhattan for their livelihood, cultural influences and style.

It is high style, too. A number of Fortune 500 companies have established corporate headquarters here, in part because their top executives like the quality of life. Real estate values outpace those in most of the country. Sophistication in all areas of life is palpable.

All the towns along this southwestern shoreline share the New York-commuter orientation, but differences among them are discernible.

Greenwich is rich and restrictive. Probably known more than the others for its aloofness, the town is characterized by huge estates at the end of winding drives, for fine restaurants and high-fashion stores.

Norwalk is a city in its own right. It's alluring to visitors for its long-standing factory outlet shopping and its new and rejuvenated SoNo district in South Norwalk, anchored by a maritime museum and full of good restaurants and shops.

Westport is trendy and fast-paced, celebrated for writers, artists, actors and creative types among its residents. Its downtown is full of upbeat shops; early in May some of its beautiful people start their tans at Compo Beach or Sherwood Island.

Fairfield seems quieter and less oriented to New York than the rest (it borders Bridgeport to the east). But its Southport Harbor is the most charming of all and is a posh address. Also prized are homes in Fairfield's Greenfield Hill section, many of them pre-Revolutionary and some set among the gorgeous pink and white dogwood trees that turn the area into a floral fantasy for two weeks in early May.

The proximity of Long Island Sound adds special flavor to a weekend in lower Fairfield County. Despite a discouraging lack of public access, it's possible to find a few beaches to walk along and a boatyard or marina where you can sense the seasonal stirring, the first fitting out of the pleasure boat fleet. A few restaurants yield water views.

Best of all, perhaps, in catching the flavor of lower Fairfield County are the drives along winding back roads through wooded residential sections where vintage homes and New England stone fences are solid and stable amid the soft spring green of lawns and leaves.

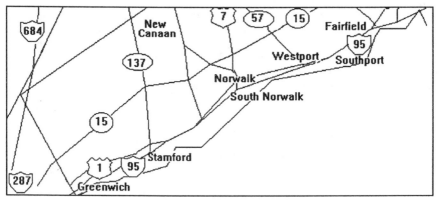

Getting There

Accessibility is one of Fairfield County's virtues. The Merritt Parkway, Route 15, is the most pleasant way to arrive, especially when the dogwoods are in bloom. Paralleling it closer to the shore is busy Interstate 95, the Connecticut Turnpike. Route 1, congested and commercial, also runs west to east through the towns we discuss here.

Metro North trains depart from Grand Central Station in New York City for all towns along the coast, making the area an easy destination for visitors to New York who want to get a taste of New England. Greyhound operates several buses daily from New York to Stamford, Norwalk and Bridgeport. The major New York airports are linked to Fairfield County by frequent limousine service.

Where to Stay

The Homestead Inn, 420 Field Point Road, Greenwich 06830, (203) 869-7500. Lessie Davison and Nancy Smith completely renovated and refurbished this 1799 inn in the exclusive Belle Haven section when they took it over in 1979. Since then they have redone two buildings out back, the Independent House and a charming little place called the Cottage, where most recently they have added a small conference center for boards-of-directors retreats. Now there are twenty-three rooms — twelve in the 1799 main house, eight in the Independent House and three in the Cottage. Although it claims an 18th-century heritage, the Homestead feels more Victorian, and its cupola on top is definitely a 19th-century addition. Eclectic would be the way to describe the furnishings, a mix of antiques with contemporary touches. There's nothing old-fashioned about the bathrooms, which adjoin all rooms; those in the Independent House, in fact, have bidets. Color TVs, clock radios, telephones, good bedside reading lamps with three-way bulbs, bowls of low-calorie candies and bathrobes are standard. Skylights in many rooms and in one bathroom let in the light. A canopied bed makes the Bride's Room a favorite of many; we also like the Sleigh Bed Room with its antique sleigh beds and the Robin Suite, which has a sitting room with original hand stenciling of robins on the walls. In the cottage, the two-room suite with cathedral ceiling is an especially airy spot. Rooms in the Independent House have access to porches. The main inn harbors cozy nooks, especially a fireplaced reading area with a window seat upholstered in deep green. LaGrange, the inn's dining room (see Where to Eat), is one of the best in Fairfield County. Inn guests enjoy continental breakfast there with homemade muffins and croissants and — if they are hungry — they may order a full meal. Doubles, $127 to $152; suites, $167 to $175.

The Cotswold Inn, 76 Myrtle Ave., Westport 06880, (203) 226-3766. This is one of the most sophisticated B&Bs we've seen, which is appropriate, given its location at the eastern edge of Westport's downtown, with all those marvelous stores and restaurants within walking distance. You drive behind a stone house and up a driveway to a clapboard cottage tucked back from the street, which was actually built as a bed and breakfast in an English country style by local builder Richard Montanaro, resident innkeeper with his wife Lorna. Each of the four rooms (one a two-room suite that can accommodate three persons) is distinctively furnished and decorated and each has a large bath. The Wheeler Suite, in apricot and white, includes a fireplace, a canopy bed and an adjoining room with a single pine sleigh bed tucked against the wall. The other three rooms have such furnishings as Queen Anne armchairs, Chippendale loveseats and Deerfield lolling chairs and, in the spacious main-floor Bedford Room, a sitting area, writing table and "mule chest." All rooms have large closets and TVs sequestered

Cotswold Inn is tucked away off residential street near downtown Westport.

in armoires. The light stain on the woodwork and the light oak and pine pieces add to an airy, upbeat feeling — cheery even on the rainy day we first visited. The Montanaros serve a continental-plus breakfast (fresh fruit, cereal, yogurt, plus scrambled eggs in a chafing dish on weekends) in a bright breakfast area off the kitchen or outdoors. Tea and wine are complimentary for house guests in the afternoon. Classical music, fresh flowers, bedside mints and a roaring fire in the parlor on chilly evenings are the norm. Doubles, $175 to $200; suite, $225.

The Stanton House Inn, 76 Maple Ave., Greenwich 06830, (203) 869-2110. On two-plus acres not far from the center of town, this imposing white inn is run by Tog Pearson, who grew up in town, and his wife Doreen, who hails from nearby Norwalk. Doreen has redecorated all the rooms of the former boarding house with taste and pleasant touches. The 25 guest rooms are hard to find them since they are located off meandering hallways and there is a sense of the house having been added onto and rearranged several times. All rooms are individually decorated with a tendency toward the Victorian period. The main floor contains high-ceilinged public rooms, including a spacious main parlor and a nice breakfast room with individual tables and windsor chairs, where a continental-plus breakfast is served to guests. Muffins, bagels, danish pastry, fresh fruit, cereal and beverages are set out buffet-style on a table in the center. Most rooms come with color TVs and phones; they have bare wood floors, area rugs and desks where business people can work during the week. The Queen Suite with pink walls, rose flowered Austrian shades, an old-fashioned tub with french shower, and a kitchen area with microwave oven and wet bar is especially nice. Two new two-room suites on the fourth floor have dormered windows and unusual roof lines. Tea, coffee or iced tea are often served in the afternoon and guests enjoy an outdoor patio. Doubles, $72 to $82; suites, $130.

Hyatt Regency Greenwich, 1800 East Putnam Ave., Old Greenwich 06870, (203) 637-1234. This French Norman-style hotel, which opened in 1986 virtually on the Stamford-Greenwich line, is fortress-like and imposing as you approach from Route 1. Inside, the skylit atrium with a bar and restaurant and a goldfish-filled brook offers a different feeling. On a brisk April day, the atrium area was warm and salubrious.

Favored by business travelers, the hotel has 353 guest rooms on four floors, plus a health club and pool. The Regency Club concierge floor offers a private room where guests may eat breakfast, have tea or sip a cocktail. **Conde's,** the main dining room, serves dinner nightly ($8 to $23) in a paneled, clubby atmosphere off the skylit atrium. Doubles, $174; weekends, $99.

Silvermine Tavern, 194 Perry Ave., Norwalk 06850, (203) 847-4558. If you want a traditional old-style inn out in the country, this may be for you. The original part of the homey structure dates back 200 years and the setting, on a millpond in the rural Silvermine section north of Norwalk, is picturesque. Ten guest rooms with private bath are located in the main white inn with pink shutters or across the street in a steeply staired annex behind the Country Store, another of the attractions on the property. Rooms 5 and 6 in the annex, where we once stayed with our children, now have canopy beds. Innkeeper Frank Whitman Jr. oversees the sprawling inn filled with antiques, primitive portraits and old tavern signs. The costumed figure of Miss Abigail is the well-known mannequin in the early American cocktail lounge. The several dining rooms and a spectacular outdoor deck overlook the millpond and the Silvermine River waterfall. The restaurant is famed for its honey buns, prime rib, lobster pie and rich, smooth ice creams. Contemporary options have been added lately to the traditional dinner menu ($14.50 to $22.95). You can't beat the ambience, with brick or wood floors and tables set with homespun placemats, and you can eat outdoors in nice weather. Continental breakfast is complimentary to guests. Doubles, $87 to $92

The Westport Inn, 1595 Post Road East, Westport 06880, (203) 259-5236 or (800) 446-8997. The location is good for this motel-type inn, which has undergone a massive renovation lately. Now there's a second building behind the first with a large mauve and gray lobby, as well as a huge skylit atrium area with luxurious, oversize rooms around a large indoor pool, where chaise lounges are at the ready. The atrium is also the setting for a complimentary continental breakfast. All 116 rooms are new or have been completely upgraded, most with two queensize beds. There's a fitness center with saunas. Meals are served in **The Hearth** restaurant and lounge, and a new American grill restaurant, **Chop Chop,** is located next door. Doubles, $90 to $125.

Norwalk Inn and Conference Center, 99 East Ave., Norwalk 06851, (203) 838-5531 or (800) 873-2392. This smallish (71 rooms) inn, near the green in Norwalk, is situated back from the road. It includes an appealing outdoor pool and patio. The well-regarded restaurant, **Adam's Rib,** specializes in beef. The location is fairly convenient to Norwalk's discount shopping district as well as SoNo, the renovated historic area near the water, although it's not close enough for walking. Doubles, $60 to $67.

Courtyard by Marriott, 474 Main Ave., Norwalk 06851, (203) 849-9111. With an indoor pool, exercise room and restaurant, this motor inn off Route 7 just north of the Merritt Parkway is particularly popular. The 145 rooms and suites, most with kingsize beds, open onto an interior courtyard patio or balcony. Doubles, $74 to $94; suites, $94 to $114.

Norwalk Holiday Inn, 789 Connecticut Ave., Norwalk 06854, (203) 853-3477. Astride U.S. Route 1 just above I-95, this eight-story motor inn is conveniently located. The 258 rooms contain kingsize or two double beds and the usual Holiday Inn accoutrements. Facilities include an indoor pool and sauna, a coffee shop and a full-service restaurant. Doubles, $93.

The Inn at National Hall, 2 Post Road West, Westport 06880, (203) 221-1351. Four years in the works, a handsome three-story brick building with green trim beside the Saugatuck River was being readied for opening in mid-1993 as a deluxe inn and restaurant. The developer is Arthur Tauck of Tauck Tours of Westport, a leading tour

310

Boats await summer stirrings in Southport Harbor.

company headquartered across the street. General manager Nick Carter said the inn faciliity would be unrivaled in Fairfield County, containing fifteen elegant guest rooms with private baths. Seven were to be suites, four of them with loft bedrooms. **Restaurant Zanghi** was scheduled to open first with contemporary French and Italian cuisine under the aegis of former Long Island restaurateur Nicola Zanghi. The restored 1873 structure, part of Westport's National Hall boardwalk and historic district, is on the National Register of Historic Places. It originally was the First National Bank and later a newspaper office and furniture store. Rooms were to start at $250, including breakfast.

Seeing and Doing

Because a warm spring day lures us out of doors as surely as an inclement one keeps us in, we've started with a sampling of Fairfield County's outdoor attractions.

The Dogwood Festival, Old Academy and Bronson Roads, Greenfield Hill, Fairfield, (203) 259-5596 or 259-2128. The festival is a five-day celebration of the pink and white dogwood trees first planted by a surgeon in the American Revolution. Dr. Isaac Bronson transplanted hundreds of trees from his own woods to the roadsides of the town. Today, there are more than 30,000. The women of Greenfield Hill Congregational Church, which crowns the hill, have conducted the popular festival for more than 50 years. Featured are a picnic luncheon in a large tent near the church and a seated luncheon for which reservations must be made well in advance, an arts and crafts show, a bazaar with handmade items for sale, walking tours of the district with many outstanding homes, and a daily music program in the church sanctuary. The early May event runs from Saturday through Wednesday, usually around Mother's Day. Free.

Connecticut Audubon Society/Fairfield Nature Center, 2325 Burr St., Fairfield, (203) 259-6305. The state's Audubon Society prides itself on predating the national organization. The 160-acre Larsen Sanctuary contains more than six miles of boardwalk trails, including a singing and fragrance walk for the blind, handicapped and elderly. A well-regarded birdcarvers' show sometimes coincides in May with the Dogwood Festival. The sanctuary is a managed wildlife area where visitors experience woodlands, meadows, streams, marshes and ponds. Sasco Creek meanders through the property, as do, at a slightly quicker pace, joggers. The society also operates the **Birdcraft Museum,** which highlights local natural history amid a six-acre wildlife sanctuary, at 314

Unquowa Road. Museum open Saturday and Sunday, noon to 5; donation. Nature Center, Tuesday-Saturday 9:30 to 4:30; free. Larsen Sanctuary, daily dawn to dusk; adults $1, children 50 cents.

Nature Center for Environmental Activities, 10 Woodside Lane, Westport, (203) 227-7253. Two great horned owls have been residents here but the main emphasis is the flora. An unusual wildflower atrium in the museum is especially lovely in the spring; species native to southwestern Connecticut are on view. The 62-acre site contains several trails, including one for the blind. The Swamp Loop is considered the best springtime trail; it takes a half hour and exhibits quite a few wildflowers. Open Monday-Saturday 9 to 5, Sunday 1 to 4. Adults $1, children 50 cents.

Bartlett Arboretum, 151 Brookdale Road, Stamford, (203) 322-6971. The only state-owned arboretum in Connecticut is run under the aegis of the University of Connecticut. "We specialize in rhododendrons and azaleas," says a staff member; in spring there are "a lot of wildflowers." The 64 acres of natural woodlands and cultivated gardens include major collections of dwarf conifers and native herbs. Allow three hours if you walk all five miles of trails. It's connected by a trail to the Stamford Museum and Nature Center to the south. Open daily, 8:30 to sunset. Free.

Woodcock Nature Center, 56 Deer Run Road, Wilton, (203) 762-7280. Two miles of hiking trails and a swamp walk are available at this 146-acre center encompassing portions of Wilton and Ridgefield. Trails open daily, dawn to dusk; donation. **The Weir Preserve,** a Nature Conservancy property straddling the Wilton-Ridgefield border, is on its way to becoming Connecticut's first national park. Once the estate of artist J. Alden Weir, it's now occupied by another artist and his wife. You can visit this house occasionally, but there's nothing else to do yet, other than enjoy the park and its trails.

Greenwich Audubon Center, 613 Riversville Road, Greenwich, (203) 869-5272. This is one of the five nature centers maintained nationwide by the National Audubon Society (another is in Sharon). Of 485 acres, 135 comprise the Audubon-Fairchild Garden, located on North Porchuck Road. Started in the early 1900s by donor Benjamin T. Fairchild, it is a fine example of naturalistic landscaping and includes all the ferns and flowering plants native to the state. Special events include birdwalks in late April and early May. An excellent visitor center, exhibit room, gift and book shop are found here. Open Tuesday-Sunday 9 to 5. Adults $2, children $1.

Southport Harbor, Harbor Road, Southport section of Fairfield. Southport was one of the earliest designated historic districts in Connecticut and its harbor area is like a stage set from the 18th and early 19th centuries. The houses around the small and exquisite harbor are impeccably maintained and a walk here is a must. The only surviving pre-Revolutionary homestead is the William Bulkeley House at 824 Harbor Road, which was remodeled in the Federal period. Of interest are the Pequot Yacht Club at 669 Harbor Road, which was once a warehouse; 789 and 825 Harbor Road, old storehouses, now residences; the Gurdon Perry House at 780 Harbor Road, and the Austin Perry House, 712 Harbor Road, whose Corinthian portico is one of the finest of its type on an American house. The two Perry houses, with number 750 between them, form a neo-classic composition unparalleled in Fairfield County, almost an Acropolis of Southport. You can rest and reflect on benches on a grassy strip along the water. To see how the modern elite lives, continue west onto Beachside Avenue and southeast onto Sasco Hill Road past the largest waterfront estates imaginable.

Beaches

If you're near salt water, you should take a walk or two on a beach (preferably deserted). This is not easy in Fairfield County since many towns restrict their beaches to residents. An exception is Westport, where lovely **Compo Beach** may be used by non-residents, although the parking fee is steep. **Calf Pasture Beach** in Norwalk offers a similar opportunity to get near the water. Fairfield allows non-residents to use **Jennings Beach** off Fairfield Beach Road for a parking fee.

Sherwood Island State Park in Westport, one of only six state beaches, is popular with nearby New Yorkers. In the spring it's likely to be less crowded. The beach is one and a half miles long and there are two large picnic groves near the water; we were surprised to discover mussels on the rocks here. Open 8 a.m. to sunset. Parking, $6 weekends, $4 weekdays.

The Inside Story

Ogden House, 1520 Bronson Road, Fairfield, (203) 259-1598. Maintained by the Fairfield Historical Society, this 18th-century farmhouse opens for the season with the start of the Dogwood Festival. Newlyweds Jane and David Ogden moved into the two-story saltbox during the spring of 1750; it is authentically furnished to the period. A favorite stop outside is the herb garden containing more than 40 varieties. Open mid-May to mid-October, Thursdays and Sundays 1 to 4. Adults $2, children $1.

Fairfield Historical Society, 636 Old Post Road, Fairfield, (203) 259-1598. This Georgian Colonial brick building faces the Town Hall Green, where the 1770 Town Hall still functions as the center of municipal activity. This pretty section is close to Long Island Sound and less than a block from the town's oldest burial ground along Beach Road. The society's collections span 350 years of Fairfield life. In the basement, early tools and household artifacts are displayed; on the second floor is a fine exhibit of children's toys and dollhouses. The costumes are outstanding but not always on display. An interesting diorama shows Fairfield as it was on July 7, 1779, the day the British burned it to the ground. Open Monday-Friday 9:30 to 4:30, Sunday 1 to 5. Adults $1, children 50 cents.

WPA Murals, Norwalk City Hall, 125 East Ave., Norwalk, (203) 866-0202. One of the nation's largest collections of Depression-era art is contained in the atrium and adjacent corridors of City Hall, converted from the old Norwalk High School. The 23 murals and eight panels were created for Norwalk High School by five local artists under President Roosevelt's Works Progress Administration jobs effort. They are among the few nationwide to have been saved and restored. The remarkable murals portray local history through industry, recreation and landmarks, showing oyster dredging, oyster houses and Calf Pasture beach, among others. Open Monday-Friday 9 to 5 and Saturday mornings by chance. Free.

Lockwood-Mathews Mansion Museum, 295 West Ave., Norwalk, (203) 838-1434. America's first chateau was constructed in 1864-68 as the country residence of a Norwalk-born New York stockbroker, LeGrand Lockwood. And le grand a place it is indeed. The four-story, 50-room granite structure has a host of unusual features: central heating, an attic water distributing tank that supplied fourteen bathrooms and twelve water closets with hot and cold running water, fabulous interior woodworking and parquet floors. The architect was Detlef Lienau, born in Denmark, and a famous residential designer of the period. The mansion is quite unusual in that it is in the process of restoration. Part of the movie, "The Stepford Wives," was filmed here. The house was saved from extinction in 1965 by a citizens' group and is now a National Historic Landmark. Open March to mid-December, Tuesday-Friday 11 to 3, Sunday 1 to 4. Adults $5, students $3.

Silvermine Guild Arts Center, 1037 Silvermine Road, New Canaan, (203) 966-5617. Founded in 1922 as a mecca for artists, the guild operates a number of arts and crafts classes and mounts changing exhibits in the brown and white barnlike building in a rural setting. The pond with wooden footbridge out back is an attractive backdrop for large sculptures; we enjoyed the yellow iris at the water's edge. A major annual exhibition is held in June. Open Tuesday-Saturday 11 to 5, Sunday noon to 5.

Bush-Holley House, 39 Strickland Road, Greenwich, (203) 869-6899. This was another gathering spot for artists, specifically the American Impressionists of the late 19th and early 20th century, and some writers as well. The brown clapboard saltbox dates from the late 17th century but many additions, among them the double cream-colored verandas out front, came later. When the artists (including Childe Hassam) and the writers (including Willa Cather) stayed here, it was a boarding house and the center of a creative colony in the Cos Cob section of town. Today, the elevated roadbed off I-95 passes in front, marring the view of Cos Cob Harbor. Check out the Childe Hassam etchings in the dining room and the pastels and oils in other locations. The Long Room, our favorite, stretches across the rear of the house with an exceptional refectory-type table and large plant-filled windows. Maintained by the Greenwich Historical Society, the house is extremely well furnished and is one of the finest historic house museums in New England. Open Tuesday-Friday noon to 4, Sunday 1 to 4. Adults $3, children 50 cents.

Putnam Cottage, 243 East Putnam Ave., Greenwich, (203) 869-9697. George Washington visited this Revolution headquarters in 1776, and Connecticut Gen. Israel Putnam escaped from the British here in 1779. The cottage contains furniture, decorative objects and Putnam memorabilia in a setting like that of its early Knapp Tavern days. Open Wednesday, Friday and Sunday 1 to 5. Adults $2.

Fairfield County Stage Company, 25 Powers Court, Westport, (203) 227-1072. The lights are on year-round now at the 50-year-old **Westport Country Playhouse,** considered one of the finest on the summer straw-hat circuit. In the off-season, which is to say fall to spring, the Fairfield County Stage Company, a professional Equity troupe, mounts eight plays for three-week runs (among them in 1992-93, "A Christmas Carol," "The Merchant of Venice" and "Two for the Seesaw"). Performances are generally Tuesday-Friday at 8 and Saturday at 9, with matinees Wednesday at 2, Saturday at 5 and Sunday at 3. Tickets, $17 to $19.

SoNo

This area of South Norwalk by the water is gradually being restored and fine restaurants and shops are moving in. But the maritime heritage of what once was the oyster capital of the world remains; it still has a model ship-building company, sailmaking companies, a large wood-boat builder, a floatable dock manufacturer and, yes, oyster boats. New major maritime attractions are the Maritime Center at Norwalk and Sheffield Island Lighthouse.

The Maritime Center at Norwalk, 10 North Water St., Norwalk, (203) 852-0700. This $30 million project is part history exhibit, part aquarium, part IMAX theater and part re-created working waterfront. A showcase for the maritime heritage and marine life unique to Long Island Sound, it's a high-tech, hands-on place of particular appeal to the younger set. The soaring entry hall houses the Patient Lady V, a Little America's Cup winner whose 36-foot mast is tilted sideways to fit beneath the skylight. Also here are a seal tank and the fascinating 24-foot-long Tango, in which Dwight Collins of Darien pedaled 2,000 miles across the Atlantic in 1992 from St. John's, Newfoundland, to Plymouth, England, setting a world record for the fastest human-powered crossing. The heart of the center is the aquarium, where twenty marine habitats contain more than 125 species indigenous to Long Island Sound — with a bit of a stretch to the open ocean

Folks gather around seal pool for feeding session at Maritime Center.

and "travellers from the tropics" in the biggest shark tank. Youngsters like the touch tank, where they can pick up two horseshoe crabs (if they dare). Here you learn of the rock crab that if you can see the Washington Monument etched on its tummy, it's a male; if a pineapple, a female. A boat builder is at work in the Maritime History Hall, at one end of which is a large oyster bar (open weekends) and the smaller Captain's Galley snack bar. Connecticut's only large-screen IMAX theater changes its production every six months. Sharks were the featured attraction at our latest visit to the new blue "tent" room, where exhibits change every nine months. Outside along the waterfront dock is the restored Hope, the last wooden-hulled, sail-powered oyster sloop to be built on Long Island Sound. Public excursions are available in summer on the R/V Oceanic, the center's research vessel. The center is located in a restored 19th-century foundry on the west bank of the Norwalk River. Open daily 10 to 5, to 6 in summer. Adults $7.50, children $6.50; IMAX Theater, $5.50 and $4.50; combination, $11.50 and $9.50.

Sheffield Island Lighthouse, operated by the Norwalk Seaport Association at 132 Water St., is a four-level, ten-room lighthouse constructed in 1868 and located on a small island off the coast. The three-acre site is accessed by the 60-passenger shuttle boat Island Girl. Visitors travel on the Norwalk River, through the harbor to the outermost of the thirteen Norwalk Islands in Long Island Sound for a guided lighthouse tour and optional picnicking or walking along the shore. Ferry departs from the Hope Dock next to The Maritime Center two to four times daily from May 23 to Labor Day; adults $9, children $7.

New England Brewing Co., 13 Marshall St., Norwalk, (203) 866-1339. This fledgling micro-brewery in downtown Norwalk planned to move into new quarters around the corner from the Maritime Center in mid-1993. State-of-the-art beer-making equipment and 120-barrel fermentation tanks were on order to produce its best-selling Atlantic Amber, Oatmeal Stout, Pale Gold Stock Ale and Holiday Ale. A brewing museum and a restaurant and brew pub with custom beers on tap also were in the works.

Shopping in SoNo is great fun. We're intrigued by **Beadworks,** where more than

4,000 beads nestle in hundreds of boxes and where you can make your own necklace of Chinese turquoise, blue lace agate, poppy jasper or what have you. **Earth Stuff!** (toys and tools for the environment) has ecology-minded toys, books and games like Save the Forest. **Fontana** offers trendy clothes by young California designers. **Faience** for French tableware, **Wirth-Salander** for a fantastic collection of tiles, **Chelsea Crossing** for funky clothes and **Charles of SoNo** for super children's clothes and presents are others. "Yer not much if yer not Dutch," says a picture at **A Taste of Holland,** with everything Dutch from gouda cheeses to wooden shoes to windmill magnets. **Sassafras** is an interesting gift shop, and lots of goodies beckon in the windows of **European Home Products,** with its 21 jars of coffee beans and many kitchen gadgets. At the **Brookfield/SoNo Craft Center,** you can visit artists' studios and shops for paintings, hand-woven clothing, sculptured candles, dried floral arrangements and more. If you need a little fuel to keep on shopping, drop into **Cafe Ole,** a cheerful little spot where you can get a latte (the coffee comes from Seattle, coffee capital of the world) with a shot of almond or hazelnut flavoring for $1.50. The brew here was named Fairfield County's "best cup of coffee" for 1992. By summer of 1993, the owner plans to serve California smoothies and coffee granita. Another place for espresso or cappuccino is **Darien Junction Ice Cream,** which also offers carrot-cake ice cream, peach-melba yogurt and "Samoa," toasted coconut, caramel and fudge. **European Home Products** serves fancy coffees, as well. If you want something a little more hearty, **Delilands Seaport** will serve you a triple-decker blue plate sandwich (one is turkey breast and tongue) with pickles and coleslaw for $6.95. All the pastries, like almond horns with Belgian chocolate, are made in house.

More Shopping

Shopping opportunities in these Fairfield County towns boggle the mind. From antiques shops to the junkyard of a famous wrecking company to high-fashion boutiques and decorator stores, this is Valhalla. The best way is to go to any of the town centers (do not miss Greenwich and Westport) and poke on your own.

Southport Center (Pequot Avenue is the main street here) has quality stores, especially a few antiques shops. The Fairfield Women's Exchange operates the finest shop of its sort we've seen.

United House Wrecking, 535 Hope St., Stamford (Exit 9 off I-95), is five acres of relics and nostalgia; you may find bits of stained glass from a demolished church, a balustrade of an old house or a lighting fixture that has seen better days. Interior decorators are known to poke around here; cast a creative eye on the merchandise and you may wind up with an appropriate addition for your own home. Open Monday-Saturday 9:30 to 5:30, Sunday noon to 5.

Actress June Havoc spearheaded and lent her name to **Cannondale Village,** a nifty addition to the shopping scene off Route 7 in Wilton. The grouping of pre-Civil War restored farm buildings, post office and a mill contains antiques and gift shops and the **Schoolhouse Cafe and Grill. Penny Ha' Penny** is ever-so-British; other special shops include **Annabel Green Flowers** and **Green Willow Antiques.**

Stroll along Greenwich Avenue, the main shopping street in Greenwich, and you might think you were on Madison Avenue on New York's Upper East Side, but for the lack of high-rises. Another small-town touch: friendly traffic patrolmen are posted at each corner, keeping pedestrians and vehicles moving. The store window displays exude big-city glamour. There are the requisite **Banana Republic, Laura Ashley, Gap, Benetton** and **Polo-Ralph Lauren** chain stores, as well as an old-line **Woolworth's** and a hardware store gone upscale. One-of-a-kind stores abound: **Irresistibles** stocks great sweaters among other women's apparel and **Now-a-Days** has casual clothing. **The Naked Zebra** offers high-style gifts, while **Applewood's** purveys all-natural products from Devon, England, including a line of fruit-flavored soaps that smell wonderful. **Rags** is anything but. The spirit and style of southern France prevails at **French Country Living.** We could fall for all the lovely clothes at **Amanda Fielding,** opposite a Putnam Avenue block of fashion that goes from **Ann Taylor** to **Talbots.** Stunning contemporary gifts are featured at **New Horizons.** Check out the lush **Astral Sweaters** from northern Italy. Clothing and gifts are featured at **Handblock,** while **Canyon Road** carries everything Southwest, from sandalwood soap to a purse we coveted with an egret on it (however, the $275 pricetag was about $225 too much). Cups of cappuccino go for $2 and $3.50 at **The Coffee Tree** — how the prices increase in Greenwich! But you still can get a breakfast of eggs, sausage, homefries, toast and coffee for $2.95 at **Gourmet Galley.**

Old Greenwich is lovely. The drive past the Perrot Library and Binney Park is worthwhile and the park is especially lovely in the spring when its stands of forsythia are in bloom. There's a variety of good shops beyond the railroad overpass.

Norwalk is a center for discount shopping. The **Factory Outlets at Norwalk,** 11 Rowan St. off East Avenue, contains two dozen outlets; we understand people come from all over for the Dooney & Burke leather handbags at the **Company Store.** We'd gladly head any time to **Bed, Bath & Beyond,** which seems to be mostly beyond: marvelous selections of placemats, china sets, lamps, household appliances and gadgets stacked ten feet high. Other favorites here are **Sabatier** for premium French cutlery, **Tanner** and **Harve Benard** for women's apparel, **Royal Doulton** china, **Top of the Line Cosmetics & Fragrances** and **Star Baby** for cute children's things. We used to visit the large **Loehmann's** and **Decker's** along West Avenue for women's and men's clothing at bargain prices, long before they branched outward. **Clark's Factory Shoe Outlet, Shoe Mart** and **R.C. Gibson Co.** for paper products are other standouts.

Called the "Disneyland of Supermarkets," **Stew Leonard's** on Westport Avenue (Route 1 east) in Norwalk is worth a trip just for the fun of it. Nearly 100,000 customers go through this enormous dairy and grocery store each week. In the heart of the store is a glass-enclosed dairy plant.

Other markets to visit include two locations of **Hay Day,** an upscale and pricey farm market with the kinds of plants and flowers, exotic fruits and vegetables, made-up dinners, spreads, desserts and much more the folks who live in the mansions around here might buy. Many of the spreads are set out for tasting. We bought a shepherd's pie to take home for dinner and it was outstanding. One market is on the Post Road in Westport and another on East Putnam Avenue in Greenwich. Another (the biggest and best, with a cafe and wine store, too) opened recently upcounty in Ridgefield.

Westport's two-block-long Main Street "has become a mall lately," in the words of a local innkeeper. The chains seem to have taken over at the expense of local shopkeepers. The litany is impressive: **Barneys New York, Eddie Bauer, Benetton, Banana Republic, The Gap, Laura Ashley, Ann Taylor, Coach, J.Crew, Williams-Sonoma** and who knows next. The bright pink **Remarkable Book Shop,** with its Left Bank book sale carried on in pink wood bins out front, the posh **Lillian August** home furnishings and accessories, the tiny but interesting **Clementine** gift shop and a couple of **Henry Lehr** clothing stores are some of the local names still here. There's also a showroom for **Simon Pearce,** the Irish glass blower based in Quechee, Vt.

The Fairfield Store, ever so elegant in the heart of Fairfield, purveys fashionable clothing for men and women, gifts and children's apparel, advertising on New York radio and keeping up with the times where other department stores have failed.

Where to Eat

Some of the best restaurants in the country are found in Fairfield County and there are lots of them.

Bertrand, 253 Greenwich Ave., Greenwich, (203) 661-4459. Frenchman Christian Bertrand, who was executive chef at Lutece in New York for twenty years, and his wife Michelle now have their own restaurant, and it is smashing. Located in the former Greenstreet restaurant — before that, the Putnam Bank & Trust — this establishment is beautifully done in pale apricots and peaches, even to the painted brick facade and the awnings outside. The interior space beneath a vaulted ceiling with gold-tone tiled domes is spectacular. Tables on several levels are set with Villeroy & Boch china in a swirled peach design. Chairs are a French wicker in green and cream. The French dinner menu starts with such extravagances as foie gras terrine with toasted raisin brioche ($25) or a galette of Russian caviars with crab ($35). Entrees run from $21 for chicken paillard to $28.75 for sauteed lobster flambeed with Jack Daniels and sea scallops in paprika. Vegetables are a la carte ($4.50 for spring carrots or spinach). A variety of frozen souffles, homemade sorbets and creme brulee head the dessert list ($8 to $9). Prices are only slightly less stratospheric for lunch (entrees, $17.75 to $22.75). The best value is the three-course prix-fixe lunch for $25. Bertrand's has met the high expectations of the sophisticated Greenwich diner and seems to be doing everything right. Lunch, Monday-Friday noon to 2:15; dinner, Monday-Saturday 6 to 10.

La Grange, Homestead Inn, 420 Field Point Road, Greenwich, (203) 869-7500. Since Lessie Davison and Nancy Smith took over the inn, Jacques Thiebeault has been the chef in its excellent restaurant. There is a relaxed elegance to the dining rooms, which include a main room with a large brick fireplace, an enclosed porch (the most popular spot) or a smaller room, elegantly wallpapered and cozy. Mismatched chairs at tables in the main dining room, slender vases with a couple of fresh flowers, white tablecloths and white Wedgwood service plates with floral borders make for an interesting setting, but the food is what everyone raves about. Chef Thiebeault changes the menu a couple of times a year, but perennially popular is the duckling with black currant sauce and wild rice. Several selections of veal, including veal kidneys with brandy, cream and mustard or veal sauteed with chestnuts, cream and cognac, are also favorites. Medallions of lobster with vegetables in a creamy wine sauce, rack of lamb garnished with fresh vegetables and sirloin steak finished with a black peppercorn sauce are other choices, all in the $25 to $33 range. Start with escargots served with pernod and herbs, chevre warmed with garlic butter or crabmeat Belle Haven (at $16 the most expensive appetizer). For lunch ($13 to $25), choices include salad nicoise, grilled mahi-mahi, cassoulet Toulosain, pot roast with garlic potato puree and grilled lamb. Dessert could be baked apple with gingered creme anglais, creme caramel or chocolate mousse. A new three-course Sunday brunch is priced from $18 to $24. Lunch, Monday-Friday noon to 2; dinner nightly, 6 to 9:15 or 10:15; Sunday brunch, 11:30 to 2:30.

Cafe du Bec Fin, 199 Sound Beach Ave., Old Greenwich, (203) 637-2447. Sous chef Joseph Cizynski took over this wonderful little French restaurant in the center of Old Greenwich in 1986 and enhanced the outstanding fare with a new emphasis on seafood. We like the ambience here, especially the sprightly wall murals and the blue Mexican tiles on the floor. Dinner might begin with seafood gazpacho, a seafood sausage or crab crepes with corn. For entrees ($22 to $26), try any of the three salmon dishes, soft-shell crabs with hazelnuts and orange, sea scallops with a fresh crabmeat sauce or roasted veal chop in pernod sauce. Among desserts in the $8 range are a white chocolate mousse, napoleons with fresh berries, coconut and hazelnut ice cream strudel and tartlettes with

318

coffee pastry cream and grapefruit. The extensive wine list contains many affordable choices. Lunch, Tuesday-Friday noon to 2; dinner, Monday-Saturday 6 to 9 or 10.

Restaurant Jean-Louis, 61 Lewis St., Greenwich, (203) 622-8450. By now you may wonder if there is anything other than French restaurants in Greenwich, and the answer is yes, but the French ones are outstanding. In any event, this tiny spot, located on a side street just off Greenwich Avenue, is particularly well-rated. Formerly known as Guy Savoy, the restaurant is one very small, pretty room. A full mirrored wall makes it seem bigger; the tables bear white cloths over lace undercloths and fresh flowers, and diners sit on mahogany chairs. Owner-chef Jean-Louis Gerin presides in the kitchen; his American wife, Linda (daughter of renowned chef Rene Chardain), handles the front of the house. Most diners opt for the five-course menu degustation ($60, two-person minimum), which changes daily and reflects the chef's broad range. Items on the regular menu include hors d'oeuvre like Linda's favorite endive salad with American caviars and creme fraiche ($16) and New York State foie gras slices on toast ($19). Warm vichyssoise with shrimp and a vegetable and mussel soup are each $7. Entrees ($25 to $29) might include fish fillet du jour sauteed on one side and then steamed on a bed of braised endive, sauteed lobster on a bed of thin-sliced potatoes and salad, sauteed sweetbreads with foie gras and black truffle essence, and filet of beef medallions with a gratin of potatoes and vegetable. Warm apple tart with creme anglaise and praline cheesecake are among desserts, and a sampler plate brings a taste of the day's repertoire. Lunch, Friday only, noon to 2; dinner, Monday-Saturday 6 to 9 or 10.

Terra, 156 Greenwich Ave., Greenwich, (203) 629-5222. Honest food of the earth is the theme at this trendy, crowded and noisy Italian newcomer in the heart of Greenwich. Ethnic music was played rather loudly at our visit as waiters in pink button-down shirts and khaki pants (shades of the 1950s) scurried back and forth beneath a striking, muraled cylindrical ceiling. Five gourmet pizzas ($11 to $13.50) emerge from a wood-fired oven. Dinner entrees ($18.50 to $26) on the changing menu might be wood-roasted striped bass with braised fennel, sauteed grouper fillet on vegetable ragout, wood-grilled lamb steak with braised tuscan beans and wood-grilled veal chop with prosciutto and tomato-zucchini timbale. Tirami su with espresso sauce and warm walnut tart with honey gelato are among sweet endings ($6 to $6.50). The shorter lunch menu is in the same vein, with pastas and entrees priced from $9.50 to $16.50. Lunch, Monday-Saturday noon to 2:30; dinner nightly, 6 to 9:30 or 10.

miche mache, 18 South Main St., South Norwalk, (203) 838-8605. Among the new kids on the block in the lively SoNo section in 1992, this engaging establishment was getting great reviews from food critics as well as locals. Named after young chef-owner Michel (Miche) Nischan of Belgian descent, it's a lively mishmash that defies categorization. There are two light and airy dining rooms with crisp white linens and brick walls, plus a few tables in the cozy midnight-blue bar accented with artworks. Miche is a master in the kitchen. His extensive lunch menu includes almond turkey salad in a radicchio cup, wood-grilled yellowfin tuna served over mesclun lettuces, a sandwich of grilled salmon on fresh watercress with a dill and grain mustard creme fraiche, and julienned scaloppini of venison over garlic-wilted spinach with wood-grilled eggplant. Prices are in odd numbers, from $5.34 for "just a burger" to $10.82 for wood-grilled tenderloin medallions with melted gorgonzola on sourdough toast. At night, you might start with pistachio rabbit sausage or herb-fried calamari with black bean salsa. Main courses go from $14.66 for ragout of chicken and black olives over linguini to $20.88 for pepper-roasted loin of rabbit over a caramelized leek and dijon cream with garlic mashed potatoes. Or pick one of the "miche mache items" — seared tuna, blackened chicken and andouille sausage with black bean salsa and garlic mashed potatoes, $29.02 for two to four, or a miche mache of game (venison loin and rabbit sausage with garlic mashed potatoes and sauteed lentils, $34.14 for two to four). Portions are so ample and the choices so tantalizing that such desserts as creme brulee and raspberry sherbet may be redundant. Personable Miche moves from table to table seeking suggestions and notes on his menu: "If you want it and we have it...we'll do it." Now that's accommodating. Lunch, Monday-Friday noon to 2:30; dinner, Monday-Saturday 6 to 9:30 or 11.

La Provence, 86 Washington St., South Norwalk, (203) 855-8958. Host Patrick Ravanello, formerly with Guy Savoy in Greenwich, and chef Eric Holveck draw plaudits for their charming storefront bistro that looks to be straight out of the south of France. The prices have always been a good value, especially the three-course prix-fixe lunch for $12 and the three-course dinner for $19.50 — both about $10 less than if ordered separately. The former might offer fish soup, seafood quiche provencal and marquise au chocolat; the latter, pate, bouillabaisse and kirsch mousse. Even a la carte, the prices are quite un-Fairfield-like, dinner entrees running from $16 for braised chicken piperade to $18.50 for veal stew. Baked salmon with lobster sauce on a bed of fettuccine, confit of duck, roasted lamb medallions with ratatouille and flageolet beans, and sirloin steak with green pepercorn sauce, gratin potatoes and vegetables — these are the kinds of dishes that revive memories of France. Lunch, Tuesday-Friday noon to 2:30; dinner, Tuesday-Saturday 6:30 to 9:30 or 10.

Pasta Nostra, 116 Washington St., South Norwalk, (203) 854-9700. One of SoNo's great restaurants, Pasta Nostra is also a pasta store where you can buy not only freshly made pasta but also good, coarse, peasant-style Italian bread, olives, olive oil and the like. Our lunch yielded the best Italian food we've had in Connecticut, from the Italian bread with just the right crispy crust to the choclate sponge cake with raspberries and whipped cream. We reveled in appetizers ($5) of soft bel paese cheese, sliced tomato and prosciutto and a ball of robiola cheese in the middle of toasted croutons covered with a black olive spread and a fettuccine ($8) with pesto, ricotta and pinenuts. The sophisticated menu changes frequently. Among recent dinner appetizers ($7 to $9) were clams oreganata, Sicilian seafood salad and a torta of gorgonzola and mascarpone with spicy olives and sundried tomatoes. Entrees from $12 to $18 included pan-fried soft-shell crabs with linguini, scallops and linguini with garlic and olive oil, tortellini tossed with cream and pancetta, polenta with sausage and black-eye peas, and steak Marcella (for Hazen) with linguini and caramelized garlic. If you can find room for dessert, you might want to try ricotta cheesecake or cold zabaglione with strawberries in cognac. Lunch, Tuesday-Friday 11:45 to 2:45; dinner, Thursday-Saturday 6 to 9:30.

Meson Galicia, 10 Wall St., Norwalk, (203) 866-8800. Lately moved to a restored brick trolley barn, this authentic Spanish restaurant is elegant and excellent. Genuine Spanish restaurants are hard enough to find, but this one also specializes in the cuisine of northwestern Spain. Plates of wondrous Iberian specialties arrive almost too picture-perfect to disturb. The food measures up, and then some. Luncheon might be a classic paella ($9.75) or a veal stew with chestnuts and vegetables. At night, a good range of tapas is offered, as are changing entrees ($14.95 to $22.50) like grilled veal chop with wild mushrooms and oloroso sherry sauce, roasted chicken with raisins and pinenuts, and veal sweetbreads with chopped pistachios in a lingonberry sauce. A fine selection of Spanish wines is available. Desserts include the typical Spanish flan, creme Catalan, almond tart and torta de frutas. Lunch, Tuesday-Friday noon to 2; dinner, Tuesday-Saturday 6 to 10 or 11, Sunday 5 to 9.

The Last Mango, 15 North Main St., South Norwalk, (203) 855-1236. Who wouldn't be intrigued by a new place with a name like this? It's one long storefront of a room,

Good restaurants and shops have congregated along Washington Street in SoNo.

with glass over floral tablecloths and good local art on the walls. Mango-pineapple sauce comes with the grilled chicken brochette appetizer and mango-pineapple relish with the grilled swordfish. The menu is affordably priced, from $5.50 to $10.95 at lunch, $9.95 to $12.95 at dinner. It ranges widely, from zucchini burger with tahini or falafel sandwiches to cobb salad, crab cakes with spicy remoulade, bay scallops stir-fry, sauteed shrimp and scallops over black pepper fettuccine and mixed grill trio with bearnaise sauce. Open Monday-Saturday, 11 to 10.

Rattlesnake Bar & Grill, 2 South Main St., South Norwalk, (203) 852-1716. Check out the 40-foot-long rattlesnake replica that tops the bar, curls out one end and wraps around a pillar in this casual new place in quarters vacated when the Sweptaway restaurant swept away. The spare decor is done with Southwest accents and the menu follows suit. You'll find buckaroo burgers, prairie pizzas, fajitas, "sage brush and tumbleweed" salads and a handful of entrees ($9.95 to $14.95) like Texas barbecued ribs, grilled swordfish with cilantro aioli, panfried rainbow trout with tomatillo salsa verde and grilled loin of lamb with goat cheese tortilla lasagna and tangy green chile sauce. Open daily, 11 to 10.

Silver Star Restaurant-Diner, 210 Connecticut Ave., Norwalk, (203) 852-0023. This "un-diner diner that's really a restaurant" advertises the best breakfast in Fairfield County. We headed over, got past all the cigaret machines and video games in the entry atrium and settled into one of the booths near the counter. Wham. We were assaulted by cigaret smoke on all sides, moved to another booth and wham. More smoke. We asked for a non-smoking area, so the waitress opened the main dining room, a glitzy mix of high-tech in lavender, burgundy, smoked glass, mirrors and chrome. A window table was the setting in solitude for the chef's omelet (an usual combination with sauteed escarole, mushrooms, scallions and onions, $3.95) and oniony homefries. The serving was so ample that it was shared with the light eater who had ordered only toast and cappuccino (topped, horrors, with whipped cream). The breakfast menu is prodigious, as is the rest of the menu, from burgers to veal parmesan, baklava to royal banana splits. Everything is extravagant at this place built by Greek brothers in 1980 as the world's first million-dollar diner. Some diner. Open daily, 6 a.m. to 3 a.m.

Da Pietro, 36 Riverside Ave., Westport (203) 454-1213. Generally considered the best of Westport's sea of restaurants is this small, stylish dining room dressed in oak wainscoting, tapestry banners on the walls, patterned banquettes and Villeroy & Boch china. The reputation of his sophisticated European fare keeps chef-owner Pietro Scotti's two dozen seats filled. Italian opera music plays in the background as you partake of the good life. Start with bruschetta, poached mussels in a raspberry vinaigrette or an exquisite warm seafood salad with belgian endive, radicchio, baby bibb and arugula. Entrees ($15.95 to $25.95) might be braised Norwegian salmon, veal in champagne sauce, rabbit bourguignonne, roasted duck with lingonberries and calvados or saddle of lamb with garlic and leeks. The pasta dishes also are highly rated. A three-course prix-fixe dinner with several choices is $38.95. Most of the masterful desserts are served on oversize plates whose edges are whimsically sprinkled with cocoa and powdered sugar. They include fresh fruit tart on a bed of creme anglaise, cappuccino velvet cake and a rich tirami su. Dinner, Monday-Saturday 5 to 10.

Sole e Luna, 25 Powers Court, Westport, (203) 222-3808. Hidden behind the Westport Country Playhouse, this fine new Tuscan ristorante seems "out in the country," according to young owner Felton Weller. The rear bar section opens onto a garden and deck and the main dining room opens onto a charming courtyard patio with a view of the park-like Barrons estate. Except for the tiled entry heading toward a window onto the kitchen with a table displaying the day's antipasti in front, the interior is simplicity itself. The large, soaring dining room with rustic posts and beams occupies what once was a tannery. White-clothed tables are well spaced and track lights and modern wall sconces provide subdued illumination. The only color comes from the food, starting with great peasant bread you dip in extra-virgin olive oil poured in a saucer. For lunch, we liked the robust white elephant bean and plum tomato soup topped by parmesan croutons ($5) and a special of air-dried beef with grilled radicchio, a rather paltry portion for $8.50. The grilled chicken sandwich with sundried tomatoes and arugula ($8.50) was masterful, though messy. For dinner, Felton and his wife Diana recommend the boneless stuffed quail roasted in the wood-fired oven, the osso buco and the lamb shanks among entrees priced from $18 to $23.50. Favorite starters ($5.50 to $9) are fresh squid grilled over fruitwood, wild mushrooms sauteed with fresh mozzarella and mixed game sausage of wild boar, venison and rabbit, served over polenta. The extensive wine list covers all price ranges except low. Lunch, Monday-Friday 11:30 to 3; dinner, nightly, 5:30 to 10 or 11; Sunday, brunch 11:30 to 3, dinner, 4 to 9.

Cafe Christina, 1 Main St., Westport 06880, (203) 221-7950. This is one beautiful restaurant, from the light and airy murals on the soft Mediterranean-colored walls to the clay pots of colorful flowers on each table, from the handpainted faux tabletops to the pillars and trellises overhead. Particularly striking are the trompe l'oeil windows at the top of the stairway and the Etruscan murals in the ladies' room. All the artists and decorators are given credit on the inside of the menu. You'd never guess this was the old Westport library, reopened in 1992 by New York restaurateurs William Galvin and Philip Murray. Chef Christine Galvin oversees a short menu combining specialties from southern France and northern Italy. Dinner entrees ($14 to $21) include grilled swordfish with grilled onions, trevisio, escarole and new potatatoes; roasted salmon with basmati rice and spinach; roast breast and confit of duck with cabbage, onions and caramelized apples; spaghettini with fennel sausage, broccoli rabe and pecorino romano, and ravioli with braised veal, vegetables, wild mushrooms and smoked caciocavallo cheese. Among starters ($6.50 to $7.50) are risotto fritter with grilled portobello mushrooms and arugula, and shaved fennel salad with prosciutto, parmesan, mushrooms and white truffle oil. Both also appear on the lunch menu, which ranges from $7.50 for pizzas, a hamburger or a grilled chicken sandwich to $15 for grilled swordfish or steak with frites. The grilled salmon salad with capers, olives and arugula appealed on the opening menu. Lunch, Tuesday-Friday 11:45 to 2:30, Saturday and Sunday to 3; dinner, Tuesday-Sunday 5:45 or 6 to 9:45 or 10:45.

Chez Pierre, 146 Main St., Westport, (203) 227-5295. In an age — and an area — of fast-paced, oft-changing life, perhaps it is the longevity of Chez Pierre that seems so comforting. There is solace in rediscovering this French bistro, reached by climbing a set of stairs from Westport's busy shopping district. Inside, red and white checked curtains, dark wooden beams, pierced tin lights, fireplaces and the aromas of hearty foods are inviting. For more than 25 years, Chez Pierre has been catering to its faithful clientele with traditional and good French fare. French onion soup, always on the menu, is served in a crock, hot and hearty. At lunch ($6.95 to $11.50), you might have an omelet, shrimp provencal, grilled salmon with stir-fried cabbage or a "rustic" salad of chicken, garlic sausage, parma ham, roasted peppers, flageolets, black olives and artichokes. Escargots, biegnets of shrimp piquant and salmon carpaccio are among appetizers. Creme caramel, peach melba, mousse au chocolat and a coupe romanoff au kirsch are classic desserts. For dinner, entrees run $15.75 to $24 for such items as veal sweetbreads, grilled loin lamb chops or duckling l'orange. A cafe menu is served in the bar Tuesday-Saturday 5 to 9:30. Lunch, Tuesday-Saturday from noon; dinner, Tuesday-Saturday from 6; Sunday brunch, 11 to 3.

Le Chambord, 1572 Post Road East, Westport, (203) 255-2654. Another classic French restaurant in a time warp, Le Chambord is still run by chef-owner Oscar Basler, who has developed a loyal following in more than twenty years at the same location. Two romantic dining rooms have trellised walls and tablecloths in peach, wall sconces for soft lighting and fresh flowers on the tables. There's an a la carte menu ($15.95 to $22), but the best deal is the complete dinner, three courses with an ample range of choices from $22.95 to $31.95, depending on the entree. You might start with a mousse of scallops in a green and garlicky mayonnaise, duck pate au poivre vert, quiche lorraine, marinated herring or artichokes vinaigrette. Seafood dishes include swordfish steak with bearnaise sauce, coho salmon with beurre blanc, fresh steamed twin lobsters or scampi provencal. Other choices might be duckling a l'orange, veal fillet dijonnaise, coq au vin and broiled boneless quail with raisins and wild rice. Grand marnier souffle, peach melba, crepes suzette for two, chocolate mousse and country cheesecake are favored desserts. Lunch, Monday-Friday noon to 1:30; dinner, Monday-Saturday 5:30 to 9.

Onion Alley, 42 Main St., Westport, (203) 226-0794. Down an alley and sequestered in an old onion warehouse is this casual spot. It's a charming barn of a place with artifacts on the paneled walls, tables and benches of wood and a loft overhead. The all-day menu combines soups, salads, sandwiches, pizzas, burgers and omelets in the $4.50 to $7.95 range with a handful of stir-fries and dinner entrees, $12.95 to $14.95. Try the grilled chicken with sundried tomato dressing over mixed greens and chevre or blackened Norwegian salmon with orange-mango chutney. Out front are delectable-looking salads to go in the **Food Company Deli** and desserts in season at the **Ice Cream Company.** A deck on the roof is used in summer. The owners also operate a sister restaurant, **The Wild Scallion,** at 480 Westport Ave. in Norwalk. Open daily, 11:30 to 10 or 11:30.

Soup's On, 111 Main St., Westport, (203) 227-2227. Perfect for lunching and takeout is this tiny establishment with a large deli case, tables for 24, bar stools at a counter and a changing blackboard menu. Oversize bowls of soup — perhaps french onion, beef and watercress, New England clam chowder or gazpacho — go for $7.50 with salad and bread. You also can order salads and heartier meals like turkey chili, macaroni and cheese, beef stew and mushroom-scallop quiche, $6.95 to $8.95. Key lime pie and apple crisp are favored desserts. There's a wine and beer license. Open daily 9:30 to 9 or 9:30, Sunday to 5.

Centro, 1435 Post Road, Fairfield, (203) 255-1210. You enter this trendy Italian eatery through a takeout area and pass a deli counter that gives one pause. You may be tempted by all the pastas or the bellagio — a sandwich of grilled chicken, bacon, avocado, lettuce, tomato and pesto mayo, packed to go for $3.25. And you can pick up a dinner of homemade pasta with sauce, caesar salad, Italian bread and marinated olives, also a bargain at $11.95 for two. Proceed onward to the long, narrow and nicely whimsical dining room with trompe l'oeil columns. Here we lunched memorably on a chicken pancetta salad with a powerful garlic and olive-oil dressing and a tasty farfalle al forno with three cheeses, sausages and peas. These were so filling we could only look longingly at the tirami su and the sweet potato pecan pie served up for dessert at the next table. The menu offers gourmet pizzas and sandwiches in the $6.50 to $7.95 range, four versions of carpaccio and luscious pastas for $6.95 to $8.95 at lunch, $10.95 to $14.95 (for red pepper spaghetti scampi) at dinner. The dinner menu adds entrees from the grill (also $10.95 to $14.95), among them shrimp wrapped with prosciutto, Sicilian sausage, marinated chicken with pesto butter and sirloin steak with balsamic vinegar. The owners also operate a newer Centro in a mill at 328 Pemberwick Road in the Glenville section of Greenwich. Lunch, Monday-Saturday 11:30 to 3; dinner nightly, 5 to 10 or 11.

Gregory's, 1599 Post Road, Fairfield, (203) 259-7417. We lunched at this small, inventive restaurant one chilly, gray April Saturday, our party of three taking over the one nice round window table where we could watch the passing scene on Fairfield's main drag. The narrow little spot has a front room with pale pink walls, off-white wainscoting, botanical prints on the walls, bare wood floors and interesting wood columns. The room out back with the bar is dark and cozy, painted a deep blue-gray and with a black and white tile floor. We passed on the soups (black bean and french onion) in favor of special entrees ($6.95 to $8.95): a cajun chicken and andouille sausage crepe and shrimp strudel, as well as an open-face turkey sandwich on rye with tomato and sprouts. The hot entrees were served with bright yellow couscous and sprigs of fresh dill. Other choices might be flatbread pizza, fajita sandwich or a charred steak salad. In the evening, entrees run from $13.95 for mandarin chicken to $17.50 for shrimp and scallops on a bed of bok choy or Long Island duckling with sundried cherry sauce. Among desserts are creme brulee and a white chocolate plum torte. Lunch, Monday-Saturday 11:30 to 3; dinner nightly, 5:30 to 10 or 11.

Breakaway, 2316 Post Road, Fairfield, (203) 255-0026. Breakaway is such an unpretentious place, and that's why the crowds like it. At a recent Saturday lunchtime you could barely squeeze into the small restaurant. The facade is a crazy mix of purples and greens. Breakaway satisfies the most basic of urges: you can get hamburgers plain, with American, Swiss, cheddar or mozzarella, with sauteed mushrooms, chili or jalapeno peppers. Then there are the "sensations" ($9.95 to $16.95), including grilled chicken, barbecued baby back ribs or barbecued combo, mixed grill and fresh seafood dishes, most served with steak fries and house salad. People rave about the fish and chips. Salads include chicken waldorf, cobb, taco and Greek ($5.95 to $7.95). Sandwiches aren't fancy but are filling. The "Royal Gorge: is a mountain of turkey, Canadian bacon, tomatoes, melted Swiss and Russian dressing for $6.95. Open daily, 11:30 to 10 or 11.

FOR MORE INFORMATION: Yankee Heritage Tourism District, 297 West Ave., Norwalk, Conn. 06850, (203) 854-7825 or (800) 866-7925.

21  Spring

Minuteman Statue stands sentry on Battle Green in Lexington.

Writers and Revolutionaries

Lexington and Concord, Mass.

Lexington and Concord. Just say the words and your patriotic blood stirs. As little as any American may know about his country's history, he has usually heard of the Battle of Lexington and Concord, which literally started the Revolutionary War the morning after Paul Revere's ride.

The battle was April 19, 1775, and because of it the two towns northwest of Boston are linked irrevocably. They take an understandable pride in that past. Not only do they stage re-enactments and parades each year to commemorate the events of the famous battle, but they've also preserved, for the visitor and for themselves, precious reminders of their feisty resistance to the British.

Lexington and Concord are not towns that have failed to emerge from the past, however. Proud and protective as they are of it, these Boston suburbs are thriving areas whose residents work in sophisticated 20th-century industries.

Their shops are tasteful, their homes gorgeous and their residents savvy. Their traffic can be horrendous at rush hour; Route 128, which rings Boston and swings close to Lexington, is infamous. Still, there is a sense here not only of preserving the past, but of living comfortably with it. And there is more to it than the Revolution.

In Concord, there are the writers. Possibly the richest town of its size in America in terms of literary output, it was home to Ralph Waldo Emerson, Henry David Thoreau, Nathaniel Hawthorne and Louisa May Alcott — all at the same time.

That was in the mid-1800s, and the writers found in this gently wooded town just the right atmosphere for their ideas. Happily, the homes and famed literary sites of the Concord authors are preserved and opened to the public as shrines.

And there is the Concord grape. Ephraim Wales Bull started with a wild Lambrusca grape and wound up with the purple variety that is so widely used today. His house on Lexington Road, known as the "Grapevine Cottage," is noted with an historic marker. A descendant of the original vine still lives.

In a way, much of the area is a shrine. You have the sense when you are there of walking on hallowed ground.

Students of early American architecture are delighted by the many fine examples of 18th- and 19th-century homes in both Lexington and Concord. It is a joy to view them at any season of the year.

Still, we're inclined to agree with the woman, a Thoreau scholar, who urged us one January day to "come back in the spring to Walden Pond; it's best then."

We've been back in the spring and we agree. There are lilacs in Lexington and dogwoods in Concord; there is the soft spring green not only at Walden, but in all of the parkland and wooded areas preserved as Minute Man National Park. There are the April celebrations for Patriots Day (including the nearby Boston Marathon). There are sun-softened days for canoeing on the Concord, the Sudbury and the Assabet rivers, which converge in Concord. This is the time to walk in the hillside hush of Sleepy Hollow Cemetery, where the authors lie.

A spring holiday from school is a good time to bring your children along, for we've never yet seen kids who didn't love to hear stirring stories of battles, to practice with their own make-believe muskets or to take home a souvenir tri-cornered hat.

In these times of uncertain national spirit, we can go back to Lexington and Concord, lest we forget.

Getting There

Lexington and Concord are located about twenty miles northwest of Boston and are easily reached by major automobile routes. Route 2, the Mohawk Trail, which crosses Massachusetts from west to east, goes right through Concord. Lexington is located near Route 128, the inner beltway around Boston. Concord and Lexington are linked by Route 2A, the Battle Road followed by Paul Revere on his famous Midnight Ride.

Trains run between Concord and Boston's North Station on the Boston & Maine line. Route 2 is the route followed by buses from western Massachusetts to Acton and West Concord.

Most major airlines, domestic and international, serve Boston.

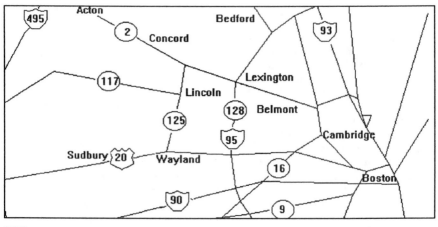

Where to Stay

It used to be that you could scarcely find an old house turned into an inn in the area, but the situation is improving. Concord has three B&Bs of interest. Longfellow's Wayside Inn in South Sudbury is within striking distance. Lexington hasn't a single venerable inn right in town. We prefer to stay in Concord because the town is quieter and more authentically kept; it's easy enough to make the trip to Revolutionary War sites and restaurants in Lexington.

Hawthorne Inn, 462 Lexington Road (Route 2A), Concord 01742, (508) 369-5610. Dating from 1870, this pale pink stucco house with lavender and deep pink trim is on the Battle Road in Concord. If its location didn't recommend it, the fine furnishings and warm hospitality of its innkeepers — Gregory Burch and Marilyn Mudry, husband and wife — would. Since we first stayed here in 1979, the inn has been updated, redesigned and redecorated so that each room is a treasure. All seven rooms, three on the main level and four on the second floor, have private baths. Six have double beds, one of which uses a handmade linen tablecloth as a canopy; one has maple twin beds that were originally rope beds. Almost all are covered with quilts made by Marilyn. Furnishings include items from the Sheraton, Federal and Victorian periods; bare wood floors are polished to a shine. We like the bay window and fireplace in the Emerson Room, and the black wallpaper with honeysuckles and the red bathroom in the Walden Room. Guests enjoy a common room where there's frequently a fire in the hearth. Gregory is an artist whose stunning contemporary pieces adorn the walls throughout. Marilyn serves homemade breads and fresh fruits for continental breakfast, taken at a long table in the dining room. "People love the pound cake that we make," says she. Sometimes there are cookies at check-in (if the couple's three children haven't reached the cookie jar first). Cribs and cradles are available for families. Doubles, $110 to $160.

The Colonial Inn, On the Green, Concord 01742, (508) 369-9200 or (800) 370-9200. Deep gray with white trim and dating from the early 1700s, this old inn meets the expectations of those who want a real early American inn, on a village green, with an old-fashioned dining room. There's even tea served in the afternoon. Innkeeper Jurgen Demisch, born in Germany, took over the hotel in the late 1980s after much experience with the Omni hotel chain. Since then, it has been upgraded throughout. Most of the 60 air-conditioned rooms are furnished with a period look and have four-poster beds, wide floorboards and beamed ceilings; all come with private baths, telephones and color television. Those in the main inn are a bit larger and more elegantly appointed than the seven in the adjoining Prescott Wing, which are decorated in country style. John Thoreau, grandfather of Henry David, lived in that part of the inn that houses the offices and the Thoreau Room. The main dining room, with beamed ceilings and wooden columns, is cozy, with lamps flickering on wood posts. Tablecloths are white and napkins a Colonial blue; the chairs are a comfortable captain's style with rust-colored leather seats. The Village Forge is a popular cocktail lounge, just the place to order a hot toddy. Doubles, $85 to $140.

Anderson-Wheeler Homestead, 154 Fitchburg Tpke., Concord 01742, (508) 369-3756 or (800) 338-3756. Innkeeper David Anderson was born in this large Victorian home, built in 1890, which he and his wife Charlotte opened as a B&B in the mid-1980s. After raising their seven children in the house, having a few guests didn't seem like much extra work. The original dark varnished wood is seen extensively throughout the main floor where guests breakfast in the dining room, read or chat as they sip sherry in the parlor, and warm their bones in a fireplaced library, which has a bowl of nuts to crack and a VCR for watching movies. Five rooms, three on the second floor that share two baths and two on the third floor sharing one bath, have been nicely decorated. We like the Blue Room with kingsize bed, fireplace and a view of the Sudbury River. The Peach Room on the third floor has a window seat perfect for curling up with a book. And the shower on the third floor is great — a large glassed-in enclosure in a room with skylights and plenty of space. Guests enjoy a continental-plus breakfast with two kinds of muffins or breads, fresh fruit, and hot or cold cereal. While the house has seen lots of living and is three miles from Concord center, it offers a good alternative for the guest who isn't too fussy. Doubles, $65.

Longfellow's Wayside Inn, Wayside Inn Road, South Sudbury 01776, (508) 443-1776. America's oldest inn, or so it claims, has ten guest rooms with a mix of king, queen, double and twin beds. They are decorated in Colonial style and proudly claim no TV or radio, and they tend to be booked far in advance. Henry Wadsworth Longfellow spent a night in one of the rooms, then wrote *Tales of a Wayside Inn,* but no one seems to know exactly which room he used. The pleasure of staying here is enhanced by the Colonial dining room (see Where to Eat) and the Martha Mary chapel on the grounds, where you're likely to witness a wedding, since more than 400 are held here annually. It was the Ford Foundation that so generously restored the inn, the oldest section of which is the Old Barroom, dating from 1702. Now it is operated by a non-profit trust. Antiques and charm abound and the rates are reasonable, especially when you consider that a full breakfast is included. Doubles, $85.

Battle Green Inn, 1720 Massachusetts Ave., Lexington 02173, (617) 862-6100 or (800) 343-0235. Renovated in 1987, this establishment smack dab in the center of Lexington — with a red neon sign — is a good choice, well-priced for its location and its amenities. Inside the complex (with parking below) are 96 guest rooms with reproduction furnishings and mostly four-poster beds. Some small rooms have baths with shower only. A plant-filled atrium contains a heated pool under a large skylighted roof. In front of the doors to each unit are white picket fences. Unfinished country pine furniture in the lobby is particularly attractive, and you can get coffee and donuts there in the morning. Doubles, $56 to $59; a large efficiency with living room, bedroom and kitchen is $105.

Sheraton Tara Lexington Inn, 727 Marrett Road, Lexington 02173, (617) 862-8700. Conveniently located between Concord and Lexington, this attractive two-story motel's 119 rooms were renovated in 1991. Most rooms contain two double or queensize beds and reproduction period furniture. A simple lobby with Chippendale-style loveseats is quite pleasant. There are a dining room and lounge, exercise room and outdoor pool. Doubles, $99 to $139.

Howard Johnson Lodge, Routes 2 and 2A, Concord 01742, (508) 369-6100. This 106-room lodge is typical of the chain, but it is very well-kept and there's a good Italian restaurant, Papa-Razzi, right next door. A jacuzzi accommodating four and a small fitness center are available, as is an outdoor swimming pool. Doubles, $70 to $88.

This Old House B&B, 12 Plainfield St., Lexington 02173, (617) 861-7057. Three attractive guest rooms, all with up-to-date baths, are found in this B&B named for the PBS television special. Half of a side-by-side duplex, it was renovated by the show's crews in 1988. Located about two miles south of Lexington center, the front of the house retains some of its 1909 features and woodwork; toward the rear is a large addition with skylights and decks. Innkeeper Mary Van Sinek serves breakfast at a large table in the dining room. Guests enjoy a television-equipped sitting room on the main floor or an upstairs book nook with a window seat. A refrigerator and microwave are available upstairs for guests. Two bedrooms are on the second floor, one with twin beds and the other, a double. A handicapped-accessible single is on the main floor. Doubles, $70.

Monument marks historic site at Old North Bridge.

Bed and Breakfast in Cambridge and Greater Boston, Box 665, Cambridge 02140, (617) 576-2112. Accommodations in private homes and apartments are offered through this B&B service. At last check, rooms in this area were available in Lexington, Lincoln and Bedford. Doubles, $60 to $85.

Places of Interest

Food for thought takes precedence over the bodily sort when you're in Concord and Lexington. The battle that started the American Revolution is commemorated by a Massachusetts state holiday, Patriots Day, on the Monday closest to April 19. That's also the day of the famed Boston Marathon. Lexington and Concord stage special events.

In addition to Revolutionary War sites in both towns, Concord is renowned for its literary lights and landmarks. Other special places, not specifically connected with revolutionaries or writers, are also worth a visit. And the shopping is interesting.

Revolutionary Sites

Start in Lexington, which is where the British did, early on that chilly, April morning more than 200 years ago. Appropriately, Lexington's common is known as Battle Green, and this is where it all began. Some 800 troops marched onto the green to be met by a tiny band of 50 Minutemen. When they refused to disperse as ordered, the British opened fire, killing eight and wounding ten. The others scattered and the British went on to Concord's North Bridge.

The Chamber of Commerce Visitors Center, in a Colonial house just off the green, is open daily 9 to 5 (shorter hours in winter).

The **Minuteman Statue** on the Battle Green, erected in 1900, was done by the Boston sculptor, Henry Hudson Kitson. The base is rough fieldstones, raising the statue to a symbolically appropriate height.

The **Lexington Historical Society,** (617) 861-0928, operates three historic houses on or near Battle Green. All are open mid-April through October, daily 10 to 5, Sunday 1 to 5. Adults $2.50 each house, children 50 cents; combination ticket $4.50.

Buckman Tavern, across from the Green, dates from 1710 and served as the rendezvous for the Minutemen before the April 19 battle. Among the bullet holes lodged in the structure is one that marred the front door during the first shots of the Revolution. The interior today appears much as it did in 1775. The original seven-foot-wide taproom fireplace and a portrait of John Buckman, the tavern proprietor, are of interest.

The **Hancock-Clarke House** nearby on Hancock Street is where Paul Revere alerted Samuel Adams and John Hancock during the night of April 18, 1775, that the British were coming. The house, built around 1698, served as the parsonage for the Rev. John Hancock, grandfather of the Revolutionary statesman with the famous signature. At the time of the famous battle, Hancock and Adams were visiting the Rev. Jonas Clarke, another minister, here. The house contains furnishings and portraits owned by the Hancock and Clarke families.

The **Munroe Tavern** at 1332 Massachusetts Ave. was used as headquarters and as a hospital by the retreating British after their surprise defeat in Concord. Dating from 1695, the house also was visited by George Washington in 1798 when he was traveling through New England, and visitors can see the southeast room on the second floor where he stopped. The tavern is kept as a museum of home life in Colonial times.

All around Battle Green are stellar examples of 18th- and 19th-century houses and churches, and a walk is highly recommended. You might want to look in at the **Old Burying Ground** at the rear of the First Parish Church behind the green, where the oldest stone is dated 1690.

Minute Man National Historical Park, (617) 862-7753. This is a misnomer for this "park" is really a number of different sites, exhibition areas and historic markers commemorating the famous battle. Among the units:

Battle Road Unit, Route 2A, Lexington, approximately half a mile east of Route 128. The visitor center is open daily 9 to 5 except January-March. A 22-minute film about the battle is shown here.

Paul Revere Marker, a short distance down the road toward Concord, marks the site where Revere's famous ride ended. Revere was forced from his horse by a group of six British soldiers. One of the men traveling with him, Dr. Samuel Prescott, escaped and carried the alarm the rest of the way to Concord.

North Bridge Unit off Monument Street, Concord. The wooden North Bridge over the slow-moving Concord River is a source of pride for Concordians and all Americans. About 400 Minutemen were waiting for the 200 British soldiers who arrived about 7 o'clock in the morning on April 19. The Americans were not only ready and willing to fight, but their observances of Indian methods, especially firing from behind trees, made them able as well. The British retreated before long.

When we visited, canoeists paddled along the river beneath the bridge, visitors picnicked nearby and a couple in Colonial dress answered questions — an entrancing scene. Park rangers lecture periodically.

Concord's historic **Minuteman Statue,** sculpted by the famous Daniel Chester French, is on the path just beyond North Bridge. French is buried in Concord in Sleepy Hollow Cemetery, the final resting place of most of Concord's literary greats. A museum, the **North Bridge Visitor Center,** (508) 369-6993, is on the hill above the

Minuteman statue at North Bridge.

North Bridge and can be reached by footpath or by car from Liberty Street. It's open daily year-round.

The **Wright Tavern** in Concord center near Monument Square was the place where the British commanders Col. Francis Smith and Maj. John Pitcairn made their headquarters while the British occupied Concord. It now houses an unusual gift shop (see Shopping).

Concord Museum, 200 Lexington Road, Concord 01742, (508) 369-9609. This is one of the finest small museums we've visited. A large expansion in 1991 added considerable space for changing exhibitions and made the place handicapped-accessible. It also added an orientation theater. For the Revolutionary War buff, there is a splendid diorama of the fight at Concord's old North Bridge, which heightens the visitor's understanding of the event. You'll also find one of the two lanterns that were hung in the spire of Boston's Old North Church on the night of Paul Revere's ride. But there is much more. Fifteen period rooms, arranged in sequence from 1680-1860, vividly depict the growth and evolution of one of America's most significant early communities. From the stark "keeping room" to the Empire Parlor, the decorative arts and domestic artifacts, either owned by Concord-area residents or made by Concord craftsmen, are attractively displayed. The study of Ralph Waldo Emerson, furnished as it was at the time of his death, was brought to the museum from his house across the street. The Thoreau Room, which was due to be moved to make way for more memorabilia, contains the bed he made, the flute he played at Walden Pond, his spyglass, walking stick and snowshoes. Alcott memorabilia includes a copper kettle used by Louisa when she was a nurse in the Civil War. If you have time to visit only one museum in Concord, this should be it. Open Monday-Saturday 10 to 5, Sunday 1 to 5; slightly reduced hours January-March. Adults $5, children $2.

Patriots Day Events

Lexington, Concord and the State of Massachusetts have had trouble getting their acts together on the celebration of the famous day. A few years ago, the state moved the traditional anniversary of the battle to the Monday closest to April 19 to make a three-day holiday. Things got confusing, however, because Lexington and Concord had always celebrated the event on the actual anniversary and were reluctant to change.

For a while, one town was celebrating on the 19th and the other was going with the state, which made it impossible for the visitor to do both in one day. To be sure of what is going on the year you plan to visit, check with the local Chambers of Commerce after January.

What happens?

Lexington re-enacts the original battle with the British on the Battle Green at 6 a.m.; natives say this is the most fun of any of the celebrations. A small local parade follows in which Girl Scouts, Boy Scouts and other civic groups participate. In the early afternoon, a larger parade with floats, marching fife and drum corps units, town officals — the works — makes its way down Massachusetts Avenue for a couple of hours.

Concord has a spirited parade that usually begins around 9 a.m. at the North Bridge. Groups gather and then march into the center of town. One of the civic clubs sometimes sponsors a pancake breakfast until noon.

The Literary Legacy

Concord's literary heritage is incredibly rich and, as you walk around town, it's easy to imagine the 19th-century writers feeling at home here. The very air seems rarified. The old homes are beautiful but not pretentious, and the nearby hills and woods were places in which the writers might ponder the issues of the world and the age. Concord today is not so different from the Concord of Emerson, Hawthorne, Thoreau and the Alcotts; one imagines them resting in peace in Sleepy Hollow Cemetery.

School of Philosophy at The Orchard House.

The Orchard House, Lexington Road (Route 2A), Concord, (508) 369-4118. The Alcott family came here in 1857 when Louisa May, author of *Little Women,* was already in her mid-twenties. Her father, Bronson, a great friend of Emerson's and one of the Transcendentalists of the early 19th century, spent a year having two early 18th-century houses on the site joined together and renovated. The Alcotts lived here for twenty years; the house became the setting for *Little Women,* the most widely published children's book in the world. We like Louisa's "mood pillow," a sausage-shaped pillow on the living room sofa; the author would let the rest of the family know when she was not in a good mood by putting the pillow in a certain position and they would leave her alone. Upstairs are costumes used by the Alcott girls (then young women) when they gave their famous plays. Louisa's sister, May, was an accomplished artist who had a studio in the house; the visitor may view some of her works. Outside is the **School of Philosophy,** a barn-like structure for the school started by Alcott and Emerson in 1879. Great thinkers of the day studied and spoke here; the spirit is continued in summer evening events sponsored by the school. In front of the house are the fruit trees from which it took its name. Guided tours of the house and grounds are given April-November, daily 10 to 4:30, Sunday 1 to 4:30. Adults $4, children $2.50.

The Wayside, Lexington Road, Concord, (508) 369-6975. The Alcotts stayed here while their own Orchard House, down the road a few hundred feet, was being renovated. But the house is more closely connected with Nathaniel Hawthorne, who lived here in 1852-53 and from 1860 until his death in 1864. Although originally only four rooms, the house now rambles in different directions. Hawthorne added the third-floor study with large chimney and gables. Some years after the Hawthornes, the house was bought by publisher Daniel Lothrop, whose wife, Margaret Sidney, was author of the *Five Little Peppers* series. Open late spring to October, Friday-Tuesday 10 to 5; tours on the hour. Adults $2, children free.

Emerson House, Cambridge Turnpike, Concord, (508) 369-2236. This great white house was Ralph Waldo Emerson's home from 1835-1882 and contains a wealth of family memorabilia. The study is a replica since the genuine articles are across the street at the Concord Museum, but there's plenty of authenticity here among the books, personal effects and furniture. A guided tour takes about a half hour. Open mid-April through October, Thursday-Saturday 10 to 4:30, Sundays 2 to 4:30. Adults $3.50, children $2.

The Old Manse, Monument Street, next to the North Bridge, Concord (508) 369-3909. This was the home of Concord's early ministers, including the Rev. William Emerson, grandfather of Ralph Waldo, who was living here on April 19, 1775. Ralph Waldo Emerson also lived here at various times. Here also Nathaniel Hawthorne brought his bride, Sophia Peabody. The house is marvelously restored and filled with original furnishings from several generations of descendants of Mrs. William Emerson. Charming mementos of the Hawthorne residency are the inscriptions on several window panes, cut by Sophia's diamond ring. The Hawthornes called the house "their Eden" and referrred to each other as Adam and Eve in their early nuptial bliss. Set far back from the road, the house was the inspiration for Hawthorne's *Mosses from an Old Manse,* which he wrote on a tiny board desk in an upstairs back bedroom. Open mid-April to May 31, weekends only; June-October, daily except Tuesday 10 to 5, Sunday 1 to 5. Adults $4, children $2.50.

The Thoreau Lyceum, 156 Belknap St., near the Concord Depot, Concord (508) 369-5912. This house is undistinguished except for the site, which is next to that on which one of the houses occupied by the Thoreau family stood. That house was destroyed by fire. Allow at least an hour if you have a guide as learned and as much a fan of Thoreau's as was ours. Thoreau memorabilia here include actual surveyor's maps he made, dried botanical specimens (he mounted more than 1,000, we were told), the desk at which he is believed to have written *Walden* and some of his father's company's pencils. Out back is a replica of the cabin at Walden Pond, a shrine for Thoreau followers, of which there are thousands — our guide said more foreigners visit here than Americans. Did you know Thoreau changed his name from David Henry to Henry David while he was a student at Harvard? Or that he is the only one of the famous Concord authors actually born in the town? The Lyceum, run by the private Thoreau Society, sells used and new books related to Thoreau and the Transcendentalists. A visit here is recommended before seeing Walden Pond and the site of Thoreau's cabin. Open daily 10 to 5, Sunday 2 to 5. Closed January and open weekends only in February and March. Adults $2, children 50 cents.

Walden Pond, Route 126 (Walden Street), a half mile south of Route 2, Concord. You can follow the white-circled Ts on the trees to the site of Thoreau's cabin, an easy walk along the water's edge. Thoreau lived here for two years from 1845 to 1847, producing the classic work, *Walden*. The site, rediscovered in 1945, is marked by a circle of stones. Nearby is the plaque with Thoreau's famous words on his reasons for the experiment: "I went to the woods because I wished to live deliberately, to front only the essential facts of life, and see if I could not learn what it had to teach and not, when I came to die, discover that I had not lived." The area is now a state reservation. Concord kids swim off the dock at the entrance to the spring-fed pond; we encountered some skinny dippers in a cove as we walked the path to the cottage site one warm May day. The swimming is seasonal, but you can walk to the cottage site anytime. There's a reproduction of Thoreau's cottage — fully furnished — next to the parking lot across the road from the pond. Parking, $5.

Concord Free Library, junction of Main Street and Sudbury Road, Concord (508) 369-5324. This is some library — not only a lovely building, built in 1873, but a repository for collections by the Concord authors in special cabinetry in the lobby. Busts of the authors, four by Daniel Chester French, are here, as is a case containing Thoreau's surveying instruments and pieces of the original cabin at Walden Pond. The oak-paneled reading room provides just the right atmosphere for scholarly research. There's a fine diorama of old Concord, a collection of editions of Walden in many languages and, of course, works of Emerson, Alcott and Hawthorne. Upstairs in the balcony art gallery are changing exhibits. Open Monday-Thursday 9 to 9, Friday 9 to 6, Saturday 9 to 5, Sunday 2 to 5 except summer.

Sleepy Hollow Cemetery, Route 62 (Bedford Street), Concord. Concordians like to stroll with their friends or their dogs through this large, hilly cemetery near the center of town. Enter the main vehicle gates (the second set of stone and wrought-iron gates from the center of town) to reach Authors Ridge and you can find the graves of the Thoreau family, the Alcotts, the Emersons, the Hawthornes and sculptor Daniel Chester French, whose stone says he left us "a heritage of beauty."

Other Sights and Sites

The **Grapevine Cottage** at 491 Lexington Road, Concord, was the home of Ephraim Wales Bull, who planted the seeds of a wild Lambrusca grape found growing on the hillside. After three generations it became, in 1840, the famous Concord grape. The house is privately owned; you can stop at the gate outside to read the plaque and see the small grape arbor by the side of the house. Many Concord families chauvinistically grow the Concord grape in their yards.

Museum of Our National Heritage, Marrett Road, Lexington, (617) 861-6559. This Bicentennial gift to the nation from the Scottish Rite Freemasons is unusual in that they generally put their money into hospitals and medical centers. Since its opening in 1975, the sprawling brick place (four galleries, two atria, a large auditorium) has presented all sorts of exhibits from one on Amish quilts to a major one from the British Library on Sir Francis Drake. Focusing on changing exhibits, the museum has only two permanent galleries, one devoted to the heritage of revolutionary Lexington, "Let It Begin Here," and another to the history of the Masons, of which Benjamin Franklin was a member. Special auditorium events are scheduled frequently on Sunday afternoons. A large gift shop contains wares from other museums, such as Old Sturbridge Village, in addition to its own items. The contemporary building somehow fits into Colonial Lexington quite comfortably. Open daily 10 to 5, Sundays noon to 5. Free.

DeCordova Museum, Sandy Pond Road, Lincoln (617) 259-8355. Given the questionable taste and worth of his private collection, the art museum that honors Julian DeCordova is not only a monument, it is almost a miracle. In DeCordova's turreted hilltop mansion, the museum presents the art of living New England artists — the only museum in the country to so concentrate. The exhibitions are generally very good. The 35-acre site is stunning and the museum uses it well for summer band concerts in an open-air amphitheater and several other special events, and for displaying contemporary sculpture. It is a great place to stroll or picnic. Open Tuesday-Thursday 10 to 5, Friday 10 to 9, Saturday and Sunday noon to 5. Adults, $4; children, $3.

Drumlin Farm, Route 117, Lincoln, (617) 259-9807. Part of the Massachusetts

Canoeists paddle along river near Old North Bridge.

Audubon Society, whose headquarters is across the street, this 220-acre New England farm with animals is a delight for youngsters. There are changing programs according to the season, walking and hiking trails, a picnic area and the animals, mostly of the barnyard variety. What is really special for adults here is the gift shop, one of the best conservation and nature-oriented ones we've seen. There are family programs and usually hayrides every Saturday and Sunday. Open Tuesday-Sunday 9 to 5. Adults $5, children $3.50.

A Canoe Trip

A spring trip to this area really ought to include a canoe trip down the Concord, Assabet or Sudbury rivers (they all come together here). Such a trip — only a longer one — was immortalized by Thoreau in his first published book, *A Week On the Concord and Merrimack Rivers.*

Rent a canoe from the South Bridge Boat House, Main Street, Concord (508) 369-9438, a beehive of activity on a sunny spring or summer day. It's open April-October, Tuesday-Friday noon to 6, weekends and holidays 9 to 6. You can paddle to North Bridge — we found this especially fun and scenic on a warm spring day — or you can go off for more than twenty miles of water travel.

Shopping

Lexington is about twice the size of Concord in terms of population, but has about half as much interesting shopping from our point of view.

One bright spot is **La Tienda,** a little Mexican shop on Meriam Street off Massachusetts Avenue. It's a non-profit venture that benefits Lexington's sister city in Mexico, Dolores Hidalgo. Brass angels carrying candles come in three sizes and make wonderful Christmas gifts. We also liked the Christmas trees in bright colors and nifty pillows, jewelry and wall decorations. Lexington's relationship with its Mexican sister city has continued for more than 25 years, kept alive by a very interested group of citizens.

The **Candy Castle** on Massachusetts Avenue and **The Balloon Shop** are both places hard to pass with young children. The latter carries unusual toys. **Goodies to Go** is a gourmet deli with luscious baked goods; it sells wonderful scones from Concord Teacakes in Concord, but makes most of its own baked goods and salads. At the **Coffee Connection** on Mass. Ave., you can buy from a wide selection of coffees and teas or stop for a cup of cappuccino or espresso and a homemade muffin or croissant. The place is always mobbed and the aroma of coffee is wonderfully enticing. **Steve's** sells very good ice cream, just a few doors away.

In Concord, check out the **Wright Tavern,** Monument Square, which is not only an historic building but a good place to browse. The five downstairs rooms are operated as the Tri-Con Shop, a non-profit shop run by the women of Trinitarian Congregational Church. Actually, the building is owned by the Unitarians; talk about ecumenism! One of our favorite rooms is the one with paper and party goods, but you also can get your child a tri-corner hat in the room devoted to historically oriented souvenirs. China, pewter, brass and table goods are also sold.

The pewter is magnificent at **John Anthony's** pewter shop in the basement of The Colonial Inn. You can buy mugs that say Concord or, if you want to break the bank, a beautiful coffee and tea service. There are also great gifts, not all pewter, like baskets and teddy bears, and a nice selection of cards.

The **Concord Depot** on Thoreau Street stocks quilts, pottery, placemats and napkins, toys and paper goods, all of the highest quality. Across the street, **Spice & Grain** has more kinds of tea for sale than we've seen under one roof. The **Mary Curtis Shop** in Concord carries local New England crafts, plus special items like opals from Australia. **Montagu's** also has a great range of gifts. **The Concord Shop** is the last word in kitchen shops. **Concord Hand Designs** has some interesting dried flower arrangements and wreaths. Gourmet goodies can be found at **The Cheese Shop** and great china and glassware at **Cooley's Marco Polo. The Concord Bookshop** on Main Street is a good place to buy your reading material. And don't forget the gift shops at the literary sites and the Concord Museum.

In West Concord, you can visit a couple of unusual factory outlets. The **Potting Shed** is the outlet for Dedham Pottery, manufacturers of that very special crackle glaze pottery with bunnies on it. We bought a plate for deviled eggs, with the dearest bunny sitting in the center, and used it for an Easter Sunday brunch with friends. At the outlet we also found a new pattern, the Concord Grape.

Also in West Concord is the outlet store for a mail-order business called **bear-in-mind.** This is the ultimate shop for the teddy bear lover, and you can buy not only bears but T-shirts, aprons, books and more with bears on them.

Where to Eat

Aigo Bistro, 84 Thoreau St., Concord, (508) 371-1333. New in 1992, this restaurant at the Concord Depot is owned by Moncef Meddeb, the mastermind who opened the fantastic L'Espalier in Boston a few years back, and Pierre Jospe. The chef, Ana Sortun, is highly praised. The two dining rooms are done in a sophisticated Mediterranean style. The front room overlooks the railroad tracks below and in the back room is a huge contemporary painting reminiscent of a Mediterranean village by the sea. Tangerine pink walls and bright green trim add to the feeling of sunny southern climes; the word "Aigo" is an ancient Provencal word for garlic, a much-used ingredient in many of the Mediterranean-inspired foods here. At lunch, you might start with "Aigo Bouido," a roasted garlic and squash soup, served with grilled bread. The house salad ($4.50) is greens dressed with balsamic vinaigrette and cabrales cheese. Lunch entrees ($6 to $8) include grilled chicken breast on focaccia with Moroccan eggplant relish and greens, spicy chorizo sausage on country bread with apple-onion relish, and Aigo codcakes with pinenuts and raisins served with tomato-saffron sauce and crispy fried onions. In the evening, consider starting with a tapas plate of roasted peppers, sweet onions, Spanish-style salads and marinated goat cheese, grilled stuffed squid with chorizo, almonds and breadcrumbs, or seared tuna with Moroccan chermoula, green olives and eggplant chips. Among entrees ($15 to $17) are braised lamb shanks with flageolets, tomato, and rosemary and chick pea polenta; roasted veal shoulder stuffed with leeks, sage and juniper, and grilled duck breast with Spanish mole sauce, roasted acorn squash and wilted chicory. The lamb shanks and veal dishes are among the most requested, we hear. If you have room for dessert, try red wine flan, chocolate mousse with an orange tuile cookie or poached fruit in a daily special preparation, all $5.95. Lunch, Monday-Friday 11:30 to 2:30; dinner nightly, 5:30 to 10.

Le Bellecoeur, 10 Muzzey St., Lexington, (617) 861-9400. The influence of Dutch owner Frans van Berkhout is felt throughout for, while not in the kitchen, he runs a tight ship and demands excellence. Success over sixteen years indicates he's doing things right. We dined here early on a Saturday evening with two children when they were little, and the accommodating waitress allowed them to share an order of tournedos. The soup of the day was puree of Mongol, something we find too rarely available. Since then, van Berkhout has continued to offer a formal dining experience in the rear dining room, but has changed the front room to the **Cafe Bellecoeur** with lighter fare and a more relaxed atmosphere. At lunchtime, when the same menu is available both in front and back, you can eat either in the more lively bistro atmosphere or in the romantic, pink-clothed room with fresh flowers. There's a good selection of salads, including caesar with or without grilled chicken, a chalupa salad in a fried flour tortilla shell or a cafe garden salad. Or you might start with Mediterranean seafood chowder, panfried oysters or pumpkin raviolis. Sandwiches include grilled chicken breast; entrees ($7 to $8.50) might be vegetarian lasagna, garlic and rosemary roasted half-chicken, and braised duck on fettuccine. Two menus are available in the evening. In the cafe, a prix-fixe dinner is an affordable $12.50 and includes any appetizer and entree or any entree and dessert. You also can order a la carte; all entrees are $8.95. Possibilities are baked goat cheese with tomatoes and basil or cod cakes with caper sauce to start; veal ragout in red wine sauce or penne pasta Mediterranean for the main course, and a brownie with ice cream or creme caramel to finish. In the main dining room, entrees ($16 to $22) include roast pork loin stuffed with nuts, raisins and apricots and served with smoky pink lentils, loin of lamb with rosemary sauce, white beans and stewed root vegetables, and steak au poivre with shallot fricassee. Lunch, Monday-Friday 11:30 to 2; dinner, Monday-Saturday 5:30 to 9:30.

Chez Claude, 5 Strawberry Hill Road (Route 2A), Acton, (508) 263-3325. Claude Miquel, the chef-owner of this charming little French restaurant ensconced in an old red house, maintains his popularity in the area more than twenty years after opening. Striped floral wallpaper in one of the three nice-size dining rooms and plain white linens, with a single white candle on each table, provided a pleasant atmosphere one chilly Friday evening for dinner on classic French fare. Among the hors d'oeuvre at dinner, you might try escargots bourguignonne, Claude's homemade country meat pate or french onion soup. Such classic entrees as coq au vin, roast duck with orange sauce, crepes filled with shrimp, scallops and lobster, and frogs' legs in garlic butter are available. They include potato, vegetable, salad and coffee and are priced from $13.50 to $39 for chateaubriand for two. Dessert possibilities are creme caramel, poire belle

Longfellow's Wayside Inn claims to be America's oldest.

helene, strawberries romanoff and almond pie. At lunchtime, entrees range from $8 to $10 for chicken livers, shrimp salad and breast of chicken in a champagne-mushroom sauce. Lunch, Tuesday-Friday noon to 2; dinner, Monday-Saturday 6 to 9:30.

Le Lyonnais, 416 Great Road, Route 2A, Acton, (508) 263-9068. Not far from Chez Claude, this is another classic French restaurant revered by its clientele. Gerard LaBrasse presides over the kitchen in the snug white house with four dining rooms, at least one with a fireplace. White cloths and napkins set the scene for traditional French food. A prix-fixe dinner with five courses for $19.95 is offered daily with a limited choice of entrees; among those available when we stopped in were roast cornish hen with tarragon, duckling in an unsweetened sauce with olives, and breast of chicken with a white wine cream sauce and mushrooms. Hors d'oeuvre ($2 to $5) include a plate of mixed hot and cold French specialties, onion soup, an anchovy and tomato salad and eggs with mayonnaise. Entrees ($12 to $20) might be crepes du jour, brook trout with mushrooms, frogs' legs with herbs and garlic, coq au vin and sweetbreads (which must be ordered in advance). The ambitious list also includes tenderloin bearnaise, rack of lamb and chateaubriand for two. For lunch on Thursday you might try a Mediterranean pasta, paella Marseillaise or coquilles St. Jacques ($7.50 to $10). Lunch, Thursday noon to 2:30; dinner nightly, 5:30 to 9:30.

Walden Station, 24 Walden St., Concord, (508) 371-2233. This fun restaurant in an old fire station is one of those BPBW (brass, plants, brick and wood) places, but it's a pleasant environment and the firefighting theme is not overdone. You can enter from the rear (directly from a municipal parking lot), where an old red fire engine marks the spot, or from busy Walden Street. The narrow restaurant contains a bar in the center, with dining areas at either end. The all-day menu is nicely varied. We enjoyed the thick, spicy turkey gumbo soup with bits of Louisiana hot sausage. Chicken caesar or beef fajita salads are lighter entree options ($7 to $8) and you can always get a six-ounce station burger, $4.95 with optional extras. Other sandwiches include the Vermonter (roasted turkey breast topped with homemade stuffing and an orange-cranberry relish served hot with turkey gravy), the Georges Bank fish sandwich, deep-fried and topped with lemon-basil tartar sauce, and the Firehouse steak sandwich, mesquite-grilled with horseradish and garlic dressing. Other options ($6 to $13) are turkey pot pie, shepherd's pie, Louisiana roast pork (baked with andouille sausage dressing and served with gingersnap gravy), vegetarian lasagna, country skewered lamb and New Orleans seafood etouffee. Because it's smack in the middle of Concord's shopping district, Walden Station tends to be crowded at lunchtime. Open daily, 11:30 to midnight.

The Colonial Inn, Monument Square, Concord, (508) 369-2373. A cozy Colonial environment is the setting for some well-regarded food of late. Among the dishes the inn is known for are chicken pie and prime rib. Also offered as dinner entrees ($15 to $20) are baked scrod, broiled scallops, veal marsala, rack of lamb dijonnaise and lobster pie. Appetizers ($5 to $7) include clams on the half shell, shrimp cocktail, mussels marinara, a country pate and fresh fruit cup. New England clam chowder and baked onion soup are offered along with a soup of the day. A $16.95 brunch is offered on Sundays with the added attraction of a Boston actress playing the part of poet Emily Dickinson — no, she wasn't from Concord, but who's to quibble? A lighter menu, served daily from 11:30 in the two rustic lounges, includes chicken fingers, potato skins, club sandwich, burgers, tortellini shrimp salad and the like. Broiled twin beef kabobs on this menu are $11.95. Tea is served in the afternoon, beginning at 2:30, Sunday at 3:30. High tea costs $12.75, Colonial tea, $8.25, and light tea (with scones, pastries and jams), $5.75. The high tea includes five courses, with scones, pates, sandwiches, fresh berries and cream and pastries. Lunch daily, 11:30 to 2:30; dinner, 5 to 9.

Longfellow's Wayside Inn, Route 20, South Sudbury, (508) 443-1776. This is the kind of Colonial dining spot that everyone gets into the mood for once in a while. Hordes of visitors seem to get into the mood on nice Sundays and the place is usually mobbed for Sunday dinner. The menu changes daily but generally includes tried-and-true favorites, things your grandmother used to make. For lunch ($8 to $12), you might select Yankee pot roast, chicken pie, fried scallops, stuffed fillet of sole or New England boiled dinner. Appetizers include fresh pressed apple cider, frosted fruit shrub, cranberry juice, fresh fruit cup with sherbet and marinated herring. Among dessert selections are deep-dish apple pie with spiced whipped cream, baked Indian pudding, strawberry shortcake, parfaits, pecan pie and custard pudding. Complete dinners are priced in the $15 to $20 range, except for baked stuffed or boiled lobster. Other choices might be poached salmon with hollandaise sauce, filet mignon, prime rib or jumbo baked shrimp. The food is consistent, and people return again and again to enjoy it in the exceptional surroundings. The dining room is simply and honestly furnished; the bare wood floors, gold cloths and napkins, and floral china convey a sense of the old days. We rather like the cozy Tap Room with brown and white checked tablecloths and less din. Lunch, Monday-Saturday 11:30 to 3; dinner, 5 to 9, Sunday noon to 8.

Sweet Peppers, 20 Waltham St., Lexington, (617) 862-1880. This spot has had a number of different owners and styles, but since 1991 the Italian bistro known as Sweet Peppers has been drawing in crowds. The white clapboard facade is a bit misleading; inside the place throbs with bright colors and the feel of a Mediterranean cafe. A large one, at that, for there are three dining rooms upstairs, two of them quite large, and two more, plus a bar, on the ground floor. We like the atmosphere: floral printed tablecloths, brightly painted and distressed windsor-style chairs, vibrant murals of Italian street and market scenes, hanging garlic and chianti bottles — even umbrellas advertising mineral water over a few tables. We wish we could be quite as enthusiastic about our meals, but the bread — which should have been outstanding — was unimpressive and service was slow. The menus for both lunch and dinner are quite ambitious, offering pizzas, pastas, salads and entrees. At lunchtime, we tried a good tuscan lamb ragout and shrimp scampi linguini, the latter pronounced a mite bland. Locals praise the grilled chicken sandwich with roasted peppers, prosciutto and provolone served with a honey-dijon sauce on a grilled roll. Pizzas, all twelve inches and costing $7 to $11, are made with mozzarella, provolone and parmesan as well as fresh plum tomatoes. Entrees at lunchtime are $9 to $11; in the evening, $9 to $14. Lunch, Monday-Saturday 11:30 to 4; dinner, 5 to 10; Sunday, brunch 11:30 to 3, dinner 5 to 9.

The Yangtze River Restaurant, 25 Depot Square, Lexington, (617) 861-6030. For more than fifteen years, this Chinese restaurant has been commanding loyalty from its followers. The food is Szechuan-Mandarin on one side of the menu, Polynesian on the other. Beyond an off-putting bar just as you walk in, the decor is rather contemporary with lots of wood and plants. High ratings by Boston's restaurant critics are displayed prominently. Among the Chinese offerings are house specials, including General Tsao's chicken with watercress, sesame beef with broccoli, yunan shrimp with black bean sauce and hunan lamb for $16 or $17. Other items, priced from $9 to $14, include all the regulars plus plum-flavored duck or Peking duck, which is $28. A lunchtime buffet for $5.75 weekdays is appreciated by business people. You also can order from the regular menu. Open daily, 11:30 to 9:15, weekends to 10:15.

Lemon Grass, 1710 Massachusetts Ave., Lexington, (617) 862-3530. Nothing but praise is heard for this Thai restaurant, which opened in 1990 in the center of town. Fan-back rattan chairs and tables with white tablecloths and bright green placemats are placed in a bright open space with soft pink walls. At lunchtime, you can start with Siam rolls (crispy spring rolls served in a white turnip sauce) or satay (chicken or beef barbecued on skewers and served with peanut sauce). Hot and sour shrimp soup, chicken coconut soup and a large list of "rice dishes" — from chicken pineapple (sauteed with pineapple, snow peas, tomatoes, onions and curry powder) to beef panang (sauteed sirloin in a Thai curry with lemon leaves, mushrooms, basil leaves and walnuts) are in the $5 to $7 range. In the evening, try wild boar basil (actually pork pan-fried with mushrooms, green peppercorns, fresh basil and hot chile peppers) or seafood bouquet (steamed shrimp, scallops, squid, crabmeat and other fish in a broth), priced from $9 to $14. Lunch, Monday-Friday 11:30 to 3; dinner, Monday-Saturday 5 to 9:30.

One Meriam, 1 Meriam St., Lexington, (617) 862-3006. Sandwiches, salads and soups are served up in this small, bustling restaurant conveniently located near most of the historic sites around Battle Green. Popular for breakfast and lunch, the restaurant is bright and open with cane chairs at wood tables. The menu is quite ambitious, considering the size of the place, and you can get breakfast — from pancakes to omelets — all day long. Sandwiches, soups and salads also are offered at lunchtime in the $5 to $7 range. Open Monday-Friday 7 to 3, Saturday 8 to 3.

Willow Pond Kitchen, Lexington Road (Route 2A), Concord, (508) 369-6529. This low gray roadside building with the huge beer sign over the entrance may not look promising, but it is. Locals not only fill the large parking lot but enthusiastically recommend the place. Old wooden booths, muskets mounted on beams, a TV over the bar and a counter where you can get a quick bite make this really down home. The walls and ceiling are pale green and the curtains change periodically, but somehow it all works, even the plastic ketchup bottles on the tables. Seafood is a prime draw and you can get whole fried clams for $10.95 or baked shrimp pie for $9.35 off the dinner menu. A hamburger is about $2.50, a BLT $2.45 and a grilled cheese, $2.15. Other favorites are beef stew, franks and beans, chili, homemade bread pudding and pecan pie, all at reasonable prices. Beer and wine are available. Open daily, 11 to 11, Sunday 1 to 11.

The tiny **Concord Deli** on Main Street, Concord, has been gaining a following. It's tucked down a flight of stairs from the street, holding just a few tables. A Greek-American couple offers Greek foods and pastries.

FOR MORE INFORMATION: Concord Chamber of Commerce, Wright Tavern, Monument Square, Concord, (508) 369-3120. Lexington Chamber of Commerce Visitor Center, half block east of Lexington Green, (617) 862-1450.

Cornelius Vanderbilt's Breakers occupies grand site along the ocean.

Water and Wealth

Newport, R.I.

Fabulous mansions from the Gilded Age, the Newport Jazz Festival, the America's Cup races — all have given Newport a cachet perhaps unmatched in the Northeast.

The fortuitous combination of water and wealth have made Newport probably the single most varied town in New England. Here in one roughly ten-mile-square area are seashore, history, architecture, culture, affluence, shops and restaurants in both variety and quantity that would be the envy of cities many times its size.

History alone makes Newport worth visiting. As an early seaport dating to 1639, the town contains more pre-Revolutionary houses than any other in America. Most are restored, signed and lived-in, some are open to the public, and all are a delight to view on walking tours through the Point or Historic Hill.

The wealth of history was refined during Newport's second heyday following the Civil War. The Astors, Vanderbilts, Morgans and other leading families built their summer "cottages" above the ocean along Bellevue Avenue, creating a society resort unmatched for glitter and opulence. Now opened to the public, America's largest collection of what Europeans would call palaces can keep a visitor enthralled (and occasionally appalled) for several days.

What links both eras of Newport's history and makes it so engaging for today's visitor is, of course, the water. Newport is at the southern tip of Aquidneck Island, surrounded by water on three sides. The restored waterfront areas off America's Cup Avenue and Lower Thames Street are great for browsing, shopping and viewing sailing ships and fishing vessels. Out Ocean Drive is today's version of the mansions — large homes (some strikingly contemporary) showing that Newport hasn't lost its glory — and the rocky shoreline is good for fishing, hiking or bicycling expeditions. Just east of town are excellent beaches for swimming and surfing.

Newport offers so much to see that you run the risk of seeing rather than doing. So do the mansions along the newly repaved and restored Bellevue Avenue, walk the Cliff Walk, bicycle the Ocean Drive, visit old Touro Synagogue and Green Animals topiary garden, take the self-guided history tours, try the seafood, poke through the shops, ogle the yachts, swim in the ocean and revel in all that is Newport.

But note: as an old, island city, Newport wasn't built for large numbers of visitors. In summer and on weekends, the town is jammed. The streets are narrow and many are one-way — you can find yourself going nowhere in circles, so you may want to abandon your car, particularly in the downtown area, which is eminently strollable anyway. Also, for a resort of such magnitude, Newport has not kept up with the demand for accommodations at peak periods. So book far in advance, or pick an off-season weekend, say in December, when the town decks itself out for Christmas in style, or better yet in spring, when the azaleas and rhododendrons burst forth in all their seaside glory.

Getting There

Its island location has cut Newport off from the mainstream. Bonanza Bus Lines serves the city direct, arriving at the new Gateway Visitors Center at 23 America's Cup Ave. Amtrak serves Providence, and major airlines fly into T.F. Green State Airport in Warwick, outside Providence. Most visitors arrive by car, taking the Jamestown-Newport Bridge from the west ($2 toll) or Routes 114 and 138 from the east. And, of course, you can arrive on your own yacht — what better way to savor the water and wealth of Newport?

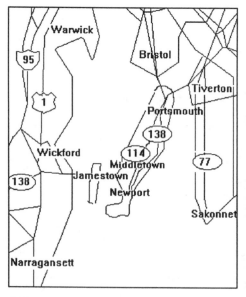

Where to Stay

Newport offers an enormous array of accommodations, from hotels to B&Bs. Lower-priced chain motels are located just north of the city in Middletown.

Big and Busy

Newport Islander Doubletree Hotel, Goat Island, Newport 02840, (401) 849-2600 or (800) 528-0444. Formerly the Sheraton Islander, this was acquired in 1991 by the Doubletree chain. It promptly invested $4 million in renovations to an already spiffy 253-room hotel, conference center and family resort (bring quarters for the kids, who like all the pinball machines and video games). Although it is unfortunately not quite within walking distance of the downtown area, its setting on Goat Island is magnificent and its architecture unusual (natives call it the grain elevator). A focal point is the huge indoor pool area, light and bright, with glass walls, high arched glass roof and a bar on an upper level where you can watch the swimmers. Try not to occupy a room opening onto the pool area as we once did, or you may have to endure the pool lights shining in your window all night (in desperation, we tacked the two bedspreads over the window, but that didn't help much). Much better are the deluxe rooms with whirlpool baths and waterfront balconies in the newer Captain's Quarters wing that we occupied during a conference a couple of years back. The Islander also has racquetball and tennis courts and an outdoor saltwater pool. For sustenance, there are the cheery **Sunset Cafe** coffee shop and lobster restaurant, where you can get meals and snacks at most times of the day, and the renovated **Windward** dining room. The latter is well regarded locally, particularly for its lavish salad bar featuring shrimp or crab legs, which comes with dinner entrees ($14.95 to $21.95) or can be taken separately ($10.95 for all you can eat). **Rodger's Roost** is a stylish rooftop cocktail lounge. Doubles, $149 to $229.

Newport Marriott Hotel, 25 America's Cup Ave., Newport 02840, (401) 849-1000 or (800) 458-3066. Newport's biggest hotel opened in 1988 after a year's delay and a change in ownership (it was started as a Holiday Inn Crowne Plaza, and the guest rooms are smaller than the Marriott would have built). On Long Wharf, between the harbor and the new Gateway Center, this is billed as one of the Marriott chain's top ten resort hotels. The 315 guest rooms surround a five-story atrium, which often is used for parties and can get noisy. The indoor swimming pool includes an outdoor sun deck. Health facilities include a whirlpool, sauna and exercise center with Universal equipment and four racquetball courts. **J.W.'s Sea Grill and Oyster Bar** offers all-purpose dining all day, while **Cafe del Mare** serves northern Italian cuisine in the $12.50 to $20.50 range. The lounge was designed to be Newport's liveliest nightclub. Doubles, $179 to $229.

Newport Harbor Hotel & Marina, 49 America's Cup Ave., Newport 02840, (401) 847-9000 or (800) 955-2558. The new ownership of the former Treadway hotel/motor inn that fell on hard times has renovated all 133 rooms on four floors. Decor is nicely nautical in blue and white, the stripes in the bedspreads being repeated in the draperies. In-room coffee makers and hair dryers are pluses. About half the rooms face the water and have private balconies; the rest overlook the parking lot. Facilities include an indoor pool, saunas and a 60-slip marina. The location is one of Newport's best, in the thick of the downtown action near Bowen's and Bannister's wharves. Three meals a day are served in **Waverleys,** a restaurant and bar in several sections. There's frequently live entertainment in Waverleys or the Coconuts Comedy Club. Doubles, $165 to $225.

The Newport Bay Club and Hotel, 337 Thames St., Box 1440, Newport 02840, (401) 849-8600. Probably the nicest of the many harborfront time-sharing resorts, this has 36 large, luxurious units, ranging from one-bedroom suites to two-bedroom townhouses. The old General Electric mill retains its high wood ceilings and paneling. Each condominium-style unit contains a kitchenette or full kitchen, a large living room with pullout bed and dining area, a queensize bedroom and a marble bathroom with jacuzzi tub. The fourth-floor townhouses have balconies upstairs and down, with side views of the harbor. Continental breakfast is served. Downstairs in the Perry Mill Marketplace are retail shops and the Thames Street Pub, a restaurant and disco. Suites, $155 to $255; townhouses, $295 to $375.

Inn on Long Wharf, 142 Long Wharf, Newport 02840, (401) 847-7800 or (800) 225-3522. One of five time-sharing hotels run locally by Inn Group Hotels, this offers 40 suites, all facing the harbor. Even the elevator, enclosed in a wall of glass, yields a water view. Most suites are entered through the bedroom; beyond are a kitchenette with refrigerator and microwave opposite a marble bathroom with double jacuzzi, and a living room with pullout queensize sofa. Corner suites are billed as superior in that you enter the living rooms first and both they and the bedrooms are larger and share water views. In the second-floor **Smuggler's Landing,** a wraparound restaurant in pink and black, you feel as if you're right out over the water. The exotic Polynesian-Caribbean island menu is one of Newport's more interesting; among entrees priced from $12.95 to $22.95, the curried fettuccine with shrimp won an award for the most creative sauce in a pasta contest. Gene Oliver's entertainment at the piano bar is a weekend highlight in summer. Doubles, $150 to $225.

Mill Street Inn, 75 Mill St., Newport 02840, (401) 849-9500. Inn purists might find this inn austere, but we rather like its European atmosphere. A 19th-century brick mill restored in 1985 and now listed on the National Register of Historic Places, it has 23 deluxe guest suites. The vast expanses of white walls are fine backdrops for contemporary paintings and posters, modern sofas and chairs, industrial gray carpeting, vases filled with fresh flowers, wet bars and television sets. In a few rooms, original brick walls and beams tone down some of the white. Beds are queensize, fans whir on the ceilings, and baths are gleamingly white-tiled with pedestal sinks. Eight duplex townhouses on the second floor have living room down and bedroom above, opening onto decks raised just *nough so you can sit on the chairs and still see the distant water and the Jamestown bridge. Pastries and coffee are served in a basement breakfast room with stone walls and built-in benches. Doubles, $135 to $225.

Small and Personal

Cliffside Inn, 2 Seaview Ave., Newport 02840, (401) 847-1811 or (800) 845-1811. Among the most alluring of Newport's upscale B&Bs is this Victorian charmer, nicely upgraded by new owner Winthrop Baker. The summer villa built in 1880 by a governor of Maryland contains twelve rooms and suites, the four largest of which he considers "clearly room for room the best in Newport." Three have jacuzzi baths and sitting areas with TVs. The inn's many floor-to-ceiling and bay windows bathe the rooms with light, blending an airy Laura Ashley freshness with rich Victoriana. Guests enjoy afternoon refreshments in a large fireplaced parlor or on the wide front veranda, from which the ocean can be glimpsed down the street. Resident innkeepers Annette and Norbert Mede serve a lavish breakfast that could include walnut pancakes, strawberry crepes or eggs benedict. Doubles, $125 to $175; suites, $205. No smoking.

Elm Tree Cottage, 336 Gibbs Ave., Newport 02840, (401) 849-1610 or (800) 882-3356. Here is one beautiful "cottage," a shingle-style mansion built in 1882 a block from the water for the daughter of Unitarian clergyman William Ellery Channing. Guests enjoy an acre of landscaped grounds, a huge living room, a morning garden room and a handsome bar room furnished in wicker. The five upstairs guest rooms are no slouches, either, particularly the 1,000-square-foot master bedroom with a canopied kingsize bed and two sitting areas, one in front of the fireplace. Almost as inviting is the new main-floor library bedroom, lovely in wine and teal colors. Two plush chairs face a TV and guests are helping fill the room's shelves with favorite books. Personable innkeepers Priscilla and Tom Malone, who occupy the third floor with their three young daughters, also design and execute handsome stained-glass pieces. Breakfast by candlelight is an event in the large dining room. Ours started with juice and homemade oatmeal in a dish decorated with five varieties of dried leaves and culminated in delicious pumpkin waffles. Doubles, $135 to $225. No smoking.

Suite at The Francis Malbone House.

The Francis Malbone House, 392 Thames St., Newport 02840, (401) 846-0392. Local investors transformed a former nursing home and physician's residence into one of Newport's most elegant B&Bs in 1990. Eight corner rooms on the second and third floors come with private baths and antique queensize beds with monogrammed duvet covers. A queensize bed faces the TV in the sunken main-floor suite, fashioned from the former doctor's office. Two main-floor guest parlors and a library-TV room, all with fireplacres, are unusually inviting. At one spring visit, the rooms abounded with a profusion of colorful house plants, from African violets to hibiscus to hydrangeas. Out back is a courtyard with a fountain and a large, shady lawn where you'd hardly know you were in downtown Newport. Innkeepers Jim Maher and Will Dewey, both of whom are into cooking, serve a full breakfast at a long, linen-covered table in the dining room. The main course might be raspberry french toast, quiche or belgian waffles. The inn's owners, who also run a Providence catering service, were about to reopen our favorite Crest Farm grocery store and deli at 43 Memorial Blvd. as the even fancier Market on the Boulevard at our latest visit. Doubles, $125 to $155; suite, $225. No smoking.

The Victorian Ladies, 63 Memorial Blvd., Newport 02840, (401) 849-9960. These two Victorian beauties, one behind the other, are among the most comfortable of their genre. A prevailing pink and blue color scheme and striking window treatments characterize the eleven guest rooms, all with private baths, television sets and a light, uncluttered look. Innkeepers Helene and Donald O'Neill serve a full breakfast in the dining room of the front house, which also has a small parlor. In 1991, the O'Neills added two deluxe suites upstairs in the rear caretaker's cottage. A secluded courtyard and gazebo are pleasant places to relax on a nice day. Doubles, $125 to $165.

The Inn at Old Beach, 19 Old Beach Road, Newport 02840, (401) 849-3479. A residential location with a big back yard commends this romantic B&B opened in 1989 by Luke and Cyndi Murray. In the main house they offer five guest rooms with private baths, named after flowers and furnished with whimsy in various English country styles. Lately, the Murrays moved with their newborn son to a rear carriage house, where they were about to add two more guest rooms upstairs. The room they vacated on the main floor was converted into a guest living room to supplement the small front parlor. A continental breakfast is served in the dining room or outside on a porch and brick patio overlooking the gazebo and lily pond in the back yard. Doubles, $125 to $130.

Wayside, Bellevue Avenue, Newport 02840, (401) 847-0302. If you want to stay in a Newport mansion, this beige brick summer cottage almost across from the Elms and just down the street from the homes of the Astors and Vanderbilts fits the bill. And the bill won't break your bankbook. Al and Dorothy Post have converted the mansion into a low-key B&B with ten guest rooms, all with private baths and TVs. Lately they have updated the bathrooms and spiffed up the bedrooms, which are spacious and comfortable. Twelve-foot-high ceilings, canopy beds and crystal knobs on the doors are among the extravagant touches. The most prized accommodation is in the main-floor library, big enough for a kingsize bed, two sofas and a chair and now boasting two french doors that cost more than his first house, says Al. It's a steal for $125 a night. A continental breakfast is served in the family dining room off a magnificent entry foyer with oak parquet floor, paneled walls and a fifteen-foot-high ceiling. There's a swimming pool out back for guests. Wayside welcomes children and accepts single-night reservations. Doubles, $95 to $125.

The InnTowne, 6 Mary St., Newport 02840, (401) 846-9200 or (800) 457-7803. This inn built in 1980 after a fire destroyed the original structure is aptly named. It couldn't be more in town, just off Thames Steet, its side rooms facing the busy main street and those on the third and fourth floors catching a glimpse of the harbor. Built and furnished by Betty and Paul McEnroe of the famed Inn at Castle Hill, it was sold in 1991 and the old Restoration House annex was converted into time-sharing. The remaining nineteen guest rooms with private baths are nicely decorated in colorful and contemporary matching fabrics (right down to the shower curtains and wastebaskets), thick carpeting, canopy beds, upholstered wing chairs and wicker furniture. The inn has a delightful rooftop sun deck, and downstairs are a sitting room and a small dining room for afternoon tea and continental breakfast. Doubles, $115 to $165.

The Melville House, 39 Clarke St., Newport 02840, (401) 847-0640. Typical but a cut above many of Newport's ubiquitous small B&Bs, this cozy 1750 Colonial has seven rooms, five with private bath and all decorated in Colonial style with stenciling done by innkeeper Rita Rogers. She and husband Sam serve a continental-plus breakfast of juice, homemade granola (which they have packaged for sale to guests), yogurt and muffins in the small breakfast room. Guests gather for sherry hour in the fireplaced sitting room. This is a place to immerse yourself in history, the location is good for walking to practically anywhere downtown, and there's off-street parking. Doubles, $85 to $100. Closed January and February.

Where to Eat

Newport is a place for eating, and the best restaurants in town tend to be elegant, expensive and crowded. Reservations and dressy attire are suggested for dinner. But Newport has many casual restaurants as well, with newcomers popping up like spring flowers.

The Black Pearl, Bannister's Wharf, (401) 846-5264. You can sit under the Cinzano umbrellas and watch the world go by while you enjoy some of the best clam chowder ever, thick and dill-laced ($2.50 a cup, $4.50 a bowl). You also can enjoy a pearlburger ($5.95), served with mint salad in pita bread and good fries, plus a variety of other sandwiches, salads and desserts. Inside, the tavern is cozy, dark and noisy, usually with a line of people waiting for seats, and the fare is basically the same as outside, with a few heartier entrees available at lunch or dinner. Desserts are delectable, especially the Black Pearl cheesecake followed by cappuccino laced with kahlua and courvoisier. The Commodore Room, the highly rated formal dining room facing the harbor, serves contemporary cuisine, with dinner entrees ($16.50 to $26) like sauteed soft-shell crabs, grey sole meuniere, salmon steak with mustard-dill hollandaise, breast of duck with green peppercorn sauce, breast of pheasant with perigueux sauce and rack of lamb. More than 1,500 meals a day in summer come forth from what must be one of the world's tiniest kitchens. Tavern and outdoor cafe open daily from 11; dinner in Commodore Room, 6 to 11.

Typical Bellevue Avenue summer cottage takes in guests as Wayside.

The Place, 28 Washington Square, (401) 847-0116. This new adjunct of Yesterday's, a pubby Washington Square institution, was opened in 1992 by its owners as a showcase for their longtime chef, Alex Daglis. He obliges with the most exciting cuisine in Newport, served stylishly at white-clothed tables on two levels of a long, narrow dining room and accompanied by "flights" of wine, such as four kinds of sauvignon blanc for $11. Folks rave about the changing entrees, priced from $14.95 for grilled creole chicken to $22.95 for Caribbean lobster with snow peas and black angel-hair pasta. But we never got beyond the appetizers, so tantalizing that we shared and made a meal of five. The shrimp and corn tamales, the exquisite scallops with cranberries and ginger, the gratin of wild mushrooms, and raviolis of smoked chicken and goat cheese were mere warmups for a salad of smoked pheasant with poached pears and hazelnuts. Each was gorgeously presented on black octagonal plates. An apple crepe with apple sorbet was a crowning finale. Dinner nightly, 5:30 to 10 or 11.

White Horse Tavern, Marlborough and Farewell Streets, (401) 846-3600. The historic ambience of the country's oldest operating tavern, elegantly restored by the Preservation Society some years back, draws a well-heeled following. Chef Christopher Hawver's food is equal to the elegant setting, which we find particularly appealing in the off-season when the fireplaces are lit. Dinner entrees ($21 to $33) include Thai poached shrimp, sauteed sweetbreads over fettuccine with an olive-cream sauce, beef wellington, grilled tenderloin of veal with fresh gnocchi and tournedos of beef with grilled sweet peppers and mushrooms. For most, this is special-occasion dining, topped off by such masterful desserts as a three-cherry tart on a chocolate crust in a pool of vanilla cream sauce or triple silk torte on a bed of raspberry melba. Lunch, Monday-Saturday noon to 3; dinner nightly, 6 to 10; Sunday brunch, noon to 3. Closed Tuesday in winter.

La Petite Auberge, 19 Charles St., (401) 849-6669. On two floors in the historic Stephen Decatur House, Roger Putier serves classic French fare from an extensive menu in five small and elegant dining rooms where lace tablecloths are layered over pale blue or gold linen. There's also a rose-trellised courtyard where meals are served outdoors in season. The sauces are heavenly — from the escargots with cepes, a house specialty, to our entrees of veal with morels and cream sauce and two tender pink lamb chops, also with cepes and an intense brown sauce. Appetizers and soups are $5.95 to $8.50 (for smoked salmon). Entrees range from $17.95 for chicken with apples to $23 for beef wellington. The excellent wine list is nicely priced, and desserts are mostly classics like crepes suzette and cherries jubilee. Dinner, Monday-Saturday 6 to 10, Sunday 5 to 9.

Le Bistro, Bowen's Wharf, (401) 849-7778. An elegant decor in the second- and third-floor dining rooms with glimpses of the harbor and creative American cuisine commend this French bistro, long owned by chef John Philcox and now in partnership with the owner of the Wharf Deli below. We've enjoyed a fine salad nicoise ($6.25) and a classic bouillabaisse ($9.95) from a luncheon menu on which everything looks good. Dinner entrees are priced from $9.95 for Burgundy-style sausage with hot potato salad to $16.95 for sea scallops meuniere, plus nightly specials up to $22.95 for such treats as grilled swordfish provencal, grilled antelope steak with pumpkin pancakes and leg of lamb braised with chestnuts and wild mushrooms. We can vouch for the veal kidneys in port and the roast duck in a red cream sauce with endives. The convivial third-floor bar serves light fare and is crowded all day and evening. Lunch, 11:30 to 2; dinner nightly from 6; Sunday brunch.

Scales and Shells, 527 Thames St., Newport, (401) 846-3474. Almost as fast as seafood can be unloaded from the docks out back, retired sea captain Andy Ackerman and his staff cook up a storm in an open kitchen near the door of this casual restaurant, a huge success since its opening in 1988. Plain and exotic seafood, simply prepared but presented with style, comes in many guises. The blackboard menu on the wall lists the offerings, from mussels marinara ($9.95) to lobster fra diavolo ($36.95 for two). There are mesquite-grilled shrimp, tuna and bluefish with cilantro salsa ($8.95 to $16.50), but no non-seafood items at all. A raw bar offers fresh goodies near the entry, and there's a good wine list. Dinner, Monday-Saturday 5 to 9 or 10, Sunday 4 to 9. No credit cards.

The Mooring, Sayer's Wharf, (401) 846-2260. A casual spot with outdoor dining on a brick patio under blue umbrellas or a canopied upper deck brightened by colorful geraniums, the Mooring has about the best water location around, thanks to its former incarnation as the New York Yacht Club station. The inside is all blue and nautical, with a fireplace ablaze in the off-season. The lines for meals can get long, but you could stop in during off-hours for a gin and tonic, a bowl of prize-winning clam chowder, or coffee and a piece of orange ambrosia pie. The mix-and-match menu ranges from $6.40 for sandwiches to $20.90 for top-priced dinner entrees. The steak and seafood fare is standard, but the setting is rewarding. Open daily, 11:30 to 9 or 10; fewer days in winter.

Sea Fare's American Cafe, Brick Market Place, (401) 849-9188. The former Dave & Eddie's seafood grill and raw bar gave way in 1992 to this seafood cafe run by the folks from Sea Fare Inn, a luxurious restaurant in nearby Portsmouth. Owner George Karousos's son Ted oversees the Newport operation, which is more casual and features pizzas baked in a wood-burning brick oven from Italy. The menu ranges widely, from smoked salmon and baked oysters as appetizers through fishermen's and octopus salads to pastas and grills. Prices run from $9.95 for baked stuffed scrod to $18.95 for lobster stuffed with veal, the Sea Fare's version of "the perfect surf and turf." Open daily, 11 a.m. to midnight; Sunday brunch, 9:30 to 2.

Pronto, 464 Thames St., (401) 847-5251. Dark and cozy, with candles flickering and palm trees soaring beneath a pressed-tin ceiling, this is a place for romance. Owner Janne Osean oversees a with-it Italian menu listing such pastas ($9.25 to $12.50) as fettuccine with four cheeses and farfalle with shiitake mushrooms, calamata olives, spinach, roasted red peppers, pinenuts and chevre. A few specials are available at dinner, perhaps pan-roasted salmon with red bell-pepper vinaigrette and lentil salad, seared sea scallops with chanterelles on a bed of braised endive and leeks, and grilled beef tenderloin with herb-roasted potatoes, $14 to $18. Grilled pizzas, bruschetta and pastas are in the $5.75 to $8.50 range at lunch. Sunday breakfast yields treats like eggs copenhagen, banana pancakes, crisp johnnycakes with scrambled eggs and huevos rancheros, $4.75 to $7.25. Lunch, Monday-Saturday 11:30 to 4, Sunday noon to 4; dinner, 5 to 10:30 or 11; Sunday breakfast, 8 to noon.

Rhumb Line, 62 Bridge St., (401) 849-6950. A bistro-like place in the historic Point section of Newport, this has a cozy feeling, with oriental rugs dotted around the wide-plank floors, an old piano in one corner and a wood stove in another, old-fashioned lamps and woven tablecloths. Even the bar stools bear hooked rug cushions. Waitresses in bermuda shorts dart by with chowders, salads and burgers with huge steakfries. Prices are moderate, and many wines are available by the glass. Entrees like curried chicken madras, wiener schnitzel, scallops with pesto and filet mignon are priced from $13.95 to $18.95 at night. Although there's an outdoor cafe, the Rhumb Line seems more appealing in the off-season than on a hot summer's day when you might rather be outdoors near the water. Lunch, 11:30 to 3, weekends to 5; dinner, 5 to 10 or 10:30; Sunday brunch, noon to 4.

Music Hall Cafe, 250 Thames St., (401) 848-2330. The historic Music Hall building erected in 1894 was converted into a restaurant with music-hall overtones in 1992. Borrowing a page from the days when the old Italian-American Club staged dances on the third floor, the cafe presents country music on Wednesday nights, jazz on Thursdays, bluegrass on Fridays and special events as the occasion demands. An artist was at work during the transformation here: the faux stone walls inside the entry look real, as do the windows handpainted on the stucco and brick walls; a water fountain with tiles appears positively three-dimensional. A pleasant Southwest decor is the backdrop for a lengthy Mexican-American menu supplemented by oodles of blackboard specials. Barbecued pork ribs, fajitas, chicken Santa Fe, Southwest crab cakes and mixed grill are typical fare, priced from $5.75 to $9 at lunch, $9.25 to $15.50 at night. Lunch daily, 11:30 to 2:30; dinner nightly from 5:30.

Brick Alley Pub & Restaurant, 140 Thames St., (401) 849-6334. We don't know which is more dizzying: the bar with its mirrors and memorabilia, or the sixteen-page menu, which blows the mind. No matter. This establishment with a neat rear courtyard is locally esteemed for good food at pleasant prices. We can't begin to detail the fare; suffice to say that there's half a page for nachos and another half for potato skins, a full page for soup and salad buffet, two for sandwiches and two for dinner specials (from $11.95 for pastas to $16.95 for steak au poivre). Open daily, 11 to 10 or 11.

A few other choices: **The 509 Grill** opened in 1992 in the space formerly occupied by Southern Cross and later Amsterdam's Rotisserie. The Amsterdam's connection remains, despite the name change, and the menu favors flame-roasted chicken dishes in the $10 range, seafood salad and grilled delmonico steak. Dinner, Tuesday-Sunday 5 to 11; Sunday brunch.

The International Cafe, 677 Thames St., is run simply by chef-caterer Fred Almanzor, who serves foods from around the world at remarkably low prices ($6.50 to $12.25, each a dollar less for petite sizes). The eclectic menu lists a few of the chef's native Philippine dishes. Besides the twenty-plus entrees, you can get sandwiches or appetizers as a main dish. Dinner nightly except Tuesday from 4:30. BYOB.

Anthony's Shore Dinner Hall, on Waites Wharf off Lower Thames Street, is the kind of down-home, family waterfront spot that Newport has lacked. A huge enclosed lobster pound with garage-size doors opening onto the harbor, it offers a one-pound lobster for $8.95, as well as chowder, mussels, fish and chips and hot dogs for the kids.

Busy Bannister's Wharf waterfront scene takes in shops, restaurants and outdoor cafes.

A full lobster boil is $19.95. Sit at picnic tables and chow down. Open April-October, daily from noon to 10 or 11.

Ocean Breeze Cafe at 580 Thames St. purveys gourmet coffees and teas, baked goods and an array of salads and sandwiches. Neither the grilled chicken sandwich nor the Islander (chorizo with grilled peppers and onions), both $6.95, were as memorable as the black raspberry cheesecake.

The Wharf Delicatessen & Raw Bar, 37 Bowens Wharf, is good for casual dining in a mob scene. Salads, sandwiches and smoked fish plates are in the $4 to $6 range.

If you are in the Bellevue Avenue area, a good place for breakfast or lunch is **Cappuccino's** at 92 William St. Here at tiny marble tables you can munch on salads, quiches and delectable desserts like orange crunch trifle with triple sec.

The best pasta dishes in town can be had at **Puerini's,** 24 Memorial Blvd., a small cafe that has the locals lined up outside. How about an entree of sole stuffed with lobster, pinenuts, brie and sundried tomatoes, followed by tartuffo? Dinner nightly from 4.

Shopping

Like the restaurants, the shops in Newport come and go, but every year there seem to be more. You can have fun window-shopping, or you can be a big spender here. The main shopping areas are along Bellevue Avenue, where some of the more established shops cater to the descendants of the 400, Brick Market Place and Thames Street downtown, and the restored waterfront around Bowen's and Bannister's wharves. Increasingly, lower Thames Street is populated by interesting shops all the way out to the new Wellington Square, and Spring Street is dotted with galleries and boutiques.

Along Bellevue Avenue you will find **Talbots** with colorful and tailored apparel for women, **Michael Hayes** for elegant clothes for men, women and children, the **Cole-Haan Company Store, The Linen Shop** and **Cabbages & Kings** for gifts and antiques of appeal to those who still live in Newport "cottages."

Brick Market Place is a complex of restaurants, condominiums and shops, among them the **Mole Hole** and **Indesign** for gifts, **Island Canvas, the Chocolate Soldier,**

Davison's of Bermuda and **The Book Bay.** At the head of Thames Street is a huge new **Benetton,** strategically located not far from **The Gap.** The **Arnold Art Store** at 210 Thames had a remarkabe display of cow art at our visit.

Over at Bowen's and Banister's wharves, the aroma drifting through the door may draw you into the **Cookie Jar** for chocolate chip, oatmeal raisin or gingersnap cookies. **Operculum** has a wondrous selection of shells, and the **Crabtree & Evelyn** and **Laura Ashley** stores uphold tradition. Great rabbits dance around the **Spring Pottery.** We also like **Irish Imports Ltd.** for wools and linens, **Timberland** for rugged clothing, **Frillz** for handpainted clothing, **Miko** for accessories and **Marblehead Handprints** for colorful silk-screened prints. **A Cocoa Bean** offers ice cream and specialty foods.

Check out lower Thames Street for places like **Tropea-Puerini,** which carries great pottery, frames and jewelry. **Thames Street Pottery** has some fine items from the Southwest. **Pastabilities** purveys fifteen flavors of pasta, including rosemary and thyme. **Flying Colors** stocks colorful wind socks. Avant-garde gifts are available at **Erica Zap Collection** and handknit sweaters and interesting gifts at **New Moon Boutique.** The **Armchair Sailor** marine bookstore has moved into expanded quarters. The native American and Western arts and crafts at **Tribal Pride** are fascinating. **Tea & Herb Essence** is the place for dozens of tea blends and herbal health-care products.

Newport also has many antiques shops, most in the Spring Street area around Queen Anne's Square. This quaint, up-and-coming street also is notable for **The Spring Street Collection,** where the owner knits the children's sweaters and makes all the beautiful wreaths and flower arrangements. We liked the padded stars hanging from the ceiling at **Handmaids,** home of contemporary crafts and a neat handpainted table. **The Liberty Tree** sells good folk art. Outerware from around the world and Eskimo arts and crafts are featured in side-by-side stores, **Indian Territory** and **Native American Trading Company.**

The Mansions

Nowhere in this country can such a concentration of palatial mansions be found, and few visitors fail to take in at least one of the six acquired and operated by the Preservation Society of Newport County. Most popular of all is Cornelius Vanderbilt's Breakers, first leased to the society in 1948 by his daughter — 45 years later, more than four million people have gone inside to gape at its opulence.

Most mansions are strung along **Bellevue Avenue,** newly paved with concrete and lined with brick sidewalks, gas lights and utility poles with a period look. A parade and three days of parties and concerts marked the rededication of Bellevue Avenue, a once-a-century event, in June 1992. The mansions have been illuminated by floodlights at night since.

Whether or not you like the way the four hundred lived (and some of the tales about the ostentatiousness of it all could make one ill), it must have been a fabulous era when a hostess could give a ten-course dinner party for more than 100 dogs belonging to friends (the dogs came in party dress to dinner at the Marble House). It's hard to believe the mansions were occupied only two months of the year and were considered summer cottages. The "cottage" we like best — and one that is often skipped — is the early Victorian Kingscote, which is smaller and not so overwhelming.

Prices for the Preservation Society facilities: The Breakers, adults $7.50, children six through eleven, $3.50. The Elms, $7 and $3. Marble House, Chateau-sur-Mer, Rosecliff and Kingscote, $6 and $3. Combination tickets good for all six plus Hunter House and Green Animals topiary farm are $32.50 for adults, $10 for children; mansions only, $25.50 and $8.

Schedule: All mansions are open daily May-September from 10 to 5 for guided tours; the Breakers is open until 6 from July 4 to Labor Day. The Breakers, Marble House and Rosecliff are open daily from 10 to 5 in April and October, also the Elms in October, while the others are open weekends only. Marble House and Chateau-sur-Mer are open weekends and most holidays from 10 to 4, November-March.

The Breakers, Ochre Point Avenue at Ruggles Avenue. Richard Morris Hunt, the architect who designed many public buildings, modeled Cornelius Vanderbilt's residence after a northern Italian palace. Built in a mere two years (1893-95), it was an

extravagant place for a man described as quiet, kind and a pillar of his church — ironically, he was disabled by a stroke in 1896, was unable really to enjoy his summer home, and died in 1899. Tour highlights are the lower and upper loggias (from the upper you can see the Elizabeth Islands far out to sea on a clear day), the 45-foot-high Great Hall, an immense tapestry on the landing of the grand staircase (softly illuminated by a stained-glass ceiling), a magnificent 42-by-58-foot dining room, and a music room totally executed in Paris and shipped to this country. Upstairs, the bedrooms are comparatively modest, but the bathtubs had a choice of fresh or salt water. Also on view are the kitchens and butler's pantries, an area bigger than most houses.

Entrance to Marble House.

Rosecliff, Bellevue Avenue. Rosecliff's romantic reputation wasn't hurt by the fact that "The Great Gatsby" wooed Mia Farrow here. It was designed by Stanford White to resemble the Grand Trianon of Louis XIV in Versailles, and finished in 1900 for Mrs. Hermann Oelrichs, an heiress whose father made his fortune in Virginia City as one of a partnership that struck the Comstock Lode. She was considered one of the three great hostesses of Newport and is said to have spent $25,000 each summer on perfume to fill the light fixtures. The living room could double as a ballroom — at 80 by 40 feet, it was the largest in Newport and was the scene of many lavish balls. The grand staircase is graceful, heart-shaped and appropriately romantic looking. Rosecliff is sometimes rented for various functions; we enjoyed cocktails on the terrace during a New England press convention some years ago and felt elegant indeed.

The Elms, Bellevue Avenue. Built in 1901 for coal baron Edward J. Berwind by Philadelphia architect Horace Trumbauer in the classical style of 18th-century France, this palatial structure is considered one of the finest homes in America, partly because of its balanced plan. It doesn't exactly have a lived-in look; in fact, the Elms is more like a museum, with some furniture on loan from the Metropolitan. The conservatory is perfectly charming, bright and cheerful, with a marble fountain, statues in the corners and a gigantic marble urn. As befits a coal baron, Mr. Berwind had tracks for a coal car under his house; the car could be pushed out to the road where it would be filled with coal, thus ensuring no unsightly coal delivery on the property. He also generated his own electricity. The grounds are thought to be the finest of the Newport mansions, with a sunken garden, marble teahouses, fountains, and labeled trees and shrubs.

Kingscote, Bellevue Avenue. A picturesque cottage in the Gothic Revival style, Kingscote is one of the very early summer residences remaining, having been built in

1839. A McKim, Mead and White dining room was added in a new wing in 1881. We think it is one of the nicest rooms of all the mansions, decorated with Tiffany glass tiles and stained-glass panels of dahlias. Since one of the two owners of the house was in the China trade, there's a fabulous collection of Chinese export ware. The house was left to the Preservation Society in 1972, with most of its furnishings intact. It looks lived-in and thoroughly livable.

Marble House, Bellevue Avenue. Considered the most sumptuous of the "cottages," Marble House was completed in 1892 for William K. Vanderbilt and designed by Richard Morris Hunt. All the original Louis XIV furnishings are here, the ballroom is practically covered in gold, and this is where the party for all the dogs was given. It's modeled after the Petit Trianon at Versailles.

Chateau-sur-Mer, Bellevue Avenue. The original villa here was built in 1852 but was extensively redone by Richard Morris Hunt twenty years later. William Wetmore, who made a fortune in the China trade, was the first owner. His son, George Peabody Wetmore, a Rhode Island governor and senator, inherited it, and his daughter Edith lived here until her death in 1968. It is considered a fine example of lavish Victorian architecture and, although the interior is quite dark, at least it feels lived in. A collection of Victorian toys enchants younger visitors.

Several other mansions are open to visitors under private ownership: **The Astors' Beechwood** at 580 Bellevue Ave., built in 1851 as an Italian seaside villa, was purchased in 1880 by the William Backhouse Astors, at the time the richest family in America. Mrs. Astor coined the phrase "the 400," because that's how many her ballroom in New York could hold. In 1890 she took $2 million, went to the Continent and had sent back to her mansion a music room from France, a dining room from an English manor house, and a ballroom that is a replica of one in a Viennese palace. Mrs. Astor had 281 diamonds in her stomacher and looked like a walking chandelier, according to our tour guide. The house is the newest to be restored and opened to the public; the owners have tracked down many of the original furnishings. Adults $7, children $4.25. Tours daily, 10 to 5, early June through November.

Belcourt Castle, the Bellevue Avenue home of Oliver Hazard Perry Belmont, was built at a cost of $3 million by (who else?) Richard Morris Hunt in the style of Louis XIII's palace. Since 1956, the castle has been the home of the Tinney family and a place to display their fabulous art collection from 33 countries. There's a fine collection of stained glass and a golden coronation coach that weighs four tons — imagine what that would be worth these days! Costumed guides take you around, and you can stay for tea. Adults $6.50, children $2. Open daily, 9 to 5, Memorial Day to mid-October; rest of year, daily 10 to 4, January by appointment.

Hammersmith Farm, Ocean Drive. With much more of a country feeling than most Newport mansions, Hammersmith Farm also has one of the nicer settings — across the island on a hill next to Fort Adams, overlooking a meadow to Narragansett Bay and beyond to Jamestown. Jacqueline Bouvier Kennedy Onassis spent childhood summers in this airy home, and President Kennedy used one of the second-floor rooms as a summer Oval Office. Tour guides are well-versed in anecdotes about the Kennedys and the Auchincloss family, owners of Hammersmith since the late 19th century, until it was sold to a group of businessmen in 1978 and opened to the public. Caroline and John Jr. summered here too, Caroline with her famous pony Macaroni.

Don't miss the beautiful tiled fireplaces in almost every room, the fabulous flower arrangements, the glimpse of monogrammed linen in Mrs. Auchincloss's bedroom (her bed is turned down to show it) and, our favorite, the huge deck room, where surely a crowd of grownups and children could find their own spaces.

The grounds are worth a stroll, with formal gardens created by Frederick Law Olmsted. Trees and shrubs are labeled. A small gift shop is in the old children's playhouse, with a greenhouse attached. As well as plants, seedlings and bulbs, you can buy the book by Jackie and her sister Lee about a trip they took to Europe as young girls, *One Special Summer,* plus oriental china, and pickles and jams. The shop is especially heavy on all sorts of candy, some in fancy boxes. The tour takes about an hour, costs $6 (children $3) and the house is open daily from 10 to 5 (to 7 in summer) from April to mid-November, weekends from mid-March and to end of November.

Things to Do

There is so much to see and do in Newport that it would take many days and more space than we have available to cover everything. Free local publications like *Newport This Week* and the *Pineapple Post* can clue you in to timely events.

Tours. The **Newport Trolley** departs from the Gateway Visitors Center on the hour daily from 10 to 3, June-September, and makes sixteen stops at Newport's leading attractions. You can hop on and off as many times a day as you want for $7.50 (children $3.50). **Viking Tours of Newport,** 847-6921, offers a variety of bus tours, departing from the Gateway Visitors Center at 23 America's Cup Ave. and lasting from 90 minutes to four hours. It also offers one-hour harbor cruises from Goat Island Marina on its 140-passenger Viking Queen. Several enterprises rent tape cassettes for driving tours of Newport, available at the Visitors Center. Harbor tours and sailboat cruises are provided by any number of boats around the downtown wharves. The **Old Colony & Newport Railway** runs eight-mile excursions along Narragansett Bay to Green Animals topiary garden in Portsmouth on weekends in season. The fancy **Newport Star Clipper** dinner train follows the same path nightly at 7.

Ocean Drive should not be missed, whether you go by car, bike or moped (the latter two can be rented from several places). It offers miles of spectacular scenery, rocky points with crashing surf, views of many privately owned mansions and striking contemporary homes, the fabled Bailey's Beach where the 400 swam (and still do), and refreshing ocean breezes. The lovely Brenton State Park is along the drive and a favorite of sunset-watchers; you can park free and picnic on the rocks there.

The Cliff Walk. For an intimate look at the crashing ocean and also at the backs of the mansions, the three-and-a-half-mile Cliff Walk is a must. In late spring, wild roses lend their fragrance to the salty air. You can get onto the walk at several points; many people start at the foot of Narragansett Avenue, where you walk down to the ocean on the Forty Steps. When we did the walk some years ago, we found the first couple of miles easy because it was well maintained, but the latter part unkempt and difficult (and we had torn stockings to show for it); we hear this section has been upgraded. We had to pass through a couple of dark and slimy tunnels and were welcomed (?) at the Doris Duke estate by a surly looking guard with a gun who stood behind the chain-link fence, accompanied by the fiercest looking and sounding dogs we have ever seen.

Fort Adams State Park, at the start of Ocean Drive, is open daily during daylight hours (out-of-staters, $1) for picnicking, swimming, fishing and guided tours. Named for President John Adams, the fort was begun during the Revolution and is one of the largest seacoast fortifications in the country. The hilly point juts into the bay and provides as good a vantage point today for yacht-watching as it did for soldiers defending their country. Tours and period garrison drills are given in the summer.

The Museum of Yachting, Fort Adams State Park, 847-1018. Opened in 1985 in a 19th-century granite building on a point at the end of Fort Adams, this fledgling museum showcases the history of yachting and yacht racing. The Hall of Ships displays old wooden boats beneath a model of a boat that won the first America's Cup. In the harbor is the museum's prized Shamrock V. The last of the famed J-boats, it's called the largest floating ship of its kind in the world. The small museum, designed to appeal to laymen as well as sailors, gives a feeling for this aspect of Newport's heritage. Open mid-May through October, daily 10 to 5. Adults $3.

Green Animals, Cory Lane off Route 114, Portsmouth, 847-1000. The topiary is terrific at Green Animals, which is run by the Preservation Society just north of Newport. On view in the gardens are 80 trees and shrubs sculpted into shapes of a donkey, bear, ostrich, horse and rider, camel, mountain goat and the like. The animals are

The Cliff Walk.

formed of California privet; the geometric figures and ornamental designs of golden and American boxwoods. The charming small estate that slopes toward Narragansett Bay also includes dahlia and vegetable gardens, espaliered fruit trees, a grape arbor, and a gift and garden shop where you can buy forms to make your own topiary, plants and Salt Marsh Pottery. Open daily 10 to 5, May-October. Adults $6, children $3.

Beaching. The Newport area has plenty of places where you can stretch out on the sand. Of course, the water is rather chilly except in July and August. **King Park** on Wellington Avenue in town is on the sheltered harbor with green lawns for sitting, a raft with slides, free bathhouses and swings; it's a good beach for children. **Easton's Beach,** also known as First Beach, is a three-quarter-mile-long strand from the Cliff Walk at Memorial Boulevard to the Middletown line. It's being restored and raised onto piers following the destruction caused by the tidal surge from Hurricane Bob in 1991; Victorian bathhouses will be part of the turn-of-the-century look. The amusement area includes bumper boats and mini-golf. Beach admission is $5 per vehicle weekdays, $10 weekends. Just beyond Easton's are Second Beach and Third Beach in Middletown. Third Beach offers the island's best windsurfing.

A Wealth of History

Newport has more than 400 buildings dating from the Colonial era, all within walking distance of the Visitors Center. A few places not to miss:

Touro Synagogue, 27 Touro St. A home of worship for Congregation Jeshuat Israel, this is a National Historic Site, the oldest place of Jewish worship in the United States. Built in 1763 in classic Georgian style, the simple but beautifully proportioned exterior — cream brick with a trim of dark brown — hides an ornate interior in which twelve Ionic columns, representing the tribes of Israel, support a gallery where women in this Orthodox congregation sit. The Torah dates from 1658. The synagogue has a fascinating history, which you can learn from free guided tours, late June to Labor Day, Sunday-Friday 10 to 5; mid-May to mid-June and Labor Day to mid-October, Sunday-Friday 1 to 3; rest of year, Sunday 1 to 3.

Trinity Church, corner of Church and Spring Streets. Nicely framed by the spruced-up Queen Anne Square rising from America's Cup Avenue and restored in 1987, Rhode Island's first Anglican church was built in 1726 from designs by Christopher Wren. Its

graceful white spire is a Newport landmark. It has the second oldest organ in the country, two Tiffany windows and a triple-deck wineglass pulpit. Church is open free, Monday-Saturday 10 to 4 and Sunday noon to 4 in summer; afternoons in spring and fall; other times by appointment.

St. Mary's Church, corner of Spring Street and Memorial Boulevard, is the oldest Catholic parish in Rhode Island. Work was begun on the Gothic-style red stone church in 1848. The church is most famous as the site of the 1953 wedding of Jacqueline Bouvier to John F. Kennedy. The Kennedys summered in Newport in 1961, attending Mass on Sundays. A brass marker on the tenth pew, right side facing the altar, designates it as theirs. Open daily except Sunday, 9 to 4.

Hunter House, 54 Washington St. Restored by the Preservation Society, Hunter House is an outstanding example of Georgian architecture and is considered one of the ten finest Colonial homes in America. Beside the harbor, it was built for a wealthy merchant family in 1748, and its collection of early Rhode Island furniture crafted by the famous Goddard and Townsend families in mahogany and walnut is priceless. Open May-September, daily 10 to 5; weekends in April and October. Adults $6, children $3.

Colony House, Washington Square. Built in 1739 in the style of an English manor house, this handsome brick building was the center of governmental affairs for 160 years. Rhode Island was the first colony in 1776 to declare its independence and in May, the Declaration of Independence was read from its balcony. The building, still used for public ceremonies, has a full-length Gilbert Stuart portrait of George Washington, who met here with Rochambeau during the Revolutionary War. Open mid-June to Labor Day, Monday-Saturday 10 to 4 and Sunday noon to 4; rest of year by appointment. Free.

Redwood Library and Atheneum, 50 Bellevue Ave. Designed in 1748 by the arrchitect who did Touro Synagogue, this is the nation's oldest lending library. It contains countless valuable books and a fine collection of early American paintings, including seven by Rhode Islander Gilbert Stuart. Almost across the street in **Touro Park** is the **Old Stone Mill,** a 26-foot-high landmark that some think is a Viking church tower predating Columbus's voyage; others think it is the remains of Gov. Benedict Arnold's 17th-century windmill. Library open Monday-Saturday 9:30 to 5 or 5:30. Free.

International Tennis Hall of Fame, 194 Bellevue Ave., 846-4567. This place in the historic Newport Casino is one that tennis buffs won't want to miss. The casino, built in 1880 by Stanford White, is considered the cradle of American lawn tennis, and the National Men's Singles Championships were held here from 1881 to 1914. A gracious Victorian air lingers. This still is home to major tournaments like the annual Hall of Fame tennis championships played on the world's oldest grass courts in early July. The world's largest tennis museum includes the Davis Cup Theater, where old tennis films are shown. The public may play tennis on twelve grass courts or three indoor courts in season. Open daily, 10 to 5. Adults $5, children $2.50, family $10.

FOR MORE INFORMATION: Newport Gateway Visitors Center, 23 America's Cup Ave., (401) 849-8098 or (800) 326-6030. Preservation Society of Newport County, 118 Mill St., Newport 02840, (401) 847-1000.

Brick sidewalk, iron fence and facade of 1789 house on Pleasant Street.

Restorations and Restaurants

Portsmouth, N.H.

For a small city (population, 25,900), Portsmouth packs a wallop. As New Hampshire's first settlement, it has a rich historic tradition and takes great pride in its past. What it also has, and what makes it such fun for today's visitor, is a lively present. Waterfront redevelopment, the restoration of its historic homes, interesting restaurants and good places to stay all make Portsmouth exciting.

The town's original name was Strawbery Banke, an impulsive and appropriate choice by English settlers who arrived in 1630 and found wild strawberries growing in profusion on the banks of the Piscataqua River. Twenty-three years later, the town was renamed Portsmouth.

The old name lives in a fine historic restoration in the city's South End. There a dilapidated but potentially rich neighborhood was saved from almost certain destruction in the 1950s. A few interested locals pleaded with the federal government not to raze buildings for the construction of subsidized rental apartments, but to help fund the restoration instead. The resulting Strawbery Banke celebrates its 30th anniversary in 1994.

"Adaptive re-use" is a phrase used by Strawbery Banke Inc. as it attempts to make this museum more than just a 9 to 5 affair — one where craftsmen and a few complementary businesses might also reside. There are a boat shop and a leather craftsman, for example.

Elsewhere in Portsmouth the same spirit of restoration exists. The entire city seems bent on the renovation and adaptation of its vintage houses and buildings, and it has plenty to work on. After all, the reason the city was settled so early was because of the deep-water port it offered, and those early sea captains built some great homes.

Several of Portsmouth's beautiful houses from the 18th and 19th centuries are open to the public as museums. The 1763 Moffatt-Ladd House, with its original formal English gardens out back, and the John Paul Jones House, built in 1758, are two of our favorites. Jones, whose ringing words, "I have not yet begun to fight," have inspired scores of schoolboys, rented rooms in town on two occasions while he oversaw the construction of vessels for the Revolutionary War.

Red tugboats, commercial fishing vessels, sightseeing boats, pleasure craft and the massive defense ships of the Portsmouth Naval Shipyard (located across the Piscataqua River in Kittery, Me.) ply Portsmouth's harbor. The river is the second fastest tidal river in the U.S. navigable by ship, with six knots the average current and a nine-foot tidal range. It is fun to sit outdoors on restaurant decks, or inside by windows in cooler weather, and check the action.

Portsmouth is cultural. Theater, chamber music, choral groups, artists and craftsmen lend their talents to the vibrancy of the city. While these aspects make Portsmouth a great place to visit, more and more people want to live here, too.

In the spring, this city by the sea is an especially good destination. That's the time when the idea of being near the water has special appeal, and yet a cozy bed and breakfast appeals as well. Portsmouth can supply both experiences and more.

Getting There

Portsmouth is located at New Hampshire's most northerly seacoast point. It is easily reached by automobile via coastal Route 1 or Interstate 95. Greyhound buses stop in the center of town at Market Square. The closest major airport is Logan International in Boston; limousine service between Logan and Portsmouth is provided frequently.

Where to Stay

Accommodations are varied in Portsmouth. The city boasts several charming B&Bs in vintage homes and a larger Victorian-era inn that appeals to business people as well

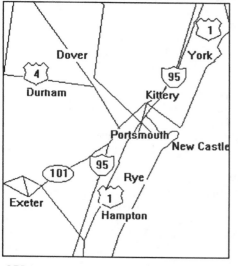

as travelers. A new Sheraton hotel on the waterfront and several good motels at the Portsmouth Traffic Circle off I-95 provide more lodging choices. Rates in the motels change seasonally, and the Sheraton offers a weekend package.

The Martin Hill Inn, 404 Islington St., Portsmouth 03801, (603) 436-2287. What a charmer this place is! The first of Portsmouth's B&Bs, it is run with great care by Jane and Paul Harnden, corporate dropouts who probably work as hard at innkeeping as they ever did in the so-called business world. Seven air-conditioned rooms with private baths in two buildings are tastefully decorated with mostly period furnishings. The two yellow

Queen Anne Victorian theme prevails at The Sise Inn.

buildings are linked by an exquisite city garden, an oasis of coolness and color on a warm day, where the Harndens were also thinking of constructing a water garden. The inn is on a busy street, a couple of miles from the historic waterfront section of town, but once here, you're in a world of your own. Williamsburg wallpapers, oriental rugs and canopied beds strike the right note for Portsmouth. The Harndens furnish their own brand of wildflower and glycerine soaps, which can be purchased in gift packs as keepsakes. We like the suite with a greenhouse in the Guest House; for a change of pace, it features rattan furniture and lush plants. Breakfast, served in a dining room with lovely Sheraton furniture, is delicious. Blueberry pecan pancakes, omelets and baked apples are among the Harndens' most popular items. Doubles, $75 to $95.

The Sise Inn, 40 Court St., Portsmouth 03801, (603) 433-1200 or (800) 232-4667. This small luxury inn with 32 air-conditioned guest rooms is owned by Someplace Different Inc., a Canadian organization. Opened in 1986, this was the first in the United States; the second is the Capt. Daniel Stone Inn in Brunswick, Me. According to innkeeper Carl Jensen, the house was built in 1881 by businessman John Sise as a family home. There are ten rooms in the original building and the rest are in a new addition. All have private baths, wall-to-wall carpeting and color TVs hidden in armoires. The mood is Queen Anne Victorian and there are great oak beds, skylights, overhead fans and a different wallpaper (usually flowered) in each room. Room 203 has a fireplace and sitting area and is particularly attractive; the fireplaces, however, are only to be looked at. A few bathrooms contain whirlpool tubs. The inn is notable for the amount of richly varnished butternut wood in the lobby. A Victorian-style parlor is comfortable and a cheerful breakfast room offers a continental-plus breakfast with yogurt, muffins, bagels, cereals and fruits. Newspapers are complimentary. Doubles, $100 to $175.

The Inn at Strawbery Banke, 314 Court St., Portsmouth 03801, (603) 436-7242 or (800) 428-3933. The location of this inn is perfect: right in the downtown section and a short walk to Strawbery Banke or the historic waterfront and shopping area. Once you pull your car into the adjacent parking lot, you may not need it again. Sally

O'Donnell, the innkeeper, works with a small staff to keep things shipshape. All seven guest rooms have private baths. Ours on the second floor was done in blue and white and was large and airy, with a queen and a single bed. This is an old house, though, with narrow hallways and somewhat steep staircases. Guests enjoy a pleasant parlor with loads of books in floor-to-ceiling bookcases. Breakfast is served in a sunny breakfast room. Ours was juice, cantaloupe slices, bacon and eggs and the best homemade bread, toasted — plenty to fill us up for a day of touring. Doubles, $75 to $85.

The Inn at Christian Shore, 335 Maplewood Ave., Portsmouth 03801, (603) 431-6770. Three former antiques dealers, Tom Towey, Louis Sochia and Charles Litchfield, have run this attractive B&B for fifteen years. The house is a short drive from the historic downtown area. Of the six well-appointed guest rooms, four have private baths and two share. One on the main floor contains a canopy bed. All are air-conditioned. The breakfast room is unusually attractive with a large central table and several deuces with wing chairs by the windows, and an enormous collection of rabbits in all guises. The flowers here are gorgeous from spring through early fall; Tom is the gardener. Breakfasts are complete and might even include steak. There are always fresh muffins, two favorites being the blueberry and the black raspberry. Doubles, $75.

Sheraton Portsmouth Hotel & Conference Center, 250 Market St., Portsmouth 03801, (603) 431-2300. Built in 1988, this is the newest kid on a very good block. The brick hotel has been built high enough so that there's a view of the working waterfront and the Piscataqua River from the main lobby and the dining area, which is at the waterview end. While the building seems a bit imposing from the outside, inside the color scheme of green, peach and mauve is most restful and furnishings are traditional and comfortable. The 148 rooms with kingsize or two double beds offer cable TV and HBO. Several penthouse and townhouse suites with one or two bedrooms, kitchen and living room with fireplace are available for extended stays. There are an indoor pool and sauna and a fitness center. A nightclub, Enticements, offers something to do in the evening. Doubles, $109 to $139; condominium suites, $200 to $350.

Susse Chalet Hotel, 650 Borthwick Ave. Ext., Portsmouth 03801, (603) 436-6363. We've been very pleased with accommodations and service at this member of the national motel chain located at the Portsmouth circle. There's a rather nice outdoor pool for warm-weather stays, and the motel is set back off a side road so that it seems quieter than some. Most of the 105 rooms contain two double beds. A continental breakfast is available in the lobby. Doubles, $54.70 to $59.70.

Anchorage Inn, 417 Woodbury Ave., Portsmouth 03801, (603) 431-8111 or (800) 370-8111. Also at the Portsmouth Circle, this is an especially attractive motel, member of a small group. A jaunty red awning out front and colorful plantings set the tone. Some of the 93 rooms have kingize beds, others have extra-long doubles, and several have two beds. Deluxe suites contain living room, bedroom and bathroom with a whirlpool tub. A complimentary continental breakfast is served in the attractive cafe, **Sweet Dreams,** which also opens in the evening for light supper items such as fish and chips. There's a small indoor pool. Doubles, $60 to $75.

Holiday Inn, 300 Woodbury Ave., Portsmouth 03801, (603) 431-8000. This motel at the Portsmouth Circle has been around for a long time, but it's looking better than ever since a complete upgrading in 1991-92. All 138 rooms were renovated and **Cranberry's** restaurant got a facelift, too. There are king, queen and standard double rooms available. A small outdoor pool is, unfortunately, right next to the front parking area. Doubles, $97.95 to $105.95.

An **Econo Lodge** and a **Howard Johnson's** also are available at the Portsmouth Circle.

Historic Restorations

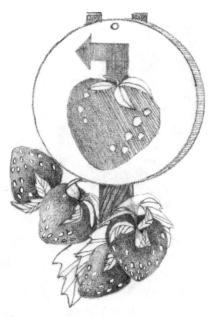

Historic restorations abound in Portsmouth. More than 40 houses are open to the public in one fashion or another. The greatest concentration is in Strawbery Banke.

Strawbery Banke, Marcy Street, (603) 433-1100. Salvaged from demolition and urban renewal in the 1950s, this ten-acre site calls itself a museum in progress, and that is part of its appeal. Not only are there eight furnished houses of several time periods, but also on-site archaeological excavations, landscape reconstruction and building restorations as officials seek to renew the area piece by piece. Opened in 1990, for example, was the Rider-Wood House, built around 1800 and furnished to interpret the daily life of a widow around 1830. All but one house, the Goodwin Mansion, are on their original sites, which makes Strawbery Banke particularly authentic. Interpreters lead orientation tours a couple of times a day, but basically it's a do-it-yourself, walk-through deal, and with the museum's illustrated map in hand, you'll have no trouble. Take time to see the boat builder, the potter, the weaver, and anything else that's going on while you're there. New England Gardening Day in June is one of several special events planned throughout the season. The Dunaway Store is a gift shop where you can pick up all sorts of quasi-historic items. If you're hungry, good food is available at **The Washington Street Eatery,** a Colonial-style lunchroom where you can get home-baked muffins, soups, sandwiches and luscious desserts (you can also tote your own lunch and picnic at Strawbery Banke). Open daily 10 to 5, May-October. Adults $9, children $5, family $25. Tickets can be used for two consecutive days.

Moffatt-Ladd House, 154 Market St., (603) 436-8221. If you can visit only one historic house while you are in Portsmouth, make it this. A copy of an English manor house, it is beautifully situated high on the banks of the Piscataqua River and it is not hard to imagine lawns extending to the water's edge, as they once did. Today, Market Street interrupts the line, but out back extensive English gardens remain much as they were. The gardens may be visited separately from the house. The house was built in 1763 as a wedding gift from John Moffatt, an English sea captain, to his son. Later it was the home of John's son-in-law, Gen. William Whipple, a signer of the Declaration of Independence. Visitors are treated to three floors of exceptional 18th-century furnishings. The design of the house is unusual, from the cellar with its great brick arches leading to a secret passageway that once went to the wharves, all the way up to rooms with extra-deep fireplaces allowing for spacious closets on each side (a novelty in their day). Next door is the 1823 Counting House where Moffatt and Ladd cargoes were laded; out back is an old-fashioned herb garden. A used-book sale is conducted on an ongoing basis in the Coach House. Open June 15 to Oct. 15, Monday-Saturday 10 to 4, Sunday 2 to 5. Adults $4, children $1. Gardens only, $1.

John Paul Jones House, 43 Middle St., (603) 436-8240. John Paul Jones, the naval hero, was a bachelor who never owned a house. But he made this lovely yellow gambrel-roofed house his headquarters during two lengthy stays in Portsmouth. Sarah

Moffatt-Ladd House is among the most imposing in Portsmouth.

Wentworth Purcell, a widow, rented Jones a room in 1776-77 when he was in town to oversee construction of the sloop, Ranger, and again in 1781-82 when he returned for the building of the America. A handsome man (note the bust of Jones in the house), he is reputed to have turned a few pretty heads during his stay. The second-floor room he occupied is a memorial. The house has been headquarters of the Portsmouth Historical Society for many years and contains rich local collections. You'll love the costumes, the collection of canes in which weapons are concealed and items from ships that were dismantled in Portsmouth. The kids will, too. On July 6, the anniversary of John Paul Jones's birth, the society hosts a birthday party. Open mid-May to mid-October, Monday-Saturday 10 to 4 until July 1 and then daily. Adults $4, children $1.

Wentworth-Coolidge Mansion, Little Harbor Road, (603) 436-6607. This rambling yellow clapboard structure of 42 rooms is situated on a point of land with a great view of Portsmouth Harbor. It was originally the home of Benning Wentworth, New Hampshire's royal governor from 1741 to 1767, and contains the council chamber where the state's first provincial government conducted its affairs in the turbulent pre-Revolutionary War period. Today, the governor's council meets annually in the room, making the trek from Concord. It is a handsome space, with low corner cupboards, unique to the house, and a splendid table surrounded by beautiful walnut Queen Anne chairs. A glass chandelier hangs overhead. When Benning Wentworth died in 1770, his widow married Michael Wentworth, a retired British Army colonel. They made the mansion a hospitable social center, entertaining George Washington here in 1789. The house's many subsequent owners made changes and added rooms that contribute to its eclectic but not unattractive appearance. The grounds contain the oldest lilacs original to their property in the United States. A tour takes about an hour and is most interesting, although there's relatively little furniture in the house, which is viewed primarily for its construction and history. Open June 20 to Labor Day, daily 10 to 5; Memorial Day to June 20, weekends only. Adults $2.50.

Wentworth-Gardner House, Mechanic Street, (603) 436-4406. Considered one of the most nearly perfect examples of Georgian architecture in America, this house had an interesting succession of owners, beginning with a member of the ubiquitous Wentworth family and including the Metropolitan Museum of Art, which at one time planned to move it to New York's Central Park. The carving throughout the interior required fourteen months to complete. Among items of interest are the great fireplace in the kitchen, original Dutch tiles and the spinning attic on the third floor. Open June to mid-October, Tuesday-Saturday 2 to 4. Adults $4, children $3.

Warner House, 150 Daniel St., (603) 436-5909. This house is considered the finest example in New England of a brick urban mansion of the early 18th century. Among its treasures: six mural paintings on the staircase wall, an early example of marbleization in the dining room and a lightning rod on the west wall, said to have been installed under the supervision of Benjamin Franklin in 1762. From 1748-54 it was the home of Gov. Benning Wentworth, who seems to have lived only in the best places. A guided tour takes 45 minutes to an hour. Open mid-June to end of October, Tuesday-Saturday 10 to 4. Adults $4, children $2.

Other historic houses include the **Gov. John Langdon House,** the **Rundlet-May House** and the **Jackson House,** oldest in New Hampshire, all operated by the Society for the Preservation of New England Antiquities, (603) 436-3205.

Seeing and Doing

Walking. Portsmouth is a city for walkers. Its streets are narrow, its houses and shops easily viewable, and some of its sidewalks brick. One popular area for walkers is the Market Street-Ceres Street area near the riverfront, where there are many shops and restaurants. Check out the red tugboats tied up by Ceres Street docks; they symbolize the city and are used to aid ships coming up the river. A map from the Chamber of Commerce is invaluable.

One walk we like begins at the Portsmouth Public Library on Islington Street (there's a public parking lot nearby). Walk along Middle Street to State Street and down State to Pleasant, passing the John Paul Jones House along the way. Follow Pleasant Street all the way to Marcy. Pass a park to the right and follow it down to Mill Pond. Look at old houses, among them, at 346 Pleasant St., the **Gov. John Wentworth House,** the official residence of New Hampshire's last royal governor. Nearby is the Pleasant Street Cemetery dating from 1753. Turn left onto Marcy Street, which leads past Strawbery Banke on the left and Prescott Park on the right.

Prescott Park is located in an area that was once one of the seamiest in the city. Two civic-minded sisters, Mary and Josie Prescott, began to beautify the waterfront in the 1930s by establishing the oldest section of the park. They willed their fortunes for its further development. Formal gardens, with lighted fountains, have long been an attraction. The Prescott Park Arts Festival operates all summer long with a variety of special events, musical, theatrical and otherwise. The gardens — a joint venture between the park and the University of New Hampshire's Cooperative Extension Service — are a place for trying new floral varieties, including annuals.

Picnicking is permitted in Prescott Park. An even better spot is **Four Tree Island,** within walking distance from the park across a short bridge that leads from Marcy Street to Pierce Island and then via causeway to the little island. There are sturdy picnic tables under shelters, all with views of waterfront activity.

Isles of Shoals. Ten miles off the coast of Portsmouth lie nine rocky islands first charted by Capt. John Smith when he sailed past in 1614. They were included on his now-famous map of the New England coast, and were subsequently used for many summers by European fishermen, who were attracted by the "shoals" or schools of fish. In the 1800s they became famous as summer resorts, especially the two largest, Appledore and Star islands. The most famous daughter of the islands was the poet Celia Thaxter, born in Portsmouth and raised out on the isles, where her father was the first innkeeper on Appledore. To his hotel, the Appledore House, Celia attracted many artistic and literary figures of the day, including Nathaniel Hawthorne, James Russell Lowell, Childe Hassam and Henry Ward Beecher.

Since early in this century, Star Island has operated as a religious conference center under the Congregational and Unitarian churches. The legends and lore of the barren islands are fascinating and you can hear them aboard the ships operated by the **Isles of Shoals Steamship Co.**, Steamship Dock at 315 Market St., (603) 431-5500 or (800) 441-4620. Frequent sailings operate from spring to early fall. Whale-watch cruises also are offered. While a regular Isles of Shoals cruise costs $12 (children $7) and takes about three hours, we suggest the "Star Island Stopover," which leaves at 11 and returns before 5. This allows you to alight on Star Island and spend a few hours exploring. Adults $16, children $9. Bring a picnic lunch or buy a snack on the island. Reservations are recommended, especially on weekends.

The Shoals Room at the Portsmouth Public Library on Islington Street is a great follow-up to your cruise through the islands. Ask the reference librarian to admit you to the upstairs room where the Shoals Collection is kept.

Portsmouth Harbor Cruises, 64 Ceres St., (603) 436-8084 or (800) 776-0915. The narrated cruise down the Piscataqua River and around the island of New Castle is informative and amusing at times. Ours was particularly oriented to the importance of the Portsmouth Naval Shipyard, especially during World War II. You'll see what's left of the great resort, Wentworth-by-the-Sea, from the water. Cruises leave mid-June through Labor Day on Tuesday-Sunday at 10, also at noon daily except Wednesday and Saturday, when they go to the Isles of Shoals. There are also a 3 p.m. cruise on Monday, Wednesday and Saturday, a daily cocktail cruise at 5:30 and a sunset cruise at 7. Harbor cruises take about 90 minutes. Adults $8.50, children $6.

Horse and Carriage Rides. The Portsmouth Livery Co., (603) 427-0044, operates horse and carriage rides in the downtown waterfront area and near Prescott Park. From May through October, day and evening sightseeing tours start at noon. Several different tours are offered, ranging from $15 to $35 per group. A special picnic ride for two includes a tour, a round trip to a scenic picnic area and food for $65.

Forts. Several forts are located along the Atlantic coast and the banks of the river. One of the most pleasant vistas of sea and coast is enjoyed from **Fort McClary** in nearby Kittery Point, Me. The site contains a six-sided blockhouse commanding impressive views of the coast and the river's mouth. The fort and grounds are maintained as a state park. Attractive paths lead to the edge of the bluff looking down on the sea. Picnicking is permitted. To reach the fort, take U.S. Route 1 to Kittery, then Route 103 or Kittery Point Road to the fort.

Fort Constitution on the island of New Castle is particularly popular with young boys who like to climb around fortifications.

The town of **New Castle** is very old and many of the houses sport dates from the 1700s. Riding or biking through offers visual treats. You can stop at **Great Island Common,** a large, recently developed seacoast park with a vista of open ocean. Also in New Castle was the late, great Wentworth-by-the-Sea resort. Its great white hulk still towers, ghostlike, above the sea as a series of owners keep coming up with plans, then discarding them. Its golf course is still in use.

Wentworth-Gardner House, as viewed from Piscataqua River.

Swimming. Portsmouth does not have a good beach. You must go south to Hampton or Rye or north to the coast of Maine for saltwater swimming.

For the kids. The Children's Museum of Portsmouth, 280 Marcy St., (603) 436-3853. This special museum, just for the youngsters in your group, is not far from Strawbery Banke. Occupying the historic Old South Meeting House, it offers hands-on exhibits, workshops and demonstrations, and changing programs. "The Primary Place" is a great space for toddlers. Open Tuesday-Saturday 10 to 5, Sunday 1 to 5; also Monday in summer. Admission $3.50.

U.S.S. Albacore, Albacore Park, Exit 7 off I-95, (603) 436-3680. This 1,200-ton research vessel built at the Portsmouth Naval Shipyard in 1952 and retired from service in 1972 was an experimental sub that carried a crew of 55. The exhibit, with the Albacore in permanent drydock, opened in 1986. Following a brief film in the Visitor Center, visitors take guided tours of the cramped sleeping quarters, the engine room and the navigation station. The teardrop hull design was considered innovative. Open daily, 9:30 to 5:30. Adults $4, children $2, family $10.

Shopping

People love to shop in Portsmouth's boutiques. Across the river in Kittery you'll find many discount outlets.

Market, Ceres and Bow streets have most of the individualized small shops in Portsmouth. We like the **Cat House** with every kind of feline item imaginable, from stuffed cats to refrigerator magnets in the shape of cats. **Macro World** on Market Street offers all sorts of items for the ecology-minded; we especially liked stuffed and huggable globes, birds' nests and shower curtains showing the night sky.

Jester's Collectibles is filled with harlequin dolls, masks, marionettes, dolls and other items with a theatrical bent. **Fair Skies** on Market Street carries creatively designed clothes, both sportswear and dresses. Nearby, **Gallery 33** has creative pottery, things like papier mache sneakers, and more. The new **J.T. Lee** on Ceres Street has great clothes with the Zoe label.

Serendipity on Pleasant Street stocks wonderful clothing, jewelry and gift items.

Don't miss the back room with animal-shaped wooden napkin rings and other household items.

North of Kittery, Route 1 is lined with **factory outlets.** Among them are Boston Trader Kids, Crazy Horse, Brooks Brothers, Timberland shoes, Gant, Puma, Izod, Evan Picone, I West shoes and Guess jeans. There are also factory stores for Dansk, Royal Doulton, Waterford and Wedgwood.

Wining and Dining

Bostonians regularly travel to Portsmouth for dinner and the city has become known for its restaurants. Here are a few of our favorites.

L'Auberge, 96 Bridge St., (603) 436-2377. This smallish, one-room restaurant in an old house, run by Francois Rolland and his wife Kathy, is patronized mostly by locals. The few tourists who manage to find it are usually delighted. All the old classics are offered on the menu, a throwback to the 1950s and '60s. We were a bit surprised to find Pepperidge Farm goldfish in a little bowl that said "Pepperidge Farm" on each candlelit table, but that's a small quibble. Dark green napkins contrast with white tablecloths; walls are white above the wainscoting and deep violet below, but the soft lighting allows everything to blend nicely. French plates are displayed on the walls. We found both the chicken chasseur and the sweetbreads sauteed with mushrooms and marsala excellent. Accompaniments were fresh green beans and scalloped potatoes. Small individual caesar salads were fine and a bottle of Chateau St. Michelle fume blanc was a perfect accompaniment. Our only disappointment was the chocolate mousse; the delicious chocolate truffles that accompany the check would have sufficed. Other entrees ($13 to $21) include tournedos bordelaise, steak au poivre flambe, chateaubriand and roast duck with orange sauce. Service is attentive but not cloying and you are not rushed. Lunch, Tuesday-Friday 11:30 to 1:30; dinner, Tuesday-Saturday 5 to 10; Sunday brunch, 11:30 to 3.

The Blue Strawbery, 29 Ceres St., (603) 431-6420. This inventive restaurant in a narrow restored ship's chandlery across from the waterfront was the first of an eventual wave of exciting restaurants to become established in Portsmouth. James Haller was the most famous of the chef-partners; he went on to write a cookbook and was frequently on TV. Now another of the originals, Gene Brown, runs the restaurant. Although it fell out of favor with locals for a time, it is considered very good again indeed. The format remains basically the same: nine freshly prepared dishes in six courses are served for a fixed price ($38). Entrees always include the choice of a fish, a fowl and a meat, and dishes are prized for their creativity. The choice of soups, for example, recently included champagne, pickled thyme and artichoke heart in a cream base. Appetizers could be phyllo pastry stuffed with spiced pork on Southern Comfort barbecue sauce or escargots baked in a garlic and whiskey butter with toast rounds. Entrees were beef wellington with a lightly gingered madeira and mushroom sauce, half a partly boned duck roasted with a green peppercorn, honey and lemon glaze, and salmon, sea scallops and shrimp baked in a duxelle with pernod lime butter. The restaurant's hallmark dessert is strawberries with brown sugar and sour cream. This is culinary show biz at its best. Dinner by reservation, nightly at 7:30 in summer, additional seating Saturday at 6; Sunday dinner at 6 only. Closed Monday-Wednesday rest of year. No credit cards.

Anthony's Al Dente, Custom House Cellar, 59 Penhallow St., (603) 436-2527. More than ten years ago, Ruth Rutherford (with the help of chef Tony Catalina) opened this wonderful spot downstairs in the stone-walled cellar of the Federal building that was Portsmouth's Custom House from 1816 to 1850. The environment is enchanting:

Red tugboats are frequent sight along Piscataqua River.

oriental rugs on the floor, wood tables with windsor chairs, candlelight and fresh flowers. The menu changed in 1992 to reflect today's eating habits; instead of expecting diners to have pasta as the "first main course" followed by another entree, the new pink menu lists two divisions of main courses: pasta and seafood or meat. Of course, there are still some terrific appetizers, including funghi trifolati (sauteed mushrooms with pancetta, garlic and brandy served on a pastry round) or poulet grille (grilled chicken served with sliced pears and walnuts and topped with a roquefort dressing). Pastas remain the rage here. Fettuccine verde primavera con arsella combines scallops, carrots and broccoli with spinach fettuccine in a light alfredo sauce; salmone al forno tops baked fillet of salmon with red pepper-basil pesto on mixed julienned vegetables and angel-hair pasta. Among entrees ($10 to $17), try lamb steak with a lemon sauce, baked stuffed chicken with pistachio sauce or any of the daily specials. Desserts are things like zuppa inglese, almond cake with amaretto whipped cream and ricotta cheesecake. Dinner, Tuesday-Saturday 5:45 to 10, Sunday 5 to 9.

The Depot, Market Square, (603 427-0600). Tony Catalina, who was the Anthony of Anthony's al Dente, then moved to the State Street Saloon and had everyone flocking after him. Now he runs his own show at The Depot in Market Square and suddenly, but not surprisingly, its stock is up. Tony is proud to serve inventive and tasty cuisine at rock-bottom prices. "I want to run a place my friends can eat at," he says. Open for three meals daily, the attractive storefront restaurant with a railroad motif manages to please almost everybody. Breakfast includes homemade granola, breakfast sandwiches (like scrambled eggs with cheddar, bacon or ham on a croissant with Depot potatoes for $3.95), omelets, french toast, and banana or blueberry pancakes. Salads and sandwiches are stressed for lunch. At night, most entrees cost $7 and include such delights as chicken cacciatore, Tony's chicken (sauteed boneless breast with prosciutto and artichoke hearts in a pesto-cream sauce) and pork tenderloin marsala. For $8.50 you can break the bank and get roast lamb with garlic and rosemary, served with wild porcini mushroom sauce. Get there early if you don't want to wait in line. Breakfast, 7:30 to 11:30; lunch, 11:30 to 2:30; dinner, 5 to 9.

367

The Grotto, 73 Pleasant St., (603) 436-1373. This sunny Mediterranean restaurant, new in 1991, was opened by the owners of the nearby State Street Saloon. Known for good Italian and Greek food at rational prices, the restaurant features bright wall murals by Shane Baker that are reminiscent of Greek isles and Italian coasts. Stucco walls, a skylit ceiling and sleek black chairs at marble tables add to a sophisticated, warm and bright decor. Lunch specials might be a souvlaka sandwich for $4.95, Greek pastitsio for $5.95 (add a buck for rice or salad), spanakopita, meatball sub or sauteed chicken with a basil pesto. At night, most entrees are under $10, with steak oscar the most expensive at $13.95. Choices include eleven fettuccine dishes, four tortellinis and eight spaghettis. You can get eggplant parmigiana in two guises (tomato sauce or meat sauce). Besides a zillion chicken dishes, there are seafood, steak and Greek specialties, including a Greek sampler (lamb and chicken shish kabob, stuffed cabbage and grape leaves and grilled locanico) for $10.95. We didn't spy any Greek offerings on the pedestrian wine list. Lunch, Thursday-Sunday 11:30 to 3; dinner nightly, 5 to 10.

Hi Bombay! 86 Pleasant St., (603) 427-1436. This rather sophisticated Indian restaurant — with a sister emporium in Portland, Me. — was new to Portsmouth in 1991 but was very highly spoken of almost immediately. Burgundy and green are the restful colors in the dining room and high-backed carved and upholstered chairs add a touch of elegance. The exhaustive menu includes seven Indian breads such as paratha (a flaky layered bread sweetened with butter) and onion kulcha (mild unleavened bread filled with onions and spices). Rikki Tikki Tavi is an appetizer described as "a pocket of spiced vegetables deep fried." Among entrees in the $7.50 to $10 range are chicken tandoori, shrimp, lamb or taj biryani (all made with basmati rice), lamb curry (mild, regular or hot) and lamb bhuna (grilled pieces simmered in a light sauce with Himalayan herbs, tomatoes and bell pepper). A lengthy list of vegetarian dishes includes raj mah (kidney beans in a robust tomato-based sauce of ginger, garlic, tumeric and other herbs) and malai kofta (balls of freshly minced vegetables simmered in cardamom, saffron, garlic, cashews and a light cream sauce). In addition to Darjeeling tea or a mango milkshake, you can get King Fisher beer from India. Lunch daily, 11 to 3; dinner, 5 to 10.

The Oar House, 55 Ceres St., (603) 436-4025. Dick Gallant's popular restaurant across the street from the waterfront draws crowds because of the location and the ambience, as much as the food. The restaurant is ensconced in what was once a warehouse for a major local merchant. Brick walls, candles in hurricane lamps and eclectic furnishings — believe it or not, one table features the brass headboard and footboard of a bed — add charm. Photos of ships on the walls and stained-glass lamps over the bar are other appealing touches. A small deck, across the street and overlooking the river, is crowded on warm days. Always on the menu are clam chowder and onion soup au gratin. Sandwiches and light entrees like seafood fettuccine are available at noon. For dinner (entrees $16 to $20), try bouillabaisse, seafood-stuffed shrimp, baked haddock or the Oar House Delight (shrimp, scallops and fresh fish lightly sauteed and topped with sour cream and seasoned crumbs, then browned in the oven). There is also a raw bar. The restaurant's bloody mary won a Seacoast contest. Lunch daily, 11:30 to 2:30; dinner, 5 to 9 or 10.

The Dolphin Striker, 15 Bow St., (603) 431-5222. Two new owners, Paul Schafer (who was in the restaurant business in Gloucester) and Peter DiZoglio, were bringing this restaurant back to its former fame after taking over in 1991. Seafood with a bit of Italian and French flavor was being stressed. Especially popular were entrees like fettuccine portofino and lobster and scallop-stuffed ravioli in cream sauce. Among other dinner entrees ($12 to $18) were swordfish schafer (stuffed with sauteed leeks, basil and mozzarella cheese and served with a lemon butter sauce), chicken bolonnaisse (a double breast layered with ham, sage, swiss cheese and served with a mushroom demi-glaze) and tortellini carbonara. The place looks much as it always did — Colonial in feel with hurricane lamps flickering in the evening. Around the corner and down one level is the adjoining **Spring Hill Tavern** with stone walls and lots of wood and brass. A light menu is served in the tavern. Lunch daily, 11:30 to 2; dinner, 5 to 9 or 10; Sunday brunch, noon to 4.

Outdoor dining in Portsmouth.

The Codfish, The Hill, (603) 431-8503. Spanish tapas plus pizza, soups, pastas and such other dishes as New York sirloin or shrimp prosciutto ($10 to $14) are among the varied entree choices at this longtime resident of Portsmouth. Located in the 1810 Nutter-Rymes House in an area of the city that has been much renovated, The Codfish also features music virtually every night and jazz on Sundays. Owners Charles and Dorry Richmond have a good thing going, offering a little something for everyone. The bar is on the first floor; the pretty dining rooms are upstairs. Open daily, 11:30 to 11.

Karen's, 105 Daniel St., (603) 431-1948. First Karen Weiss taught school for a couple of years, then took a job making and selling ice cream during the summer vacation. That intrigued her so much that instead of returning to school, she stayed in the food business, soon opening her own little spot. It's been fourteen years and she is still at it. Locals and visitors love Karen's for breakfast, lunch and dinner. In a narrow old building near the historic district, the restaurant has bare wood floors, stenciled walls and a blackboard menu above the fireplace. Tables are wood and chairs are mismatched, but the food is fabulous. The tiny but well-organized kitchen whips up luncheon specialties ($3 to $5.95) like Karen's Favorite (sauteed red onion, tomato, mushroom, artichoke hearts and spinach on pita bread with melted cheddar) and a wonderful Greek salad pita loaded with feta. The sandwiches come with a choice of potato salad or black bean salad; the black bean is out of this world. Grilled fish, salmon en papilotte and grilled eggplant with polenta are possibilities for dinner ($8 to $12.50). Breakfast and lunch, Monday-Saturday; dinner, Thursday-Saturday 6 to 10; Sunday brunch, 8 to 2. BYOB. No credit cards.

Cafe Brioche in Market Square has wondrous pastries and baked goods; you can sit at a little ice cream table outside or indoors and have a real European-style repast. **Belle Peppers** is a good deli/gourmet food store that has picnic lunches to go. **Cafe Mirabelle** on Bridge Street is another restaurant worthy of your attention, as is **Strawbery Court** in the downtown area.

FOR MORE INFORMATION: Greater Portsmouth Chamber of Commerce, 500 Market St., Portsmouth, N.H. 03801, (603) 436-1118.

Casco Castle overlooks boats in South Freeport harbor.

Main Street and More

Freeport and the Harpswells, Maine

Every year, nearly four million people from around the world make the pilgrimage to the big, plain building with the canoes and kayaks out front, something of a landmark in the center of Freeport. It's the famous 24-hour-a-day retail store of L.L. Bean, purveyors of goods for the outdoorsman and symbol to many of the Maine mystique. They may only have heard of Freeport from Bean's ubiquitous mail-order catalogs, but they're coming to mecca — many in search of nostalgia, of simpler times, of basic virtues and values. It's as much a mecca in springtime for parents getting their youngsters outfitted for summer camp as it is for affluent urbanites seeking to get back to the earth, if only through a Bean jacket.

And what a shopping mecca it is. All those pilgrims have turned Bean's into the second most frequented tourist destination in the state (after Acadia National Park). In their wake in the last ten years have popped up more than 125 outlet stores, two dozen inns and B&Bs, a dozen restaurants, and assorted peripheral services and attractions.

It wasn't always thus. Once a thriving shipbuilding center and later a mill town, 200-year-old Freeport had fallen on hard times in the mid-20th century. It harbored Bean's eccentric factory and mail-order house, where hunters would stop on their way to the woods, but that was about all. The Bean retail store emerged from relative obscurity only in the 1970s, and began inflating into its current gargantuan state in the 1980s.

Freeporters point to 1981 as the start of the town's latter-day tourism boom, which they consider a mixed blessing. Fire had destroyed Leighton's 5 & 10, and into its rebuilt quarters across from L.L. Bean moved a Dansk outlet center. More outlets were to follow. Their situation in Freeport, however, was determined by a two-year legal battle involving McDonald's, which sought to install golden arches in place of one of Freeport's finest remaining 19th-cenury mansions. Opponents, united in what they called a Mac Attack, forged a compromise. McDonald's could sell its hamburgers, but only if it restored the interior and retained the facade of the 1855 William Gore House. So it is that thousands of Big Macs are consumed in Freeport in a Colonial setting, that Banana Republic occupies a most un-Banana-Republic-like, two-story Federal brick edifice, and The Gap is located in a white contemporary colossus. Tight zoning and management helped the small town of 6,900 residents spurn the Kittery and Ellsworth strip looks in favor of a village downtown appearance patterned after that of Camden.

Where shoppers converge, food and lodging are sure to follow. Jameson Tavern, where the papers were signed forging Maine as a separate state in 1820, was turned into a restaurant next door to L.L. Bean — a coincidence its owner likened to having the hot dog franchise at Fenway Park. Two native Maine sisters who had a thriving lodging operation in Connecticut recognized the opporunity in Freeport and eventually expanded a five-room B&B into the first-class Harraseeket Inn and restaurant. Smaller B&Bs emerged as well.

There's more to Freeport than Bean's and its expanding Main Street — a fact overlooked by most visitors. Head down to gracious South Freeport and a picturesque working harbor far removed in place and spirit from what the rest of us call Freeport and oldtimers know as Freeport Square or Freeport Corner. Explore the byways of Porter's Landing, Lower Mast Landing and the other settlements along Freeport's hidden coastline. Enjoy the waterside walking trails at Wolf Neck Woods State Park, the wildlife at Mast Landing Sanctuary, the swimming and camping at Winslow Memorial Park.

If that piques your interest, head a few miles east to the Harpswells, rural fingers of land stretching south from Brunswick into northern Casco Bay. Great, Orr's and Bailey islands, connected by bridges, make up one finger. Harpswell Neck forms another. This is the unspoiled Maine of old, the natural state you expect far Down East but not along the southwestern coast. Hidden coves, ocean vistas, quaint hamlets and lobster pounds

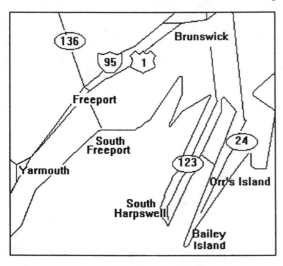

portray the Maine you came for, the one you suspected lies miles beyond the portals of L.L. Bean. But here it is, just outside.

Freeport and the Harpswells are at their best in spring, before the hordes arrive.

Getting There

Freeport straddles coastal Route 1 just off I-95, about eighteen miles east of Portland. The Harpswells extend south of Route 1 at Brunswick, a college town six miles northeast of Freeport.

A car is a necessity in both areas, although traffic and parking can be a problem in Freeport at peak shopping periods.

Air service is available into Portland International Jetport. Greyhound buses serve Portland as well.

Freeport

Seeing and Doing

The draw for most visitors is shopping, specifically L.L. Bean. Be advised: beyond Main Street is another Freeport with often-bypassed attractions.

Shopping

L.L. Bean. Leon Leonwood Bean's legacy is the stuff of retailing legends. From his brother's clothing store across the street from what is now the Bean retail store, late-blooming outdoorsman "L.L." — as he was called — invented at age 40 the Maine hunting shoe, a practical boot with rubber bottoms and leather uppers that's still Bean's best-seller (243,000 pairs a year). Bean was a master at mail-order, promising uncon-

ditional guarantees and free delivery along with value, the assurance of personal testing and plenty of homespun charm. Bean designed many of the goods himself and tried them out personally on the trails. Although mail-order remains the fastest-growing component of the business, it is retailing that is most evident in Freeport these days. The early factory/mail-order business located conveniently above the local post office developed a retail adjunct when sportsmen would stop for licenses and equipment at all hours. That prompted L.L. to throw away the key in 1951 and stay open for business 24 hours a day. Following his death in 1967, the Bean enterprise prospered under grandson Leon Gorman from sales of $4 million to $600 million a year. Though the original Bean building was removed in 1977 for parking space, the various addi-

tions L.L. built over the decades comprise half of today's 125,000-square-foot, three-level structure that includes skylights, atriums and a stocked trout pond beneath the main staircase. Although goods for the outdoorsman remain foremost, Bean's now carries 75,000 items — far more than are pictured in the 22 catalogs mailed annually to 114 million customers. Totes, books, Adirondack chairs, Maine foods, clothing, footwear, sports equipment, bicycles — you name it, and if it fits L.L.'s vision, Bean's carries it. Never more so than after Lisa Birnbach's *The Official Preppy Handbook* made L.L. Bean the bearer of preppy tidings. Bean's sales increased a record 42 percent in 1981. But as Leon Gorman noted, Bean's had suddenly become fashionable at the expense of function. While new customers were buying Bean's products, they were buying them for the wrong reasons. The preppy bubble burst and in 1983, Bean's sales increase flattened to 6 percent. Threatened with being passed by as last year's fashion house, Bean rededicated itself to the family and to the outdoors. The store is open 24 hours a day, 365 days a year.

Other Retailing. The 1981 fire at Leighton's 5 & 10 coincided with Bean's changing emphasis and marked the emergence of Freeport as a shopping destination. A Dansk outlet moved into the rebuilt Leighton building across Freeport Square from Bean's, and Freeport's revitalized Main Street was on its way with Cole-Haan shoes, Hathaway shirts, Cannon towels, Frye boots and Deering ice cream in the vanguard. Freeport's recent advertising as Maine's answer to Rodeo Drive is far-fetched; more credible is its claim to be "the Maine village quality goods made famous." Downtown Freeport avoided the strip mentality of Kittery, Ellsworth and North Conway, though a bit of that is evident on the outskirts along Route 1 south. It also shunned the outlet image of its counterparts. Twenty percent of the 125 (and growing) retailers here aren't factory outlets at all; these include **Praxis** and **Abacus** for outstanding crafts, **Edgecomb Potters** for fine pottery and **Santa Fe** for Southwest jewelry, clothes and the like. Most of the others feature first-quality items (no seconds) at prices that aren't particular bargains. Some have outlet corners or floors (Bean's factory store is tucked away off Depot Street). Ten to fifteen new retailers enter the Freeport market every year and five to ten leave as the merchandising mix evolves, according to the Freeport Merchants Association.

Freeport considers itself unique in having the only **Laura Ashley** outlet, as well as a **Fanny Farmer** outlet. A **Brooks Brothers** factory store occupies a prime space along Bow Street. Some of the most imposing along Main Street are **The Gap, Benetton, Banana Republic** and **Mikasa,** three floors crammed full of china, silver and more. We also liked the **Bleyle, Gant, Evan-Picone** and **Patagonia** stores. Unexpectedly prominent on the prime corner next to L.L. Bean is the Mobil service station, where gasoline was priced 5 percent higher than the prevailing norm at our latest visit. Also no bargain is the **Ben & Jerry's** ice cream store right in front of Bean's, where patrons are often lined up ten deep to order a small cone for $2.25. There seem to be as many sidewalk food vendors per corner as in midtown Manhattan; the hot dog cart across the street from Bean's is managed and operated by students from Freeport High School. The best deal we saw was two hot dogs for $1.85 at **Depot Street Caboose.**

If you suffer from crowds, avoid Freeport at peak hours on busy shopping days. We happened by on a cloudy, non-beach weekday in early August to find ourselves embroiled in Freeport's biggest day ever — an estimated 25,000 people. Vehicles were bumper-to-bumper along Main Street between exits from I-95. Cars cruised for parking spaces blocks away from downtown. Pedestrians, who have the right of way in crosswalks, kept traffic at a standstill and made negotiating the sidewalks difficult.

Other Attractions

South Freeport. The focal point of a 19th-century boom in shipbuilding and still a working harbor, this is now a fashionable residential area and yachting center. We first discovered there was more to Freeport than Main Street a few years ago when we set out for a lobster roll at Harraseeket Lunch & Lobster Co. The surprises yielded by the rural route there were exceeded only by the sights of the gracious homes and the picturesque harbor at the end. Our latest visit coincided with the South Freeport Summer Festival, three days of art shows, craft sales and feasting (lobster dinner, $8; chicken barbecue, $7) inside and out at the South Freeport United Church of Christ. Other than the harbor, the town's best known landmark is **Casco Castle,** a 100-foot-high stone tower — all that remains of a large summer hotel destroyed by fire in 1914.

Atlantic Seal Cruises (865-6112), an old, 28-passenger Coast Guard cruiser, departs

Harraseeket Inn offers food and lodging near center of Freeport.

from the town wharf in South Freeport on a variety of daily excursions. Most popular are three-hour tours at 9 and 1:30 out seven miles to **Eagle Island,** a state park where the boat pauses for an hour to let passengers explore the seventeen-acre island and visit the museum/home of Admiral Robert E. Peary, the first man to reach the North Pole. Photos and artifacts from his Arctic explorations are displayed in his summer home along with a collection of mounted Arctic and Maine birds. The state of Maine and the National Geographic Society restored the home's library. Captain Tom Ring hauls his lobster traps on the return voyage. The Atlantic Seal also offers seal and osprey watches and dinner cruises to Chebeague Island on various summer evenings. Adults $20, children $15. Also leaving from the wharf on several trips daily is a mail boat to Bustin's Island (passengers, $5).

Wolf Neck Woods State Park, Wolf Neck Road, Freeport. Five miles of hiking trails and lovely, secluded picnic sites are the attractions of this 200-acre property along the Harraseeket River and Casco Bay. "To the uninitiated, all of this may appear as nothing more than a collection of trees and brush," notes the display board. You learn that the forests of Wolf Neck represent a unique collection of ecological and local climatic conditions. Some of the white pine trees are thought to have been used by the British Navy as masts for their sailing ships. That led to the name for nearby Mast Landing and gave the unusual shape to Freeport Square, the triangle opposite L.L. Bean, where the logs were given extra turning room as they were hauled to the waterfront. People can swim off the Casco Bay trail, spot the pair of osprey that make the Googins Island sanctuary their home, and dig up to a peck of clams from the salt marsh when the tide is out. The park is open daily from 9 to sunset, Memorial Day through Labor Day; fee for parking. Upon leaving, drive farther down Wolf Neck Road through huge pines that resemble a redwood forest to the University of Southern Maine's working farm and

Smith Stone House, whose landscaped grounds yield a view of Casco Bay on one side and South Freeport's Casco Castle on the other.

Mast Landing Sanctuary, Upper Mast Landing Road, Freeport. The Maine Audubon Society operates this 140-acre sanctuary amid fields and streams. A favorite attraction is a mill stream cascading over a dam into the tidal salt marshes of the Harraseeket River estuary. Visitors see shorebirds, deer and porcupines from two miles of marked trails. Open daily, dawn to dusk; donation.

Other choice spots include **Winslow Memorial Park,** Staples Point Road, South Freeport, a 90-acre municipal park with a good sandy beach (the area's nine-foot tides are such that there's swimming at high tide only), a grassy picnicking area and a campground. The Freeport Historical Society at the Harrington House on Freeport's Main Street can give directions for a scenic walk out to its **Pettingill Farm,** an old saltbox farmhouse on a saltwater farm. **Good Earth Farm** at 55 Pleasant Hill Road, Freeport, purveys all kinds of dried flowers and herbs. Commercial attractions are the **North American Wildlife Expo,** Route 1 south of Freeport, billed as the largest wildlife museum of its kind on the East Coast, and **Desert of Maine,** 100 acres of sand dunes that evolved from pastureland that lost its topsoil.

A short excursion takes visitors just across the town line to **Lower Falls Landing,** a commercial complex and marina beside the Royal River in Yarmouth. Here are a handful of stores and **The Cannery,** a good seafood restaurant run by the owners of the Waterfront restaurant in Camden and much recommended by Freeport innkeepers.

Where to Stay

Harraseeket Inn, 162 Main St., Freeport 04032, (207) 865-9377 or (800) 342-6423. Nancy Gray and Jody Dyer, two sisters from South Portland who built the thriving Inn at Mystic complex in Connecticut, saw what was happening back in their home state in 1983 and started assembling property for a badly needed full-service inn and gathering spot in the center of Freeport. They started with an elegant five-room B&B in 1984 and, in 1989, added a three-story, 49-room inn and restaurant. Such was the response (77 percent year-round occupancy rate in 1992) that the Harraseeket was planning to add an enclosed swimming pool and eight more rooms in two other structures on the property. In the main inn, standard accommodations offer one queensize or two double beds with blue and white fabric half-canopies, wing chairs and baskets of Lord & Mayfair toiletries in the bathrooms. Deluxe rooms contain fireplaces and jacuzzis, wet bars and TVs hidden in armoires. Chocolates come with turndown service at night. Excellent meals are available in the Maine Dining Room or the Broad Arrow Tavern (see Where to Eat). A full breakfast buffet and an elaborate afternoon tea in the attractive living room are included in the rates. Doubles, $135 to $175; suites, $225.

181 Main Street Bed & Breakfast, 181 Main St., Freeport 04032, (207) 865-1226. David Cates and Ed Hasset renovated this 1840 Greek Revival House into a B&B in 1986. Theirs was one of the first along an outer Main Street stretch that is now chock-a-block B&Bs. They offer seven upstairs guest rooms with private baths, all attractively furnished but rather small, as rooms in some historic homes are apt to be. Guests spread out in twin front parlors, one containing quite a collection of ceramic animals in a sideboard and a long coffee table made of glass atop an old ship's rope bed. The other is more like a library with a TV. The partners serve a breakfast to remember in two dining rooms dressed with calico tablecloths and Hitchcock chairs. The day we visited, it included a choice of juices, cranberry coffee cake, blueberry pancakes with sausage, poached pear with yogurt sauce and fresh fruit. An asset here is the secluded swimming pool in the long back yard. Doubles, $95.

Porter's Landing Bed & Breakfast, 70 South St., Freeport 04032, (207) 865-4488. A rural location and suave accommodations recommend this B&B on five shady acres. Peter and Barbara Griffin, parents of three young children, turned the wood shop attached to their classic 1830 Greek Revival home into three guest rooms, a spiffy living-dining room and a library loft in 1989. The soaring space gave their architect lots of room and angles; witness the stairway and landing leading to the skylit, third-floor library hideaway. All three rooms on the second floor have private baths. They are furnished simply but elegantly and contain interesting art. Lemonade and banana bread might be served in the afternoon. Breakfast involves fresh fruit, homemade granola and perhaps belgian waffles, egg ramekins or cheese omelets. Doubles, $90. No smoking.

The Kendall Tavern Bed & Breakfast, 213 Main St., Freeport 04032, (207) 865-1338. Big bucks went into the renovation of this old farmhouse by three California men in 1991. The landscaped grounds are welcoming, as are two small fireplaced living rooms, one with a TV cosseted in a corner armoire. Wonderful paintings adorn a breakfast room set with seven tables for two, where a fruit course, muffins and pancakes or a mushroom omelet might be served. Upstairs are five fairly small bedrooms with queensize beds and two with twins, each with private bath and most with attractive bed coverings. At the rear of the main floor is a large indoor whirlpool tub for guests' use. Doubles, $100 to $110.

Isaac Randall House, 5 Independence Drive, Freeport 04032, (207) 865-9295. Spirited conversation is the norm in the country kitchen of this rambling farmhouse, once a stop on the Underground Railroad as slaves made their way to Canada. Here is where new owners Cynba and Shannon Ryan prepare breakfast for guests at two sittings around a large table above a rug painted on the floor. Quiche, huevos rancheros or orange-almond french toast could be the fare. The house has eight homey guest rooms, six with private baths and several outfitted with day beds that make them good for families. The two nicest are in the rear. The Pine Room offers a queen bed and an antique copper tub. Above is the large Loft, with sloping ceiling, skylights, a draped kingsize bed, TV, oriental rattan furniture and an enormous, two-section bathroom with a rattan chair. Besides the kitchen focal point, there's a Victorian sitting room with TV on the second floor, plus a kitchenette where soft drinks, cheese and crackers are kept for guests. The B&B is located on five rural acres, with a parked train car and a pond out back. Guests are scarcely aware of the presence of the sprawling L.L. Bean office and distribution center across the street. Doubles, $70 to $105.

Holbrook Inn, 7 Holbrook St., Freeport 04032, (207) 865-6693. Only one house separates the 100-year-old Victorian home of retired Freeporters Ralph and Bea Routhier from the busy Main Street shopping area. But the side yard, which Ralph tends to lovingly, is turned the other way and Bea's three spotless guest rooms are air-conditioned and equipped with TVs, queensize four-poster beds and private baths. Lest the amenities mislead: this is not a typical B&B layout. The two main rooms on the second floor amount to a two-bedroom suite with a living room and a kitchen attesting to its former status as an apartment. The other room at the rear has a small wicker sitting room downstairs off the office and a bedroom with two stenciled rockers and a shower bath upstairs. At a polished round table in an airy breakfast room, Bea serves a hearty breakfast that might include french toast or scrambled eggs. Doubles, $75. No smoking. No credit cards.

The Bagley House, Route 136, RR 3, Box 269C, Freeport 04032, (207) 865-6566 or

(800) 765-1772. One look at the expansive, eat-in kitchen with its free-standing fireplace, beehive oven and two arch kettles was enough for Sig Knudsen. The ex-Freeporter decided on the spot to buy the oldest (1772) house in Durham, just across the Freeport town line, after spending twenty years as a social worker, ten of them with the Inuit in southwest Alaska. Personable Sig, a great host, offers five spacious bedrooms with private baths. Three possess custom-made beds fashioned by a local craftsman and quilts hand-sewn by Sig's sister. The upstairs Nook with unusual low-slung windows harbors a double and a three-quarter bed, good for families. Guests gather in a fireplaced living room or a library with a huge collection of reading material. Sig serves quite a breakfast at a long table beside the fireplace in the rear kitchen off his quarters. He might whip up a decadent french toast made with crois-

Little Island Motel at Orr's Island.

sants and triple sec, or serve scrambled eggs with nasturtiums, calendula blossoms and baked beans. At our visit, Sig had decided to sail his boat around the world and had the inn up for sale. Doubles, $95.

Atlantic Seal Bed & Breakfast, Main Street, Box 146, South Freeport 04078, (207) 865-6112. Freeport's only B&B on the water, this is the lifelong home of Tom Ring, a tugboat captain by trade, and his wife Gaila. Theirs is a house full of nautical memorabilia and antiques, among them an antique sextant, an original clipper ship painting over the fireplace and old ship models made by his grandfather and showcased in a lighted corner cabinet. The Rings offer three bedrooms. Largest is the Dash, with windows on three sides, a queensize and a double bed, TV and a private bath with a deep, oversize jacuzzi and a separate shower. Two smaller rooms that share a bath also afford views of the Harraseeket River. The rear deck overlooking the water holds some of the striking modern wood slat chairs made by Tom's father. Tom lets guests use a rowboat at high tide, and offers a discount on his morning Atlantic Seal excursions to Eagle Island. He traps the lobsters that go into the Rings' trademark lobster omelets for breakfast. Doubles, $65 to $125.

Coastline Inn, Route 1, Freeport 04032, (207) 865-3777. One of a small Maine motel chain, this has 109 rooms with two double, one double or one kingsize bed and standard motel furnishings. The rooms are air-conditioned, have no balconies, and the windows don't open. In winter, these would be quite adequate but in spring or summer, who wants to be in Maine in a place where you can't sit outside or open the windows? At least the room configuration puts guests away from the highway, which is more than we can say for the Super 8 squashed between Route 1 and I-95 across the street. Doubles, $72.95 to $74.95.

Where to Eat

Harraseeket Inn, 162 Main St., Freeport, (207) 865-9377. Talented Maine chef Sam Hayward closed his acclaimed 22 Lincoln restaurant in Brunswick in 1991 and was lured to the Harraseeket to become executive chef. It was a fortunate match for both innkeeper Nancy Gray and for Sam, who wanted to spend more time with his young family and reveled in the inn's state-of-the-art, two-story kitchen, which he calls "a tremendous piano to play on." Sam quickly won rave reviews for his creative fare, both upstairs in the three elegant rooms of the Maine Dining Room and downstairs in the Broad Arrow Tavern. Sam is at his best when he turns his creativity toward local products, from wild mushrooms to Maine game. Consider one summer night's specials ($21.95 to $24.95): striped bass fillet with chanterelles and tart apples, ragout of Atlantic shellfish with cognac and fennel, and two-texture duckling with Saskatoon berries. Knowing gourmands opt for his $39.95 prix-fixe dinner, a legacy of 22 Lincoln and yielding at our visit a "chartreuse" of smoked salmon with crabmeat and caviar, a feuilletée of fresh morels, a salad of Maine mesclun with edible flowers, the aforementioned duckling dish and three homemade sorbets with berries and berry coulis. The tavern menu is nicely priced, and the luncheon buffet spread is a cut above the norm. Lunch daily, 11:30 to 2:30; dinner nightly, 5:30 to 9.

Fiddlehead Farm, 15 Independence Drive, Freeport, (207) 865-0466. This expanding rural homestead across from the L.L. Bean distribution center offers some of Freeport's most highly touted cuisine. Chef-owners Chris and Laura Washburn acquired their culinary skills at restaurants across the country before returning to her native Maine to acquire the former Sebastian's, renaming it and adding a country cafe out back. The farmhouse interior is cozy and properly historic; for lunch, we're partial to the small, canopied outdoor deck, somewhat dwarfed lately by the new cafe. Here at our latest visit we enjoyed fish chowder and the Fiddlehead Farm salad ($6.95), spinach with dried cranberries, feta cheese and turkey, and the restaurant's "famous grilled turkey club" ($5.95), which turned out not to be a three-decker club but simply a regular sandwich, albeit excellent. The dinner menu changes nightly. The limited selections run from $12.95 for roast chicken with raspberry chutney to $20.95 for lobster strudel served with a wild mushroom and cognac cream. Basic breakfasts and lunches and homestyle dinners are served in the intimate Country Cafe. Lunch, Monday-Friday 11 to 3; dinner nightly, 5 to 9. Cafe open daily from 6 or 7 a.m. to 8 p.m.

Jameson Tavern, 115 Main St., Freeport, (207) 865-4196. With a location next to L.L. Bean and an historic setting proclaimed as the birthplace of Maine, how could this place miss? A plaque outside denotes it as the site in 1820 of the signing of the papers that separated Maine from Massachusetts. A selection of menus steers hundreds of patrons on a busy day to the dark and intimate dining rooms, the rear tap room and the large outdoor deck alongside. This is not a place for leisurely dining, and the steakhouse menu encourages turnover of tables by limiting appetizers and desserts. Dinner entrees run from $11.50 for sauteed sirloin tips to $16.75 for seafood fettuccine alfredo. Side dishes like coleslaw, sauteed mushrooms and vegetable of the day are extra. Burgers are priced at $3.95, plus extras. Tap room serves daily from 11:30 to 10 or 11; dining room, lunch or Sunday brunch, 11:30 to 2:30; dinner, 5 to 9.

China Rose, 10 School St., Freeport, (207) 865-6882. Leave it to Freeport to turn up a Chinese restaurant that earned 4 1/2 stars for food from the Maine Sunday Telegram reviewer shortly after it opened in 1992. Unusual dishes, attractively presented, are served in a serene, two-level dining room pretty in pink and black. Among them are a seafood hot and sour soup, shrimp and scallops sauteed in Mala sauce, sizzling seafood wor bar and lobster with ginger and scallions. Prices are moderate ($7.50 to $13.95, except $22.95 for Peking duck). Lunch daily, 11 to 3; dinner to 9:30 or 10.

The Muddy Rudder, Route 1, Yarmouth, (207) 846-3082. Just across the narrow Cousins River from Freeport is this large and surprisingly spiffy restaurant and lounge

Eating lobster by the water is attraction at Harraseeket Lunch & Lobster Company.

where the first-thing-you-see bar gives little hint of the cut-above food to come. We like the jaunty outdoor deck overlooking the Great Salt Marsh and the dining room with large windows beside, but the 250-seat establishment includes some interior tables as well. New management in 1992 produced a new look and food that was winning good reviews. The menu is one of those something-for-everyone encyclopedias, offering for dinner a range from broiled scrod with a blackened mayonnaise and shrimp creole over pasta to grilled halibut, swordfish kabob and fisherman platter, $10.95 to $14.95. There are some good-sounding salads and sandwiches for lunch, and seafood benedict ($7.25) is a highlight of the weekend brunch. Live piano music is played in the bar at night. Open daily from 11 to midnight; weekend brunch, 9 to 1.

The Blue Onion, Lower Main Street, Freeport, (207) 865-9396. The owners welcome patrons to "the restaurant that love built," allow no alcohol and close on Sundays. Many folks like the shady outdoor deck and the home-style interior where mismatched cloths cover the tables. Dinner entrees ($8.95 to $13.95) run the gamut from chicken maximillian and baked haddock to lobster pie, veal marsala and steak au poivre. The homemade desserts are something else, from raspberry fudge cake to a strawberry-banana-amaretto concoction with ice cream. Lunch, 11 to 4, dinner to 9; breakfast in summer, 7 to 10:30. Closed Sunday.

The Corsican Restaurant, 9 Mechanic St., Freeport, (207) 865-9421. Plain as plain can be but ever-popular is this offshoot of a Brunswick pizza and vegetarian eatery. For lunch, you might choose a vegetarian calzone with cheese for $4.95, a crabmeat pizza for $9.95 or any number of salads or sandwiches. Dinnertime adds such entrees ($10.95 to $12.95) as haddock a la grecque, chicken marsala and broiled salmon. There are no beef dishes beyond a meatball sub. Beer and wine are available. Open daily, 11 to 9.

Harraseeket Lunch & Lobster Company, Town Wharf, South Freeport, (207) 865-4888. This is the one we'd been waiting for. Family-run and astride the fishing pier, it serves typical lobster-pound and seafood fare inside and out. It's at its best for lunch, when you can sit outside and watch the harbor goings-on; nighttime is apt to get busy and buggy. Our latest lunch included a delicious clam chowder, a clam roll on a toasted bun and a clam burger for under $10. The two weighty lobsters we took home for dinner in a special icebox cost an additional $22. Last we knew, hot dogs were going for $1.25, lobster rolls for $8.95 and the specialty basket of fried clams for $9.25. Open daily, 11 to 9. BYOB. No credit cards.

The Harpswells

Diametrically opposed to Freeport's Main Street and what it represents are the Harpswells, the collective name for the fingers of land stretching into Casco Bay south of Brunswick and embracing Great Island, Orr's Island, Bailey Island and Harpswell Neck. The three islands are attached one to the other and the mainland by short bridges and, because of their narrowness, cast a thoroughly watery aspect. Bailey, the most seaward of the islands, is said to be the most popular of Casco Bay's 365 Calendar Islands because of its accessibility, though only a relative few venture down there. Harpswell Neck is a peninsula leading from Brunswick and, because of its width, lacks a watery feeling except at the ends of roads leading off Route 123 or at the neck's far end near South Harpswell.

The Harpswells — with their solitude, their scenery and their stability reflecting Maine as it used to be — are the perfect antidote to the frenzy of Freeport. Anyone partial to the water would be advised to make them their base for exploring the area.

Seeing and Doing

What's there to do? Not much, which is precisely the lure for those in the know. A few inns, motels and B&Bs offer lodging of the old school, the lobster houses provide sustenance, the fishing villages and working harbors add charm, the seaside air is exhilarating, and rockbound coves and inlets pop up at almost every turn. The Casco Bay Lines out of Portland runs a six-hour cruise to Bailey Island; as round-trip passengers lay over here, others board for a 90-minute nature cruise past nearby islands (noon daily from Cook's Marina; adults $7, children $3). Explore the shoreline, dig clams, walk or bike along the back roads, browse at one of the Harpswell Craft Guild's member galleries or the new Orr's Island Mini Mall, four shops in a small house-like structure. If you want more, the shops of Freeport are less than 45 minutes' drive away. Where Freeport has action, the Harpswells have, well, character.

You'll notice that on an early-morning walk, many others are out walking, too. Folks exchange pleasantries, and even wave to the occasional motorist who happens by. You marvel at the piles of lobster traps, some stunning seaside homes interspersed between the prevailing weatherbeaten cottages, the old fishing boats that give Mackerel Cove the look of Nova Scotia, and the passing lobster boats hauling in their bounty. You stop outside All Saints By the Sea, a tiny Episcopal chapel that is most un-chapel-like, a shingled cottage without so much as a steeple. A sign points the way to **Giant Stairs,** a five-minute walk past wild rose and bayberry bushes along a bluff resembling Ogunquit's Marginal Way. Just when you think you won't find the stairs, a family who preceded say you've arrived. Their youngsters are scrambling on the massive stone steps that march down to the open ocean. A plaque at the top relates that these were given to their native town in 1910 by Capt. William Henry Sinnett and his wife Joanna. The preceding family, who have summered for years on Bailey Island, point out the jagged Pinnacle Rock, advise of Thunder Hole and Pirate's Cove and Land's End beyond, and tell how the locals go out by small boat to trade with Russian fishermen on trawlers just beyond the lighthouse. You drive down to Land's End, where a statue of a lobsterman rises outside an unlikely-looking gift shop. All this is a Maine experience for you.

Where to Stay

Little Island Motel, RD 1, Box 15, Orr's Island 04066, (207) 833-2392. "Please drive slowly — duck crossing," advises the sign at the entrance to the spit of land jutting into

Fishing shack at Mackerel Cove, Bailey Island.

the water off Lowell's Cove Road. Beyond is an inviting small complex billed by owner Jo Atlass as "the intimate resort." It includes a seven-room, chalet-style motel with decks right over the water and two more private units at either end of her house opposite. A carved duck and a lobster trap are outside each door. The rooms we saw had small sitting areas with cable TV and mini-refrigerators, but most appealing were the decks, given privacy by canvas screens between each unit. Ducks emerged from under the trees and waddled up to a shady sitting area with a barbecue and picnic tables beside the water. Jo puts out a complimentary continental buffet breakfast in her home: lots of fresh fruits, muffins, croissants, jams, cereals, and ham and cheeese biscuits. She also operates a small shop called the Gull's Nest, which stocks Maine handcrafts and rather suave gifts. Doubles, $104 to $108.

Senter Bed & Breakfast, Route 123, South Harpswell 04079, (207) 833-2874. Location, location, location. And personality, personality, personality. These are the attributes of the relaxed B&B run by Albert Senter, a 70-something bachelor who moved to a large contemporary house on three acres overlooking Harpswell Sound in 1979 and found it so lonesome he started taking in guests. It's an unlikely role for patrician Mr. Senter, who with his seven siblings ran the eight-store Senter department store chain, one store for each child. His was the downtown Brunswick flagship, which was about to close its doors for good at our 1992 visit, the inevitable victim of the outlets of Freeport and the malls of Brunswick. His comfortable year-round house, very much geared to its magnificent hillside setting, is a treat: three guest rooms with private baths and the peaceful soliloqy of waves lapping at the shore all night, a modern living room with TV and windows onto the water, a seaside deck topped by a vine-covered trellis, and remarkable gardens that the host embellishes from two greenhouses. A stairway descends from the lawn to the water. Arriving without reservations after phoning without answer all day, we and a Florida couple had the house to ourselves upon checking in with the woman who greeted us. She's the tenant in the walkout basement apartment, and said she thought the owner had gone to dinner at the Driftwood Inn — as had been his custom every night since he built a cottage across the way at Land's

End, Bailey Island (a two-bedroom cottage he now rents out for $450 a week). When he hadn't returned by 10:30 and couldn't be located, we all went to bed. Next morning, Mr. Senter was in the kitchen cooking breakfast, most apologetic that a last-minute dinner invitation had prevented him from greeting his unexpected guests. That breakfast included choice of cereals, blueberry muffins "with berries I picked myself up the road" and a "dropped egg" on toast. Prunes and homemade oatmeal, endless coffee and lots of conversation with a prominent native Mainer were offered. Staying here, we found, is like visiting a well-to-do Yankee grandfather's home, one that happens to occupy a slice of paradise by the sea. Doubles, $70.

Harpswell Inn, 141 Lookout Point Road, RR1, Box 141, South Harpswell 04079, (207) 833-5509. A handsome 1761 structure that once served as the cookhouse for the famed Lookout Point Shipyard has been renovated into an up-and-coming B&B. Bill and Susan Menz, Connecticut natives who tired of corporate life in Houston, acquired the old Lookout Point House in 1991 and set about its restoration; visiting when we were there was a woman who had grown up in the house and couldn't believe the changes. The inn has twelve bedrooms, three with private baths; the others have sinks in the rooms and shared baths. Rooms are stylishly outfitted and decorated. The prized main-floor Rackliffe Room is all blue and yellow with peacock wallpaper. The Lilac Suite has Laura Ashley print wallpaper and draperies and a loveseat. A smaller favorite is the rear Bowdoin Room, resembling a college dorm room and bearing all sorts of memorabilia from Bill's days at Bowdoin College in Brunswick. The Texas Room on the third floor sports a queensize bed with longhorns above. Youngsters like to pull the chain at the top of the staircase to ring the rooftop bell that summoned hungry shipbuilders to their meals back in the 1860s. Much of the main floor is given over to a "great" room, which has a huge fieldstone fireplace, a grand piano, comfortable seating and windows almost to the floor. Breakfast in a large dining room might bring Swedish pancakes, waffles with caramelized strawberry sauce, french toast triage (regular, orange and caramelized fruit), omelets or sausage and cheese casserole. Doubles, $58 to $100.

The Driftwood Inn, Bailey Island 04003, (207) 833-5461. A simple, old-fashioned place, this complex of shingled buildings perched beside the water at Land's End has been around for more than 75 years and has done very nicely, thank you. The Conrad family offer five housekeeping cabins and 26 double and single guest rooms in three houses, most sharing one bathroom per floor. Four rooms in one house contain half-baths. Each house includes a common room and a porch that takes full advantage of the view toward the open ocean. A saltwater swimming pool ensconced in the rocks is popular with children. Meals are served at a single seating in an open-timbered dining room with windows onto the water on two sides. Outside diners may come for breakfast ($4.50) at 8 or dinner ($10) at 6. The single-choice menu yields roast pork on Monday, lamb on Wednesday, steak or lobster on Friday and turkey dinner on Sunday. Doubles, $60 EP, $100 MAP; $540 weekly, MAP. No credit cards. Closed mid-October to May.

Bailey Island Motel, Route 24, Bailey Island 04003, (207) 844-2886. Idyllically located on a grassy, shady waterside property beside the last cribstone bridge in existence at the entrance to Bailey Island, this two-story motel has ten rooms. Five on the second floor were renovated in 1990 and are quite serviceable. We stayed in 1992 in one of the first-floor rooms that needed the upgrading planned by owners Harold and Cathy Dayton for the following winter. We spent several hours on the grounds, relaxing in chairs beside Casco Bay in the evening and eating a complimentary breakfast of coffee and Cathy's homemade strawberry muffins at a picnic table on a shady knoll affording views of both bay and Harpswell Sound beyond the cribstone bridge. The

Lawn at Senter Bed & Breakfast slopes down to Harpswell Sound.

bridge was built with granite blocks laid in honeycomb fashion without cement to let the area's nine-foot tides flow through. Doubles, $75. No credit cards.

Orr's Island Bed & Breakfast, Route 24, Box 561, Orr's Island 04066, (207) 833-2940. Lovely landscaped grounds and gardens sloping down to Long Cove, a huge raised sun deck and a rambling contemporary house. These draw overnight guests to the home of Sandy and Colin Robinson, who opened in 1991 when "the rooms became available and I needed something to do," in Sandy's words. Two upstairs bedrooms vacated by their offspring share a large bath and a cathedral-ceilinged family room with a TV. Guests sometimes join the Robinsons in their modern living room, and eat a full breakfast in a skylit kitchen-dining area or on the deck. You can swim from the dock in Long Cove when the tide's in; otherwise, as is the case with shallow places in the area when the water disappears, the mud flats are good for clamming. Doubles, $60.

Where to Eat

J. Hathaways' Restaurant & Tavern, Route 123, Harpswell Center, (207) 833-5305. In an area where seafood and lobster houses reign, this chef-owned restaurant has stood out since 1984. The dinner menu changes frequently in the Maine farmhouse with dark Colonial decor. Choices ($8.95 to $11.95) might include haddock with herbed meringue, baked scallops, pork spareribs, charbroiled ham steak with a side dish of stewed apples and raisins or honey-mustard chicken. Prime rib is available on Saturday, and fish and chips every night. Among desserts are lime mousse pie, grapenut custard and fudge walnut pie. Dinner, Tuesday-Saturday 5 to 9, Sunday 4 to 8.

Richard's, Route 123, North Harpswell, (207) 729-9673. "Auf Wiedersehen," says the sign as you leave the old schoolhouse that in 1988 became Richard's, serving European and American cuisine. Chef-owner Richard Gnauck of Germany, longtime chef at the Stowe House in Brunswick, wows regulars with his wiener schnitzel, bratwurst, sauerbraten and other German specialties. The continental-American side of the menu turns up items like veal oscar, tournedos rossini and lamb medallions sauteed with Dutch peppers, straw mushrooms and honey-mustard sauce, all nicely priced from $8.85 to $15.45. A list of imported beers includes the renowned Belgian Framboise for a hefty $7.25, and Richard offers quite a few German wines. A collection of beer steins tops a divider in the high-ceilinged room; more tables are on a wraparound deck outside. Lunch, Tuesday-Sunday 11:30 to 2; dinner, Tuesday-Saturday 5 to 9, Sunday to 8.

Jack Baker's Oceanview Restaurant, Route 24, Bailey Island, (207) 833-5366. Our favorite Rock Ovens restaurant, long a beacon of culinary creativity beside the cribstone bridge, had given way to the Oceanview at our last visit and we weren't sure what to expect. The decor remained the same, and oil lamps flickered and Vivaldi played as we watched the moonlight dance on the waves of Casco Bay. The menu is mostly seafood, from $8.95 for baked scrod to $19.95 for a shore dinner. Lasagna, chicken pot pie and fettuccine alfredo are the only non-fish dishes. We did not expect so sensational a house salad of leaf lettuce bearing cheese, salami, garbanzo beans, black olives and a mustard-garlic dressing or the really great rolls and corn fritters. The garlic shrimp on a bed of fettuccine, billed on the menu as something special for $9.95, turned out to be just that. The only disappointment was Maine crab cakes ($10.95) that were deep-fried rather than sauteed and were much too overdone. Boiled red potatoes and sauteed summer squashes came with. A bottle of Entre Deux Mers cost $11.50. With rum raisin ice cream for dessert, the total tab came to $40, not bad for one of our better dinners in a while. The adjacent dock with a shack serving hamburgers and lobster rolls looks like a neat place for lunch. Lunch, 11:30 to 4; dinner, 4 to 9 or 10.

Log Cabin Restaurant, Route 24, Bailey Island, (207) 833-5546. Original owner Sue Favreau took back the cavernous Log Cabin in 1992 after leasing it for four years to Jack Baker (see above). She and her family did some modest upgrading, but the high-ceilinged interior that looks like a log cabin remains, complete with a moosehead over the fireplace. Enclosed porches yield additional seating with water views. The extensive menu is priced from $9.95 for chicken teriyaki to $22.95 for a shore dinner. The food is straightforward and the fare predictable. Soups, sandwiches and four entrees, including chicken pot pie and quiche with salad, are offered at lunchtime. Open daily, 11:30 to 9:30. Closed November-February.

Cook's Lobster House, Bailey Island, (207) 833-6641. Folks come from all over the Harpswells for the fresh seafood and lobster at this oldtimer in a marina on a point surrounded by water and open year-round. With windows on three sides, the main dining room is an expanse of low pine booths with a lamp on every table. Outside is Moby's Deck, a raw bar serving light food and drinks. The dinner menu is priced from $11.45 for fish or shrimp to $17.95 for sauteed lobster. Four shore dinners are $20.95 to $23.95. Blackboard specials when we were there were grilled swordfish and fried oysters. A lobster roll was $8.95 and boiled lobster, $9.45. Dinner nightly to 9.

Estes Lobster House, Route 123, South Harpswell, (207) 833-6340. Here is a huge, two-story barn of a place on a spit of land with water on both sides. You order at a large counter near the entrance, pick up your meal served on paper plates with wimpy plastic implements, and take a seat in a couple of long, nondescript rooms or, our choice, at picnic tables outside. The mosquitoes were fierce only for ten minutes around dusk, and the manager obliged by providing a couple of citronella candles (well, we were the only ones outside on a slow night and the inside was nearly empty). Estes was pushing its original triple lobster plate for $19.95, but we stuck with the lobster pie (lots of lobster, topped with stuffing) and a really good seafood medley (baked haddock, shrimp and scallops), both with french fries and $13.95. A bottle of our own wine, candlelight and a gorgeous sunset made for quite a picnic, but next time we'll bring our own cutlery. Open daily, 11 to 9. Closed mid-October to May.

Dolphin Marina and Restaurant, Basin Point, South Harpswell, (207) 833-6000. Local folks pour in for three meals a day at this small, pine-paneled restaurant with a counter, eight tables, two booths, an attempt at a store and the best fish chowder around.

Outdoor tables at Jack Baker's Oceanview Restaurant.

We can vouch for the chowder, absolutely delectable and containing more fish than chowder. Also great for lunch was the lobster stew ($9.95), accompanied, rather strangely, by a blueberry muffin that we took home for breakfast the next day. Although it was lunchtime, the value enticed one of us to try the complete dinner ($9.95) of clam strips, chowder, salad (with pepper-parmesan dressing on the side), french fries, rainbow sherbet and coffee, ending up thoroughly sated. No wonder the oldtimers come here for their midday meal. There's no liquor, and iced tea seems to be the beverage of choice. The windows also don't open, and one of us found the air so stifling she thought she was going to faint. Imagine, all that sea air and those water views and you're stuck behind storm windows. But is it ever popular. Open daily, 8 to 8.

Holbrook's Lobster Wharf & Snack Bar, Cundy's Harbor, (207) 725-5697. A favorite haunt of Brunswick restaurateurs and others in the know is this spot beside Cundy's Harbor. You sit at picnic tables on the wharf and see everybody you know, says our local informant who thinks it's the best place going. Concert pianist Martin Perry and Broadway stage dancer Henry D'Allessandris came up to be part of the Maine State Theater and decided to stay. They run a quality, summery lunch place and their lobsters, salads and desserts are first-rate, particularly the steamed chocolate pudding. Open daily for lunch and dinner; seasonal.

Simply Chris, Route 24, Bailey Island. Geraniums are painted on the door of this simple eatery. It's sandwiched between a market and Frenchy's Fresh Fish, not far from the fire department and the Catholic chapel (weekly Mass at 5:30 p.m. Saturday) in what passes for downtown Bailey Island. At four tables inside and out on a side deck, Chris Theberge whips up fancy-for-the-area breakfasts, from blueberry pancakes to omelets. The fisherman's breakfast combines eggs and pancakes for $6.25, and the island brunch ($7.50) adds a ribeye steak. We'd settle for the breakfast sandwich ($4.75) of fried egg, cheese and Canadian bacon on grilled homemade bread with homefries. Breakfast daily except Tuesday, 7 to noon, Sunday to 1.

FOR MORE INFORMATION: Freeport Merchants Association, Box 452, Freeport, Me. (04032, (207) 865-1212. The state-run Yarmouth Information Center along Route 1 at Exit 17 off I-95 has considerable information on Freeport and environs.

Index

390

Also by Wood Pond Press

Waterside Escapes in the Northeast. The latest book by Betsy Wittemann and Nancy Webster relates the best lodging, dining, attractions and activities in 36 great waterside vacation spots from Chesapeake Bay to Cape Breton Island, from the Thousand Islands to Martha's Vineyard. Everything you need to know for a day trip, a weekend or a week near the water is told the way you want to know it. Published in 1987; revised and expanded in 1991. 442 pages to discover and enjoy. $13.95.

The Best of Daytripping & Dining. Another book by Betsy Wittemann and Nancy Webster, this is a companion to their original Southern New England and all-New England editions. It pairs 25 featured daytrips with 25 choice restaurants, among 200 other suggestions of sites to visit and places to eat, in Southern New England and nearby New York. Published in 1985; revised in 1989. 210 pages of good ideas. $9.95.

Getaways for Gourmets in the Northeast. The first book by Nancy Webster and Richard Woodworth appeals to the gourmet in all of us. It guides you to the best dining, lodging, specialty food shops and culinary attractions in 22 areas from the Brandywine Valley to Montreal, the Finger Lakes to Nantucket. Published in 1984; fully revised and expanded in 1988 and 1991. 514 pages to read and savor. $14.95.

Inn Spots & Special Places in New England. Much more than an inn guide, this guide by Nancy Webster and Richard Woodworth tells you where to go, stay, eat and enjoy in the region's choicest places. Focusing on 32 special destination areas, it details the best inns and B&Bs, restaurants, sights to see and things to do. Published in 1986; revised and expanded in 1989 and 1992. 452 pages of timely ideas. $13.95.

Inn Spots & Special Places/New York and Mid-Atlantic. The second volume in the series, the newest book by Nancy Webster and Richard Woodworth guides you to the best in 30 of the Mid-Atlantic region's choicest areas, from New York to Virginia. Published in 1992. 424 pages of great ideas. $13.95.

The Restaurants of New England. This book by Nancy Webster and Richard Woodworth is the most comprehensive guide to restaurants throughout New England. The authors detail menu offerings, atmosphere, hours and prices for more than 1,000 restaurants. Published in 1990. 394 pages of thorough information. $12.95.

The Originals in Their Fields

These books may be ordered from your local bookstore or direct from the publisher, pre-paid, plus $1.50 handling for each book. Connecticut residents add sales tax.

Wood Pond Press
365 Ridgewood Road
West Hartford, Conn. 06107
(203) 521-0389